Anger, Hostility, and Aggression: Assessment, Prevention, and Intervention Strategies for Youth

Anger, Hostility, and Aggression: Assessment, Prevention, and Intervention Strategies for Youth

Edited by

Michael Furlong
University of California at Santa Barbara
Graduate School of Education

Douglas Smith
Chaminade University
Department of Psychology
Honolulu, Hawaii

Clinical Psychology Publishing Co., Inc.
4 Conant Square
Brandon, Vermont 05733

Library of Congress Cataloging–in–Publication Data

Anger, hostility, and aggression: assessment, prevention, and intervention strategies for youth / edited by Michael J. Furlong, Douglas C. Smith.
p. cm.
Includes bibliographical references and index.
ISBN 0-88422-151-2
1. Aggressiveness (Psychology) in children. 2. Anger in children. 3. Aggressiveness (Psychology) in adolescence. 4. Anger in adolescence. 5. Hostility (Psychology) I. Furlong, Michael J., 1951– . II, Smith, Douglas C., 1951– .
RJ506.A35A54 1994
618.92'89--dc20 93-35857
CIP

Library of Congress Catalog Card Number: 93-35857

ISBN: 0–88422–151–2

CPPC 4 Conant Square
Brandon, Vermont 05733

Cover design: Sue Thomas
Layout and graphic design: Michael Furlong
Editorial consultant: Jane Todorski

Printed in the United States of America.

For our children:

May they attend schools that are safe, secure, and peaceful…

Leiana, Devin, Damon, Nikki, Alexandra, Christopher, Adam, Kathryn, Ellise, David, Ellen, Emily, Daniel, Michael, Brandy, Sarah, Sabastian, Sean, Taylor, Matthew, Evan, Jake, Nicolas, Christopher, Sara, Brandon, Rosa, Jamell, Madeline, Emma, Ashley, Bubba, Kalie, Anna, Michaela, Miles, Elizabeth, Marie, Brian, Jeremy, Meagan, Christen, Brittany, Sean, Dexter, Diego, Kristen, Justin, Kyle, Rachael, Shelley, Evan, Rebekka, James, Christopher, Tanya, Tamara, Todd, Tasha, Scott, Brent, Randy, Eddie, Adam, Jared, and all the kids at Englishton Park

Table of Contents

Contributors

Kenyon F. Chan, Ph.D., is currently Professor and Chair of the Department of Asian American Studies at California State University, Northridge. Mailing address: CSUN, Department of Asian American Studies, 18111 Nordhoff Street, Northridge, CA 91330.

Gregory J. Eaken is a doctoral student in the School Psychology Program at Indiana University Bloomington. Mailing address: Indiana University, School of Education, 910 State Road 46 Bypass, Bloomington, IN, 47405.

Marcy Feldman, M.Ed., is a school psychologist employed by the Los Angeles Unified School District.

Jay Fortman, Ph.D., is a school psychologist in the Goleta Union School District and an adjunct Lecturer in the Graduate School of Education at the University of California, Santa Barbara. Mailing address: Goleta Union School District, 401 North Fairview Ave., Goleta, CA 93117.

Michael Furlong, Ph.D., is an Associate Professor in the Graduate School of Education—Counseling/Clinical/School Psychology Program, at the University of California, Santa Barbara. He is President-elect of the California Association of School Psychologists. Mailing address: UCSB, Education, Santa Barbara, CA 93106.

Thomas Huberty, Ph.D., is an Associate Professor in the School Psychology Program at Indiana University Bloomington. Mailing address: Indiana University, School of Education, 910 State Road 46 Bypass, Bloomington, IN, 47405.

Cynthia Ann Hudley, Ph.D., is an Assistant Professor in the Graduate School of Education at the University of California, Santa Barbara. Mailing address: UCSB, Education, Santa Barbara, CA 93106.

Mitchell Karno is a doctoral student in the Counseling/Clinical/School Psychology Program at the University of California, Santa Barbara. Mailing address: UCSB, Education, Santa Barbara, CA 93106.

James Larson, Ph.D., is currently an Assistant Professor in the Psychology Department at the University of Wisconsin–Whitewater, where he is also Coordinator of the School Psychology Program. Mailing address: Psychology Department, University of Wisconsin–Whitewater, Whitewater WI 53190.

Ellen Lewis, Ph.D., presently manages integrated work and community living programs for the Institute for Applied Behavior Analysis. Mailing address: IABA, N. Lantana, Suite 245, Camarillo, CA 93010.

William McLain, M.A., works for Tri-Counties Regional Center conducting research on quality assurance systems, providing resource development, and coordinating quality assurance activities. Mailing address: Tri-Counties Regional Center, 5464 Carpinteria Ave., Suite B, Carpinteria, CA 93013.

Gloria Miller, Ph.D., is a Professor in the Department of Psychology at the University of South Carolina. Mailing address: U of SC, Department of Psychology, Barnwell College Blvd., Columbia, SC, 29208.

María Guadalupe Morales, M.Ed., is a school psychologist for the Oxnard Elementary School District, Oxnard, California.

Gale Morrison, Ph.D., is an Associate Professor in the Graduate School Of Education at the University of California, Santa Barbara. She is the coordinator of the school psychology specialization and is affiliated with the Development and Disability Program. Mailing address: UCSB, Education, Santa Barbara, CA 93106.

Rebecca Norton, M.Ed., is a school psychologist for the Santa Barbara School Districts, Santa Barbara, California.

W. S. Carlos Poston II, Ph.D., is a licensed health & rehabilitation psychologist. He recently completed an advanced fellowship in Health Psychology and Behavioral Medicine at Wilford Hall Medical Center in San Antonio, Texas. Mailing address, UCSB, CCSP-Education, Santa Barbara, CA 93106.

Michael Pullis, Ph.D., is a Professor in the Department of Special Education at the University of Missouri, Columbia. Mailing address: University of Missouri, Department of Special Education, Columbia, MO 65211.

Monica Sandowicz is a former teacher and is currently a doctoral student in the Counseling/Clinical/School Psychology Program at the University of California, Santa Barbara. Mailing address: UCSB, Education, Santa Barbara, CA 93106.

Douglas Smith, Ph.D., is the Director of the Master of Counseling Psychology Program at Chaminade University and Lecturer at the University of Hawaii, Manoa. Mailing Address: Chaminade University, MSCP, 3140 Waialae Ave., Honolulu, HI 96816.

Stephanie Stein, Ph.D., is an Assistant Professor in the Psychology Department at Central Washington University in Ellensberg, WA. Mailing address: Central Washington University, Psychology, Ellensberg, 98926.

PREFACE

The idea for this book was born as we were discussing our professional struggles to help children with serious emotional disturbances. It turned out that we both had experiences with a student much like Kimo (pseudonym). Kimo was big and burly, frequently used four-letter words to punctuate his opinions, and often crashed and bumped into other students only to announce, "Watch where you're going, $@3$&!!!!" In our discussions, it became more clear that Kimo's behavior was often not in reaction to specific trigger events, but due to a pervasive, chronic anger he seemed to carry with him. As we began to inform ourselves more about the role that anger plays in the lives of youth, we came to appreciate fully the complexities of issues involved in the experience and expression of anger. After we organized some of our research to share with our colleagues at conferences, we were somewhat surprised to see that this topic always drew large groups. Our discussions with these colleagues (school psychologists, special education teachers, school social workers, school counselors) revealed their pressing need for information about how to help youth with anger-related problems. This book was developed to address this perceived need.

We do not have to look far to see evidence of the great necessity in our society of helping youth learn how to handle their anger more effectively and express it in less violent ways. As is usually our custom when writing or speaking about youth and violence, we only have to go to the day's paper to get an example emphasizing this point. In today's *Los Angeles Times* (September 26, 1993) there is an article entitled, "Everyone Should Be Scared." It presents the results of a survey of high school students who were asked about their fear of violence on their school campuses. It highlights the feelings of one boy who was shot 2 weeks earlier while registering for classes—it was his first day of high school. After spending more than a week in intensive care he offered this perspective: "School should be a place to learn. It's a place where you can study hard and be somebody in your life, a place for you to get a good education. Not a place where you can get killed" (pp. D1-D3).

The experience of this Los Angeles area high school student is unfortunately not unusual (Furlong & Morrison, in press). Although violent crimes overall are not dramatically increasing in the United States, homicides among youth, particularly with handguns, have increased over the past several years. Homicide is now the #1 killer of young African-American males, and the homicide rate for all young American males is perversely high. During 1987, for example, there were 4,223 homicides of males ages 15–24 in the United States compared with just 398 in 14 other industrial countries combined (Fingerhut & Kleinman, 1990). Circumstances such as these influenced high school students in a recent national survey to indicate that violence is increasing in the streets (86%), in their schools (73%), and even in their homes (47%) (Harris, 1993). It is not surprising, therefore, that one of the Educate America 2000 goals (#6) is to create safe, disciplined, and drug-free schools. In addition, the Centers for Disease Control and Prevention is implementing efforts to achieve several of the Healthy People 2000 goals that pertain to youth violence (reducing weapons-related deaths, reducing weapons carrying, reducing the frequency of physical fights, and increasing the number of youth receiving conflict resolution training).

We believe that educators and mental health professionals who consult in school settings share a dual responsibility in helping society achieve these goals. First, comprehensive programs need to be developed, wherever possible, to reduce school violence risk factors. Second, we need to assume a leadership role in helping our youth learn the skills and knowledge they will need as adults to contribute to the reduction of violence in American society. We have come to believe that this effort is something that involves all educators and all students—this is not just about identifying youth who are aggressive and providing them with treatment. It is more fundamentally about helping our youth to manage their angry emotions, hostile attitudes, and tendencies to aggressive reactions more effectively. In fact, if we were to retitle this book, it might be appropriately called, "Helping ALL Youth Manage Anger, Hostility, and Aggression."

In this book, we have compiled information for intervention programs for youth who are felt to exhibit behaviors associated with conduct disorders or antisocial behavior patterns. It is important to note, however, that we feel the information is equally applicable for those engaged in the important task of developing prevention programs for youth anger management and aggression control. We have found, for example, that youth harboring chronic hostile attitudes are not uniquely those who are aggressive—some youth maintain a hostile world outlook but do not exhibit it as obviously as Kimo in our example above.

In attempting to provide a resource book for educators and mental health professionals who work in school settings, we have had the wonderful opportunity to work with a varied group of professionals. These authors provide a complementary blend of theory and empirical research findings about the role of anger, hostility, and aggression in youth. Several chapters are written by practitioners who provide a valued, balanced perspective for those chapters that present more traditional reviews of empirical findings. The content, structure, and organization of this book represent our belief that practitioners want information that has high utility, but they also want to be informed about the research findings that support prevention and intervention programs. We hope that our effort to strike a balance between practicality and professional-scientific review has been successful and that the material in this book will support your efforts to help ALL children more effectively manage their angry emotions and the cognitions and behaviors associated with them.

Michael J. Furlong
Santa Barbara, California

Douglas C. Smith
Honolulu, Hawaii

REFERENCES

Fingerhut, L. A., & Kleinman, J. C. (1990). International and interstate comparisons of homicide among young males. *Journal of the American Medical Association, 263*(24), 3292-3295.

Furlong, M. J., & Morrison, G. M. (in press). Introduction to miniseries: School violence and safety in perspective. *School Psychology Review.*

Harris, L. (1993). *A survey of experiences, perceptions, and apprehensions about guns among young people in America.* Prepared for the Harvard School of Public Health under a grant from the Joyce Foundations. New York: LH Associates.

Los Angeles Times. (1993, September 26). Everyone should be scared. D1-D3.

INTRODUCTION

PREVALENCE, DEFINITIONAL, AND CONCEPTUAL ISSUES

Michael J. Furlong and Douglas C. Smith

In the wake of recent urban unrest, most notably the civil unrest in Los Angeles, along with continued increasing violence in schools and society as a whole, researchers and clinicians in the social sciences have begun to focus on the role of anger and hostility as predictors of aggressive behavior among youth. It is a common perception today that violent behavior has reached epidemic proportions in our country and we are constantly bombarded by media accounts of yet another and more terrifying incident of gratuitous violence in the streets.

Schools too can no longer be regarded as "islands of safety" in this vast sea of impending danger (Furlong, Morrison, & Clontz, 1991, 1993; Harrington-Leuker, 1992). As early as 1978, the National Institute of Education, in its report entitled "Violent Schools - Safe Schools; The Safe School Study Report to the Congress" (National Institute of Education, 1978), indicated that:

- Approximately 282,000 students are physically attacked in America's secondary schools each month.
- Almost 8% of urban junior and senior high school students missed at least one day of classes a month because they were afraid to go to school.
- Nearly 5,200 of the nation's million secondary school teachers are physically attacked at school each month.

- Estimates of the annual cost of school crime, including vandalism, run from $50 million to $600 million (Turner, 1991).

More recent data from the National Crime Survey, 1985–1988 (National School Safety Center, 1991) revealed that almost half of the 1.9 million violent crimes committed each year against youth aged 12 to 19 occur on or around school grounds. Approximately 67 of every 1,000 teenagers in this country experience violent crimes each year and 12% of these crimes involve an offender with a weapon. Survey data from the Illinois Criminal Justice Information Authority indicated that 1 in 12 students had been the victim of a physical attack during the last school year and almost one third stated that they had, at some time during their high school career, brought a weapon to school for protection (National School Safety Center, 1991). It is also apparent that recent statistics reflect a significant upsurge in violent crimes on school campuses. In the Dade County (Florida) Public Schools, assaults in 1989–90 were up 9% over the previous year and robberies and thefts were up 12% (Crime Prevention Coalition, 1992). In Detroit, attacks against teachers increased 900% from 1985 to 1990, and 464 assaults against teachers were committed in New York City schools in 1989–90, up 34.9% over the previous year. A most sobering fact is that Stone (1993) reports 36 incidents of shootings or significant gun assaults on school campuses nationwide between September 7, 1992 and May 28, 1993. See Furlong (1994) and Furlong and Morrison (in press) for a detailed analysis of youth and school violence.

In response to the stress created by increasing violence, states such as California, Florida, South Carolina, and Minnesota have established school violence advisory panels to identify critical school safety needs and to set an agenda for training school personnel to be better prepared to respond to school violence. In addition, the American Psychological Association will shortly release a report by its own Youth and Violence Task Force.

At this point, it is difficult to know the extent to which increasing acts of violence are attributable to hostile attitudes or angry feelings. Nonetheless, the sheer frequency and nature of aggressive acts committed by both adults and children, along with society's reaction to such violence, argue convincingly for the need to expand preventative programs that specifically target aggressive behavior across a broad spectrum of attitudes, cognitions, and experiences and which themselves are further shaped by a wide range of contextual variables. The role of anger in such a framework is clearly worthy of further consideration.

DEFINITIONAL ISSUES

Physical and verbal aggression constitute one possible consequence of angry feelings; however, not all anger results in aggressive acts toward others, and aggressive behaviors are sometimes performed in the absence of emotional arousal (Berkowitz, 1990). Vitiello, Behar, Hunt, Stoff, and Ricciuti (1990) have distinguished between "predatory" and "affective" aggression. As the label implies, predatory aggression is thought to be planned, malicious, and designed with a clearly defined goal in mind. As such, it is similar to what Dodge (1991) calls "proactive" aggression, what Berkowitz (1990) labels "instrumental" aggression, and what Gadpaille (1984) labels "hostile" or "violent" aggression. Affective aggression, on the other hand, is generally regarded as an impulsive display of violent behavior that is perhaps less goal-oriented and more reactive in nature, often in response to perceived transgressions on the part of others. We argue that these constitute two distinct types of aggressive expressions and demand specific strategies in terms of both assessment and intervention. See Furlong & Smith (Chapter 7) for further discussion of this distinction.

Additionally, high degrees of emotional arousal, including arousal of anger, do not necessarily correspond to observable aggressive episodes (Spiro, 1978). At least two other possibilities exist. One is that anger and/or aggressive behavior may be suppressed or regulated through a variety of defense-oriented mechanisms (e.g., rationalization, denial) or through application of moral, conventional, or societal restrictions against such behavior (Miller & Sperry, 1987). Alternatively, anger may be expressed in nonaggressive, socially acceptable ways, often viewed as assertive in nature, which may vary markedly from culture to culture and even within cultural contexts (Averill, 1982; Gadpaille, 1984).

Numerous researchers (Barefoot, 1992; Musante, MacDougall, Dembroski, & Costa, 1989; Spielberger et al., 1985; Spielberger, Krasner, & Solomon, 1988) have commented on the multidimensional nature of anger and have identified three distinct components corresponding to cognitive, affective, and behavioral dimensions. These components, definitions, and key terms are depicted in Table I.1.

The cognitive or attitudinal component includes various negative beliefs about others and society at large such that the world is viewed as a threatening, dangerous place and others are perceived as antagonistic, selfish, untrustworthy, and potentially harmful. Barefoot (1992) refers to this constellation of beliefs as a "cynical world view." Similarly, Spielberger et al. (1985, 1988) describe the attitudes associated with this view, and particularly the attribution of negative intent on the part of others, as a pattern of "generalized hostility." Hostility and cynicism, though not necessarily interchangeable, have become popular and useful terms for describing the cognitive/attitudinal component of anger and have been linked to a wide range of negative physical and health-related outcomes including high blood pressure, coronary heart disease, and gastrointestinal difficulties (Barefoot, Dahlstrom, & Williams, 1983; Dembroski, MacDougall, Costa, & Grandits, 1989; Matthews, Glass, Rosenman, & Bortner, 1977; Shekelle, Gale, Ostfeld, & Paul, 1983; Williams & Williams, 1993).

The behavioral component of anger includes physical and verbal aggression as well as other antagonistic and hurtful responses. Additionally, anger may be expressed in more socially appropriate ways such as through assertive behavior or ritualistic aggression exemplified in some athletic events. Both Musante et al. (1989) and Spielberger et al. (1988) use the term "anger expression" to refer to behavioral manifestations of anger; this descriptor is preferable to aggression because it includes a much wider spectrum of coping responses in addition to the aforementioned aggressive responses. The affective component of anger includes emotional states ranging from mild annoyance to intense rage. Spielberger et al. (1988) label this range of emotions as the "experience" of anger. This term is general enough to include both affective and physiological aspects of arousal. For example, anger is often associated with sympathetic responses such as increased heart rate, higher blood pressure, pupil dilation, and shallow breathing (Williams & Williams, 1993).

Throughout this volume, the terms "anger," hostility," and "aggression" will be synonymous with emotional, cognitive or attitudinal, and behavioral components. It is becoming increasingly clear that anger should be viewed as a multidimensional construct composed of internal experiences and cognitions, more stable and consistent belief systems or attitudes, and a wide range of observable behaviors. Additionally, Barefoot (1992) suggests that although the different forms of anger may covary among individuals, it is conceivable that one may experience these various components either singularly or in various combinations. One could, for example, harbor general negative thoughts about others in the absence of angry emotions or overt aggressive behavior (Gadpaille, 1984). In stark contrast, a youth may murder someone in a drive-by shooting with little or no immediate emotional arousal.

TABLE I.1. COMPONENTS OF ANGER

Anger Components	Definitions	Key Terms
Anger Experience		
I. Emotional or Affective	• Refers to the range of feelings or emotional reactions experienced as a result of interference, goal-blocking, negative feedback, etc.	• Anger and its derivatives (e.g., annoyance, irritation, disgust, fury, rage, etc.)
Hostile Attitudes		
IIA. Situational	• Refers to social-cognitive processes whereby one interprets social situations and the actions of others in biased or inaccurate ways. Often this is situation- or person-specific.	• Social cognition, social intelligence, attributions, perceptions of intentionality
IIB. Chronic	• Refers to a belief system that characterizes the world and others as antogonistic, threatening, and inherently bad. This is a well-developed system of beliefs that essentially comprises a personality-like trait.	• Hostility, cynical outlook, cynicism
Anger Expression		
IIIA. Expression - Positive	• Refers to socially appropriate means of expressing anger and frustration.	• Coping responses, problem-solving
IIIB. Expression - Negative	• Refers to socially inappropriate methods for expressing anger and frustration.	• Physical and verbal aggression, passive-aggressive behavior
IIIC. Expression - Withdrawal	• Refers to denial and/or stifling of angry feelings and expression either positive or negative of it.	• Supression, repression

OVERVIEW AND STRUCTURAL FRAMEWORK

The purpose of this volume is to provide a comprehensive overview of the role of anger, hostility, and aggression in the lives of youth, with a particular emphasis on school-related behavior and learning problems. What is of critical importance for clinicians and educators who work with youth to understand is that the creation of prevention or intervention programs should be based upon a complex conceptualization of the factors affecting youth's anger. To help practitioners work toward this objective, Section I presents core concepts and issues about youth anger. Section II presents general information about the importance of understanding the contexts that can influence a youth's experience and expression of anger. Section III provides detailed information about projective, behavioral, and rating scale procedures to assess anger. Finally, Section IV presents descriptions of five different approaches that can be used in prevention or intervention programs.

To assist the reader in developing a framework from which to glean information from the book we offer the diagrams shown in Figures I.1. and I.2. Figure I.1 illustrates various factors that can broadly influence a program designed to increase a specific child's ability to experience and express anger in constructive ways. With respect to these broader influences on youth anger, Poston, Norton and Morales (Chapter 3) focus on possible biological influences on anger and aggression; Miller (Chapter 4) discusses the family's role in affecting anger; Pullis (Chapter 5) focuses on the school classroom setting; and Chan (Chapter 6) examines the role that cultural and economic forces can play in the way in which anger is experienced and expressed.

Figure I.2 illustrates a framework that can be used to guide the identification of a child's needs with respect to anger experience, anger expression, and hostile attitudes (attitude filter). The assessment and intervention chapters included in this book were selected to provide information about specific aspects of this framework. The careful, high-quality work of Hudley (Chapter 10) documents the effectiveness of the BrainPower program, a reattribution training program for youth who have difficulty processing social interaction information as shown in portions #1, #2, and #3 of Figure I.2. The review of social skill training programs by Morrison and Sandowicz (Chapter 11) provides invaluable information about interventions for youth who have difficulty with portions #6 and #7 of the framework. These youth may have difficulty developing and selecting prosocial

FIGURE I.1. CONTEXTUAL INFLUENCES FOR PREVENTION/INTERVENTION OF ANGER, HOSTILITY, AND AGGRESSION.

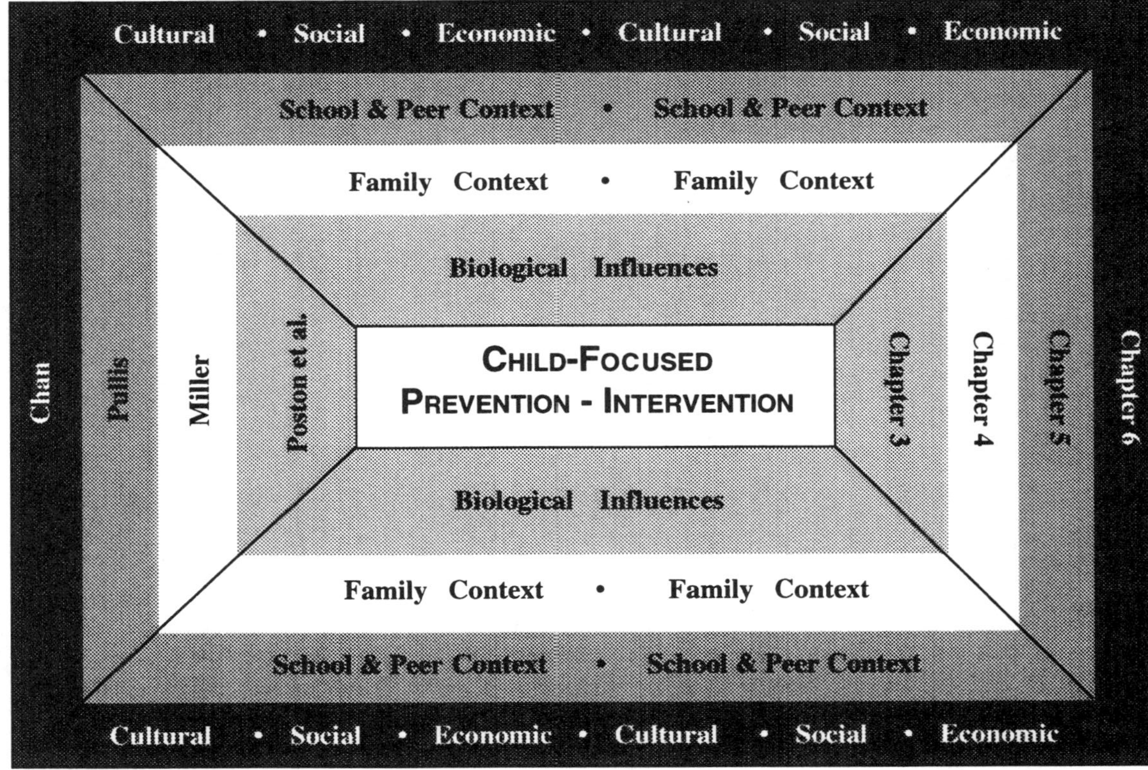

FIGURE I.2. ORGANIZATIONAL FRAMEWORK FOR PREVENTION/INTERVENTION PROGRAM PLANNING.

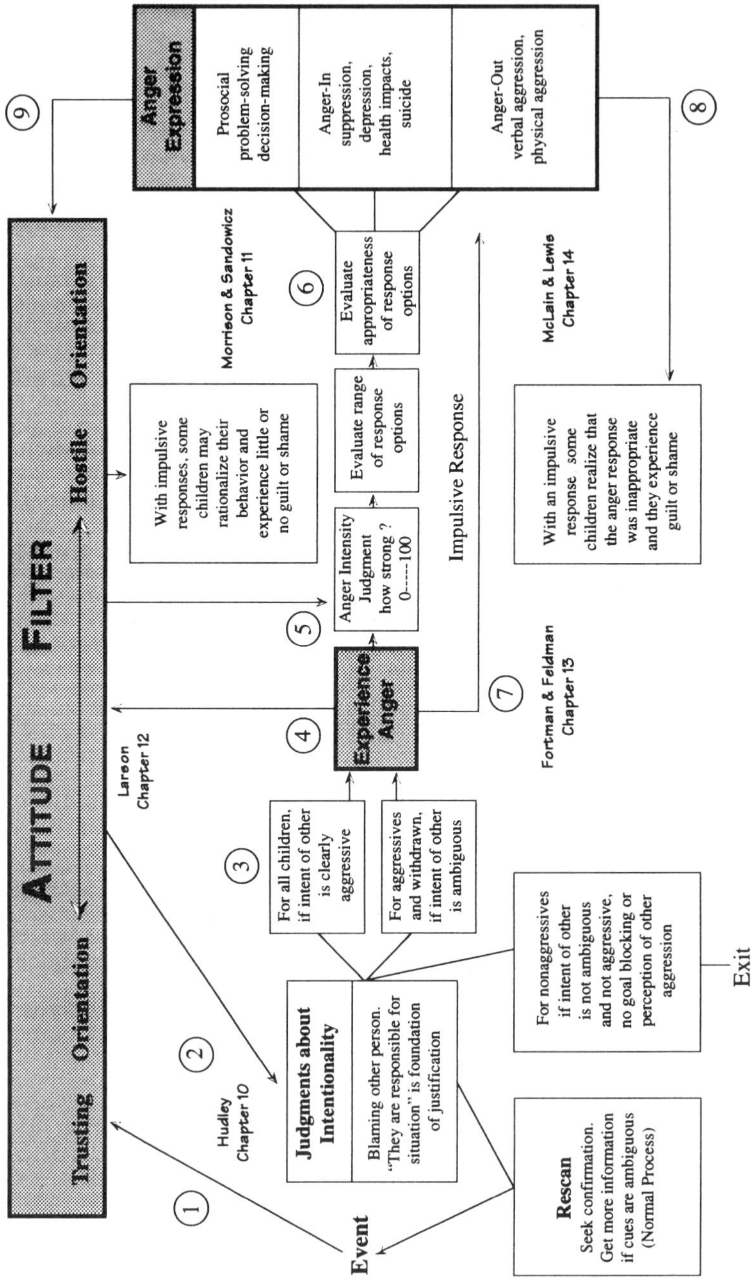

ways in which to express anger that they may experience. The very practical work by Larson (Chapter 12) presents information about how to carry out an anger group intervention based on cognitive-behavioral principles. This work offers useful insights for working with youth whose perceptions of others or events are negatively influenced by a hostile attitude. Fortman and Feldman (Chapter 13) present practical suggestions about how to help youth whose experience of anger is affected by impulsive expression, #7, #8, and #9 in Figure I.2. Finally, McLain & Lewis (Chapter 14) provide guidance for using an eclectic anger management program when working with youth who have developmental delays

In closing, we want to emphasize that the framework shown in Figures I.1 and I.2 is intended to convey the notion that various levels of intervention are possible when a youth is having anger-related difficulties. Assessment, prevention, and intervention strategies should be selected based upon each youth's particular strengths and deficits related to the cognitive, affective, and expressive aspects of anger.

REFERENCES

Averill, J. R. (1982). *Anger and aggression: An essay on emotion.* New York: Springer-Verlag.

Barefoot, J. C. (1992). Developments in the measurement of hostility. In H.S. Friedman (Ed.), *Hostility, coping, & health* (pp. 13-31). Washington, DC: American Psychological Association.

Barefoot, J. D., Dahlstrom, W. G., & Williams, R. B. (1983). Hostility, CHD incidence and total morality: A 25-year follow-up study of 255 physicians. *Psychosomatic Medicine, 45,* 59-63.

Berkowitz, L. (1990). On the formation and regulation of anger and aggression. *American Psychologist, 45,* 494-503.

Crime Prevention Coalition. (1992). Dade County schools target gun violence. *The Catalyst, 12,* 1-2.

Dembroski, T. M., MacDougall, J. M., Costa, P. T., & Grandits, G. A. (1989). Components of hostility as predictors of sudden death and myocardial infarction in the Multiple Risk Factor Intervention Trial. *Psychosomatic Medicine, 51,* 514-522.

Dodge, K. A. (1991). The structure and function of reactive and proactive aggression. In D. Peppler & K. Rubin (Eds.), *The development and treatment of childhood aggression* (pp. 201-218.). Hillsdale, NJ: Lawrence Erlbaum.

Furlong, M. J. (1994, Winter).Evaluating school violence trends. *School Safety,* p. 23-27.

Furlong, M. J., Morrison, R. M., & Clontz, D. (1991). Broadening the scope of school safety. *School Safety,* Spring, 8-11.

Furlong, M. J., Morrison, R. M., & Clontz, D. (1993). Planning principles for safe schools. *School Safety,* Spring, 23-27.

Gadpaille, W. J. (1984). Adolescent aggression from the perspective of cultural anthropology. In C. P. Keith (Ed.), *The aggressive adolescent: Clinical perspectives* (pp. 432-454). New York: Collier MacMillan.

Harrington-Lueker, D. (1992). Blown away by school violence. *The American School Board Journal, 179,* 20-26.

Matthews, K. A., Glass, D. C., Rosenman, R. H., & Bortner, R. W. (1977). Competitive drive, Pattern A, and coronary heart disease: A further analysis of some data from the Western Collaborative Group Study. *Journal of Chronic Diseases, 30,* 489-498.

Miller, P., & Sperry, L. L. (1987). The socialization of anger and aggression. *Merrill-Palmer Quarterly, 33,* 1-3.

Morrison, G. M., Furlong, M. J., & Morrison, R. M. (in press). School violence to school safety: Redefining the issue for school psychologists. *School Psychology Review.*

Musante, L., MacDougall, J. M., Dembroski, T. M., & Costa, P. T. (1989). Potential for hostility, anger-in and the two dimensions of anger. *Health Psychology, 8,* 343-354.

National School Safety Center. (1991, October). Annual study shows 3 million crimes on school campuses. *School Safety Update,* 1-2.

Shekelle, R. B., Gale, M., Ostfeld, A. M., & Paul, O. (1983). Hostility, risk of coronary heart disease, and mortality. *Psychosomatic Medicine, 45,* 109-114.

Spielberger, C. D., Johnson, E. H., Russell, S. E., Crane, R. J., Jacobs, G. A., & Worden. T. J. (1985). The experience and expression of anger: Construction and validation of an anger expression scale. In M. A. Chesney & R. H. Rosenman (Eds.), *Anger and hostility in cardiovascular and behavioral disorders* (pp. 5-29). New York: Hemisphere.

Spielberger, C.D., Krasner, S.S., & Solomon, E.P. (1988). The experience, expression, and control of anger. In M. P. Janisse (Ed.), *Health psychology: Individual differences and stress* (pp. 89-108). New York: SpringerVerlag.

Spiro, M. E. (1978). Culture and human nature. In G. D. Spindler (Ed.), *The making of psychological anthropology* (pp. 331-359). Berkeley, CA: University of California Press.

Stone, A. (1993, June 3). Kids, guns: 'It's shoot or be shot.' *USA Today,* lA, 2A, 6A.

Turner, B. (1991). Children are our future. *School Safety,* Spring, 4-7.

Vitiello, B., Behar, D., Hunt, J., Stoff, D., & Ricciuti, A. (1990). Subtyping aggression in children and adolescents. *Journal of Neuropsychology and Clinical Neurosciences, 2,* 189-192.

Williams, R., & Williams, V. (1993). *Anger kills.* New York: Times Books.

SECTION I

CORE CONCEPTS OF ANGER, HOSTILITY, AND AGGRESSION IN YOUTH

This section of the book presents key definitional and conceptual issues that are important to understanding anger in the lives of youth. Chapter 1, by Smith and Furlong, discusses research pertaining to how anger, hostility, and aggression impact the lives of both children and adults. A particular emphasis of this chapter is the idea that anger can have a negative impact on the lives of many youth, not just those who express their anger through aggression. Physical, emotional, social, and cultural impacts are presented. Chapter 2, by Hudley, presents a review of research about how children's attributional reasoning processes can affect aggressive behavior. This theoretic perspective is highlighted because it is one of the few aspects of youth anger and aggression that has received careful research attention.

1 CORRELATES OF ANGER, HOSTILITY, AND AGGRESSION IN CHILDREN AND ADOLESCENTS

Douglas C. Smith and Michael J. Furlong

INTRODUCTION

The origins, manifestation, and regulation of anger have long been of interest to philosophers, theologians, and historians who have been intrigued by this complex human emotion. In the wake of recent urban unrest, most notably the Los Angeles rebellion, along with continued increasing violence in schools and society at large, researchers and clinicians in the social sciences have begun to focus on the role of anger and hostility as predictors of aggressive behavior among youth. Although viewed by many as a primary emotion (Izard, 1977; Madow, 1972), surprisingly little is known about the subjective experience of anger, its developmental sequence, and factors involved in its expression or suppression. This is the case despite the fact that anger and its regulation may play a crucial role in many aspects of one's life including interpersonal relationships, physical and mental well-being, vocational success, and general life satisfaction (Diamond, 1982; Friedman, 1992; Novaco, 1975; Williams & Williams, 1993).

The purpose of this chapter is to review research relating anger, hostility, and aggression to a wide range of outcome variables including physical and emotional health status, social relationships, and academic performance. As will be seen, much of the research is correlational in nature, making causal interpretations problematic. Nonetheless, an impressive body of data continues to accumulate implicating components of anger, hostility, and aggression in the development and manifestation of a variety of physical and emotional problems including cardiovascular disorders, internalizing and externalizing problems of adjustment, negative social status, and poor school performance. We will review results of studies that examine these relationships with particular emphasis on child and adolescent findings.

Anger and Physical Health

In this section, we briefly review the large body of data that has accumulated linking various components of anger to a wide range of health concerns including hypertension, coronary heart disease (CHD), cancer, gastrointestinal difficulties, and asthma. The relationship between anger and hypertension was initially hypothesized by Alexander (1939), who speculated that chronic activation of the autonomic and cardiovascular system was responsible for increases in blood pressure, and this was particularly likely to occur when angry feelings were habitually suppressed. In the past several years, findings from both prospective and cross-sectional studies have lent credibility to the notion that frequent and intense arousal of angry feelings and hostile attitudes and cognitions increases one's risk for physical illness including CHD and particularly hypertension and atherosclerosis (Dembroski, MacDougall, Costa, & Grandits, 1989; Friedman, 1991; Hokanson & Sheter, 1961; Kahn, Medalie, Neufeld, Riss, & Goldbourt, 1972; Shekelle, Gale, Ostfeld, & Paul, 1983; Siegel, 1984; Williams & Barefoot, 1988; Williams, Haney, Lee, Kong, Blumenthal, & Whalen, 1980; Williams & Williams, 1993) and cancer (Derogatis, Abeloff, & Melisaratos, 1979; Shekelle et al., 1983). Perhaps less well substantiated, but gaining support in the literature, is the notion that suppression of angry feelings is the real culprit in this linkage (Barefoot, 1992; Diamond, 1982; Harburg, Blakelock, & Roeper, 1979).

Two oft-cited major prospective studies linking the Type A behavior pattern (Friedman & Rosenman, 1959), which includes characteristics like competitiveness, high need for achievement, hurried pace, and frequent expressions of anger and hostility, to CHD were conducted in California and Massachusetts. The first of these, the Western Collaborative Group Study (Rosenman et al., 1975; Rosenman et al., 1964), followed a group of 3,500 middle-aged males and, controlling for such factors as age, blood pressure, cigarette smoking, and serum cholesterol level, demonstrated that those subjects classified as Type A on the basis of personality assessment were more than twice as likely as those classified as Type B to develop coronary heart disease. Further, the aspect of Type A most often implicated in this finding was the presence of high levels of anger and hostility (Matthews, Glass, Rosenman, & Bortner, 1977; Siegel, 1985; Williams & Williams, 1993). The Framingham Heart Study (Haynes, Feinlieb, & Kannel, 1978; Haynes, Feinlieb, Levine, Scotch & Kannel, 1980), a second major prospective study, indicated that those individuals tending to suppress or withhold expression of angry feelings were at high risk for CHD.

The relationship between Type A personality traits in children and various psychophysiological measures has been the subject of studies by several investigators. Lawler, Allen, Critcher, and Standard (1981) studied 11- and 12-year-old children classified as Type A or B on the basis of either behavioral measures or observer ratings. Type A children, in general, demonstrated higher systolic blood pressure levels and greater heart rate and blood pressure reactivity during competitive tasks accompanied by small monetary incentives than did Type B children. Matthews and Jennings (1984) studied cardiovascular reactivity to a set of competitive computer games in a sample of 4th- and 5th-grade boys, again classified as Type A or B on the basis of structured interviews and observer ratings. Results again suggested greater heart rate and blood pressure reactivity during the course of a competitive game for Type A boys. Finally, Lundberg (1983) measured blood pressure and heart rate changes during physically and emotionally challenging games in a sample of 3- to 6-year-old boys. Consistent with other findings, boys classified as Type A on the basis of observers' ratings tended to show greater blood pressure reactivity on physically challenging tasks than Type B boys. Taken together, the results of these studies support the idea that certain psychophysiological responses thought to be characteristic of CHD may have their origin in behavior patterns established relatively early in life.

In the past decade, numerous studies have further investigated the hypothesized relationship between anger, hostility, and aggression and physical illness. Barefoot, Dahlstrom, and Williams (1983), in a 25-year follow-up study of 255 male physicians who were administered the Minnesota Multiphasic Personality Inventory (MMPI), found those subjects scoring above the median on the Cook-Medly Hostility (Ho) scale (Cook & Medley, 1954) to be six times more likely to die of all causes over the course of the study than those scoring below the median. Similarly, Barefoot et al. (1987) used the suspiciousness scale of the Sixteen Factor Personality

Questionnaire (Cattell, Eber, & Tatsuoka, 1970) to significantly predict 15-year mortality risk in a sample of males and females.

In a study of 288 male factory workers between the ages of 10 and 65, Siegel (1992) utilized the Multidimensional Anger Inventory (MAI) (Siegel, 1986), which assesses emotional, attitudinal, and behavioral components of anger. The criterion variable in this case was diastolic blood pressure. Included in the regression equation, in addition to the anger measures, was a self-report measure of anxiety, the State-Trait Anxiety Inventory (Spielberger, Gorsuch, & Lushene, 1970). Results indicated that the combination of high hostile outlook and high anxiety was significantly, though modestly, related to higher blood pressure readings. In another study of 364 female children and adolescents, ages 10 to 17, Siegel (1992) tested the relationship between anger (again measured by the MAI), stress, self-esteem, and measures of both physical and mental health. Although all zero-order correlations reached statistical significance, partial correlations revealed that only stress was significantly related to physical health when the effects of the other variables were parceled out ($r = .24, p > .0001$). For the mental health outcome variable (in this case depression), partial correlations indicated that high anger and stress and low self-esteem each contributed significantly and uniquely to the prediction of depression.

In a large-scale (5,115 subjects) investigation of the relationship between hostility and "consumptive behaviors" reported by Scherwitz and Rugilies (1992), high scores on the Ho Scale were significantly and positively related to cigarette and marijuana use, alcohol intake among drinkers, caloric intake, and extent of obesity. In general, high hostility scores were more prevalent among African-Americans in the sample, those with less education, males, and younger subjects. Hostility scores were not significantly correlated with caffeine use, amount of exercise, use of leisure time, and cholesterol level. Nonetheless, the authors suggest that individuals experiencing high levels of hostility tend to engage more readily in consumptive life-styles marked by excessive eating, drinking, smoking, and substance abuse (Williams & Williams, 1993), all of which are vulnerability markers for youth.

The question of whether it is more detrimental physically to express or suppress angry feelings has been the subject of numerous investigations, primarily by researchers within medical settings. As mentioned earlier, Alexander (1939) hypothesized that suppression of angry feelings was primarily responsible for chronic activation of the cardiovascular system and resulting elevations in blood pressure. Psychodynamically oriented theorists have long described a repressive personality type who frequently defends him/herself against threatening feelings such as anxiety or anger by employing a wide assortment of defense mechanisms designed to deny, distort, or otherwise minimize unwanted affects (Emmons, 1992). Funkenstein, King, and Drolette (1954) introduced the terms "anger-in" and "anger-out" to refer to the two extremes by which one handles angry feelings. *Anger-In* refers to the tendency to suppress emotional reactions or to direct negative affect toward the self (e.g., blame oneself for negative outcomes; Averill, 1982; Tavris, 1982). *Anger-Out* refers to the tendency to express anger either verbally or nonverbally toward others or the environment (Spielberger, Johnson, Russell, Crane, Jacobs, & Worden, 1985). Several investigators (Gentry, Chesney, Gary, Hall, & Harburg, 1982; Harburg et al., 1979) have found higher blood pressure levels and greater degrees of hypertension among individuals prone to express their anger inwardly versus those prone to express their anger outwardly.

In early studies examining anger expression, Hokanson (1961a, 1961b) and Hokanson and Burgess (1962) found increases in blood pressure as a result of frustration within laboratory settings, but corresponding decreases in blood pressure for their male subjects given an opportunity to aggress against equal- or low-status perpetrators. When the perpetrator was high status or fear of retaliation was relatively high, subjects engaged in less counteraggression and blood pressure generally remained high. It may be that hypertensive individuals experience high levels of guilt with regard to aggression and thereby suppress such behavior, thus failing to experience a subsequent release of tension. Interestingly, aggressive counterresponses were not effective in reducing blood pressure for female subjects. It may be that social and cultural expectations mitigating against overtly aggressive behavior in females actually increase levels of guilt for females choosing to vent their anger in this manner.

Prospective data from the Framingham study cited earlier (Haynes et al., 1980) also suggested that men who denied expressing anger were at substantially higher risk for CHD than their more expressive peers. Barefoot (1992), utilizing a structured interview format, found a strong association between "indirect" expressions of hostility and heart disease among males. Further, there is a growing body of evidence (see Pennebaker, 1992, and Emmons, 1992, for reviews) that chronic repression of negative affect, including anger, may be related to a broader range of negative health consequences including cancer, asthma, excessive cholesterol levels, ulcers, irritable bowel syndrome, and insomnia. Conversely, when individuals are taught to verbalize or write about frustrating experiences and negative feelings, there is a greater likelihood of symptom remission or reduction.

Not all studies have supported the proposition that direct expression of one's anger serves to reduce tension and enhance facets of physical and mental health. Some investigators have suggested that anger expression, even when done in socially appropriate ways, serves to justify and perhaps exacerbate angry feelings. Mallick and McCandless (1966) found that children who were encouraged to express their anger toward peers who had upset them, later disliked the offending peer more than a control group who were not allowed to express anger. Similarly, Ebbesen, Duncan, and Konecni (1975) measured attitudes toward their employers among groups of aerospace workers who had been recently laid off. Those workers who were encouraged to ventilate their angry feelings maintained higher degrees of anger thereafter than workers who did not ventilate. In some situations, then, it appears that expressing anger may serve to increase rather than decrease emotional arousal, thus contradicting the commonly held notion that anger release is desirable, as in the steam kettle analogy. Furthermore, engaging in anger-expressive behaviors, particularly of a more violent nature, may result in guilt which may further exacerbate angry feelings (McKay, Rogers, & McKay, 1989). Siegel's (1992) study of male factory workers discussed earlier in this chapter supports this perspective because she found that outward expression of anger was related to low levels of blood pressure only when it was accompanied by low anxiety as well. Harburg et al. (1973) also found a lower prevalence of hypertension in high anger-out subjects, again only when accompanied by low guilt.

Siegel (1992) and others (e.g., Antonovsky, 1990) argue that the relationship between anger expression and physical disorders must be examined in the context of intervening psychosocial variables. Such variables as low self-esteem, lack of social support networks, and emotional reactions such as guilt or anxiety may serve to make one particularly vulnerable to the effects of anger expression or suppression. Additionally, the relationship between anger expression/suppression and both physical and mental health may not be linear in nature (Scherwitz & Rugulies, 1992). Harburg et al. (1979), for example, speculated that those most at risk for health problems are at each extreme of the anger expression/suppression continuum. Further, it is likely that chronically angry or hostile individuals both express and suppress significant amounts of anger, thus confounding studies attempting to classify individuals as essentially anger "suppressors" or anger "expressors."

In an effort to better specify the complex nature of anger and its associated variables, Siegel (1985) has proposed that anger and its effects on health be examined within a multidimensional framework. Within her model, anger experience can be measured in terms of its frequency, duration, magnitude, and range of anger-producing situations. Hostile outlook and mode of anger expression/suppression can also be included in a multidimensional assessment (see Furlong and Smith, Chapter 7 for a discussion of multidimensional anger assessment). The advantage of such a system would be to provide a more detailed and specific analysis of anger, presumably increasing predictive utility and providing greater treatment specificity.

Recently, Smith and Christensen (1992) have proposed four explanatory models purporting to clarify the relationships between dimensions of anger and hostility and various indices of physical health. Briefly, these are as follows:

Psychophysiological reactivity model. This model suggests that high hostile persons experience elevated levels of cardiovascular and endocrine responses, which may contribute to development of disease. Current research suggests that this link may exist for anger problems of an interpersonal nature but is not necessarily true for impersonal problems.

Psychosocial vulnerability model. This model suggests that high hostile persons may experience a greater number of interpersonal conflicts with others both at home and at work or school. As a result, these individuals have fewer and less stable social support networks, which may also contribute to development of disease.

Transactional model. High hostile individuals tend to elicit similar reactions from others. Thus, a reciprocal relationship is established that tends to confirm the individual's view of the world as an uncaring place. This, in turn, leads to greater levels of stress and conflict.

Health behavior model. People who experience high degrees of hostility tend to have less healthy life-styles. They tend to smoke and drink more, exercise less, and otherwise engage in unhealthy behaviors.

Smith and Christensen's framework stresses the complexity and interactional nature of the relationship between hostility and health factors. High degrees of anger and hostility are often associated with interpersonal difficulties, lack of social support, problems with self-esteem, high levels of stress, and poor coping skills. Future studies need to address these mediating variables and, at the same time, specify which dimensions of anger are being measured. The majority of studies have relied on subjects' self-reports of anger and hostility. More naturalistic studies are needed that examine anger experience, attitudes, and the behaviors associated with them as well as developmental studies of anger in children.

It seems apparent now, however, that enough is known about anger's association with adult health outcomes to provide significant incentive for those working with youth who manifest anger-related problems. Adult life-styles associated with chronic anger are established in childhood and adolescence. Youth who are disturbing to adults because of aggression or other anger-related externalizing conditions need more than corrective procedures intended to change "bad attitudes." The health-related research cited here suggests that these individuals may be prone to have significant long-term emotional and physical health needs that can be overlooked because of the more obvious disturbing effects of their behavior. Further-more, there are other youth who may not be disturbing to adults, but for whom anger also has long-term negative developmental effects. For these youth, anger may be consistently repressed and lead to the formation of a habitual pattern of keeping anger in, which may have even more detrimental health outcomes. In summary, both increased levels of violence in our society and negative health/developmental effects provide good reasons to help youth learn how to cope more effectively with the cognitive, affective, and behavioral components of anger.

Anger and Emotional Status

Anger in the DSM–III–R. Anger is a noteworthy characteristic in a wide range of adult and childhood psychiatric disorders. Interestingly, despite its status as a primary human emotion, high frequency of occurrence, and potentially debilitating effects on social and psychological adjustment, anger and its related disorders have a less than prominent place in mental health diagnostic systems. Within the *Diagnostic and Statistical Manual of Mental Disorders III-Revised (DSM-III-R;* American Psychiatric Associa-tion, 1987) there is no major category of anger-related affective disorders rivaling those of other major emotional dysfunctions (i.e., mood disorders and anxiety disorders). Rather, anger symptomatology is interwoven within a broad spectrum of disorders prominent in both children and adolescents. Table 1.1 presents anger-related symptomatology of *DSM-III-R* disorders, including diagnostic criteria and associated features and descriptors, that are applicable to youth. An inspection of the table reveals that irritability is a prominent feature of all the major mood disorders including bipolar disor-ders and depressive disorders. Additionally, negativistic or antisocial behavior and aggression are associated features of adolescent mood disorders. In adjustment disorders involving disturbance of emotions or conduct, often there is violation of the rights of others including aggressive behavior or persistent anger. In many of the personality disorders, which may be applicable to older adolescents, hostile attitudes or violent, aggressive behavior, and inappropriate or intense anger are common characteristics. This applies to the following personality disorders: paranoid, antisocial, borderline, histrionic, narcissistic, and borderline. Aggressiveness, poor impulse control, and intense anger and hostility are likewise characteristic of a broad range of disorders involving abuse or withdrawal from alcohol or other drugs. Clearly, this is a diagnostic category of extreme importance for those working with adolescents. Intermittent explosive disorder is defined primarily by discrete episodes of loss of control of aggressive impulses. In children and adolescents, both oppositional and conduct disorders are defined primarily by aggressive or destructive behaviors, temper tantrums, and high degrees of anger and resentment. Finally, both separation anxiety disorder and elective mutism in children often result in temper tantrums and other forms of oppositional behaviors. In examining the diagnostic categories, it becomes clear that the emotional experience of anger, hostile attitudes/cognitions, and aggressive behavior are frequently characteristics of a wide range of childhood and adolescent psychiatric disorders.

Anger and comorbidity. Given this broad manifestation of anger as a diagnostic symptom, we now review some empirical work about the "comorbidity" of anger and depression, disruptive behavior disorders, and school achievement.

Garber, Quiggle, Danak, and Dodge (1991) define comorbidity as *"the co-occurrence of two or more syndromes in the same individual at the same point in time"* (p. 226). With regard to anger and its components, comorbidity has been studied in populations diagnosed as depressed (Altman & Gotlib, 1988; Edelbrock & Achenbach, 1980; Marriage, Fine, Moretti, & Haley, 1986; Riley, Treiber, & Woods, 1989), anxious (McCranie, 1971), hyperactive (Sanberg, Wieselberg, & Shaffer, 1980; Shapiro & Garfinkel, 1986), and learning disabled (Cornwall & Bawden, 1992; Keilitz & Dunivant, 1986; Larson, 1988). In an effort to focus on those studies with primary relevance to children and adolescents, we will limit our discussion to comorbidity between anger and both depression and school learning problems.

Garber et al. (1991) reviewed a number of studies assessing the degree of comorbidity between conduct disorders, which normally have a highly

DSM-III-R Diagnostic Code	Mental Disorder	Diagnostic Criteria	Associated Features and Descriptions
Mood Disorders (Depressive)			
296.2x	Major depression, single episode	1) Irritable mood	• Irritability, negativistic or frankly antisocial behavior; grouchiness and aggression; sulkiness
296.3x	Major depression, recurrent	Same	
300.40	Dysthymia	Same	
Mood Disorders (Bipolar)			
296.6x	Bipolar disorder, mixed	1) Irritable mood	• Irritability, negativistic or frankly antisocial behavior; grouchiness and aggression; sulkiness, labile mood with rapid shifts to anger
296.4x	Bipolar disorder, manic	Same	
296.5x	Bipolar disorder, depressed	Same	
301.13	Cyclothymia	Same	
Dissociative Disorders			
300.13	Psychogenic fugue	None	• Occasional outbursts of violence against property or another person
Adjustment Disorders			
309.30	Adjustment disorder with disturbance of conduct	None	• Anger • Violation of rights of others or societal norms, e.g., fighting
309.40	Adjustment disorder with mixed disturbance of emotional conduct	None	
309.28	Adjustment disorder with mixed emotional features	None	
Personality Disorders			
301.00	Paranoid Personality Disorder	1) Expects, without sufficient basis, to be exploited or harmed by others 2) Reads hidden demeaning or threatening meanings into benign remarks or events	• None

Table 1.1. DSM-III-R Anger-Related Diagnostic Symptoms and Characteristics for Children and Adolescents.

DSM-III-R Diagnostic Code	Mental Disorder	Diagnostic Criteria	Associated Features and Descriptions
		3) Bears grudges or is unforgiving of insults or slights 4) Is easily slighted and quick to react with anger or to counterattack	
301.70	Antisocial Personality Disorder	1) Is irritable and aggressive, as indicated by repeated physical fights or assaults including spouse- or child-beating 2) Lacks remorse (feels justified in having hurt, mistreated, or stolen from another)	• Violation of the rights of others of major age-appropriate, societal norms, e.g., vandalism, fighting
301.83	Borderline Personality Disorder	1) Affective instability-irritability 2) Inappropriate, intense anger or lack of control of anger, e.g., frequent displays of temper, constant anger, recurrent physical fights	• Anger • Usually argumentative and exaggerate difficulties; have a tendency to counterattack when they perceive any threat; often viewed as hostile, stubborn, and defensive • Conviction that others are hostile toward them
301.50	Histrionic Personality Disorder	1) Expresses emotion with inappropriate exaggeration, e.g., has temper tantrums	• None

DSM-III-R Diagnostic Code	Mental Disorder	Diagnostic Criteria	Associated Features and Descriptions
301.81	Narcissistic Personality Disorder	1) Reacts to criticism with feelings of rage, shame, or humiliation	• None
301.84	Passive Aggressive Personality Disorder	1) Becomes sulky, irritable, or argumentative when asked to do something he or she does not want to do	• When unable to control others, a situation, or the environment, they often ruminate about the situation and become angry, although the anger is usually not expressed directly
Impulse Control Disorders			
312.34	Intermittent Explosive Disorder	1) Several discrete episodes of loss of control of aggressive impulses resulting in several assaultive acts or destruction of property 2) The degree of aggressiveness expressed during the episodes is grossly out of proportion to any precipitating psychosocial stressors	• Violent or aggressive behavior is common, and restraint may be required
Organic Mental Syndromes and Disorders			
292.81	Cocaine Delirium	1) Irritability, frustration, or anger	• Irritability
292.11	Cocaine Delusional Disorder		• Same
292.00	Nicotine withdrawal		• Same
292.00	Opioid withdrawal		• Same
303.00	Alcohol Intoxication		• Same

DSM-III-R Diagnostic Code	Mental Disorder	Diagnostic Criteria	Associated Features and Descriptions
Disruptive Behavior Disorders			
314.01	Attention-deficit Hyperactivity Disorder (ADHD)	None	• Temper outbursts and low frustration tolerance, e.g., butts into other children's games
312.20 312.00 312.90	Conduct Disorder, Group Conduct Disorder, Solitary Aggressive Conduct Disorder, Undifferentiated	1) Deliberate firesetting 2) Deliberate destruction of others' property 3) Forced sexual activity 4) Used weapons in more than one fight and/or frequent initiation of physical fights 5) Has been physically cruel to people 6) Stealing with confrontation	• Physical aggression is common, initiates aggression, poor frustration tolerance, temper outbursts, provocative recklessness, impulsiveness
313.81	Oppositional Defiant Disorder	1) Frequently lose tempers 2) Often angry, resentful, and easily annoyed by others 3) Low frustration tolerance and temper outbursts; irritability	• Low frustration tolerance and temper outbursts; irritability
Anxiety Disorders of Childhood or Adolescents			
309.21	Separation Anxiety Disorder	None	• Temper tantrums or crying, pleading with parents not to leave
Other Disorders of Infancy of Adolescents			
313.23	Elective Mutism	None	• Negativism, temper tantrums, or other oppositional behavior may be observed

From American Psychiatric Association. (1987). *Diagnostic and statistical manual of mental disorders* (3rd ed., rev.). Washington, DC: Author. Copyright 1987 American Psychiatric Association. Adapted by permission.

aggressive component, and depression in children from 5 to 18 years old. The majority of these studies begin with a population of clinically depressed youngsters and subsequently examine the co-occurrence of conduct disorder. Rates of comorbidity in these studies showed that between 8% and 37% of the youngsters who were diagnosed as depressed also carried a diagnosis of conduct disorders. It is not clear from these data how many of the depressed youth may have been eligible for a primary or secondary diagnosis of conduct disorder but had not as yet been so diagnosed. Given this possibility, it is likely that the percentages reported by Garber et al. are a low estimate of the degree of overlap between these diagnoses. In a few studies reviewed by Garber et al. (1991), investigators began with a population of conduct-disordered youth and calculated the percentage of them having an additional diagnosis of depression. These studies reported a comorbidity range of between 10% and 30%. Again, this is likely to be a low estimate of actual comorbidity because some youngsters with a conduct disorder who fit the *DSM-III-R* criteria for a mood disorder may simply have been overlooked.

In addition to understanding the extent of comorbidity within clinical populations, it is important to develop an awareness of the characteristics of children who fit such a profile. Garber et al. (1991) studied social-cognitive processes of 220 children (grades 3-6) attending public schools who, although not carrying a psychiatric diagnosis, were categorized as high on the Aggression subscale of the Child Behavior Checklist (CBCL) (Achenbach & Edelbrock, 1983, 1986) and also scored high on the parent version of the Children Depression Inventory (Kovacs & Beck, 1977), or a depression scale based on the teacher version of the CBCL. Findings indicated that students identified as scoring high on both aggression and depression showed information-processing patterns that were similar to those demonstrated by either aggressive or depressed youngsters. That is, they tended to view others with hostile intent and either endorse aggression or withdrawal as response options in social problem situations. Additionally, the comorbid group tended to generate more "pure affect" responses; that is, they tended to report how they would "feel" in response to questions about how they would react in problem situations. Finally, children high in both aggression and depression tended to have lower expectations for success utilizing assertive responses and higher expectations for success utilizing aggressive responses than children classified solely as high in depression or aggression. Overall, it appears that children identified as both depressed and aggressive share some common social-cognitive patterns with children scoring high on either factor, but also may tend to demonstrate more severe processing errors in their understanding of social situations.

The relationship between anger and depression has a rich history in psychodynamic theory. Within this view, anger is a response to increased tension, discomfort, or frustration and serves as a means of release from this tension (Rubin, 1969). However, anger is often perceived as a negative emotion and is blocked or suppressed for a variety of reasons. Defense mechanisms such as denial, projection, displacement, and rationalization are used to suppress anger. According to psychodynamic theory, suppression of anger can result in anxiety, depression, and other psychological and physical conditions, including many of those discussed earlier in this chapter. Riley et al. (1989) examined the relationship between anger and depression in normal, clinically depressed, and post traumatic stress disordered (PTSD) adult samples. Using Siegel's (1985) Multidimensional Anger Inventory, results indicated greater suppression of anger on the part of the depressed group than either PTSD or normal samples. Depressed subjects also tended to express anger at or below the level of normal subjects. The authors interpreted their study as lending support to the psychodynamic view that depression is associated with an inhibition or suppression of angry feelings.

An alternative view of the relationship between anger and depression has been put forth by Berkowitz (1989). According to this cognitive-neoassociationistic theory, negative affect (e.g., depression) can stimulate anger arousal and aggressive behavior. In this view, both internal events, such as cognitive distortions, and external events, such as insults or provocation by others, can trigger anger and aggression. A study reported by Hyman and Grush (1986) involved 80 undergraduate males who were classified as either impulsive or reflective. Subjects either were praised or criticized by a confederate and then subjected to a laboratory procedure designed to induce either feelings of depression or neutral mood. The dependent measure in this study was the amount of aggression displayed by the subjects toward a confederat. Results lend general support to Berkowitz's model of anger and aggression arousal. As expected, subjects who were provoked aggressed more than those who were unprovoked. Impulsive subjects who were depressed tended to display the greatest amount of aggression toward the confederate. Although external provocation is clearly one source of aggressive behavior, it appears that internal states, as well as self-control factors, also play major roles in determining the extent and duration of aggression.

Anger and Social and Educational Status

The difficulties in interpersonal relationships experienced by angry, aggressive children have been well documented in the literature (Asher & Gottman, 1981; Bierman, 1986; Cantrell & Prinz, 1985; Shantz, 1986). Aggressive children are often avoided or rejected be peers. Further, aggressive, antisocial behavior appears to be a relatively stable trait, with aggressive children often continuing to exhibit aggressive behaviors throughout their lives (Loeber, 1991; Olweus, 1979).

Although reasons for rejection of aggressive, angry children by their peers are undoubtedly varied and complex, much of the current research in this area has focused on social information processing deficits. Aggressive children display a range of specific cognitive deficits and/or differences including limited problem-solving skills, poor social reasoning, lack of empathy, and poor perspective-taking. Dodge and his colleagues, for example, have noted the occurrence of hostile attributional biases in the response styles of aggressive boys (Dodge, Bates, & Pettit, 1990; Dodge & Coie, 1987). (See Hudley, Chapter 2, Chan, Chapter 6, and Morrison and Sandowicz, Chapter 11, for a more detailed discussion of social-cognitive deficits among aggressive children.)

Patterson and colleagues (Patterson, 1982; Patterson, DeBaryshe, & Ramsey, 1989) have emphasized the role of family factors in the etiology of aggressive, antisocial behavior. In general, the families of aggressive, hostile children are often characterized by instability, high levels of stress, lack of consistency and a punitive approach to transgressions (Bierman, Coie, Dodge, Greenberg, Lochman, & McMahon, 1992; Dodge et al., 1990). Patterson (1982) hypothesizes that, due to lack of resources, knowledge, and support, parents within dysfunctional families often fail to consistently set limits for their children's behavior. Without such limits, children tend to behave in ways that frustrate and draw the ire of parents. As the frustration and tension mounts, parents are likely to respond in highly punitive ways. Thus begins an escalating cycle of violence in which parent and child alternately behave in aversive ways toward each other and toward others in the family. The child is likely to incorporate this pattern of responding in interactions outside of the family as well, including interactions with peers. Such a style of responding is likely to be met with resistance and/or withdrawal on the part of others. As the child is rejected or ignored by peers, he or she may develop a view of the world as a hostile, rejecting place.

In terms of the relationship between anger and school achievement, it has been hypothesized that students with learning problems evidence greater anger and frustration with regard to school. In a study of children manifesting serious learning and behavior problems, Smith, Adelman, Nelson, Taylor, and Phares (1987) found a significant relationship between severity of learning problems and anger as measured by the School Anger Inventory (reviewed in Chapter 7). Those students with the most severe learning problems presumably experienced greater degrees of frustration with regard to school. However, the relationship between school anger and problematic behaviors, as measured by both parent and teacher ratings, yielded only modest positive correlations.

In a study comparing learning disabled (LD) and normally achieving children in a public school setting, Smith, Adelman, Nelson, and Taylor (1988) again found higher degrees of anger arousal among the LD students than non-LD students. Additionally, LD students were rated by both parents and teachers as manifesting a greater number of problem behaviors at school.

In a review of studies examining the relationship between reading disabilities and aggression and other behavior problems in elementary school children, Cornwall and Bawden (1992) concluded that the pressure of a reading disability is NOT a necessary or sufficient condition to produce aggressive behavior. Findings from cross-sectional research were inconsistent, showing only modest correlations between reading problems (defined as a significant discrepancy between measured intelligence and reading achievement) and aggressive behavior (as measured by parent-, teacher-, or self-report). Extent of reading problems was also a poor predictor of aggressive and antisocial behavior among high school students. The authors point out a number of problems in the current research including (a) a small number of studies utilizing female subjects, (b) a tendency to focus primarily on externalizing disorders, and (c) the lack of attention to mediating variables such as language disorders. Since all of the studies reviewed focused on anger expression, there is little to offer in terms of clarification between other dimensions of anger (i.e., emotional, attitudinal, and reading problems). Additionally, reading problems are only one specific academic concern, albeit an important one. Future studies examining the relationship between anger and school performance need to assess anger dimensions as well as academic achievement and problem behavior more broadly.

Summary

As this brief review suggests, the affective, cognitive, and behavioral manifestations of anger are associated with numerous personal, social, and health problems. There is good reason, therefore, to help youth to learn how to manage this basic human emotion because it negatively impacts many aspects of their childhood development and because it is associated with life-long problems.

REFERENCES

Achenbach, T.M., & Edelbrock, C.S. (1983). *Manual for the Child Behavior Checklist and Revised Child Behavior Profile.* Burlington, VT: Department of Psychiatry, University of Vermont.

Achenbach, T. M., & Edelbrock, C. S. (1986). *Manual for the Teacher's Report Form and Teacher Version of the Child Behavior Profile.* Burlington, VT: Department of Psychiatry, University of Vermont.

Alexander, F. (1939). Emotional factors in essential hypertension: Presentation of tentative hypothesis. *Psychosomatic Medicine, 1,* 173-179.

Altman, E. D., & Gotlib, I. H. (1988). The social behavior of depressed children: An observational study. *Journal of Abnormal Child Psychology, 16,* 29-44.

American Psychiatric Association. (1987). *Diagnostic and statistical manual of mental disorders* (3rd ed., rev.). Washington, DC: Author.

Antonovsky, A. (1990). Personality and health: Testing the sense of coherence model. In H. S. Friedman (Ed.), *Personality and disease* (pp. 155-177). New York: John Wiley.

Asher, S. R., & Gottman, J. M. (Eds.) (1981). *The development of children's friendships.* New York: Cambridge University Press.

Averill, J. R. (1982). *Anger and aggression: An essay on emotion.* New York: Springer-Verlag.

Barefoot, J. C. (1992). Developments in the measurement of hostility. In H. S. Friedman (Ed.), *Hostility, coping, & health* (pp. 13-31). Washington, DC: American Psychological Association.

Barefoot, J. C., Dahlstrom, W. G., & Williams, R. B. (1983). Hostility, CHD incidence and total mortality: A 25-year follow-up study of 255 physicians. *Psychosomatic Medicine, 45,* 59-63.

Barefoot, J. C., Siegler, I. C., Nowlin, J. B., Peterson, B. L., Haney, T. L., & Williams, R. B. (1987). Suspiciousness, health, and mortality: A follow-up study of 500 older adults. *Psychosomatic Medicine, 49,* 450-457.

Berkowitz, L. (1989). Frustration-aggression hypothesis: Examination and reformation. *Psychological Bulletin, 106,* 59-73.

Bierman, K. L. (1986). Conflict, aggression, and peer status: An observational study. *Child Development, 57,* 1322-1332.

Bierman, K. L., Coie, J. D., Didge, K. A., Greenberg, M. T., Lochman, J. E., & McMahon, R. J. (1992). A developmental and clinical model for the prevention of conduct disorders: The FAST track program. *Development and Psychopathology, 4,* 509-527.

Cantrell, V. L., & Prinz, R. J. (1985). Multiple perspectives of rejected, neglected, and accepted children: Relation between sociometric status and behavioral characteristics. *Journal of Consulting and Clinical Psychology, 53,* 884-889.

Cattell, R. B., Eber, H. W., & Tatsuoka, M. M. (1970). *Handbook for the Sixteen Factor Personality Questionnaire.* Champaign, IL: Institute for Personality and Ability Testing.

Cook, W. W., & Medley, D. M. (1954). Proposed hostility and pharisaic-virtue scales for the MMPI. *Journal of Applied Psychology, 38,* 414-418.

Cornwall, A., & Bawden, H. N. (1992). Reading disabilities and aggression: A critical review. *Journal of Learning Disabilities, 25,* 281-288.

Dembroski, T. M., MacDougall, J. M., Costa, P. T., & Grandits, G. A. (1989). Components of hostility as predictors of sudden death and myocardial infarction in the Multiple Risk Factor Intervention Trial. *Psychosomatic Medicine, 51,* 514-522.

Derogatis, L. R., Abeloff, M. D., & Melisaratos, N. (1979). Psychological coping mechanisms and survival time in metastatic breast cancer. *Journal of the American Medical Association, 242,* 1504-1508.

Diamond, E. L. (1982). The role of anger and hostility in essential hypertension and coronary heart disease. *Psychological Bulletin, 92,* 410-433.

Dodge, K. A., Bates, J. E., & Pettit, G. S. (1990). Mechanisms in the cycle of violence. *Science, 250,* 1678-1683.

Dodge, K. A., & Coie, J. D. (1987). Social-information-processing factors in reactive and proactive aggression in children's peer group. *Journal of Personality and Social Psychology, 53,* 1146-1158.

Ebbesen, E., Duncan, B., & Konecni, V. (1975). The effects of context of verbal aggression on future verbal aggression: A field experiment. *Journal of Experimental Psychology, 11,* 192-204.

Edelbrock, C. S., & Achenbach, T. M. (1980). A typology of child behavior profile patterns: Distribution and correlates for disturbed children aged 6-16. *Journal of Abnormal Child Psychology, 8,* 441-470.

Emmons, R. A. (1992). The repressive personality and social support. In H. S. Friedman (Eds.); *Hostility, coping & health* (pp. 141-150). Washington, DC: American Psychological Association.

Friedman, H. S. (1991). *Self-healing personality: Why some people achieve health and others succumb to illness.* New York: Henry Holt.

Friedman, H. S. (1992). *Hostility, coping, & health.* Washington, DC: American Psychological Association.

Friedman, M., & Rosenman, R. H. (1959). Association of specific overt behavior pattern with blood and cardiovascular findings. *Journal of the American Medical Association, 169,* 1286-1296.

Funkenstein, D. H., King, S. H., & Drolette, M. E. (1954). The direction of anger during a laboratory stress-inducing situation. *Psychosomatic Medicine, 16,* 404-413.

Garber, J., Quiggle, N. L., Panak, W., & Dodge, K. A. (1991). Aggression and depression in children: Comorbidity, specificity, and social cognitive processing. In D. Cicchetti & S. L. Toth (Eds.), Rochester Symposium on Developmental Psychopathology (Vol. 2), *Internalizing and externalizing expression of dysfunction* (pp. 225-264). Hillsdale, NJ: Lawrence Erlbaum.

Gentry, W. D., Chesney, A. D., Gary, H. E., Hall, R. P., & Harburg, E. (1982). Habitual anger-coping styles: I. Effect on mean blood pressure and risk for essential hypertension. *Psychosomatic Medicine, 44,* 195-202.

Harburg, E., Blakelock, E. H., & Roeper, P. J. (1979). Resentful and reflective coping with arbitrary authority and blood pressure: Detroit. *Psychosomatic Medicine, 41,* 189-202.

Harburg, E., Erfurt, J. C., Haunstein, L. S., Chape, C., Schull, W. J., & Schork, M. A. (1973). Socio-ecological stress, suppressed hostility, skin color, and black-white male blood pressure: Detroit. *Psychosomatic Medicine, 35*, 276-296.

Haynes, S. G., Feinleib, M., & Kannel, W. B. (1978). The relationship of psychosocial factors to coronary heart disease in the Framingham study: II: Prevalence of coronary heart disease. *American Journal of Epidemiology, 197*, 384-401.

Haynes, S. G., Feinleib, M., Levine, S., Scotch, N., & Kannel, W. B. (1980). The relationship of psychosocial factors to coronary heart disease in the Framingham study: III: Eight-year incidence of coronary heart disease. *American Journal of Epidemiology, 111,* 37-58.

Hokanson, J. E. (1961a). The effects of frustration and anxiety on overt aggression. *Journal of Abnormal Psychology, 62*, 346-35.

Hokanson, J. E. (1961b). Vascular and psychogalvanic effects of experimentally aroused anger. *Journal of Personality, 29,* 30-39.

Hokanson, J. E., & Burgess, M. (1962). The effect of status, type of frustration, and aggression on vascular processes. *Journal of Abnormal and Social Psychology, 65,* 232-237.

Hokanson, J. E., & Sheter, S. (1961). The effect of overt aggression on physiological arousal. *Journal of Abnormal and Social Psychology, 63,* 446-448.

Hynan, D. J., & Grush, J. E. (1986). Effects of impulsivity, depression, provocation, and time on aggressive behavior. *Journal of Research in Personality, 20,* 158-171.

Izard, C. E. (1977). *Human emotions.* New York: Plenum Press.

Kahn, H. A., Medalie, J. H., Neufeld, H. N., Riss, E., & Goldbourt, U. (1972). The incidence of hypertension and associated factors: The Israeli ischemic heart disease study. *American Heart Journal, 84,* 171-182.

Keilitz, I., & Dunivant, N. (1986). The relationship between learning disability and juvenile delinquency: Current state of knowledge. *Remedial and Special Education, 7,* 18-26.

Kovacs, M., & Beck, A. T. (1977). An empirical-clinical approach toward a definition of childhood depression. In J. G. Schulterbrandt & A. Raskin (Eds.), *Depression in childhood: Diagnosis, treatment, and conceptual models.* New York: Raven.

Larson, K. A. (1988). A research review and alternative hypothesis explaining the link between learning disability and delinquency. *Journal of Learning Disabilities, 21*, 357-363, 369.

Lawler, K. A., Allen, M. T., Critcher, E. C., & Stanford, B. A (1981). The relationship of physiological responses to the coronary-prone behavior pattern in children. *Journal of Behavioral Medicine, 4,* 203-216.

Loeber, R. (1991). Antisocial behavior: More enduring than chageable? *Journal of the American Academy of Child Psychiatry,30,* 393-397.

Lundberg, M. (1983). Note on Type A behavior and cardiovascular responses to challenge in 3-6-year-old children. *Journal of Psychosomatic Research, 27,* 39-42.

Madow, L. (1972). *Anger.* New York: Macmillan.

Mallick, S. K., & McCandless, B. R. (1966). A study of catharsis aggression. *Journal of Personality and Social Psychology, 4,* 591-596.

Marriage, K., Fine, S., Moretti, M., & Haley, G. (1986). Relationship between depression and conduct disorder in children and adolescents. *Journal of the American Academy of Child Psychiatry, 25,* 687-691.

Matthews, K. A., Glass, D. C., Rosenman, R. H., & Bortner, R. W. (1977). Competitive drive, Pattern A, and coronary heart disease: A further analysis of some data from the Western Collaborative Group Study. *Journal of Chronic Diseases, 30,* 489-498.

Matthews, K. A., & Jennings, J. R. (1984). Cardiovascular responses of boys exhibiting the Type A behavior pattern. *Psychosomatic Medicine, 46,* 484-497.

McCraine, E. J. (1971). Depression, anxiety, and hostility. *Psychiatry Quarterly, 15,* 117-133.

McKay, M., Rogers, P. D., & McKay, J. (1989). *When anger hurts.* Oakland, CA: New Harbinger.

Novaco, R. W. (1975). *Anger control: The development and evaluation of an experimental treatment.* Lexington, MA: Lexington Books.

Olweus, D. (1979). Stability of aggressive reaction patterns in males: A review. *Psychological Bulletin, 86,* 852-857.

Patterson, G. R. (1982). *Coercive family processes.* Eugene, OR: Castalia.

Patterson, G. R., DeBarysky, B. D., & Ramsey, E. (1989). A developmental perspective on antisocial behavior. *American Psychologist, 44,* 329–335.

Pennebaker, J. W. (1992). Inhibition as the linchpin of health. In H. S. Friedman (Ed.), *Hostility, coping, & health.* Washington, DC: American Psychological Association.

Riley, W. T., Treiber, E. A., & Woods, M. G. (1989). Anger and hostility in depression. *Journal of Nervous and Mental Disease, 177,* 668-674.

Rosenman, R. H., Brand, R. J., Jenkins, C.D., Friedman, H. S., Strauss, R., & Wurm, M. (1975). Coronary heart disease in the Western Collaborative Group Study: Final follow-up experience of 8 1/2 years. *Journal of the American Medical Association, 233,* 872-877.

Rosenman, R. H., Friedman, H. S., Strauss, R., Wurm, M., Kositchek, C., Hahn, W., & Werthessen, T. (1964). A predictive study of coronary heart disease: The Western Collaborative Group Study. *Journal of the American Medical Association, 189,* 15-22.

Rubin, I. R. (1969). *The angry book.* New York: Collier.

Sandberg. S. T., Wieselberg, M., & Schaffer, D. (1980). Hyperkinetic and conduct problem children in a primary school population: Some epidemiological considerations. *Journal of Child Psychology and Psychiatry, 31,* 393-411.

Shantz, D. W. (1986). Conflict, aggression, and peer status: An observational study. *Child Development, 57,* 1322-1332.

Shapiro, S. K., & Garfinkel, B. D. (1986). The occurrence of behavior disorders in children: The interdependence of attention deficit disorder and conduct disorder. *Journal of the American Academy of Child Psychiatry, 25,* 809-819.

Scherwitz, L., & Rugilies, R. (1992). Life-style and hostility. In H. S. Friedman (Ed.), *Hostility, coping & health* (pp. 77-98). Washington, DC: American Psychological Association.

Shekelle, R. B., Gale, M., Ostfeld, A. M., & Paul, O. (1983). Hostility, risk of coronary heart disease, and mortality. *Psychosomatic Medicine, 45,* 109-114.

Siegel, J. M. (1984). Anger and cardiovascular risk in adolescents. *Health Psychology, 3,* 293-313.

Siegel, J. M. (1985). The measurement of anger as a multidimensional construct. In M. A. Chesney & R. H. Rosenman (Eds.), *Anger and hostility in cardiovascular and behavioral disorders* (pp. 59-82). New York: Hemisphere.

Siegel, J. M. (1986). The multidimensional anger inventory. *Journal of Personality and Social Psychology, 51,* 191-200.

Siegel, J. M. (1992). Anger and cardiovascular health. In H S. Friedman (Ed.), *Hostility, coping, & health* (pp. 49-64). Washington, DC: American Psychological Association.

Smith, D. C., Adelman, H. S., Nelson, P., Taylor, L., & Phares, V. (1987). Perceived control at school and problem behavior and attitudes. *Journal of School Psychology, 25,* 167-176.

Smith, D. C,. Adelman, H. A., Nelson, P., & Taylor, L. (1988). Anger, perceived control, and school behavior among students with learning problems. *Journal of Child Psychology and Psychiatry, 29,* 517-522.

Smith, T. W., & Christensen, A. J. (1992). Hostility, health, and social contexts. In H. S. Friedman (Ed.), *Hostility, coping, & health* (pp. 33-48). Washington, DC: American Psychological Association.

Spielberger, C.D., Gorsuch, R. L., & Lushene, R. E. (1970). *Manual for the State-Trait Anxiety Inventory.* Palo Alto, CA: Consulting Psychologists Press.

Spielberger, C. D., Johnson, E. H., Russell, S. E., Crane, R. J., Jacobs, G. A., & Werden, T. J. (1985). The experience and expression of anger: Construction of an anger expression scale. In M. A. Chesney & R. H. Rosenman (Eds.), *Anger and hostility in cardiovascular and behavioral disorders* (pp. 5-30). New York: Hemisphere.

Tavris, C. (1982). *Anger, the misunderstood emotion.* New York: Simon & Schuster.

Williams, R. B., & Barefoot, J. C. (1988). Coronary-prone behavior: The emerging role of the hostility complex. In B. K. Houston & C. R. Snyder (Eds.), *Type A behavior pattern* (pp. 189-211). New York: Wiley.

Williams, R. B., Haney, T. L., Lee, K. L., Kong, Y., Blumenthal, J. A., & Whalen, R. E. (1980). Type A behavior, hostility, and coronary atherosclerosis. *Psychosomatic Medicine, 42,* 539-550.

2 PERCEPTIONS OF INTENTIONALITY, FEELINGS OF ANGER, AND REACTIVE AGGRESSION

Cynthia Ann Hudley

Excessive displays of aggression in childhood merit the attention of research and practice "because of the developmental continuity in patterns of aggressive behavior" (Feshbach & Fraczek, 1979, p. 2). Excessive levels of aggressive behavior in childhood have been found to be extremely stable over time (Kazdin, 1987; Lefkowitz, Eron, Walder, & Huesmann, 1977; Olweus, 1979) and to presage a host of negative developmental outcomes. Youth who display deviant levels of aggression in school settings, males in particular, have been found to manifest significantly higher rates of juvenile delinquency (Loeber & Stouthamer-Loeber, 1987), poor overall school adjustment, greater than average rates of school drop out, and higher than average rates of referral for clinical mental health interventions (Cox & Gunn, 1980; Kupersmidt & Coie, 1990). In fact, surveys of child guidance clinic populations have determined that "excessive and inappropriate aggression poses one of the most common and serious problems of children referred for treatment" (Nasby, Hayden, & DePaulo, 1980, p. 460).

Among developmental psychologists, one of the more active perspectives in the study of childhood aggression has been research on the relationship between causal attributions and aggressive behavior. According to attribution theory, one typical cognitive activity performed by individuals in social situations is the effort to understand why others behave as they do, and how those behaviors are related to the outcomes experienced in the situation. A causal attribution occurs when an individual interprets the behavior of others (Weiner, 1986). In essence, the individual's attribution answers a question about why a given interpersonal outcome has occurred. These causal explanations provide the impetus for behavior and facilitate decision making among alternative courses of action (Kelley, 1973). It seems evident that attributions may be internal mediators for human aggressive behaviors (Park & Slaby, 1983).

This chapter reviews empirical and theoretical evidence concerning attributional differences between aggressive and nonaggressive boys. Findings are summarized in Table 2.1. Research typically identifies two distinct types of aggression, related to motivations underlying behavior: instrumental aggression (behavior directed toward attaining objects, privileges, positions, or activities) and reactive, retaliatory, or hostile aggression (behavior provoked in response to the actions of another) (Dodge & Coie, 1987; Hinde & Groebel, 1989). This review will confine itself to consideration of the display of hostile, reactive aggression. Applying principles of attribution theory to the reduction of childhood reactive aggression should be especially fruitful because research in this area has focused almost entirely on children and adolescents. Thus a great deal is known about the attributional antecedents of reactive aggression among children.

STUDIES IDENTIFYING A COGNITIVE BIAS TO INFER HOSTILITY

Children are typically able to use social information in order to distinguish between acts of accident and intent by age 5 or 6 (Shantz, 1983). However, Nasby et al. (1980) were among the first to suggest that extremely aggressive children might inappropriately attribute hostile intent to others regardless of the presented social cues. Emotionally disturbed boys (of average intelligence) at a residential treatment center labeled a series of 40 facial photographs, each depicting a strong emotion (e.g., jealous anger), accompanied by two situational labels (e.g., "she is angry that someone is late"). Four distinct categories of emotions were represented, created by crossing two bipolar dimensions: positivity-negativity and dominance-submission. For example, among negative emotions, sadness represents submission whereas hostility is related to dominance. Errors favoring negative-dominant responses were interpreted as an attributional bias to infer hostility. Results yielded a significant, positive correlation between staff ratings of aggressiveness and percent of negative-dominant errors.

Table 2.1. Summary of Studies Investigating Attributional Bias and Reactive Aggression.

Author	Method	Characteristics of Aggressive Subjects
Nasby, Hayden, & DePaulo (1980)	Photo identification	Higher rate of errors inferring hostility
Dodge (1980)	Puzzle assembly task	Rated ambiguous situations equal to hostile situations
Dodge & Newman (1981)	Detective game	Responded more rapidly, used fewer prepared cues for decision making
Dodge & Frame (1982)	Paper-pencil scenarios video interviews playgroup observations	More likely to attribute hostile intent, more likely to retaliate aggressively, anticipate hostility toward self only
Dodge & Somberg (1987)	Video hypothetical scenarios viewed with or without threat from peer	More likely to attribute hostile intent, more likely to respond aggressively, greater disruption of processing under threat conditions
Dodge & Tomlin (1987)	Audio hypothetical scenarios	Poor recall of benign cues, limited use of presented information when determining peer's intent
Waas (1988)	Paper-pencil scenarios	More aggressive response choices
Sancilio, Plumert, & Hartup (1989)	Paper-pencil scenarios	No differences in aggresson toward friends vs. nonfriends
Graham, Hudley, & Williams (1992)	Paper-pencil scenarios	Higher levels of reported anger, less consistency among thought, affect, and behavior

Another landmark study (Dodge, 1980), one that initiated an entire program of research by Kenneth Dodge and colleagues on social cognitions of aggressive youth, reported similar findings with very different subjects and procedures. His point of departure was the extensive findings from moral judgment research which indicated the importance of interpreting the intent of others in selecting behavioral responses (cf. Rule, 1974). Dodge suggested that the inappropriate expression of reactive aggression may be related to one's inability to judge correctly the intentions of others and integrate intention information into behavioral choice. He hypothesized that, given a negative interpersonal outcome, the aggressive child would most likely misattribute hostile intent and retaliate aggressively against a peer's ambiguously intended behavior. Aggressive and nonaggressive participants (elementary school boys) in a puzzle assembly task were given the opportunity to dismantle an unseen peer's puzzle after they believed this person had dismantled their work. The unseen peer's intent (actually an audio recording) was manipulated to be either accidental, hostile, or ambiguous. In comparing behavior across the three types of intent, aggressive boys treated the ambiguous situation equivalent to the hostile situation, and were relatively less aggressive in response to the accidental situation. Among nonaggressive boys, behavior was similar in the ambiguous and accidental conditions, and relatively more aggressive in the hostile condition.

Dodge, Murphy and Buchsbaum (1984) also explored the related question of whether all children displaying deviant social behavior have difficulty discerning the intentions of others. Using a series of videotaped vignettes with elementary school boys, they found that all subjects could accurately discern hostile intent, but average children scored better than both aggressive and withdrawn children on discerning prosocial and accidental intent. Errors for all groups most often incorrectly presumed hostility. Thus the deviant groups were more likely to assign hostile intent incorrectly because they made more errors overall than the normal groups (Dodge et al., 1984, p. 168). Misattribution of hostile intent may lead to either inappropriate retaliatory aggression or social withdrawal, but this chapter will focus only on the former behavior. These findings draw a clear relationship between an inability to perceive benign intentions in others accurately and high levels of aggressive behavior.

EXPLORING THE NATURE OF BIASED PROCESSING

Building on the results of Dodge's initial investigation, Dodge and Newman (1981) found that aggressive boys misjudged the intentions of peers because they responded quickly and ignored available relevant social cues. In this study, boys participated in a "detective game" in which they requested clues to make judgments of a peer's intent in hypothetical scenarios. Aggressive children appeared to make judgments and select behaviors in accordance with the information processing notion of "perceptual readiness" (Dodge & Newman, 1981, p. 375), that is, a predisposition for an attribution based on past experience or learning. Rather than using social information contained in the available cues, they based their cognitions and subsequent behavioral choices on their belief that peers would behave aggressively.

Dodge and Frame (1982) used hypothetical scenarios, videotaped interviews of unknown peers, and observations of playgroups in a laboratory setting in a series of three interrelated studies intended to provide further illumination of attributional bias. These studies found that the bias in aggressive boys is a paranoid expectancy of hostile intent that they believe to be directed toward themselves personally, not a generalized or cynical expectancy of peers' hostility towards all others. It is interesting to note that, all subjects, aggressive and nonaggressive alike, attributed a hostile intention five times more often to peers they perceived to be aggressive than to nonaggressive peers. All subjects were also more likely to propose aggressive retaliation against aggressive targets than to nonaggressive targets. Thus, children known to be aggressive were more likely to receive hostile attributions and to be the objects of retaliatory aggression. Conversely, aggressive children were more likely to attribute hostile intent to others, and due to this hostile attributional bias, were more likely to retaliate aggressively in inappropriate circumstances. This process set up a self-fulfilling cycle in which peer nominated aggressive boys both initiated and received far more aggressive acts than did other boys. The aggressive boys, however, initiated "many more aggressive acts" than they received (Dodge & Frame, 1982, p. 633) (see Figure 2.1).

After viewing the videotaped interviews, aggressive boys "recalled" and "recognized" hostile and benign statements more frequently even though they actually had not been part of the interviews nor present on the video. These intrusion errors suggest a cognitive deficit similar to the inhibition deficit found in impulsive boys (Dodge & Frame, 1982). Aggressive boys failed to inhibit highly available hostile cognitive responses, regardless of the presence of disconfirming cues. In other words, these boys' responses were based on predetermined beliefs about the intentions of peers rather than available social information.

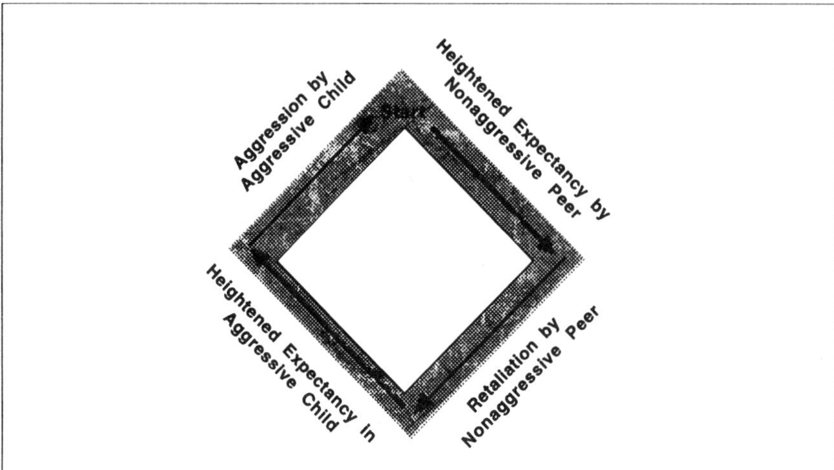

Figure 2.1. Cycle of Aggressive Behavior and Peer Expectancy

Cognitive biases peculiar to aggressive boys were further elaborated by Dodge and Tomlin (1987). Elementary school aggressive boys who listened to audiotaped stories describing the behavior of a peer were no better at recalling hostile cues than were nonaggressive boys. They were, however, significantly worse at recalling benign cues. Further, they ignored cues presented in the interview and judged the peer's intentions based on their own past experiences 24% of the time, compared to 14% of the time for nonaggressive boys.

Kelley's (1973) process model of causal attribution proposes a cognitive construct, causal schema, which allows individuals to make judgments based on limited cue input. This construct is strikingly similar to the behavior described in attribution research (Dodge & Frame, 1982; Dodge & Newman, 1981; Dodge & Tomlin, 1987). Perhaps aggressive boys are prematurely invoking hostile causal schemata in some situations rather than reflectively processing available cues.

Waas (1988) demonstrated that all children utilize consistency information (i.e., data pertaining to their past relationship with a peer) more than distinctiveness (i.e., a peer's past relations with others) when judging behavior directed to themselves. Highly aggressive children, however, were most aggressive in their response choices, regardless of the presented social information. That is, even when social cues indicated benign intent, aggressives more often than nonaggressives chose to respond aggressively. Taken together, the work by Waas and Dodge and colleagues suggests a transactional relationship among expectancy, bias, and inappropriate reactive aggression. It appears that hostile bias is shaped by aggressive children's tendency to respond based on past personal experience rather than all available social cues.

THE INFLUENCE OF AFFECT ON ATTRIBUTIONAL BIAS

Until quite recently, little attention was paid to the role of affect in these obviously emotionally charged, aggressive peer interactions. Dodge and Somberg (1987) speculated that perhaps those children who display inappropriate retaliatory aggression are those who are especially affectively aroused in interpersonal situations involving negative outcomes. Alternatively, affective arousal may be especially disruptive of unbiased attributional processing for these children. Instead, the aggressive child may employ causal schemata to interpret events, using the most immediately available cognitive cues, primarily hostile, and invoking the most cognitively available response—aggressive retaliation.

Threatening stimuli are especially likely to distort the social cognitive processing of children who are the least skillful processors (Dodge, 1991). Previous work (Dodge et al., 1984) established that socially deviant children are less skillful at intention cue detection than are their normal peers. Thus, it was hypothesized that attributional differences between aggressive and nonaggressive children would be greater under conditions of threat than under relaxed conditions.

The normal laboratory setting became the relaxed condition. The statement of an aggressive male peer (a confederate) threatening to initiate a conflict with the subject when they left the lab constituted the threat condition. The participants "overheard" this statement (an audio recording) when the experimenter was out of the room. Male aggressive and nonaggressive subjects in grades 3-5 individually viewed videotaped vignettes in which one child caused a negative outcome for another with hostile, accidental, prosocial, or ambiguous intent. The subjects' task was to identify the intent of the provocateur and specify a behavioral response.

Both groups were extremely accurate at detecting hostile intentions. For detection of prosocial intent, the aggressive group made significantly more errors of presumed hostility in both relaxed and threatening conditions. Skill in detection of accidental and ambiguous intent showed distinct decrements for the aggressive group under threat conditions compared to relaxed conditions. Nonaggressives did not differ in the threatening and relaxed conditions. Behavioral responses, though related to all subjects' interpretation of presented intent, were less predictable for aggressive boys. Aggressive boys were more likely to respond behaviorally in an arbitrary and predetermined (primarily hostile) manner regardless of the attribution of intent or the presence or absence of threat (see Table 2.2). This finding is similar to Waas' (1988) response bias and the explanation of perceptual readiness offered by Dodge and Newman (1981).

As expected, the threat manipulation did indeed disrupt the attributional accuracy and skillful intention detection of the aggressive, but not the nonaggressive boys. A threatening interaction might exert a debilitating influence on subsequent attributional accuracy such that a cognitive schema "threat from peers" becomes highly salient, adversely affecting immediate social cognitive processing. The effects may be most often demonstrated by aggressive boys perhaps because they are more likely than nonaggressives to possess such a schema (Dodge & Somberg, 1987). Alternatively, aggressive boys may have learned that "negative affect in oneself is associated with hostility in others" (Dodge & Somberg, 1987, p. 221) thus leading to more biased attributions and selective recall under conditions of negative affect. Other questions remain, as well. Were only aggressive children experiencing a negative affect? Were aggressive children more highly aroused, and their cognitive processes thus more severely disrupted? Clearly, the mediating role of affective arousal and affective valence in children's attributions requires further explanation.

One positive affective mediator of children's attributions and behavior was addressed by Sancilio, Plumert, and Hartup (1989), who investigated how friendship can act as a determinant of attributions and behavior. They suggested that children may favorably bias their attributions, or they may alter their behavioral responses in a more conciliatory direction, in provocation situations involving friends.

Aggressive and nonaggressive third- and fifth-grade boys were read hypothetical scenarios of a peer interaction that resulted in a negative outcome, but the intent of the peer in the story was ambiguous. The identities of the peer instigator and the target child in the story were varied to be either friend, aggressive nonfriend, nonaggressive nonfriend, or self, with the exception that instigators were never self. When the self was the target (i.e., children were told to imagine that the negative outcome was happening to them personally), aggressive children attributed more hostile intent and predicted more aggressive responses than did nonaggressive children, regardless of whether the instigator was a friend or not. When the instigator

TABLE 2.2. SUMMARY OF DODGE & SOMBERG (1987) FINDINGS

Condition	Aggressive	Nonaggressive
Ambiguous	Decreased accuracy under threat	No change in accuracy
Accidental	Decreased accuracy under threat	No change in accuracy
Prosocial	Inaccurate judgments of hostility in both conditions	No change in accuracy
Hostile	No change in accuracy	No change in accuracy

in the story was not directing action toward the self, no differences were found between the aggressive and nonaggressive children, consistent with previous findings (Dodge & Frame, 1982). For all subjects, hostile responses followed attributions of hostile intent directed to the self 77% of the time and hostile responses followed attributions of nonhostile intent 44% of the time. Aggressive subjects more often endorsed hostile responses, regardless of their prior attributions than did nonaggressives, again consistent with prior research (Waas, 1988). Thus a hallmark of aggresive youth appears to be their tendency toward inappropriate reactive aggression when interacting with others, be they friend or foe. In fact, peer-directed aggression has been consistently associated with peer rejection, and this is especially true for boys (Coie, Dodge, & Kupersmidt, 1990).

Friendship was postulated to be the mediator of social cognitions and behaviors, but somewhat surprisingly, Sancilio et al. (1989) did not find support for this hypothesis. Subjects were no more likely to respond aggressively to nonfriends than to friends. One possible interpretation is that their stories involved friends and nonfriends, rather than liked and disliked peers (Sancilio et al., 1989). We might assume that friends were liked, but there is no basis for assuming that peers identified as nonfriends by the methods used here were necessarily disliked. It is possible that the label "disliking" may generate more negative affect (possibly anger) than the label "nonfriend." Such an interpretation would be consistent with Imamoglu's (1975) findings. In her work, children rated peers as more disliked when their behavior was portrayed as deliberately hostile than when portrayed as accidental.

Another recent investigation (Graham, Hudley, & Williams, 1992) directly investigated the mediational role of anger. They tested the hypothesis that, in negative outcome situations, perceived intentionality elicits anger which then serves as a direct motivator of aggressive retaliation. This attribution affect—behavior linkage was tested with a series of hypothetical scenarios of peer interaction, in which the intent of the peer was presented as either hostile, prosocial, accidental, or ambiguous. Subjects were asked to judge the peer's intent, rate the level of anger they would feel, and rate a series of behavioral alternatives ranging from "do something nice for him" to "have it out right then and there." Participants were male (n = 74) and female (n = 14) middle school students identified as aggressive or nonaggressive by a combination of teacher ratings and peer nominations.

Consistent with Dodge's (1980) initial findings, aggressive students' judgments of the peer's intent were significantly more hostile than nonaggressives' judgments only in the ambiguous scenarios. On the other hand, aggressive youth reported feeling significantly more angry than nonaggressives, independent of the peer's intent. These findings are counter to Waas (1988), who found no differences in reported anger between aggressive and nonaggressive children. However, consistent with Waas' (1988) data, these aggressive youth were significantly more likely to endorse aggressive responses (e.g., "have it out") regardless of the attributional cues. Although causal modeling analyses supported the thinking-feeling-behavior motivational sequence, the relationships were much more consistent for nonaggressive than aggressive subjects, similar to the Dodge and Somberg (1987) findings. For example, an alternative feeling-thinking-behavior model fit the aggressive subjects' data from the ambiguous scenario equally as well. Aggressive students may be as likely to engage in an angry outburst before considering intention information as to decide on the purposefulness of others' behavior before becoming angered. Thus the relationship between attributions, affect, and aggression is not fully clarified by these data either.

In summary, several studies have examined how affect can act as a mediator between thoughts and aggressive behavior and suggest that attributional processes can be disrupted in affectively charged situations. In the absence of logical reasoning from evidence, children may invoke schemata to interpret and respond to negative interpersonal situations, relying less on presented cues and more on preexisting expectancies and beliefs about causality. Perhaps only highly aggressive children are invoking schemata. Or, perhaps all children do so in potential conflict situations, and the schemata of aggressives are qualitatively different. Research by Waas (1988) indicated that all children experience equal levels of anger, but Graham et al. (1992) have found that aggressives report more anger than nonaggressives. Dodge and Somberg (1987) demonstrate that under potential conflict conditions, aggressive children suffer greater decrements in their processing abilities than their peers, which also suggests a mediational role for affective arousal. Thus, the role of affect, though obviously important, is far from clarified at this juncture. Let us turn now to a brief discussion of the theoretical models that have been proffered to explain the roots of excessive reactive aggression, to determine if theory can provide order to this diverse body of empirical observation.

THEORIES OF COGNITION, AFFECT, AND BEHAVIOR

Drawing on a substantial body of empirical findings, Dodge (1986) proposed a model of social information processing composed of five sequential steps. Unskillful or biased processing (whether conscious or unconscious) at any given step enhances "the probability that the child will behave in a deviant, possibly aggressive way" (p. 83).

Step 1: Receiving and Perceiving Social Input

Implied in this step is the ability to search the environment actively for appropriate cues and distinguish those that are relevant or appropriate (Park & Slaby, 1983).

Step 2: Interpretation

This step is "often indistinguishable from the first" (Dodge, 1986, p. 85). Now the child must meaningfully understand the cues by integrating them with memories of past experiences. If not enough information has been encoded, the child returns to step one to seek out more cues actively via a feedback loop.

Step 3: Response Search

Once the situation has been interpreted, in the third step, response search decision rules acquired through learning and direct experience are invoked to access reasonable responses in the behavioral repertoire.

Step 4: Response Decision

The child must next choose the optimal response from among the possibilities by evaluating probable consequences in the given context and based on the child's behavioral capabilities.

Step 5: Response Enactment

In the final step, the child acts out the chosen behavioral response. It is important to note that the model is presumed to be transactional in that the child monitors the effects of behavior stemming from the fifth step, utilizing these cues as new input from the environment and repeating the five-step information-processing sequence until the desired effect is achieved.

The proposed model clearly predicts a number of the effects reported in the body of literature reviewed here. Unskillful apprehension of social cues is associated with deviant behavior (Dodge et al., 1984; Nasby et al., 1980), as predicted at step one of the model, as is an inadequate search for relevant cues (Dodge & Newman, 1981). Problems with cue interpretation have been manifested by a robust bias to infer hostility on the part of extremely aggressive (e.g., Dodge, 1980; Dodge & Frame, 1982; Graham et al., 1992) and withdrawn (Dodge & Coie, 1987) children. Only Waas (1988) reported no interpretive bias, perhaps because children's responses were influenced by highly salient social cues present in his stories. The presence of bias only when outcomes are directed to the self is not explicitly accounted for by this model, but it can be assumed bias occurs because aggressive children's interpretation process is less skillful when they are the target rather than the observer.

Dodge (1986) first suggested several cognitive factors that could lead to incompetent responding, including processing overloads, cognitive biases, and deficits in interpreting and utilizing relevant cues. However, the additional questions raised by Graham et al. (1992), Dodge and Somberg (1987), and Sancilio et al. (1989) regarding the role of affect in the social cognitive processing of aggressive youth remain unclear. Most recently Dodge (1991) has acknowledged that deficiency and begun to explore the central role of emotion in social behavior by formulating an expanded model of the relation between emotion and social information processing.

Ferguson and Rule (1983) have proposed an attributionally based model of anger and aggression. Their model is founded on the assumption that reactive anger and retaliatory aggression result from the discrepancy between the actor's perceived harmful intent and what the perceiver believes should have occurred.

First a perceiver (or target) of harm decides on the actor's causal responsibility at three levels: intentionality, avoidability, and motive. Was the harm intended? If not, was it foreseeable? And if intended, were the actor's motives malevolent? The perceiver discerns and integrates available social cues with preexisting expectancies about the actor to assign responsibility and thus classify the actor's behavior as "accidental, foreseeable, nonmalevolently intended, or malevolently intended" (Ferguson & Rule, 1983, p. 43). The perceiver then compares this assessment to a judgment about what ought to have happened. These "ought" judgments may be specified by the perceiver's own value system, or by someone else (e.g., the legal system). In any case, at the point of comparison, if a discrepancy is detected, anger results. Hostile, retaliatory aggression results from anger generated by the detection of a discrepancy. Thus Ferguson and Rule's model accounts for retaliatory aggression with a combination of cognition and affect, with affect being the mediator between cognition and behavior.

For example, consider a child who has been pushed in the hallway by a schoolmate. The child might ask himself, "Did the person do this on purpose?" "Did he see me standing here?" "Was he trying to knock me down?" In deciding on the answers to these questions, the child might consider his past relationship with the peer (e.g., an argument earlier), the condition of the hall (e.g., crowded), and the observable behavior of the peer (e.g., not looking where he is going, or rushing). Once the child evaluates the provocation (e.g., "It's crowded, and he is talking to someone instead of paying attention to where he is going"), he decides on the appropriateness of the peer's actions (e.g., "He ought to be careful and pay attention like the rest of us."). In this example, anger is likely due to the discrepancy between perceived carelessness and the need to be mindful of the rights of others. The child might be expected to display verbal or physical aggression in this instance.

The research reviewed here is somewhat consistent with Ferguson and Rule's model of aggression. The hostile attributional bias and the robust reputation effect are accounted for in the process of assigning causal responsibility. Affective arousal also explains why the bias to infer hostile intent emerges only in situations where self is the target. "The perceiver's degree of involvement in the situation is also likely to have an effect on the ought standard adopted by the perceiver" (p. 61) due to arousal generated by the direct experience of harm, as Dodge and Frame (1982) also suggested. Thus, a lesser degree of harm is needed to generate a sufficient discrepancy to invoke retaliation when the self is the target. Though the incorporation of affect increases the power of this model to explain the presence and workings of the hostile attributional bias, the reciprocal influences of cognition and affect in determining aggressive behavior, as investigated by

Graham et al. (1992) and Dodge and Somberg (1987), remain to be specified.

PERCEIVED CONTROL AND AGGRESSIVE BEHAVIOR

I would also propose a somewhat more parsimonious model of the attributional determinants of aggression (see also Graham et al., 1992; Graham & Hudley, 1992; Hudley, 1991). Based on the formulations of Weiner (1986, 1991), attributions of intentionality are linked to behavior through the mediating role of emotion. In a negative (or an unexpected) outcome situation, individuals are hypothesized to undergo a causal search to explain that outcome. Causal attributions have been found consistently (Sobol & Earn, 1985; Weiner, 1986)) to share at least three common properties, or causal dimensions: locus, stability, and controllability.

The locus dimension describes the perceived cause as internal or external to the perceiver (e.g., low ability vs. noisy distractions as an explanation for failing a test). Stability defines whether the cause is perceived as enduring or temporary (e.g., low ability vs. not studying hard enough). The dimension of interest to the study of aggression is perceived controllability, also referred to as intentionality in the childhood aggression literature. Perceived controllability is defined here as the extent to which a given individual can be considered responsible for a given social outcome. In a negative outcome situation, if one of the parties to the interaction attributes that outcome to causes controllable by the other party, s/he will believe that the other party deliberately caused her/him harm.

Controllability influences behavior toward others through the mediating influence of emotion, in a motivational sequence of thought to emotion to action. Once negative outcomes accruing to the self are attributed to causes perceived as controllable by others (e.g., a homework assignment is deliberately destroyed by a peer), anger is elicited, and one possible behavioral response is aggression (Weiner, 1986). Attributing blame to others has been empirically linked to experienced anger (Weiner, Graham, & Chandler, 1982), and the linkages between attributions of hostile intent, feelings of anger, and retaliatory aggression have been described previously (Graham et al., 1992).

Thus when a child presumes that the causes of a negative outcome are controllable by a peer partner in the interaction, that child will attribute hostile intentions to the peer. When a negative peer interaction is perceived as intentional, feelings of anger will be directed to that peer. In contrast, if the negative interaction is perceived as resulting from unintentional causes, anger should not be aimed at the peer partner. The degree of anger directed toward the peer will determine the extent of retaliatory aggression exhibited by the child target.

Attributional bias would therefore be explained as perceiving negative social outcomes to be highly controllable by others. Perhaps aggressive young males are more likely to perceive causes of negative interactions to be controllable by the peer(s) with whom they are interacting, rather than of accidental or uncontrollable origin. Such a possibility would explain the heightened anger reported by aggressive youngsters (Graham et al., 1992). However, among excessively aggressive youngsters, the thinking-feeling-acting linkage is less consistent and predictable (Dodge & Somberg, 1987; Waas, 1988), especially in situations of attributional ambiguity (Graham et al., 1992). Thus, though anger appears to serve as a mediator between thought and action in competent social information processing, when the process is distorted, affect may be operating to destabilize, rather than regulate, subsequent behavior.

SUMMARY AND CONCLUDING COMMENTS

A great many of the attributional differences between aggressive and nonaggressive young males have been delineated, as demonstrated by the body of literature presented here. Aggressive youth display a bias to infer hostile intent in others in ambiguous interpersonal situations. This bias is characterized by poor intention detection skills, a more rapid rate of social decision making, limited attention to social cues, schema-based social decision-making, and a response bias toward a much higher level of aggressive retaliation. Their biased judgments seem to appear, however, only when negative social outcomes are directed at themselves. A presumption of hostility from peers reflects to some degree the actual social experiences of boys with a reputation for aggression. Because they more often display aggressive behavior, they are more often the target of aggression from peers (Dodge & Frame, 1982).

However, these findings are almost entirely correlational in nature. Although it is apparent that peer-directed reactive aggression and an attributional bias to presume hostility go hand-in-hand, it is difficult to determine which is cause and which effect. Perhaps children with cognitive biases are more likely to react aggressively. It is equally plausible, however, that some aggressive children develop biases after differential treatment from peers. Or, perhaps some third variable (parental beliefs, for example) leads to both cognitive bias and heightened reactive aggression. It requires an experimental manipulation of cognitive bias and an assessment of subsequent behavior to accurately determine if biased attributions generate retaliatory aggressive behavior. Such an intervention has been created and evaluated, and is described elsewhere in this volume.

REFERENCES

Coie, J., Dodge, K., & Kupersmidt, J. (1990). Peer group behavior and social status. In S. Asher & J. Coie (Eds.), *Peer rejection in childhood* (pp. 17-59). New York: Cambridge University Press.

Cox, R., & Gunn, W. (1980). Interpersonal skills in the schools: Assessment and curriculum development. In D. Rathjen & J. Foreyt (Eds.), *Social competence: Interventions for children and adults* (pp. 113-132). New York: Pergamon Press.

Dodge, K. (1980). Social cognition and children's aggressive behavior. *Child Development, 51*, 162-170.

Dodge, K. (1986). A social information processing model of social competence in children. In M. Perlmutter (Ed.), *The Minnesota symposium on child psychology* (pp. 77-126). Hillsdale, NJ: Lawrence Erlbaum.

Dodge, K. (1991). Emotion and social information processing. In J. Garber & K. Dodge (Eds.), *The development of emotion regulation and dysregulation* (pp. 159-181). New York: Cambridge University Press.

Dodge, K., & Coie, J. (1987). Social information processing factors in reactive and proactive aggression in children's peer groups. *Journal of Personality and Social Psychology, 53*, 1146-1158.

Dodge, K., & Frame, C. (1982). Social cognitive biases and deficits in aggressive boys. *Child Development, 53*, 620-635.

Dodge, K., Murphy, R., & Buchsbaum, K. (1984). The assessment of intention cue detection skills in children. *Child Development, 55*, 163-173.

Dodge, K., & Newman, J. (1981). Biased decision-making processes in aggressive boys. *Journal of Abnormal Psychology, 90*, 375-379.

Dodge, K., & Somberg, D. (1987). Hostile attributional biases among aggressive boys are exacerbated under conditions of threat to the self. *Child Development, 58*, 213-224.

Dodge, K., & Tomlin, A. (1987). Utilization of self-schema as a mechanism of interpersonal bias in aggressive children. *Social Cognition, 5*, 280-300.

Ferguson, T., & Rule, B. (1983). An attributional perspective on anger and aggression. In R. Green & E. Donnerstein (Ed.), *Aggression: Theoretical and empirical reviews* (pp. 41-74). New York: Academic Press.

Feshbach, S., & Fraczek, A. (1979). Changing aggression: The need and the approach. In S. Feshbach & A. Fraczek (Ed.), *Aggression and behavior change: Biological and social processes* (pp. 1-5). New York: Praeger Press.

Graham, S., & Hudley, C. (1992). An attributional approach to aggression in African-American children. In D. Schunk & J. L. Meece (Eds.), *Student perceptions in the classroom: Causes and consequences* (pp. 75-94). Hillsdale, NJ: Lawrence Erlbaum Associates.

Graham, S., Hudley, C., & Williams, E. (1992). Attributional and emotional determinants of aggression in African-American and Latino young adolescents. *Developmental Psychology, 28*, 731-740.

Hinde, R., & Groebel, J. (1989). The problem of aggression. In J. Groebel & R. Hinde (Eds.), *Aggression and war: Their biological and social bases* (pp. 3-9). Cambridge: Cambridge University Press.

Hudley, C. (1991). *An attribution retraining program to reduce peer directed aggession among African-American male elementary school students* [Unpublished doctoral dissertation]. UCLA.

Imamoglu, E. O. (1975). Children's awareness and usage of intention cues. *Child Development, 46*, 39-45.

Kazdin, A. (1987). *Conduct disorders in childhood and adolescence.* Newbury Park, CA: Sage.

Kelley, H. (1973). The process of causal attribution. *American Psychologist, 28*, 107-128.

Kupersmidt, J., & Coie, J. (1990). Preadolescent peer status, aggression, and school adjustment as predictors of externalizing problems in adolescence. *Child Development, 61*, 1350-1362.

Lefkowitz, M., Eron, L., Walder, L., & Huesmann, L. (1977). *Growing up to be violent: A longitudinal study of the development of aggression.* New York: Pergamon.

Loeber, R., & Stouthamer-Loeber, M. (1987). Prediction. In H. Quay (Ed.), *Handbook of juvenile delinquency* (pp. 325-382). New York: Wiley.

Nasby, W., Hayden, B., & DePaulo, B. (1980). Attributional bias among aggressive boys to interpret unambiguous social stimuli as displays of hostility. *Journal of Abnormal Psychology, 89*, 459-468.

Olweus, D. (1979). Stability of aggressive reaction patterns in males: A review. *Psychological Bulletin, 86*, 852-875.

Park, R., & Slaby, R. (1983). The development of aggression. In P. Mussen (Ed.), *Handbook of child psychology* (pp. 547-642). New York: Wiley.

Rule, B. (1974). The hostile and instrumental functions of human aggression. In J. De Wit & W. Hartup (Eds.), *Determinants and origins of aggressive behavior* (pp. 125-146). The Hague: Mouton.

Sancilio, M., Plumert, J., & Hartup, W. (1989). Friendship and aggressiveness as determinants of conflict outcomes in middle childhood. *Developmental Psychology, 25*, 812-819.

Shantz, C. (1983). Social cognition. In P. Mussen (Ed.), *Handbook of child psychology* (pp. 495-547). New York: Wiley.

Sobol, M., & Earn, B. (1985). Assessment of children's attributions for social experiences: Implications for social skills training. In B. Schneider, K. Rubin, & J. Ledingham (Eds.), *Children's peer relations: Issues in assessment and intervention* (pp. 93-110). New York: Springer-Verlag.

Waas, G. (1988). Social attributional biases of peer-rejected and aggressive children. *Child Development, 59*, 969-975.

Weiner, B. (1986). *An attributional theory of motivation and emotion*. New York: Springer-Verlag.

Weiner, B. (1991). On perceiving the other as responsible. In R. Dientsbier (Ed.), *Nebraska symposium on motivation* (pp. 165-198). Lincoln: University of Nebraska Press.

Weiner, B., Graham, S., & Chandler, C. (1982). Pity, anger and guilt: An attributional analysis. *Personality and Social Psychology Bulletin, 8*, 226-232.

SECTION II

CONTEXTUAL INFLUENCES ON YOUTH ANGER, HOSTILITY, AND AGGRESSION

Recently some controversy has surrounded national research agendas emphasizing the role individual personal characteristics play in the expression of violent, aggressive behavior. Given this controversy, we feel it is important to become familiar with how research informs us about the association between key contextual conditions and anger, hostility, and aggression. In doing so, it is not our intent to place primary explanatory power on any specific contextual factors. Nonetheless, it is important to consider these factors when designing an anger prevention/ intervention program. The authors, for example, had a situation in which an incarcerated youth was being evaluated for aggressive behavior. School and probation officials perceived this youth to be unpredictable and dangerous. Although it is true that aggressive behavior was present, investigation disclosed that the youth had "put on" 30 pounds during the previous summer to "beef up" for football. Further investigation revealed that this was due to abuse of steroids, which provided another factor to understand the angry, aggressive behavior being observed. If we had initiated an anger control program, however well-conceived, without attending to the young man's steroid abuse, the probability of a successful outcome would have been diminished. Section II includes chapters that focus on *physical* and *biological* factors (Poston, Norton, & Morales, Chapter 3) related to the expression of anger or aggressive behaviors. Other chapters focus on influences that are particularly salient to the lives of youth: *family* (Miller, Chapter 4), the *classroom* setting (Pullis, Chapter 5), and *sociocultural* factors (Chan, Chapter 6). The importance of understanding contextual factors associated with aggression is emphasized in the preliminary report of the Youth Violence Task Force to the American Psychological Association. This report described a "trajectory" toward violence among youth who experience multiple risks in family, peer, and other social relationships.

3 BIOLOGICAL INFLUENCES ON ANGER AND HOSTILITY

W. S. Carlos Poston, Rebecca Norton, and
María Guadalupe Morales

DEFINING ANGER, HOSTILITY, AND AGGRESSION

The purpose of this chapter is to discuss the various ways that biology can affect the expression of anger in children. It is not within the scope of this chapter to present an exhaustive review of the literature regarding anger and children's aggression; our purpose is rather to focus more succinctly on ways that children's expressions of anger might be influenced by their biology. Although biological factors may not play as large an explanatory role in anger expression as do learning and culture (Achenbach, 1982; Berkowitz, 1990; Johnson, 1972), school psychologists should be aware of possible biological factors that might influence the expression of anger and aggression in children.

Before proceeding further, it is instructive to distinguish between anger and aggression. Anger is an emotion that Webster's Dictionary (Merriam-Webster, 1988) defines as "a feeling of great displeasure, hostility, indignation, or exasperation: wrath" (p. 107). Anger is a feeling that can include some unpleasant thoughts, physical feelings, and behaviors, including hostility, but it does not necessarily include inappropriate or destructive behavior. As Schaefer and Millman (1981) note, there is a place for anger, appropriately expressed. They go on to suggest ways that children might be taught and encouraged to express their anger in socially appropriate ways, such as verbally expressing their feelings and being assertive. The key to this is the word *appropriate*. It is unlikely that school psychologists will receive referrals for children who express their anger in "socially appropriate" ways. It is when children express their anger in ways that are not socially sanctioned that it becomes problematic. This is particularly the case when the expression of anger manifests itself as aggression.

Webster's Dictionary (Merriam-Webster, 1988) defines aggression as "the initiation of forceful, usually hostile, action against another: attack; hostile action or behavior" (p. 86). The focus of this definition is on hostile behavior, or what is done. Although the emotion of anger may set the stage for aggressive behavior, this behavior is not the only possible outcome. The question, then, is how biology influences the expression of anger, or more specifically, how it influences aggressive behavior. This is a tough question, because aggression is often difficult to define. A related definitional problem is that the expression of a particular behavior, in this case aggression, is often assumed to be a fixed property in an individual, rather than a complex process that arises from the interaction of biological, psychological, interpersonal, and environmental factors (Lewontin, Rose, & Kamin, 1984).

Similarly, as Moyer (1983) and Piacente (1986) have observed, aggression is not a unitary construct. It includes many types of behaviors, ranging from behaviors that are essential to survival to blatant destruction and

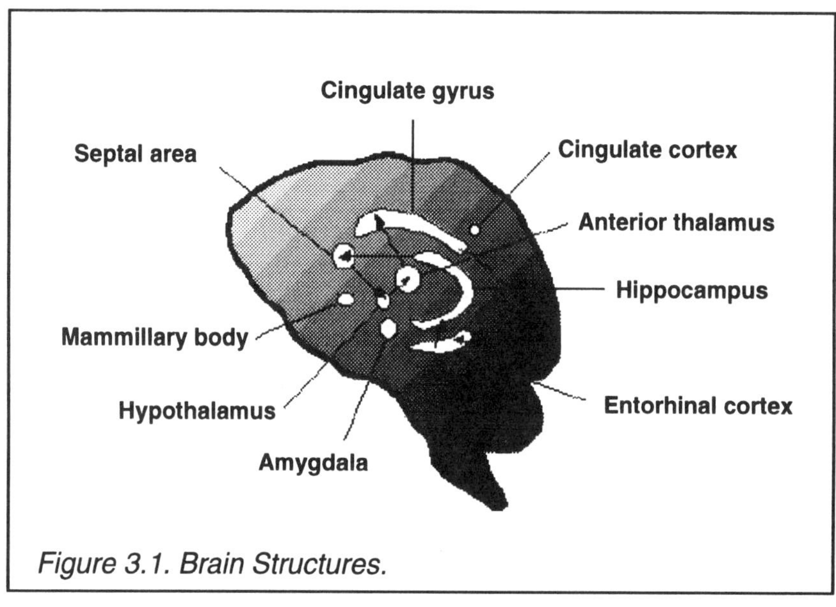

Figure 3.1. Brain Structures.

heinous violence. Although it is usually assumed that most aggressive behavior has a psychosocial or environmental basis, not all aggressive behavior can be accounted for by these factors (Piacente, 1986). Aggressive behavior is a complex mixture of biological factors and environmental factors. Thus, it is important also to examine biological factors that could precipitate and/or influence aggressive behavior.

In the remainder of this chapter, we will (a) examine the anatomical structures of the brain that appear to play a role in the regulation of aggressive behavior and how damage to these areas influences behavior; (b) examine the effects of legal and illegal drugs on both the expression and inhibition of aggressive behavior; (c) explore the role of hormones, the stress response, and diet on aggression; and (d) evaluate the influence of developmental and genetic factors on aggression.

BRAIN-RELATED INFLUENCES

Brain Anatomy and Physiology

The limbic system is thought to be the primary brain structure involved in the regulation of aggressive behavior (Berkowitz, 1990; Johnson, 1972; Pincus & Tucker, 1985). The limbic system is made up of a series of structures in the lower cerebrum and upper brain stem that appear to be involved in the regulation of most motivated behavior. The limbic system is composed of the following structures: the thalamus, epithalamus, hypothalamus, and mammillary bodies; the cingulum; the septal area and nuclei; and the hippocampus, amygdala, and uncus (Pincus & Tucker, 1985). The limbic system appears to have a strong influence on the regulation of aggressive behavior, but it's action is also regulated by the neocortex because experimental stimulation does not cause aggressive or rage reactions (Johnson, 1972; Piacente, 1986). (See Figure 3.1).

Brain Damage/Traumatic Brain Injury

It has long been known that damage to some of these areas of the brain is associated with a resultant increase in aggressive behavior and difficulty with impulse control (Lezak, 1983; Pincus & Tucker, 1985). This information was primarily derived from animal ablation studies, brain stimulation studies with animals and humans, and clinical observation and evaluation of brain-injured individuals and individuals receiving psychosurgery. This research yielded evidence that the limbic area influences memory, learning, emotional states (such as rage and anger), and aggressive behavior. Although it is not within the scope of this chapter to address all of the effects of injury or lesions to the brain, particularly the limbic system, it should be noted that the evidence from animal experiments and clinical observation suggests that a relationship between the neocortex, the limbic system, and violence is extensive (Moyer, 1983; Pincus & Tucker, 1985). For example, decortication of cats causes rage reactions, as does destruction of the ventral medial nucleus of the hypothalamus or the septum (often referred to as "septal rage"). In addition, bilateral lesioning of the temporal lobes, including the hippocampus and the amygdala, is associated with decreased aggression, hypersexuality, visual confusion, and is referred to as Kluver-Bucy Syndrome (Johnson, 1972). Finally, damage to the frontal lobe (referred to as "frontal lobe syndrome") can result in inability to control rage and violent behavior in a large number of patients with this type of damage (Silver & Yudofsky, 1987). Traumatic head injury is a major contributor to a wide variety of neurological and neuropsychological disorders and the leading cause of death in pediatric populations. Although precise incidence estimates are not readily available, due to differences in data collection and criteria in epidemiological studies, Fletcher and Levin (1988) present reviews that give estimates of 220 per 100,000 children (0.22%). Suffice it to say, a wide variety of behaviors have been reported in connection with mild, moderate, and severe traumatic brain injury (TBI), brain damage associated with tumors, and cerebral vascular accidents (CVA), such as irritability, attentional deficits, hypersensitivity, and increases in aggressive behaviors (Begali, 1987; Silver & Yudofsky, 1987). In addition, several retrospective studies have demonstrated a relationship between increased violent behavior and neurological impairment in juvenile offenders. Pincus and Tucker's (1985) review led them to conclude that extremely violent juvenile offenders differed in several ways from their less violent peers. More specifically, violent juveniles were more likely to manifest major and minor signs of neurological impairment including complex partial seizures; they were more likely to experience paranoid ideations; and they were more likely to have witnessed extreme violence and/or suffered abuse.

Additionally, there is some evidence to suggest attentional deficits may predispose some to aggressive and/or other delinquent behavior as adolescents (Pincus & Tucker, 1985). Although these studies present possible biological factors that might influence the expression of aggressive behavior, they suffer from fairly obvious confounds, such as the fact that most are retrospective in nature and cannot attest to causality. Many of these studies examined biological, as well as social variables, and did not control well for social/cultural influences. Finally, the existence, incidence, and nature of conditions such as attentional deficits and hyperactivity are still debated topics (Henker & Whalen, 1989; McGuinness, 1985).

In general, only moderate to severe cases of TBI have been linked with aggressive or hostile types of behaviors. It is important to note that direct causal relationships between TBI and aggressive behavior cannot be assumed because many other factors may also play a role. These other factors can include:

- *constitutional factors* (e.g., prior, latent conditions or problematic personality traits may be expressed or intensified following the injury),
- *secondary handicaps* related to the injury,
- *lowered intellectual functioning* as a result of the injury,
- *predisposition to disturbance*, and
- *psychosocial deprivation* (e.g., parents with lower income often cannot afford comprehensive rehabilitation programs, parents with already existent marital problems, etc.).

Additionally, it is important to note that the type of disturbance is affected by the site of injury, lateralization of the injury, age at the time of injury, and gender, with males showing a greater risk for increased irritability and acting out. The rate at which psychological disturbances arise, including aggressive behavior, is influenced by the severity of the injury, the type of injury, premorbid behavioral status, psychosocial status, emotional stability of parents, and prior intellectual and academic status (Begali, 1987).

When considering TBI or brain damage as a possible factor in children's aggressive behavior, it is important to remember several things. First, true pathology is rare, or said another way, not all individuals with brain damage experience problems with explosive rage and not all cases of aggressive behavior or explosive rage can be explained by brain damage (Tavris, 1989). In a review of a large study of head-injured patients ($N = 2{,}000$), Tavris (1989) found that only 0.5% of the subjects had spontaneous rage attacks.

Another important factor to note is that the study of abnormal rage (as the result of brain damage) will not necessarily lead to an understanding of aggressive behavior that does not result from brain damage. Said another way, pathology does not explain normality (Tavris, 1989). Similarly, although the limbic system and damage to its components has been the focus of much of the research, it is does not imply that the limbic system is the only area of origin for anger and aggression (Tavris, 1989) because premeditated violence for revenge and profit has been committed by individuals without any known brain damage. Finally, it is important to remember that physiology and anatomy need an environment, because behavior does not occur in a vacuum. As Tavris (1989) stated, "there is no such thing as a rage circuit that is unresponsive to, or independent of, environment and learning" (p. 78). It is critical to appreciate that there are important interactions between physiology, cognition, emotion, learning, and behavior when examining aggressiveness. The existence of a lesion in a part area of the brain will not necessarily lead to aggressive behavior because all of the above factors play a significant role in displays. It is most important to evaluate the problematic behavior functionally for possible behavioral and pharmacological management, because the actual site of the lesion does not necessarily play a large role in the management of the problematic behavior (Lezak, 1983).

DRUG INFLUENCES

Licit Drugs

When discussing the subject of drugs and violence, or how certain drugs may affect the expression of aggressive behavior, one is struck by numerous deficiencies in the literature, such as methodological issues in evaluating drug research (e.g., the lack of active placebos, problems with keeping clinical trials blind, small numbers of subjects, etc.), the problem of defining legal vs. illegal drugs, and the overly reductionistic approaches to studying a very complex phenomenon. In spite of these problems, in this section we will attempt to examine how both legal and illegal drugs can play a role in the expression of aggressive behavior. We will not attempt to cover the specific pharmacology or hypothesized mechanisms of action of these drugs because there are many adequate textbooks on pharmacology and psychopharmacology already in existence and to do so would be beyond the scope of our expertise. Instead, it is our intention to provide educators and psychologists with a brief introduction to the manner in which drugs they might encounter in the schools might influence a child's propensity for violent behavior.

Alcohol. There are several legal drugs that have been hypothesized to have an effect on the incidence of aggressive behavior, usually in adults.

Because alcohol misuse and abuse is one of our country's most serious drug problems, and it is estimated that there are 1.3 million teenagers and preteens who drink to excess (Schaefer & Millman, 1981), it is not surprising that a good portion of the research has focused on the effect of alcohol on behavior. Alcohol is one of the few drugs that is known to precipitate or exacerbate incidents of violence in individuals with a past history of violent behavior (Mckim, 1986; Naranjo & Bremer, 1993; Pincus & Tucker, 1985). It is thought that alcohol, which is a central nervous system depressant, may have this effect because it appears to decrease an individual's ability to make good judgments, as well as causing disinhibition of impulsiveness and aggression, although experimental studies have not shown a consistent direct effect in the absence of environmental factors and personality variables (Mckim, 1986; Naranjo & Bremer, 1993). Thus, it may be the interaction of the physiological effects of alcohol, along with an environment supportive of violence and aggression, learning history, and personality variables, that lead to increases in violence and crime (Johnson, 1972).

Caffeine. Another legal drug that has a hypothesized relationship with aggression is caffeine, which is a central nervous system stimulant. Carmel (1991) reviewed a study that showed, after the removal of caffeine from patients' diets, a 29% decrease in the incidence of violent and destructive behavior in a state hospital setting. It is interesting to note that Carmel (1991) attempted to explain these findings by examining the incidence of violent behavior during the same period of time in another state hospital setting; caffeine use was not restricted for the residents of the second state hospital. The results of this study were similar to those in the first study; during that particular period of time, there was a similar drop in violence (26%), but because caffeine use was unchanged, it is unlikely that decreasing caffeine use was the explanatory factor in the first study's results. Carmel (1991) notes that many factors, such as changes in the patient census and changes in staff and reporting procedures, might account for the lowered incidence of violent behavior. The point to be made here, as Carmel (1991) states so aptly, is that the literature is mixed regarding the effects of caffeine on aggression and psychotic illness. Although there may be some health reasons to minimize caffeine use, related to conditions like hypertension, there is not a substantial amount of evidence to conclude that caffeine is related to increased aggression.

Steroids. Steroid use has been the subject of much controversy in recent years (Schrof, 1992; Yesalis, Kennedy, Kopstein, & Bahrke, 1993).

Here is an example of the difficulty in defining a drug as legal or illegal because steroids are technically legal when prescribed as indicated, but illegal when used the way many people are using them now, specifically as athletic performance-enhancing drugs. It has been estimated that 1 million Americans, about half of whom are adolescents, mostly boys, use black-market steroids (Schrof, 1992). Steroid use, whether for extensive or brief periods of time, affects the muscles, sex organs, and the brain and nervous system of the user.

Although it is still debatable whether steroids actually influence athletic performance, it has been reported, in a comprehensive review of the available literature, that some steroid users (up to 30%) experience greater feelings of aggression and hostility, and greater incidence of angry outbursts (often referred to as "roid rages") (Haupt & Rovere, 1984; Schrof, 1992; Uzych, 1992). Conversely, Bahrke, Wright, O'Connor, Strauss, and Catlin (1990) did not find any differences in the amounts of hostility, aggression, tension, or anxiety reported by steroid users and nonusers on a standardized symptom checklist. Again, it appears that due to the dearth of research, and to flaws with the current research, no definitive statement can be made about the relationship between steroids and aggressive behavior except that such a relationship might exist.

Drug treatments. Another group of legal drugs found to have an impact on the expression of aggression are drugs that are often used to treat aggressiveness in institutional settings. A number of drugs have been found to be useful in managing aggressive outbursts in various institutionalized populations, including brain injured patients, psychotic patients, juvenile offenders, and developmentally disabled patients. It is not within the scope of this chapter to discuss the specific regimens, the ethical issues, the efficacy, or the actual mechanism of action of drug management procedures. We are only attempting to review which drugs are most commonly used to manage aggressive behavior. Antipsychotics (e.g., Thorazine®, Haldol®), which are essentially very potent tranquilizers, are used to decrease violence in psychotic patients, but not in nonpsychotic offenders (Johnson, 1972; Pincus & Tucker, 1985). These drugs tend to produce some problematic side effects when used for long periods of time, such as tardive dyskensia, akasthesia, and a range of sedation, depending on the drug used and the patient response (Kaplan & Saddock, 1989). It is interesting to note that milder sedatives, such as barbiturates and benzodiazepines, have been of limited use because near anesthetic doses are needed to eliminate violence and they have problematic side effects and addictive potential (Johnson, 1972; Kaplan & Saddock, 1989).

Numerous authors have documented the effects of lithium therapy on aggressive behavior in adolescents and children (Sheard, 1975; Siassi, 1982; Vetro, Szentistvayi, Pallag, Vargha, & Szilard, 1985; Worrall, 1977). These studies have tended to find that lithium therapy decreases hyperaggressivity, unprovoked aggressive acts, and excited states. This finding has not been conclusive, however, as Worrall (1977) notes that the administration of lithium was not successful with all patients. Many of these studies did not find statistically significant results, and many had very small sample sizes. Mattes (1986) notes that lithium has also been associated with increased aggressive behavior. In addition, Breggin (1991) reviewed research that examined the effects of lithium on normal volunteers and found that normal volunteers experienced a general dulling and blunting of personality functions and cognitive processes, increased drowsiness, and impaired work ability. Taken together, it is not clear whether lithium is a viable treatment method for aggressive behavior, but this is understandable because aggressive behavior is multidimensional and multifactorial, the biological mechanisms of aggression are not well understood, and lithium's mechanism of action is not known (Kaplan & Saddock, 1989).

There are several drugs that have reportedly been found to decrease temper outbursts in brain-damaged populations. Propranolol (Inderal®) is a beta blocker, currently used to control hypertension. Propranolol has been used to control anger outbursts in both brain-injured and non-brain-injured populations (Greendyke & Kanter, 1986; Mansheim, 1981; Mattes, 1986; Ratey, Morrill, & Oxenkrug, 1983). Unfortunately, most of these articles are case presentations and not controlled studies. Drugs like carbamazepine (Tegretol®—an anticonvulsant) have been used to control rages and aggressive behavior in Kluver-Bucy/temporal lobe damaged patients with rage attacks and patients with epilepsy (Mattes, 1986; Stewart, 1985). Again, these articles tend to present case studies and are not well-controlled studies.

Finally, moderate levels of legally prescribed stimulants have been reported to control hyperactivity and aggression in adolescents and children, whereas high levels have been found to increase problematic behavior (Henker & Whalen, 1989; Mattes, 1986). The usefulness and efficacy of these drugs (such as Ritalin®) is still a debated topic—with long-term use, as documented in some longitudinal studies, showing some deterioration in several of the touted positive effects (Breggin, 1991; McGuinness, 1985).

All of these studies point to the inadequacies of viewing multifactorial behaviors, such as anger and aggression, from an overly reductionistic viewpoint and attempting to control aggressive behavior biologically when the target behavior is complex and the role of biological determinants is not well understood. In addition, as Pincus and Tucker (1985) note, "it seems intuitively unlikely that anticonvulsant, antipsychotic, or beta-blocking medications would work in individuals whose violent behavior is semiadaptive, predatory, or motivated by loyalty to a cause, even if brain damage were a factor" (p. 93).

Conclusions about licit drugs. From the above discussion, it is apparent that the licit drugs reviewed can have an impact on an individual's behavior, in both increasing ***and*** decreasing the probability of aggressive behavior. On the other hand, it is also apparent that there is not a unicausal relationship between drug presence and aggression. It is very important to examine the environmental, social, affective, and cognitive factors that also have an influence on aggressive behavior.

Illicit Drugs

Now we shift our focus to illegal/illicit drugs and examine the literature that has explored the relationship between aggressive behavior and the use of marijuana (cannabis), other hallucinogens, and stimulants. It is important to keep in mind that direct causal relationships between the use of a particular drug and aggressive behavior have not been demonstrated, but that drug effects on behavior are multifactorial and can depend on the specific physiological action of the drug, prior learning, the environment, and so on (Achenbach, 1982; Schaefer & Millman, 1981).

Marijuana and other hallucinogens. Marijuana, a hallucinogen, is the most widely used illicit drug in the United States and it has been estimated that between 35%–50% of high school and college students have used it at least once (Achenbach, 1982; Schaefer & Millman, 1981). As with other drugs, the effects of marijuana vary with the user's expectations, personality, and circumstances of use (Achenbach, 1982). In general, the subjective effects are a feeling of mild intoxication, loosening of inhibitions, increased self-confidence, and uncontrollable hilarity or crying, as well as other well documented psychological and neuropsychological effects (Achenbach, 1982).

With regard to aggression and anger, several studies have reported contradictory findings. Hendin, Pollinger, Ulman, and Carr (1981) found that adolescents reported using marijuana to reduce their feelings of anger.

In addition, the teenagers reported that it helped them overcome rage and control violent impulses. In a similar vein, Hendin and Haas (1985) found that the college students they interviewed reported that marijuana relieved their feelings of tension, and that they used it to ease feelings of chronic anger and frustration. Unfortunately, these studies relied exclusively on interview data, which can be fraught with self-report bias. In stark contrast to the above findings, Stoner (1988) found that individuals who used marijuana frequently expressed more aggression when motivated by angry feelings than did nonusers or occasional users. In addition, Achenbach (1982) reviewed several longitudinal studies on drug use and social problems and discovered that there is a documented relationship between early marijuana use and later social problems, including an increased tendency to have a police record for nondrug offenses and more reported violent behavior in young, Black, urban males. This points to the multifactorial nature of anger and aggression and the varying roles that social/environmental, psychological, and biological factors play in this complex phenomenon.

Other hallucinogens have been documented to have an impact on the expression of aggressive and violent behavior, but it is not a simplistic causal relationship. LSD (lysergic acid diethylamide) is the next most widely use hallucinogen and has been documented to cause hallucinations, delusions, and disorientation, some terrifying enough to precipitate violent behavior and suicide attempts (Schaefer & Millman, 1981). PCP (phencyclidine), an animal tranquilizer, has been documented as causing intense perceptual disturbances, depersonalization, disorganization, and, in some individuals, violent and suicidal behavior (Achenbach, 1982).

Stimulants. The most widely abused stimulants are cocaine, PCP, and other amphetamines, which act by stimulating the central nervous system to increase activity and alertness and speed up bodily processes (Mckim, 1986; Schaefer & Millman, 1981). The abuse of these drugs is associated with increased nervous system activity, emotional reactivity, and physiological arousal, and in some individuals, psychotic symptoms including paranoia and disorganized thinking (Mckim, 1986; Yudofsky, Silver, & Hales, 1993). A few analog and self-report studies have found a relationship between cocaine use and aggressive behavior (Manschreck, 1993; Miller, Gold, & Mahler, 1991). Licata, Taylor, Berman, and Cranston (1993) also found that subjects who were given increased doses of cocaine reacted more aggressively in an analog study. Additionally, McCardle and Fishbein (1989) found a relationship between self-reported violence and reported PCP use. Even so, they also found that behavioral responses to PCP varied, depending on the background and personality characteristics of the PCP users. Consistent with this, other literature does not indicate a strong relationship between their specific use and incidence of anger and aggressive behavior (Achenbach, 1982; Mckim, 1986; Schaefer & Millman, 1981). We see again that anger and aggressive behavior is multifactorial and the expression of aggressive behavior requires a combination of environmental support, appropriate learning and personality variables, and, in some cases, physiological/biological priming.

Emotional status and illicit drug use. Finally, although the discussion of the effects of drugs has thus far focused on legal and illegal drugs and their role in increasing or decreasing an individual's propensity for inappropriate expressions of anger, it is also instructive to examine how anger might influence drug use. Swaim, Oetting, Edwards, and Beauvais (1989) examined emotional variables that might play a role in adolescent drug use. Using a path analysis model, they found that teenagers with emotional problems, particularly anger, had a higher chance of associating with peers who use drugs and who encourage drug use. Additionally, Brook, Whiteman, Cohen, and Tanaka (1992) found that childhood aggression and parental sociopathy affected later drug use. A shortcoming of the Swaim et al. (1989) and Brook et al. (1992) studies is that they are based on correlational data, so causal inferences are not possible, but they do suggest that anger may have a role in increasing teens' opportunities to develop associations with drug users and possibly increase their drug involvement.

Conclusions about illicit drugs. This review speaks to the complex nature of anger and aggression, in that not only might drug use and effects play a role in anger and inappropriate anger expression, but anger may play a role in developing drug use. The reviewed research points to the heterogeneous nature and multifactorial causes of aggressive behavior.

DIETARY INFLUENCES

Malnutrition

The role of dietary factors and nutrition on behavior has long been an area of interest and speculation (Story & Rosen, 1987). Conditions such as undernutrition, nutrient deficiency, nutritional excesses, and meal skipping have been correlated with problems of cognition, mood, behavioral, or neurological function, and physical growth (Lozoff, 1989; Story & Rosen, 1987). Several investigators have attempted to explore the relationship between nutritional/dietary factors and the expression of anger/aggression.

Story and Rosen (1987), in a review article, noted that iron deficiency has an undetermined relationship with juvenile delinquency. It has been found that iron deficiency occurs in twice as many incarcerated adolescents as in nonjailed peers, but this result is confounded by the fact that trace metal deficiencies are much more likely to occur in the context of poverty, disadvantaged economic and social conditions, and environmental deprivation—conditions experienced by greater proportions of teenage offenders (Lozoff, 1989).

Less confusingly, starvation and the resultant hypoglycemia (low blood glucose levels) has been associated with anger outbursts and irritability (Piacente, 1986; Story et al., 1987), but again, there are multiple nutritional deficiencies associated with starvation, as well as numerous environmental and social factors. Finally, Story et al. (1987) note that tryptophan, a naturally occurring amino acid commonly found in cheese and a serotonin precursor (serotonin, a neurotransmitter, is thought to play a role in arousal and sleep, pain sensation, mood, and aggression), has been found to reduce aggression in some populations, such as aggressive schizophrenic males. In addition, thiamine-deficient diets, which impair the production of serotonin, appear to play a role in precipitating aggressive behavior. Similarly, Kitahara (1986) found that when cultural and social differences are minimal, low tryptophan ratios (and thus, theoretically, low serotonin levels), are associated with high homicide rates in western and southern European populations. On the other hand, Kitahara (1986) also found that social and cultural differences play much more significant roles in homicides. In addition, Piacente (1986) warns that these findings may tend to present an oversimplified picture, because they do not take into account the complexity of brain anatomy and function, the interaction of neurotransmitters, and their differing effects on the receptor synapses.

Sugar

Schoenthaler and Doraz (1983), in a quasi-experimental study, reduced antisocial behavior by 48% in juvenile detention home occupants by making nutritional improvements, such as reducing the quantity of sugar in food, beverages, and snacks. Unfortunately, the Schoenthaler et al. (1983) study suffers from several important problems, including a small sample size, limited generalizability, and difficulties with distinguishing between sugar type, amount, and utilization patterns (e.g., fruit juices were substituted for soft drinks). It is important to note that both soft drinks and fruit drinks have high sugar contents and the sucrose in the soft drinks actually has a lower glycemic index—ability to raise blood glucose—than some fruit juices. In addition, there was a failure to test the "blindness" of their double-blind study, as well as to control for other variables that might explain the changes, such as a priori group differences.

There is a great body of evidence that diet is not a significant factor in aggressive behavior, which led Story et al. (1987) to conclude that the available scientific evidence indicates that diet is not a primary factor in the mediating of problematic adolescent behaviors, including aggression. Consistent with this conclusion, Kruesi et al. (1987) found that sugar loading did not increase aggression or activity in preschool children. This is consistent with a recent review of the literature by Furlong and Poston (1992), which found inconclusive evidence for any relationship between sugar and problematic behavior in children.

ENDOCRINE AND NERVOUS SYSTEM INFLUENCES

Androgenic Hormonal Influences

Although clear relationships between androgenic (sex-related) hormones and aggression have been demonstrated in lower animals, in humans the relationship is less clear (Buchanan, Eccles, & Becker, 1992; O'Carroll & Bancroft, 1985). In males, androgenic hormones are primarily produced in the male gonads and testosterone is the main androgenic hormone, whereas in females the main source of androgenic hormones is the adrenal glands (Carlson, 1986). Several studies have attempted to examine the relationship between testosterone levels and aggressive behavior. Testosterone is produced in the Leydig cells of the testes and plays a role in spermatogenesis and production of secondary sexual characteristics in males (Andreoli, Carpenter, Plum, & Smith, 1990). Inoff-Germain et al. (1988) investigated the relationship between adolescents' hormone levels and anger/aggressive behavior. Using the logic that adolescent males and females at different levels of puberty are likely to be experiencing disruption of their past levels of hormonal equilibrium (their androgen levels should be increased the further into puberty they are), they interviewed the adolescents and their families with regard to how anger was expressed by youth . Their results indicated that the older the male adolescent (i.e., the higher the pubertal stage), the less likely he was to show no anger when aggressed against and the more likely he was to express anger and aggressive behavior. There were no significant findings for female adolescents, except that they had significantly lower levels of testosterone than males (Inoff-Germain et al., 1988).

Supportive evidence for the role of testosterone in the expression of aggressive behavior comes from both research on the treatment of male sexual offenders and animal studies. For example, in Moyer's (1983) review of the literature, he notes that castration and the administration of estrogens, progesterones, and/or antiandrogens have been found to decrease expressions of anger and aggressiveness in male offender populations. Similarly, men with XYY syndrome (a sex chromosome disorder) tend to have higher rates of criminal behavior and juvenile delinquency as well as a higher rate of testosterone synthesis (Piacente, 1986). Finally, Piacente (1986) also notes that castration of mammals results in the reduction of fighting and aggressive displays.

In contrast to the above results, Piacente (1986) notes that there is much species variation in castration results and that castration appears to affect the behavior of male higher primates and humans less; it is also known that excessive levels of testosterone actually suppress fighting and aggressive behavior. In addition, Piacente (1986) notes that attempts to substantiate the notion that higher testosterone levels correlate with violence (rape) have not been successful. Similarly, Buchanan et al. (1992), in their major review of the literature, concluded that whereas androgenic hormones might have activating effects in the expression of aggressive behavior in adolescents, factors such as changing roles, sociocultural expectations, and the timing of puberty are much more likely to explain aggression or delinquent behavior.

Another often-noted confound is that testosterone levels can be increased temporarily by activity level or exercise (Picante, 1986). Achenbach's (1982) review also contests the simplistic relationship between XYY syndrome, testosterone levels, and violence by noting many confounds with this research, such as the facts that the overall proportion of males with XYY syndrome is very low (< 0.11%), the number of XYY males who are incarcerated is low, the crimes they commit are not particularly aggressive, and the total proportion of crime they commit is low. He also notes that males with XYY syndrome have lower levels of intellectual functioning (IQs), and this may account for their elevated levels of incarceration in comparison to the general population. Additionally, as much as 90% of the males with XYY syndrome remain outside of mental hospitals and penal institutions (Pincus & Tucker, 1985).

O'Carroll and Bancroft (1985) found in a case study that a patient who was previously aggressively reactive to high doses of testosterone showed no increase in aggressive outbursts when his testosterone levels were gradually increased and hospital staff raters were kept blind to the dosages of testosterone administered. On an interesting note, women who suffer from PMS (premenstrual syndrome) are more likely to report more feelings of irritability, hostility, and violent acts premenstrually. This is interesting because testosterone is not known to play a role in PMS and women tend to have significantly lower testosterone levels than men (Andreoli et al., 1990; Moyer, 1983). Additionally, it should be noted that only a small number of women (20% or less) suffer severe and disruptive PMS symptoms (Andreoli et al., 1990). This all leads to the repetitively emphasized point that aggressive behavior is complex in origin, many factors play a role in precipitating aggression, and even those individuals with a significant biological predisposition are not necessarily prone to engage in angry or aggressive behavior unless learning, personological, interpersonal, and environmental factors support it.

Finally, although the link between nuerochemistry and hostility is not known completely, recent findings are showing an association between low levels of serotonin in the central nervous system fluid and high scores on psychological measures of hostility (Williams & Williams, 1993). This possible relationship warrents close monitoring.

Stress-Related Influences

Current data suggest that a complex relationship exists between stress, physiological arousal, and aggressive behavior. As Moyer (1983) notes, it is known that prolonged frustration and stress are important variables in inducing aggressive behavior. Physiologically, it is known that stress initiates activation of several biological pathways, including the nervous system, the respiratory system, the circulatory/cardiovascular system, the musculoskeletal system, the endocrine system, the gastrointestinal system, and the immune system, to name a few (Snyder, 1989). In addition, the stress response appears to be mediated by the nervous system, the endocrine system, and the immune system. Immediate physiological responses are mediated by the autonomic nervous system (ANS), which controls basic bodily processes, such as heart rate, digestion, respiration, and blood pressure. Activation of this system under stress is commonly referred to as sympathetic arousal or the "fight or flight" response, because the increased arousal prepares the body for dealing with a stressor (e.g., rapid heart rate and respirations, decreased peripheral blood flow, increased muscle tension, and increased arousal and vigilance).

The endocrine system, via the adrenal medulla (the adrenal gland is on top of the kidney), maintains the short-lived sympathetic arousal by releasing epinephrine (E) and norepinephrine (NE), which maintain increased physiological arousal for an hour or more (Snyder, 1989). Thus, when a child gets upset, it is often difficult for him or her to calm down quickly, due to the endocrine-mediated effects of arousal. This leads to a very important point about stress-related aggression: It is common for people to experience stressors, some chronic, on a routine basis. On the other hand, it is not common for children or adults to act aggressively in response to all the stressors they encounter in daily life. It is evident that stress and all possible responses, including aggression, are centrally mediated (Snyder, 1989). This means that the way children learn to think about stress and how they appraise a stressor, as well as the availability and effectiveness of their coping options, in addition to personality factors, biological predisposition, and situational factors, play a role in their ultimate behavioral response.

GENETIC INFLUENCES

Sex Chromosome Influences

As was previously noted, one of the most examined genetic factors that was felt to have a relationship to aggressive behavior was the sex chromosome disorder XYY syndrome. Although it was initially believed that males with this syndrome were highly predisposed towards aggression, further research has generated alternative explanations that have already been discussed (Achenbach, 1982). Another genetic condition that is related to sex chromosome abnormalities is Klinefelter's Syndrome. Individuals with this syndrome are genetic males who have two or more X chromosomes, in addition to their Y chromosome (Andreoli et al., 1990). The only reason that this condition is mentioned is that males with this syndrome have been found to have lower than normal levels of testosterone. As a result of the extra X chromosome, their testes are underdeveloped and they are infertile, as well as behaviorally passive. Although this may seem to support the notion that testosterone has an important influence on behavior, the literature already covered in the previous section presents a much more complex relationship between testosterone and the expression of aggressive behavior.

Other Genetic Factors

Primary research areas that have attempted to examine the relationship between genetic factors and aggressive behavior include investigations that relate genetic factors to temperament; aggressive, delinquent, and criminal behavior; and the study of the genetic basis and developmental course of sociopathy. Tavris (1989) notes that twin studies have demonstrated strong correlations for particular aspects of infant and child temperament, including emotionality, sociability, level of activity, and impulsivity. These four areas of personality are believed to have strong hereditary components. On the other hand, Tavris (1989) also notes that inherited predispositions are diffuse and generalized and may only provide a reaction range, in which environmental, learning factor, and situational variables play a greater role in determining behavioral outcome. In fact, Tavris (1989) goes on to note that "efforts to demonstrate emotional consistency from infancy through childhood to adulthood are contradictory and inconclusive" (p. 84) With regards to aggression in particular, there is some evidence that aggressive behavior in boys shows some developmental stability (Achenbach, 1982). In contrast, the correlation between early and later aggression in girls is generally low, which may be due to societal and cultural pressures against aggressiveness in girls. In addition, the increased stability of aggression in boys may be partially due to the interaction between their body types (boys have greater muscularity, which may make aggressive behavior more effective, and thus more reinforcing) and rewards associated with successful use of aggressive behavior (Achenbach, 1982).

Finally, Ghodsian-Carpey and Baker (1987) did not find any significant differences between mothers' ratings of monozygotic and dizygotic twins on report measures of aggressive behavior. They go on to note studies investigating the relationship between aggression and genetics have had inconclusive results. In general, these relationships again point to the complex relationship between biology, psychology, and environment in the expression of anger and aggressive behavior.

Delinquent/criminal behavior and sociopathy, which can include aggressive behavior, have also been thought to have genetic influences. A few studies have indicated that a genetic influence in regard to criminal behavior exists (Brennan, Mednick, & Kandel, 1991). These studies include monozygotic and dizygotic twin studies, as well as adoption studies. In general, they have revealed somewhat higher concordance rates for criminal behavior in identical twins than in fraternal twins or children who were adopted (Brennan et al., 1991; Plomin, 1989). In contrast, Plomin (1989) also notes that whereas the concordance rate for identical twins is generally higher in the reviewed studies (87%), the concordance rate for fraternal twins, who share no more genetic material than any set of siblings, was also quite high

(72%), indicating slight genetic influence and significant environmental similarities. Finally, antisocial behavior in childhood has usually been a predictor of adult sociopathy, but numerous other factors also play a role in the development of antisocial behavior, including learning, personality, and environmental factors (Achenbach, 1982).

DEVELOPMENTAL INFLUENCES

Prenatal and Perinatal Factors

There has been much speculation about how prenatal factors might influence behavior. The prenatal period can be viewed as the time around conception or the first few weeks of pregnancy and prenatal risks comprise those factors that are associated with more serious developmental consequences (Kopp & Kaler, 1989). Prenatal risk factors can include adverse events and environments, harmful agents, and chronic or acute maternal conditions. There is currently much speculation about what factors might affect a fetus before birth. Kopp and Kaler (1989), in a review article on developmental risks in infancy, identified the emergence of a new field called behavioral teratology, which focuses on the behavioral effects of prenatal and perinatal damage to the brain. One prenatal condition that is known to cause substantial damage to the brain is the abuse of alcohol during pregnancy, which often results in fetal alcohol syndrome (FAS). Full-blown FAS, which may occur in 12 live births per 100,000 in the United States (Kaplan & Saddock, 1989), is thought to cause substantial developmental problems, such as mental retardation and postnatal growth retardation, characteristic facial malformations, and nonspecific minor and major malformations (Kaplan & Saddock, 1989; Pincus & Tucker, 1985).

Although FAS is not necessarily known to play a role in aggressive behavior and not all children born to alcohol-abusing mothers show FAS (Kopp & Kaler, 1989; Pincus &Tucker, 1985), it is not known whether there might be a relationship between other behavior problems, including aggression, and maternal drug and alcohol use, making this an important area for longitudinal research. In addition, a host of other factors, including pollutants, viral infections, and adverse environmental conditions could pose prenatal risks (Kopp & Kaler, 1989).

The perinatal period is the time frame that overlaps the prenatal period and postnatal life. Perinatal risks have been defined as any condition or symptom that might stress the fetus or neonate (Kopp & Kaler, 1989). Brennan et al. (1991) suggest that certain perinatal factors such as obstetrical difficulties could play a role in criminal behavior. In fact, they found a positive relationship between individuals with serious offense records and perinatal difficulties. Unfortunately, retrospective studies like this suffer from significant problems, including numerous confounds that cannot be adequately controlled in a post-hoc fashion and correlational designs that do not allow causal inference.

CONCLUSIONS

In this chapter, we have presented various biological factors that may influence children's expressions of anger and aggressive behavior. In spite of the definitional difficulties mentioned in the beginning of the chapter, we have examined how different biological variables may play a role in aggressive behavior. We have stressed that nonbiological factors such as environment, family, learning history, and personality often play a primary role in the development and expression of anger and aggressive behavior. Nonetheless, it is important to examine biological influences because some conditions occur infrequently but with obvious behavioral effects (e.g., traumatic brain injury or fetal alcohol syndrome), others have suspected but unspecified effects (e.g., XYY syndrome or steroid use), and yet others are occurring with increasing frequency (e.g., alcohol abuse, stimulant abuse, and stress-related factors). For these reasons educators and psychologists need to become more aware and knowledgeable of the complex ways in which biology influences human behavior. We have also emphasized the complex and interactional nature of these biological factors with other elements, including personality variables, cognitive/learning histories, interpersonal and social factors, and environmental factors, in determining the expression of anger and aggressive behavior. Finally, and most important, we have emphasized the complex nature of anger and aggressive behavior, the difficulties inherent in studying such complex phenomena, and the need for further research using sophisticated and less reductionistic and simplistic models. This is necessary so that more useful and compassionate conceptualizations and approaches to treatment are available for educators and psychologists and for the children they serve.

REFERENCES

Achenbach, T. (1982). *Developmental psychopathology.* New York: John Wiley & Sons.

Andreoli, T., Carpenter, C., Plum, F., & Smith, L. (1990). *Cecil's essentials of medicine* (2nd ed.). Philadelphia: W. B. Saunders.

Bahrke, M., Wright, J., O'Connor, J., Strauss, R., & Catlin, D. (1990). Selected psychological characteristics of anabolic-androgenic steroid users. *The New England Journal of Medicine, 323*, 834-835.

Begali, V. (1987). Psychiatric and psychosocial sequelae of traumatic head injury: Educational implications. In V. Begali (Ed.), *Head injury in children and adolescents: A resource and review for school and allied professionals* (pp. 82-90). Brandon, VT: Clinical Psychology Publishing Co.

Berkowitz, L. (1990). On the formation and regulation of anger and aggression. *American Psychologist, 45,* 494-503.

Breggin, P. (1991). *Toxic psychiatry.* New York: St. Martin's Press.

Brennan, P., Mednick, S., & Kandel, E. (1991). Congenital determinants of violent and property offending. In D. J. Pepler & K. H. Rubin (Eds.), *The development and treatment of childhood aggression* (pp. 81-92). Hillsdale, NJ: Lawrence Erlbaum.

Brook, J. S., Whiteman, M., Cohen, P., & Tanaka, J. S. (1992). Childhood precursors of adolescent drug use: A longitudinal analysis. *Genetic, Social, and General Psychology Monographs, 188,* 195-213.

Buchanan, C., Eccles, J., & Becker, J. (1992). Are adolescents the victims of raging hormones: Evidence for activational effects of hormones on moods and behavior at adolescence. *Psychological Bulletin, 111*, 62-107.

Carlson, N. (1986). *Physiology of behavior* (3rd ed.). Boston, MA: Allyn and Bacon.

Carmel, H. (1991). Caffeine and aggression. *Hospital and Community Psychiatry, 42*, 637-639.

Fletcher, J., & Levin, H. (1988). Neurobehavioral effects of brain injury in children. In D. K., Routh (Ed.), *Handbook of pediatric psychology* (pp. 258-295). New York: Guilford Press.

Furlong, M. J., & Poston, W. S. C. (1992). *Sugar's effect of children's behavior: The sweet trooth.* Paper presented at the annual meeting of the California Association of School Psychologists, San Francisco, CA.

Ghodsian-Carpey, J., & Baker, L. A. (1987). Genetic and environmental influences on aggression in 4- to 7-year-old twins. *Aggressive Behavior, 13,* 173-186.

Greendyke, R., & Kanter, D. (1986). Therapeutic effects of pindolol on behavioral disturbances associated with organic brain disease: A double-blind study. *Journal of Clinical Psychiatry*, *47*, 423-426.

Haupt, H., & Rovere, G. (1984). Anabolic steroids: A review of the literature. *The American Journal of Sports Medicine*, *12*, 469-484.

Hendin, H., & Haas, P. (1985). The adaptive significance of chronic marijuana use for adolescents and adults. *Advances in Alcohol and Substance Abuse*, *4*, 99-115.

Hendin, H., Pollinger, A., Ulman, R., & Carr, A. (1981). The functions of marijuana abuse for adolescents. *American Journal of Drug and Alcohol Abuse, 8*, 441-456.

Henker, B., & Whalen, C. (1989). Hyperactivity and attention deficits. *American Psychologist, 44*, 216-233.

Inoff-Germain, G., Arnold, G., Nottelmann, E., Jusman, E., Butler, G., & Chrousos, G. (1988). Relations between hormone levels and observational measures of aggressive behavior of young adolescents in family interactions. *Developmental Psychology, 24*, 129-139.

Johnson, R. (1972). *Aggression in man and animals*. Philadelphia: W. B. Saunders.

Kaplan, H., & Saddock, B. (1989). *Comprehensive textbook of psychiatry* (2nd ed.). Baltimore, MD: Williams and Wilkins.

Kitahara, M. (1986). Dietary tryptophan ratio and homicide in western and southern Europe. *Journal of Orthomolecular Medicine, 1*, 13-16.

Kopp, C., & Kaler, S. (1989). Risk in infancy. *American Psychologist, 44*, 224-230.

Kruesi, M., Rapoport, J., Cummings, E., Berg, C., Ismond, D., Flament, M., Yarrow, M., & Zahn-Waxler, C. (1987). Effects of sugar and aspartame on aggression and activity in children. *American Journal of Psychiatry, 144*, 1487-1490.

Lewontin, R., Rose, S., & Kamin, C. (1984). *Not in our genes*. New York: Pantheon Press.

Lezak, M. (1983). *Neuropsychological assessment* (2nd ed.). New York: Oxford University Press.

Licata, A., Taylor, S., Berman, M., & Cranston, J. (1993). Effects of cocaine on human aggression. *Pharmacology, Biochemistry and Behavior, 45*, 549-552.

Lozoff, B. (1989). Nutrition and behavior. *American Psychologist, 44*, 231-236.

Manschreck, T. C. (1993). The treatment of cocaine abuse. *Psychiatric Quarterly, 64*, 183-197.

Mansheim, P. (1981). Treatment with propranolol of the behavioral sequelae of brain damage. *Journal of Clinical Psychiatry, 42*, 132.

Mattes, J. (1986). Psychopharmacology of temper outbursts: A review. *The Journal of Nervous and Mental Disease, 174*, 464-470.

McCardle, L., & Fishbein, D. H. (1989). The self-reported effects of PCP on human aggression. *Addictive Behaviors, 14*, 465-472.

McGuinness, D. (1985). *When children don't learn.* New York: Basic Books.

Mckim, W. A. (1986). *Drugs and behavior: An introduction to behavior pharmacology*. Englewood Cliffs, NJ: Prentice-Hall.

Merriam-Webster. (1988). *Webster's new Riverside university dictionary.* Boston, MA: The Riverside Publishing Co.

Miller, N. S., Gold, M. S., & Mahler, J. C. (1991). Violent behaviors associated with cocaine use: Possible pharmacological mechanisms. *International Journal of Addictions, 26*, 1077-1088.

Moyer, K. (1983). The physiology of motivation: Aggression as a model. *G. Stanley Hall Lecture Series, 3*, 119-137.

Naranjo, C. A., & Bremer, K. E. (1993). Behavioral correlates of alcohol intoxication. *Addiction, 88*, 25-35.

O'Carroll, R., & Bancroft, J. (1985). Androgens and aggression in man: A controlled case study. *Aggressive Behavior, 11*, 1-7.

Piacente, G. (1986). Aggression. *Neuropsychiatry, 9*, 329-339.

Pincus, J., & Tucker, G. (1985). *Behavioral neurology.* New York: Oxford University Press.

Plomin, R. (1989). Environment and genes. *American Psychologist, 44*, 105-111.

Ratey, J., Morrill, R., & Oxenkrug, G. (1983). Use of propranolol for provoked and unprovoked episodes of rage. *American Journal of Psychiatry, 140*, 1356-1357.

Schaefer, C., & Millman, H. (1981). *How to help children with common problems.* New York: Van Nostrand Reinhold.

Schoenthaler, S., & Doraz, W. (1983). Types of offenses which can be reduced in an institutional setting using nutritional intervention: A preliminary empirical evaluation. *International Journal of Biosocial Research, 4*, 74- 84.

Schrof, J. (1992, June 1). Pumped up. *U.S. News and World Report,* pp. 55-63.

Sheard, M. (1975). Lithium in the treatment of aggression. *The Journal of Nervous and Mental Disease, 160*, 108-118.

Siassi, I. (1982). Lithium treatment of impulsive behavior in children. *Journal of Clinical Psychiatry, 43*, 482-484.

Silver, J., & Yudofsky, S. (1987). Aggressive behavior in patients with neuropsychiatric disorders. *Psychiatric Annals, 17*, 367-370.

Snyder, J. (1989). *Health psychology and behavioral medicine.* Englewood Cliffs, NY: Prentice-Hall.

Stewart, J. (1985). Carbamazepine treatment of a patient with Kluver-Bucy syndrome. *Journal of Clinical Psychiatry, 46*, 496-497.

Stoner, S. (1988). Undergraduate marijuana use and anger. *The Journal of Psychology, 122*, 343-347.

Story, M., & Rosen, G. (1987). Diet and adolescent behavior. *Psychiatric Annals, 17*, 811-817.

Swaim, R., Oetting, E., Edwards, R., & Beauvais, F. (1989). Links from emotional distress to adolescent drug use: A path model. *Journal of Consulting and Clinical Psychology, 57*, 227-231.

Tavris, C. (1989). *Anger: The misunderstood emotion.* New York: Simon and Schuster.

Uzych, L. (1992). Anabolic-androgenic steroids and psychiatric-related effects: A review. *Canadian Journal of Psychiatry, 37*, 23-28.

Vetro, A., Szentistvayi, I., Pallag, L., Vargha, M., & Szilard, J. (1985). Therapeutic experience with lithium in childhood aggressivity. *Pharmacopsychiatry, 14*, 121-127.

Williams, R., & Williams, V. (1993). *Anger kills.* New York Times Books.

Worrall, E. (1977). The antiaggressive effects of lithium. In F. Johnson & S. Johnson (Eds.), *Lithium in medical practice* (pp. 69-77). Blackburn, Lancashire: MTP Press Limited.

Yesalis, C. E., Kennedy, N. J., Kopstein, A. N., & Bahrke, M. S. (1993) Anabolic-androgenic steroid use in the United States. *Journal of the American Medical Association, 270*, 1217-1221.

Yudofsky, S. C., Silver, J. M., & Hales, R. E. (1993). Cocaine and aggressive behavior: Neurobiological and clinical perspectives. *Bulletin of the Menniger Clinic, 57*, 218-226.

4 ENHANCING FAMILY-BASED INTERVENTIONS FOR MANAGING CHILDHOOD ANGER AND AGGRESSION

Gloria E. Miller

INTRODUCTION

The regulation and control of anger constitute a normal aspect of social development with many forms of expression. Kazdin, Rodgers, Colbus, and Seigel (1987) recently have identified at least two behavioral dimensions associated with anger that are closely tied to the development of antisocial behavior in children. The first dimension represents behavior of an overtly aggressive nature that typically involves physical or verbal assaults. John, whose entry into and transitions within his fourth-grade classroom are nothing short of cataclysmic, is representative of this aggressive dimension. His teachers complain that he carelessly rams into people, impulsively takes objects, and taunts or interrupts other children during daily routines. The second dimension reflects internalized hostile attitudes and perceptual reactions not necessarily tied to specific acts of aggression. Joan's behaviors are more reflective of this cognitive and affective dimension. She has been referred by her third-grade teacher because she complains no one likes her, resents any attention given to other children, and engages in covert forms of retaliation towards adults and peers (e.g., lying, nonconfrontative theft). Constellations of such disruptive aggressive or hostile reactions that persist 6 months or longer, result in a variety of antisocial acts, and cause significant disruption across multiple settings reflect serious childhood conduct problems that when left untreated have poor developmental prognosis (Kazdin, 1987; Kelso & Stewart, 1986; Loeber & Dishion, 1984; Wells & Forehand, 1985).

Children like John and Joan represent a significant portion of referrals facing educational and mental health professionals. Recent estimates indicate between 5% to 10% of the children in the general population (Costello, 1989; Rutter, Cox, Tupling, Berger, & Yule, 1975) and over 50% of all children referred for clinical services (Patterson, 1982; Robins, 1981) evidence significant problems of aggression and hostility. These behaviors are on the rise for both males and females (Loeber, 1990) and may have contributed to the dramatic increase over the past two decades in the number of children diagnosed as emotionally disturbed (U.S. Department of Education, 1989) and in the reported acts of a violent, assaultive, or destructive nature that occur within school and community settings (Galloway, Ball, Blomfield, & Seyd, 1982; Rubel, 1978; Bastian & Taylor, 1991).

Problems stemming from uncontrolled expressions of anger and aggression are among the most prevalent and serious complaints made by parents and educators of young children (McGee, Silva, & Williams, 1983). Continued expressions of indiscriminate anger towards others that extend across a variety of settings clearly put a child at risk for a multitude of negative outcomes, including: limited social skills (Dodge, 1980, 1986), peer rejection (Cantrell & Prinz, 1985; Coie, Dodge, & Coppotelli, 1982; Shinn, Ramsey, Walker, O'Neil, & Steiber, 1987), academic difficulties (Hawkins & Lishner, 1987; Patterson, DeBaryshe, & Ramsey, 1989), and later involvement in antisocial acts of both an overt (i.e., assaults and destructive acts) and covert nature (i.e., truancy, theft, and substance abuse) (Loeber & Schmaling, 1985a, 1985b; Loeber & Stouthamer-Loeber, 1987; Robins & Ratcliff, 1980). Strong connections also are found between internalized anger and expressions of revenge in reaction to perceptions of having been wronged (Emmons, 1992). As a result, children with high levels of internalized or externalized anger have the highest probability of being referred to special education programs (McMahon, 1984; Walker, Reavis, Rhode, & Jenson, 1985).

Loeber (1990) recently suggested that aggressive and hostile reactions are part of a developmental trajectory of antisocial behavior. The progression begins with initial parental accounts of early temperamental difficulties, followed by increased reports of impulsivity and inattention, incidents of hostility and aggression, inappropriate interpersonal relations, academic deficiencies, and finally association with an antisocial peer group that predicates delinquent behavior (Loeber, 1990; Loeber & Dishion, 1983; Loeber & Stouthamer-Loeber, 1986). Persistent angry behavior that violates societal norms is linked to other problems in adolescence, including serious mental disorders, drug abuse, teen pregnancy, and school dropout (Elliot, Huizinga, & Ageton, 1985; Loeber, 1988; Robins, 1978, 1986). Unfortunately, by the time such children reach the late elementary grades misconduct patterns are quite stable and resistant to change (Rutter & Giller, 1983). That many disenfranchised adolescents and incarcerated adults report similar behavioral progressions has led to the conclusion that serious problems associated with aggression and anger in childhood may worsen in adulthood for almost half of these cases (Kelso & Stewart, 1986; McCord, 1983; Olweus, 1979; Robins & Ratcliff, 1980; Rutter, 1985).

The implication of such findings is that interventions to alleviate maladaptive expressions of anger and aggression in childhood are essential to prevent an escalation to antisocial behavior during adolescence (Hawkins & Lishner, 1987). Early intervention and prevention make even more sense when one considers the cost of serving delinquent youth who account for a disproportionate number of criminal offenders (Farrington, 1983). Moreover, established behavior patterns in adolescence are considered highly resistant to change (Farrington, Ohlin, & Wilson, 1986; Loeber, Dishion, & Patterson, 1984). Clearly, the prevalence, stability, and deleterious psychological, social, and economic repercussions associated with persistent childhood aggression and hostility provide strong justification for early intervention.

One of the promising approaches to meet the needs of at-risk children and to prevent more serious antisocial outcomes during adolescence is structured family-based intervention (Dumas, 1989; Kazdin, 1987; Miller & Prinz, 1990). A family intervention focus is supported by the strong links found between family antecedent factors and the prevalence of childhood conduct problems (Farrington, 1978; Olweus, 1980; Patterson & Stouthamer-Loeber, 1984; Rutter, 1978; Rutter & Giller, 1983). Dysfunctional interactions within the family environment are hypothesized to be a critical link in the progression of aggressive behaviors across settings and time (Patterson, 1986; Vuchin, Bank, & Patterson, 1992). The disturbed interpersonal relations a child exhibits in the family are assumed to spill over into school settings, to disrupt relations with peers and teachers, to impede academic progress, and finally to increase a child's association with antisocial peer groups (Dishion, 1990; Dishion, Patterson, Stoolmiller, & Skinner, 1991).

School professionals are in a unique position to provide and/or facilitate the delivery of family-based services. Historically, however, the family has not been a primary context within which school professionals have operated. In fact, the majority of school interventions offered for at-risk children are directed at the individual child with minimal parent involvement beyond the assessment phase. Such a child-focused and school-bound orientation may be due to restrictive role delineations, practical constraints, or perceived lack of expertise in providing family-based interventions. It is clear, however, that recent public policy changes mandated by PL 99-457 and the growing impetus to enhance school–home partnerships have heightened the importance of early intervention and created a movement towards family-based service delivery models within school settings (Conoley, 1987, 1989).

The main purpose of the present chapter is to provide an overview of family-based approaches for working with children who exhibit serious problems of anger, hostility, and aggression. Initially, critical components of structured parent training interventions will be reviewed because of their documented empirical success and wide adoption in school and clinical settings. Such interventions emphasize parents as critical therapeutic change agents in the modification of children's behavior and focus on behavioral management skills, communicative competence, and social interactions. Major obstacles that limit the effectiveness of structured parent training will be presented. Finally, specific recommendations will be forwarded to enhance service delivery to families within an ecological framework.

STRUCTURED PARENT TRAINING

Structured parent training programs endorse therapeutic guidelines and principles that are rooted in behavioral (Becker, 1971) and social learning theories (Bandura, 1977, 1986). The central premise behind such approaches is that child behavior is acquired and maintained primarily through social exchanges between parents and children. The seminal work of Gerald Patterson and his colleagues was instrumental in uncovering specific disturbances in parent–child interactions that contributed to child misconduct (Patterson, 1979, 1982; Patterson & Brodsky, 1966; Patterson, Chamberlain, & Reid, 1982; Patterson & Reid, 1973; Reid & Patterson, in press). These findings led to the development of a variety of programs targeted towards changing the contingencies and communication processes operating within a family (Alexander, Barton, Schiavo, & Parsons, 1976; Barkley, 1987; Blechman, 1984; Fleishman, Horne, & Arthur, 1983; Forehand & McMahon, 1981; Patterson & Forgatch, 1987; Patterson, Reid, Jones, & Conger, 1975).

Although the reciprocal nature of interpersonal relations within the family has been recognized, emphasis is placed on the role of the parent in affecting changes in child behavior. Because parents are considered the primary social change agents for their children, a primary goal is to strengthen parental child management skills (Kazdin, 1987). Parents learn strategies for improving prosocial and reducing inappropriate child behavior. These skills are generally taught through a prescribed set of therapeutic activities; however, the course and timing of such activities are matched to the initial competence and unique needs of each family. Parent participation is elicited through supportive coaching and directive methods, such as role-play, discussion, modeling, in vivo practice, home practice assignments, and guided feedback.

Components of Structured Parent Training

At least six critical parental competencies are stressed in structured parent training approaches but the sequence and emphasis given to particular content may vary across different programs.

Tracking, labeling, and pinpointing. An initial goal of many structured parent training programs is to improve parents' monitoring of a variety of overt and covert child misbehaviors and to increase the consistency with which such behaviors are observed (Patterson & Dishion, 1985; Reid, 1975; Reid & Patterson, 1976a). Assignments are given to heighten awareness of what occurs before and after a child's transgression. Parents also learn to replace global, overinclusive, and general descriptions of child behavior (e.g., "He is a terror. He drives me crazy. He never does what he is told") with precise, action-oriented behaviors targeted for change (e.g., "He does not complete chores and often teases his brother"). Such labeling specificity allows parents to track and evaluate changes in child behavior more accurately and facilitates subsequent therapeutic efforts (Patterson & Reid, 1973; Patterson et al., 1975).

Emphasis on positive child behavior. Parents are next taught about the importance of providing greater attention to desirable than to undesired child behavior (Dumas & Wahler, 1985). Parents learn that a disproportionate amount of negative attention (e.g., yelling or screaming) in reaction to inappropriate child behavior can lead to an escalation of punitive actions and to coercive exchanges (Dumas & Wahler, 1985). Thus, a primary goal is to heighten parental observance of prosocial child behaviors in a contingent, consistent, and proactive manner and to thereby increase overall parental approval (Patterson, 1982). Parents are coached to shift their attention primarily to appropriate child behaviors and are given practice in the effective use of social reinforcement. Labeled praise is emphasized that specifies a precise desired behavior (e.g., "I like the way you put all the toys away when I said it was time to go"). Global praise (e.g., "Nice job"), double-edged praise (e.g., "You listened so well this time, why can't you always listen like this"), and nagging (e.g., "You need to get one more, you can do it, almost there, come on one more") are discouraged. Finally, parents are assisted in finding age-appropriate enjoyable activities to share with their child at home in order to promote greater opportunities for pleasant adult–child interactions. These procedures also help to ensure that the child becomes an established source of reinforcement for the parent.

Appropriate commands. Another important aspect of training is to increase parents' understanding of developmentally appropriate expectations, rules, and consequences for child behavior and to teach how to give effective commands (Forehand & McMahon, 1981; Patterson & Reid, 1973). Specific attention is given to enhancing parents' ability to gain child compliance through the use of clear, concise requests and directives. That is, instead of simply telling a child to "clean-up," parents learn to give age-appropriate, distinct commands that communicate measurable steps towards compliance (e.g., "Please pick up all the toys on the floor and put them in the box near the steps"). Parents also are taught to avoid interrogative commands and requests that do not specify precise behavioral responses (e.g., "Can you pick those up?") and to allow sufficient time for compliance before issuing new requests. Instruction in "commanding" includes extensive use of role playing and modeling. In addition, in vivo practice is employed where parents are coached while interacting with their child.

Effective discipline. The importance of consistent, nonphysical disciplinary procedures and follow-through is stressed in all structured parent training programs (Patterson, 1982; Patterson & Brodsky, 1966; Patterson & Reid, 1984). Parents are introduced to a variety of disciplinary approaches that can be applied to reduce noncompliance and inappropriate child behavior. The goal is to shift parents from either excessively lax discipline or an overreliance on physical punishment, towards dependence on simple, routine, nonemotional management procedures that target specific and highly aversive child behaviors (Arnold, O'Leary, Wolff, & Acker, 1991). Typically, parents are taught age- appropriate reinforcement removal strategies, such as ignoring, time-out, and response cost. Discipline procedures are thoroughly discussed, modeled, and extensively role-played. In addition, all newly learned procedures are employed directly in a session with both the parent and child present. Such explicit practice and feedback are warranted before in-home use is recommended.

Extensive discussion, demonstration, role-playing, and in vivo coaching are particularly important when parents are learning time-out procedures. Parents first must acknowledge that a high level of support and reinforcement for the child is necessary for time-out to be effective. Once parents understand the rationale behind time-out, an appropriate time-out "place" is designated and a minimum criterion for the duration of the time-out is established (i.e., between 5 to 10 minutes). Next, parents learn how to administer and release a child from time-out through a series of structured steps (Roberts, 1982). A child's inappropriate behavior is initially recognized with a clear warning of the impending time-out (e.g., "If you do not stop taking your sister's book, then you will have to sit in the chair"). Further transgressions are immediately followed by the calm placement of the child in a designated time-out (e.g., "Tom, you did not return your sister's book. You will have to sit in the chair until I tell you to get out"). The time-out period is ended only if the child is composed at the end the prespecified period. Any other child behavior (e.g., yelling, whining) that occurs at the end of the period results in an extension of the time-out (e.g., "You are not calm yet, you must stay in the chair until I ask you to come out"). Upon release, parents are taught to reissue original requests and to reinforce immediately all attempts towards compliance.

As parents master these new skills and procedures, concomitant discussions are held on how to handle potential obstacles and problems that may arise when using disciplinary procedures at home or in the community. Parents develop explicit contingencies for managing aversive child behaviors in a consistent manner no matter what the situation or context. Most important, emphasis is placed on employing disciplinary techniques in conjunction with procedures to reinforce prosocial child behaviors. The ultimate goal is to get parents to ensure that good things happen when their child acts responsibly and that certain sanctions routinely are administered for inappropriate behavior.

Clear communication. Another overriding goal of structured parent training is to foster effective modes of personal communication between family members, especially surrounding specific child behavior problems (Blechman, 1984; Patterson, 1979). In fact, Blechman and her colleagues (Blechman & McEnroe, 1985; Blechman, Tinsley, Carella, & McEnroe, 1985) have hypothesized that a child's acquisition of appropriate coping responses and subsequent social competence is influenced by how effectively family members exchange information, influence each other's behavior, and resolve problems. In general, effective communication skills are stressed

(Blechman, 1985, 1990), including how to listen actively, empathize and reflect another person's concerns, state personal viewpoints and concerns, and engage in mutual problem solving. Successful actions to reduce and resolve conflict between parents and children are reviewed. Parents who report experiencing high levels of stress or anxiety during conflict situations with their child also are introduced to personal coping strategies (e.g., thought stopping, self-instruction, relaxation training) (Fleishman et al., 1983). Such personal coping strategies are especially helpful when parents are feeling depressed, guilty, and/or out-of-control or if it appears that child misbehavior is a cue for such negative emotional reactions.

Trouble shooting and generalization. Because the transfer of newly learned child management skills is not likely to occur spontaneously (Stokes & Baer, 1977), generalization is stressed throughout training but becomes the focal point of final sessions. Self-control techniques (e.g., self-recording, self-evaluation, self-reinforcement) are often incorporated directly into training sessions by having parents practice both newly learned parenting skills and self-monitoring strategies (Wells & Forehand, 1985). In addition, parents discuss potential areas of future concern and rehearse how to utilize newly acquired skills within new settings (e.g., how to employ time-out when at a public restaurant). The goal is to improve parents' ability to foresee problems and plan for appropriate actions. Strategies for "setting-up" success are reviewed, such as preparing a child for what to expect and designating reasonable standards of behavior before entering into new situations. Moreover, collaboration between home and school is stressed. Parents role-play and then arrange situations in which they communicate to others about their child's needs. The emphasis is on increasing parents' confidence and competence to initiate and coordinate specific behavioral contingencies across home and school settings. Actual assignments are given that allow for reasonable demonstrations of success in the transfer of skills across settings. The goal is to ensure that before termination, parents feel secure in their ability to handle future problems and to coordinate child management procedures across settings.

OBSTACLES TO STRUCTURED PARENT TRAINING

The efficacy of structured parent training has been substantiated in a large number of well-designed studies (see Dumas, 1989, and Kazdin, 1987, for excellent reviews of this literature). In fact, empirical demonstrations have supported positive child outcomes, treatment generalization, and maintenance (Baum & Forehand, 1981; Forehand, Rodgers, McMahon, Wells, & Griest, 1981; Patterson et al., 1982; Patterson & Fleishman, 1979). However, major challenges to the implementation and overall efficacy of structured parent training have been posed, especially in regard to working with at-risk families.

Limited Effectiveness and Engagement

Concerns have been raised about the social significance of structured parent training because of limited evidence of generalized improvements or long-term effectiveness (Kazdin, 1990; Patterson & Fleishman, 1979). Less than favorable outcomes have been reported for a substantial number of families across a variety of settings (Bernal, Kinnert, & Schults, 1980; McMahon & Forehand, 1984; Reid & Patterson, 1976b; Sanders & James, 1983). Two related concerns facing practitioners who offer structured intervention programs are the likelihood of inadequate participation (Prinz & Miller, in press) and limited adherence to newly learned routines (Meichenbaum & Turk, 1987). Such engagement difficulties are commonly reflected in behaviors such as premature drop out, sporadic attendance, insufficient interaction, resistance during treatment, or lack of follow-through on homework assignments (Dumas, 1984c; Firestone & Witt, 1982; Webster-Stratton, 1985). Helping agents commonly report that such behaviors are the fundamental barriers to successful family and individual outcomes (Bernal, 1988; Blechman et al., 1981; Kazdin, 1990; Meichenbaum & Turk, 1987). Attrition occurs in anywhere between 50% to 75% of families referred to clinics because of child aggression or anger (Singh, Janes, & Schechtman, 1982). Unfortunately, families who terminate prematurely typically are those in greatest need (Kazdin, 1990; McMahon, Forehand, Griest, & Wells, 1981; Prinz & Miller, in press).

Mismatched Expectations

Parents and consultants may hold very different beliefs and ideas about the efficacy or value of intervention procedures or the overall goals of an intervention (Reimers & Wacker, 1988; Sigel, 1985). Often these expectations are based on misconceptions, faulty information, distortions, or cultural attitudes (Meichenbaum & Turk, 1987). Such differences when left unspoken can lead to dissatisfaction and disengagement. For example, the application of direct, instructive procedures found in structured family training is not an easy task with at-risk families (Chamberlain & Baldwin, 1987). Parents often do not expect the active involvement or the time and effort required to practice and role-play newly learned parenting skills. Nor do parents expect to make significant changes in personal behaviors and household routines (Bernal, 1988). Oftentimes, such attitudes lead to the determination that the inconveniences and perceived negative side effects outweigh the potential benefits of continuing in treatment. Parents often show signs of resistance when the techniques under discussion are not seen as relevant to their own child's problem (Chamberlain, Patterson, Reid, Kavanagh, & Forgatch, 1984). In fact, parents and children are likely to have constructed implicit hypotheses regarding the causes and possible cures for the targeted problems that have a considerable impact on treatment engagement and adherence (Meichenbaum & Turk, 1987). For instance, Patterson and Forgatch (1985) found that verbal exchanges by helping agents intended to educate and inform parents about potential contributors to child misbehavior led to systematic in-session increases in parental resistance. Because families typically seek help in response to a crisis, there is an increased expectation for immediate solutions to eliminate aversive child behaviors. As a result, parents may be hesitant to focus initial attention on improving positive child behaviors in order to reduce inappropriate behaviors and may show impatience with the seemingly slow pace of progress. Moreover, parents often enter treatment with strong feelings of self-defeat and self-doubt in relation to parenting skills. Thus, pessimism, skepticism, and hopelessness frequently are encountered when introducing new approaches to child management. Such consumer attitudes may prevent parents from investing the necessary amount of energy to adopt new skills and may hinder further adherence and cooperation, especially when in conflict with the trainer's attitudes (Bernal, 1988; McMahon & Forehand, 1984; Reimers & Wacker, 1988).

Interference from Contextual Factors

Structured parent training approaches focus primarily on improving parents' child management skills, yet personal and contextual factors have been found to contribute directly to antisocial behavior and to interfere with personal adjustment (Henggeler, 1991a; Tolan, 1988; Tolan, Cromwell, & Brasswell, 1986; West & Prinz, 1987). In fact, personal problems (e.g., health, depression, drug dependency), socioeconomic disadvantage (e.g., poverty, unemployment), and social stressors (e.g., limited or aversive social networks, marital discord) have deleterious effects on parental competence (Brody & Forehand, 1985; Dumas & Wahler, 1983, 1985; McMahon et al., 1981; Pianta & Egeland, 1990) and child behavior (Garmezy, 1983). Stressful living conditions have been hypothesized to erode the social bonding process needed for the adoption of prosocial behaviors and attitudes during adolescence and adulthood (Elliot et al., 1985; Patterson & Dishion, 1985). These ideas are supported by the fact that aversive contextual factors exacerbate dysfunctional family interactions (Wahler, 1980a, 1980b) and lead to serious disruptions in parent–child relationships (Pianta & Egeland, 1990). In fact, child misconduct may be intensified as a consequence of stressful life events because it disrupts parents' vigilance and attention to child behavior (Dumas, 1986a; Wahler & Dumas, 1989). Multiply stressed parents often find it difficult to accurately monitor their child's behavior (Dumas, 1986b; Wahler & Dumas, 1987a,b). Stressful environmental conditions and concomitant family problems also decrease the likelihood that parents will become active participants in interventions (McMahon, Forehand, Griest, & Wells, 1981). Multiply stressed parents may not have the support or motivation necessary to assimilate new interaction patterns or child management skills (Brody & Forehand, 1985; Griest & Forehand, 1982; Wahler & Dumas, 1989). As a consequence, there is a reduced probability of both short-term (Brody & Forehand, 1985; Dumas & Wahler, 1983; Webster-Stratton, 1985) and long-term (Bernal, 1988; Forehand, Wells, McMahon, Griest, & Rodgers, 1982; Kazdin, 1990) intervention success.

Restricted Focus

A final concern with structured parent training is its singular focus on deficient parenting determinants of antisocial behavior. Henggeler (1989) has argued convincingly that the limited outcomes associated with prior family-based interventions may be due to the fact that past interventions have addressed only a small portion of the factors that contribute to serious antisocial behaviors. A growing body of literature has arisen that emphasizes the multidimensional causes of delinquency and antisocial behavior (Henggeler, 1991a). Researchers have pointed to the strong contribution of peer rejection and academic deficiencies in explaining the ontology of antisocial behavior (Loeber, 1990; Patterson & Dishion, 1985). Antisocial behavior also has been strongly related to important characteristics of the school system and community (Henggeler, 1989). Most recently, researchers have emphasized the role of personal belief systems, perceptions, and attributions in the development of dysfunctional social behavior (Bandura,

1977, 1986; Dodge, 1980). Some social cognitive biases and deficiencies have been linked to problems in the modulation of aggression or anger in both children and adults, including the ability to appraise environmental cues accurately, make attributions, generate possible courses of action, and evaluate expected consequences of actions (Dodge & Frame, 1982; Lochman, 1987; Sigel, McGillicuddy-DeLisi, & Goodnow, 1992). For example, Lochman (1987) found that nonaggressive children assumed greater personal blame for aggression in early stages of conflict whereas aggressive children tended to blame others. Similar attributional biases may also affect the parents of nonaggressive and aggressive children (Ricardo & Baum, 1991).

ECOLOGICAL EXPANSIONS OF FAMILY-BASED INTERVENTIONS

The limitations associated with structured parent training have led to recent recommendations to broaden our conceptualization of family-based service delivery (Dumas, 1984b, 1986b; Henggeler & Borduin, 1990; Mash, 1989; Miller & Prinz, 1990). In fact, a growing body of literature exists where specific attempts have been made to enhance the long-term success of family interventions for seriously at-risk youth (Brunk, Henggeler, & Whelan, 1987; Dadds, Schwarts, & Sanders, 1987; Griest et al., 1982; Henggeler, Rodick, Borduin, Hanson, Watson, & Urey, 1986; Prinz &

Figure 14.1. Considerations in Ecological Expansion of Family-Based Interventions

- ✓Adopt a multisystemic orientation
- ✓Attend to consumer expectations and social cognitions
- ✓Emphasize strengths and adaptive coping
- ✓Consider family circumstances
- ✓Foster a collaborative environment
- ✓Design culturally sensitive interventions
- ✓Initiate interagency coordination and follow-up services

Miller, in press; Wahler & Dumas, 1989). Proposed enhancement efforts have evolved within a ecological framework where child disorders are conceptualized as embedded within constellations of dynamic, interconnected systems and subsystems (Bronfenbrenner, 1979). From an ecological perspective, child behavior is best understood when consideration is given to the primary contexts in which the child resides (the most important of which is the family unit) and the numerous and reciprocal sources of influence that impact on the child and family (Bronfenbrenner, 1986).

Interventions designed within an ecological framework focus on flexible change strategies to foster adherence and to optimize family and child improvements. General principles and guidelines form the foundation of such an intervention perspective rather than highly specific or routine therapeutic techniques (Henggeler & Borduin, 1990). At least seven critical principles guide the successful implementation of ecological expansions of family-based interventions (see Figure 14.1).

1. Adopt a Multisystemic Orientation

A major characteristic of enhanced family-based services is that all relevant interpersonal relationships within and beyond the family system are considered fundamental to change. Unlike structured parent training, which focuses on parenting skills and the parent-child dyad, assessment is broadened to address personal, family, and community adjustment factors that contribute to child misbehavior (Henggeler, 1991b; Henggeler & Borduin, 1990). Intervention efforts seek to improve individual deficiencies, strengthen interpersonal relationships, and advocate for links between family, peer, school, and community environments. The goal is to fortify connections between all subsystems that affect the child and family and to alleviate stressful environmental conditions that affect such relations (Bronfenbrenner, 1986; Henggeler, Melton, & Smith, in press). Instead of one intervention approach, a wide array of services are offered to improve multiple aspects of personal and family functioning (e.g., parent training, individual counseling, marital therapy, academic tutoring, positive peer group involvement; Griest et al., 1982). Interventions are selected strategically on an as-needed basis to match the developmental status of the child and family (Belsky, 1984). Changes are targeted across multiple domains (i.e., affective, behavioral, cognitive, physiological) and across the diverse settings in which children and parents function (e.g., home, school, peer group, community, workplace; Henggeler, Melton, & Smith, in press).

2. Attend to Consumer Expectations and Social Cognitions

Another therapeutic principle common across efforts to improve family-based services is the greater acknowledgment of the role of personal beliefs, expectations, and social cognitive processes (Meichenbaum & Turk, 1987). Reduced compliance and limited behavioral outcomes have been strongly associated with mismatched ideas about expected roles, activities, and goals of treatment between consumers and helping agents (Baekeland & Lundwall, 1975; Karoly, 1980; Miller, 1985; Pajares, 1992). Many potential sources of misalignment can exist between parents' and professionals' expectations for family interventions, including (a) the lack of focus on alternative life problems not directly related to child behavior, (b) the assignment of tasks outside of sessions, (c) the expected level of parent involvement and interaction, and (d) the educative nature of most training programs (Miller & Prinz, 1990). Moreover, dysfunctional attributions and other social cognitive processes may seriously jeopardize therapeutic progress (Dodge, 1986; Michelson, 1987). For example, children may fail to comprehend that parents' actions follow logically from their own behavior and may view parents' legitimate disciplinary attempts as aggressive, purposefully antagonistic, or as a perceived injustice. A child's inaccurate or incomplete interpretation of parental overtures or directives may lead to hostile attributions regarding a parent's sincere attempt to resolve conflict. Such inappropriate child responses tend to reduce further application of positive parenting skills. Similarly, biased or deficient parental attributions or beliefs may lead to rejections of a partner's or child's attempts to change.

These issues have contributed to the increased recognition of the importance of the parent–helper relationship and the need to access personal belief systems and expectations specifically in order to strengthen commitment and adherence to intervention procedures (Meichenbaum & Turk, 1987). As a result, greater attention is given to forging a strong alliance with families and to creating an atmosphere of openness where parents feel their concerns and ideas will be heard (Hoen-Saric et al., 1964; Wahler & Dumas, 1989). An important goal of initial sessions is to encourage discussion of prior experiences with and personal feelings about seeking help (e.g., guilt, discouragement, self-doubt), attributions and ideas about the cause of their child's misbehavior (e.g., "He's just a boy, I don't know why his mother gets so upset"), and concerns not directly related to child management (e.g.; health problems, feelings of depression, work pressures, conflicts with relatives, Prinz & Miller, in press). Moreover, continued attempts are made to address consumer expectations through specific prompts that elicit: (a) ongoing perceptions and reservations about the efficacy and usefulness of an intervention (e.g., "It sounds like there are many things that will stand in the way of this plan"; "I would like to hear your concerns and misgivings about this"; "How do you see this fitting in with your daily activities?"), (b) negative personal perceptions and frustrations (e.g., "Most parents I have worked with report that they feel awkward and uncomfortable when they first decide to shift attention to prosocial behavior. I am wondering if this has been your experience too?"), and (c) alternative life and personal concerns (e.g., "How are things going? Last week you mentioned your mother was in the hospital, how has this affected you and your family?"). Finally, procedures are used to identify and challenge deficient attributions, to improve cognitive problem-solving processes, and to engage children and parents in reciprocal behaviors supportive of each other's attempts to change (Hughes, 1988; Kelly, Embry, & Baer, 1979; Lochman, White, & Wayland, 1991).

3. Emphasize Strengths and Adaptive Coping

One other characteristic of enhancement efforts is the conception that dysfunctional family interactions are performance rather than skill deficits (Dumas, 1989). From this perspective, child and family disturbances are considered situations where inadequate coping skills have been blocked. Intervention efforts are designed to support healthy interpersonal functioning and to accentuate personal assets and strengths as opposed to focusing primarily on deficit skills (Hawkins & Catalano, 1992; Shure & Spivack, 1987). Steps are taken to bolster protective factors already operating in the family in order to minimize specific risk behaviors and to increase the overall well-being of family members (Zeitlin, Williamson, & Rosenblatt, 1987). There is a strong emphasis on empowerment strategies (Rose & Black, 1985) that seek to improve effective decision-making processes and general adaptive competencies while working towards the reduction of inappropriate behaviors and the adoption of new skills. Families are encouraged and reinforced for their previous attempts to meet challenges within the environment (Dunst, Trivette, & Deal, 1988). Efforts also are directed at getting parents to utilize existing resources further and to strengthen their informal (i.e., family, friends, neighbors, colleagues) and formal (i.e., community groups, professional providers) sources of social support (Wilson & Tolson, 1990). In general, the focus of service delivery shifts from efforts to improve deficient parenting skills towards efforts to enhance adaptive coping, develop adaptive interpersonal strengths, build social support networks, and link parents with valuable service providers (Hegar, 1989; Trute & Hauch, 1988). As an example of such an adaptive approach, parents could learn how to insulate a child from poor peer influences by coordinating multiple resources for the child (e.g., get the child placed in a new classroom, or increase the child's involvement with a prosocial peer group).

4. Consider Family Circumstances

A fourth principle central to successful ecological expansion efforts is the design of interventions that are responsive to family values, needs, and routines (Paget, 1991). Peterson (1984) has suggested that family adaptation is jointly determined by the number of stressors and hardships piled up on a family, the environmental resources of the family, and the family's perception of the harmfulness of these stressors. Increased demands on the family system already struggling with significant outside demands have been associated with greater severity of child problems (McCubbin, 1988; McCubbin & Patterson, 1983; Vincent & Salisbury, 1988). Clearly, a major challenge facing practitioners working with multiproblem families is how to design interventions that encourage self-sufficiency without adding undue stress to the family (Conoley, 1987). Time is required to identify and alleviate potent sources of parental and family stress (DeFrain, 1989). Fisher and Fagot (1991) have recently identified at least three critical components within families: interpersonal tension, financial problems, and child-rearing difficulties. Ultimately, success depends on finding ways to provide support without forgetting that parents are family members with many responsibilities and needs (Turnbull & Turnbull, 1986). Attempts to reduce stress on the family have included specific steps to "fit" interventions into the family's daily routines (Rainforth & Salisbury, 1988), to offer services during flexible hours in the community or at a family's home, and to assist with transportation and child care (Conoley, 1989; Henggeler & Borduin, 1990).

5. Foster a Collaborative Environment

A fifth enhancement principle is that initial endeavors must focus on establishing an equal footing with parents (Chamberlain & Baldwin, 1987). Positive communication between parents and school professionals is critical to the formation of supportive and dynamic home–school partnerships where parents are encouraged to become active participants in a decision-making process. Parents must be made to feel welcome and that their views are respected. A self-confident, yet flexible interpersonal style is critical to building a collaborative professional environment where parents feel empowered to contribute to solving their child's problems (Turnbull, 1983). Conjoint consultation approaches have been most effective in achieving these goals (Sheridan & Kratochwill, in press; Sheridan, Kratochwill, & Elliot, 1990). A collaborative environment is compromised by a professional demeanor that conveys impatience, disorganization, a lack of empathy, or superiority and by beliefs that parents are less knowledgeable about, are less vested in, or are the cause of a child's behavior problem (Darling, 1991). Besides planning sessions so as to reduce the probability of any disruptions, Meichenbaum and Turk (1987) recommend that enhanced collaboration is obtained when time is taken to introduce oneself fully; to explore all parental concerns, expectations, and goals; to explain the rationale for suggested interventions; to answer all questions; to elicit personal fears, preferences, and reservations; to anticipate possible side effects and inconveniences; to negotiate all decisions; and to customize all intervention plans. Moreover, practitioners must have the capacity to persist even in the face of initial resistance and high levels of conflict. A great deal of professional perseverance is necessary to build trust and convince parents who have experienced past disappointments with social agencies of the practitioner's sincere concern and commitment (Flick, 1988). Routine supervision and peer support has also been endorsed as a necessity for professionals who work with difficult family cases (Chamberlain & Ray, 1988).

6. Design Culturally Sensitive Interventions

Ecological intervention efforts must be culturally relevant and sensitive to the identity and motivations of all family members (Phinney, 1990; Wilson & Tolson, 1990). This requires an informed understanding of the cultural contexts within which families exist, including the family's dominant attitudes, expectations, and life-style characteristics (Rios & Gutierrez, 1986). It also requires that professionals develop an increased awareness of personal attitudes, beliefs, and interaction styles that can impact on their working relationship with families from diverse cultural backgrounds (Atkinson, Morten, & Sue, 1992; Chamberlain & Ray, 1988). For example, attitudinal differences regarding verbal and physical aggression are common between professionals, children, and parents, especially when families reside in impoverished settings impacted by crime and violence. Aggression in such contexts may be tolerated as an adaptive rather than a problematic behavior with adverse consequences because it is viewed as necessary for surviving neighborhood violence (e.g., as when acting-out behavior is viewed as successful coping or as an attempt to demonstrate independence) (Prinz & Miller, 1991). Moreover, different perspectives can exist about what constitutes effective parenting (e.g., as when improved parental monitoring is seen as prying or as excessive meddling). Substantial dialogue is required to elicit various standpoints about targets of change. Intervention goals must be jointly determined to fit the perspective of all involved individuals (e.g., a rationale for improved parental monitoring could emphasize the child's susceptibility to peer influence; Heffer & Kelly, 1987). Finally, continued assessments of the acceptability of intervention efforts should be obtained from all involved individuals (Hall & Didier, 1987; Kazdin, 1980; Reimers, Wacker, & Koeppl, 1987).

7. Initiate Interagency Coordination and Follow-up Services

A final feature of ecological enhancement efforts is the emphasis on coordinated case management between home, school, and community agencies. Substantial time is taken to ensure that basic family needs are met by hooking the family into sources of social, therapeutic, and economic assistance (e.g., referrals to marriage counselors; obtaining food stamps or other economic aid; arranging for adequate housing; coordinating with vocational rehabilitation; Hawkins & Catalano, 1992). Efforts are then taken to coordinate and integrate all adjunctive services into a cohesive, practical, and effective intervention plan. The ultimate goal is to empower families to acquire needed community resources that foster future success and independence (Dunst, Trivette, & Deal, 1988). A strong appreciation of and collaboration with local community resources is necessary in order to best meet the needs of seriously at-risk families (Conoley, 1989). Finally, as proposed by Kazdin (1987), durable improvements in family functioning may be best achieved by considering childhood aggression and hostility as a chronic health problem that requires careful monitoring over long periods of time. Regular booster sessions and routine follow-up efforts (e.g., mailings or phone contact) are seen as integral to successful family-based interventions (Durlack, 1985; Henggeler & Borduin, 1990).

CONCLUSIONS AND FUTURE DIRECTIONS

The strong links found between childhood aggression and hostility and later evidence of maladjustment during adolescence underline the critical need for preventative efforts designed to alleviate such behaviors in early childhood (Kazdin, 1987; Patterson, 1986). The consistent relationships found between social interactions within the family and severe antisocial behaviors in childhood clearly emphasize the importance of parental involvement in any early intervention effort (Vuchin et al., 1992). Although structured parent training approaches have a long history of success in reducing severe childhood hostility and aggression (Patterson, 1982), too often these procedures are accompanied by complaints of insufficient parental involvement, early termination, and less than optimal long-term success (Miller & Prinz, 1990).

Recommendations to improve the efficacy of family-based interventions have evolved within an ecological framework where structured parent training is viewed as one potential component of an array of prevention and supplemental services. The idea behind ecological enhancement efforts is to design multisystemic family-based interventions that are culturally sensitive and responsive to family values, needs, and routines (Henggeler & Borduin, 1990). Supportive and dynamic home–school partnerships, coordinated case management efforts, and careful monitoring over extended periods of time are critical attributes of such expanded family interventions (Carlson & Sincavage, 1987; Hegar, 1989). One prevailing conclusion to be drawn from existing work is that no simple formula exists to ensure success with all families or with all children (Brandt, 1989). Practitioners must be sensitive to unique individual characteristics as well as to combinations of situational and contextual factors that can impact upon the success of family interventions (Conoley, 1987).

School professionals, and school psychologists in particular, are in a unique position to provide ecological family-based services to decrease hostile and aggressive behaviors in children and adolescents (Miller & Prinz, 1990). In fact, such efforts may be viewed most appropriately as a primary prevention approach where emphasis is placed on averting predictable mental health problems in individuals not yet evidencing severe maladjustment (i.e., reducing the number of new cases of antisocial behavior) (Durlack, 1985). Such proactive efforts must be designed to emphasize psychological wellness, facilitate personal competencies, and foster health-promotion attitudes and may require the alteration of regulations, policies, and relationships within and between the major environments that affect children and families (Cowan, 1980; Seidman, 1987). Unfortunately, there are many practical and philosophical barriers to the wide adoption of preventative family-based efforts in school settings (Cochran & Brassard, 1979; Conoley, 1987; Wilson & Tolson, 1990). Considerable administrative support in the form of reduced case loads, more flexible role expectations, supportive supervision, and continued professional training are fundamental to the successful implementation of ecological interventions (Conoley, 1989). Notwithstanding the considerable expenditures of time and energy, the poor prognosis for these children and the economic, social, and personal costs associated with serious hostility, anger, and aggression clearly warrant our continued commitment to enhance service to such at-risk families.

REFERENCES

Alexander, J. F., Barton, C., Schiavo, R. S., & Parsons, B. V. (1976). Systems behavioral intervention with families of delinquents: Therapist characteristics, family behavior, and outcome. *Journal of Consulting and Clinical Psychology, 44,* 656-664.

Atkinson, D. R., Morten, G., & Sue, D. W. (1992). *Counseling American minorities: A cross-cultural perspective* (4th ed.). Indianapolis, IN: WCB Brown & Benchmark.

Baekeland, F., & Lundwall, L. (1975). Dropping out of treatment: A critical review. *Psychological Bulletin, 82,* 738-783.

Bandura, A. (1977). *Social learning theory.* Englewood Cliffs, NJ: Prentice-Hall.

Bandura, A. (1986). *Social foundations of thought and action.* Englewood Cliffs, NJ: Prentice-Hall.

Barkley, R. A. (1987). *Defiant children: A clinician's manual for parent training.* New York: Guilford Press.

Bastian, L. D., & Taylor, B. M. (1991). *School crime: A national crime victimization survey report.* Washington, DC: U.S. Department of Justice, Office of Justice Programs, Bureau of Justice Statistics (#NCJ 1311645).

Baum, C. G., & Forehand, R. (1981). Long-term follow-up assessment of parent training by use of multiple-outcome measures. *Behavior Therapy, 12,* 643-652.

Becker, W. C. (1971). *Parents are teachers: A child management program.* Champaign, IL: Research Press.

Belsky, J. (1984). The determinants of parenting: A process model. *Child Development, 55,* 83-96.

Bernal, M. E. (1988). Consumer issues in parent training. In R. F. Dangel & R. A. Polster (Eds.), *Parent training: Foundations of research and practice* (pp. 477-500). New York: Guilford.

Bernal, M. E., Kinnert, M. D., & Schults, L. A. (1980). Outcome evaluation of behavioral parent training and client centered parent counseling for children with conduct problems. *Journal of Applied Behavior Analysis, 13,* 677-691.

Blechman, E. A. (1984). Competent parents, competent children: Behavioral objectives of parent training. In R. F. Dangel & R. A. Polster (Eds.), *Parent training* (pp. 34-66). New York: Guilford.

Blechman, E. A. (1985). *Solving child behavior problems at home and at school.* Champaign, IL: Research Press.

Blechman, E. A. (1990). Effective communication: Enabling the multi-problem family to change. In P. Cowan & M. Hetherington (Eds.), *Advances in family research* (Vol. 2, pp. 219-244). Hillsdale, NJ: Erlbaum.

Blechman, E. A., Budd, K. S., Christophersen, E. R., Sukula, S., Wahler, R., Embry, L. H., Kogan, K., O'Leary, K. D., & Riner, L. S. (1981). Engagement in behavioral family therapy: A multisite investigation. *Behavior Therapy, 12,* 461-472.

Blechman, E. A., & McEnroe, M. J. (1985). Effective family problem solving. Special issue: Family development. *Child Development, 56,* 429-437.

Blechman, E. A., Tinsley, B., Carella, E. T., & McEnroe, M. J. (1985). Childhood competence and behavior problems. *Journal of Abnormal Psychology, 94,* 70-77.

Brandt, R. S. (Ed.). (1989). Strengthening partnerships with parents and community [Special issue]. *Educational Leadership, 47* (2).

Brody, G. H., & Forehand, R. (1985). The efficacy of parent training with mentally distressed and nondistressed mothers. A multi-method assessment. *Behavior Research and Therapy, 23,* 291-296.

Bronfenbrenner, U. (1979). *The ecology of human development.* Cambridge, MA: Harvard University Press.

Bronfenbrenner, U. (1986). Alienation and the four worlds of childhood. *Phi Delta Kappan,* 430-436.

Brunk, M., Henggeler, S. W., & Whelan, J. P. (1987). A comparison of multisystemic therapy and parent training in the brief treatment of child abuse and neglect. *Journal of Consulting and Clinical Psychology, 55,* 171-178.

Cantrell, V. L., & Prinz, R. J. (1985). Multiple perspectives of rejected, neglected, and accepted children: Relationship between sociometric status and behavioral characteristics. *Journal of Consulting and Clinical Psychology, 53,* 884-889.

Carlson, C. I., & Sincavage, J. M. (1987). Family-oriented school psychology practice: Results of a national survey of NASP members. *School Psychology Review, 16,* 519-526.

Chamberlain, P., & Baldwin, D. V. (1987). Client resistance to parent training: Its therapeutic management. In T. R. Kratochwill (Ed.), *Advances in school psychology* (Vol. 6, pp. 131-171). New York: Plenum.

Chamberlain, P., Patterson, G., Reid, J., Kavanagh, K., & Forgatch, M. (1984). Observation of client resistance. *Behavior Therapy, 15,* 144-155.

Chamberlain, P., & Ray, J. (1988). The therapy process code: A multidimensional system for observing therapist and client interactions in family treatment. In R. J. Prinz (Ed.), *Advances in behavioral assessment of children and families* (Vol. 4, pp. 189-217). Greenwich, CT: JAI Press.

Cochran, M. M., & Brassard, J. A. (1979). Child development and personal social networks. *Child Development, 50,* 601-616.

Coie, J. D., Dodge, K. A., & Coppotelli, H. (1982). Dimensions and types of peer status: A cross-age perspective. *Developmental Psychology, 18,* 557-570.

Conoley, J. C. (1987). Schools and families: Theoretical and practical bridges. *Professional School Psychology, 2*(3), 191-203.

Conoley, J. C. (1989). The school psychologist as a community/family service provider. In R. C. D'Amato & R. S. Dean (Eds.), *The school psychologist in nontraditional settings: Integrating clients, services, and settings* (pp. 33-65). Hillsdale, NJ: Lawrence Erlbaum.

Costello, E. J. (1989). Developments in child psychiatric epidemiology. *Journal of the American Academy of Child and Adolescent Psychiatry, 28,* 836-841.

Cowan, E. L. (1980). The wooing of primary prevention. *American Journal of Community Psychology, 8,* 258-284.

Daads, M. R., Schwarts, S., & Sanders, M. R. (1987). Marital discord and treatment outcome in behavioral treatment of child conduct disorders.

Journal of Consulting and Clinical Psychology, 55, 396-403.

Darling, R. B. (1991). Parent-professional interaction: The roots of misunderstanding. In M. Seligman (Ed.), *The family with a handicapped child* (pp. 119-149). Needham Heights, MA: Allyn and Bacon.

DeFrain, J. (1989). The healthy family: Is it possible? In M. J. Fine (Ed.), *The second handbook on parent education: Contemporary perspectives* (pp. 53-74). San Diego, CA: Academic Press.

Dishion, T. J., (1990). The family ecology of boys' peer relations in middle childhood. *Child Development, 61,* 874-892.

Dishion, T. J., Patterson, G. R., Stoolmiller, M., & Skinner, M. L. (1991). Family, school, and behavioral antecedents to early adolescent involvement with antisocial peers. *Developmental Psychology, 27*(1), 172-180.

Dodge, K. A., (1980). Social cognition and children's aggressive behavior. *Child Development, 51,* 162-170.

Dodge, K. A. (1986). A social information processing model of social competence in children. In M. Perlmutter (Ed.), *The Minnesota Symposia on Child Psychology: XVIII Cognitive perspectives on children's social and behavioral development* (pp. 77-125). Hillsdale, NJ: Erlbaum.

Dodge, K. A., & Frame, C. C. (1982). Social cognitive biases and deficits in aggressive boys. *Child Development, 53,* 163-173.

Dumas, J. E. (1984a). Child, adult-interactional, and socioeconomic setting events as predictors of parent training outcome. *Education and Treatment of Children, 7,* 351-364.

Dumas, J. E. (1984b). Indiscriminate mothering: Empirical findings and theoretical speculations. *Advances in Behavior Research and Therapy, 6,* 13-27.

Dumas, J. E. (1984c). Interactional correlates of treatment outcome in behavioral parent training. *Journal of Consulting and Clinical Psychology, 52,* 946-954.

Dumas, J. E. (1986a). Indirect influence of maternal social contacts on mother-child interactions: A setting event analysis. *Journal of Abnormal Child Psychology, 14,* 205-216.

Dumas, J. E. (1986b). Parental perception and treatment outcome in families of aggressive children: A causal model. *Behavior Therapy, 17,* 420-432.

Dumas, J. E. (1989). Treating antisocial behavior in children: Child and family approaches. *Clinical Psychology Review, 2,* 197-222.

Dumas, J. E., & Wahler, R. G. (1983). Predictors of treatment outcome in parent training: Mother insularity and socioeconomic disadvantage.

Behavioral Assessment, 5, 301-313.

Dumas, J. E., & Wahler, R. G. (1985). Indiscriminate mothering as a contextual factor in aggressive-oppositional child behavior: "Damned if you do and damned if you don't." *Journal of Abnormal Child Psychology, 13,* 1-17.

Dunst, C. J., Trivette, C. M., & Deal, A. (1988). *Enabling and empowering families: Principles and guidelines for practice.* Cambridge, MA: Brookline.

Durlack, J.A. (1985). Primary prevention of school maladjustment. *Journal of Consulting and Clinical Psychology, 53,* 623-630.

Elliot, D. S., Huizinga, D., & Ageton, S. S. (1985). *Explaining delinquency and drug use.* Beverly Hills, CA: Sage.

Emmons, R. A. (1992, August). *Revenge: Individual differences and correlates.* Presented at the 100th Annual Convention of the American Psychological Association, Washington, DC.

Farrington, D. P. (1978). The family background of aggressive youths. In L. A. Hersov & M. Berger (Eds.), *Aggression and antisocial behavior in children and adolescence* (pp. 73-93). Oxford, England: Pergamon.

Farrington, D. P. (1983). Offending from 10 to 25 years of age. In K. T. Van Dusen & S. A. Mednick (Eds.), *Prospective studies of crime and delinquency* (pp. 17-37). Boston: Kluwer-Nijhoff.

Farrington, D. P., Ohlin, L. E., & Wilson, J. Q. (1986). *Understanding and controlling crime: Toward a new research strategy.* New York: Springer-Verlag.

Firestone, P., & Witt, J. E. (1982). Characteristics of families completing and prematurely discontinuing behavioral parent training. *Journal of Pediatric Psychology, 7,* 209-222.

Fisher, P. A., & Fagot, B. I. (1991). *Components of family stress in high-risk and normative samples: A factor analytic study.* Paper presented at the 25th annual meeting of The Association for Advancement of Behavior Therapy.

Fleishman, M. J., Horne, A. M., & Arthur, J. L. (1983). *Troubled families: A treatment program.* Champaign, IL: Research Press.

Flick, S. N (1988). Managing attrition in clinical research. *Clinical Psychology Review, 8,* 499-515.

Forehand, R., & McMahon, R. (1981). *Helping the noncompliant child: A clinician's guide to parent training.* New York: Guilford Press.

Forehand, R., Rodgers, T., McMahon, R., Wells, K., & Griest, D. (1981). Teaching parents to modify child behavior problems: An examination of some follow-up data. *Journal of Pediatric Psychology, 6,* 313-322.

Forehand, R., Wells, K., McMahon, R., Griest, D., & Rodgers., T. (1982). Side effects of parent counseling on marital satisfaction. *Journal of Counseling Psychology, 29,* 104-107.

Galloway, D. R., Ball, T., Blomfield, D., & Seyd, R. (1982). *Schools and disruptive behavior.* London, England: Longman.

Garmezy, N. (1983). Stressors in childhood. In N. Garmezy & M. Rutter (Eds.), *Stress, coping and development* (pp. 43-84). New York: McGraw-Hill.

Griest, D. L., & Forehand, R. (1982). How can I get any parent training done with all these other problems going on? The role of family variables in child behavior therapy. *Child and Family Behavior Therapy, 4,* 73-80.

Griest, D. L., Forehand, R., Rogers, T., Breiner, J., Furey, W., & Williams, C. A. (1982). Effects of parent enhancement theory on the treatment outcome and generalization of a parent training program. *Behavior Research and Therapy, 20,* 429-436.

Hall, C., & Didier, E. (1987). Acceptability and utilization of frequently-cited intervention strategies. *Psychology in the Schools, 24,* 153-161.

Hawkins, J. D., & Catalano, R. F. (1992). *Communities that care: Action for drug abuse prevention.* San Francisco, CA: Jossey-Bass.

Hawkins, J. D., & Lishner, D. (1987). Etiology and prevention of antisocial behavior in children and adolescents. In D. H. Crowell, I. M. Evans, & C. R. O'Donnel (Eds.), *Childhood aggression and violence: Sources of influence, prevention and control* (pp. 263-282). New York: Plenum Press.

Heffer, R., & Kelly, M. (1987). Mothers' acceptance of behavioral interventions for children: The influence of parent race and income. *Behavior Therapy, 18,* 153-164.

Hegar, R. L. (1989). Empowerment-based practice with children. *Social Science Review, 63,* 372-383.

Henggeler, S. W. (1989). *Delinquency in adolescence.* Newbury Park, CA: Sage.

Henggeler, S. W. (199la). Multidimensional causal models of delinquent behavior. In R. Cohen & A. Siegel (Eds.), *Context and development* (pp. 211-231). Hillsdale, NJ: Erlbaum.

Henggeler, S. W. (199lb). *Treating conduct problems in children and adolescents: An overview of the multisystemic approach with guidelines for intervention design and implementation.* Columbia, SC: South Carolina Department of Mental Health.

Henggeler, S. W., & Borduin, C. M. (1990). *Family therapy and beyond: A multisystemic approach to treating behavior problems of children and adolescents.* Pacific Grove, CA: Brooks/Cole.

Henggeler, S. W., Melton, G. B., & Smith, L. A. (in press). Family preservation using multisystemic therapy: An effective alternative to incarcerating serious juvenile offenders. *Journal of Consulting and Clinical Psychology.*

Henggeler, S. W., Rodick, J. D., Borduin, C. M., Hanson, C. L., Watson, S. M., & Urey, J. R. (1986). Multisystemic treatment of juvenile offenders: Effects on adolescent behavior and family interaction. *Developmental Psychology, 22,* 132-141.

Hoen-Saric, R., Frank, J. D., Imber, S. D., Nash, E. H., Stone, A. R., & Battle, C. C. (1964). Systemic preparation of patients for psychotherapy: Effects of therapy behavior and outcome. *Journal of Psychiatric Research, 2,* 267-281.

Hughes, J. N. (1988). *Cognitive behavior therapy with children in schools.* New York: Pergamon Press.

Karoly, P. (1980). Person variables in therapeutic change and development. In P. Karoly & J. J. Steffen (Eds.), *Improving the long-term effects of psychotherapy* (pp. 195-261). New York: Gardner Press.

Kazdin, A. E. (1980). Acceptability of alternative treatments for deviant child behavior. *Journal of Applied Behavior Analysis, 13,* 259-273.

Kazdin, A. E. (1987). *Conduct disorders in childhood and adolescence.* Newbury Park, CA: Sage.

Kazdin, A. E. (1990). Premature termination from treatment among children referred for antisocial behavior. *Journal of Child Psychology and Psychiatry, 31,* 415-425.

Kazdin, A. E., Rodgers, A., Colbus, D., & Siegel, T. (1987). Children's Hostility Inventory: Measurement of aggression and hostility in psychiatric inpatient children. *Journal of Clinical Child Psychology, 16,* 320-328.

Kelly, M. L., Embry, L. H., & Baer, D. M. (1979). Skills for child management and family support: Training parents for maintenance. *Behavior Modification, 3,* 373-396.

Kelso, J., & Stewart, M. A. (1986). Factors which predict the persistence of aggressive conduct disorder. *Journal of Consulting and Clinical Psychology, 27,* 77-86.

Lochman, J. E. (1987). Self and peer perceptions and attributional biases of aggressive and nonaggressive boys in dyadic interactions. *Journal of*

Consulting and Clinical Psychology, 55, 404-410.

Lochman, J. E., White, K. J., & Wayland, K. K. (1991). Cognitive-behavioral assessment and treatment with aggressive children. In P. C. Kendall (Ed.), *Child and adolescent therapy: Cognitive-behavioral procedures* (pp. 25-65). New York: Guilford Press.

Loeber, R. (1988). The natural history of juvenile conduct problems, delinquency, and associated substance use: Evidence for developmental progressions. In B. B. Lahey & A. E. Kazdin (Eds.), *Advances in clinical child psychology* (Vol. 11, pp. 73-124). New York: Plenum.

Loeber, R. (1990). Development and risk factors of juvenile antisocial behavior and delinquency. *Clinical Psychology Review, 10,* 1-42.

Loeber, R., & Dishion, T. J. (1983). Early predictors of male delinquency: A review. *Psychological Bulletin, 94,* 68-99.

Loeber, R., & Dishion, T. J. (1984). Boys who fight at home and school: Family conditions influencing cross-setting consistency. *Journal of Consulting and Clinical Psychology, 52,* 759-768.

Loeber, R., Dishion, T. J., & Patterson, G. R. (1984). Multiple gating: A multistage assessment procedure for identifying youths at risk for delinquency. *Joumal of Research on Crime and Delinquency, 21,* 7-32.

Loeber, R., & Schmaling, K. B. (1985a). The utility of differentiating between mixed and pure forms of antisocial child behavior. *Journal of Abnormal Child Psychology, 13,* 315-335.

Loeber, R., & Schmaling, K. B. (1985b). Empirical evidence for overt and covert patterns of antisocial conduct problems. *Joumal of Abnormal Child Psychology, 13,* 337-352.

Loeber, R., & Stouthamer-Loeber, M. (1986). Family factors as correlates and predictors of juvenile conduct problems and delinquency. In M. Tonry & N. Morris (Eds.), *Crime and justice* (Vol. 7, pp. 29-149). Chicago: University of Chicago Press.

Loeber, R., & Stouthamer-Loeber, M. (1987). Prediction. In H. C. Quay (Ed.), *Handbook of juvenile delinquency* (pp. 325-382). New York: Wiley.

Mash, E. J. (1989). Treatment of child and family disturbance: A behavioral-systems perspective. In E. J. Mash & R. A. Barkley (Eds.), *Treatment of childhood disorders* (pp. 3-36). New York: Guilford Press.

McCord, J. (1983). A longitudinal study of aggression and antisocial behavior. In K. T. VanDusen & S. A. Mednick (Eds.), *Antecedents of aggression and antisocial behavior.* Boston, MA: Kluwer-Nijhoff.

McCubbin, J. (1988). Parental behavior in the cycle of aggression. *Psychiatry,*

51, 14-23.

McGee, R., Silva, P. A., & Williams, S. (1983). Parents' and teachers' perceptions of behavior problems in seven year old children. *The Exceptional Child, 30,* 151-161.

McMahon, R. J. (1984). Behavioral checklists and rating scales. In T. H. Ollendick & M. Hersen (Eds.), *Child behavioral assessment: Principles and procedures* (pp. 80-105). New York: Pergamon.

McMahon, R. J., & Forehand, R. (1984). Parent training for the non-compliant child: Treatment outcome, generalization, and adjunctive therapy procedures. In R. F. Dangel & R. A. Polster (Eds.), *Parent training* (pp. 298-328). New York: Guilford Press.

McMahon, R. J., Forehand, R., Griest, D. L., & Wells, K. C. (1981). Who drops out of treatment during parent behavioral training? *Behavioral Counseling Quarterly, 1,* 79-85.

Meichenbaum, D., & Turk, D. C. (1987). *Facilitating treatment adherence: A practitioners guidebook.* New York: Plenum Press.

Michelson, L. (1987). Cognitive-behavioral strategies in prevention and treatment of antisocial disorders in children and adolescents. In J. D. Burchard & S. N. Burchard (Eds.), *Prevention of delinquent behavior* (pp. 190-219). Beverly Hills, CA: Sage.

Miller, G. E., & Prinz, R. J. (1990). The enhancement of social learning family interventions for childhood conduct disorder. *Psychological Bulletin, 108,* 291-307.

Miller, W. R. (1985). Motivation for treatment: A review with special emphasis on alcoholism. *Psychological Bulletin, 98,* 84-107.

O'Leary, S.G., Wolff, L.S., & Acker, M.M. (1991). *The Parenting Scale: A brief measure of parenting effectiveness.* Poster presented at the 25th annual meeting of the Association for the Advancement of Behavior Therapy, New York.

Olweus, D. (1979). Stability of aggressive reaction patterns in males: A review. *Psychological Bulletin, 86,* 852-857.

Olweus, D. (1980). Familial and temperamental determinants of aggressive behavior in adolescent boys: A causal analysis. *Developmental Psychology, 6,* 644-660.

Paget, K. D. (1991). Early interventions and treatment acceptability: Multiple perspectives for improving service delivery in home settings. *Topics in Early Childhood Special Education, 11*(2), 1-17.

Pajares, M. F. (1992). Teachers' beliefs and educational research: Cleaning up a messy construct. *Review of Educational Research, 62*(3), 307-332.

Patterson, G. R. (1979). A performance theory for coercive family interaction. In R. B. Cairns (Ed.), *The analysis of social interactions: Methods, issues and illustrations* (pp. 119-157). Hillsdale, NJ: Lawrence Erlbaum.

Patterson, G. R. (1982). *Coercive family processes.* Eugene, OR: Castalia.

Patterson, G. R. (1986). Performance models for antisocial boys. *American Psychologist, 41*, 432-444.

Patterson, G. R., & Brodsky, G. (1966). A behavior modification programme for a child with multiple problem behaviors. *Journal of Child Psychology and Psychiatry, 7,* 277-295.

Patterson, G. R., Chamberlain, P., & Reid, J. B. (1982). A comparative evaluation of parent training procedures. *Behavior Therapy, 13,* 638-650.

Patterson, G. R., DeBaryshe, B. D., & Ramsey, E. (1989). A developmental perspective on antisocial behavior. *American Psychologist, 44,* 329-335.

Patterson, G. R., & Dishion, T. J. (1985). Contributions of family and peers to delinquency. *Criminology, 23,* 63-79.

Patterson, G. R., & Fleishman, M. J. (1979). Maintenance of treatment effects? Some considerations concerning family systems and follow-up data. *Behavior Therapy, 1,* 168-185.

Patterson, G. R., & Forgatch, M. S. (1985). Therapist behavior as a determinant for client noncompliance: A paradox for the behavior modifier. *Journal of Consulting and Clinical Psychology, 53,* 846-851.

Patterson, G. R., & Forgatch, M. (1987). *Parents and adolescents: Living together.* Eugene, OR: Castalia.

Patterson, G. R., & Reid, J. B. (1973). Intervention for families of aggressive boys: A replication study. *Behavior Research and Therapy, 11,* 383-394.

Patterson, G. R., & Reid, J. B. (1984). Social interactional processes within the family: The study of the moment-by-moment family transactions in which human social development is embedded. *Journal of Applied Developmental Psychology, 5,* 237-262.

Patterson, G. R., Reid, J. B., Jones, R. R., & Conger, R. E. (1975). *A social learning intervention. Vol. 1: Families with aggressive children.* Eugene, OR: Castalia.

Patterson, G. R., & Stouthamer-Loeber, M. (1984). The correlation of family management practices and delinquency. *Child Development, 55,* 1299-1307.

Peterson, P. (1984). Effects of moderator variables in reducing stress outcome in mothers of children with handicaps. *Journal of Psychosomatic Research, 28*(4), 337-344.

Phinney, J. S. (1990). Ethnic identity in adolescents and adults: Review of research. *Psychological Bulletin, 108,* 499-514.

Pianta, R. C., & Egeland, B. (1990). Life stress and parenting outcomes in a disadvantaged sample: Results of the mother-child interaction project. *Journal of Clinical Child Psychology, 19,* 329-336.

Prinz, R. J., & Miller, G. E. (1991). Issues in understanding and treating childhood conduct problems in disadvantaged populations. *Journal of Clinical Child Psychology, 19,* 329-336.

Prinz, R. J., & Miller, G. E. (in press). Family-based treatment for childhood antisocial behavior: Experimental influences on dropout and engagement. *Journal of Consulting and Clinical Psychology.*

Rainforth, B., & Salisbury, C. L. (1988). Functional home programs: A model for therapists. *Topics in Early Childhood Special Education, 7*(4), 33-45.

Reid, J. B. (1975). The child who steals. In G. R. Patterson, J. B. Reid, R. R. Jones, & R. E. Conger (Eds.), *A social learning approach to family intervention: The socially aggressive child* (pp. 135-138). Eugene, OR: Castalia.

Reid, J. B., & Patterson, G. R. (1976a). The modification of aggression and stealing behavior of boys in a home setting. In E. Ribes-Inesta & A. Bandura (Eds.), *Analysis of delinquency and aggression* (pp. 123-145). Princeton, NJ: Erlbaum.

Reid, J. B., & Patterson, G. R. (1976b). Follow-up analyses of a behavioral treatment program for boys with conduct problems: A reply to Kent. *Journal of Consulting and Clinical Psychology, 44,* 299-302.

Reid, J. B., & Patterson, G. R. (in press). The development of antisocial behavior problems in childhood and adolescence. *European Journal of Personality.*

Reimers, T. M., & Wacker, D. (1988). Parents' ratings of the acceptability of behavioral treatment recommendations made in an outpatient clinic: A preliminary analysis of the influence of treatment effectiveness. *Behavioral Disorders, 14,* 7-15.

Reimers, T. M., Wacker, D. P., & Koeppl, G. (1987). Acceptability of behavioral interventions: A review of the literature. *School Psychology Review, 16,* 212-227.

Ricardo, I. B., & Baum, C. G. (1991). *Interpersonal problem-solving abilities of rejected boys and their mothers.* Paper presented at the Annual Convention of the Association for the Advancement of Behavior Therapy.

Rios, J. D., & Gutierrez, J. M. (1986). Parent training with nontraditional families: An unresolved issue. *Child and Family Behavior Therapy, 7,* 33-45.

Roberts, M. W. (1982). The effects of warned versus unwarned time-out procedures on child noncompliance. *Child and Family Behavior Therapy, 4,* 37-53.

Robins, L. N. (1978). Sturdy childhood predictors of adult antisocial behavior: Replications from longitudinal studies. *Psychological Medicine, 8,* 611-622.

Robins, L. N. (1981). Epidemiological approaches to natural history research: Antisocial disorders in children. *Journal of the American Academy of Child Psychiatry, 20,* 566-580.

Robins, L. N. (1986). Changes in conduct disorder over time. In D. C. Farran & J. D. McKinney (Eds.), *Risk in intellectual and psychosocial development* (pp. 227-259). Orlando, FL: Academic Press.

Robins, L. N., & Ratcliff, K. S. (1980). Childhood conduct disorders and later arrest. In L. N. Robins, P. Clayton, & J. Wing (Eds.), *Social consequences of psychiatric illness* (pp. 248-263). New York: Brunner/Mazel.

Rose, S. M., & Black, B. L. (1985). *Advocacy and empowerment: Mental health care in the community.* Boston, MA: Routledge & Kegan Paul.

Rubel, B. (1978). *HEW's Safe School Study: What it says and what it means for teachers and administrators.* College Park, MD: Institute for Reduction of Crime, Inc.

Rutter, M. (1978). Family, area and school influences in the genesis of conduct disorder. In L. A. Hersov, M. Berger, & D. Schaffer (Eds.), *Aggression and antisocial behavior in childhood and adolescence* (pp. 95-113). New York: Pergamon.

Rutter, M. (1985). Classification. In M. Rutter & L. Hersov (Eds.), *Child and adolescent psychiatry: Modern approaches* (2nd ed., pp. 304-321). Oxford, England: Blackwell.

Rutter, M., Cox, A., Tupling, C., Berger, M., & Yule, M. (1975). Attainment and adjustment in two geographical areas: The prevalence of psychiatric disorders. *British Journal of Psychiatry, 126,* 493-509.

Rutter, M., & Giller, H. (1983). *Juvenile delinquency: Trends and perspectives.* New York: Penguin.

Sanders, M. R., & James, J. E. (1983). The modification of parent behavior: A review of generalization and maintenance. *Behavior Modification, 7,* 3-27.

Seidman, E. (1987). Toward a framework for primary prevention research.

In J. A. Steinberg & M. M. Silverman (Eds.), *Preventing mental disorders: A research perspective* (pp. 2-19). Rockville, MD: National Institute of Mental Health.

Sheridan, S. M., & Kratochwill, T. R. (in press). Behavioral parent-teacher consultation: Conceptual and research considerations. *Journal of School Psychology.*

Sheridan, S. M., Kratochwill, T. R., & Elliot, S. N. (1990). Behavioral consultation with parents and teachers: Applications with socially withdrawn children. *School Psychology Review, 19,* 33-52.

Shinn, M. R., Ramsey, E., Walker, H. M., O'Neil, R. E., & Steiber, S. (1987). Antisocial behavior in school settings: Initial differences in an at-risk and normal population. *Journal of Special Education, 21,* 69-84.

Shure, M. & Spivack, G. (1987). Competence-building as an approach to prevention of dysfunction: The ICPS model. In J. A. Steinberg & M. M. Silverman (Eds.), *Preventing mental disorders: A research perspective* (pp. 124-139). Rockville, MD: National Institute of Mental Health.

Sigel, I. E. (1985). A conceptual analysis of beliefs. In I. E. Sigel (Ed.), *Parental belief systems: The psychological consequences for children* (pp. 345-371). Hillsdale, NJ: Erlbaum.

Sigel, I. E., McGillicuddy-DeLisi, P. & Goodnow, J. J. (1992). *Parental belief systems: The psychological consequences for children.* Hillsdale, NJ: LEA.

Singh, H., Janes, C. L., & Schechtman, J. M. (1982). Problem children's treatment attrition and parents' perception of the diagnostic evaluation. *Journal of Psychiatric Treatment Evaluation, 4,* 257-263.

Stokes, T. F., & Baer, D. M. (1977). An implicit technology of generalization. *Journal of Applied Behavior Analysis, 10,* 349-367.

Tolan, P. H. (1988). Socioeconomic, family, and social stress correlates of adolescent antisocial and delinquent behavior. *Journal of Abnormal Child Psychology, 16,* 317-331.

Tolan, P. H., Cromwell, R. E., & Brasswell, M. (1986). Family therapy with delinquents: A critical review of the literature. *Family Process, 25,* 619-650.

Trute, B., & Hauch, C. (1988). Social network attributes of families with positive adaptation to the birth of a developmentally disabled child. *Canadian Journal of Community Mental Health, 7,* 5-16.

Turnbull, A. P. (1983). Parent-professional interactions. In M. E. Snell (Ed.), *Systematic instruction of the moderately and severely handicapped* (2nd ed., pp. 18-43). Columbus, OH: Charles E. Merrill.

Turnbull, A. P., & Turnbull, H. R. (1986). *Families, professionals, and exceptionality: A special partnership.* Columbus, OH: Charles E. Merrill.

U. S. Department of Education. (1989). *Youth indicators. 1988.* Washington, DC: Government Printing Office.

Vincent, L. J., & Salisbury, C. L. (1988). Changing economic and social influences on family involvement. *Topics in Early Childhood Special Education, 8,* 48-59.

Vuchin, S., Bank, L., & Patterson, G. R. (1992). Parenting, peers, and the stability of antisocial behavior in preadolescent boys. *Developmental Psychology, 28,* 510-521.

Wahler, R. G. (1980a). The insular mother: Her problems in parent-child treatment. *Journal of Applied Behavior Analysis, 13,* 207-219.

Wahler, R. G. (1980b). The multiply entrapped parent: Obstacles to change in parent-child problems. In J. P. Vincent (Ed.), *Advances in family intervention, assessment, and theory* (Vol. 1, pp. 33-61). Greenwich, CT: JAI Press.

Wahler, R. G., & Dumas, J. E. (1987a). Family factors in childhood psychology: Toward a coercion-neglect model. In T. Jacob (Ed.), *Family interaction and psychopathology: Theories, methods and findings* (pp. 581-627). New York: Plenum.

Wahler, R. G., & Dumas, J. E. (1987b). Stimulus class determinants of mother-child coercive interchanges in multi-distressed families: Assessment and intervention. In J. D. Burchard & S. N. Burchard (Eds.), *Prevention of delinquent behavior* (pp. 190-219). Beverly Hills, CA: Sage.

Wahler, R. G., & Dumas, J. E. (1989). Attentional problems in dysfunctional mother-child interactions: An interbehavioral model. *Psychological Bulletin, 105,* 116-130.

Walker, H. M., Reavis, H. K., Rhode, G., & Jenson, W. R. (1985). A conceptual model for delivery of behavioral services to behavior disordered children in educational settings. In P. Bornstein & A. Kazdin (Eds.), *Handbook of clinical behavior therapy with children* (pp. 700-741). Homewood, IL: The Dorsey Press.

Webster-Stratton, C. (1985). Predictors of treatment outcome in parent training for conduct disordered children. *Behavior Therapy, 16,* 223-243.

Wells, K. C., & Forehand, R. (1985). Conduct and oppositional disorders. In P. Bornstein & A. Kazdin (Eds.), *Handbook of clinical behavior therapy with children* (pp. 218-265). Homewood, IL: The Dorsey Press.

West, M. O., & Prinz, R. J. (1987). Parental alcoholism and childhood psychopathology. *Psychological Bulletin, 102,* 204-218.

Wilson, M. N., & Tolson, T. F. (1990). Familial support in the Black community. Special issue: The stresses of parenting. *Journal of Clinical Child Psychology, 19,* 347-355.

Zeitlin, S., Williamson, G. G., & Rosenblatt, W. P. (1987). The coping with stress model: A counseling approach for families with a handicapped child. *Journal of Counseling and Development, 43,* 443-446.

5 A MODEL FOR HELPING TEACHERS IMPLEMENT CLASSROOM-BASED ANGER INTERVENTION PROGRAMS

Michael Pullis

Angry and hostile children and youth often behave in disruptive, resistant, or troubling ways in classrooms such that they either (a) are constantly being punished by school officials or (b) are referred for and placed in special education programs for students with serious emotional disturbance (SED). Prolonged and serious problems may result in more restrictive and segregated placements (alternative or residential programs), further away from the realities of "mainstream" school, family, and community life.

It has been argued that such a range of placements or continuum of services is necessary in order to meet the severe and complex needs of both students who have exhibited serious anger-based psychological and behavioral problems and their families. Although this may be true, it is also important to note that waiting until such problems are serious enough to warrant therapeutic interventions from special education and/or mental health professionals has been shown to have some serious long-term implications. Data from evaluations of special education programs for SED students have been interpreted to indicate that these students have a very high drop-out rate (Knitzer, Steinberg, & Fleisch, 1990) and that their transition to adult life is fraught with continuing problems and conflicts (Frank, Sitlington, & Carson, 1991; Neel, Meadows, Levine, & Edgar, 1988). From the psychological literature, the adult prognosis for youth exhibiting antisocial behavior and conduct disorders (common manifestations of anger and hostility) also has been shown to be very problematic (Kazdin,

1987). It appears that more concerted efforts directed towards primary and secondary prevention and earlier intervention are needed, are more likely to be successful than tertiary programs aimed at therapeutic or educational responses for youth with chronic problems that attempt to bring them "back to health," and are more cost efficient.

Knoff and Batsche (1990) argued that schools, within broad-based community mental health services, are the most appropriate place for such prevention and early intervention efforts to be focused. Central then to these processes are teachers, in both regular and special education, who must become knowledgeable and skilled as well as be provided with the opportunities and support necessary to address the complex and serious issues of working with angry and hostile youth. Although both teachers and mental health professionals (therapists, school psychologists, etc.) should collaborate, it is teachers who have a more natural and more sustained relationship with children and adolescents. They are in a unique position, if trained and supported appropriately, to exert a tremendous positive influence on the development of their troubled students (Morse, 1992).

OVERVIEW AND USES

This chapter contains four sections that can be viewed as a general model of strategic classroom elements for interventions with angry and hostile students. The first section presents an overview of some prerequisite knowledge bases and attitudes for dealing effectively with these students. Part two covers some of the organizational or contextual components of classroom-based programs. The third part is focused on instructional and problem-solving options. The final section presents a discussion of motivational or incentive options including some perspectives on the role and uses of punishment within intervention programs. Although the sections are separated for the purposes of presentation and discussion, in practice programs must be designed that integrate the various components in meaningful and therapeutically beneficial ways for the intended students.

There are a number of potential uses or applications of a model such as the one presented here. It could be used as part of the curriculum for the preparation of teachers, administrators, school psychologists, and mental health workers. If all of these professionals' initial preparation contained sound coverage of school-based intervention issues, collaboration would be enhanced. School personnel could use the model as a broad blueprint for program planning or design for at-risk or special education students. School psychologists could use the general model as a framework to plan consultations with teachers, to structure integrated inservice development programs, or to assist with the evaluation of programs. Finally, at an individual level, teachers could use the components of the model in the formulation of IEPs for students who have exhibited significant adjustment problems due to their chronic anger and hostility problems.

KNOWLEDGE BASES AND ATTITUDES

Anger/Hostility Development

The ability to intervene sensitively and effectively with angry/hostile students requires a comprehensive and deep understanding of the developmental processes for these frustrated and often discouraged children. Teachers working in prevention or intervention programs must comprehend the fundamental and complex nature of individual developmental factors, experiential factors, and ecological factors pertinent in the development of ingrained patterns of anger and hostility.

In order to explore the complexities involved in these developmental processes, the author has used the concept of "schemas" in the preparation of teachers of students with SED. This idiosyncratic notion of schema is roughly defined as an integrated set of thoughts, feelings, and behaviors constructed by the individual over time and through experiences, regarding predictions about or behavioral reactions to certain situations or domains of situations (social, academic, etc.). The concept incorporates (rather loosely) ideas from the triadic reciprocality model of Bandura (1986), some notions from object relations theory (Blatt & Lerner, 1983), and some of the developmental constructivist principles of Piaget. This definition allows for consideration of individual differences (in the broad sense of both biological and experiential uniqueness) as well as the roles that SES, gender, and cultural variables may play in the cognitive, emotional, and sociobehavioral development of children. It has been used to help teachers learn to examine the complexities of development of social and emotional problems. It is a conceptualization that is quite consistent with several of the key themes presented in the first section of this book.

Anger and hostility may be expressed or manifested in many forms within the classroom setting. Most often these schemas have been associated with externalizing disorders (Achenbach, 1985) or with conduct disorders (Kazdin, 1987). However, as noted by Smith and Furlong (Chapter 1), anger and hostility may also be linked to internalizing disorders such as depression, withdrawal, and passive-aggressive resistance or reluctance. All of these manifestations are of concern and, at a practical level, are very disruptive to classroom learning and interactions. Teachers need to be able to understand and decode accurately these various superficial expressions of underlying anger and hostility.

Case study—Gus, age 12. As an example of schemas and their ingrained nature, a case study is used to illustrate our discussion. A teacher or clinician could probably predict the personal, social, and motivational schemas of this boy. Gus, a 12-year-old, has had a long history of family and school problems. He has earned a neglected social status due to consistently aggressive interactions with peers. Adults have reported him to be verbally aggressive, uncooperative, and disruptive in school. He has been viewed as impulsive in both social and academic situations. He is average intellectually but earns very poor grades and will seldom complete his class or homework assignments. School officials have used a variety of discipline techniques including loss of privileges, detentions, suspensions, parent conferences, extra monitoring, and removal from the classroom via in-school suspensions.

Comprehensive and sensitive assessment would likely yield the following schema profile. In the personal area, Gus's self-concept or identity includes the views that he is a tough trouble-maker. He does not view himself as a friend to others because he has to show people that he is tough and cannot be controlled or pushed around by other students or adults. He believes either that he is not a competent student or that school holds no real meaning for him any longer. It is likely that his self-esteem is quite low in the social and learning domains. With respect to self-control, there is little evidence that he can manage his angry feelings about others and the demands of school nor has he developed age-appropriate skills of self-management or impulse control.

In the social area he essentially has negative feelings about relationships and interactions with others. In terms of the work on social cognitive bias by Dodge and Somberg (1987) and Hudley (Chapter 10), he anticipates trouble and hostility from others in the school environment. This attributional bias leads him to continue to be defensive through the use of aggressive and resistant behavior. In addition, the removal or separation strategies used by the school have not helped him learn any new skills for successfully negotiating social situations with classmates or authority figures.

Finally, his achievement motivation is very low. There may have been a time when he cared about learning and put forth a reasonable amount of effort to complete assigned tasks. Tasks now have become another occasion for failure and negative feelings both from him and the adults who are continuously disappointed and frustrated with him. Tasks are now viewed more as compliance situations than learning or skills development opportunities. As is the case with many young adolescents, he questions the value, relevance, or utility of academic assignments. He sees no chance for success and very little meaning in the work that he is ordered to complete. He speaks angrily of the day he turns 16 so that he can drop out of school.

Gus has created from his school experiences a set of personal, social, and motivational schemas that are extremely negative and highly resistant to change. How he thinks, feels, and behaves in the academic and social demand structure of school consistently puts him in conflict with that environment. In order to help him construct new schemas, serious, sensitive, multifaceted, and long-term interventions will be required.

As noted earlier, schemas are developed and become ingrained as both predictions about and reactions to situations or domains of situations. Although many angry and hostile children may bring these schemas to the school setting as a result of family interaction patterns (e.g., Patterson, 1982), it is worth remembering that Kauffman (1989) and others have suggested that schools may maintain existing schemas or actually elicit anger and hostility from students because of instructional and management approaches that are inappropriate (McCaslin & Good, 1992). Schools can be very demanding places, where conformity, compliance, competition, and sustained effort are expected for long periods of time within large, diverse social groupings. Put simply, they are fraught with opportunities for stress and conflict (Wood & Long, 1991).

Pullis (1988) noted that schools and teachers can have a significant influence (positive or negative) on students' schemas about themselves, others, and learning. He viewed personal schemas (self-concept, self-esteem, and self-control) as being constantly impacted by academic and social interactions. Likewise, social schemas (social cognition, feelings about relationships with peers and adults, and social or pragmatic skills) are critical in school life. Demands for academic performance can also influence schemas regarding identity, values or perceived relevance of schooling, attributions, and general motivation to achieve. The schema notion can thus be applied as a tool to examine and understand the interactions or relationships between individual developmental problems and school or teacher factors.

Too often, teachers are presented with approaches, techniques, or options almost in isolation from the complex developmental variables that they are supposed to influence or the ecological context within which those strategies may be utilized. If they have not mastered a fundamental knowledge and understanding of anger and hostility development, teachers cannot possibly make important choices and decisions regarding intervention strategies.

Intervention Decision Making

In order to make effective decisions about intervention with these kinds of students, teachers must become knowledgeable of specific uses for information about anger and hostility that become applied to basic teaching processes. These processes, noted in Figure 5.1, are assessment, planning, implementation, and evaluation. As described in the assessment chapters in this volume, there are a variety of methods of measurement or assessment that need to be used in planning and evaluating programs for both groups and individual students. Functional assessment of the cognitive, emotional, and behavioral aspects of anger and hostility requires careful coordination of methods, assessors, and environments. Teachers will play an important role in both the assessment and evaluation processes and thus need to be familiar with the various methodologies. Planning and implementation activities will be influenced by the teachers' knowledge about a wide range of therapeutic, instructional, and curricular options that are tied to the assessment areas. Later in this chapter, a range of contextual, instructional, and motivational options will be presented as the knowledge base for intervention decision making. At this point (either in preparation or inservice training), teachers would be exposed to the theoretical background and practical research base for the various approaches.

Attitudes and Orientations

Dealing with angry/hostile students certainly requires knowledge about development and about tools or techniques for intervention. However, actual delivery of that knowledge requires intervening with these students in an educational or therapeutic manner; in consistent, healthy ways, on a daily basis (several hours per day); for prolonged periods of time (175–195 days per school year); in groups of captured kids (mandatory attendance) who have a very wide range of emotionally based behavioral difficulties; and in a demanding environment that has often meant personal, social, and academic frustration and failure for the students. Quite a challenging situation! Clearly, more than conceptual knowledge is required here.

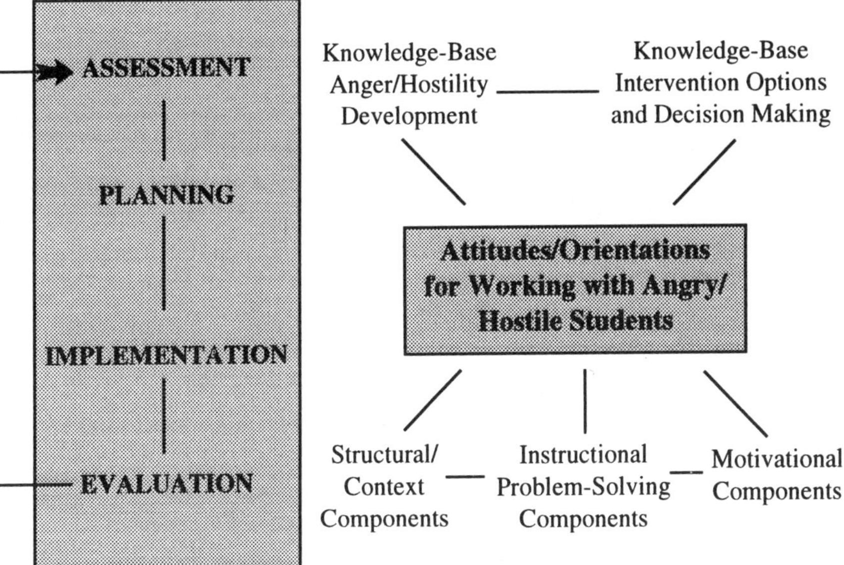

Figure 5.1. Model for Classroom-Based Anger-Aggression Interventions.

Professionals have to want to do this kind of work because they are convinced that (a) it is important, (b) their communities and schools agree and support them, and (c) they can have some influence or degree of success with these students. Although it is important to recruit individuals who possess these beliefs or values, it is also critical that information about certain types of attitudes and orientations be presented, discussed, and "sold" to these teachers so that they integrate it into their working philosophy. What follows is a brief discussion of two broad attitudinal themes—empathy and patience—that have been used by the author in the preparation of teachers of students with SED.

Morgan (1991) maintains that the most fundamental element of working with troubled students is empathy, which she defines as the ability to understand what the child is experiencing at an emotional level and to communicate that understanding. If this can be accomplished, students can begin to feel understood and accepted, notwithstanding the unacceptable nature of many of their classroom behaviors. Establishing such rapport with these students seems a critical part of the teacher–student relationship. Although touted by many as a crucial part of developing effective therapeutic and educational relationships, empathy may not be as easy to achieve as it is to write about. At a very basic demographic level, teachers of SED students, very predominantly white, non-Hispanic, middle-class females (McManus & Kauffman, 1991; Pullis, 1992), are quite different from the children and youth that they serve. Embedded within these classification variables are substantive cultural, class, and gender differences. The teachers' history of experiences with and beliefs about anger and conflict often do not put them in a position to achieve empathy easily with their students. This reinforces all the more strongly the importance of a thorough understanding of the dynamics of anger and hostility development. This knowledge, along with each teacher's own experiences with anger and frustration, can be used to create a genuine basis for empathy. Thus, interpersonal relationship attitudes,as exemplified by this brief discussion of empathy, are important in the preparation of teachers to work with these types of students.

Another broad attitudinal theme regards patience. Although often discussed as a personality trait or disposition, patience, at least from a training perspective, may be conceptualized more concretely in terms of its basis in knowledge and reality orientation. Many topics can be discussed under this broad theme, such as: (a) knowledge and acceptance of the ingrained and erratic nature of the students' problems and behaviors; (b) acceptance of the inevitability of conflict in the classroom; (c) knowledge that the students are behaving in the ways that they are because that is what they have learned about life and relationships; (d) acceptance of the belief that it is OK to have problems and difficult feelings; (e) perspective that conflict and problems are an opportunity to learn something; (f) acceptance that teachers play only one part in the students' lives; and (g) acceptance that change processes are long-term, complicated, and unstable for the most part. In general, this theme of patience creates the opportunity to discuss two interrelated areas of concern to teachers. The first has to do with understanding and accepting the realities of the child's problems. The second area, which is predicated on the first, concerns the realities of intervention work with these students. Being patient when working with problems of this nature requires reasonable expectations for both the student and the teacher regarding the dynamics and timelines of change. Failure to accept the realities of the child's problems and expectations regarding either rapid (spontaneous) change on the part of students or quick "magic" cures on the part of teachers leaves both vulnerable to disappointments and frustrations. These negative feelings, held by either or both parties, can undermine their relationship and hinder progress towards the goal of healthy change.

The final part of integrating these attitudinal themes involves a translation of these notions into a working orientation that can guide a teacher's perspectives, choices, and motivation. This working orientation can be thought of as a frame of reference for intervention. Pullis (1988) outlined a positive approach for dealing with negative classroom behaviors such as aggression, noncooperation, or poor task completion. He contrasted this positive, shaping approach with a punitive or disciplinary one to illustrate the importance of "framing" to intervention practices. In essence, teachers define the approaches they will take based on how they frame the problem. If negative behaviors are viewed as discipline problems then the strategies chosen will likely be aimed at quickly eliminating the problem and are often punitive, aversive, and coercive in nature. There is a strong probability that these are precisely the ways that parents and teachers have responded to the child's problems in the past and the likelihood is that the child's negative schemas are fortified and maintained rather than changed. These punitive reactions carry little of the empathy and patience themes presented above.

In contrast, framing anger and hostility problems in a shaping or therapeutic teaching perspective leads to a very different set of choices and motivations. This approach is focused on creating opportunities for positive replacement of old schemas. As such, this orientation begins with a thorough assessment and acceptance of the student's problems and a realistic sense that complex changes require time and support. This perspective assumes that new skills need to be taught explicitly and consistently. Finally, this approach highlights the importance of encouragement and reinforcement in the processes of changing angry, hostile schemas about others and achievement. Fundamentally, this perspective challenges teachers to create positive learning environments and social relationships with students who often have negative feelings about both. In summary, helping teachers learn how to deal effectively with angry or hostile students has to begin at the knowledge and attitudinal levels. Understanding the complex dynamics of anger and hostility development creates an appropriate background for beginning to examine intervention options and strategies. Knowledge in both of these areas then is "filtered" through each teacher's beliefs and values regarding the realities of the day-to-day work involved with these students. Finally, teachers have to examine and integrate the knowledge and attitudinal factors into a working orientation that guides their decision-making and teaching practices. Both the technical and professional/personal aspects of this complex process can be dealt with only through careful preparation or inservice development.

STRUCTURAL/CONTEXTUAL COMPONENTS

Classroom-based interventions essentially attempt to take a natural environment for students and teachers and modify it in ways that facilitate therapeutic interactions and change. As such, specific intervention techniques are "housed" or take place within a broader social and academic context. Therefore, a significant part of planning programs for angry/hostile students is creating a classroom context within which personal, social, and academic changes can be facilitated. Although there are any number of strategies for classroom design, four areas thought to be critical for angry students are addressed in this section—emotional climate, rules or expectations, academic and social opportunities, and teacher–student relationships.

Emotional Climate

Because the problems of chronically angry students emanate from strong negative emotions as well as from a set of expectations or perceptions of hostility about their school environment, it is appropriate for teachers to ask questions about the feeling state or emotional climate of their classrooms. Extending the concept of empathy noted earlier, teachers should ask, "*What does it feel like for this cynical, angry student to be in this classroom every day? How do this program and I make this child feel? How do I want kids to feel while they are with me? What type of emotional climate will help me reach the goals we have for this student?*" Attempting to answer questions like these can guide some of the teacher's decision making or choices. A major goal for these students has to be trust, because many of them "trust" only that people will continue to hurt them or try to control them. Changing these ingrained perceptions and expectations as well as helping these students develop new behavioral skills or strategies involves some risk on their part. Their history certainly tells them not to trust others or try new ways of relating. The necessary risk taking the teacher asks the child to make must occur within an appropriate emotional climate. The critical aspects of such a climate of risk taking and change can be summarized into the following four themes:

- Students can change only in an environment where they feel safe. That is, they should feel little or no threat to their physical and psychological self.
- Students need to feel supported and encouraged as they struggle to change their views, feelings, and behaviors.

- Students will change only in an environment that has relevance to them. Social and academic efforts will take place only if the students see them as possible and beneficial.
- Students will participate in a program only if they are involved in it and have some degree of control or some choices regarding their goals and daily activities.

Attempting to address these themes through classroom design strategies can help the teacher focus on practical issues such as rules, academic or vocational content and opportunities, and teacher–student interactions. If students can feel safe and supported in an environment or program that they have some say in and that they perceive to be useful, then the teacher indeed has created an emotional climate that will support the therapeutic goals of his/her program.

Rules or Expectations

The fundamental themes or objectives of a classroom are conveyed within the rules or expectations for behavior that are established by the teacher and the students. These rules or "rights and responsibilities" (Reinhart, 1991) set the parameters or limits for behavior, within which teachers and students will do their work. As such they are a structural component of the class, guiding the choices made by the students, and they are the basis for teachers' decisions regarding group or classroom management, shaping, and discipline reactions to individuals (Jones & Jones, 1990).

Keeping in mind the themes of safety, support, relevance, and involvement, the teacher should work with the students to develop rules regarding the basic purposes of the classroom and program *[involvement]*. This would include rights and responsibilities regarding academic and therapeutic or behavioral "work" and productivity—expectations for each individual student as well as the rights of others, both classmates and the teacher, to complete their work *[relevance]*. A second rule area should address the expectation for respect of the property and feelings of other individuals in the class *[safety]* as well as a minimum expectation to leave others alone if not to be cooperative and encouraging to others *[support]*. A final area should cover the classroom's materials, equipment, and environment (furniture, decorations, "pollution," etc.).

In each rule area students should become aware, through discussions and even role playing, what their rights and responsibilities are and *why* those rules are in place. Their active involvement in the process of creating "our" classroom should assist in a clear comprehension of the expectations. The teacher can then assume that behavioral problems are not the result of misunderstandings or confusion about expectations. Involvement of this nature also should enhance the students' motivation to try to live within these (essentially their) guidelines. Contrast this with the more likely past experiences of students (at least in their view) where teachers imposed rules, demanded complete and immediate compliance, and punished students as a way of "teaching" them about the rules.

In addition to classroom rules, the daily activities and interactions within the program need to be structured and predictable by having a well-designed schedule and routines. Organization of class time (schedule) and development of routines to handle daily chores, movement (transitions), and learning activities (lessons, homework, group, etc.) helps provide a supportive environment. The "clinical" issue here is to create enough structure from an efficiency standpoint to facilitate a productive working environment but not to overroutinize or overstructure the program so that it "feels" unduly restrictive. Similar to classroom rules, it is recommended that students help (where appropriate) with the initial creation and ongoing adjustments to the class schedule and routine.

Both rules and routines should be established collectively at the very beginning of the year. There should be a reasonable period of adjustment when the focus is on the appropriate teaching and re-teaching of these structural aspects of the classroom. The expectations and daily routines should be quite explicit and the students should understand the underlying purposes for their creation.

Academic and Social Opportunities

The orchestration of an organized and purposeful classroom structure or context creates the opportunities for meaningful learning both as an individual and as a member of a group of students. The teacher needs to design a wide range of types of learning activities and lessons where the students can be successful in acquiring personally relevant academic, vocational, and social skills. Thus, the "content" of the day, supported by an adequate structure, should address the fundamental concerns of schooling and the therapeutic objectives of the program as well as each student's IEP. Angry/hostile students who have had negative achievement experiences and negative social interactions need to learn how to participate responsibly in a variety of situations. The teacher needs to be creative in the development of individualized work, dyadic activities (peer tutoring), small-group interactions, and whole-class lessons (cooperative learning) across a range of academic and/or vocational subjects. Having an appropriate "mix" of activity structures requires and allows the students to learn personal responsibility for their own progress, assist others in their learning, and play a role in the completion of work done by a group. If designed well and implemented with a good deal of support, the students can learn a variety of both academic and social cooperation skills that can address their current problems as well as life needs as adults.

Brendtro, Brokenleg, and Van Bockern (1990) address, in a particularly insightful way, the need to create "reclaiming" environments that contain important learning and social opportunities for at-risk youth. Their views, based on traditional Native American principles of child-rearing, urge teachers and other child-care workers to offer students opportunities to experience (a) *belonging* through participation in constructive relationships, (b) *mastery* through meaningful achievement, (c) *independence* through the acquisition of self-discipline, and (d) *generosity* through assisting others. These authors maintain that positive, reinforcing relationships and learning activities are much more likely to be successful than the more typical control-oriented programs for angry youth. Teachers could use these themes both to create and evaluate efforts at affording their angry/hostile students with a program abundant in significant academic and social opportunities.

Teacher–Student Relationships

Daily work with chronically angry/hostile students is intensely interpersonal in nature. The fact that many of these students have relationship difficulties highlights the importance of teachers being able to break through former schemas and patterns to develop new, productive adult–child interactions. In addition, virtually every major approach to therapy recognizes the critical nature of the therapeutic relationship as both unique interpersonal dynamics and as a context within which changes can take place. Although teachers are not therapists in any sense of the 1-hour therapy session conceptualization (role or strategies for analysis), they most assuredly can and do engage in therapeutic interactions with troubled students.

Central to these relationship concerns are themes noted earlier. These would include aspects of relating such as empathy, trust, patience, and respect for the struggles that students are experiencing. Somewhat more tangible aspects of teacher–student relationships that have been identified include teachers as role models and teachers' communication strategies. Kauffman (1989, Chapter 19) emphasized the importance of teachers serving as a model for their students. More specifically, he suggested that teachers, under very challenging conditions, must be a model of self-control. They must let students see that there are alternative ways to experience and express feelings and to handle conflict situations. Kauffman cited Hobbs (1966) in describing the characteristics of a good teacher-counselor. These include being a decent individual with a clear set of personal and professional values who is able to participate in relationships in healthy ways.

The commerce of any relationship is communication—the sharing of ideas and feelings through messages and listening. Teachers need to convey understanding of and respect for students in the things they say and, just as important, in how they listen (Faber & Mazlish, 1980; Jones & Jones, 1990). Communication skills are critical at all levels of classroom interactions—routine classroom talk, directions or instructions for assignments, presenting lessons or demonstrations, questioning for comprehension, feedback about academic tasks and behavior, "personal" chats, problem solving, or conflict resolution. A very important part of teachers' initial training and ongoing professional development is their acquisition and refinement of effective communication skills with "relationship-reluctant" students.

These structural or contextual components of an effective classroom-based program set the stage for the more direct intervention work on the problems experienced by these students. It is within the context of a safe, predictable, supportive, and relevant learning environment that the difficult and complex work of therapeutic change more likely can take place.

INSTRUCTIONAL/PROBLEM-SOLVING COMPONENTS

Helping angry students interpret their world with less hostility, manage their negative emotions, and begin to master the complicated processes of cooperative social interaction and problem solving is the real core of classroom-based interventions. Continuing with the earlier themes of schemas and shaping, it is clear that interventions must (a) be multifaceted in nature, addressing cognitive, emotional, and behavioral processes; (b) involve direct and explicit instruction in skill development, (c) be carried out consistently (daily) and over long periods of time, and (d) entail practice and extension activities so that the changes are both durable and generalized to relevant situations in the classroom and beyond.

The content of these direct intervention approaches, for each individual student and/or the group of students, should be determined from the assessment that involves professionals, parents, and the students themselves. Following a brief discussion of the basic logic of these interventions, a description and examples of four critical components of skill development and their application—self-control or self-management, social interaction or pragmatic communication, problem solving, and generalization strategies, as discussed in Chapters10–14, will be presented.

Angry students need to acquire and be able to use a wide range of skills that allows them to decrease the frequency and manage the intensity of their negative feelings in both academic tasks and in social interaction situations. This implies that they need access to cognitive strategies that can help them override or manage strong emotions that are often the source of impulsive and nonproductive behavioral choices. Thus, the basic logic for intervention includes helping students learn skills to reduce initial feelings associated with perceived stressful academic or social demands and to manage ongoing emotions in order to use rational and age-appropriate academic and social strategies. Managing feelings and developing strategic behaviors both must be addressed and can actually reinforce each other. Controlled feelings allow access to good decision making and increase the likelihood of successful negotiation of the situation. If, however, the student does not have adequate academic or social skills, then the temporary "calm" will not be sustained as the child is likely to flounder in the situation and become more threatened and upset. Likewise, as students develop a wider repertoire of skills and begin to experience some successes, then they are more likely to acquire more confidence about their ability to handle the situation. This confidence should begin to reduce the perceptions of hostility or threat embedded in situations, reducing the arousal level of the feelings associated with the situation, and making it more likely that the feelings-management skills can be successful. As they learn to manage their feelings and the daily learning and social demands of the classroom successfully, their schemas can begin to change in more positive directions.

Self-Control

A major goal area for intervention for angry/hostile students is self-control or self-management. For over two decades intervention work in the area of verbal mediation has resulted in a variety of skills development approaches that can be used successfully in classroom settings (Nelson,

Smith, Young, & Dodd, 1991). The verbal mediation or self-talk approaches range from complicated, multifaceted curricular approaches (Fagen, Long, & Stevens, 1975; Goldstein & Glick, 1987; Workman, 1982) to specific strategies for particular situations. The central goal of such approaches is to help students learn to gain control over strong emotions and to regulate their behavior in strategic ways. Common elements across these approaches include: (a) teaching students to read and interpret provoking situations or triggers in more realistic ways; (b) helping students develop strategies for recognizing and managing feelings primarily through relaxation and thought-stopping approaches; and (c) assisting students in learning strategic coping skills for sustaining their attention, effort, and thinking through problem-solving and self-reinforcement strategies. Typical methods for teaching these skills are through modeling, practice,and reinforcement procedures or other variations of cognitive-behavioral methods (Kendall & Braswell, 1985).

Social Skills

Because many problems experienced by angry/hostile students are exhibited in interpersonal situations (with classmates, teachers, and administrators), enhancing these students' repertoire of social skills is critical to their improvement in school. A variety of comprehensive curricular materials is available to teachers to help guide their intervention efforts in this area. These materials would include instruction focused on enhanced pragmatic language skills (Wiig & Bray, 1983, 1984) where students learn to use language functionally in typical and problematic interpersonal situations. Another broad area would include standard or conventional social behaviors expected in school and other situations (Walker et al., 1983). Finally, some curricular or training approaches contain social areas particularly pertinent for angry/hostile youth such as parts of Aggression Replacement Training by Goldstein and Glick (1987). The social or structured learning component of this program contains two sections on "Skill Alternatives to Aggression" and "Skills for Dealing with Stress." Thus, the content of these programs can range from quite generic in nature to skills specific to our target population.

Most of the instructional methods used for language and social skills instruction are grounded in social learning theory conceptualizations that call for a modeling or coaching format. This would include (a) a discussion of the situation and tactics that might be successful, (b) modeling of the skill by the teacher and/or a peer, (c) guided practice opportunities through role playing, and (d) extensive and constructive performance feedback.

Problem Solving

In addition to direct instruction in self-control and social skills which are often quite "scripted" lessons or activities, teachers can also model and teach problem-solving skills to their students. These can be taught separately as skill instruction and/or they can be used in a more integrated fashion to handle problems that arise during daily social interactions or academic situations. Again, there are many approaches to problem solving from which teachers may choose and these vary in terms of their goals and their complexity. Fairly straightforward compromise and problem resolution strategies can be found in *Teacher Effectiveness Training* (TET) by Gordon (1974) and in Faber and Mazlish's *How to Talk so Kids Will Listen and Listen so Kids Will Talk* (1980, Chapter 3). Problem-solving approaches that contain more therapeutic goals such as expression of feelings, values, decisions, and insight can be found in the work by Glasser (1965, 1985) in his explication of reality therapy for classroom use or the *Life Space Interview* (LSI) (Wood & Long, 1990). It should be noted that these more complicated strategies require more training and supervision.

At the heart of problem-solving approaches are the notions of mutuality and flexibility. Mutuality means that both teachers and students can, and actually have a responsibility to, work cooperatively on classroom problems and that teachers can model and support the development of problem-solving skills. As the students learn these skills they will be in a better position to address with flexibility the nuances and complexities of normal daily problems.

There are four basic components involved in these problem-solving methods. First, there is a description and analysis of the problem situation where events, interpretations, and emotions might be discussed. Second, there is some type of brainstorming to arrive at a range of options or choices that the student has. This would also include some predictions or anticipatory analysis of what would happen in each case. Here the student must learn to look ahead to examine the effects of their choices on other people. Third, there is the development of a plan that entails elaborating on the choices explored and creating a rather explicit scheme for managing the problem in a more productive manner. Here, too, the student normally makes a commitment to see the plan through and the teacher commits to providing encouragement, guidance, and support. Finally, the process involves ongoing evaluations, discussions, and modifications as necessary. The mutuality noted above implies that the teacher will stick with the student as they struggle to try to manage the problem situation.

Maintenance and Generalization

All three skill areas should be included in each IEP and addressed through explicit, segregated instructional activities and times. Furthermore, the skills must be extended from the teaching or training sessions to real and relevant situations for the students. Although another professional such as a counselor or a school psychologist may conduct these skill development activities, the teacher should play a role in the planning of the activities and assuredly has to be involved in the extensions of the skills to other situations.

The consistent finding that skills, especially skills that are required under stressful or emotional circumstances, do not readily transfer from the training situation means that specific plans need to be developed to assure maintenance and generalization of the self-control, social skills, and problem-solving skills. The students need to learn to discriminate situations that are similar to the training activities and to recall the sequence of steps or operations that might be successful for them. The teacher can play a major role in these processes. First, they can help choose situations and skills that are socially relevant and that are likely to have positive outcomes for the student. They can follow-up on the skills being taught by modeling or prompting their use in the daily academic and social activities of the classroom, using "teachable moments" to help students transfer their skills. They can encourage and reinforce the skills or approximations of the skills (shaping) in the classroom as well as in other parts of the school. Finally, they can inform other teachers, administrators, and parents about what the student is trying to learn so that these important people can also reinforce the new skills. Taken together, the self-control, social, and problem-solving skills components represent the explicit therapeutic intervention portion of the classroom-based model. Although sometimes contrasted or viewed as incompatible, the behavioral or social learning theory approaches and the more cognitive, insight-oriented strategies can be used together effectively within a comprehensive classroom program (Jones, 1992). The classroom teacher plays a very critical role in virtually all aspects of the therapeutic program from assessment and planning to instruction and follow-through for generalization.

MOTIVATIONAL COMPONENTS

It has been asserted throughout this chapter that motivation, both intrinsic and extrinsic, plays an important role in the classroom-based model. It has been suggested that the classroom has to be a positive learning environment where students can be successful and experience a good deal of reinforcement for their academic and social efforts and progress. Angry/hostile students need to see the benefits of the risks and changes that they are being asked to make and they need to feel the positive rewards of those efforts in consistent and tangible ways. On balance, then, the classroom has to be a reinforcement-rich environment, both socially and academically.

That assertion notwithstanding, the realities are that these students will still engage in hostile and inappropriate behavior, quite likely for long periods time (old schemas change slowly!). The teacher must make decisions as to how to react to classroom misbehavior and problems in order to maintain a safe, orderly environment as well as to help the students learn that those types of behavior are not acceptable or efficient any longer. Furthermore, the types of behavior and interactions these students exhibit are very likely to elicit emotions such as frustration, anger, or disappointment that have led and can lead teachers to respond in very restrictive and coercive ways, often the reactions the students have elicited before and that maintain their negative views and interaction patterns with authority figures. Thus, teachers of these students must be very cognizant of their own feelings and reactions. This begs the question of the role of negative consequences and punishment in such a classroom setting.

Although it is a truism that children and youth need to experience the consequences of their actions, when applied to angry/hostile students this bromide typically means they need to be punished for their bad behavior. In a therapeutic classroom environment this notion needs to be thought through very carefully with an eye towards the earlier concepts of positive development of new schemas. Thus, consequences for problematic behavior should be tied to the classroom rules and their reasons (purposes) that the students helped develop. They also need to be linked to the skill development activities occurring in the classroom. Thus, the entire school day is consistent and cohesive with respect to the expected "new" behaviors that the students are trying to learn (shaping of replacement behavior). The themes of productivity, cooperation, rights, and responsibilities should be at the core of the classroom discipline approaches.

When students do engage in behavior that is not consistent with the agreed-upon rules then the teacher needs to stop and discuss the behavior and explain clearly why it is a problem. It may be necessary to describe or demonstrate an appropriate behavior and to explain how that choice is a better or more productive one for the student or the class. It is probably more useful to approach first infractions of this nature as an instructional problem for the teacher ("What am I trying to help them learn here?") and as a memory problem for the student ("He/she must have a difficult time remembering all the new things that we are trying to help him/her learn!"). Central to these initial reactions is a philosophy that inductive reasoning or authoritative discipline methods that focus on an explanation regarding the behavior are more productive in the long term for the student (Dornbusch, Ritter, Leiderman, Roberts, & Fraleigh, 1987).

After the teacher has spoken with the student about the problem and a possible "better" choice, they can also indicate to the student that if the inappropriate behavior continues there will be a consequence such as separation or removal from the group for a time, restitution for some damage, or delay of reinforcement (intrinsic or tangible) that could be gained by behaving in an appropriate, productive manner. In all cases the consequence should be logically linked to the nature of the problem behavior and the theme or rule that the student is violating. In no case should the punishment be hostile, physical, or unrelated to the problem behavior (Patterson, 1986). These power-assertive discipline techniques will likely increase the negative behavior exhibited by the student and can significantly damage the teacher–student relationship (Kauffman, 1989).

The net positive effects of such an approach to problematic behaviors are many. First, there are indeed consequences linked to the child's behavior. However, these consequences are both logical within the classroom rule agreements and they are predictable as the teacher has specified them in the initial conversation. By helping the student to see why her or his behavior is problematic and by suggesting an improvement, the teacher has given the child one chance, provided a valid reason for the need to change behavior, and reminded the student about her or his choices and responsibilities in the classroom. Delaying the negative consequence until a second infraction or continuation of the behavior (a) prevents the teacher from making "snap" judgments (often lamentable), (b) signals to the student that the teacher will indeed maintain limits and hold to his or her word, and (c) eliminates arguments that the student didn't know that there was a problem or that the consequence wasn't known. This type of approach can address some of these student issues or perceptions of overcontrolling, inconsistent, or hostile authority figures and still allows the teacher to feel fair and firm in dealing with classroom discipline problems.

If such an approach is used within a reinforcement-rich, positive classroom environment where students have ample opportunities to improve academically and socially, then the students will learn that there are indeed consequences for their actions. By design, they can learn that there are benefits to trying out new ways of thinking and behaving. They can come to believe that they are capable of academic improvement, that they can cooperate with classmates, and that there are adults who have positive expectations about them. These teachers are caring, supportive, and will "push" them; not around, but towards better skills and more satisfying, productive relationships and lives.

SUMMARY

The daily work with angry/hostile students is an important and complex challenge for teachers and other school personnel. The model presented in this chapter indicates that there are many areas of knowledge and specialized methods that these professionals must master in order to create and implement a program that can successfully address the needs of these troubled youth. In addition to the technical information regarding the development of anger and hostility as well as information regarding classroom design and intervention strategies, the work is intensely interpersonal in nature. Thus, teachers, who in this model do the bulk of the work, must have adequate preparation and ongoing inservice support at both technical and personal/professional levels.

The schools, as a reflection of their community, must ultimately see the value in these students' lives and recognize the very real losses accrued when the problems they have developed are ignored, viewed with contempt, or result in them being pushed out of school. These negative, cynical reactions do no good, perpetuate the views and problems of these students, and portend troubled and even dangerous lives for a clearly growing number of our country's young people.

REFERENCES

Achenbach, T. M. (1985). *Assessment and taxonomy of child and adolescent psychopathology*. Beverly Hills, CA: Sage.

Bandura, A. (1986). *Social foundations of thought and action: A social cognitive theory.* Englewood Cliffs, NJ: Prentice-Hall.

Blatt, S., & Lerner, H. (1983). Psychodynamic perspectives on personality theory. In M. Hersen, A. Kazdin, & A. Bellack (Eds.), *The clinical psychology handbook* (pp. 87-106). New York: Pergamon.

Brendtro, L., Brokenleg, M., & Van Bockern, S. (1990). *Reclaiming youth at risk: Our hope for the future.* Bloomington, IN: National Educational Service.

Dodge, K., & Somberg, D. (1987). Hostile attributional biases among aggressive boys are exacerbated under conditions of threat to self. *Child Development, 58,* 213-224.

Dornbusch, S., Ritter, P., Leiderman, P., Roberts, D., & Fraleigh, M. (1987). The relation of parent style to adolescent school performance. *Child Development, 58,* 1244-1257.

Faber, A., & Mazlish, E. (1980). *How to talk so kids will listen and listen so kids will talk.* New York: Avon.

Fagen, S., Long, N., & Stevens, D. (1975). *Teaching children self-control: Preventing emotional and learning problems in the elementary school.* Columbus, OH: Charles E. Merrill.

Frank, A., Sitlington, P., & Carson, R. (1991). Transition of adolescents with behavioral disorders—is it successful? *Behavioral Disorders, 16,* 180-191.

Glasser, W. (1965). *Reality therapy.* New York: Harper and Row.

Glasser, W. (1985). *Control theory in the classroom.* New York: Harper and Row.

Goldstein, A., & Glick, B. (1987). *Aggression replacement training: A comprehensive intervention for aggressive youth.* Champaign, IL: Research Press.

Gordon, T. (1974). *Teacher effectiveness training.* New York: Wyden.

Hobbs, N. (1966). Helping the disturbed child: Psychological and ecological strategies. *American Psychologist, 21,* 1105-1115.

Jones, V. (1992). Integrating behavioral and insight-oriented treatment in school based programs for seriously emotionally disturbed students. *Behavioral Disorders, 17,* 225-236.

Jones, V., & Jones, L. (1990). *Comprehensive classroom management: Motivating and managing students.* Boston: Allyn and Bacon.

Kauffman, J. (1989). *Characteristics of behavior disorders of children and youth.* Columbus, OH: Merrill.

Kazdin, A. (1987). *Conduct disorders in childhood and adolescence.* Beverly Hills, CA: Sage.

Kendall, P., & Braswell, L. (1985). *Cognitive-behavioral therapy for impulsive children.* New York: Guilford.

Knitzer, J., Steinberg, Z., & Fleisch, B. (1990). *At the schoolhouse door: An examination of programs and policies for children with behavioral and emotional problems.* New York: Bank Street College.

Knoff, H., & Batsche, G. (1990). The place of the school in community mental health services for children: A necessary interdependence. *The Journal of Mental Health Administration, 17,* 122-130.

McCaslin, M., & Good, T. (1992). Compliant cognition: The misalliance of management and instructional goals in current school reform. *Educational Researcher, 21,* 4-17.

McManus, M., & Kauffman, J. (1991). Working conditions of teachers of students with behavioral disorders: A national survey. *Behavioral Disorders, 16,* 247-259.

Morgan, S. (1991). The fundamental element of the teaching process: Empathy. In S. Morgan & J. Reinhart (Eds.), *Interventions for students with emotional disorders* (pp. 31-49). Austin: Pro-Ed.

Morse, W. (1992). Mental health professionals and teachers: How do the twain meet? *Beyond Behavior, 3,* 12-20.

Neel, R., Meadows, N., Levine, P., & Edgar, E. (1988). What happens after special education: A statewide follow-up study of secondary students who have behavioral disorders. *Behavioral Disorders, 13,* 209-216.

Nelson, J., Smith, D., Young, R., & Dodd, J. (1991). A review of self-management outcome research conducted with students who exhibit behavioral disorders. *Behavioral Disorders, 16,* 169-179.

Patterson, G. R. (1982). *Coercive family process.* Eugene, OR: Castalia.

Patterson, G. R. (1986). Performance models for antisocial boys. *American Psychologist, 41,* 432-444.

Pullis, M. (1988). Using affective and motivational factors as a basis for classroom interventions. In D. K. Reid (Ed.), *Teaching the learning disabled: A cognitive developmental approach* (pp. 97-115). Boston: Allyn and Bacon.

Pullis, M. (1992). An analysis of the occupational stress of teachers of the behaviorally disordered: Sources, effects, and strategies for coping. *Behavioral Disorders, 17,* 191- 201.

Reinhart, J. (1991). Organization of the environment. In S. Morgan & J. Reinhart (Eds.), *Interventions for students with emotional disorders* (pp. 51-77). Austin: Pro-Ed.

Walker, H., McConnell, S., Holmes, D., Todis, B., Walker, J., & Golden, N. (1983). *The Walker social skills curriculum.* Austin: Pro-Ed.

Wiig, E., & Bray, C. (1983). *Let's talk for children.* Columbus, OH: Charles E. Merrill.

Wiig, E., & Bray, C. (1984). *Let's talk intermediate level.* Columbus, OH: Charles E. Merrill.

Wood, M., & Long, N. (1991). *Life space intervention: Talking with children and youth in crisis.* Austin: Pro-Ed.

Workman, E. (1982). *Teaching behavioral self-control to students.* Austin: Pro-Ed.

6 SOCIOCULTURAL ASPECTS OF ANGER: IMPACT ON MINORITY CHILDREN

Kenyon F. Chan

The challenge of this chapter is to examine the literature on anger and children and to analyze its applicability to minority children. In addition, the chapter links anger literature to research on the influence of the sociocultural context on development and presents some strategies for intervention. First, a context for the research review that follows is provided.

SOCIOCULTURAL CLIMATE OF MINORITY YOUTH

A Chinese-American girl was enrolling in first grade in a suburban school in Los Angeles. Her European-American teacher claimed that her name, Rai-ling, was too difficult to pronounce, so her teacher told her that she needed an "American" name and promptly renamed her Mary. The girl was a fourth-generation Asian American.

A white child was overheard telling a black child, "You have dirty skin! I don't want to play with you anymore." The white child's mother had explained to her child that African Americans had skin the color of dirt, except they couldn't wash it off. The white child had concluded that his

The author would like to thank the editors and Drs. Shirley Hune, Deborah Stipek, and Aimee Dorr for their thoughtful review of early versions of this chapter. Thanks are also extended to Ms. Barbara Miyagawa for her assistance in the preparation of this manuscript. Errors and omissions are the sole responsibility of the author.

African-American friend was always dirty and therefore inferior to himself. The teacher was dumbfounded, but did not intercede. [1]

A Mexican-American boy was selected by his teacher to give a speech in front of the whole school in celebration of Thanksgiving. He gave a stirring address and was applauded by the entire school. Afterwards, the principal lavished praise on the young boy and told the audience that she hoped the other "Mexican" kids in the audience would learn to speak English like this boy. She did not realize that this boy grew up in a third-generation, fully bilingual Mexican-American family who instill pride in his bilingual abilities.

These examples of social encounters might seem rather trivial to some readers. Certainly, the white child, the classroom teacher, and the principal did not intend to insult these minority children. Nor did they maliciously intend to make these children feel unwanted or undesirable. Yet, the effects of these incidents make these children feel that their backgrounds and cultures are less "American" than others. These subtle wounds of racism inflict pain and hurt to the developing minority child. They provide a sociocultural climate for minority children in the United States that results in feelings of anger and rage unique to the minority experience.

Outbursts of anger, aggression, and violence in our urban schools have become common occurrences. Teachers and school administrators are faced with the task of resolving conflicts that are often provoked by something as simple as the color of a child's tennis shoes and may escalate to the use of a gun on the school grounds. Certainly the drama, if not the frequency, of such events, has drawn our attention and concern.

The urban unrest experienced in the summer of 1965 and again in the spring of 1992 suggest an underlying foundation of anger in minority communities, particularly the African-American community, that is not fully explained by current psychological theories of anger and aggression. In the spring of 1991, the world witnessed a videotape of a shocking beating of an African-American motorist by members of the Los Angeles police

---

[1] This anecdote was provided by Dr. Karen Hill-Scott.

[2] Three of the four officers charged in the Rodney King beating were acquitted of all state charges. One officer was acquitted of all charges but one, for which he will undergo a second trial. All were later found guilty of Federal charges of civil rights abuses under color of authority.

department. One year later, after a lengthy and well-publicized trial of the officers involved, a jury acquitted the officers of all charges.[2] This verdict ignited a full-scale riot in the minority areas of Los Angeles. The depth and breadth of anger displayed by the African-American community was a symptom of an underlying rage described in the sociological literature over 25 years ago (Grier & Cobb, 1968).

The dramatic impact on the American public of media images of urban areas burning and people looting and violently attacking innocent bystanders was quite profound. Although the media often provided the impression that the unrest was largely limited to the African-American community, the 1992 unrest in Los Angeles was a multicultural event. In fact, postriot analysis revealed that the greatest number of arrests were among Latinos (Lieberman, 1992).

The 1992 unrest recalled Gunnar Myrdal's (1944/1962) classic analysis of American society completed nearly 50 years ago and the Kerner Commission report (U.S. Kerner Commission, 1968), which both drew attention to white racism in America and a society divided by race and class. Once again in 1992, government agencies launched intensive investigations and "intervention" programs to quell any further disturbances (for example, the much publicized *Rebuild L.A.* initiative). Social scientists and educators pondered their possible roles in rebuilding urban areas in the aftermath of the civil disturbances (Steinberg, Lyon, & Vaiana, 1992). Yet, although the drama of an occasional urban riot might draw immediate political and media attention over a short period of time, the symptoms of discontent and despair are quite evident even after the political spotlight shifts to another crisis.

Accounts of trouble and discontent among minority youth are well documented. High rates of gang activity and gang-related deaths, teenage suicide, teenage pregnancies, drop-out rates, alcohol and substance abuse, and teenage homicides are only a few of the challenging problems faced by those interested in the lives of minority youth, particularly in urban areas. It is important to note that these signs of a lost generation of youth are not confined exclusively to African-American youth but are also widespread among Latino, Asian-American, and Native American youth as well (Hechinger, 1992). These problems are evidence of a smoldering rage pervading minority communities that can infect these youth with feelings of despair, anger, and powerlessness so deep that their only outlet is self-destructive behavior and increasing violence so descriptive of alienated minority youth in the United States.

Interest in the development of minority children is partly a product of observed differences between minority children and what is perceived as the standard child, generally defined as white, middle-class, and male. Minority children, specifically African-American, Latino, Asian-American, and Native American children, have been a major challenge to American educators for many decades. Except for Asian Americans who are falsely seen as a successful "model minority" (see Sue and Okazaki, 1990 and Suzuki, 1989), minority children are often described in troubled terms with regard to school achievement, school behavior, school outcome, and many other school measurements.

The term "minority" in this chapter refers to the traditionally underserved and historically underrepresented persons in our society including individuals from African-American, Asian-American, Latino, and Native American backgrounds. In contrast, the term "white" refers to persons who are of European descent, often referred to as Caucasian, and who historically have been given greater privileges, prestige, and access to resources in this society making them more powerful.

Anger and Minority Children

An examination of the psychological literature on anger and aggression is quite limited in explaining the depth and intensity of angry feelings expressed by ethnic minority communities. Most empirical research and writing on the development of anger in children examine anger as a transitory short-term state and suggest that anger has important universal characteristics. Something happens that a person interprets as personally hostile, noxious, or threatening and a person will feel anger that dissipates over time. A response to the noxious stimulus may or may not be activated. In addition, some empirical researchers remove the study of emotions from real-life contexts to reducing emotions to their "purest" essence.

Even if reducing emotions to pure laboratory events were warranted, it still might be important to test empirical theories using a variety of sampling groups, including ethnic minorities. Yet, the published research in the psychological literature makes scant mention of subjects from minority group backgrounds. Recently, Graham (1992) concluded that less than 3.5% of all the published studies in a select group of prestigious psychological journals from 1970–1989 mentioned African Americans as primary subjects of the investigations. A similar content analysis investigating the inclusion of subjects from Asian-American, Latino, or Native American ancestry would likely result in an even more limited number of research studies.

So when charged with reviewing a body of psychological literature as it pertains to ethnic minorities in America, one is faced with the discovery of very little literature and lots of fundamental questions. Does the lack of empirical research on ethnic minorities imply that current research, primarily focused on white children, is applicable to all children regardless of ethnic background, socioeconomic status, or sociocultural experience? Does the lack of research on minority children imply that different experiences are not determinants of emotional behavior? Clearly, the answers to these questions rest in the level of analysis or focus of the research. Looking at anger as a short-lived and stimulus-related emotion, it is likely that minority children experience anger in the same physiological way as other children experience this emotion. An unpleasant event, a noxious stimuli, or an unfair action on the part of another is likely to provoke an angry feeling in minority children just as it might in white children.

Berkowitz (1990) is one of the prime experimental psychology theorists examining anger and aggression at a micro level. Over years of laboratory experimentation, using primarily college students as subjects, Berkowitz has developed a "cognitive-neoassociationistic" analysis of anger. Reduced to its most pure stimulus-response form, Berkowitz suggests that unpleasant stimuli give rise to negative affects which "activate ideas, memories, and expressive-motor reactions associated with anger and aggression as well as rudimentary angry feelings" (Berkowitz, 1990, p. 494). Although no specific research could be identified that tested the universality of Berkowitz's analysis, it seems unlikely that cultural or socioeconomic differences among individuals would lead one to predict differences in experiencing anger at this level.

Cross-cultural psychologists and anthropologists have documented universal emotions across many cultures. All cultures have language to describe emotions and recognize similar emotional stimuli (Lutz & White, 1986; McGuire & Troisi, 1990; Russell, 1991). Insults, unfair treatment, threat, and confrontation seem to provoke angry responses around the world. McGuire and Troisi (1990) suggested that anger was a basic, fundamental emotion and an outcome of human evolution. Sadness, happiness, contempt, and fright also have universal emotional responses.

Although people in all cultures react and feel emotions, the expression and intensity of the display of emotions have cultural-specific characteristics (Ekman, 1982; Lutz & White, 1986; Scheff, 1985). Indeed, Matsumoto and Ekman (1989) pointed out that whereas the recognition of emotion in the human face appears universal, cultures differ in the rules and intensity by which emotions are displayed. Ekman (1972) found that Japanese subjects may not display emotions when in the presence of an authority figure, whereas American subjects were not inhibited in their display of emotion. Further, cultures may differ in which emotions are encouraged and which are inhibited. For example, Levy (1984) found that Tahitians had many words describing forms of anger and irritability and relatively few words describing sadness and grief.

From basic research on anger, it can be concluded that most people, including minority children, are likely to recognize anger-provoking stimuli that are straightforward and generally universal in interpretation. However, the interpretation and reaction to universal stimuli and, perhaps, the recognition, interpretation, and reaction to ambiguous social stimuli for minority children may be quite different from white children. Anger, as an emotion, is certainly universal, but what provokes anger and how it is displayed and reacted to by individuals from different cultural backgrounds requires greater explanation.

Social Cognitive Model of Anger

Review of social cognition research provides some possible explanations for observed differences in the expression or display of emotions across cultures. From a social cognition point of view, emotions like anger are a product of a complex response system. (In this book, Chapters 2 and 10 by Hudley present more detailed information about social cognition and anger in youth.) For the purpose of discussion in this chapter, a brief review of Dodge's (1986) emotional response involved with anger is offered. He suggests that emotional behavioral response is a five-step process including (a) Encoding, (b) Representation, (c) Response Search, (d) Response Decision, and (e) Enactment.

Step 1. At the *encoding step* a person attends to the social cues in the environment. A child recognizes and attends to appropriate social signals that stimulate his or her response system. For example, when a child hears a peer say, "You have dirty skin. I don't want to play with you anymore," the child is likely to recognize this social cue as directed at him or her and attend to the cue.

Step 2. During step two, the *representation step,* Dodge suggests that individuals must integrate the observed information with past experiences and come to some understanding of the meaning of the behavior observed or determine that more information is needed about the meaning of the peer's social behavior. In our example, at this stage, the target child attempts to integrate the peer's remarks with past experiences and evaluate the intent of the remark—was it an insulting or rejecting remark or was it a benign remark meant only in the context of the moment? Was the comment justified? That is, "Do I have dirty skin and should I go wash?" Or, was the peer referring to something else? The child may look for other social cues like body language, facial expression, or the physical context to help interpret the social cue.

Step 3. In the third step, the child *searches for possible responses* based on the interpretation concluded in the previous step and on the repertoire of responses developed by the child. If, for example, our target child interprets the statement by the peer as benign or neutral, the child could ignore the encounter or respond indifferently in a verbal or nonverbal manner. If on the other hand, the target child evaluates the peer's intent as hostile or insulting, the target child may choose more negative responses such as returning a verbal insult.

Step 4. Ideally, Dodge suggests that a child generates many response alternatives in the third step and in the fourth step *evaluates the potential consequences* for the proposed responses. One response may be more effective in a particular situation, whereas another response would be more effective in another situation. Our target child may decide that hitting the peer may not be effective because a teacher is standing nearby, whereas if a teacher was not present, perhaps hitting would be a viable option. Evaluating response alternatives is founded, in part, on past experiences. A child may have learned through past experiences that hitting another child is not an acceptable behavior or that a particular emotional response is not acceptable to powerful others in the environment.

Step 5. Finally, in the *enactment step,* the child responds to the social cue using available verbal and motor skills. One monitors one's own behavior and the responses generated by the behavior that loop back to the beginning of the social cognitive process. In our example, the target child may decide that more information is needed and respond by asking the peer to clarify the provoking remark. The child's response, then, sets the stage for further encoding of information generating more processing of information.

Dodge sees this entire process as dynamic and transactional with information being encoded and responses being generated quickly and efficiently within the developmental abilities, experiences, and capabilities of the child.

Implications for minority children. This social cognitive view of the social process generates some interesting possibilities in understanding the unique development of anger in minority children. During the encoding step, a child is required to learn to be alert to social cues and signals and to distinguish between relevant and irrelevant cues. For the minority child, this demands attention to the routine social cues experienced by most individuals and to dangerous or demeaning race-related social cues as well. Unlike other children, minority children must develop an awareness of how their race and ethnic background often evoke negative responses by other more powerful individuals. The sociocultural context of their lives is complicated by experiences of prejudice and discrimination.

In our example presented earlier, if the target child was a minority child, that child would be more attentive to racially motivated social cues than other children. He or she is likely to interpret that "dirty skin" referred to the pigmentation of the skin rather than some aspect of personal hygiene. A general sense of powerlessness or a history of experiencing or observing negative social cues will generate heightened attentiveness and perceptions of danger.

Further, in step two, minority children integrate social cues into an experience bank, or what Dodge (1986) refers to as a "data base," which is quite different from other children. The interpretation by minority children of social cues is mediated by not only their general experience and development as children, but by their experiences in a society that treats members of their group differently from others. Experiences or observations of discrimination, racial slurs, rejection based on race, and other forms of racist acts mediate the interpretation of even the most innocent social cue and make the minority child more alert to potential danger or insult.

Because our target child has personally experienced social rejection as a result of his or her minority status, that social history will influence the interpretation of social cues differently in situations where difference in race is a factor. A rejecting or even neutral social cue by a white peer will be interpreted very differently by a minority child than it would be if the child was from the same ethnic background. The minority child will be more attentive to the racial overlay in almost all social encounters.

In the third and fourth steps of this social cognitive model, searching for and evaluating possible responses are also mediated by the minority experience. Minority children learn that there are certain limited responses to negative social cues based on their race. Although minority children may believe that these negative social cues are unfair and unjust, direct responses to racist acts often are heavily sanctioned by the dominant culture or evoke even more shrill responses.

Therefore, although a minority child may want to respond in an overt and openly angry way, the social context and dominance of race relations may mediate the response. Referring to our earlier examples, what was Railing to say to her teacher who arbitrarily changed her name? Or, how could the young Mexican-American orator respond to his principal when she indirectly insulted an aspect of his heritage? How is a young African-American child going to defend himself against the racial lesson promoted by his peer's mother and reinforced by the silence of the observing teacher? Angry responses by minorities to racist acts are often dismissed by others as "overly sensitive" or overly militant to warrant any serious regard. The inability to dissipate angry feelings by overt, direct, and effective actions may give rise to a reservoir of angry and hostile feelings turned inward in the form of self-hate or uncontrollable explosions of anger or rage.

A long history of experiencing and observing unfair treatment based on one's race accompanied with few effective behavioral remedies to challenge discriminatory treatment raises questions about the long-term consequences of internalized anger and rage. Some of the answers concerning these long-term consequences lie in a better understanding of the sociocultural context of anger.

Sociocultural Context of Anger

Emotions, specifically anger, do not occur in isolation of the sociocultural environment in which a person lives. Emotions, like all human functioning, are moderated by the environment or social ecology surrounding the individual. Therefore, unless one believes that minority individuals biologically experience emotions differently, it is the sociocultural context of anger that will produce the most fruitful understanding of the differences between minority and white children in the development and expression of anger.

The sociocultural environment is a carefully chosen concept. It defines an environment with both social and cultural components. Every child's development is influenced by the social and cultural context in which the child resides. The social context refers to the societal and political environment surrounding children, while the cultural context refers to the shared values, norms, and behaviors of a group of people with whom the child shares an affiliation and alliance. Both of these contextual environments influence the development of children in significant ways (Chan, 1983; Chan & Rueda, 1979) and are certain to influence the notion of the social cognitive process described by Dodge (1986).

The most influential aspect of the social environment that affects minority children is the informal rules of social dominance and subordination in race relations in America. Comer (1989) and others (Skillings & Dobbins, 1991; Spencer & Markstrom-Adams, 1990) suggest that the historical subdominant position forced on minorities in America (i.e., racism in the United States) places minority children at risk of mental health and educational problems.

In its most technical sense, the term "racism" is defined as the subordination of one people by another people on the basis of racial or physical characteristics. The dominant group creates a minority group by constructing a social image of the "other" as inferior to themselves allowing the dominant group to feel comfortable with disparity in power, wealth, and influence in their favor. Racism justifies powerfulness as a right over other people based on physical features such as skin color. It serves to immobilize the victims by making them feel powerless.

The history of race relations in the United States is a history of domination or control by the powerful over the powerless. As mentioned earlier, 50 years ago, Myrdal (1944/1962) noted the conflict between American ideals of equality and justice with America's despicable treatment of African Americans. More recently, Omi and Winant (1986) concluded that the history of race relations in the United States is a history where "Native Americans faced genocide, blacks were subjected to racial slavery, Mexicans were invaded and colonized, and Asians faced exclusion" (p. 6). Unfortunately, the legacy of this history continues today.

Less than 30 years ago, non-white children were required to attend segregated and deficient schools. Their parents were excluded from the full richness of the work environment, and their families faced housing discrimination and segregation. Now in 1994, evidence of racism is much less overt. The social and judicial transformation of the 1960s and 1970s has made overt institutional racism illegal. Minority children may now attend integrated schools. Their parents, at least overtly, may not be discriminated against in the workplace. Minority families may now seek housing in almost any neighborhood they can afford and public accommodations are generally integrated. Yet, minorities continue to face inadequate education, housing, employment, and health care.

While overt forms of racism have diminished, covert or symbolic forms of racism still remain (Sears, 1988). Sears and Kinder (Kinder & Sears, 1981; Sears, 1988) propose that "old-fashioned racism" has been replaced by a much more subtle form of racism which uses traditional American values, particularly individualism, and anti-black feelings to continue to dominate African Americans. Their analysis can certainly be applied to other minority groups as well.

Modern "symbolic racism" acknowledges the unfairness of segregated public accommodations and schools. It supports an end to overt job and housing discrimination. Symbolic racism explains the continued level of racial inequality as a function of the African American's lack of American values such as "individualism, self-reliance, the work ethic, obedience, and discipline" (Kinder & Sears, 1981, p. 416). Applying this logic to all minorities, this modern version of racism concludes that the problems of minorities are not the fault of the dominant society or racist social policies. Nor are they manifestations of biological inferiority. Rather, symbolic or covert racism implies that America is "color-blind" and that the problems of America's minorities center on the content of their character and cultural values which inhibit minorities from fully realizing their potential in this land of equality and individual freedom. Programs like affirmative action in the workplace or in university admissions are no longer necessary, so the argument goes. Jobs and schooling should be based on merit alone and should not discriminate against whites. The conclusion is that all should compete on an open and level playing field within our society.

Indeed, as mentioned earlier, Asian Americans are often erroneously proclaimed by white society as an example of "the model minority" because they are perceived as hard working, obedient, and disciplined (Sue & Okazaki, 1990; Suzuki, 1989). Asian Americans have fought against this stereotype of their communities because it both ignores the anti-Asian history they have experienced in the United States and is used to separate them from the struggles of other minorities (see Chan, 1991 and Takaki, 1989). Further, it neglects serious social problems found among many of the subgroups that makeup the Asian-American community and disregards the growing level of anti-Asian violence in the United States (U.S. Commission on Civil Rights, 1992).

Modern symbolic racism concludes that if minorities do not succeed in America it is because they are lazy, lack discipline, lack American values, or are otherwise morally insufficient; in a phrase, "it is their fault." For those who do succeed, it is because they have the proper values and culture which accordingly match those of the dominant white society. Symbolic racism ignores the fact that the playing field is not level and has never been level. It shifts the blame squarely on the shoulders of minority communities. This "blame the victim" explanation for social inequities is reminiscent of the "culture of poverty" explanations of the 1970s (see, for example, Ryan, 1971).

Racism is not just an interesting sociological construct. Racism has a direct effect on a child's development and may impede the natural development of a minority child (Comer, 1989; Fordham & Ogbu, 1986). As children experience their social world they are as much an observer as they are a participant. They observe how they are treated by others and how their actions are responded to by others. They observe how other children and adults interact and learn who they are as a product of how others treat them (Damon, 1977).

Like all children, as minority children grow up they observe many positive models and experience love and devotion from their parents and family. The difference between the development of minority children and children from the dominant mainstream community is that minority children find limits and barriers to their development as a product of racism.

Fordham and Ogbu (1986) argue that "one major reason black students do poorly in school is that they experience inordinate ambivalence and affective dissonance in regard to academic effort and success" (p. 177). They conclude that the development of an "oppositional collective or social identity" and an "oppositional cultural frame of reference" are adaptive mechanisms to protect minority group members collectively from the wounds of racism. Because of ill treatment and discrimination by the dominant society, minorities must reject the accoutrements of the dominant society including definitions of success and achievement in order to maintain their own character and self-esteem.

In more simple terms, when someone is beating you down physically or emotionally, it is difficult to take on their values as your own even if many are adaptive and positive. "Acting white" would be the last thing a victimized minority person would want to do even if it meant failing in school. "Acting white" might lead to peer group rejection and loss of cultural or ethnic identity.

Minorities are trapped, then, between maintaining their oppositional and collective response to racist treatment and accepting definitions of success that would appear to be "acting white." This process of oppositional social identity and oppositional frame of reference begins early in life.

Children are aware of ethnic differences as early as 1 year old and at least by 3 years old (Abound, 1987; Goodman, 1964; Katz, 1976, 1987; Spencer, 1987). By early childhood, children have learned to distinguish themselves from other children on the basis of race and gender. In a review of research, Spencer and Markstrom-Adams (1990) concluded that ethnic children are able to identify race and specifically identify membership in their own racial group by the preschool years and, more disturbing, ethnic children have developed a positive bias for whites as opposed to their own ethnic affiliation by that same age period.

Attempts at developing positive African-American identity, such as the Afrocentric historical movement (see, for example, Asante, 1991), are often met with harsh and unrelenting criticism from mainstream society (see, for example, Hughes, 1992, and Schlesinger, 1992). The same desires for strong ethnic affiliation by Mexican Americans, Native Americans, and Asian Americans are also seen by mainstream America as anti-American and attacked as part of the "politically correct" movement which is seen as a threat to the integrity of the "our American" culture.

The effects of racism on minority children's development dampen self-development and confidence and may account for why minority children are often found to report feelings of greater powerlessness when compared to dominant culture children (Funk & Wise, 1989). The wounds of racism are quite subtle and are carried by children like grains of sand, added one by one, eventually weighing children down beyond their capacity to carry the sand and to grow emotionally and intellectually as well.

All children would like to grow up feeling safe and secure knowing that their parents will care for them and protect them. All children would like to grow up with a positive view of themselves and their families. For minority children, however, they observe their parents' inability to combat racial discrimination and prejudice. They observe their parents in subservient roles with, for most part, little hope of escaping their plight. They observe, with a helpless feeling of inadequacy, the beating of an African American at the hands of police authority without any consequences for the officers involved.

Minority children are also bombarded with television and advertising images almost devoid of depictions of minorities in positive and constructive roles. If one were to rely solely on news accounts of minority communities, one might easily conclude that most African Americans are poor and/or criminals. Most Mexican Americans are illegal aliens. Asian Americans are all foreign born and overly studious, while Native Americans exist only in the past or are missing completely. The early development of a positive bias for whites by minorities may be an ominous sign of the rejection of themselves and their parents in favor of the more powerful white model.

The sociocultural context provides a personal history of racism and negative social experiences that differentiate minority children from children of the dominant culture. Incidents of racial discrimination or hurtful remarks and rejections form a fundamental sense of powerlessness and victimization that is often difficult to overcome. This history of powerlessness in the face of racism moderates how minority children interpret social cues, social interactions, and the range of possible social responses available to them. Within the social cognitive perspective, the negative history of racism would certainly moderate one's interpretation of social cues, the pool of available responses, and the assessment of the impact of considered actions. For minority children, negative or even neutral social cues are interpreted within the context of their experiences with racism. Their emotional responses are moderated by what they deem as possible given their seemingly powerless status. Their evaluation of their actions will be tempered by their relative feelings of powerlessness. Ultimately, the wounds of racism are not only a powerful sociocultural source that differentiates the experiences of minority children and white children, but helps explain differences in their social behavior and mental health in the school setting.

Racism and Mental Health

A number of theorists have suggested that racism poses serious mental health problems for both the majority (Skillings & Dobbins, 1991) and minority (Comer, 1989; Fordham & Ogbu, 1986; Root, 1992) communities. Root (1992) argues that the impact of racism and sexism on minorities and women is a form of psychological trauma. The wounds of racist and sexist acts are viewed as forms of trauma that attack and weaken the ego just like other forms of trauma that affect the ego. Given this perspective, an examination of the effects of racism on psychological development is instructive in understanding its impact on anger in minority children.

It is well recognized that there are many life events that cause psychological harm. The death of a parent, experiencing rape or physical violence, witnessing an automobile accident, or watching parents argue are all examples of life events that may affect a child's development. Traumatic life events may be experienced directly by a child, for instance, a brutal slap by a parent, or may be experienced indirectly, like watching a news report of a war in a foreign country. These experiences are incorporated into the child's understanding of the world and will affect his or her own interpretation of the world.

Experiencing racism forces minority children to question their self-worth and makes them feel vulnerable to external dominant forces outside the control of their parents and themselves. A young child worrying about the color of his skin begins to wonder what other personal features might also be "wrong" and why skin color determines social rank. A young child asked to change her name to a more "American" sounding name is forced to wonder what is wrong with her name and what is wrong with her parents for giving her such a "bad" name. The almost complete absence of positive minority role models in textbooks, television, and advertising forces minority children to wonder if people who look like them belong to this society or not.

Minority children, like all children, grow up with the inherent notion that the world is fair and adults, particularly parents, are always right. Yet, frequently minority children are faced with racist acts or witness their parents subjected to racist domination or hear how their culture lacks family values. Consequently, these children are forced to resolve the cognitive dissonance caused by the conflict between their notion that the world is fair and the fact that the more powerful dominant society is not fair in its treatment of minorities. Further, they must resolve the conflict between the notion that their parents are all powerful with their experience that sometimes their parents and other significant adults cannot protect them from racist harm.

The common occurrence of race-related graffiti on school walls provides a vivid example of the cognitive conflicts faced by minority children. Hateful slogans directed at all minority groups are found quite easily on the walls of school bathrooms or carved on table tops by young vandals. Offensive terms such as "nigger," "slant-eyed gook," and "wetbacks" are only examples of this racist vocabulary. Neither parents nor school officials can protect children against encountering such emotion-laden terms. School officials certainly do not condone such behavior and, in fact, most teachers try to teach children the principles of equality and respect for our diversity (see, for example, Derman-Sparks and ABC Task Force, 1989).

How do children resolve the conflict between what they are taught about equality and diversity and what they see on the school bathroom walls? It is reasonable to assume that when confronted with racist acts one would react with anger. Applying Dodge's (1986) perspective, a racist social stimulus is likely to be encoded and evaluated by the target individual within the context of his or her social history. Indeed, Armstead, Lawler, Gorden, and Cross (1989) reported that showing excerpts of films of racist situations not only provoked anger in African Americans but was associated with high blood pressure as well. Broman and Johnson (1988) concluded that African-American adults described high levels of negative life stress that were associated with high levels of anger and health problems.

Experiencing each racist act singularly is not necessarily an overwhelmingly traumatic event by itself. Rather, it is the accumulation of such experiences and the inability to prevent or ameliorate such traumas that begin to weigh heavily on a child's psychic development and certainly his or her interpretation of the social world. Such trauma is subtle and indirect and, as Root (1992) suggested, subtle and indirect racist trauma have an insidious and cumulative effect on development.

Experience of racist acts is integrated with past social experiences and observations. Given this accumulated experience, minority children search for strategies to respond to the assault. Yet, direct response by victims of racism is often not possible. The dominant-subordinate character of racist acts and often the indirect and anonymous nature of these experiences make the direct expression of anger quite difficult and often unwise. Racial teasing or dehumanizing remarks may go unchallenged by the less powerful victim. Anger over graffiti accumulates with few avenues for expression. As Root (1992) concluded, targets of racist acts must internalize their wounds and control their outward response often for fear for their own safety. Still other researchers have noted a relationship between racism and the high suicide rates found among African-American teenagers (Baker, 1990; Dillihay, 1989; Spaights & Simpson, 1986). The suicide rates for Chinese Americans and Japanese Americans are 36% and 54%, respectively, higher than the national average (Rigdon, 1991).

Evidence of this internalization of wounds can be found in early childhood. Since the classic studies by Clark and Clark (1940), researchers have demonstrated the "racial identity dissonance" among African-American children (see Spencer, 1987, and Spencer and Markstrom-Adams, 1990). African-American children may have positive views of themselves but prefer white characteristics over black characteristics. This dissonance can be interpreted as early awareness of racial preference, privilege, and power of the white "standard" observed by African-American children.

Spencer (1987) concluded that while African-American parents can help their children develop positive self-concepts, these children still grow up in disadvantaged environments and outside the mainstream of American life. That disadvantaged environment, supported by institutional barriers and racism, results in the logical preference by African-American preschoolers for the mainstream culture and behavior. Because no research is available on other minority groups, one can only surmise that a similar pattern of racial identity dissonance may be found for other minority children.

Racism, then, has a negative effect on children's mental health. Traumatic racist acts accumulate and become a part of the socialization history of a minority child. Responses to this accumulation of trauma result in unresolved feelings of anger, frustration, anxiety, and powerlessness. This accumulation may be at the root of explosive displays of rage seen in some individuals that seem out of proportion to the precipitating event.

Fordham and Ogbu (1986) linked the self-destructive behavior often characteristic of minority youth to traumatic racism. Unmotivated school performance, high drop-out rates, high teenage pregnancy rates, substance abuse, gang activities, violence, and other problems associated with alienated youth may be products of unresolved anger and rage resulting from racist wounds experienced throughout their lives. Perhaps the explosive rage of an entire community is a product of internalized anger and unresolved powerlessness thrust upon minority communities by decades of discrimination, prejudice, and exploitation.

Even successful minority youth, of whom there are many, may suffer the ill effects of racism in other ways. Their ability to cope more positively with the trauma of racism is a result of many factors ranging from strong family support, strong religious support, and generally strong ego on the positive side to overidentification with the aggressor or deep repression of anger on the negative side. Much research on this topic is needed.

Children from different minority cultures are likely to express the effects of racist wounds and anger differently. Research is required to determine which "display" rules operate within a given community or family. For some Asian-American children perhaps "putting their heads down" and plowing through the trauma are acceptable coping behaviors. For some African-American children,more open defiance is supported by friends and family. For some Native American and Latino children, isolating themselves from the white world may be a culturally acceptable form of adaptation. Concentrated research on this topic also deserves attention.

Finally, the explosive rage displayed by some minority students is often misunderstood by teachers. If teachers view anger as only a short-term temporal event, disproportionate explosive rage would seem puzzling indeed. What appears to be overreaction to the precipitous stimulus may be instead explosive release of smoldering feelings held by children as a result of unresolved cumulative, racially motivated experiences. Rather than viewing explosive anger or apparently inappropriate anger as an individual behavioral problem, such behavior is equally likely to be an adaptive reaction to a history of negative racist experiences that provokes feelings which rest largely unresolved and unexpressed. Much of this speculation deserves careful research and attention.

What Can Educators Do Now?

Racism in the classroom may be even more subtle than in the rest of a child's life. Teachers, for the most part, are dedicated individuals with the best of intentions for every child in their classrooms. Yet teachers, too, contribute to the weight of racism for minority children. Teachers are often ill-equipped to handle race bias in their classrooms. Teachers often ignore racial conflicts between children, which gives minority children the feeling that acts of racism against them must be acceptable and that somehow it must be their fault because the teacher does nothing to intervene. Minority children are powerless to stop the wounds.

The vignettes that opened this chapter are examples of thoughtless but sometimes well-intentioned acts. They are noted by children as minor discomforts, unfairness, stress, and the feeling that they don't quite "belong." They add up, however, to help children define which Americans are "acceptable" and which are marginal or unacceptable.

In the absence of concrete research, experiments, or intervention projects, one can only speculate about possible actions educators can implement to help minority children with the anger associated with traumatic racism. Some educators have attempted bold and exciting methods to combat racism in schools (see, for example, Derman-Sparks & ABC Task Force, 1989). Perhaps these preliminary guidelines can be presented while we wait for more definitive research to develop.

Recognize subtle racism. Racism is an important overlay in the lives of minority children. Overt acts of racism are relatively easy to recognize. Educators, however, must recognize the more subtle nature of covert and symbolic racism. Insults and social slights are defined by the victim not the perpetrator.

Intervene. Racism is uncontrollable by minority children and their effects accumulate over time. Anger, frustration, anxiety, and a sense of powerlessness are a result of this accumulated trauma. Therefore, educators must intervene when they witness unfair behavior. Teachers should clearly communicate to their children that discrimination or prejudice of any kind will not be tolerated in their classrooms.

Discuss racism. Educators should openly discuss racism and fairness with children. They should help children identify unfairness and discrimination in the world around them. Teachers should discuss racism found in textbooks, readings, films, and other aspects of the curriculum.

Transform curricula. More than simply "celebrating diversity," educators should understand and teach cultural and racial differences and similarities. Having a "tacos" or "won ton" day does not teach children about Mexican Americans or Chinese Americans. Textbooks, pictures on bulletin boards, test materials, and other aspects of the curriculum must express the diversity of American life. Curricula must be transformed and values should be inclusive rather than exclusive (see, for example, Hernandez, 1989).

Adjust pedagogy. Educators should realize there is more than one way of teaching and should recognize differences in learning styles and adjust their pedagogy to enhance the culturally different styles of their students. Cooperative learning, peer teaching, and utilizing community resources are important elements in diversifying one's pedagogical style (see, for example, Chan & Rueda, 1979).

Recognize roots causes of anger expression. Educators should reinterpret disruptive or angry behavior as potentially signs of alienation and trauma. Although disruptive behavior or violent outbursts are still not acceptable, the root causes of the behavior may be a result of the trauma of racism rather than some inherent characteristic of the child.

Involve the family. Involving parents, grandparents, uncles and aunts, and other members of the family in the education of minority children may help demonstrate respect for minority families.

Institute anti-bias policy. Educators should institute an anti-bias policy in their schools, their communities, and their personal lives. An anti-bias policy in one's classroom is not enough. Rather, educators must learn to recognize their own biases and prejudices in the classroom and in their lives in general. Educators might ask themselves how many truly multicultural personal friendships do they actually have? How have their actions promoted or inhibited an anti-bias environment in their lives?

Be sensitive to individual needs. Educators should expect that all children will express the wounds of racism differently. Cultural differences will result in culturally defined expressions of emotions and anger and the successful minority child is just as much at risk of the underlying effects of traumatic racism as the alienated disruptive child.

Redefine academic success. Finally, academic success and life success should not be defined as "acting white" but should be the right of all children from every culture. Academic success should be redefined to include minority role models, parental and community support, multicultural understanding, and the integration of school life with community life.

REFERENCES

Abound, F. (1987). The development of ethnic self-identification and attitudes. In J. Phinney & M. Rotheram (Eds.), *Children's ethnic socialization* (32-55). Newbury Park, CA: Sage.

Armstead, C., Lawler, K., Gorden, G., & Cross, J. (1989). Relationship of racial stressors to blood pressure responses and anger expression in Black college students. Special Issue: Race, reactivity, and blood pressure regulation. *Health Psychology, 8*, 541-556.

Asante, M. (1991). The Afrocentric idea in education. *Journal of Negro Education, 60*, 170-180.

Baker, F. (1990). Black youth suicide: Literature review with a focus on prevention. *Journal of the National Medical Association, 82*, 495-507.

Berkowitz, L. (1990). On the formation and regulation of anger and aggression: A cognitive-neoassociationistic analysis. *American Psychologist, 45*, 494-503 .

Broman, C., & Johnson, E. (1988). Anger expression and life stress among Blacks: Their role in physical health. *Journal of the National Medical Association, 80,* 1329-1334.

Chan, K. (1983). Limited English speaking, handicapped, and poor: Triple threat in childhood. In M. Chu-Chang (Ed.), *Asian and Pacific perspectives in bilingual education: Comparative research* (pp. 153-171). New York: Teachers College Press.

Chan, K ., & Rueda, R. (1979). Culture and poverty: Separate but equal. *Exceptional Children, 45*, 422-428.

Chan, S. (1991). *Asian Americans: An interpretive history.* Boston: Twayne.

Clark, K., & Clark, M. (1940). Skin color as a factor in racial identification and preferences in Negro children. *Journal of Negro Education, 19*, 341-358.

Comer, J. (1989). Racism and the education of young children. *Teachers College Record, 90*, 352-361.

Damon, W. (1977). *The social world of the child.* San Francisco: Jossey- Bass.

Derman-Sparks, L., & ABC Task Force. (1989). *Anti-bias curriculum: Tools for empowering young children.* Washington, DC: National Association for the Education of Young Children.

Dillihay, T. (1989). Suicide in Black children. *Psychiatric Forum, 15*, 24-27.

Dodge, K. (1986). A social information processing model of social competence in children. In M. Perlmutter (Ed.), *Cognitive perspectives on children's social and behavioral development. The Minnesota Symposium on Child Psychology, (Vol. 18).* Hillsdale, NJ: Lawrence Erlbaum.

Ekman, P. (1972). Universal and cultural differences in facial expressions of emotions. In J. K. Cole (Ed.), *Nebraska Symposium on Motivation, 1971* (pp. 207-283). Lincoln: University of Nebraska Press.

Ekman, P. (Ed.). (1982). *Emotion in the human face* (2nd ed.). New York: Cambridge University Press.

Fordham, S., & Ogbu, J. (1986). Black students' school success: Coping with the "burden of 'acting white.' " *The Urban Review, 18*, 176-206.

Funk, A., & Wise, G. (1989). Anomie, powerlessness, and exchange: Parallel sources of deviance. *Deviant Behavior, 10*, 53-60.

Goodman, M. (1964). *Race awareness in young children* (rev. ed.). New York: Collier.

Graham, S. (1992). "Most of the subjects were white and middle class:" Trends in published research on African Americans in selected APA journals, 1970-1989. *American Psychologist. 47*, 629-639.

Grier, W., & Cobb, P. (1968). *Black rage.* New York: Basic Books.

Hechinger, F. (1992). *Fateful choices.* New York: Carnegie Corp.

Hernandez, H. (1989). *Multicultural education: A teacher's guide to content and process.* Columbus: Charles E. Merrill.

Hughes, R. (1992). The fraying of America. *Time, 139(5),* pp. 44, 46.

Katz, P. (1976). The acquisition of racial attitudes in children. In P. Katz (Ed.), *Towards the elimination of racism* (pp. 125-154.) New York: Pergamon.

Katz, P. (1987). Developmental and social processes in ethnic attitudes and self-identification. In J. Phinney & M. Rotheram (Eds.), *Children's ethnic socialization* (pp. 92-99). Newbury Park, CA: Sage.

Kinder, D., & Sears, D. (1981). Prejudice and politics: Symbolic racism versus racial threats to the good life. *Journal of Personality and Social Psychology, 40,* 414-431.

Levy, R. (1984). The emotions in comparative perspective. In K. R. Scherer & P. Ekman (Eds.), *Approaches to emotions* (pp. 397-412). Hillsdale, NJ: Erlbaum.

Lieberman, P. (1992, June 8). 51% of riot arrests were Latino, study says. *Los Angeles Times,* p. 3.

Lutz, C., & White, G. (1986). The anthropology of emotions. *Annual Review of Anthropology, 15,* 405-436.

Matsumoto, D., & Ekman, P. (1989). American-Japanese cultural differences in intensity ratings of facial expressions of emotion. *Motivation and Emotion, 13,* 143-157.

McGuire, M., & Troisi, A. (1990). Anger: An evolutionary view. In R. Plutchik & H. Kellerman (Eds.), *Emotion: Theory, research and experience Vol 5.: Emotion psychopathology and psychotherapy* (pp. 43-57). New York: Academic Press.

Myrdal, G. (1944/1962). *An American dilemma: The Negro problem and modern democracy.* New York: Harper and Row.

Omi, M., & Winant, H. (1986). *Racial formation in the United States from 1960's to the 1980's.* New York: Routledge & Kegan Paul.

Rigdon, J. (1991, July 10). Exploding myth: Asian-American youth suffer a rising toll from heavy pressures. *Wall Street Journal,* p. 1, 5.

Root, M. (1992). Reconstructing the impact of trauma on personality. In L. Brown & M. Ballou (Eds.), *Personality and psychopathology: Feminist reappraisals* (pp. 229-265). New York: Guilford Press.

Russell, J. (1991). Culture and the categorization of emotions. *Psychological Bulletin, 110,* 426-450.

Ryan, W. (1971). *Blaming the victim.* New York: Pantheon.

Scheff, T. (1985). Universal expressive needs: A critique and a theory. Special Issue: The sociology of emotions. *Symbolic Interaction, 8,* 241-262.

Schlesinger, A., Jr. (1992). *The disuniting of America.* New York: Norton.

Sears, D. (1988). Symbolic racism. In P. Katz & D. Taylor (Eds.), *Eliminating racism* (pp. 53-84). New York: Plenum Press.

Skillings, J., & Dobbins, J. (1991). Racism as a disease: Etiology and treatment implications. *Journal of Counseling & Development, 70,* 206-212.

Spaights, E., & Simpson, G. (1986). Some unique causes of Black suicide. *Psychology: A Quarterly Journal of Human Behavior, 23,* 1-5.

Spencer, M., & Markstrom-Adams, C. (1990). Identity processes among racial and ethnic minority children in America. *Child Development, 61,* 290-310.

Spencer, M. (1987). Black children's ethnic identity formation: Risk and resilience of castelike minorities. In J. Phinney & M. Rotheram (Eds.), *Children's ethnic socialization* (pp. 103-116). Newbury Park, CA: Sage.

Steinberg, J. B., Lyon, D., & Vaiana, M. (Eds.). (1992). *Urban America policy choice for Los Angeles and the nation.* Santa Monica: RAND.

Sue, S., & Okazaki, S. (1990). Asian-American educational achievements: A phenomenon in search of an explanation. *American Psychologist, 45,* 913-920.

Suzuki, B. (1989). Asian Americans as the "model minority": Outdoing whites? Or media hype? *Change, 21,* 13-17.

Takaki, R. (1989) *Strangers from a different shore: A history of Asian Americans.* New York: Penguin Books.

U.S. Commission on Civil Rights. (1992). *Civil rights issues facing Asian Americans in the 1990's.* Washington, DC: U.S. Commission on Civil Rights.

U.S. Kerner Commission. (1968). *The Kerner report: The 1968 report of the National Advisory Commission.* New York: Pantheon.

SECTION III

ASSESSMENT APPROACHES FOR ANGER, HOSTILITY, AND AGGRESSION

This section of the book presents three complementary approaches to the assessment of anger, hostility, and aggression in children and adolescents. Chapter 7 (Furlong & Smith) presents a detailed review of various self-report and rating scales that focus specifically on the affective, cognitive, or behavioral aspects of anger. These instruments will be an essential component of any comprehensive assessment of a youth's anger-related feelings, thoughts, and actions. In addition, it is essential to document carefully the manifestations of specific aggressive behaviors, particularly in school settings. Chapter 8 (Stein & Karno) provides a practical guide for conducting observations of anger-related behaviors. Some readers will be interested in placing such assessments into a more general evaluation model that takes into account individual personality characteristics; such an approach is presented in Chapter 9 (Huberty & Eaken). Although not all readers of this book will conduct in-depth anger assessments, we believe it is very important for all professionals to be aware of various assessment options so that they can participate meaningfully in collaborative screening and prescriptive evaluations. Such evaluations provide essential information when creating individual strategies to help a child cope more effectively with the conditions in his or her life associated with the experience and expression of anger.

7 ASSESSMENT OF YOUTH'S ANGER, HOSTILITY, AND AGGRESSION USING SELF-REPORT AND RATING SCALES

Michael J. Furlong and Douglas C. Smith

INTRODUCTION

Chapter Objectives

Anger-related assessments in school and clinical settings often include self-report and rating scale instruments in addition to projective and behavioral approaches discussed in later chapters. In this chapter, we begin with a brief discussion of some general psychometric and administration considerations to keep in mind when using any self-report or rating scale instrument. The core of the chapter describes instruments that assess affective, cognitive, and behavioral aspects of anger.

This chapter is not merely a review of broad-based child rating scales that contain subscales labeled "aggression" or "aggressive." The Achenbach rating scales (Achenbach, 1991a, 1991b, 1991c), for example, have such a subscale. A review of the item content of such "aggression" subscales often finds items that focus on anger expression behaviors (e.g., hitting), but also general conduct disorder behaviors (e.g., stealing). Such instruments have an essential role in any comprehensive youth evaluation (see McConaughy, 1993), but space concerns do not permit a detailed review of these scales. The reader is referred to Martin, Hooper, and Snow (1986), McMahon (1984), Witt, Cavell, Heffer, Carey, and Martens (1988), and Witt, Heffer, and Pfeiffer (1990) for critical reviews of broad-based behavior scales. The reader is also referred to the brief discussions of anger and aggression assessment presented by Bowers (1987), Witt et al. (1990), and Zlomke and Piersel (1987).

Nor does this chapter review various narrow-band rating or self-report scales that tap constructs related to anger or aggression scales, such as the Social Skills Rating Scale (Gresham & Elliott, 1991; see reviews by Furlong & Karno, in press; McLean, 1992) or the Conners Teacher Rating Scale (Conners, 1990). A few broad-based instruments are reviewed if they contain specific subscales that measure a unique aspect of anger, as is the case for the Minnesota Multiphasic Personality Inventory—Adolescent version (MMPI-A; Butcher et al., 1992). In such instances, only the relevant subscales are discussed.

This chapter reviews various instruments that specifically assess youth's experience of angry emotions, hostile or cynical cognitions associated with those emotions, and the behaviors (internal and external) they use to express their anger. Both commercially produced materials and research instruments are reviewed.

Appropriate Use of Self-Report and Rating Scales

A distinction can be made between behavioral checklists and rating scales based on whether they emphasize specific, distinct behaviors (checklists) or summary impressions formed after observing a child's behavior across time and perhaps settings (rating scales). McMahon (1984) argues that rating scales using "generally" worded items are prone to more bias than scales using items that describe "specific" behaviors. He argues that rating scales are best used for screening, intervention selection, identification of behavioral variation across settings, and program outcome evaluation.

Martin (1988), Martin et al. (1986), Finch and Rogers (1984), McMahon (1984), and Witt et al. (1990) provide reviews of rating scales focusing on general personality, anxiety, fears, types of reinforcement, life events/stress, self-esteem, social behavior, and locus of control. Some of these instruments contain subscales labeled "aggression" or "conduct disorder," but they were not designed specifically to measure anger-related constructs. In these reviews only the Children's Inventory of Anger (Finch, Saylor, & Nelson, 1987) and the Matson Evaluation of Social Skills for Youth (MESSY; Matson et al., 1980), reviewed in this chapter, were briefly discussed by Witt et al. (1990). These reviews, nonetheless, provide particularly good summaries of the general advantages and disadvantages to

TABLE 7.1. CONSIDERATIONS WHEN USING SELF-REPORT AND RATING SCALES.

ADVANTAGES OF USING SELF-REPORT AND RATING SCALES

- Easily provide multiple perspectives.
- Ensure that many behaviors are not inadvertently ignored by raters.
- Structured format increases objectivity and reliability.
- Ecological validity increases as more informants/settings are used.
- Collect a lot of information efficiently.
- Contradictions among raters may identify setting-specific behavior.
- Provide information when children can or will not cooperate.
- Raters are often particularly motivated to respond.

CAUTIONS OF USING SELF-REPORT AND RATING SCALES

- Rater perceptions are filtered—they do not report "objective" reality.
- Appropriate norms are often unavailable.
- Halo effects can occur—no discrimination among behaviors.
- Leniency effects can influence ratings—there is a bias to be tough or easy, regardless of who or what is being rated.
- Central tendency bias can influence ratings when the informant avoids using the extreme ends of the rating scale.
- Self-serving bias can influence ratings in which there is a tendency for individuals to rate themselves above average on positive personal traits.
- Social desirability can affect self-reports on negative emotions and behaviors.
- Ratings are often given equal weight even though some raters have more intimate awareness of a child's behavior.
- Many informant rating scales do not have an internal reliability check as do self-report rating scales.
- Long- and short-term memory limitations may influence responses.
- Items may not be worded in ways that generate strong emotional reactions, particularly important in anger-related scales.
- Heuristics of information processing, such as illusory correlation, may bias judgments about the occurrence of certain behaviors.
- Low agreement across raters.
- Validity and applicability of anger scales across diverse groups of children has not been well-established.

consider when using any of the anger self-report or rating scales reviewed in this chapter (see Table 7.1).

Model for using self-report and rating scales. Martin et al. (1986) define a rating scale as "any paper and pencil device whereby one assesses the behavior of that individual based on his or her observation of the child or adolescent over an extended period of time" (p. 309). There is a close relationship between rating scales and observational procedures, as discussed by Stein and Karno (Chapter 8). Observational procedures focus on recording situation-specific behaviors that presumably are unfiltered by the observer. Rating scales, in contrast, request information about behaviors and, to greater or lesser degrees, request global judgments to be made about the behaviors. Thus, for example, in behavioral observation we look for specific instances of a child kicking other children, whereas rating scales typically ask someone who has intensive contact with the child how often they have observed the child kicking other children. Self-report procedures can be considered a subgroup of rating scales with the important distinction that the ratings are provided by the individual being evaluated, not by others.

Beitchman and Corrandini (1988) and Cutchen and Simpson (1993) review research suggesting that teachers' and mental health professionals' behavior ratings may have a number of biasing factors. In particular, studies show more variability by teacher and school than by social and psychological variables. For this reason, they emphasize the importance of providing a multimodal assessment that includes children's ratings of their own behavior. The same bias may potentially affect parent ratings.

Another potentially biasing influence is that self-report rating scales often include only conflict situations with few prosocial situations described in the item stems. To address this issue and the other concerns mentioned above, other questions need to be asked when using self-reports with youth:

- Can younger children understand the items?
- Should they be read to the child?
- How does reading the items affect the psychometric characteristics of the scale?
- Do younger children have the cognitive maturity to evaluate their feelings, thoughts, and actions in complex ways?
- How are child self-reports influenced by reactions to recent events?
- Can enduring traits of children be measured?
- Are children willing to disclose the same types or levels of behavior that parents or teachers may be able to report?

FIGURE 7.1. MODEL FOR ANGER ASSESSMENT USING SELF-REPORT AND RATING SCALES

SETTING	HOME	SCHOOL	PEER GROUP
SOURCE	Parents	Teachers	Peers
INSTRUMENTS	Anger Experience	Hostile Attitude	Anger Expression

From Martin, R. P., Hooper, S., & Snow, J. (1986). Behavior rating scale approaches to personality assessment in children and adolescents. In H. E. Knoff (Ed.), *The assessment of child and adolescent personality* (pp. 309-352). New York: Guilford. Copyright 1986 by Guilford Press. Adapted by permission.

Martin et al. (1986) suggest that rating scale data should be collected across *settings* (home, school, clinical, community, etc.), *sources* (parents, teachers, counselors, administrators, etc.), and with *multiple instruments*. However, it will usually be impractical to collect rating scale responses in all combinations of these three areas, although it is a worthwhile goal to pursue and following it will assure that an assessment of any child will not be based on unrepresentative, isolated data. In the context of anger-related assessment, we have modified Martin et al.'s (1986) model as shown in Figure 7.1.

Obviously, an assessment that addresses all combinations of settings, sources, and domains of anger may not be practical. In practice, one minimally needs to collect information from multiple sources. With evaluation issues related to anger, hostility, and aggression it is important to attend to emotional, cognitive, and behavioral/coping components. Martin et al. (1986) also recommend summing same-scale rating instruments across sources and settings into an "aggregate score." We do not recommend this practice because for most anger scales the norms are not sufficiently well developed to support cross-scale comparisons.

The reader needs to keep in mind that there has been more research evaluating the reliability and validity of adult anger scales than youth scales (e.g., Friedman, 1992; Williams, Barefoot, & Shekelle, 1985). Furthermore, many of the instruments for youth are just modifications of adult instruments (e.g., Caine, Foulds, & Hope, 1967; Evans & Strangeland, 1971; Novaco, 1975, 1979; Philip, 1968, 1969; Zelin, Adler, & Myerson, 1972). Aggression research has overshadowed anger research, and in some instances these two constructs have been confused (Biaggio, 1980) and the labels have been used by researchers rather loosely. The reader is cautioned therefore to examine the item content of an instrument to evaluate its appropriateness for a specific purpose.

In the following section we review the instruments listed in Table 7.2. They are organized into the following three basic categories: (a) self-report instruments, (b) analog self-report instruments, and (c) rating scales. In addition, several scales that do not directly address anger issues are reviewed because of their potentially important role in developing an understanding of a youth's anger-related experiences.

TABLE 7.2. LISTING OF ANGER-RELATED SCALES.

INSTRUMENT	KEY RERFERENCES	AGE	# OF ITEMS	RESPONSE	ANGER EXPERIENCE	HOSTILE ATTITUDE	ANGER EXPRESSION	SCALE TYPE
Buss-Durkee Hostility Inventory (BDHI)	Biaggio et al. (1989) Buss & Durkee (1957) Morrison et al. (1975) Treiber et al. (1989)	14–adult	66 (without the Guilt subscale)	True-False	Irritability	Resentment Suspicion	Assault Verbal Hostility Indirect Hostility Negativism	Self-Report
Buss-Durkee Hostility Inventory (BDHI-C) Child Version	Treiber et al. (1989)	7–10 presumably could be used with older children as well	13	True-False	Expressive Hostility		Experienced Anger	Self-Report
State-Trait Anger Expression Inventory (STAXI)	Spielberger (1988)	12–18	44	4-point Likert 1 = Not at all ... 4 = Very much so State Anger 1 = Almost never 4 = Almost always Trait Anger and Anger Expression subscales	State Anger 10 items	Trait Anger 10 items	Anger-In 8 items Anger-Out 8 items Anger Control 8 items Anger Expression composite score	Self-Report

(Continued)

Instrument	Key Rerferences	Age	# of Items	Response	Anger Experience	Hostile Attitude	Anger Expression	Scale Type
Pediatric Anger Expression Scale (PAES)	Jacobs et al. (1989)	4th- & 5th graders	15	3-point 1 = Hardly ever 2 = Sometimes 3 = Often	None	None	Anger-out Anger-control Anger-reflection Anger-suppression	Self-Report (Modeled after the STAXI)
Multidimensional Anger Inventory (MAI)	Siegel (1985) Siegel (1992)	15+ (Developed with college students, has been used with high school students)	38	5-point Likert 1 = completely undescriptive... 5 = completely descriptive	Range of Anger Eliciting Situations	Hostile Outlook	Anger-In Anger-Out	Self-Report
Children's Inventory of Anger (CIA)	Finch et al. (1987) Finch & Eastman (1983) Frentz et al. (1991) Shapiro et al. (1985) Shoemaker et al. (1986)	9–16 4th-grade reading level	71 Range = 71–284 Modification of Novaco Anger Inventory (adult scale)	1 = Don't Care to 5 = Furious Uses "Happy Face" ☺ visual cues	Items measure intensity of anger reaction to "provoking" situations... "How angry would you get if..."	None	None	Self-Report

(Continued)

School Ager Inventory (SAI)	Heavy et al. (1989) D.C. Smith et al. (1987) D.C. Smith et al. (1988)	9–18	24 Range = 26–216	1 = Don't care 6 = I'm furious Uses "Happy Face" visual cues Modification of CIA response scale	Peer Annoyances Peer-Teacher Problems Moral Infractions Teacher Antagonism	None	Anger Provocation Anger Level	Self-Report Content focuses on school conflict situations
Minnesota Multiphasic Personality Inventory - Adolescent (MMPI-A)	Butcher (1992) Butcher et al. (1992) Butcher & Williams (1992) Williams et al. (1992)	14–18	478 on total instrument	True-False	None	Cynicism Content Scale (23 Items)	Anger Content Scale (17 items)	Self-Report
Olweus Rating Scales	Mattson et al. (1980) Moskowitz & Schwartzman (1987) Olweus (1991) Olweus et al. (1980) Waas & French (1986)	School-Aged					Verbal Aggression Physical Aggression	Self-Report (Developed for bullying research conducted in Norway)
Predatory Aggression Subtype Scale (PASS)	Slabby & Guerra (1988)	15–18	18		None	1. Legitimacy 2. Increases Self-Esteem 3. Avoid Negative Image 4. Victim Deserves 5. Victims Don't Suffer	None	Self-Report

(continued)

Instrument	Key Rerferences	Age	# of Items	Response	Anger Experience	Hostile Attitude	Anger Expression	Scale Type
Children's Action Tendency Scale (CATS)	Deluty (1979) Deluty (1981a) Deluty (1981b) Deluty (1983) Deluty (1984a) Deluty (1984b) Williamson & McKenzie (1988) Williamson et al. (198x)	Grades 3–6 (probably appropriate for Grades 7–8)	Originally 13, a 10-item version has also been used	Forced-choice pairs of assertive, aggressive, and passive responses to presented scenarios	None	None	Aggressive Passive Assertive	Self-Report Analog
Children's Assertive Behavior Scale (CABS)	Michelson & Wood (1982) Wood et al. (1978)	Grades 3–6	27 Absolute value of response. Range 0 = assertive 54 = most "unassertive"	5-point (-2 to +2) Child presented scenario selects from among 5 responses ranging from very passive to assertive to very aggressive	None	None	Total Assertion Score	Self-Report Analog

(Continued)

Children's Assertion Inventory	Ollendick (1984) Scanlon & Ollendick (1986)	Grades 3–6	14	True-False Child indicates if he/she would respond as described in scenario	None	None	Postive response negative response	Self-Report Analog
Play Entry Assertion/ Aggression Scale (PEAAS)	Morrison (1989)	Grades 3–6	8 Representing passive assertive or aggressive strategies for play entry	3-point 1 = no 2 = maybe 3 = yes	None	None	Passive Assertive Aggressive	Self-Report Analog
Children's Hostility Inventory (CHI)	Kazdin et al (1987) Kolko et al. (1985)	5–17 research norms for 6–12-year-olds	38 Range = 0–38	True-False	Irritability	Resentment Suspicion	Assaultivess Verbal hostility Indirect expression of hostility Negativism	Rating Scale (Parent)
Becomes Angry Scale	Siegel (1984) Siegel & Leitch (1984)	Grades 6–12	19	Presence - absence of behaviors during an interview	Anger situations	None	Frequent Anger Out	Rating Scale (Interviewer responds)

(continued)

Instrument	Key Rerferences	Age	# of items	Response	Anger Experience	Hostile Attitude	Anger Expression	Scale Type
Matthews Youth Test for Health (MYTH)	Matthews & Angulo (1980) Siegman et al. (1990) Woodall & Matthews (1989)	Grades 2–12	17	5-point 1 = extremely uncharacteristic 5 = extremely characteristic	None	None	Aggression factor	Rating Scale (Teacher)
Interview for Aggressive Behavior IAB	Kazdin & Esveldt-Dawson (1986)	6–13	30	5-point 1 = None at all 5 = Very much	Some items, no specific scale	None	Arguing Fighting subscale	Rating Scale (Parent)
Aggression Scale	Vitiello et al. (1990)	10–18	10	Yes - No (behavior present or absent)	None	None	Predatory Affective	Rating Scale (nurses and aides inpatient setting)
Matson Evaluation of Social Skills for Youngsters (MESSY)	Matson et al. (1983) Spence & Liddle (1990)	4–18	62 items		None	None	Aggressive - Antisocial Subscale (18 items from total) Appropriate Social Skills	Rating Scale

(Continued)

School Social Behavior Scale (SSBS)	Merrell (1993)	K–6 norms 7–12 norms	33 Scale B Antisocial Behavior (there is a companion Social Competence scale)	5-point Likert 1 = Never ... 5 = Frequently	None	None	Hostile-irritable Antisocial-aggressive Demanding-disruptive	Rating Scale (Teacher)
School Behavior Checklist (SBC)	Miller (1977)	Form A1: 4–6 Form A2: 7–13	Form A1:104 Form A2: 96	True-False Is behavior "descriptive" of the child	None	Hostile Isolation subscale	Aggression subscale	Rating Scale (Teacher)
Pupil Evaluation Inventory (PEI)	Pekarik et al. (1976)	Grades 1–8	35	True-False Matrix format with each child in class rated on 35 items	None	Items # 4, 7, 12, 16, 23, 27, 29, 31, 34	Aggression Factor	Rating Scale Sociometric (Peers)
Assessment Scale for Sociometric Evaluation of Secondary-School Students (ASSESS)	Prinz et al. (1978)	Grades 9–12	45	True-False Matrix format with each child in class rated on 45 items	None	None	Aggression-disruptiveness	Rating Scale Sociometric (Peers)

(continued)

Instrument	Key Rerferences	Age	# of Items	Response	Anger Experience	Hostile Attitude	Anger Expression	Scale Type
Peer Nomination Inventory (PNI)	Landau & Millich (1985) Milich & Landau (1984) Perry & Perry (1974) Wiggins & Winder (1961)	Grade K version Grade 3–6 Version	K version 12 (uses photos) 3–6 version 22	Give name of student in class who is most like descriptor given in item	None	None	Some items ask for who is mean, fights, bossy, gets mad	Rating Scale Sociometric (Peers)
Peer Nomination of Anger Control Problems (PNACP)	Finch et al. (1987)		40	Give name of student in class who is most like descriptor given in item	None	None	Some items ask for who gets angry easily… who fights with smaller children	Rating Scale Sociometric (Peers)
Marlowe Crown Social Desirability Scale Children's Version MCSD-C	Crandall et al. (1965)	Grades 3–12	48	True-false	N/A	Measures tendency to have a desirability response bias, less willing to admit angry thoughts and behaviors	N/A	Self-Report

SELF-REPORT INSTRUMENTS

Buss-Durkee Hostility Inventory (BDHI)

Buss and Durkee (1957) developed the BDHI because of a need for a multidimensional index of hostility, which they hypothesized was a precursor of aggression. The BDHI was one of the first psychometrically developed hostility scales and it has been widely used in research studies. Although used predominantly with adults, it has application for older adolescents and has recently inspired the development of other instruments.

The initial scale had 105 items and was administered to 159 college students in a pilot study. Items were revised, new items added, and a 94-item version administered to another sample of 120 college students. Items were included in a final set of 75 items if they had a scoring rate of 15%–85% for males or females and an item-total correlation of .40 or higher. A true–false response scale was used, so the range of scores is 0–75. The score obtained by the college males ($M = 30.9$; $SD = 10.2$) was higher than that obtained by the females ($M = 27.7$; $SD = 8.8$) (Buss & Durkee, 1957). For a review of the BDHI with adults see Veliocer, Govia, Cherico, & Corriveau (1985).

The structure of the BDHI originally included the following subscales (sample items are presented below; see the Appendix for all 75 items):

- **Assault Subscale:** Physical violence against others. This includes getting into fights with others but not destroying objects. Sample item: 25. *If someone hits me first, I let him have it.*
- **Indirect Hostility Subscale:** Indirect aggressive behaviors like malicious gossip or practical jokes, attacks by devious means. Undirected aggression, such as temper tantrums and slamming doors, discharge of negative affect against no one in particular; it is a diffuse rage reaction that has no direction. Sample item: 18. *When I am angry, I sometimes sulk.*
- **Irritability:** A readiness to explode with negative affect at the slightest provocation. This includes quick temper, grouchiness, and rudeness. Sample item: 4. *I lose my temper easily but get over it quickly.*
- **Negativism:** Oppositional behavior, usually directed against authority. This involves a refusal to cooperate that may vary from passive noncompliance to open rebellion against rules or conventions. Sample item: 36. *When people are bossy, I take my time just to show them.*

- **Resentment:** Jealousy and hatred of others. This refers to a feeling of anger at the world over real or fantasized mistreatment. Sample item: 37. *Almost every week I see someone I dislike.*
- **Suspicion:** Projection of hostility on to others. This varies from merely being distrustful and wary of people to beliefs that others are being derogatory or are planning harm. Sample item: 46. *My motto is "Never trust strangers."*
- **Verbal Hostility:** Negative affect expressed in both style and content of speech. Style includes arguing, shouting, and screaming; content includes threats, curses, and being overcritical. Sample item: 23. *I can't help getting into arguments when people disagree with me.*

A Guilt subscale was originally included, but subsequent research has generally questioned its utility in anger assessment (e.g., Biaggio, Supplee, & Curtis, 1981).

Morrison, Chaffin, and Chase (1975) provide epidemiological information about hostility among adolescents. This study focuses on the responses of 438 high school students (ages 14–18) from a southern U.S. community. The sample included both white and African-American students, as well as 62 residents in a university psychiatric unit. The results showed that 14- to 15-year-old boys from middle- and low-socioeconomic class obtained the highest total score. Overall, the students in the psychiatric unit had a total BDHI score (34.7) that was just slightly higher than that of the high school sample (33.9). There was a tendency for the female patients and the high school students to obtain slightly higher scores. One complication in this study was that the students signed their response sheets. Due to the influence of social desirability, it is possible that the information derived from these students is lower than would be obtained from other groups of students. In addition, differences related to the socioeconomic and racial backgrounds of the students were found, suggesting that users should be particularly sensitive to diversity issues when using the BDHI with adolescents. Because the Morrison et al. (1975) study provides the only available data regarding adolescent responses to the BDHI, their data have been transformed into T-scores and presented in Table 7.3. These norms are for the BDHI Total score minus the nine Guilt items, so the score range is 0–66.

There has been little research examining the use of the BDHI with adolescents. However, extensive research with adults shows good convergent validity (Riley & Treiber, 1989) and those with high scores are not as likely to engage in constructive social actions in role-play situations (Biaggio et al., 1981). In contrast, the BDHI is susceptible to "faking bad" (Riley & Treiber, 1989), and responses are inversely related with social desirability measures (Biaggio et al., 1981; Buss & Durkee, 1957; Selby, 1984). Moderate to high negative correlations (range = -.44 to -.68) between the BDHI Total score and the Marlowe-Crowne Social Desirability Scale (Crowne & Marlowe, 1960) have been reported in various studies (Leibowitz, 1968). Biaggio et al. (1981) point out that those who score high on social desirability scales are not those who are likely to cover up their responses on anger inventories. Individuals who score low on social desirability scales tend to be more resentful or hostile in experimental situations when they receive "unjust" treatment (Novaco, 1975). This leads us to expect a negative correlation between anger expression and social desirability.

Evidence of divergent validity (different from other constructs) is not well established (Riley & Treiber, 1989), and construct validity is inconsistent. Veliocer et al. (1985) report that the factor structure of the BDHI does not hold up across different adult samples or when the response scale is changed from the usual true–false format to a 7-point scale. It does appear, however, that the Resentment and Suspicion subscales consistently measure aspects of hostile attitudes. Given the well-established history of the BDHI in clinical research, it can be used as part of a comprehensive evaluation of youth's anger. It should be integrated into a systematic interview process, but it should not be used in isolation to make diagnostic or program placement decisions.

Buss-Durkee Hostility Inventory—Children's Version (BDHI-C)

Treiber et al. (1989) extended the use of the BDHI to children. Drawing upon earlier factor analytic studies of the BDHI (Saronson, 1961; Siegman, Dembroski, & Ringel, 1987), they developed a scale for children that taps the "experience component" of hostility, which is derived from the BDHI Resentment and Suspicion subscales. They also assessed the "expression component" of hostility, which is derived from the Assaultiveness, Irritability, Verbal Aggression, and Indirect Aggression subscales of the BDHI. Using items with the highest point biserial correlations, they created a modified BDHI for elementary school children (7 to 10 years old). A true–false response scale is used. The subscales and a sample item are as follows (all items are shown in the Appendix):

TABLE 7.3. BDHI T-SCORES FOR HIGH SCHOOL STUDENTS.

Raw Score	Female	Male	Raw Score	Female	Male
0	11	15	34	49	49
1	12	16	35	50	50
2	13	17	36	51	51
3	14	18	37	52	52
4	15	19	38	53	53
5	16	20	39	54	54
6	17	21	40	56	55
7	18	22	41	57	56
8	20	23	42	58	57
9	21	24	43	59	58
10	22	25	44	60	59
11	23	26	45	61	60
12	24	27	46	62	61
13	25	28	47	63	62
14	26	29	48	65	63
15	27	30	49	66	64
16	29	31	50	67	65
17	30	32	51	68	66
18	31	33	52	69	67
19	32	34	53	70	68
20	33	35	54	71	69
21	34	36	55	72	70
22	35	37	56	74	71
23	36	38	57	75	72
24	38	39	58	76	73
25	39	40	59	77	74
26	40	41	60	78	75
27	41	42	61	79	76
28	42	43	62	80	77
29	43	44	63	81	78
30	44	45	64	83	79
31	45	46	65	84	80
32	47	47	66	85	81
33	48	48			

Derived from data presented in Morrison et al. (1975). Aggression in adolescence: Use of the Buss-Durkee Inventory. *Southern Medical Journal, 68,* 431-436. Nine Guilt subscale items were not included so the maximum score is 66.

- **Expressive Hostility** (Expressive Anger in this chapter)
  Sample item: 1. *When people yell at me, I yell back.*
- **Experienced Anger** (Hostile Attitude in this chapter)
  Sample item: 11. *I think people usually have a hidden reason for doing something nice for me.*

Treiber et al. (1989) report a stability coefficient of .57 for the child version of the BDHI over an unspecified time period—no internal consistency reliabilities were reported. Unpublished concurrent validity coefficients are reported for "expressed hostility" (.28), "self-reported anger" (.44), and "parental ratings of negative peer interactions with expressed hostility" (.28). Evidence of the scale's reliability and validity is sketchy.

Treiber et al. (1989) administered the Expressive and Experienced Hostility scales to elementary school children, and 1 week later blood pressure readings were taken. The results showed that children with high scores on the Expressive Hostility scale had higher diastolic and systolic blood pressure readings and there was a negative relationship with Experienced Anger. However, these relationships were small and were reduced when height and weight were partialed out, so the relationship between high scores on the children's version of the BDHI and physiological measures is also not well established.

State-Trait Anger Expression Inventory (STAXI)

Spielberger (1988a, 1988b; Spielberger, Crane, Kearns, Pellegrin, & Johnson, 1991; Spielberger, Jacobs, Russell, & Crane, 1983; Spielberger et al., 1985; Spielberger, Krasner, & Solomon, 1988) discusses the early development of what was later to become the State-Trait Anger Expression Inventory (STAXI). Initially, the objective was to develop a bipolar scale that reflected anger expressed outwardly (AX/Out) and anger expressed inwardly (AX/In). This scale was pilot tested with a group of 1,114 high school students (Johnson, 1984) and submitted to a factor analysis. This revealed that the AX/Out and AX/In could be considered independent scales. In addition, some items had negative loadings on both the AX/Out and AX/In factors. These items' content focused on statements reflecting coping with anger. Based upon these early analyses, the Anger Expression scale was reduced to 20 items (10 items each for AX/Out and AX/In) and an 8-item anger control subscale was added.

The current research version of the STAXI includes 44 items that measure anger experience and expression through the following subscales, which are empirically supported by factor analyses (example items are):

- **State Anger** (10 items) *I feel irritated*
- **Trait Anger** (10 items) *I have a fiery temper*
- **Anger-in** (8 items) *I pout or sulk*
- **Anger-out** (8 items) *I make sarcastic remarks to others*
- **Anger-control** (8 items) *I am patient with others*

The Trait Anger subscale can be broken down further to derive Angry Temperament (e.g., *I am quick tempered*) and Angry Reaction (e.g., *I feel infuriated when I do a good job and get a poor evaluation*) scores. All of the subscales use a 4-point response format that asks the respondent to indicate either how intense their anger is (State-Anger) or how often they experience feelings or behaviors related to anger (Trait-Anger, Anger-in, Anger-out, and Anger-Control).

The STAXI is the only self-report anger inventory that includes normative data for a large sample of youth, a fact that led Feindler (1991) to recommend its use with adolescents. T-scores for each of the subscales are provided based upon the responses of 2,469 youth ages 12–18. These data show that these youth obtained higher scores on both Anger-in and Anger-out than samples of college students and non-college adults. It is important to note that the scores of adolescent males and females were comparable. In addition, there is a developmental trend in which both State- and Trait-Anger decrease from adolescence through middle adulthood. Although the STAXI norm sample for youth is quite sizeable, it was drawn from only nine Florida counties, so its validity across geographic regions in the U.S. is unknown. In addition, no information about the diversity of the sample is provided, thus the validity of its use with youth from low socioeconomic and various racial/ethnic groups is unknown.

For the adolescent norm group, the alpha reliabilities of the State-Anger, Trait-Anger, Anger-Temperament, and Anger-in subscales are in the moderate to high range (.82–.90). In contrast, the alpha coefficients for Anger-Reaction and Anger-out are lower (.65–.75). Construct and concurrent validity information is unavailable for youth, but comparable analyses with adult samples show that STAXI scores are positively correlated with the BDHI. Johnson (1984) also found that the Anger-in subscale correlated .47 with systolic blood pressure in a large sample of high school males.

Pediatric Anger Expression Scale (PAES)

The Pediatric Anger Expression Scale (Jacobs, Phelps, & Rohrs, 1989) was designed to assess children's "mechanism" of anger expression. Like the STAXI for adults and adolescents, the PAES presumes that anger expression is multidimensional. This scale consists of 15 items selected to measure a child's perception of how frequently she or he expresses anger. A 3-point response scale is used (1 = hardly ever; 2 = sometimes; 3 = often). The instrument was tested with a sample of 284 unreferred fourth- and fifth-grade children and their responses subjected to factor analysis. The results indicated that four, rather than two factors (i.e., anger-in and anger-out), was the best organization of these 15 items. The factors across both boys and girls, the alpha reliability coefficients [in brackets], and their respective items were as follows:

- **Anger-out** [.74] *(I show my anger, I do things like slam doors, I attack whatever it is that makes me angry, I say mean things, I lose my temper)*;
- **Anger-control** [.68] *(I control my temper, I keep calm, I calm down faster than most people)*;
- **Anger-reflection** [.63] *(I talk to someone until I feel better, I stop to think and don't get more angry than I already am, I do something totally different until I calm down, I try to calmly settle the problem)*; and
- **Anger-suppression** [.67] *(I hold my anger in, I get mad inside but don't show it)*.

High scores indicate more frequently reported use of each type of anger expression. Reflecting this scoring procedure, the correlations between Anger-out and Anger-control (-.58), Anger-reflection (-.25), and Anger-suppression, (-.33) were all negative. Correlations among the latter three subscales were all positive. Males obtained significantly higher scores than females on Anger-out and lower scores on Anger-reflection. The mean scores obtained by the boys and girls on each of the four factors are shown in Table 7.4. These values can be used for general comparison purposes, but do not meet stringent requirements for valid norms or decision making.

Evidence of convergent validity was supported by high correlations between Anger-out and another measure of trait anger for both boys (.74) and girls (.71). Divergent validity was supported by lower correlations of Anger-out with a measure of trait anxiety for boys (.46) and girls (.49); however, these latter correlations were significant, suggesting that there is overlap in the traits being assessed.

In summary, the PAES fills an important niche in the assessment of young children's anger because it provides a structured procedure to ask their opinions about how often they use certain types of anger expression.

This information may be compared with ratings provided by adult observers and systematic behavioral observations. Jacobs et al. (1989), however, caution that the scale is still in the developmental stage and should be used with appropriate care.

Multidimensional Anger Inventory (MAI)

Siegel (1984, 1986, 1992) developed the MAI as an inventory that was "sensitive to the multidimensionality of the anger construct" (p. 192). It measures emotional (frequency, duration, magnitude), cognitive (hostile outlook), and behavioral (range of anger-eliciting situations) aspects of anger. Items were drawn (some were modified) from various anger and personality inventories (e.g., Buss & Durkee, 1957; Edwards, 1966; Novaco, 1975; Rosenman, 1985), and some were developed specifically for this inventory.

Thirty-eight items were included in the developmental version. A 5-point response scale was used ranging from 1 = "completely undescriptive" to 5 = "completed descriptive" of the respondent. The 10 MAI subscales and sample items are as follows:

- **Frequency:** *I tend to get angry more frequently than most people.*
- **Duration:** *When I get angry, I stay angry for hours.*
- **Magnitude:** *Other people seem to get angrier than I do in similar*

TABLE 7.4. MEAN SCORES AND STANDARD DEVIATIONS FOR PEDIATRIC ANGER ASSESSMENT SCALE.

		Anger-out	Anger-control	Anger-reflection	Anger-suppression
Females	M	8.34	6.27	10.39	3.95
	SD	2.51	1.59	2.21	1.18
Males	M	9.24	6.21	9.64	3.75
	SD	2.44	1.63	2.46	1.27
Maximum		15	9	15	6

From Jacobs et al. (1989), Assessment of anger expression in children: The Pediatric Anger Expression Scale. *Personality and Individual Differences, 10,* 59-65. Copyright 1989 Pergamon Press. Adapted by permission.

circumstances.

- **Anger-in:** *I harbor grudges that I don't tell anyone about.*
- **Anger-out:** *I try to get even when I'm angry with someone.*
- **Guilt:** *I feel guilty about expressing my anger.*
- **Brood:** *Once I let people know I'm angry, I can't put it out of my mind.*
- **Anger-discuss:** *I try to talk over problems with people without letting them know I'm angry.*
- **Hostile outlook:** *I am secretly quite critical of others.*
- **Range of anger-eliciting situations:** *I get angry when someone lets me down.*

In an initial evaluation of the MAI's reliability and validity, Siegel (1986) administered it to two samples: 198 college students and 288 male factory workers. The college students concurrently were administered brief versions of the Buss-Durkee Hostility Inventory, the Harburg Anger-In/Anger-Out Scale, and the Novaco Anger Inventory. The factory sample concurrently completed the Jenkins Activity Survey (Jenkins, Rosenman, & Zyzanski, 1974), and the A-trait subscale of the State-Trait Anxiety Inventory (Spielberger, Gorsuch, & Lushene, 1970).

The results of separate principal-components factor analyses with varimax rotation for the college student and factory worker samples each produced five similar factors: (a) Anger-Arousal, (b) Range of Anger-Eliciting Situations, (c) Hostile Outlook, (d) Anger-In, and (e) Anger-Out. Guilt items were not included in the final scale. As a result of the factor analyses, 13 items were dropped leaving a total of 25 items.

Test-retest stability for 60 college students across a 3- to 4-week period was favorable, .75 (Siegel, 1986). The alpha coefficient for the 25-item version Total score was .88; subscale reliabilities ranged from .51 (Anger-Out, with only 2 items) to .83 (Anger-Arousal, with 8 items). Validity was checked by examining correlations between the MAI subscales and other scales measuring similar constructs. Generally, the highest correlations were found in the expected direction. Some findings of note are that, in general, college students had higher scores than the factory workers and males scored higher than females on Anger-Arousal. Anxiety measures correlated moderately with Anger-Arousal and Anger-In ($r = .54$).

Furlong, Smith, and Boles (1993) and Philaber and Furlong (1992) have examined the properties of the Hostile Outlook subscale of the MAI with two samples of adolescents: (a) a large sample of nearly 5,000 junior and senior high school students, and (b) a sample of 278 adolescents identified as being vulnerable for school failure. The students responded to the six Hostile Outlook items (range of scores 6–30; items shown in Figure 7.2) that were modified to be appropriate for a school setting and embedded in a broader survey asking their opinions about their school's safety. The results indicated that the reliability of the Hostile Outlook subscale was just .47; this is identical to that reported for a sample of college students (Siegel, 1986). No significant differences were found between boys and girls but significant differences were found when comparisons were made across five racial/ethnic groups. Post hoc comparisons indicated that Asian-American students obtained lower scores than the white and the American Indian students. All other group Total score differences were nonsignificant. The mean score obtained by this large sample of students was 18.6 (*SD* = 3.7; *SEM* = .05). These scores were essentially normally distributed. It is interesting to note that, contrary to our expectations, at-risk students who were experiencing academic and social difficulties obtained a nearly identical score. Philaber and Furlong (1992) administered the same subscale to a sample of 278 seventh- and ninth-graders who had been identified as being

FIGURE 7.2. SCHOOL-BASED HOSTILITY SCALE ITEMS.

1. I am secretly quite critical of others.
2. I have met many people at school who are supposed to be smart, but who are no better than I am.
3. Some of my friends have habits that bother me very much.
4. At school people talk about me behind my back.
5. People can bother me just by being around.
6. I am on my guard with people who are friendlier than I expect.

RESPONSE SCALE

1	2	3	4	5
Strongly Disagree	Disagree	Disagree some… Agree some	Agree	Strongly Agree

at risk for academic and social difficulties based upon school grades (at least one F grade and a grade point average below 2.0) and discipline (classroom behavior or poor attendance) records. The average score obtained by these students was 17.3, which is actually lower than that of the general student sample. This suggests that the manifestation of hostile cognitions in youth may be more complex than anticipated; it is too simplistic to presume that "aggressive" or "bad" kids are the only ones who harbor hostile attitudes, or that they will be willing to admit to having hostile attitudes.

The MAI is the most comprehensively developed instrument that assesses anger from a multidimensional perspective. Given this fact, if an educator or a psychologist had to select just one instrument for use with adolescents, the MAI is the instrument of choice at this time. This comment is tempered by the MAI's limited normative data for youth and its need for additional validity studies.

Children's Inventory of Anger

The Children's Inventory of Anger (CIA; Finch et al., 1987) was developed drawing upon the work of Novaco (1975; 1979), who postulated an association between external events and anger arousal. Finch et al. acknowledge that there are three aspects of the anger arousal process that need to be considered in assessment: affect, cognition, and behavior. Yet, using the Novaco Anger Inventory as a model resulted in a scale that focuses primarily on the measurement of anger experience. [The Novaco scale presents adult-focused situations (e.g., *Someone cuts in front of you in line*) and asks the person to indicate how mad the situation would make him or her]. In addition to items from the Novaco scale, schoolchildren ("normal" and those with emotional disturbance) were interviewed and asked to describe situations that "made them angry or mad." The resulting scale contained 71 items, written at a fourth-grade reading level, describing situations that might induce anger; for example: *You brought your favorite candy bar in your lunch today but when you go to get it out, it's all melted* (item #14). Some items reflect impersonal frustrations, but most describe interpersonal hassles [e.g., *Somebody calls you chicken* (item #10)]. The items include situations that occur at home and in school settings. The complete set of items can be obtained in Finch et al. (1987, pp. 254-260).

The scale instructions ask children to imagine that the situation described in each statement is "actually happening to them" and to indicate how "angry (mad)" it would make them. A unique aspect of the CIA is that the four-choice Likert scale is represented by both verbal descriptions and

Figure 7.3. Example of Icons Used in Children's Inventory of Anger and the School Anger Inventory.

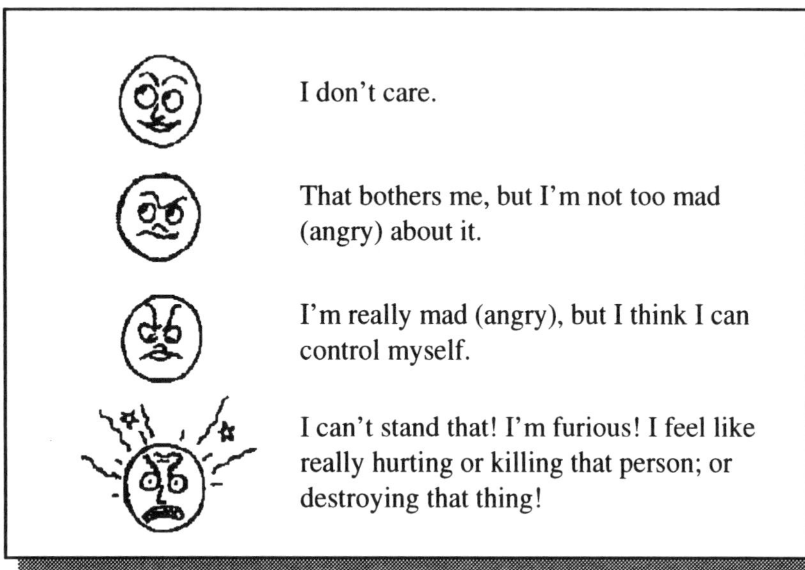

From Finch, A. J., Jr., Saylor, C. F., & Nelson, W. M. III. (1987). Assessment of anger in children. In R. J. Prinz (Ed.), Advances in behavior assessment of children and families (Vol 2., pp. 235-265). Copyright 1987 JAI Press. Adapted by permission.

stick figures with emotional expressions (see Figure 7.3 for an example). Each of the four response options is accompanied by a somewhat lengthy verbal anchor (first portion of anchor shown here). The response options are 1 = "I don't care"; 2 = "That bothers me"; 3 = "I'm really mad"; 4 = "I can't stand that! I'm furious." The total CIA score ranges from 71–284. Norms (means and standard deviations) for students in grades 4–7 are presented in Finch et al. (1987, p. 241). These norms are based upon the responses of 679 "normal" schoolchildren from Virginia; the authors suggest that these norms be used cautiously. Norms are also available for children ages 9–14 (only 8 students were 14 years old). The total scores are fairly stable by age with 9-year-olds having the highest mean score (212.3) and 12-year-olds the lowest mean score (198.5). Males tended to have higher scores than females, 205.8 and 198.3, respectively. The scores of African-American (M = 203.4, N = 223) and white (M = 201.6, N = 456) students were comparable.

Finch et al. (1987) report that the internal consistency of the CIA is well established. The K-R 20 alpha coefficient is .96 and the even-odd (.95) and split-half (.91) reliabilities were satisfactory. The stability coefficient over 3 months is .82, based on the responses of 30 psychiatric patients. Another group of 108 public school children completed the CIA at 2, 4, and 6 weeks after an initial administration. The stability coefficients were moderately favorable, but decreased a bit from week 2 (.75) to week 4 (.67) to week 6 (.63). In addition, the scores of these children were found to decrease significantly over time, suggesting that caution be exercised when the scale is used in short-term program evaluation.

In yet another reliability study, 242 youth with an emotional disturbance completed the CIA twice, separated by about 1 month (Finch et al., 1987). The internal consistency of the scale was .96 (odd-even split, Spearman-Brown corrected) and .93 (first half-second half split). The stability coefficient, however, was only .49 suggesting variability in children's anger self-reports. Finch and Eastman (1983) report the CIA's stability to be .82 (unspecified time period); split-half reliability to be .91 to .99 (varies by procedure); and the alpha coefficient to be .96. Item-to-whole correlations were .34 to .59 (90.1% of the items had correlations of .40 or higher).

Evidence of the clinical validity for the CIA is a bit mixed. Unpublished findings reported in Finch et al. (1987) indicate that its scores are not significantly different for youth with psychiatric disorders when compared to their normal peers. In this particular study, the application of the CIA with 38 residential placement children (ages 6 to 15) was examined. A cross-validation analysis was completed by collecting anger data from four sources: (a) the CIA, (b) peer nominations, (c) teacher ratings, and (d) a behavior problem checklist completed by the residential staff at the time of admission. Peer nominations were obtained from a 40-item questionnaire that described anger expression and management behaviors (for example: *Spends the least amount of time being angry*)—children were asked to identify the child on their unit who was most like each descriptor. Teacher ratings were obtained by using a cannibalized behavior checklist that gleaned anger-related items from existing child behavior rating scales. Concurrent validity coefficients with these instruments were in the moderate range (-.36 to .36). The Peer Nomination scale was significantly related to the dichotomous classification of students as either "angry" or "not angry." There was a mild association between self-reported anger, peer-nominated anger, and staff identification of anger control problems; however, teacher reports were not associated with self-reports. The authors speculate that this may have been a function of the small, controlled class setting at the residential facility.

Some preliminary work on the underlying structure of the CIA is reported by Finch et al. (1987). Factor analyses with normal and psychiatric populations have produced six and four factors, respectively. At this time, it is clear that the CIA, as one might expect with 71 items, has clusters of items reflecting more or less similar social situations (e.g., conflicts with siblings or conflicts with authority figures). The underlying structure of the CIA, however, at this time is not well known so no subscale summary scores can be derived.

In a validity study, Shapiro, Lentz, and Sofman (1985) found that the CIA was unrelated with behavioral outburst ratings compiled by classroom teachers. CIA ratings were significantly correlated only with other child ratings, not teacher ratings. Shapiro and Lentz felt that this outcome was due to the fact that the CIA asks how a child "would" feel, not "what" they would do. This may explain why it does not correlate more highly with behavioral observations and teacher ratings.

Shoemaker, Erikson, and Finch (1986) also completed a multitrait-multimethod validity study involving 51 third- and fourth-grade students. They focused specifically on the relationship between anger and depression. The students' average score on the CIA was comparable to other samples ($M = 192.8$; $SD = 30.6$). The highest correlation was between peer nomination of anger and the externalizing syndrome score from the Achenbach Teacher Rating Scale (.58). The analysis showed that 50% of the variance in ratings was attributable to subject effects, suggesting good convergent validity. In contrast, only 14% (n.s.) was attributable to a trait effect and 33% to method (rater). There was some support for the convergent validity (raters tended to give similar ratings to the same construct). However, when different constructs were compared (e.g., anger vs. depression) a similar pattern was found, so evidence of divergent validity was poor. Of all the raters, peers and teachers tended to have the highest level of agreement. Shoemaker et al. suggest that these findings raise further questions about the validity of using self-reports with children. However, it is also pointed out that without external criteria, it is difficult to conclude which ratings, children's or others', should be considered "more accurate." Along these lines, Feindler (1991) believes that the CIA measures situational antecedents and that the item content is designed more for children than adolescents.

In summary, the authors of the CIA clearly feel that this is a measure of anger experience and not anger expression. They give caution about using the CIA for clinical purposes because the substantive meaning of high scores is not totally clear at this time. In addition, most of the studies completed to date include psychiatric patients and have not been conducted with special populations in school settings. There is a need to evaluate the CIA's validity further with various categories of students.

School Anger Inventory

Smith, Adelman, Nelson, and Taylor (1988) developed the School Anger Inventory (SAI) by modifying items from the Children's Anger Inventory (Finch & Eastman, 1983; Finch et al., 1987) and developing new items. The SAI includes 24 items that sample the following components of the CIA:

- **Peer annoyances:** *11. You are trying to do your schoolwork and another student interrupts you for no good reason.*
- **Peer-teacher problems:** *8. Student brushes against you accidentally, then apologizes.*
- **School frustrations:** *4. You really try but your schoolwork just seems too hard.*
- **Moral infractions:** *16. You find out that someone has stolen something from you at school.*
- **Teacher antagonism:** *12. Your teacher tries to talk you into something you don't want to do.*

Another modification was that a 6-point Likert-type scale was used instead of a 4-point response scale (Heavy, Adelman, Nelson, & Smith, 1989). "Happy-face" type icons, similar to those used by Finch et al. (1987), provide a pictorial representation of the degree of anger associated with each response option (1 = "I don't care, that doesn't bother me" to 6 = "I can't stand that! I'm furious"). Thus, the SAI Total score ranges from 24–144.

Heavy et al. (1989) administered the SAI to students attending classes at a special education center for students with emotional and behavior problems ($N = 49$). Overall, these students received a mean total score of 57.0 ($SD = 9.8$); females ($M = 63.2$; $SD = 8.7$) had a significantly higher score than the males ($M = 55.3$; $SD = 9.5$), which is contradictory to the general pattern of males obtaining higher scores on anger instruments. The SAI's internal consistency (alpha coefficient) was .83 with a stability coefficient of .76 (time unspecified). Evidence of divergent validity was supported by the finding that it correlated -.46 with a measure of perceived academic control and .38 with magnitude of ability-reading achievement discrepancy. However, correlations with teacher and parent behavior ratings were non-significant. It is of interest that a direct relationship was found between magnitude of learning problems and anger, but not with behavioral problems. In summary, the SAI is one of the few instruments that focuses specifically on school experiences that children indicate elicit angry feelings in them. As with other anger scales reviewed in this chapter, it too requires additional validation.

MMPI-A Content Scales

Over the years a number of MMPI-derived scales for assessing anger, hostility, or aggression have been used in health psychology research with adults. Among these is the Hostility (Ho) scale (Barefoot, 1992; Barefoot, Dodge, Peterson, Dahlstrom, & Williams, 1989; Cook & Medley, 1954; Costa, Zonderman, McCrae, & Williams, 1986; Pope, Smith, & Rhodewalt, 1990; Smith & Frohm, 1985) and Megargee's Overcontrolled-Hostility (O-H) scale (Lane & Kling, 1979; Megargee & Cook, 1975; Megargee, Cook, & Mendelsohn, 1967; Truscott, 1990). Williams (1986) and Williams, Butcher, Ben-Porath, and Graham (1992), however, indicate that generalization of MMPI and MMPI-2 findings to adolescents is a questionable practice. They summarize research showing that adolescents' responses to the MMPI differ from adults in (a) the proportions endorsing specific items (differences here, for example, can be due to developmental factors), (b) code types (generally adult profile codes have not been shown to have empirical validity for adolescents), and (c) the elevation of the scales (average T-scores of 60 or higher have been found for six and five of the clinical scales for boys and girls, respectively). In addition, the responses of young women differ more from adult women's than young men's from adult men's responses (Williams et al., 1992a, 1992b). It is particularly important to note that Butcher et al. (1992, *MMPI-A Manual)* and Butcher and Williams (1992a, 1992b) do not recommend the application of MMPI code type interpretations with adolescents due to limited evidence supporting generalization of adult code patterns to youth. One exception is the 46/64 [Psychopathic Deviate (Pd) - Paranoid (Pa)] code type, which reflects severe psychopathology in adolescents, as it does in adults. Although similar content scales are also available for the MMPI using adolescent norms developed by Marks, Seeman, and Haller (1974), they should be used with caution. Even Marks et al.'s (1974) adolescent norms produce average normative T-scores of 60 or higher on three of the clinical scales for boys and one scale for girls (Butcher & Williams, 1992a, 1992b). Nonetheless, limited interpretation of specific scales is supported by the evolution of MMPI interpretation for adolescents over the years (Archer, 1987; Marks et al., 1974; Williams & Butcher, 1989a, 1989b). In doing this, Butcher and Williams (1992) suggest that MMPI-A content scale T-scores be placed into three score-range categories: high (≥65), moderate (60–64), and average (≤ 60). Scores in the high range indicate that the adolescents endorsed an unusually high number of items in comparison to those in the norm sample.

In the context of anger-related assessment, the MMPI-A retains two content scales that can be used effectively as part of a comprehensive assessment: Anger (A-ang) and Cynicism (A-cyn).

Anger (A-ang) content scale. The Anger scale contains 17 items, only 11 of which overlap with the same MMPI-2 content scale. Butcher and Williams (1992b) indicate that this content scale measures an adolescent's endorsement of items that reflect a tendency to express anger openly. Items relate primarily to observable behaviors such as fighting, throwing objects, smashing things, or yelling. Some of the items are also more generally descriptive, such as being "hot-headed." Adolescents who obtain high scores on this content scale are those who act out their anger in ways that are usually disturbing to others—parents, teachers, and other adults will frequently describe similar youth as having poor anger control. Thus, it is unlikely that this content scale will uncover novel information. However, it may prove useful in documenting the severity of an anger-control problem identified in referral concerns. The descriptors of those who obtain high scores on the Anger content scale can be used with confidence because they are empirically supported (Butcher & Williams, 1992a). It is relevant to this chapter that one of the case studies presented by Butcher and Williams (1992a) is of a young man who had no clinical elevatit ou but the MacAndrew Alcoholism (MAC-R), Alcohol Drug Problem Acknowledgment (ACK), and the Alcohol Drug Problem Proneness scales (PRO) were elevated. In addition, this adolescent, who associated with gang members, had a T-score of 75 (14 out of the 17 items were endorsed) on the Anger content scale. In this instance, the MMPI-A was sensitive to verifying the lack of emotional disturbance but the presence of socially maladjusted behavior.

Cynicism (A-cyn) content scale. The Cynicism scale contains 22 items, 21 of which overlap with the same MMPI-2 content scale. This content scale taps aspects of an adolescent's anger-related cognitions or attitudes. Those obtaining elevated T-scores endorse items expressing suspiciousness about others' intentions. They are quick to attribute hidden motivations in other's behavior, to be on guard, and distrusting of others. There is less empirical validation of this content scale so it should be used with more caution than the Anger content scale (Butcher & Williams, 1992a). Nonetheless, given its careful development associated with years of MMPI research, it is one of the best scales available to assess the cognitive component of anger in adolescents.

Olweus Scales

Olweus (1978, 1991) developed self-report scales used in research involving perpetrators and victims of school bullying. Two English versions were developed, applicable to grades 1–4 and 5–9. He describes the advantages of these scales as being that they (a) give a clear definition of bullying so each child presumably responds to the questions from a similar referent; (b) they ask students to describe victim or perpetrator experiences within a recent, specifically defined time period; (c) they use specific frequencies on the response scales (e.g., "several times a day"), not vague, imprecise response options (e.g., "often"); and (d) they request students to give their opinions about how peers, teachers, and parents respond to bullying incidents. These scales also ask about both personal experiences and perceptions of the overall school climate. Other than the School Anger Inventory, it is one of the few scales that was developed specifically for use in school settings. An example item from the scale is: *How often have you been bullied in school? (Being exposed to direct bullying or victimization with relatively open attacks on the victim.)*

Olweus (1978) developed a related scale for use in his research of bullying on school campuses. This instrument produces an overall "provoked aggressive behavior" score and is composed of two subscales: Verbal Aggression and Physical Aggression. This instrument focuses exclusively on anger expression and takes the form of asking the child to indicate how likely it is that she or he will express aggressive behavior given certain experiences at school. Examples of the items by subscale are: (a) **Verbal Aggression:** *When an adult is unfair to me, I get angry and protest;* and (b) **Physical Aggression:** *When a boy starts fighting with me, I fight back.* This scale has high ecological validity for school settings and has been used extensively in Olweus' longitudinal studies of schoolyard bullies (Olweus, 1978, 1991).

The Provoked Aggressive Behavior total score (composed of Verbal Aggression and Physical Aggression) has a moderate internal consistency reliability of .74 (Olweus, Mattsson, Schalling, & Low, 1980). The scale was developed for use with Norwegian youth and it has been used primarily in international contexts—its applicability to diverse American populations has yet to be established. Based on his longitudinal studies, Olweus argues that self-report of bullying behavior is a useful, valid method to seek this information. Early versions of the scale that included only 3 to 5 items correlated .40 -.60 with peer ratings of bullying behavior, and this finding has been replicated by subsequent research (Perry, Kusel, & Perry, 1988). This scale also asks students to give their estimation of the frequency of bullying behavior among the students in their class. These estimates were compared with the average self-reported bullying in the same classes—it was found that the class level and individual level victimization ($r = .62$) and bullying ($r = .68$) scores were highly correlated. This finding supports the validity of using self-report scales of bullying behavior. These scales have also been instrumental in research that has dispelled many myths about schoolyard bullies, among them being: bullies typically are not school failures and do not engage in bullying as compensation for a poor self-esteem. Evaluating a child's bullying behavior can be quite important as shown by the fact that children who engage in school bullying behavior are four times more likely than nonbullies to have a criminal conviction as an adult (Olweus, 1991). One shortcoming of the scales developed by Olweus is that they are not readily available outside of Finland. The scales can be purchased directly from Dr. Olweus, but the cost is such that institutional (e.g., school district) purchase is likely to be the most viable way to obtain these scales.

SELF-REPORT ANALOG MEASURES

Child's Action Tendency Scale (CATS)

The CATS (Broad, Burke, Byford, & Sims, 1986; Deluty, 1979, 1981a, b, 1983, 1984a, b, 1985) is a widely used research tool that measures how children report they would respond in conflict situations. Response options representing assertive, passive, and aggressive alternatives are included for each item. Conflict scenarios were developed by asking youth to provide answers to the questions: *I get angry when* (Aggressiveness); *I feel like giving up when* (Passiveness); and *I stand up for my rights when*

(Assertiveness). The answers were used to select 13 typical conflict situations. (In some research applications, only 10 scenarios have been used.) The students were also asked how they might respond in similar situations and their answers were used to generate assertive, passive, and aggressive response alternatives. Deluty (1979) defines assertiveness as "the ability to express, in a nonhostile manner, one's thoughts and feelings while not violating the rights and feelings of others" (p. 1061). A submissive response is "a nonhostile act that involves considering the feelings, power, or authority of others while denying one's own rights and feelings" (p. 1062). An aggressive response is "a hostile act involving self-expression at the expense of others" (p. 1062). All response alternatives were evaluated by experts, teachers, and students before inclusion in the scale.

Five of the conflict scenarios reflect peer-related conflicts with four general peer conflicts and four parent conflicts (the eight general peer and parent scenarios have no school content). The assertive, aggressive, and passive response options are presented in a forced-choice format for each of the scenarios. This means that there are three response "items" for each scenario— assertive, aggressive, and submissive options are included in two of the three "items." Thus, the Assertiveness, Aggressiveness, and Submissiveness scores each range from 0–26. As an example, if a child chooses the aggressive response each time it is paired with the assertive or submissive options, then the Aggressiveness score would be 26. For the same child, if the assertive option was always chosen over the submissive option, then the Assertiveness score would be 13 and the Submissiveness score would be 0. The sum of the three subscale scores should always be 39, the number of forced-choice options. An example of a CATS item is presented in Figure 7.4.

On the 10-item version, the split-half (with Spearman-Brown correction) internal consistency coefficients were moderate for each subscale: Aggressiveness subscale (.77), Submissiveness [aka, Passive] (.72), and Assertiveness (.63). Score stability over a 4-month period was acceptable for all subscales, although it is interesting to note that the stability coefficients were in the reverse order of the internal consistency coefficients. In this case, the Assertiveness score (.60) was more stable than the Submissiveness (.57) and the Aggressiveness (.48) scores. Girls' Assertiveness scores (.70) were more stable than boys' (.50) and the Aggressiveness scores were equally stable (.44). As with other anger-related self-report instruments, the CATS Aggressiveness (.44) and Submissiveness (.57) scores were significantly correlated with a measure of social desirability.

FIGURE 7.4. EXAMPLE OF ITEM INCLUDED IN THE CHILDREN'S ACTION TENDENCY SCALE.

Q. You're standing in line for a drink of water. A kid your age and size walks over and just shoves you out of line.
What would you do?

A. ❒Push the kid back out of line. (Aggressive alternative)
❒Tell them, "You've no right to do that." (Assertive alternative)

B. ❒Push the kid back out of line. (Aggressive alternative)
❒I'd go to the end of the line. (Passive alternative)

C. ❒Tell them, "You've no right to do that." (Assertive alternative)
❒I'd go to the end of the line. (Passive alternative)

The aggressive, assertive, and passive alternatives are paired with each other. A forced-choice procedure is used. One alternative is selected for A, B, and C (see Deluty, 1979, for more information). Copyright 1979 by R. H. Deluty. Adapted by permission.

Deluty (1979) administered the CATS to 46 parochial school third-, fourth-, and sixth-graders. Their teachers and all of their classroom peers also used a sociometric procedure to label the typical way (assertive, aggressive, submissive) each child responded to conflict. The five most aggressive and the five least aggressive children in the class were identified. The results showed that there was a positive correlation on the 13-item version between the CATS Aggressiveness score and the total Assertiveness scores ($r = .59$), peer ratings of physical aggressiveness ($r = .58$), and teacher ratings of verbal aggressiveness (r = .51), CATS Assertiveness and teacher ratings of assertiveness ($r = .30$), peer rating of submissiveness ($r = .49$), peer ratings of most submissive in the classroom ($r = .37$), and teacher ratings of submissiveness ($r = .38$). Three items (#3, #12, and #13) did not correlate well with the total external criteria, so they were dropped in this study. However, the scale has at times subsequently been used with all 13 items. This has led to confusion because some studies have used the 13-item version (Deluty, 1983; Lopesto & Deluty, 1988). In a review of the CATS,

Williamson and McKenzie (1988) mention only the 10-item version and Williamson, Moody, Granberry, Lethermon, and Blouin (1983) apparently misused the CATS (Deluty, 1984b).

Deluty (1979) cross-validated the CATS with a sample of 77 public school fourth- and fifth-graders and 17 "hyperaggressive" boys. The 10-item CATS version was used and it was found that the hyperaggressive boys obtained significantly higher Aggressiveness scores and significantly lower Assertiveness scores. Deluty (1983) also evaluated the concurrent validity of the CATS by comparing scores with systematic classroom behavioral observation of 45 third-, fourth-, and fifth-graders. Observers trained to 90% agreement looked for 32 classroom behaviors related to submissiveness (e.g., *allowing others to decide for oneself)*, assertiveness (e.g., *standing one's ground in an argument* [without any form of aggression]), and aggressiveness (e.g., *threatening to hurt others).* Observations were completed over an 8-month period in passive-structured, active-structured, and active-unstructured settings. At the end of the observation period, the CATS was group administered. The results showed differences by sex (boys higher Aggressiveness scores) and grade (higher Aggressiveness and lower Assertiveness scores for fifth-graders).

Deluty (1983) also evaluated the construct validity of the CATS in an innovative study. He screened 231 fourth-, fifth-, and sixth-graders using peer nomination and CAT scores to identify subgroups of highly aggressive, assertive, and submissive students. For some reason, in this study, only 9 randomly selected CATS conflict situations were used, and for each aggressive, assertive, and submissive item, the children were asked to rate each response option on 7-point semantic differential scales [four "evaluative" items (e.g., "good-bad") and three "potency" items (e.g., "strong-weak")]. Results showed that boys more than girls rated aggressive responses as good, strong, wise, successful, kind, and brave—the boys also rated these same descriptors lower than girls for the assertive items. The boys rated good, strong, and brave lower for the submissive response options. A similar pattern was found for "aggressives"; they rated aggressive options as more good, strong, wise, successful, and even kind. Assertive children showed a similar rating preference for the assertive response options. The patterns also show that aggressive boys were significantly more likely to indicate that aggressive options were what they "should do." This supports a view that generally aggressive and assertive youth feel justified (they are doing the right thing) in their response options. As might be expected, a similar pattern was not found for submissive children.

In another validation study, Burdett and Jensen (1983) administered the Piers-Harris Self-Concept Scale and the CATS to 229 third- and sixth-graders, and their classroom teachers completed a shortened version of the CATS for each student. The correlation between the student and teacher CATS Aggressiveness scores was only .23, indicating a mild level of correspondence between self-reported and teacher-reported aggressiveness. The correlation of the self-concept score with CATS Aggressiveness was negligible for both student (-.09) and teacher (-.04) ratings. The one exception was for the sixth-grade girls from lower socioeconomic backgrounds. For this subgroup, the correlation between self-concept and Aggressiveness was moderately negative ($r = -.41$), indicating that low self-concept scores were associated with higher CATS Aggressiveness scores. This correlation was nearly the same as the one reported by Deluty (1979, $r = -.37$). There was also a significant sex by grade interaction in which the CATS Aggressiveness scores for males decreased from grade 3 (8.7 out of 10) to grade 5 (7.2); in contrast, scores for the girls increased from grade 3 (3.5) to grade 5 (5.1). The relationship between aggressiveness and self-concept was also examined by Broad et al. (1986). They reported a nonsignificant correlation between the Coopersmith (1967) Self-Esteem Inventory and the CATS subscales. This study involved a small clinical sample, so this may be the source of the discrepancy.

Children's Assertiveness Behavior Scale (CABS)

The CABS (Michelson, 1988) was developed primarily to evaluate assertiveness training programs. The objective of this 27-item scale is to measure the social competency of youth by self-report of how they would respond in a variety of situations. A scenario is set, as in other analog assessment tools, and the child is asked to select a response from among five alternatives that best matches the way he or she believes he or she would respond. These five alternatives represent intensity level on a continuum ranging from passive to assertive: (-2) very passive, (-1) passive, (0) assertive, (+1) aggressive, and (+2) very aggressive. The absolute value of each response is summed so scores range from 0 (most assertive) to 54 (most unassertive). Assertiveness is defined as "a nonhostile act that involves self-expression and self-enhancement without violating the rights and feelings of others" (p. 103). A submissive response is "a nonhostile, unassertive act that involves considering the feelings, power, or authority of others while denying one's own rights and feelings" (p. 103). These definitions were taken from the work of Deluty (1979).

Michelson and Wood (1982) report that the CABS has an internal consistency coefficient of .89. Their study involved 51 boys and 46 girls from a rural community who tended to be from lower socioeconomic backgrounds. The strongest finding was that children who were previously identified as being aggressive obtained significantly higher Aggression scores than other children. This pattern was particularly true of boys. These results suggest that the CABS may be more valid for children who are aggressive as opposed to those who are withdrawn and repress their anger. It does not "unbind" assertiveness scores as shown by the high correlation of the Assertiveness subscale with the Aggression subscale (r = .92).

Children's Assertiveness Inventory (CAI)

The CAI (Scanlon & Ollendick, 1986) is described as a "screening" instrument for use with elementary school children. It has 14 items that describe responses to "positive" and "negative" interpersonal situations. True-False responses to the items produce a Total Assertiveness score, which can be further broken down into "Positive" situation assertiveness and "Negative" situation assertiveness. The focus on positive social situations is a unique aspect of this scale; however, it does not produce separate aggressive or submissive scores, like the CATS and the CABS. The mean total score of 10.6 (SD = 1.95) on the 14 items indicates it has a skewed distribution.

Scanlon and Ollendick (1986) conducted a study in which they compared the CAI (Ollendick, 1984), the CATS (Deluty, 1979), and the CABS (Michelson & Wood, 1982). The responses of 97 teacher-identified "aggressive," "submissive," and "assertive" fourth- and fifth-graders and their pattern of scores on all three scales were compared. Teacher nominations were based on their observations of the children's behavior at school, particularly in the classroom. Construct validity for the CAI was found in that the Positive and Negative scores were not correlated significantly (r = -.10). Evidence for convergent validity, however, was not as strong. Convergent validity coefficients with the CATS and CAI ranged from .28 to .38 (ignoring direction).

The internal consistency of this scale is low for all three scores: Positive situation assertiveness (.64), Negative situation assertiveness (64), and Total score (.44). Ollendick (1984) argues that the heterogeneous item content of the CAI reduces the scale's reliability. Nonetheless, this argument does not alleviate the impression that the CAI does not measure a clearly defined construct. One-month (.87) and 6-month (.76) stability coefficients are good and somewhat puzzlingly high given the scale's low reported internal consistency coefficients. This scale may have some utility in discriminating assertive from submissive behavior tendencies, but does not appear to be as useful as the CATS for the assessment of aggressive behavior.

Play Entry Assertion/Aggression Scale (PEAAS)

The Play Entry Assertion/Aggression Scale (PEAAS, Morrison, personal communication, January 15, 1994) was developed as part of a project designed to describe the personal expectations, social entry strategies, and attributions about specified social situations of mildly handicapped and nonhandicapped children. These specific self- and social-perception patterns were related to teacher perceptions of social characteristics and student self-perceptions. The scale was used in a study involving 95 students in grades 3–6. This group included students with average achievement scores, low achievement scores, learning disabilities, and mild mental retardation. The items included in the scale are:

- **Ideas for entering a playground social group**: *1. You want to play with a group of kids, what would you do to try to get in on their game?*
- **Ideas for retrying to enter this group upon initial rejection**: *2. You really want to play, how can you convince them?*

The child is presented with eight different response options that reflect *Passive* ("ask to play," and "wait"), *Assertive* ("tell them how good you are," "join in," and "give them your snack"), or *Aggressive* ("tell them you won't be their friend," "jump up and down or yell," and "steal the ball") ways to try and get a "friend" or "nonfriend" to play with them. The response scale used is (1 = no, 2 = maybe, and 3 = yes). Scores vary by subscale: Passive (0–6), Assertive (0–9), and Aggressive (0–9).

The interitem reliability (Cronbach's alpha) of the Aggression factor is .65 compared with .40 for the Assertion factor. Construct validity was measured by having the children complete the Child Rating Scale and the Pupil Evaluation Inventory (Pekarik, Prinz, Liebert, Weintraub, & Neale, 1976). Evidence of convergent and discriminant validity was found primarily for the Aggression subscale as it had concurrent validity coeffi-

primarily for the Aggression subscale as it had concurrent validity coefficients of -.40 with the Child Rating Scale "Acting out" subscale and .43 with the "Aggression" subscale of the Pupil Evaluation Inventory. The PEAAS is one of the few scales that addresses children's coping strategies for play entry, a common conflict situation for schoolchildren.

Slaby and Guerra Scale

Slaby and Guerra (1988) draw upon Dodge's (1986) aggression model that includes the encoding of social cues, representation and interpretation of cues, response search, response decision, and enactment. It is postulated that these steps constitute a social decision-making process that integrates anger, hostility, and aggression. In this particular study, six aspects of this model were evaluated: (a) seeking information, (b) defining the problem, (c) selecting a goal, (d) generating alternative solutions, (e) anticipating consequences, and (f) prioritizing responses. Drawing from a larger sample pool, 48 older adolescent participants (24 males and 24 females) were randomly selected from an antisocial-aggressive group (incarcerated juveniles adjudicated for a violent crime), high-aggressive high school students, and low-aggressive students (based upon PE teachers' ratings of aggression, e.g., *uses physical force to get his/her way*). The high-aggressive group received scores in the top third and the low-aggressive group received ratings in the bottom third on the screening instrument. To assess cognitive processes associated with aggression, the students were administered an adaptation of an interpersonal problem solving scale. This analog instrument has a 10-week stability of .75 to .93 across its seven submeasures. It presents scenarios such as:

You're playing on your school's softball team and have a big game coming up. You've been trying to practice as much as you can after school. One day you go outside to practice with a friend but can't find any bats. You see a guy (girl) sitting on the bench just twirling a bat around. "Hey, let me borrow that for a while," you say. "No way," says the guy (girl). After reading the vignette, the youth responds to seven different questions:

- **Problem Definition:** *What is the problem?*
- **Goal Selection:** *If you were to solve this problem, what would be your goal?*
- **Number of Facts:** *Would you need any more information? If so, what?*
- **Number of Solutions:** *What are all the ways you think you can solve*

- **Best Solution:** *What do you think is the very best solution?*
- **Second Best Solution:** *What do you think is the second best solution?*
- **Number of Consequences:** *What are all the things that might happen if you did this?*

Responses to most of the questions are summed for the number of options developed. For Problem Definition, the students were asked to choose between a hostile *(This guy/girl won't let you use his/her bat, even though he's/she's not using it.)* or nonhostile *(You don't have a bat and want to practice)* option. Similarly, for Goal Selection there were hostile *(Show the guy/girl not to mess with me)* and nonhostile *(Get a bat so you can practice)* options. Students were assigned total scores of 0, 50, or 100 depending on how many hostile options they selected.

Slaby and Guerra (1988) also developed an 18-item questionnaire about aggression beliefs, which has a 10-week stability of .86. It contains the following subscales with a sample item [alpha coefficients in brackets]:

- **Legitimacy of Aggression** (6 items) [.67]: *It's O.K. to hit someone if you just go crazy with anger.*
- **Aggression Increases Self-Esteem** (3 items) [.53]: *It's important to show everyone how tough you are by being a good fighter.*
- **Aggression Helps to Avoid a Negative Image** (3 items) [.68]: *If you back down from a fight, everyone will think you are a coward.*
- **Victims Deserve Aggression** (3 items) [.72]: *If someone gets beat up, it's usually his or her own fault.*
- **Victims Don't Suffer** (3 items) [.37]: *People who get beat up badly probably don't suffer a lot.*

The results show that, compared with low-aggressive youth, the antisocial youth (a) defined the problem scenarios with the most hostility, (b) were more likely to select hostile goals, (c) would seek less clarifying information, (d) generated fewer solutions, (e) were aware of fewer consequences, (f) were more likely to generate ineffective second solutions, (g) perceived greater legitimacy for aggression, (h) were more likely to believe that aggression raises self-esteem and avoids a negative self-image, and (i) were more likely to believe that victims of aggression don't suffer. The high-aggressive high school youths generally had response patterns in between the antisocial and the low-aggressive groups.

The correlations of Perceived Hostility were highly positive for Goal Selection (.55), a belief that aggression avoids a negative self-image (.58), and a belief that aggression increases self-esteem (.40). It had large negative correlations with the effectiveness of the best solution (-.46) and effectiveness of the second best solution (-.55). There were also gender differences—males were more likely than females to select aggressive options.

Slaby and Guerra (1988) indicate "it is unclear whether this hostile bias (among antisocial youth) represents a deficit in processing information whereby aggressive children merely assume that others' intentions would be similar to their own, presumably hostile, intentions, or whether this hostile bias reflects a more general set of 'paranoid' beliefs about others' motivations that might affect processing and interpretation of cues" (p. 587). They suggest that belief patterns may act both to support aggressive acts, but also to motivate oneself to carry out aggressive acts. This study provides a wonderful example of how cognitive aspects of anger can be included in a comprehensive assessment.

RATING SCALE INSTRUMENTS

Children's Hostility Inventory (CHI)

Kazdin, Rodgers, Colbus, and Siegel (1987) developed the Children's Hostility Inventory (CHI) by modifying the Buss-Durkee Hostility Index (BDHI). They opted to use a parent behavior rating scale format, rather than a self-report format, because parents can provide useful information about children's behavior. This format also avoided the problem of underreporting of aggression by children themselves. The CHI was initially used with a psychiatric clinic sample, but its item content is appropriate for general education pupils.

In the original developmental study, the CHI and Child Behavior Checklist (Achenbach, 1991a) were completed by the mothers (or female guardian) of 255 psychiatric inpatients. These youth were 6–12 years old and there were about three times as many boys as girls. In addition to the CHI, the students completed the Interview for Antisocial Behavior (IAB) and their previous regular school teachers completed the Aggression and Hostile Isolation portions of the School Behavior Checklist. The CHI scale itself contained 38 items assessing the same subscales as the BDHI: Assaultiveness, Indirect Expression of Hostility, Irritability, Negativism, Resentment, Suspicion, Verbal Hostility, and Guilt. The Guilt subscale was subsequently found to have low item-total score correlations so it was dropped from the data analysis. Sample items are presented below, the entire set of items can be obtained from Kazdin et al. (1987, p. 323):

- **Assaultiveness:** *S/He only hits back once in a while, even if someone hits him/her first.*
- **Indirect Expression of Hostility:** *S/He sometimes says bad things about people he/she doesn't like.*
- **Irritability:** *Sometimes people bug him/her just by being around.*
- **Negativism:** *When someone makes a rule my child doesn't like, s/he would often like to break it.*
- **Resentment:** *S/He thinks other people always seem to have good things happening to them.*
- **Suspicion:** *S/He thinks that people often say bad things about her/him behind her/his back.*
- **Verbal Hostility:** *S/He can't help getting into arguments when others don't agree with her/him.*

The CHI has acceptable internal consistency (alpha = .82; Garber, Quiggle, Panak, & Dodge, 1991, reported an alpha of .83), but reliabilities for the subscales are not provided. The construct validity of the subscales was evaluated using a principal components factor analysis—two factors emerged. The first factor was labeled Aggression (outward expression of hostility) and was composed of the Assaultiveness, Indirect Hostility, and Verbal Hostility subscales. The second factor was labeled Hostility (hostile thoughts and feelings) and was made up of the Resentment, Suspicion, and Irritability subscales. Kazdin et al. (1987) argue that Irritability should be in the Hostility factor. However, Irritability loaded .47 on the Aggression factors and .48 on the Hostility factor, so we see no compelling reason for placing it on the Hostility factor only. In addition, the Negativism subscale was not included in their final factor structure, but its loading of .34 on the Aggression factor suggests that it could be considered another type of outward expression of anger. The factor labels used by Kazdin may cause some confusion compared with other systems being used. To maintain consistency with other research, Factor I can also be considered to assess the outward expression of anger (Anger-out). Furthermore, the Irritability subscale has a high loading on the Hostility factor; this may mean that parents do not make a strong distinction between hostile attitudes and hostile emotions expressed by their children. Perhaps this may be due to parents inferring attitudes from frequent observations of agitation in their children. The CHI Resentment and Suspicion subscales were moderately correlated (.41), suggesting that they have a significant shared experience, but are distinct constructs. Further evidence to consider including Irritability in

Factor II is that the correlation between Irritability and Resentment (.51) was higher even than the one with Suspicion (.31).

Clinical validity was assessed by comparing the CHI scores of children with and without a conduct disorder diagnosis. The conduct disordered subgroup obtained significantly higher scores on all of the CHI subscales except Suspicion. The strongest differences were on those subscales assessing outward expression of anger (e.g., Verbal Hostility). The Total score for the conduct-disordered subgroup was significantly higher than for the non-conduct-disordered group.

Of particular interest is the difference between these two groups on the Resentment and Suspicion subscales, which have been found to be most consistently related with hostile attitudes. Evidence of convergent validity was found in the moderate to high correlations between CHI-Aggression and IAB–Overt Antisocial Behavior (.70) and CHI-Aggression and CBCL-Externalizing (.53). In addition, the CHI-Hostility factor was moderately correlated with IAB-Covert Antisocial Behavior (.42) and with CBCL-Internalizing (.52). These parent ratings, however, were unrelated to teacher ratings.

Evidence of divergent validity was not as strong because CHI-Hostility correlated slightly more positively with IAB-Overt Antisocial Behavior (.49) than with Covert Antisocial Behavior (.42) and with the CBCL Externalizing score (.45). Evidence for the discriminant validity of the CHI Aggression component is better than for the Hostility component. It is possible that this in part reflects the population with which the CHI scales were developed and evaluated; that is, there is a subgroup of conduct-disordered youth who also experience hostile attitudes and maintain characteristics of both internalizing and externalizing types of problems (for example, see Duchnowski, Johnson, Hall, Kutash, & Friedman, 1993).

Garber et al. (1991) present the results of another validity study involving 312 children in grades 3–6. This multitrait-multimethod analysis included self-report measures of both depression and aggression provided by the child as well as ratings provided by their parents, teachers, and peers. The CHI had a correlation of .45 with the Child Depression Inventory, which was higher than for any other comparison, showing that the source effect (i.e., the child ratings) was higher than the correlation with aggression ratings provided by other sources: teachers, parents, peers. The other sources were more consistent with one another. This may be due in part to the fact that the total CHI score was used, not factor scales. Peers and teachers tended to agree on ratings of aggression, and parents and their children tended to agree on depression ratings. There was mild evidence for discriminant and convergent validity, but rater effects were prominent. It appears that when comparing the CHI to other rating scales across informants it is necessary to keep in mind that consistency across raters is not necessarily expected (for example, see McConaughy, 1993).

Becomes Angry Scale

Siegel (1984) examined the association between anger and physical and psychological risk factors in adolescents. She collected information about physiological factors (e.g., blood pressure, serum cholesterol), psychological factors (e.g., test anxiety, self-concept, life satisfaction, and stressful life events) and correlated them with scores derived from the Becomes Angry Scale (BAS). The BAS has 19 items, an example of which is: *Has difficulty controlling anger when someone hurts him/her.* The underlying structure of the Anger Index was explored using a principal components factor analysis with varimax rotation. In this analysis, items 1, 3, 6, 7, 10, 12, 18, and 19 loaded on a first factor that was labeled Frequent Anger Out (FAO) and items 5, 9, 12, 14, and 16 loaded on a second factor that was labeled Anger Situations (AS; actually a mix of general arousal items and angry feelings elicited by specific situations). Unfortunately, no mean scores for the two factors are provided. However, there is evidence of good clinical validity. In regression analyses, the FAO and AS factor-derived scores were significantly related to health and psychological risk variables. High FAO scores were associated with elevated blood pressure, particularly for boys. Health factors such as smoking and fewer leisure activities were also positively associated with FAO scores, and students with high FAO scores reported having more test anxiety, less life satisfaction, and lower self-esteem.

This instrument is one of the few that has empirical research supporting its use with adolescents, yet the inadequate normative data available limit it to a supplemental assessment role. In addition, inclusion of items (#18 and #19) from the Adolescent Structured Interview further limits its use because of the specialized training needed to administer the ASI. Siegel (1984), however, did re-run the original regression analyses minus items 18 and 19. Similar results were found, so it appears that items 1 through 17 can be used alone. It should also be noted that item 2 was dropped from the scale because almost 9 out of 10 students said that observing the "mistreatment of others" would make them angry.

Matthews Youth Test for Health (MYTH)

Matthews and Angulo (1980; Woodall & Matthews, 1989) developed a semi-structured interview for use with children that seeks health-related Type A behavior pattern information, much as the Structured Interview (SI) (Rosenman, 1985) does for adults. In this case, concern about the reliability of self-report instruments resulted in the development of a rating scale completed by a classroom teacher—Matthews Youth Test for Health (MYTH–Form O). This Type A behavior instrument contains items tapping aggressive and "Impatient-Hostility" behavior. In its initial development, 485 teachers (grades K, 2, 4, and 6) completed a 19-item version twice over a 2-week period—2 items were eliminated because they proved to be unrelated to the other items. The items are rated on a 5-point Likert scale (1 = extremely uncharacteristic to 5 = extremely characteristic). Scores therefore range from 17 to 85, with higher scores associated with a Type A behavior pattern.

A factor analysis of the 17-item scale produced two factors accounting for 57.9% of the common variance. The first factor was associated with competitive, striving behaviors, and the second factor was associated with aggressive, impatient, and hostile items. An example of an item that is completed after completing a face-to-face interview with the child is: *When this child plays games, he/she is competitive* (the remaining items are included in the Appendix).

The aggression, impatience, hostility items (Factor II) are 3, 4, 5, 6, 8, 10, 11, 13, and 17. Factor I (Competitive) and Factor II (Impatient-Aggressive) are moderately correlated ($r = .41$), but still appear to measure distinct traits. Mean scores are stable across grade levels ranging from 51.3 ($SD = 10.4$) to 53.8 ($SD = 9.7$) for boys and 45.6 ($SD = 10.3$) to 47.9 ($SD = 7.3$) for girls. The internal consistency (alpha coefficient) for the Competitiveness (.89) and the Impatient-Aggression (.88) subscales are both adequate. Three-month stabilities of the teacher ratings were .82 for Competitiveness and .79 for Impatient-Aggression. In a follow-up validity study, Matthews and Angulo (1980) identified a group of 120 students who obtained high or low scores on the Total scale. Students were then asked to complete various psychoperceptual tasks and to engage in free play in a room that contained a *Bobo* doll. They found that the children who obtained high scores on this Type A behavior scale were in fact more competitive in play activities and engaged in more spontaneous aggressive activity with the *Bobo* doll.

Interview for Antisocial Behavior (IASB)

Kazdin and Esveldt-Dawson (1986) developed a parent rating form that was designed to assess severe forms of antisocial behavior. This scale contains 30 behaviors descriptive of various types of conduct-disordered behavior. Parents rate behaviors for both "degree" (severity) of presenting problem (1 = none at all to 5 = very much) and duration of the problem [1 = < 6 months (recent or new problem); 2 = > 6 months (long time problem); 3 = (always a problem)]. The scale yields scores for severity of problem and duration of problem. The total Antisocial score ranges from 30–240.

In the developmental study, mothers or female guardians of 264 psychiatric inpatients ages 6–13 completed the IASB. The scale was shown to have good internal consistency (alpha coefficient of .91, Spearman-Brown coefficient of .87). Clinical validity was supported by the finding that children with conduct disorders obtained higher scores than children without conduct disorders. Construct validity was demonstrated by a factor analysis that produced three interpretable factors: Arguing/Fighting (e.g., *temper tantrums, getting into fights*), Covert Antisocial Behavior (e.g., *breaking into cars, stealing from stores*), and Self-Injury (e.g., *trying to hurt him (her)self*). The items themselves primarily address anger expression content, but there are a few items focusing on anger experience (e.g., *getting mad all of a sudden*) and hostile attitudes (e.g., *a negative attitude*). The correlation between the Severity and Duration scores was .64 suggesting that parents' assessment of the severity of a youth's antisocial behaviors is related to, or perhaps reflective of, the length of time that the problem behavior has been present. A strong relationship with general hostile attitudes was also found, as shown by a correlation of .68 between the IAB Total score and the CHI Total score; and, it correlated .36 with the expression of nonverbal aggression in a behavioral role-play simulation. Concurrent validity with teacher ratings was good as shown by a high correlation with the CBCL (Teacher) Externalizing score ($r = .69$) and a low one with the Internalizing score ($r = .29$); as such it may have some utility in assessments involving the differentiation of serious emotional disturbance from social maladjustment.

Predatory Aggression Subtype Scale (PASS)

This scale was given no formal name in its original study (Vitiello, Behar, Hunt, Stoff, & Ricciuti, 1990), but given its content and measurement objectives, we have labeled it the Predatory Aggression Subtype Scale

(PASS). Drawing upon animal aggression research, Vitiello et al. (1990) argue that there are different neural pathways involved with "predatory" and "affective" aggression. Predatory refers to aggressive behavior that is "planned, profitable, and self-controlled" (p. 191)—it is similar to Dodge's (Dodge, 1991; Dodge & Coie, 1987) proactive aggression and Buss's (1966) instrumental aggression (see also Berkowitz, 1978, 1990). In contrast, affective aggression is more "impulsive, unplanned, nonprofitable, and poorly controlled" (p. 191). PASS was developed to differentiate between these two types of aggressive behavior. Originally, the scale had 16 items (8 predatory and 8 affective), but one predatory item was dropped due to a low item-total score correlation. In addition, five other items had poor interrater reliability coefficients (Kappa) that ranged from .15 to .35, so we recommend against including them in the scale. The authors, in fact, did not include these items in a cluster analysis that they completed as part of the original study.

PASS is a rating scale designed to be completed by an individual who has intimate knowledge of a child's behavior obtained through direct observation and experience. In the developmental study (Vitiello et al., 1990), this was accomplished by having nurses and staff in adolescent psychiatric residential programs complete the scale for 73 youngsters ages 10 to 18. They rated the presence (3 or more occurrences) or absence (0–2 occurrences) of the behaviors described in the items. The 10 items that we recommend for inclusion in the scale are:

- **Predatory Aggression**
  - (1) *Hides aggressive acts*
  - (2) *Can control own behavior when aggressive*
  - (3) *Very careful to protect self when aggressive*
  - (4) *Plans aggressive acts*
  - (5) *Steals*
- **Affective Aggression**
  - (6) *Nonprofitable damaging of own property*
  - (7) *Completely out of control when aggressive*
  - (8) *Exposes self to physical harm when aggressive*
  - (9) *Is aggressive without a purpose*
  - (10) *Aggression is unplanned, out of the blue*

It is interesting to note that the results of a factor analysis of these 10 items produced just one bipolar factor with the 5 predatory items having positive loadings and the 5 affective items loading negatively. The reliability of this scale was moderate, .73.

The authors suggest that a summary score be computed by subtracting the affective score (0–5) from the predatory score (0–5), thereby creating a continuum of scores ranging between -5 and +5. We do not recommend this procedure because scores near the zero midpoint are ambiguous. Using the recommended procedure, it is, of course, possible to obtain a zero score by having a zero (absence) rating on all 10 items or by endorsing all items. Nonetheless, careful use of the PASS can provide information that would help differentiate between aggressive behavior that is more planned and that which is more impulsive. The implication is that those aggressive behaviors that are more planned or predatory may respond more favorably to behavioral interventions, a distinction that has relevance to discussions about serious emotional disturbance and social maladjustment (e.g., Clarizio, 1992; Forness, 1992; Skiba & Grizzle, 1991, 1992). The application of the PASS in school and nonclinical settings will require the collection of local normative data.

School Social Behavior Scales (SSBS)

The School Social Behavior Scales (SSBS) is a general child behavior scale that evaluates aspects of positive social competence and antisocial behavior (Merrell, 1993; Merrell, Merz, Johnson, & Ring, 1992). As such, it is one of the few scales that can be used to evaluate both positive and detrimental aspects of anger-related behavior and experiences. Although this instrument was not developed specifically as an anger scale, the Antisocial Behavior component (Scale B) has an empirically supported subscale that is labeled "Hostile-Irritable." This subscale consists of 14 items describing behaviors related to anger expression (e.g., *is easily provoked; has a short fuse*), although there are two items (*blames other students for problems* and *acts as if he/she is better than others*) that appear to address cognitions or attitudes. The Social Competence scale (Scale A), in contrast, has fewer items that are relevant to anger-related assessment, but it is important to note that it does ask several questions about coping with conflicts and anger control. This scale is completed by a classroom teacher using a 5-point response scale that describes the frequency with which the behavior described in the item occurs (1 = never to 5 = frequently). Ratings are made only after being able to observe the child for at least 6 weeks.

Overall, the SSBS has excellent psychometric properties. The alpha coefficients for the Social Competence and the Antisocial Behavior scales are both .98. Subscale reliabilities range from .91 to .96, with the Hostile-

Irritable subscale having a reliability of .96. The stability coefficients of the scales (over a 3-week period) ranged from .60 to .83, with the Hostile-Irritable subscale having a coefficient of .70. As would be expected, when interrater reliabilities were evaluated (comparing special education teacher ratings to those of their classroom aides), they were found to be somewhat lower than the stability coefficients: range .53 to .83. It is important to note that, however, interrater reliability for the Hostility-Irritability subscale (.71) was equivalent to the stability coefficient. Concurrent validity coefficients with the Conners Teacher Rating Scale (Conners, 1990) and the Walker-McConnell Scale of Social Competence School Adjustment—Adolescent Version (Walker & McConnell, 1988) were moderate. The robustness of the Hostility-Irritability subscale was also supported by the results of a factor analysis in which it accounted for 61.4% of the common variance among the Antisocial Behavior scale items.

School Behavior Checklist (Hostile Isolation Subscale)

The School Behavior Checklist (SBC, Miller, 1967, 1972, 1981) is a general rating scale that focuses on positive and negative behaviors exhibited in a school setting. Form A (ages 4–6) has 104 items and Form B (ages 7–13) has 96 items. This instrument contains a general Aggression subscale (36 items on both versions) and a Hostile Isolation subscale (7 items on each version). The reliability (Form A, Form B) of the Aggression (.95, .90) subscale is high, but that of the Hostile Isolation (.58, .44) subscale is lower.

In one independent validity study, Waas (1987) had teachers complete Miller's SBC (Form A2). In addition, a sociometric rating was used to identify rejected and nonrejected students by selecting 32 children in each grade level receiving the lowest ratings. The results showed that 69% of the third-graders and 41% of the fifth-graders in the aggressive group also received SBC Aggression T-scores of 65 or greater. The same pattern was found for scores on the Hostile Isolation subscale: grade 3 aggressive ($M = 2.6$; $SD = 1.2$), grade 3 nonaggressive ($M = 0.7$; $SD = 0.8$), grade 5 aggressive ($M = 2.9$; $SD = 0.9$), and grade 5 nonaggressive ($M = 1.6$; $SD = 1.2$). The results suggest that the Aggression and Hostile Isolation subscales of the SBC have discriminant clinical validity for aggressive-rejected youth.

Teacher Anger Report

The development of the Teacher Anger Report is described in Finch et al. (1987). They indicate that this 29-item teacher checklist was created by selecting the best anger-related items from various broad-focused child behavior rating scales. Although this is purported to be a measure of anger experience, it contains items that appear also to reflect attitudinal *(has a 'chip'on shoulder)* and anger expression *(fights with other children)* components of anger. The specific items can be found in Finch et al. (1987, p. 261). There is little empirical information about this scale, so it should always be used in conjunction with other instruments.

Pupil Evaluation Inventory (PEI)

The concept behind the PEI (Pekarik et al., 1976) is that peers provide a valuable source of information about youth's anger expression because the formal and informal social interactions of children at school, after the family context, are the most important in children's lives. In brief, children more than anyone else know who is demonstrating prosocial and antisocial behaviors at school. To tap this perspective, items are presented in a item-by-student matrix format, thus, in effect, rendering the PEI into a series of true–false questionnaires for each child in a particular classroom. Pilot testing reduced the final PEI item pool to 35. Evaluation of the scale was completed using samples composed predominantly of white students in grades 1 through 9. Students complete the PEI by putting an "X" in the matrix for "everyone who fit(s) the description on the questionnaire" (p. 86). The specific items for the PEI are presented in the Appendix, on pages 248-249.

The construct validity of the PEI was examined using a principal components analysis with orthogonal rotation. Similar factor structures were derived for both boys and girls, with three factors accounting for about 61% of the variance. The first factor was labeled *Aggression* (about 37% of the variance); the second factor was labeled *Withdrawal* (about 15% of the variance); and the third factor was labeled *Likability* (about 7% of the variance). Twenty of the items (identified in bold in the Appendix) had high loadings ≥ .64 on Factor I (Aggression). The PEI includes items that measure student characteristics related to the following three empirically derived subscales (with sample item):

- **Aggression:** *Those who try to get other people into trouble.*
- **Withdrawal:** *Those who are too shy to make friends easily.*
- **Likability:** *Those who help others.*

After all children in a class complete this matrix, it is possible to assign each child a score (0 or 1) for each of the 35 items. A child's score on each factor is the percentage of students who nominated her or him on that trait.

It should be noted that Factor I was labeled Aggression, but this subscale includes items that describe behaviors associated with impulsiveness and attention seeking. In fact, only six items (9, 16, 21, 23, 29, and 31) have a content that appears to be directly related to the experience of anger, hostility, or aggression. The subscales appear to measure unique traits as shown by very low correlations between the Aggression and Withdrawal factors for boys (.08) and girls (.01). In addition, Likability had a small negative correlation with aggression (r = -.23, boys and r = -.32, girls) and withdrawal (r = -.22, boys and r = -.26, girls). Boys were rated as more aggressive than girls regardless of rater gender, and boys tended to rate other boys more positively than girls—girls rated the boys more negatively. Both Likability and Aggression ratings decreased for male and female raters from elementary school to junior high school.

For those who use this sociometric procedure, mean scores (percentages) are provided by Pekarik et al. (1967, Table II, p. 90). The distributions are skewed, with "normal" aggression scores ranging from 3%–35%. This means that it would not be unusual for a randomly selected child to be "nominated" as aggressive by as many as one fourth of their classmates. Split-half reliabilities of the factors are favorable: Aggression (mostly over .90); Likability (.59 for boys and .68 for girls). Median test-retest correlations (unspecified time) were higher for female raters than male raters: Aggression (.95, .86); Withdrawal (.91, .89); Likability (.82, .81).

The Aggression interrater correlations were high (range = .75–.92) across male and female raters at lower elementary, elementary, and junior high levels. Correlations with teacher and self ratings were also obtained. Teacher and peer Aggression ratings correlated .63 for male raters and .64 for female raters. The same pattern held when the peer Aggression ratings were compared with self-ratings, although the correlations were a bit smaller (.43 for boy raters and .48 for girl raters).

In a longitudinal validity study, Moskowitz and Schwartzman (1989) and Moskowitz, Schwartzman, and Ledingham (1985) examined adjustment during adolescence of a group of first-, fourth-, and seventh-graders. Based on PEI ratings, these youths were placed into four logical groups created by crossing the aggressive (aggressive or not aggressive) and withdrawn (withdrawn or not withdrawn) categories. After 5–7 years, it was found that the aggressive-only and aggressive-withdrawn adolescents obtained significantly lower intelligence test scores. Weak patterns pointed to more behavior problems among those in the aggressive-withdrawn group. The one area in which the aggressive-only and aggressive-withdrawn students had a great deal of difficulty was school-related problems. The pattern suggests that aggression itself has negative implications for adolescent adjustment and that its effects are compounded by child withdrawal characteristics. In a second study, medical information was obtained for 95% of the same sample some 4 years after first contact. (In Canada, virtually all children receive medical care so this could be easily accomplished.) Previously identified aggressive girls had more than twice as many medical contacts as all other groups, including aggressive males. In addition, the aggressive-only group received significantly more psychiatric treatment than all other groups. It is interesting to note that, the aggressive-withdrawn group had the lowest rate of psychiatric services. Research, such as this study by Moskowitz et al., shows that aggression in youths can be the first sign of long-term negative social, cognitive, emotional, and physical developmental concerns.

Assessment Scales for Sociometric Evaluation of Secondary-School Students (ASSESS)

The ASSESS (Prinz, Swan, Liebert, Weintrab, & Neale, 1978) is an upward extension of the Pupil Evaluation Inventory (PEI). This instrument "capture(s) important areas of high school students' social behavior" (p. 494). Interviews with students, school counselors, and the items from the PEI were used to develop an initial pool of 113 items. A very careful procedure was used to identify 45 items for five subscales: Aggression-Disruptiveness, Withdrawal, Anxiety, Social Competence, and Academic Difficulty. The items are presented to the students using a matrix format in which the items are presented on the left-hand side of the page with the names of each student in the class to be rated across the top of the page. In effect, each student in a class completes a true–false questionnaire for each other student in the class (e.g., ________ *is rude to the teacher*). An X-mark is placed in the cell associated with the names of those students for which a particular statement is considered to be true. Each student in the class receives a score on all 45 items, which is expressed as the percentage of students in the class indicating a statement was true for that child.

The five ASSESS subscales have good internal consistency characteristics with alpha coefficients ranging from .84 to .96. The 3-week stability of the subscales ranged between .72 and .91, with Aggression-Disruptive being the most stable. Furthermore, the correlation between male and female ratings by their classmates was high. The correlations for the five subscales in order were .84, .70, .72, .68, and .85. Of particular interest was the pattern of ratings on the Aggression-Disruptive subscale. In this instance, there were no significant differences across grade levels (9th through 12th), but there was a very mild significant interaction effect in which younger males were rated as more aggressive than younger females; yet in contrast, older females were rated as more aggressive than older males. Based on data provided by Prinz et al. (1978), using the very liberal criterion of +1SD defining high levels of peer-identified aggression, a senior high school student would need to be nominated by about 30% of his or her class members to be considered "aggressive" by peer designation.

Peer Nomination Inventory

The Peer Nomination Inventory was developed by Wiggins and Winder (1961) and later modified to include 22 items, 8 of which tap aggression. It is reported to be factorial-pure with content focusing on "hostile," "belligerent," and bullying behavior. In this developmental study, peers in a juvenile detention center listed all cottage residents who manifested each of the eight aggressive behaviors described in the scale. The score derived from this scale is the average percentage of peers affirming each of the eight items. Evaluation studies have been completed by Landau and Milich (1985) and Milich and Landau (1984), but this is the least documented of all sociometric rating scales of aggression.

Peer Nomination of Anger Control Problems (PNACP)

The Peer Nomination of Anger Control Problems was developed by Finch and his colleagues and reported in a validation study of the CIA (Finch et al., 1987). The instrument is easier to administer and score than other sociometric measures because each child merely lists the name of the student in their class who is "best" described by each of a list of 40 statements; for example, the student in class who *Gets angry easily*, or the student who *Fights with smaller children.* More research is needed on this instrument, but it appears that it has potential in school settings to provide ancillary information as part of a broader comprehensive anger assessment. The specific items for this scale can be found in Finch et al. (1987, p. 262).

RELATED ASSESSMENT INSTRUMENTS

Marlowe-Crowne Social Desirability Scale—Child Version (CSD)

This brief review of the CSD is offered because of the consistently high correlations found between it and other anger measures.

Crandall, Crandall, and Katkovsky (1965) developed a school-aged version of the Marlowe-Crowne Social Desirability Scale (MCSDS; Crowne & Marlowe, 1960). Inasmuch as the scores on the MCSD are highly correlated with anger, hostility, and aggression scales for adults, it is useful to evaluate the role that a social desirability response bias has on youths' responses to self-report measures. The Children's Social Desirability (CSD) scale can be used for this purpose. It consists of 48 true–false items, examples of which are: (a) *I am always respectful of older people*; (b) *I have never felt like saying unkind things to a person*; and (c) *I sometimes feel angry when I don't get my way.* Twenty of the items were taken from the adult version and modified. Children in the sixth through twelfth grades can take a pencil-and-paper version individually or in small groups. For younger children, a modified version uses a yes–no response scale, which is presented orally. The younger child version contains 47 items because a homework-related item was eliminated.

In its development, the CSD was administered to 956 students in grades 3, 6, 8, 10, and 12. Spearman-Brown adjusted reliabilities were .82 to .95 for various age and gender groups. One-month stability coefficients were .90 for the younger children and .85 for the older youth. Mean scores on the scale were highest for younger children and generally decreased with age. The mean score for the third-graders was 29.3 (out of 47 items), decreasing to 12.7 (out of 48 items) for the twelfth-graders (scores by grade level are shown in Table 7.5). The total scores obtained by the girls were 1.5 to 7.1 points higher than the boys' average scores. High scores are interpreted to express a social desirability response bias. Such youth may be reluctant to admit to negative emotions or behaviors such as anger and aggression, and this may lower scores on the self-report measures reviewed in this chapter.

CASE STUDY: DONALD, AGE 14-07, GRADE 9

Background Information

Donald was referred for this assessment during the second semester of his first year in high school. He presented with a very disheveled appearance, frequently wearing a heavy army jacket, even on warm days. School records indicated that he was at best a marginally successful student in junior high school, having received a grade point average of just 1.2. During the fall semester of the ninth grade he received a grade point average of 0.6 and had F grades in all of his classes during the spring semester of the ninth grade, at the time of the referral.

Although Donald was struggling in school, the incident that precipitated this referral was a major rage reaction at home after his father confronted him as he arrived home at 5:00 a.m. after attending a "rave" dance. His father indicated that Donald had yelled uncontrollably, hit him, threw a glass at him, and punched a hole in a wall. School records and teacher reports revealed that Donald had not been particularly disruptive in school, in fact, he was somewhat withdrawn and quiet. There had been several incidents, however, when teachers had observed him to "go nuclear" for no apparent reason. He was generally perceived by the school staff as being an unmotivated, but capable student. They attributed his poor academic performance to lack of effort and believed that his difficulties were due to a conduct disorder, and therefore he was ineligible for special services at school.

Available assessment information indicated that his scores on the Differential Abilities Scale were: Verbal Cluster (90% confidence range =

TABLE 7.5. MEANS AND STANDARD DEVIATIONS FOR THE CHILDREN'S SOCIAL DESIRABILITY SCALE.

	Boys			Girls		
Grade	*N*	*M*	*SD*	*N*	*M*	*SD*
3	54	27.7	10.8	61	30.7	9.9
4	66	18.7	10.9	49	25.8	9.7
5	53	21.8	8.8	53	23.0	9.3
6	93	17.7	8.3	73	22.1	8.8
8	69	16.0	9.1	93	17.5	8.6
10	90	13.1	6.4	93	14.6	7.3
12	52	10.7	6.8	57	14.5	7.8

From Crandall et al. (1965), A children's social desirability questionnaire. *Journal of Consulting Psychology, 29,* 27-36. Copyright 1965 by American Psychological Association. Adapted by permission.

113–130); Nonverbal Reasoning Cluster (90% confidence range = 98–113); Spatial Cluster (90% confidence range = 76–90); Reading (standard score = 145); Basic Number Skills (standard score = 90); Spelling (standard score = 80).

Referral Questions

1. Why is Donald having such extreme "rage" reactions?
2. Why has his academic performance decreased so dramatically during the past year?
3. Is he eligible for special education services?

Assessment Findings

Case history information revealed that he had a juvenile record, having been arrested for stealing bicycles, joy riding, and then merely abandoning them. He completed community service as part of his conviction for these crimes. He also admitted to engaging in "tagging" behavior in which he spray painted his monikor in culverts and concrete basins. There is no record that he ever defaced other public or private property in this way.

The information presented in this section is part of a more general comprehensive assessment that was completed. As part of this assessment, several anger assessment instruments were used. These included the MMPI-A, the State-Trait Anger Expression Inventory (STAXI), the Predatory Aggression Subtype Scale (PASS), the Achenbach Teacher's Report Form (TRF), and the Children's Social Desirability scale.

A central aspect of the referral concerns centered around Donald's extreme expressions of anger at home and to a far lesser extent at school. The parents and the school personnel had different opinions about the source of Donald's anger problems. The school characterized his concerns as being within his control and manipulation. His parents felt that even after months of family therapy he continued to express anger inappropriately. Both school personnel and his parents agreed that Donald had an anger expression problem, although they disagreed on the etiology of this behavior.

On the Children's Social Desirability scale, Donald obained a raw score of 15, which is well within the average range for his age. This suggests that it is likely that his responses were not excessively influenced by a desire to give socially acceptable answers. A brief summary of the remainder of the anger-related assessment revealed the following findings:

MMPI-A. The profile validity scales supported the validity of Donald's responses. There was a mild elevation on the Depression clinical scale (T-score = 65), but no other clinical scale elevations were noted. He did obtain elevated scores (T-score = 66) on the MacAndrew Alcoholism (MAC-R), the Adolescent-Family Problems (A-fam) (T-score = 72), the Adolescent-Anger (A-anger) (T-score = 65), and the Adolescent-Cynicism (A-cyn) (T-score = 75) content scales. Upon further investigation, it became clear that the MAC-R score was related to risk-taking behavior, but Donald denied current alcohol use, although he had experimented with drugs. The A-fam score was an accurate reflection of a high level of family discord and challenge of parental authority related to inconsistent limit setting earlier in childhood and resentment of perceived parental encroachment on personal independence. The A-anger reflected Donald's periodic wild expressions of rage. The A-cyn reflected an underlying resentment of others and suspiciousness about their motivations. In brief, the results of the MMPI-A confirmed the high level of anger-related problems that Donald was having, but also suggested that there was a significant cognitive component (hostile attitude) affecting his anger expression. In addition, the moderately elevated Depression clinical scale suggested that he was experiencing dissatisfaction with his school and family situations.

PASS. This rating scale was completed by Donald's father. His responses indicated that he had observed three or more occurrences of only one Predatory aggression behavior (stealing of the bicycles). He also indicated that all of the Affective Aggression items had been observed. He reported that Donald had smashed his Nintendo and stereo in separate fits of rage *(nonprofitable damaging of own property),* was unable to maintain control when angry even when he wanted to *(completely out of control when aggressive),* had come home several times in the past 3 months with cuts and bruises all over his body from fights *(exposes self to physical harm when aggressive),* was systematically not reinforced for aggressive acts per therapist program *(is aggressive without a purpose),* and the precipitating event for his rages was not usually clear *(aggression is unplanned, out of the blue).* In brief, the results of the PASS supported a view of Donald's problem as being less manipulative than emotionally driven. There was little evidence to support a view that his excessive expressions of anger were calculated to bring him secondary gain. In fact, he persisted in these behaviors even though they caused him significant social, academic, and familial strife.

STAXI. On the STAXI, Donald obtained the following T-score: State-Anger (51), Trait-Anger (54), Anger-In (65), Anger-Out (42), and Anger-Control (75), and Anger-Expression (57). The results indicated that he did not have any strong angry feelings at the time the assessment was completed.

He also denied expressing anger on a regular basis as reflected in a score in the average range on the Trait-Anger subscale. His patterns of scores also suggest that he tries to contain his expression of anger as reflected in his high Anger-In and low Anger-Out scores. In brief, Donald frequently experiences angry feelings, but he is not very adept at controlling these feelings or expressing them in a socially acceptable manner. Consequently, he periodically "explodes" into a rage, which he then tries to dismiss or discount.

TRF. Donald's homeroom teacher at school was asked to complete the CBCL. Of particular interest here was that he obtained elevated T-scores on both the Externalizing (64) and the Internalizing (75) scales. In discussion with his teacher, she acknowledged that his behavior was at times disruptive, but generally he was quiet and withdrawn, speaking infrequently to other students, although his behavior was not characterized as being withdrawn.

Summary of Case Study

A primary objective of this assessment was to shed light on the different views that adults had of Donald's behavior. The results of the assessment indicated that Donald frequently experienced angry feelings related to family and academic struggles. In addition, he had a lot of resentment and hostile thoughts about his parents and the inconsistent guidance and affection they had shown him. His typical way of expressing his anger was to keep it inside, but he periodically exploded into verbal and physical aggression. As a result of this assessment, a multifaceted program was created to support Donald's efforts to develop more control over his behavior. The program included continued family counseling to improve communication between Donald and his parents as well as to teach more effective parenting skills to his parents. To address the rage reactions, a program of self-monitoring and relaxation training was initiated to help Donald control his impulsive anger responses. Because he also carried hostile attitudes about his own abilities and his parents' expectations of him, a cognitive-behavior program addressed his negative belief system.

CHAPTER SUMMARY

Some authors (Kaplan, Konecni, & Novaco, 1984) suggest that the use of self-report questionnaires is declining in the assessment of youth anger and aggression. It has been the objective of this chapter to demonstrate that, contrary to this sentiment, there are a variety of useful self-report and rating scale instruments that support any comprehensive assessment where referral problems suggest that there is an anger experience, hostile attitude, or anger expression problem. Clearly, however, a comprehensive assessment does not rely on any single source of information. Thus, we strongly advocate the use of behavioral observation and projective/interview approaches when assessing anger. We do feel, nonetheless, that self-reports have an important role in a comprehensive evaluation of individuals' experience and expression of anger and the attitudes they hold that influence their coping responses.

An important point to remember when using any of the scales discussed in this chapter is that self-report measures are affected by reporting bias (Barefoot, 1992). When anger scale items are too obvious, then social desirability affects responses; thus, youth completing these scales in evaluative settings may give lower ratings. Future scale development needs to include less obvious items and intersperse positively worded items.

Although it is completely understandable that researchers and clinicians have focused on the manifestation and control of aggressive behavior in youth, this sometimes myopic focus has resulted in a dearth of information about how youth more generally experience and express anger. Some (e.g., Feindler, 1991) discuss the unnecessary and insufficient relationship between anger and aggression as if aggression is the only expression of anger that is of concern. The term *anger expression* is used here because we feel that it more accurately reflects a basic concern: How does anger affect all children, both those struggling with normal emotional and developmental concerns and those with significant problems?

Feindler (1991) discusses the importance of making a good "client–treatment" match when designing an intervention program for a specific child. Among the various factors that can affect a child's response to a program are (a) the degree to which their problems are internalized and/or externalized and (b) the reactive or impulsive nature of their anger expression. A program designed to assist a child who has a record of multiple premeditated attacks on other school children will likely be different from one designed for a child who has periodic outbursts related to poor academic performance in the classroom. Similarly, anger-related assessment of youth has as its goal an understanding of how each child experiences anger, develops attitudes and beliefs related to these experiences, and ultimately how they express and cope with their anger. This constellation of information can then be used to select the prevention/intervention components that address each child's developmental concerns.

We have progressed past simplistic conceptual frameworks with which to structure our understanding of anger and aggression. Although the three broad constructs of Anger Experience, Hostile Attitudes, and Anger Expression were used in this chapter, and have been proposed by others because of their heuristic value, each of these substructures also now appears to be multidimensional (Musante, MacDougall, Dembroski, & Costa, 1989; Siegel, 1984; Siegman et al., 1987). For this reason, users of anger scales will need to remain current on developments in this area.

REFERENCES

Achenbach, T. (1991a). *Manual for the Child Behavior Checklist/4-18 and 1991 profile*. Burlington, VT: University of Vermont, Department of Psychiatry.

Achenbach, T. (1991b). *Manual for the Teacher's Report Form and 1991 profile*. Burlington, VT: University of Vermont, Department of Psychiatry.

Achenbach, T. (1991c). *Manual for the Youth Self-Report and 1991 profile.* Burlington, VT: University of Vermont, Department of Psychiatry.

Archer, R. (1987). *Using the MMPI with adolescents.* Hillsdale, NJ: Erlbaum.

Barefoot, J. C. (1992). Developments in the measurement of hostility. In H. S. Friedman (Ed.), *Hostility coping & health* (pp. 13-31). Washington, DC: American Psychological Association.

Barefoot, J. C., Dodge, K. A., Peterson, B. L., Dahlstrom, W. G., & Williams, R. B. Jr. (1989). The Cook-Medley Hostility Scale: Item content and ability to predict survival. *Psychosomatic Medicine, 51,* 59-63.

Barefoot, J. C., Paterson, B. L., Dahlstrom, W. G., Siegel, I. C., Anderson, N. B., & Williams, R. B., Jr. (1991). Hostility patterns and health implications: Correlates of the Cook-Medley Hostility Scale scores in a national survey. *Health Psychology, 10,* 18-24.

Beitchman, J. H., & Corrandini, A. (1988). Self-report measures for use with children: A review and comment. *Journal of Clinical Psychology, 44,* 477-490.

Berkowitz, L. (1978). Is criminal violence normative behavior? Hostile and instrumental aggression and violent incidents. *Journal of Research in Crime and Delinquency, 15,* 48-161.

Berkowitz, L. (1990). On the formation and regulation of anger and aggression. *American Psychologist, 45,* 494-503.

Biaggio, M. K. (1980). Assessment of anger arousal. *Journal of Personality Assessment, 44,* 289-298.

Biaggio, M. K., Supplee, K., & Curtis, N. (1981). Reliability and validity of four anger scales. *Journal of Personality Assessment, 45,* 639-648.

Bowers, B., Jr. (1987). Children and anger. In A. Thomas & J. Grimes (Eds.), *Children's needs: Psychological perspectives* (pp. 31-36). Washington, DC: National Association of School Psychologists.

Broad, J., Burke, J., Byford, S. R., & Sims, P. (1986). Clinical application of the Children's Action Tendency Scale. *Psychological Reports, 59,* 71-74.

Burdett, K., & Jensen, L. C. (1983). Self-concept and aggressive behavior among elementary school children from two socioeconomic areas and two grade levels. *Psychology in the Schools, 20,* 370-375.

Buss, A. H. (1966). Instrumentality of aggression, feedback, and frustration as determinants of physical aggression. *Journal of Personality and Social Psychology, 3,* 153-162.

Buss, A. H., & Durkee, A. (1957). An inventory for assessing different kinds of hostility. *Journal of Consulting Psychology, 21,* 343-349.

Butcher, J., & Williams, C. (1992a). *Essentials of MMPI-2 and MMPI-A interpretation.* Minneapolis, MN: University of Minnesota Press.

Butcher, J., & Williams, C. (1992b). *User's guide to the Adolescent Interpretive Report for the MMPI-A.* Minneapolis, MN: National Computer Systems.

Butcher, J., Williams, C., Graham, J., Archer, R., Tellegen, A., Ben-Porath, Y., & Kraemmer, B. (1992). *Minnesota Multiphasic Personality Inventory for Adolescents: Manual for administration, scoring, and interpretation.* Minneapolis, MN: University of Minnesota Press.

Caine, T. M., Foulds, G. A., & Hope, K. (1967). *Manual of the Hostility and Direction of Hostility Questionnaire (HDHQ).* London: University of London Press.

Clarizio, H. (1992). Social maladjustment and emotional disturbance: Problems and positions II. *Psychology in the Schools, 29,* 331-341.

Conners, C. (1990). *Manual for the Conners Rating Scales.* Toronto: Multi-Health Systems.

Cook, W. W., & Medley, D. M. (1954). Proposed hostility and pharisaic-virtue scales for the MMPI. *Journal of Applied Psychology, 38,* 414-418.

Coopersmith, S. (1967). *The antecedents of self-esteem.* San Francisco, CA: W. H. Freeman.

Costa, P. T. Jr., Zonderman, A. B., McCrae, R. R., & Williams, R. B. Jr. (1986). Cynicism and paranoid alienation in the Cook and Medley Hostility Scale. *Psychosomatic Medicine, 48,* 283-285.

Crandall, V. C., Crandall, V. J., & Katkovsky, W. (1965). A children's social desirability questionnaire. *Journal of Consulting Psychology, 29,* 27-36.

Crowne, D. P., & Marlowe, D. (1960). A new scale of social desirability independent of psychopathology. *Journal of Consulting Psychology, 24,* 349-354.

Deluty, R. H. (1979). Children's Action Tendency Scale: A self-report measure of aggressiveness, assertiveness, and submissiveness in children. *Journal of Consulting and Clinical Psychology, 47,* 1061-1071.

Deluty, R. H. (1981a). Assertiveness in children: Some research considerations. *Journal of Clinical Child Psychology, 10,* 149-155.

Deluty, R. H. (1981b). Adaptiveness of aggressive, assertive, and submissive behavior for children. *Journal of Clinical Child Psychology, 10,* 155-158.

Deluty, R. H. (1983). Children's evaluations of aggressive, assertive, and submissive responses. *Journal of Clinical Child Psychology, 12,* 124-129.

Deluty, R. H. (1984a). Behavioral validation of the Children's Action Tendency Scale. *Journal of Behavioral Assessment, 6,* 115-130.

Deluty, R. H. (1984b). On the proper use of the Children's Action Tendency Scale: Comment onWilliamson et al.'s study. *Behavior Therapy, 15,* 426-428.

Deluty, R. H. (1985). Consistency of assertive, aggressive, and submissive behavior in children. *Journal of Personality and Social Psychology, 49,* 1054-1065.

Dodge, K. A. (1986). A social information-processing model of social competence in children. In M. Perlmutter (Ed.), *Minnesota symposium on child psychology* (Vol. 18, pp. 77-125). Hillsdale, NJ: Erlbaum.

Dodge, K. A. (1991). The structure and function of reactive and proactive aggression. In D. J. Pepler & K. H. Rubin (Eds.), *The development and treatment of childhood aggression* (pp. 201-218). Hillsdale, NJ: Lawrence Erlbaum.

Dodge, K. A., & Coie, J. D. (1987). Social-information processing factors and proactive aggression in children's peer groups. *Journal of Personality and Social Psychology, 53,* 1146-1158.

Duchnowski, A., Johnson, M., Hall, K., Kutash, K., & Friedman, R. (1993). The alternative to residential treatment study: Initial findings. *Journal of Emotional and Behavioral Disorders, 1* (1), 17-26.

Edwards, A. L. (1966). *Edwards Personality Inventory.* Chicago: Science Research Association.

Evans, D. R., & Strangeland, M. (1971). Development of a reaction inventory to measure anger.*Psychological Reports, 29,* 412-414.

Feindler, E. L. (1991). Cognitive strategies in anger control interventions for children and adolescents. In P. C. Kendall (Ed.), *Child and adolescent therapy: Cognitive-behavioral procedures* (pp. 66-97). New York: Guilford.

Finch, A. J., & Eastman, E. S. (1983). A multimethod approach to measuring anger in children. *Journal of Psychology, 115,* 55-60.

Finch, A. J., & Rodgers, T. R. (1984). Self-report instruments. In T. H. Ollendick & M. Hersen (Eds.), *Child behavioral assessment: Principles and procedures* (pp. 106-123). New York: Pergamon.

Finch, A. J., Jr., Saylor, C. F., & Nelson, W. M. III. (1987). Assessment of anger in children. In R. J. Prinz (Ed.), *Advances in behavior assessment of children and families* (Vol 2., pp. 235-265). Greenwich, CT: JAI Press.

Forness, S. (1992). Legalism versus professionalism in diagnosing SED in the public schools. *School Psychology Review, 21,* 29-34.

Friedman, H. S. (1992). Understanding hostility, coping, and health. In H. S. Friedman (Ed.), *Hostility, coping & health* (pp. 3-9). Washington, DC: American Psychological Association.

Friedman, M., & Rosenman, R. H. (1974). *Type A behavior and your heart.* New York: Knopf.

Furlong, M., & Karno, M. (in press). Review of the Social Skills Rating System. *Buros mental measurements yearbook.*

Furlong, M., Smith, D., & Boles, S. (1993). *The incidence of cynical hostility in adolescents.* Manuscript submitted for publication.

Garber, J., Quiggle, N. L., Panak, W., & Dodge, K. (1991). Aggression and depression in children: Comorbidity, specificity, and social cognitive processing. In D. Cicchetti & S. L. Toth (Eds.), Rochester Symposium on Developmental Psychopathology (Vol. 2,), *Internalizing and externalizing expression of dysfunction* (pp. 225-264). Hillsdale, NJ: Lawrence Erlbaum.

Gresham, F. M., & Elliott, S. N., (1991). *Social Skills Rating System Manual.* Circle Pines, MN: American Guidance Service.

Heavy, C., Adelman, H., Nelson, P., & Smith, D. (1989). Learning problems, anger, perceived control and misbehavior. *Journal of Learning Disabilities, 22,* 46-50, 59.

Jacobs, G. A., Phelps, M. , & Rohrs, B. (1989). Assessment of anger expression in children: The Pediatric Anger Expression Scale. *Personality and Individual Differences, 10,* 59-65.

Jenkins, C. D., Rosenman, R. H., & Zyzanski, S. (1974). Prediction of clinical coronary heart disease by a test for the coronary-prone behavior pattern. *New England Journal of Medicine, 290,* 1271-1275.

Johnson, E. H. (1984). *Anger and anxiety as determinants of elevated blood pressure in adolescents.* Unpublished doctoral dissertation. University of South Florida.

Kaplan, R., Konecni, V. J., & Novaco, R. W. (Eds.) (1984). *Aggression in children and youth.* The Hague: Martinus Nijhoff.

Kazdin, A. E., & Esveldt-Dawson, K. (1986). The Interview for Antisocial Behavior: Psychometric characteristics and concurrent validity with child psychiatric inpatients. *Journal of Psychopathology and Behavioral Assessment, 8,* 289-303.

Kazdin, A. E., Rodgers, A., Colbus, D., & Siegel, T. (1987). Children's Hostility Inventory: Measurement of aggression and hostility in psychiatric inpatient children. *Journal of Clinical Child Psychology, 16,* 320-328.

Landau, S., & Milich, R. (1985). Social status of aggressive and aggressive/withdrawn boys: A replication across age and method. *Journal of Consulting and Clinical Psychology, 53,* 141.

Lane, P. J., & Kling, J. S. (1979). Construct validation of the O-H scale of the MMPI. *Journal of Consulting and Clinical Psychology, 47,* 781-782.

Leibowitz, G. (1968). Comparison of self-report and behavioral techniques of assessing aggression. *Journal of Consulting and Clinical Psychology, 32,* 21-25.

Lopesto, C. T., & Deluty, R. H. (1988). Consistency of aggressive, assertive, and submissive behavior in male adolescents. *Journal of Social Psychology, 128*(5), 619-632.

Marks, P., Seeman, W., & Haller, D. (1974). *The actuarial use of the MMPI with adolescents and adults.* Baltimore: MD: Williams and Wilkins.

Martin, R. P. (1988). *Assessment of personality and behavior problems: Infancy through adolescence.* New York: Guilford Press.

Martin, R. P., Hooper, S.,& Snow, J. (1986). Behavior rating scale approaches to personality assessment in children and adolescents. In H. E. Knoff (Ed.), *The assessment of child and adolescent personality* (pp. 309-352). New York: Guilford.

Matson, J., Esveldt-Dawson, K., Andrasik, F., Ollendick, T., Petti, T., & Hersen, M. (1980).Direct observational generalization effects of social skills training with emotionally disturbed children. *Behavioral Therapy, 11,* 522-531.

Matthews, K. A., & Angulo, J. (1980). Measurement of the Type A behavior pattern in children: Assessment of children's competitiveness, impatience-anger, and aggression. *Child Development, 51,* 466-475.

McConaughy, S. H. (1993). Evaluating behavioral and emotional disorders with the CBCL, TRF, and YSR cross-informant scales. *Journal of Emotional and Behavior Disorders, 1,* 40-52.

McLean, D. (1992). Review of Social Skills Rating System. *Journal of Psychoeducational Assessment, 10,* 196-205.

McMahon, R. (1984). Behavioral checklists and rating scales. In T. H. Ollendick and M. Hersen (Eds.), *Child behavioral assessment.* New York: Pergamon Press.

Megargee, E. I., & Cook, P. E. (1975). Negative response bias and the MMPI Overcontrolled-Hostility scale: A response to Deiker. *Journal of Consulting and Clinical Psychology, 43,* 725-729.

Megargee, E. I., Cook, P. E., & Mendelsohn, G. A. (1967). The development and validation of an MMPI scale of Assaultiveness in overcontrolled individuals. *Journal of Abnormal Psychology, 72,* 519-528.

Merrell, K. (1993). *School Social Behavior Scales.* Brandon, VT: Clinical Psychology Publishing Company.

Merrell, K., Merz, J., Johnson, E., & Ring, E. (1992). Social competence of mildly handicapped and low-achieving students: A comparative study. *School Psychology Review, 21,* 125-137.

Michelson, L. (1988). Children's Assertive Behavior Scale. In M. Hersen & A. S. Bellack (Eds.), *Dictionary of behavioral assessment techniques* New York: Pergamon Press.

Michelson, L., & Wood, R. (1982). Development and psychometric properties of the Children's Assertive Behavior Scale. *Journal of Behavioral Assessment, 4,* 3-13.

Milich, R. (1985). Validation of inattention/overactivity and aggression ratings with classroom observations. *Journal of Consulting and Clinical Psychology, 53,* 139-140.

Milich, R., & Landau, S. (1984). A comparison of the social status and social behavior of aggressive and aggressive/withdrawn boys. *Journal of Abnormal Child Psychology, 12,* 277-288.

Miller, L. C. (1967). Louisville Behavior Checklist for Males, 6-12 years of age. *Psychological Reports, 21,* 885-896.

Miller, L. C. (1972). School Behavior Check List: An inventory of deviant behavior for elementary school children. *Journal of Consulting and Clinical Psychology, 38,* 134-144.

Miller, L. C. (1981). *School Behavior Checklist.* Los Angeles: Western Psychological Services.

Morrison, S. D., Chaffin, S., & Chase, T. V. (1975). Aggression in adolescence: Use of the Buss-Durkee Inventory. *Southern Medical Journal, 68,* 431-436.

Moskowitz, D. S. (1986). Comparison of self-reports, reports by knowledgeable informants, and behavioral observation data. *Journal of Personality, 54,* 294-317.

Moskowitz, D. S., & Schwartzman, A. E. (1989). Painting group portraits: Studying life outcomes for aggressive and withdrawn children. *Journal of Personality, 57,* 723-746.

Moskowitz, D., Schwartzman, A. E., & Ledingham, J. (1985). Stability and change in aggression and withdrawal in middle childhood and adolescence. *Journal of Abnormal Psychology, 94,* 30-41.

Musante, L., MacDougall, J. M., Dembroski, T. M., & Costa, P. T. (1989). Potential for hostility, anger-in and the two dimensions of anger. *Health Psychology, 8,* 343-354.

Novaco, R.W. (1975). *Anger control: The development and evaluation of an experimental treatment.* Lexington, MA: D.C. Health and Co.

Novaco, R.W. (1979). The cognitive relations of anger and stress. In P. Kendall & S. Hollon (Eds.), *Cognitive-behavioral interventions: Theory, research, and procedures.* New York: Academic Press.

Ollendick, T. H. (1984). Development and validation of the Children's Assertiveness Inventory. *Child & Family Therapy, 5,* 1-15.

Olweus, D. (1978). *Aggression in the schools.* New York: Wiley.

Olweus, D. (1991). Bully/victim problems among schoolchildren: Basic facts and effects of a school based intervention program. In D. Pepler & K. Rubin (Eds.), *The development and treatment of childhood aggression* (pp. 411-448). Hillsdale, NJ: Erlbaum.

Olweus, D., Mattsson, A., Schalling, D., & Low, H. (1980). Testosterone, aggression, physical, and personality dimensions in normal adolescent males. *Psychosomatic Medicine, 42,* 253-269.

Pekarik, E. G., Prinz, R. J., Liebert, D. E., Weintraub, S., & Neale, J. M. (1976). The Pupil Evaluation Inventory: A sociometric technique for assessing children's social behavior. *Journal of Abnormal Child Psychology, 4,* 83-97.

Perry, D. G., Kusel, S. J., & Perry, L. C. (1988). Victims of peer aggression. *Developmental Psychology, 24,* 807-814.

Philaber, S., & Furlong, M. (1992, July). *Klein Bottle Youth Programs case management monthly report.* Unpublished report.

Philip, A. E. (1968). The constancy of structure of a hostility questionnaire. *British Journal of Social and Clinical Psychology, 7,* 16-18.

Philip, A. E. (1969). The development and use of the Hostility and Direction of Hostility Questionnaire. *Journal of Psychosomatic Medicine, 13,* 283-287.

Pope, M. K., Smith, T. W., & Rhodewalt, F. (1990). Cognitive, behavioral, and affective correlates of the Cook and Medley cynical hostility scale. *Journal of Personality Assessment, 54,* 501-514.

Prinz, R. J., Swan, G., Liebert, D., Weintraub, S., & Neale, J. M. (1978). ASSESS: Adjustment Scales for Sociometric Evaluation of Secondary-School Students. *Journal of Abnormal Child Psychology, 6,* 493-501.

Riley, W. T., & Treiber, F. A. (1989). The validity of multidimensional self-report anger and hostility measures. *Journal of Clinical Psychology, 45,* 397-404.

Rosenman, R. H. (1985). Health consequences of anger and implications for treatment. In M. A. Chesney & R. H. Rosenman (Eds.), *Anger and hostility in cardiovascular and behavioral disorders* (pp. 103-125). Washington, DC: Hemisphere.

Scanlon, E. M., & Ollendick, T. H. (1986). Children's assertive behavior: The reliability and validity of three self-report measures. *Child and Family Behavior Therapy, 7,* 9-21.

Selby, M. J. (1984). Assessment of violence potential using measures of anger, hostility, and social desirability. *Journal of Personality Assessment, 48,* 531-544.

Shapiro, E. S., Lentz, F. E., & Sofman, R. (1985). Validity of rating scales in assessing aggressive behavior in classroom settings. *Journal of School Psychology, 23,* 69-79.

Shoemaker, O. S., Erikson, M. T., & Finch, A. J. Jr. (1986). Depression and anger in third- and fourth-grade boys: A multimethod assessment approach. *Journal of Clinical Child Psychology, 15,* 290-296.

Siegel, J. M. (1984). Anger and cardiovascular risk in adolescents. *Health*

Psychology, 3, 293-313.

Siegel, J. M. (1986). The multidimensional anger inventory. *Journal of Personality and Social Psychology, 51,* 191-200.

Siegel, J. M. (1992). Anger and cardiovascular health. In H. S. Friedman (Ed.), *Hostility, coping & health* (pp. 49-64). Washington, DC: American Psychological Association.

Siegman, A. W., Dembroski, T. M., & Ringel, N. (1987). Components of hostility and the severity of coronary artery disease. *Psychosomatic Medicine, 49,* 127-135.

Skiba, R., & Grizzle, K. (1991). The social maladjustment exclusion: Issues of definition and assessment. *School Psychology Review, 20,* 580-598.

Skiba, R., & Grizzle, K. (1992). Qualifications v. logic and data: Excluding conduct disorders from the SED definition. *School Psychology Review, 21,* 23-28.

Slaby, R. G., & Guerra, N. G. (1988). Cognitive mediators of aggression in adolescent offenders: I. Assessment. *Developmental Psychology, 24,* 580-588.

Smith, D. C., Adelman, H. S., Nelson, P., & Taylor, L. (1988). Anger, perceived control and school behavior among students with learning problems. *Journal of Child Psychology and Psychiatry, 29,* 517-522.

Smith, T. W., & Frohm, K. D. (1985). What's so unhealthy about hostility? Construct validity and psychological correlates of the Cook and Medley Ho scale. *Health Psychology, 4,* 503-520.

Spielberger, C. D. (1988a). Anger Expression Scale. In M. Hersen & A. S. Bellack (Eds.), *Dictionary of behavioral assessment techniques* (pp. 27-28). New York: Pergamon Press.

Spielberger, C. D. (1988b). *State-Trait Anger Expression Inventory: Research Edition.* Odessa, FL: Psychological Assessment Resources.

Spielberger, C. D., Crane, R. S., Kearns, W. D., Pellegrin, K. L, & Johnson, E. H. (1991). Anger and anxiety in essential hypertension. In C. D. Spielberger & I. G. Sarason (Eds.), *Stress and emotion* (Vol. 14, pp. 266-283). New York: Hemisphere/Taylor and Francis.

Spielberger, C. D., Gorsuch, R. L., & Lushene R. E. (1970). *Manual for the State-Trait Anxiety Inventory (Self-Evaluation Questionnaire).* Palo Alto, CA: Consulting Psychologist Press.

Spielberger, C. D., Jacobs, G. A., Russell, S., & Crane, R. S. (1983). Assessment of anger: The State-Trait Anger Scale. In J. N. Butcher & C. D. Spielberger (Eds.), *Advances in personality assessment* (Vol. 2, pp. 161-189). Hillsdale, NJ: Erlbaum.

Spielberger, C. D., Johnson, E. H., Russell, S. F., Crane, R.S., Jacobs, G. A., & Worden, T. J. (1985). The experience and expression of anger: Construction and validation of an anger expression scale. In M. A. Chesney & R. H. Rosenman (Eds.), *Anger and hostility in cardiovascular and behavioral disorders* (pp. 5-30). New York: Hemisphere/ McGraw-Hill.

Spielberger, C. D., Krasner, S. S., & Solomon, E. P. (1988). The experience, expression, and control of anger. In M. P. Janisse (Ed.), *Health psychology: Individual differences and stress* (pp. 89-108). New York: Springer Verlag/Publishers.

Treiber, F. A., Musante, L., Riley, W., Mabe, P. A., Carr, T., Levy, M., & Strong, W. B. (1989). The relationship between hostility and blood pressure in children. *Behavioral Medicine, 15,* 173-178.

Truscott, D. (1990). Assessment of overcontrolled hostility in adolescence. *Psychological Assessment, 2,* 145-148.

Veliocer, W. F., Govia, J. M., Cherico, N. P., & Corriveau, D. P. (1985). Item format and the structure of the Buss-Durkee Hostility Inventory. *Aggressive Behavior, 11,* 65-82.

Vitiello, B., Behar, D., Hunt, J., Stoff, D., & Ricciuti, A. (1990). Subtyping aggression in children and adolescents. *Journal of Neuropsychiatry, 2,* 189-192.

Waas, G. A. (1987). Aggressive rejected children: Implications for school psychologists. *Journal of School Psychology, 25,* 383-388.

Walker, H., & McConnell, S. (1988). *The Walker-McConnell Scale of Social Competence and School Adjustment.* Austin, TX: Pro-Ed.

Weintraub, S., Prinz, R. J., & Neale, J. M. (1978). Peer evaluations of the competence of childen vulnerable to psychopathology. *Journal of Abnormal Child Psychology, 6,* 461-473.

Wiggins, J. S., & Winder C. L. (1961). The Peer Nomination Inventory: An empirically derived sociometric measure of adjustment in preadolescent boys. *Psychology Reprints, 9,* 643-677.

Williams, C. (1986). MMPI profiles from adolescents: Interpretive strategies and treatment considerations. *Journal of Child and Adolescent Psychotherapy, 3,* 179-193.

Williams, C., & Butcher, J. (1989a). An MMPI study of adolescents: I. Empirical validity of the standard scales. *Psychological Assessment: A Journal of Consulting and Clinical Psychology, 1,* 251-259.

Williams, C., & Butcher, J. (1989b). An MMPI study of adolescents: II.

Verification and limitations of code type classifications. *Psychological Assessment: A Journal of Consulting and Clinical Psychology, 1,* 260-265.

Williams, C., Butcher, J., Ben-Porath, Y., & Graham, J. (1992). *MMPI-A content scales: Assessing psychopathology in adolescents.* Minneapolis, MN: University of Minnesota Press.

Williams, R. B., Jr., Barefoot, J. C., & Shekelle, R. B. (1985). The health consequences of hostility. In M. A. Chesney & R. H. Rosenman (Eds.), *Anger and hostility in cardiovascular and behavioral disorders* (pp. 173- 185). Washington, DC: Hemisphere.

Williamson, D. A., & McKenzie, S. J. (1988). Children's Action Tendency Scale. In M. Hersen & A. S. Bellack (Eds.), *Dictionary of behavioral assessment techniques* (pp. 102-104). New York: Pergamon.

Williamson, D. A., Moody, S., Granberry, S., Lethermon, V., & Blouin, D. (1983). Criterion related validity of a role-play social skills test for children. *Behavior Therapy, 14,* 466-481.

Witt, J. C., Cavell, T. A., Heffer, R. W., Carey, M. P., & Martens, B. K. (1988). Child self-report: Interviewing techniques and rating scales. In E. S. Shapiro & T. R. Kratochwill (Eds.), *Behavioral assessment in schools: Conceptual foundations and practical applications* (pp. 384-454). New York: Guilford.

Witt, J. C., Heffer, R. W., & Pfeiffer, J. (1990). Structured rating scales: A review of self-report and informant rating processes, procedures, and issues. In C. R. Reynolds & R. W. Kamphaus (Eds.), *Handbook of psychological and educational assessment of children: Personality, behavior, and context* (pp. 364-394). New York: Guilford.

Woodall, K. L., & Matthews, K. A. (1989). Familial environment associated with Type A behaviors and psychophysiological responses to stress in children. *Health Psychology, 8,* 403-426.

Zelin, M. L., Adler, G., & Myerson, P. G. (1972). Anger self-report: An objective questionnaire for the measurement of aggression. *Journal of Consulting and Clinical Psychology, 39,* 340.

Zlomke, L., & Piersel, W. (1987). Children and aggressive behavior. In A. Thomas & J. Grimes (Eds.), *Children's needs: Psychological perspectives* (pp. 19-27). Washington, DC: National Association of School Psychologists.

APPENDIX

Buss-Durkee Hostility Inventory

Assault Subscale (10 items)

1. I seldom strike back, even if someone hits me first. (F)
9. Once in a while I can not control my urge to harm others.
17. I can think of no good reason for ever hitting anyone. (F)
25. If someone hits me first, I let him have it.
33. Whoever insults me or my family is asking for a fight.
41. People who continually pester you are asking for a punch in the nose.
49. When I really lose my temper, I am capable of slapping someone.
57. I get into fights about as often as the next person.
65. If I have to resort to physical violence to defend my rights, I will.
70. I have known people who pushed me so far that we came to blows.

Indirect Subscale (9 items)

2. I sometimes spread gossip about people I don't like.
10. I never get mad enough to throw things. (F)
18. When I am angry, I sometimes sulk.
26. When I am mad, I sometimes slam doors.
34. I never play practical jokes. (F)
42. I sometimes pout when I don't get my own way.
50. Since the age of ten, I have never had a temper tantrum. (F)
58. I can remember being so angry that I picked up the nearest thing and broke it.
75. I sometimes show anger by banging on the table.

Irritability Subscale (11 items)

4. I lose my temper easily but get over it quickly.
11. Sometimes people bother me just by being around.
27. I am always patient with others. (F)
20. I am irritated a great deal more than people are aware of.
35. It makes my blood boil to have somebody make fun of me.
44. I often feel like a powder keg ready to explode.
52. I sometimes carry a chip on my shoulders.
60. I can't help being a little rude to people I don't like.
66. If someone doesn't treat me right, I don't let it bother me. (F)
71. I don't let a lot of unimportant things irritate me. (F)
73. Lately, I have been kind of grouchy.

Negativism Subscale (5 items)

3. Unless somebody asks me in a nice way, I won't do what they want.
12. When someone makes a rule I don't like I am tempted to break it.
19. When someone is bossy, I do the opposite of what he asks.
28. Occasionally when I am mad at someone I will give him the "silent treatment."
36. When people are bossy, I take my time just to show them.

Resentment Subscale (8 items)

5. I don't seem to get what's coming to me.
13. Other people always seem to get the breaks.
21. I don't know any people that I downright hate. (F)
29. When I look back on what's happened to me, I can't help feeling mildly resentful.
37. Almost every week I see someone I dislike.
45. Although I don't show it, I am sometimes eaten up with jealousy.
53. If I let people see the way I feel, I'd be considered a hard person to get along with.
61. At times I feel I get a raw deal out of life.

Suspicion Subscale (10 items)

6. I know that people tend to talk about me behind my back.
14. I tend to be on my guard with people who are somewhat more friendly than I expected.
22. There are a number of people who seem to dislike me very much.
30. There are a number of people who seem to be jealous of me.
38. I sometimes have the feeling that others are laughing at me.
46. My motto is "Never trust strangers."
54. I commonly wonder what hidden reason another person may have for doing something nice for me.
62. I used to think that most people told the truth but now I know otherwise.
67. I have no enemies who really wish to harm me. (F)
72. I seldom feel that people are trying to anger or insult me. (F)

Verbal Hostility Subscale (13 items)

7. When I disapprove of my friends' behavior, I let them know it.
15. I often find myself disagreeing with people.
23. I can't help getting into arguments when people disagree with me.
31. I demand that people respect my rights.

39. Even when my anger is aroused, I don't use "strong language." (F)
43. If somebody annoys me, I am apt to tell him what I think of him.
47. When people yell at me, I yell back.
51. When I get mad, I say nasty things.
55. I could not put someone in his place, even if he needed it. (F)
59. I often make threats I don't really mean to carry out.
68. When arguing, I tend to raise my voice.
63. I generally cover up my poor opinion of others. (F)
74. I would rather concede a point than get into an argument about it. (F)

Guilt Subscale (9 items)

8. The few times I have cheated, I have suffered unbearable feelings of remorse.
16. I sometimes have had thoughts which make me feel ashamed of myself.
24. People who shirk on the job must feel very guilty.
32. It depresses me that I did not do more for my parents.
40. I am concerned about being forgiven for my sins.
48. I do many things that make me feel remorseful afterwards.
56. Failure gives me a feeling of remorse.
64. When I do wrong, my conscience punishes me severely.
69. I often feel that I have not lived the right kind of life.

From Buss, A. H., & Durkee, A. (1957). An inventory for assessing different kinds of hostility. *Journal of Consulting Psychology, 21,* 343-349.

Buss-Durkee Hostility Inventory - Child Version

Expressive Hostility (expressive anger in this chapter)

1. When people yell at me, I yell back.
2. When I'm arguing, I raise my voice.
3. I would rather give in than get into an argument.
4. When I lose my temper I could easily hit someone.
5. Sometimes people upset me so much that we get into a fight.
6. I have had a temper tantrum.
7. I lose my temper easily but get over it quickly.

Experienced Anger (hostile attitude in this chapter)

8. It makes me really angry if someone makes fun of me.
9. Nice things happen to me when I deserve them.

10. I think life is fair.
11. I think people usually have a hidden reason for doing something nice for me.
12. When I think about what has happened to me in my life I feel rather upset.
13. It is important to me to be forgiven when I have done something wrong.

From Treiber, F. A., Musante, L., Riley, W., Mabe, P. A., Carr, T., Levy, M., & Strong, W. B. (1989). The relationship between hostility and blood pressure in children. *Behavioral Medicine, 15,* 173-178.

School Anger Inventory

Peer Annoyances

4. You are talking and your friend ignores you.
11. You are trying to do your schoolwork and another student interrupts you for no good reason.
18. Someone calls you a liar.
22. You are trying to do your work but other students are too noisy.

Peer-teacher Problems

3. Your friends make fun of you.
8. Student brushes against you accidentally, then apologizes.
6. Somebody calls you a bad name.
7. Your friends leave you out of an activity.
24. You want to do something but the teacher says you can't.

School Frustrations

9. Your teacher gives you more work than you are able to do.
14. You really try but your schoolwork just seems too hard.
15. Your teacher is always pointing out mistakes you made.
21. You are trying to explain something to your teacher but he/she just does not understand.

Moral Infractions

16. You find out that someone has stolen something from you at school.
19. You are playing a game at school and someone tries to cheat.
20. After you've worked really hard on a project, another student takes it from your desk and destroys it.
23. Someone in your class tells the teacher on you for doing something.

Teacher Antagonism

2. You know that you are right about something but your teacher says you are wrong.
5. Your teacher blames you for something that wasn't your fault.
12. Your teacher tries to talk you into something you don't want to do.

Becomes Angry Scale

1. Has difficulty controlling anger when someone hurts him/her.
2. Becomes angry when sees someone being mistreated.
3. Is the sort of person who is not difficult to make angry.
4. Becomes so angry that he/she feels like throwing or breaking things.
5. Gets angry if feels someone is blocking his/her plans.
6. Raises voice when gets angry.
7. Seldom gets angry about anything. (false scored)
8. Gets angry easily but gets over it quickly.
9. Gets angry with anyone who tries to restrict his/her freedom.
10. Seldom gets angry with others. (false scored)
11. Gets over angry spell very quickly. (false scored)
12. Gets angry when can't find something he/she is looking for.
13. Becomes angry when has to wait for others.
14. Gets angry if belongings are disturbed by someone.
15. Gets angry if someone tries to take advantage of his/her friendship.
16. Responds to frustration with irritation and anger.
17. Has frequent feelings of anger.
18. Showed anger when describing irritations at school.
19. Hostile during interview.

From Siegel, J. M. (1984). Anger and cardiovascular risk in children. *Health Psychology, 3,* 293-313. Copyright 1984 by Lawrence Erlbaum. Reprinted by permission.

Matthews Youth Test for Health (MYTH)

1. When this child plays games, he/she is competitive.
2. This child works quickly and energetically rather than slowly and deliberately.
3. When this child has to wait for others, he/she becomes impatient.
4. This child does things in a hurry.
5. It takes a lot to get this child angry at his/her peers.
6. This child interrupts others.

7. This child is a leader is various activities.
8. This child gets irritated easily.
9. He/she seems to perform better than usual when competing against others.
10. This child likes to argue or debate.
11. This child is patient when working with children slower than he/she is.
12. When working or playing, he/she tries to do better than other children.
13. This child can't sit still long.
14. It is important to this child to win, rather than to have fun in games or schoolwork.
15. Other children look to this child for leadership.
16. This child is competitive.
17. This child tends to get into fights.

From Matthews, K. A., & Angulo, J. (1980). Measurement of the Type A behavior pattern in children: Assessment of children's competitiveness, impatience-anger, and aggression. *Child Development, 51,* 466-475.

Pupil Evaluation Inventory (PEI)

1. Those who are taller than most.
2. Those who help others.
3. **Those who can't sit still.**
4. **Those who try to get other people into trouble.**
5. *Those who are too shy to make friends easily.*
6. *Those whose feelings are too easily hurt.*
7. **Those who act stuck-up and think that they are better than everyone else.**
8. **Those who play the clown and get others to laugh.**
9. **Those who start a fight over nothing.**
10. *Those who never seem to be having a good time.*
11. **Those who are upset when called on to answer a question in class. (Both I and II Males, only)**
12. **Those who tell other children what to do.**
13. *Those who are usually chosen last to join in group activities.*
14. Those who are liked by everyone.
15. **Those who always mess around and get into trouble.**
16. **Those who make fun of people.**
17. *Those who have very few friends.*

18. Those who do strange things.
19. Those who are your best friends.
20. Those who bother people when they are trying to work.
21. Those who get mad when they don't get their own way.
23. Those who are rude to the teacher.
24. Those who are unhappy or sad.
25. Those who are especially nice.
26. Those who act like a baby.
27. Those who are mean and cruel to other children.
28. Those who often don't want to play.
29. Those who give dirty looks.
30. Those who want to show off in front of class.
31. Those who say they can beat everybody up.
32. Those who aren't noticed much.
33. Those who exaggerate and make up stories.
34. Those who complain that nothing makes them happy.
35. Those who always seem to understand things.

Bold items Factor I: Aggression; Italicized items Factor II: Withdrawal; Other items are Factor III: Likability.

From Pekarik, E. G., Prinz, R. J., Liebert, D. E., Weintraub, S., & Neale, J. M. (1976). The Pupil Evaluation Inventory: A sociometric technique for assessing children's social behavior. *Journal of Abnormal Child Psychology, 4,* 83-97; and Weintraub, S., Prinz, R. J., & Neale, J. M. (1978). Peer evaluations of the competence of children vulnerable to psychopathology. *Journal of Abnormal Child Psychology, 6,* 461-473.

8 BEHAVIORAL OBSERVATION OF ANGER AND AGGRESSION

Stephanie Stein and Mitchell Karno

The most direct way of assessing any behavior is to observe it in the natural environment. In the case of anger and hostility, however, direct observation may not always be possible because the associated emotional state is not always manifest in a predictable outward expression of behavior. One person may become very quiet when angered, whereas another may lash out violently. Also one child may behave in a very aggressive manner in an angry response to a provocation, whereas similar aggressive behavior in a second child may not be an expression of anger at all but may instead be an attempt to dominate another person or situation. Given that there isn't a perfect fit between the expression of anger and aggression (Novaco, 1976), this chapter will proceed on the assumption that behavioral observation of aggression is still an effective way to assess anger objectively in another person. An alternative form of behavioral observation is the use of self-assessment or self-monitoring, in which the individual serves as his or her own observer. Both approaches will be explored in this chapter.

The literature reviewed in the following section reflects (a) a variety of studies using behavioral observation procedures to assess anger and/or aggression and (b) other research focusing on behavioral observation or self-monitoring procedures. No attempt has been made to review research on behavioral observation procedures exhaustively; rather, the information presented reviews key behavioral observation principles that are particularly applicable to school-based behavioral assessment of anger and aggression.

BEHAVIORAL OBSERVATION: KEY CONCEPTS

Rationale for Behavioral Observation

Behavioral observation tends to be an expensive, time-consuming procedure for assessing emotional and behavioral problems (Alessi, 1988). Rating scales, checklists, and interviews (see Furlong & Smith, Chapter 7) are much less costly in terms of time and resources. Given the differential costs of these procedures, it is clear that the use of systematic behavioral observations must be supported by a strong rationale.

One major reason for choosing behavioral observation as an assessment procedure is that it measures different behaviors from those measured through indirect assessment such as verbal reports and questionnaires. Whereas direct observation assesses the actual behavior exhibited by the child, indirect measures appear to assess others' perceptions of the child (Cone, 1978; Shapiro, Lentz, & Sofman, 1985). Though important, others' perceptions of the child are sometimes very difficult to change and may or may not alter as a result of behavioral changes in the child. Therefore, a highly valid and meaningful way of assessing behavior is to observe it directly (Hughes & Sullivan, 1988).

Another advantage of behavioral observation is that it often has direct implications for treatment. For example, if an observation indicates that a child withdraws and does not talk to others when feeling angry, then an obvious treatment goal would be to increase the frequency of assertive verbal communication with others. The child's progress towards this goal can be repeatedly measured through systematic behavioral observation.

Finally, there is a growing reform effort in public education to make assessments more authentic or outcome-based. For example, California has implemented legislation that requires schools to conduct functional behavioral assessments to address any aggressive behaviors that hinder special education students fulfilling the goals of their Individual Education Plans (IEPs) (Assembly Bill 2586, 1992).

The Relationship Between Anger and Aggression

Initial efforts at the systematic observation and study of anger date back to the 1930s (Goodenough, 1931). In this early endeavor, physical and verbal instances of nondirected energy, resistance, and retaliation were used to determine the presence of anger in children. Goodenough conducted one of the first comprehensive, behavioral assessments of anger by addressing the situations during which anger occurs, the types of behaviors displayed, the interventions used, and the subsequent effects on the child.

Further, in the vast majority of published studies on anger that use behavioral observation as a measure, the behaviors observed are either physical and/or verbal aggression (Barfield & Hutchinson, 1990; Dangel, Deschner, & Rasp, 1989; Feindler, Marriott, & Iwata, 1984; Garrison & Stolberg, 1983; Lochman, Burch, Curry, & Lampron, 1984; Schlichter & Horan, 1981; Stern & Fodor, 1989). One exception to this finding is the study by Bornstein, Bellack, and Hersen (1980) that assessed "hostile tone" in subjects. However, no definition of the hostile tone was provided for the reader. In addition, some studies have looked at "disruptive behavior," which may include aggression, but also can include a host of other behaviors such as destruction of property, hyperactivity (Goodwin & Mahoney, 1975), disturbing others, making noise (Humphrey & Karoly, 1978), inappropriate verbalizations, not attending, or being out of seat (Turkewitz, O'Leary, & Ironsmith, 1975).

Operational Definition of Anger-Related Behavior

The key to assessing a behavior effectively through direct observation procedures is to identify a clear, operational definition of the target behavior. In order for a definition to be operational, it must refer to aspects of behavior that can be directly observed and must be stated in such a way that any trained observer would be able to agree about the presence or absence of the behavior. Varied examples of the target behavior help the observer understand the range of behaviors included in the definition (Shapiro & Skinner, 1990). In addition, it is helpful if the definition provides guidelines for discriminating the target behavior of interest from other similar but nonrelevant behaviors so that the observer can also understand the limits and boundaries of the target behavior. For example, if the target behavior was aggression, the definition should be stated in such a way that the observer would record intentional acts of aggression, whether they are slugging or spitting, and not record physical harm caused through accidental means or as a result of normal participation in a play activity (Dangel et al., 1989).

The quality of the definitions of aggression and other anger-related behaviors in the literature is quite variable. The most detailed and descriptive definitions of aggression seem to come from single-subject research designs implemented with children with mental retardation (Carr, Newsom, & Binkoff, 1980; Horner, Day, Sprague, O'Brien, & Heathfield, 1991;

Luiselli & Slocumb, 1983; Mace, Page, Ivancic, & O'Brien, 1986; Slifer, Ivancic, Parrish, Page, & Burgio, 1986). Some studies provide separate definitions for verbal aggression and physical aggression (Archer, Pearson, & Westeman, 1988; Bostow & Bailey, 1969; Cummings, Iannotti, & Zahn-Waxler, 1989; Dangel et al., 1989; Feindler et al., 1984; Kettlewell & Kausch, 1983), others look at only verbal aggression (Pentz, 1980; Schlichter & Horan, 1981) or only physical aggression (Breyer & Calchera, 1971; Drabman, Spitalnik, & O'Leary, 1973; Murphy, Hutchison, & Bailey, 1983; Robin, Schneider, & Dolnick, 1976), and some include both types of behavior under the single target behavior of aggression (Forman, 1980; Shapiro et al., 1985; Sherburne, Utley, McConnell, & Gannon, 1988; Stern & Fodor, 1989; Turkewitz et al., 1975; Wilson, 1984; Zahavi & Asher, 1978).

In the literature on behavioral observation, the types of definitions given for aggression range from "aggression" (Turkewitz et al., 1975) or "physical aggression" (Humphrey & Karoly, 1978), with no further description, to extremely detailed definitions such as the one provided by Forman (1980):

> *An aggressive incident consists of the following behaviors: taking something from another child, hitting, kicking, or shoving an adult, making fun of another child, throwing an object at someone, refusing to share something, refusing to follow teacher's instructions, forcing another child to do something he or she did not want to do, hitting, kicking, or shoving a child, arguing in an angry way, cursing, or destroying someone else's property.* (pp. 595-596)

Most definitions of aggression in the literature include behaviors such as hitting, shoving, pushing, biting, kicking, scratching, pinching, hair pulling, grabbing, throwing objects at someone, self-biting, head banging, swearing, cursing, screaming, threatening, and humiliating or insulting another (Archer et al., 1988; Bostow & Bailey, 1969; Breyer & Calchera, 1971, Carr et al., 1980; Dangel et al., 1989; Feindler et al., 1984; Forman, 1980; Horner et al., 1991; Kettlewell & Kausch, 1983; Luiselli & Slocumb, 1983; Mace et al., 1986; Murphy, et al., 1983; Robin et al., 1976; Shapiro et al., 1985; Slifer et al., 1986; Zahavi & Asher, 1978). Table 8.1 provides a list of the most commonly used terms in the studies on behavioral observation of aggression. Archer et al.'s study of gender differences in aggressive behavior of children (1988) not only included terms such as

FIGURE 8.1. DEFINITIONS OF AGGRESSIVE BEHAVIOR USED IN RESEARCH STUDIES.

Study	Label Used for Behavior	Hit	Kick	Shove	Throw	Scratch	Pinch	Slap	Pull	Bite	Hair Pull	Take Object	Fight	Property Damage	Not Sharing	Insult	Swear	Threats	Argue	Curse	Yell
Archer et al. (1988)	Physical Aggression	✔	✔	✔					✔												
	Verbal Aggression															✔					
Bostow & Bailey (1969)	Aggressive Behavior	✔	✔			✔	✔			✔											
Breyer & Calchera (1971)	Aggressive Off-Task	✔		✔																	
Carr et al. (1980)	Aggressive	✔	✔			✔	✔			✔	✔										
Dangel et al. (1989)	Physical Aggression	✔	✔					✔		✔		✔									
	Verbal Aggression																✔	✔			
Feindler et al. (1984)	Mild Physical Aggression			✔	✔																
	Mild Verbal Aggression																		✔	✔	✔
	Severe Aggression												✔	✔							
Forman (1980)	Aggressive Incident	✔	✔	✔	✔							✔		✔	✔				✔	✔	
Horner et al. (1991)	Aggression or Self-Injury	✔								✔	✔										
Kettlewell & Kausch (1983)	Physical Aggression	✔	✔	✔	✔			✔		✔											
	Verbal Aggression																✔	✔			✔
Luiselli & Slocumb (1983)	Aggressive Acts	✔	✔					✔			✔										
Mace et al. (1983)	Aggression	✔	✔		✔	✔			✔	✔											
Murphy et al. (1983)	Aggression	✔	✔	✔				✔	✔												
Robin et al. (1976)	Aggressive Behavior	✔	✔		✔									✔							
Shapiro & Lentz (1985)	Aggressive Behavior				✔																
Slifer et al. (1986)	Aggression	✔	✔								✔										
Zahavi & Asher (1978)	Aggressive	✔	✔	✔								✔	✔		✔	✔					

hitting, kicking, etc., in their definition of aggression but even further defined the terms as follows:

Hit: The child beats fist or open hand on other child's head, trunk, or arms.
Kick: Kicks foot, often repeatedly, on other child's leg(s) or foot/feet.
Poke: With finger or fingers, or a sharp object (e.g., pen, paint-brush), the child prods or pokes another child forcefully, often repeatedly, in thigh, posterior, or backside.
Pull: The child pulls another child forcefully by his or her hair, ear, clothing, arms, or hands, using one or both hands; the child pulls an object held in the arms or hands of another child exerting great force in order to obtain the object.
Push: Using one or both hands the child exerts pressure on other child's body and pushes him or her backwards, forwards, or to the side; using his or her body, the child forces the other child backwards, forwards or sideways.
Wrestle: Holding arms around another child, the child wrestles, attempting to force other child to the ground; the child wrestles and rolls round with another child on the ground.
Chase: While running, the child pursues another child. (p. 384)

In order to rule out play activities, Archer et al. (1988) further specified that physical aggression must not be accompanied by a smile or laugh. Verbal aggression was defined as "insulting words or statement directed at another child" (i.e., 'God, you idiot, get away from me'; 'Stupid cow'; 'You spastic') (p. 384).

Some of the studies include aggression under a much more general definition of disruptive behavior (Goodwin & Mahoney, 1975; Humphrey & Karoly, 1978; Lochman et al., 1984). Wilson (1984) criticizes this approach of blending aggression and disruption under one behavioral category, stating that studies that combine aggression and disruptiveness in a single measure make it difficult to assess the effectiveness of treatments for aggression. Whenever possible, it is better to observe and record behavioral data on aggressiveness and disruptiveness separately so potentially different antecedents and consequences can be identified and the effectiveness of intervention strategies can be assessed. The data on the two behavioral categories can later be combined if desired, but they cannot be separated later if they are lumped together during assessment. The more specific, detailed, and precise the definitions, the more likely the observations will be accurate and reliable.

Although the bulk of the behavioral research on anger has defined the problem in terms of aggression, there are other options for operationally defining anger without simply looking at aggression. Camras (1977) used certain facial expressions categorized as aggressive to study how children defended their possession of an object. Aggressive expressions were defined to include "(a) lowered brows, (b) stare (1.5 seconds or longer), (c) face thrust forward, (d) lips pressed together, (e) both lips thrust forward, (f) lips pressed together with tightened mouth corners, and (g) nose wrinkle" (p. 1432). The results of Camras' study showed that aggressive facial expressions were related to persistent attempts to keep possession of an object.

Methods of Behavioral Observation of Anger

Behavioral observation plays a large role in the assessment and treatment of aggressive and hostile outbursts. Specifically, it is an integral part of a procedure used to determine both the underlying causes and the effectiveness of treatment for a problem behavior. This procedure, a functional analysis, has been summarized as including (a) systematic observation of the problem behavior to establish a baseline frequency, (b) systematic observation of the conditions preceding and following the behavior, with a special emphasis on antecedent cues and consequential reinforcers, (c) altering an environmental condition that is thought to be influencing the problem behavior, and (d) further observation to assess if any change in the target behavior(s) has occurred (Peterson, 1968).

The initial observation phase provides an accurate definition of the problem behavior along with a summary of its rate, intensity, and duration. Assessment of antecedents and consequences relating to the behavior offers the professional insight into what elicited the behavior and what outcome supported that behavior's occurrence. In this way, the communicative intent of the behavior for a particular child is better understood. In addition to the specific events preceding and following the problem behavior, it is important to take into account ecological elements such as the physical and social settings, the nature of instruction and activities; the type of communication that exists between students, faculty, and staff; and the level of choice and independence allowed students. Focusing on these areas may provide greater insight into why a behavior is occurring and facilitate effective manipulation of environmental conditions to reduce the problem [Assembly Bill 2586 (California), 1992]. Beyond the sources of information coming from direct observation, health records revealing medical difficulties and a look at the history of the behavior and the results of past treatment efforts also may offer a greater understanding of a child's behavior. Direct observation, interviews with family members, and reviews of pupil records and assessment reports are excellent sources of data to be used by personnel when gathering information for a functional analysis.

The final two stages of the analysis, altering the environment and assessing if the target behavior changed in its frequency, intensity, or duration, are tied directly to treatment issues, as discussed in the intervention section of this volume.

The literature on behavioral observation generally identifies five basic methods for collecting observational data: (a) narrative recording, (b) frequency/ event recording, (c) interval recording/time sampling, (d) duration or latency recording, and (e) permanent products (Alessi, 1988; Barton & Ascione, 1984; Shapiro, 1987). The type of observational used depends on a number of factors, including the rate of behavior, whether it is discrete or continuous, and the number of behaviors and/or students observed.

Narrative recording. Often the first type of observational data gathered by an observer is an anecdotal or narrative record of the target student(s) and their interactions with others (Shapiro & Skinner, 1990). The purpose of this running log is to give the observer an idea of the types and range of behaviors exhibited by the student. It also allows the observer to identify possible antecedents and consequences that may be maintaining the behavior in a particular setting (Elder, Edelstein, & Narick, 1979).

In order to be most useful, anecdotal recordings of anger and aggression in children should be based on objective, observable descriptors of behavior as much as possible (Salvia & Ysseldyke, 1991). Observer interpretations of the behavior in place of the actual description should be avoided. For example, rather than writing, "Jack was furious when Sharon took his coat," the observer would write, "Sharon grabbed Jack's coat. Jack screamed at her, roughly pulled the coat out of her arms, and hit her over the head with the coat." The second example provides a clear illustration of Jack's behavior and provides the observer a clue about the kinds of behaviors to observe (such as loud voice, physical aggression) in a more systematic way.

Galvin and Singleton (1984) developed a comprehensive narrative recording procedure to be used with their Behavior Checklist. In the classroom, they suggest that the checklist should be located near the teacher's desk so that it is readily available. Choose a single child and begin recording the occurrence of inappropriate behaviors on the checklist. At this time it is important to gather information on the presence or absence of a wide variety of behaviors. Once a broad range of inappropriate behaviors has been sampled, begin assessing the frequency of behaviors as they occur at any time. Because some behaviors may not lend themselves to measurement by frequency, measuring their duration may be more appropriate. After several weeks of assessment, the teacher can then decide which behaviors require his or her attention.

Once these important behavior areas have been determined, choose no more than two to address. This limitation is important because it may be very difficult for a child to alter too many behaviors at the same time. When observing these critical behaviors, information about who was involved in an incident, the events preceding and following the incident, how resolution occurred, and how the teacher responded is helpful to create a broader picture of a child's behavior beyond only frequencies and durations. After a period of time, determine which intervention strategies will be appropriate, based on the data collected, and implement them. Continue to monitor the child's target behaviors. Finally, compare the frequencies of the behavior before and after initiating the interventions. An example of a format for recording anecdotal observations of aggression is provided in Figure 8.1.

Although a narrative recording is a reasonable way to start an observation of a child with anger problems, by itself it is not sufficient. Additional observation procedures that can provide more systematic and measurable data are needed (Salvia & Ysseldyke, 1991).

Frequency/event recording. One simple but systematic way of recording observations of behavior is to count the frequency with which the behavior occurs within a specified time limit. Although this procedure may appear fairly straightforward, there are certain criteria that need to be present in order for a frequency count to be practical. First of all, the behavior of interest must be discrete, with a clear beginning and ending (Salvia & Ysseldyke, 1991). For example, the number of times an angry child slams a door can be counted because there is a clear end to the behavior. In contrast, the behavior of yelling may be much harder to count because it is not always clear when one incident of the behavior has stopped and another one has begun. Several researchers (Cummings et al., 1989; Shapiro et al., 1985) attempt to get around this problem of having a discrete beginning and ending when counting aggressive outbursts by defining an aggressive incident as

Anecdotal Observation

Student: Jack Brown **Activity/Setting**: Free time in classroom

Date: 10-15-93 **Time Start:** 2:15 **Time Stop**: 2:25 **Observer**: Stein

Narrative Observation: Jack is playing Monopoly with Sharon and Kevin. Jack bumps the board when reaching across, knocking over the pieces. Kevin calls Jack a "clumsy idiot." Jack frowns, straightens pieces. Kids play quietly for a few minutes. Kevin reaches over and grabs most of Jack's play money. Jack tries to grab it back and hits Kevin on the arm. Sharon laughs and grabs the rest of Jack's money. Kevin stands up, says he doesn't want to play anymore "cause Jack is cheating." Kevin and Sharon both call Jack a "cheater." Jack keeps saying, "I didn't cheat." Kevin and Sharon laugh and continue to chant " cheater." Some other kids join in. Bell rings and all the kids go to get their coats. Sharon grabs Jack's coat. Jack screams at her, roughly pulls the coat out of her arms and hits her over the head with the coat. The teacher takes Jack's arm, pulls him away, and tells him he has to stay after school.

Sequence of Behavior:

What Happened Before?	*What Did Student Do?*	*What Happened After?*
1. Playing Monopoly	Bumps board, knocks over pieces	Called "clumsy idiot"
2. Called "clumsy idiot"	Frowns, straightens pieces	Play quietly
3. Kevin grabs most of Jack's money	Tries to grab it back, hits Kevin	Sharon laughs, takes more of his money
4. Called "cheater"	Says "I didn't cheat"	Kids laugh, keep calling him cheater, others join in
5. Bell rings, Sharon grabs his coat	Screams, roughly pulls coat, hits her over head	Teacher pulls him away, Jack stays

Figure 8.1. Example of anecdotal recording of aggression.

one that has at least 30 seconds (Cummings et al., 1989) to 1 minute (Shapiro et al., 1985) of "aggressive-free" behavior following the tantrum or outburst.

Although the researchers appeared to be effective in counting the number of outbursts, their definition of the target behavior violates another criterion for frequency counts which suggests that each incident of a countable behavior should be roughly equivalent in duration. As Barton and Ascione (1984) point out, one tantrum may last just a minute or two and another may last for more than an hour. To say that a child exhibited three tantrums in a day is not very meaningful if the length of the behaviors varies greatly from incident to incident.

A third criterion for using a frequency count is to avoid counting behaviors that occur at a very high rate because it becomes very difficult to separate one occurrence of the behavior from the next and therefore observer error becomes more of a problem (Salvia & Ysseldyke, 1991). Methods of counting the number of times a child taps a pencil or drums his or her fingers are examples of impractical uses of the frequency recording procedure. In contrast, if the behavior of interest is the number of times a student hits other students during recess, this is (it is hoped) an infrequent enough behavior to allow an accurate frequency count.

The data collected through frequency recording can be stated simply as the number of times the behavior occurred during the time period. In addition, the data can be reported in terms of the rate of the behavior by dividing the number of instances by the time period. For example, if a child threw her book on the floor five times in a 15-minute observation period, the rate of book throwing would be once every 3 minutes.

Many of the studies that report behavioral observation data on aggression use a frequency recording procedure to count the number of aggressive outbursts (Dangel et al., 1989; Forman, 1980; Kettlewell & Kausche, 1983; Luiselli & Slocumb, 1983; McCullough, Huntsinger, & Nay, 1977; Murphy et al., 1983). In a somewhat different approach, Bostow and Bailey (1969) used a tape recorder to measure the verbal behavior of a woman with mental retardation who was loud and verbally abusive. The tape recorder was set so that any verbalizations or sounds above a specific threshold were recorded as "blips" on the recorder. The researchers simply kept track of the number of "blips" in a 60-minute period as a way of monitoring changes in her verbal behavior as a result of intervention.

An example of a creative use of frequency recording of aggression in the schools can be found in Murphy et al.'s (1983) study of the effects of organized games on playground aggression. Their research focused on the inappropriate, largely aggressive, behaviors of 344 K–2 children assigned to a playground prior to the beginning of the school day. Observations were conducted on aggression, property abuse, and rule violations. Aggression was defined as striking, slapping, tripping, kicking, pushing or pulling others; "karate" moves ending within 1 foot of another person; and doing anything that ends with another child falling on the ground. Initially, a system for observing large numbers of children roaming freely over a large, open area was developed. The playground was divided into three roughly equivalent "pie slices" (defined by permanent structures such as building corners or playground equipment), which were the responsibility of three separate observers. These slices on the playground were then halved and each half was monitored for alternate 15-second periods. Thus, an observer attended to only one sixth of the playground at a time, and only half of the playground was observed at any given moment. Each aggressive behavior was counted once with the use of hand counters. At the end of every 2 minutes, observers entered the frequency of incidents on their data sheets. A particular aggressive behavior directed at one child by another individual was only counted once per 15-second interval. However, more than one incident was scored if one child inflicted several types of aggression on another (e.g., one child hitting and kicking another resulted in two incidents being counted). In either the case of two children assaulting a third individual, or one child assaulting two peers, two incidents were scored. The 15-second intervals were considered independent; thus, if two children were observed to be wrestling with one another for two intervals, four incidents were scored. Using this unique observation system, the researchers were able to assess the frequency of aggressive behavior on the playground. They found that games, rope jumping, and foot racing, along with an infrequently used time-out procedure for particularly unruly behaviors, significantly reduced the frequency of inappropriate incidents.

Interval recording/time sampling. Another commonly used procedure for collecting behavioral observation data is to break the observation period down into equal time intervals and then record the presence or absence of behavior within those intervals. The interval recording method has the advantage of being useful with behaviors that are continuous (lack discrete beginnings and endings) or high frequency. In contrast, this method is not useful with behaviors that are very infrequent.

There are several procedures for collecting interval recording data. One technique, *partial interval recording,* involves recording the behavior if it occurs at any time within the interval. Although this is the most frequently used interval recording method, it has the distinct disadvantage of providing an overestimate of the occurrence of the behavior (Shapiro, 1987; Shapiro & Skinner, 1990). For example, if an observer used 1-minute intervals to observe how often one student touched other students while sitting in an assembly, the observer may find that the behavior occurred in 100% of the intervals observed, which gives the impression that the behavior occurred constantly. However, it may have only occurred for a second or two in each interval. The shorter the intervals used, the less likely that the partial-interval recording procedure will provide an overestimate of the behavior.

Several studies have reported observational data on aggression through the partial interval procedure. The use of a 10-second partial interval procedure for observing the aggressive, self-injurious, or disruptive behavior of children with mental retardation was reported in several studies (Horner et al., 1991; Mace et al., 1986). Santogrossi, O'Leary, Romanczyk, and Kaufman (1973) used 30-second intervals to observe the aggressive behavior of nine emotionally disturbed adolescent boys with high rates of disruptive and aggressive classroom behavior. Each student was observed for a 15-minute block of time. These researchers broke the observation interval into a 20-second observation period and a 10-second recording period. Building a recording-only period into an interval decreases the probability of making a recording error because the observer is able to take his or her attention away from the student briefly in order to mark the recording sheet accurately. The researchers in this study found that a token reinforcement system based on teacher ratings of behavior reduced student disruptiveness more effectively than allowing the students to self-evaluate their levels of disruptiveness.

A shorter interval of 15 seconds with no recording time was used by Archer et al. (1988) when assessing the aggressive behavior of elementary-age children to see if gender differences exist. The students were each observed for eight 5-minute blocks of time during which they were free to choose their own activity and move around the classroom. An initial period of time was allotted to facilitate the children's adjustment to the observer's presence. One half of the 5-minute blocks were in the morning and the other half were in the afternoon. The raters recorded the presence and/or absence of each category of aggressive behavior in successive 15-second intervals. Therefore, each of the eight 5-minute blocks had 20 discrete frames during which behaviors were recorded. Archer et al.'s study indicated that boys showed more physical aggression than girls and that girls demonstrated more verbal aggression than boys.

In contrast to the 15-second and 30-second intervals used by Archer et al. (1988) and Santogrossi et al. (1973), a much more taxing partial interval procedure was used by Zahavi and Asher (1978) to observe the aggressive behavior of eight preschool children. These researchers used only 6-second intervals with no recording period, rotating their observations each interval to another child. Observer error and fatigue can occur quickly in this type of observational system so the observation periods should be kept fairly short. Zahavi and Asher (1978) found that the preschoolers decreased their aggressive behavior and increased their positive prosocial behaviors when teachers explained the harmful effects of aggression and the possible benefits of alternative prosocial behaviors.

The other approach to interval recording is *whole interval recording* which requires that the behavior occur throughout the entire interval in order to be recorded (Salvia & Ysseldyke, 1991). The whole interval approach is not utilized as often because it requires continuous observation of the student and is difficult to use when observing multiple behaviors. The whole interval procedure also provides an underestimate of the behavior occurrence because if the behavior occurs for 28 seconds out of a 30-second interval it would not be recorded (Shapiro & Skinner, 1990). As with partial interval procedures, the shorter the interval, the more accurate is the estimate of behavior. No studies were found that used a whole interval procedure for assessing aggression.

Decisions about the length of observation intervals and allocation of recording time should be based on factors such as the number of behaviors and/or students being observed, the frequency of the behavior, and the extent to which other tasks place demands on the observer's time and attention. Generally, the shorter the interval, the more taxing it is on the observer. Therefore, the practitioner in the schools should select an interval size that will comfortably allow him or her to observe and record data accurately without losing too much information by having long intervals. If the observer is going to switch between a target and a comparison peer each interval, a recording period should be included to give the observer time to orient to the other student. As a general guide, the observer may wish to start with 15-second intervals that allow for 10 seconds of observation and 5 seconds of recording. The observer may decide to switch to longer intervals if this schedule is too difficult. In most cases, it is not a good idea to shorten intervals less than 10 seconds because observer error is likely to occur.

A third type of interval recording procedure, called *time sampling*, is often referred to as a separate category of observation. Although equal intervals are used in this procedure, the behavior is not observed during the interval but rather once at the onset of the interval. For example, if a playground monitor was using a 5-minute time-sampling procedure to observe the physical aggression of a student during recess, the observer may set her watch to beep every 5 minutes and at the beep look at the student to see if the target behavior was occurring at that precise moment. Time-sampling procedures are very practical for use in the schools because they do not require constant observation and therefore allow the observer to focus on other tasks as well, such as teaching or monitoring other students. Although long intervals such as 5 to 30 minutes are used often by teachers, most of the studies utilizing time-sampling methods of recording aggressive behavior used outside observers and therefore had much briefer 10-second intervals (Allen, Chinsky, Larcen, Lochman, & Selinger, 1976; Forman, 1980; Lochman et al., 1984; Santogrossi et al., 1973). It is not advisable to use time-sampling procedures, especially ones with large intervals, to observe low-frequency behaviors because it minimizes the chance that you will actually be observing the behavior when it occurs (Shapiro, 1987). For any of the interval observation procedures described here, it is important that the behavioral findings be reported in terms of the percentage of intervals observed rather than percentage of time (i.e., "Rick hit other students in 65% of the intervals observed," *not* "Rick hit other students 65% of the time"). This reporting practice minimizes the chance that the frequency of the behavior will be misinterpreted by others.

Duration or latency recording. With some low-frequency behaviors, such as tantruming, it may be more useful to record the length of the behavioral occurrence rather than just the frequency of the behavior. With duration recording, the observer starts a stopwatch with the onset of the target behavior and turns it off when the behavior stops. To use this procedure, the behavior of interest must be one that has a clear onset and end so timing can be accurate. Latency recording involves measuring the amount of time between the introduction of a stimulus and the beginning of a response by the student. Although latency recording is most frequently used in situations where the observer is measuring compliance with directions, it could also be used in anger-related studies measuring the amount of time between an antagonistic stimulus and a response by the student. The goal of the intervention may be to increase the latency of response by the student in order to decrease impulsive, aggressive responses. No studies on the use of latency recording for aggression were found. It is unlikely that latency recording of aggression will be the procedure of choice in the schools unless the practitioner is specifically looking at increasing self-control behaviors. Duration recording is more likely to be useful in assessing aggression, especially in combination with frequency recording (Pettit, Bakshi, Dodge, & Coie, 1990; Shapiro et al., 1985).

Permanent products. All of the observation procedures described so far have the potential for inadvertently altering the target behavior due to the reactive effects on the student being observed. In contrast, the observation of permanent products involves observing the lasting outcomes of the behavior and can therefore be done when the student is not present. For example, if a highly aggressive student tends to act out by destroying her or his own property, the teacher could keep a record of the number of crumpled worksheets, broken pencils, torn book pages, or any other type of destructive behavior. Although the observation of permanent products tends to be more accurate and reliable because of its lasting nature, it may not provide as valid a measure of anger because it does not allow the observer to record the situational context of the behavior, including antecedents and consequences. Several studies have used recorded consequences given for aggressive behavior as a way of monitoring aggression (Elder et al., 1979; Feindler et al., 1984). Feindler et al.'s (1984) study on aggressive and disruptive junior high students looked at the number of single and double fines given to the students as an indicator of mild and severe aggressive behavior exhibited in the classroom. The authors point out a major limitation of this approach, stating that "...the continuous archival-type data...do not reflect observed changes in discrete, aggressive responding by the adolescents but rather reflect the staff behaviors of discriminating, recording, and consequating disruptive behaviors" (p. 309).

Combined methods. Most of the methods described in this section can be combined with other methods to provide a more informative and meaningful measure of the target behavior(s). Frequency recording (if the behavior does not occur at a high rate) can often be combined with another measure such as interval recording and duration recording. Frequency within interval recording involves counting the number of behavioral occurrences within equal interval periods. This not only provides a measure of how often the behavior occurs but also the temporal pattern of the behavior (i.e., many instances occurring close together and then none for several intervals). Many studies have used a combined frequency within interval procedure for assessing aggressive behavior (Bostow & Bailey, 1969; Carr et al. 1980; Drabman et al., 1973; Humphrey & Karoly, 1978; Mace et al., 1986; Slifer et al., 1986; Turkewitz et al., 1975). Other studies have used a combination of frequency and duration recording (Pettit et al., 1990; Shapiro et al., 1985), which not only provides information on the number of occurrences and duration but also allows the observer to calculate the average length of each behavioral response. The flow chart presented in Figure 8.2 provides a guide for determining the appropriate observational method for each behavior/situation.

Important Considerations in Behavioral Observation of Anger and Aggression

There are several factors in addition to defining the behavior operationally and choosing an appropriate observation procedure that can influence the validity of behavioral observations. The effects of the observer on the student, the context of the behavior, the use of comparative peer observations, the reliability of the observation, and the use of recording devices can all impact the data collected or the conclusions regarding the data.

Reactivity of observations. Just the presence of the observer in the classroom or on the playground can alter the behavior being observed (Reid, Baldwin, Patterson, & Dishion, 1988; Shapiro & Skinner, 1990). Students are usually aware of observers and, even if they are unaware of the purpose for the observer's presence, they may behave differently around him or her. The more familiar the person is to the students within the classroom setting, the quicker the students will habituate to his or her presence and revert to their typical patterns of behavior. Therefore, observers may wish to spend some time sitting in the classroom before actually observing and recording behavior so the students can get used to their presence. Observers can further minimize the reactive nature of their presence by sitting to the side of or behind the students rather than in the front of the room and by being careful not to stare at any one student (Salvia & Ysseldyke, 1991).

Situational context. Although the primary interest of the observer may be the anger-related behavior of the student, it is also important to understand the situation or context in which the behavior occurs as well as the conditions maintaining the behavior (Green & Forehand, 1980). Particular variables to notice are the antecedents or stimulus for the behavior, the consequences of the behavior, and the setting in which the behavior occurs (i.e., math class, small group reading, lunchroom, walking to and from assemblies, etc.). Recording the antecedents and consequences of the behavior is important because it gives the observer clues about the types of interventions that may be successful with the student (Shapiro, 1987).

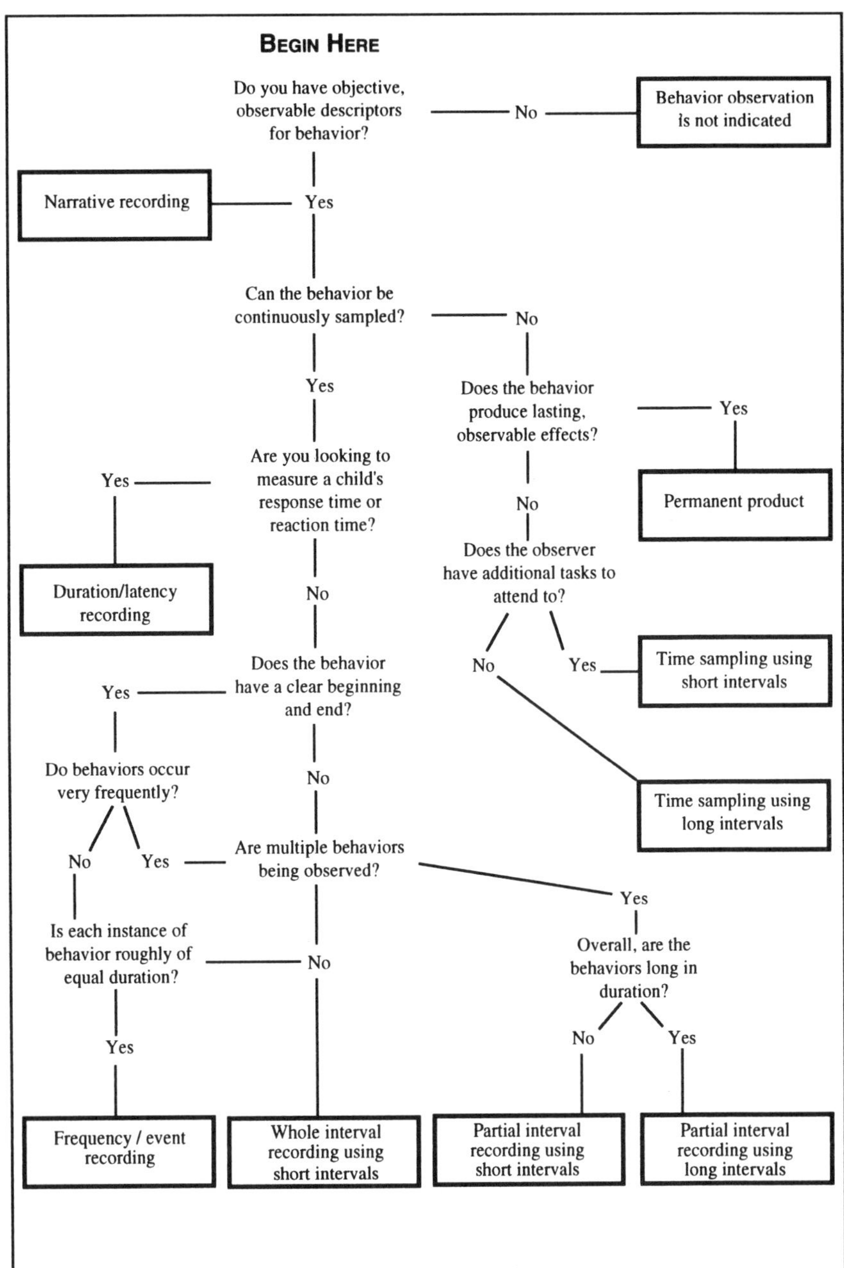

FIGURE 8.2. MODEL FOR SELECTION OF OBSERVATION METHODS.

There are several structured observation systems that are set up to allow the observer to record sequences of behavior in the classroom (Breyer & Calchera, 1971; Harris & Reid, 1981; Saudargas & Creed, 1980). Most involve a coding system for describing the type of instructional setting (large group instruction, small group instruction, individual seatwork). In addition, some look at antecedents in teacher and/or peer behaviors. Similarly, the observation systems often include information about how others respond to the target student's behavior and whether the response was positive, negative, or neutral. Most school-based observation systems are academic-related, such as on-task behaviors. However, Harris and Reid's (1981) Behavior Coding System is an interval recording procedure that looks specifically at coercive and aggressive behavior in the classroom and on the playground. The main limitations of the structured systems are that they do not necessarily focus on the behavior of interest for that particular student and they tend to require many hours of intensive observer training (Reid et al., 1988).

It is not only important to identify antecedents and consequences within a classroom environment but also to get a sample of the student's behavior in a variety of settings within the school (Shapiro, 1987). It is helpful to get information in both academic and nonacademic settings (lunchroom, recess) but also settings that differ, for example, in size of group, subject matter, or degree of structure. The more settings investigated, the more information the psychologist or teacher has about whether or not the behavioral concerns are isolated to a few conditions or generalized across a variety of conditions (Salvia & Ysseldyke, 1991).

Natural vs. controlled settings. In most cases, observers are interested in assessing naturally occurring behavior within the school environment. However, in some cases it may be more efficient to design a situation that is intentionally likely to elicit the target behavior, whether it be aggression, assertiveness, or problem-solving (Bornstein et al., 1980; Horner et al., 1991; Pentz, 1980; Pettit et al., 1990; Schlichter & Horan, 1981). The advantage of having a staged setting is that it gives the observer a greater opportunity to assess the behavior of interest. On the other hand, the staged or analogue setting may not accurately reflect the characteristics of naturally occurring events that are associated with anger and aggression and would therefore sacrifice the validity of the data collected. Most observations in the school environment would be considered observations in the natural setting, whether it be the classroom, playground, bus line, or lunchroom. However, observations during structured counseling sessions or small group lessons on social skills that explicitly involve role-playing would be considered controlled settings because the situation in which the student is to perform is artificial. Extra care needs to be taken in these situations to make the artificial situation as much like the natural situation as possible. If not, assessment of naturally occurring student behavior may be missing and generalizability of interventions would be limited.

Comparison peers. One of the important pieces of information lacking in a behavioral observation of a single student is whether or not the student's behavior is similar to or different from that of other peers. There are several different approaches one can take to gather peer comparison data within the school environment. First of all, the observer can ask the teacher to identify a *typical* student of the same sex in the classroom and then alternate observations of the target student with the typical peer on the behaviors of interest. Another procedure for selecting a comparison peer is for the observer to select a same-sex student randomly through the class list or seating chart. Instead of choosing just one comparison peer, the observer may decide to observe multiple comparison peers systematically in the classroom. For example, the observer may select six peers at random from the class. Using a 10-second partial interval recording system, the first 10-second observation would be of the target student, the second would be of the first comparison peer, then the target student, then the second comparison peer, and so forth. In a 2-minute time period, the observer would have a sample of six peers. The data for the six peers would be combined and compared to the data for the target student to see if there are differences. Similarly, the observer may choose to take a broad sample of peer behavior by periodically scanning the entire classroom to determine the number of students engaging in a particular behavior at that moment (Alessi, 1980, 1988; Forman, 1980). The main reason for observing comparison peers in addition to target students is because some of the problematic behaviors observed in the target student may actually be normative for the classroom, indicating a possible problem with overall classroom management rather than an intraindividual problem.

Interobserver reliability. An important consideration whenever one is conducting behavioral observations is assessing the reliability of the observations. Interobserver reliability refers to the degree of agreement between two independent observers who are watching the same student or situation. The main reason for calculating interobserver reliability is to confirm that the recorded observational data are due to the behavior of the student being observed rather than the biases of the person doing the observation. Observers may record inaccurate data due to preconceptions about the referred student or due to fatigue or lack of concentration. Another potential threat to reliability is observer drift (Reid et al., 1988), when observers over time gradually change their criteria for the target behavior(s). Periodic reliability checks with an independent observer help correct for errors in observation and data recording. The agreement between the observers is typically expressed as percentage of agreement, ranging from 0% to 100%.

There are several different methods for calculating interobserver reliability. For frequency recording, agreement can be calculated by dividing the higher frequency into the lower frequency. For example, if the first rater counted 10 aggressive incidents and the second rater counted 12 incidents, the interrater reliability would be: $10 \div 12 = .83$ or 83%. The major disadvantage of this method is that the observers can get high or even perfect agreement (i.e., both observed 10 incidents of physical aggression) without actually agreeing on any particular occurrence of the behavior. The 10 instances recorded by the first observer may be completely different than the 10 recorded by the second observer.

If observations are recorded by interval, interobserver reliability can be calculated on agreement for each interval, leading to a more precise index of actual agreement. Only the intervals for which both observers agreed that the behavior did or did not occur would be counted. Out of 10 intervals, if both observers agreed on behavioral occurrences of aggression in 4 intervals and nonoccurrences of aggression in 4 intervals, the total agreement would be 8 out of 10 intervals or 80%. The problem with this procedure occurs when the vast majority of the intervals are scored with nonoccurrences of the behavior. If the behavior is scored on 2 out of 20 intervals, the two observers can obtain 90% agreement without actually agreeing at all on the 2 occurrences of the behavior. To avoid spuriously high reliabilities, the observers may want to calculate interobserver reliability for occurrences of the behavior separately from interobserver reliability for nonoccurrences.

The studies on behavioral observation of aggression vary in terms of the interobserver reliability reported. Several studies did not report any interobserver reliability procedures (Feindler et al., 1984; Hamberger & Lohr, 1980; Kettlewell & Kausch, 1983; McCullough et al., 1977; Shapiro et al., 1985) and only one of these (Shapiro et al., 1985) acknowledged the lack of reliability data. Those studies that used a frequency count calculated their reliability by dividing the higher frequency into the lower frequency for the time period (Bostow & Bailey, 1969; Carr et al., 1980; Luiselli &

Slocumb, 1983; Slifer et al., 1986). Many of the studies using interval-recording procedures reported reliability data but did not specify whether the agreements were based on occurrences, nonoccurrences, or both (Dangel et al., 1989; Goodwin & Mahoney, 1975; Lochman, Lampron, Burch, & Curry, 1985; Robin et al., 1976; Schlichter & Horan, 1981; Zahavi & Asher, 1978). In contrast, a number of studies explicitly stated that reliability was calculated on the occurrences of behavior only (Bornstein et al., 1980; Drabman et al., 1973; Elder et al., 1979; Forman, 1980; Humphrey & Karoly, 1978; Santogrossi et al., 1973). Only one study reviewed in this chapter (Mace et al., 1986) reported separate reliability indexes for occurrence, nonoccurrence, and total intervals. In most cases, the reliabilities reported in these published studies were adequate to excellent (80% to 100%), although some were quite low (below 30%).

Although it is likely that most observations that occur within the school do *not* include data on interobserver reliability, it is strongly recommended that school practitioners make a point of starting to collect reliability data on a regular basis. The federal guidelines for the assessment of students for special education explicitly state that assessment measures should be reliable and valid for the purpose for which they are being used. The same expectations hold true for behavioral observations. A psychologist who states that a child's aggressive behavior is occurring at twice the rate of his or her peers needs to have reliable data to support this statement. The reliability data can be collected by training another staff member in the school in the use of observation procedures and in the behavioral definitions being utilized. Both observers need to observe the same student at the exact same time in order to compare their results, but they should not stand so close that they can see what the other observer is recording. Observers should aim for reliability of 80% or greater. Low reliability suggests that more training is necessary and/or that the behavioral definition needs to be modified so it is more specific. Adding a range of examples of behaviors that should be recorded and those that should *not* be recorded may help increase the reliability of the observations. Finally, if low reliability is a problem, the observers may want to reduce the complexity of their observation system. The more complex the observational procedure in terms of the number of behaviors being observed and interval length, the more likely that reliability problems will occur (Reid et al., 1988).

Recording apparatus. There are several items that can help make the observer's job a bit easier. First of all, it is quite helpful to have an observation form written out ahead of time that includes boxes for each observation interval, a list of behavioral codes for recording data, and a place to write narrative notes during the observation. An example of a generic interval observation form is presented in Figure 8.3; a second example of this form is completed for the case study. Some observation systems come with pre-made observation recording forms. Alternatively, the observer can usually develop a template for an observation form that is flexible enough in structure to use for a variety of observations.

Self-Monitoring of Anger

Another viable option for assessing anger through observation is to rely on self-observation or self-monitoring, in which the student observes his or her own behavior and/or affect and provides systematic objective records of these observations (Cone, 1978; Gardner & Cole, 1988; Shapiro, 1984). Self-monitoring is particularly appealing in assessing anger (Novaco, 1976, 1977; Schlichter & Horan, 1981) because much of the experience of anger is internal and therefore unavailable for direct observation by an outside party.

Training students to self-monitor. In order for students to monitor their anger and aggressive behavior effectively, they must be given some specific training on identifying and recognizing the relevant behaviors (Garrison & Stolberg, 1983) as well as procedures for recording their observations. The relevant behaviors must be clearly defined, along with a range of examples. For the purposes of this section, behavior is used in a more general way to describe any relevant target of self-observation, including overt behaviors, cognitions, emotions, and physiological symptoms. In the case of observing overt behavior, the student can be trained using the same kind of objective definition as outside observers use when conducting behavioral observations. However, definitions of internal, covert states such as angry feelings or thoughts are more difficult to specify. In many cases, the definition will be dependent on how the students verbalize the specific thoughts, emotions, and physiological changes that they notice when they experience anger (McCullough et al., 1977). Specific individual physiological signs may be particularly relevant in developing a definition of anger for the student. For example, Ben may identify anger as a tight feeling in his stomach along with a rapidly increasing heart rate. On the other hand, Shannon may experience tense shoulder and neck muscles and a flushed face when she is angry. As much as possible, it is necessary to get a complete description of the behavioral, physiological, emotional,

Student Observation

Student: Activity/Setting:

Date: Time Start: Time Stop: Observer:

Interval Length: Behavioral Codes:

Observation Method: Partial Interval =
Whole Interval =
Time Sampling =

Definition of Behavior:

Comments

Figure 8.3 Generic interval observation redording form.

and cognitive changes accompanying anger in the student in order to define the behavior thoroughly.

Once the student and the school psychologist are both clear on the behavioral signs associated with anger, the student needs to be a given a simple and unobtrusive method for recording his or her observations. Many times this will involve a recording form taped to the student's desk or the use of other recording devices such as a wrist counter (Shapiro, 1984) or the transferring of small tokens or objects from one pocket to another. The recording device needs to be obvious enough to serve as a cue for self-monitoring without being so obtrusive that it embarrasses the student or distracts from the teaching process (Gardner & Cole, 1988). If students are expected to monitor their anger in multiple settings, the data collection device must be portable.

Self-monitoring procedures. The observation systems applicable to self-monitoring are similar to those used by external observers. Initially, the student may be asked to keep a narrative record or behavioral diary of their anger and the circumstances surrounding the experience of anger (Dangel et al., 1989). The narrative comments can provide valuable cues about the definition of anger for the student as well as possible antecedents and consequences (Gardner & Cole, 1988). As with narrative recordings by outside observers, the student's narrative description is helpful but generally not sufficient for assessing the target behaviors because it does not provide a consistent and systematic measure. Therefore, more systematic procedures such as frequency counts and time sampling can be implemented by the student in self-monitoring of anger.

Students may be asked to keep a frequency count of behaviors they exhibit or of feelings or thoughts that they experience during the school day (Shapiro, 1987). The frequency count is recommended for behaviors that are fairly low-frequency, short in duration, and discrete (Gardner & Cole, 1988). The self-monitoring of emotions or physiological changes may be difficult to do using this procedure because of the unclear beginning and end and the potentially long duration of the behaviors. On the other hand, overt behaviors such as hitting or pencil-snapping or internal negative thoughts such as "that's not fair" may be more amenable to frequency counts. For continuous or high-frequency behaviors, the student may be trained to use a time-sampling procedure. The student is given a periodic signal or cue at which time he or she does a brief self-check to see if any of the behaviors associated with anger are present at that moment and then records the presence or absence of these behaviors.

Accuracy of self-monitoring data. One major methodological concern regarding the use of self-monitoring as an assessment tool is the accuracy of the data collected by the student (Gardner & Cole, 1988; Santogrossi et al., 1973; Shapiro, 1984; Wilson, 1984). When overt behaviors are being assessed, the most preferable measure of accuracy is to compare the student's self-recordings with those made by an outside observer. However, if the target behaviors are covert thoughts or emotions, the observations of the external observer may or may not be relevant. The observer may note only one incident of overt aggression during an observation period whereas the student may report several episodes of anger identified through cognitions and physiological symptoms.

Another alternative to assessing accuracy of self-monitoring is to use some sort of permanent product measure. In the case of anger, relevant permanent products could be counting damaged or destroyed materials such as broken pencils, crumpled worksheets, etc. However, there is still the problem of matching an overt behavioral outcome to the measurements of an internal state. Physiological recording devices such as galvanic skin monitors and heart rate monitors can be used to measure the physiological aspects of anger but may not be practical for use in a classroom setting.

The accuracy of self-monitoring data is influenced by many factors, including the type of recording device used, the student's awareness of accuracy checks, reinforcement of the student for accurate self-monitoring, and the positive or negative valence of the behavior being monitored. Negatively valanced behaviors tend to be less accurately self-monitored than are positively valanced behaviors, possibly due to the subject's negative self-evaluation when the behavior is observed and subsequent reluctance to record the data (Gardner & Cole, 1988; Kanfer, 1977). Because behaviors associated with anger and hostility are considered negative by most people, accuracy of self-monitored anger may be less than optimal.

Reactivity in self-monitoring. In addition to concerns about assessments of accuracy, self-monitoring data are subject to a great deal of reactivity on the part of the student. Just the process of noticing one's own state of anger can alter the immediate experience of the anger. The reactive nature of self-monitoring is one reason why it is frequently used as an intervention procedure. However, the reactivity makes self-monitoring less reliable as an assessment tool. Generally, self-monitoring decreases the frequency of undesirable behaviors while increasing the frequency of desirable behaviors (Gardner & Cole, 1988).

The self-monitoring of anger has a definite appeal because it recognizes the fact that much of the experience of anger is internal and only available for self-observation. However, because of the problems with assessing accuracy and the reactive nature of the process, self-monitoring as an assessment tool may not provide the level of precise and accurate information desired for measurement purposes. Therefore, it is recommended that self-monitoring procedures, if used, should be supplemented with direct assessments of observable behavior by an outside observer.

Visual Analysis of Findings

Once observational data collection is complete, the means by which it is reviewed or analyzed is important as it may greatly influence interpretation of the findings. Visual analysis of graphed data is a method frequently used in single-subject assessments to determine the meaning of results. However, this approach is susceptible to bias in that it is based largely on common sense.

Furlong and Wampold (1981) outlined four issues to be considered when making visual inferences about the effects of an intervention on temporal changes in behavior. The issues are as follows: (a) Are the data reliable? (b) Did the observed behavior change when the intervention was in effect? (c) Were the observed changes in behavior meaningful and important? and (d) Will the intervention produce similar results in other children?

For the first issue, it must be determined if the behavior frequency or duration is consistent within the intervention phases or nonintervention phases (i.e., Is the rate of behavior steady when it is first being measured or does it fluctuate greatly?). The second issue addresses whether the intervention produced the desired reduction in behavior or if another factor was influencing change. For the third issue, the observer must ask whether the effects were immediate or delayed, and whether they were permanent or temporary. Finally, the fourth issue questions whether the intervention will reduce problem behaviors in other children in the classroom as well. By asking these questions of the results, visual appraisal of data will more accurately assess the impact and utility of a particular intervention.

The following case example illustrates how direct behavioral observation can be used to assess a child with anger-related difficulties.

PRACTICAL APPLICATION OF BEHAVIORAL OBSERVATION: A CASE EXAMPLE: KENNY, AGE 9

Student: Kenny Smith
Date of Birth: 2-20-84
Age: 9 yr., 2 mo.
Report Date: 4-30-93
Psychologist: S. Stein
Evaluation Dates: 4-20, 4/21, 4/23, 4/27
Grade: 3rd
Referral Source: Ms. Appleton (teacher)

Reason for Referral

Kenny was referred for behavioral assessment by his third-grade teacher because of frequent "angry outbursts" directed at other students during recess. A review of his school records and group achievement test scores indicates that he is functioning within the average range in all academic areas.

Definition of Target Behavior

The teacher reports that although Kenny is a good student in the classroom, he is an "emotional wreck" on the playground. The teacher states that she can safely predict that Kenny will be at the center of any major fight during morning recess. She has attempted to decrease Kenny's playground tantrums by lecturing him about fighting, making him stay by her side during recess or keeping him inside. In each case he promises to "be good" the next time but invariably "blows up" when he is given another chance.

When asked to describe what happens when Kenny "blows up" or has an "angry outburst," the teacher reports that he typically hits other students, screams, curses, and cries. The other children respond by taunting him and calling him a "big baby."

In order to gather more information about the problem behavior, the school psychologist observed Kenny for 15 minutes during morning recess on 4/20/93 using a narrative recording procedure where she wrote down what Kenny did during recess as well as how others interacted with him (Figure 8.4).

Based on this observation and the teacher's description, the psychologist and teacher agreed that the target behavior of "angry outburst" should be defined as any action intended to harm another including hitting, pushing, kicking, biting, throwing objects at another, damage to someone else's property, taking objects/toys away from another without their consent, teasing, taunting, swearing, cursing, screaming, or crying. It does not include accidental harm done to another person or to property (e.g., stepping back and accidentally stepping on someone's foot or knocking over a chair).

Summary of Systematic Observations

Because the target behavior selected for observation may or may not have a clear beginning and ending, the school psychologist decided to use a 15-second partial-interval recording procedure, with 10 seconds for observation and 5 seconds for recording. The psychologist decided to conduct five observations—three during recess, one during P.E., and one during free time in the classroom. The nonrecess settings were chosen because they represented other school situations in which Kenny was likely to interact with his peers. The observations varied in length, ranging from 15 minutes in the classroom to 30 minutes during lunch recess. In each setting, the school psychologist observed two other male peers who were nearby Kenny. Kenny was observed during the first and third intervals each minute, while the school psychologist took turns observing the other two peers during the second and fourth intervals. An example of the observation form for 4/21/93 is presented in Figure 8.5. The school counselor also observed once during morning recess in order to assess interobserver reliability. The results of the observations are summarized in Figure 8.6 in terms of the percentage of intervals in which the target behaviors were observed.

The interobserver reliability for the recess observation on 4/27 was calculated for agreement on occurrences (82%), agreement on nonoccurrences (89%), and total agreement (86%). These figures suggest that the observations were reliable.

The results of these observations clarified several factors regarding Kenny's angry outbursts with peers. First of all, it is clear that Kenny behaves much differently than his peers in regard to angry outbursts during morning recess. He was observed engaging in the target behavior 58% to 68% of the intervals observed versus the 19% to 22% for his peers. Second, Kenny's behavior during lunch recess, P.E., and free time in class is either the same or very similar to that of other boys in the setting. Although the precise antecedents and consequences for Kenny's angry outbursts have not been identified, several tentative hypotheses can be formed. One possibility is that Kenny has more difficulty interacting with older students (morning

Anecdotal Observation

Student: Kenny Smith Activity/Setting: Morning Recess

Date: 4-20-93 Time Start: 10:05 Time Stop: 10:20 Observer: Stein

Narrative Observation: Kenny runs on field after a soccer game has started. He stands at the side of the field. The soccer ball comes near, he grabs it and kicks it away from the field. A boy pushes Kenny down. Kenny runs on to the field yelling, "I'm playing forward."

Sequence of Behavior:

What Happened Before?	*What Did Student Do?*	*What Happened After?*
1. Soccer game	Runs on field	Watches alone
2. Ball near K.	Kicks ball away	Girls laugh at K.
3. Boy pushes K.	K. pushes back	Boys yell at K.
4. K. told to leave	K. kicks boy	Boy chases K.
5. Game restarts	K. pushes girls	Kids run to K.
6. Kids run to K.	K. hits others	Teacher grabs K.
7. K. taken to office	K. cries	Boys call K. a "crybaby"

Figure 8.4 Narrative observation of Kenny.

Student Observation

Student: Kenny Smith Activity/Setting: Morning Recess

Date: 4-20-93 Time Start: 10:03 Time Stop: 10:23 Observer: Karno

Interval Length: 10" observe; 5 " record Behavioral Codes:

Observation Method: Partial Interval X = Angry outburst
Whole Interval 0 = No angry outburst
Time Sampling___ = ________________

Definition of Behavior: Angry outburst = any action intended to harm another: hitting, pushing, kicking, biting, damage to property, taking toys, teasing, swearing.

Kenny	Peer 1	Kenny	Peer 2	Kenny	Peer 3	Comments
O	O	O	O	X	O	Tries to join soccer game
X	X	X	X	X	O	Teases girl, pulls hair
O	O	O	O	X	O	Pushes, watches game
O	X	X	O	X	O	Swears at a boy
X	O	O	O	X	X	Pushing
X	O	O	O	X	O	Takes ball
X	X	X	O	O	O	Pushing match with boy
X	O	X	O	X	X	Swearing
X	O	X	X	X	O	Trips boy, hit by boy
O	O	X	O	X	O	Name calling
X	X	X	O	O	O	Hits boy
O	O	X	O	O	O	Name calling
X	X	O	O	X	O	Pushing
X	O					**Kenny = 27/40 = 68%** **Peers = 9 /40 = 22%**

Figure 8.5 ***Observation of Kenny using 15-second partial interval recording and peer comparison.***

recess) than students his own age or younger. Another hypothesis is that Kenny lacks the necessary social skills for initiating play with others and therefore has the greatest difficulty in situations such as morning recess when he wants to join the activity of others. Each structured observation also included some narrative comments from the observer regarding the setting and the activities occurring during the observation. During the two morning recess observations, Kenny attempted to join in some games that were already in progress. Most of his difficulties seemed to be centered around joining into the games. In contrast, in the lunch recess period, Kenny was one of the first kids on the playground and had the playground equipment already checked out. The other kids approached him and asked him if they could play so he did not have to initiate any peer interactions. Additional functional analyses of Kenny's morning recess interactions can confirm or disconfirm these initial hypotheses.

The hypothesis that Kenny's angry outbursts are related to a lack of initiating skills is further supported by observations in P.E. and free time where aggressive behavior is also more likely to occur. During the P.E. observation, the teacher assigned the students to teams and gave them positions to play within the team so Kenny did not have to ask to join in. Similarly, Kenny did not have to approach other students during free play in the classroom because he used that time to play on the computer by himself. In both settings, Kenny's behavior was the same, or less problematic than his peers.

Further assessment of Kenny's ability to join in group activities appropriately could be conducted by delaying Kenny prior to lunch recess until other students have had a chance to get onto the playground and start games. If Kenny has the same problem during lunch recess, the psychologist can then rule out the factor that Kenny just gets along better with younger kids. In addition to looking at the antecedents of Kenny's outbursts, educators will want to alter systematically the consequences that occur after Kenny's outbursts (kids teasing him, going to the office, getting attention from others) to see which are maintaining his behavior. Some of the possible interventions might include social skills training in how to join groups appropriately (see Morrison & Sandowicz, Chapter 11), developing appropriate alternatives to aggression, teaching Kenny to identify the behavioral and physiological cues that occur prior to his problematic behavior, setting up a consistent staff plan to deal with Kenny's behavior, and training a subset of his peers to reinforce appropriate peer interactions.

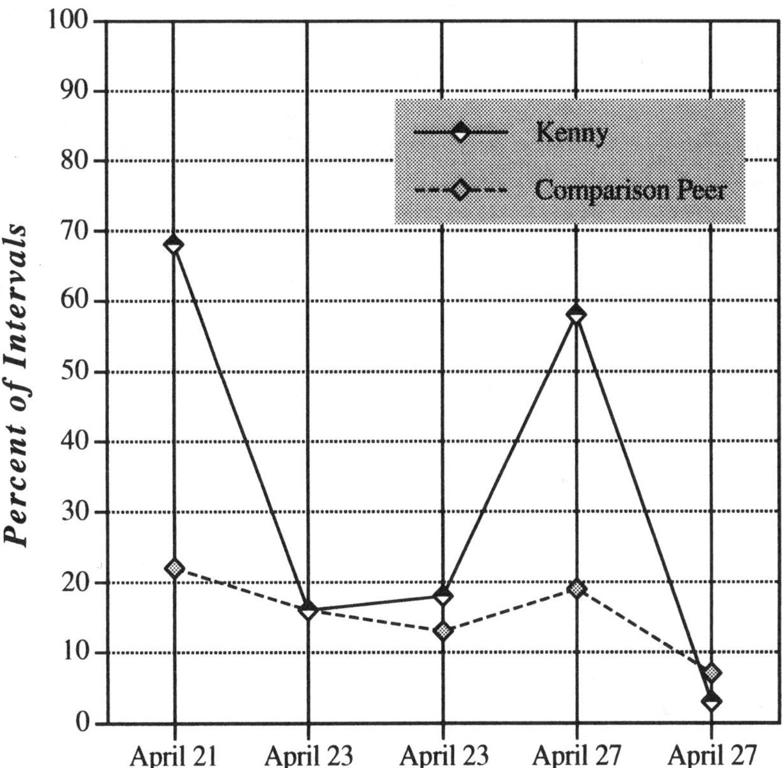

Observation Periods

AM Recess (3rd-5th) 20-minutes	PE Class (3rd) 18-minutes	Lunch Recess (1st-3rd)	AM Recess (3rd-5th) 18-minutes	Free Time (3rd class) 15-minutes
• K. tries to join ongoing soccer game	• Teacher assigns teams and positions kickball	• K. first on playground has soccer ball	• K. disrupts softball game	• K. Plays with computer

FIGURE 8.6 PERCENT OF INTERVALS WITH ANGRY OUTBURSTS FOR KENNY AND COMPARISON PEER.

SUMMARY

Behavioral observation of anger and aggression problems in the school is an important component of the assessment process. Although much of the experience of anger may be internal, there are often outward manifestations of anger in the form of physical or verbal aggression that can be systematically observed by others. Prior to conducting an observation, it is essential to have a clear, operational definition of the behavior(s) to be observed. After conducting an initial narrative record of behavior, the observer needs to decide whether to observe the behavior(s) using the procedures of frequency count, interval recording, time sampling, duration, latency, or measurement of permanent products. Choice of the most appropriate observation procedure depends on characteristics of the behavior being observed (i.e., frequency, duration, continuity) as well as competing demands placed on the observer (i.e., teaching, observing multiple behaviors, etc.).

Important considerations to keep in mind when conducting an observation include minimizing the reactivity of your observation and paying attention to antecedents and consequences of the behavior as well as other situational variables, such as whether the setting is natural or contrived. Whenever possible, it is a wise idea to collect data on comparison peers as well as the target student so you can determine how discrepant the student is from others in the same setting. It is also strongly recommended that school practitioners make a point to collect interobserver reliability data on a sample of their observations to ensure that the results are accurate. There are a variety of recording devices, including general and specific observation record forms, that can be useful in conducting an observational assessment of anger and aggression. Visual analysis of the observational data collected through these procedures will be most useful for planning and evaluating interventions if the practitioner follows specific guidelines for interpreting graphed single-subject data.

Self-monitoring by the student provides an alternate way of assessing the aspects of anger that are difficult to assess through outside observers (i.e., physical sensations, muscular tension, emotions). However, the problems of determining the accuracy of self-monitoring data as well as the reactivity of this procedure limit its usefulness as an assessment tool without the additional information provided through the direct assessment of observable behavior.

REFERENCES

Alessi, G. J. (1980). Behavioral observation for the school psychologist: Responsive-discrepancy model. *School Psychology Review, 9,* 31-45.

Alessi, G. J. (1988). Direct observation methods for emotional/behavioral problems. In E. S. Shapiro & T. R. Kratochwill (Eds.), *Behavioral assessment in schools: Conceptual foundations and practical applications* (pp. 14-75). New York: Guilford.

Allen, G. J., Chinsky, J. M., Larcen, S. W., Lochman, J. E., & Selinger, H. V. (1976). *Community psychology and the schools: A behaviorally oriented multilevel preventive approach.* Hillsdale, NJ: Lawrence Erlbaum.

Archer, J., Pearson, N. A., & Westeman, K. E. (1988). Aggressive behaviour of children aged 6-11: Gender differences and their magnitude. *British Journal of Social Psychology, 27,* 371-384.

Assembly Bill 2586. (1992). *Proposed regulations for implementation of education code.* California State Assembly.

Barfield, C. K., & Hutchinson, M. A. (1990). Observations of adolescent anger and an anger control group in residential day treatment. *Residential Treatment for Children and Youth, 7,* 45-58.

Barton, E. J., & Ascione, F. R. (1984). Direct observation. In T. H. Ollendick & M. Hersen (Eds.), *Child behavioral assessment: Principles and procedures* (pp. 166-194). New York: Pergamon.

Bornstein, M., Bellack, A. S., & Hersen, M. (1980). Social skills training for highly aggressive children. *Behavior Modification, 4,* 173-186.

Bostow, D. E., & Bailey, J. B. (1969). Modification of severe disruptive and aggressive behavior using brief timeout and reinforcement procedures. *Journal of Applied Behavior Analysis, 2,* 31-37.

Breyer, N. L., & Calchera, D. J. (1971). A behavioral observation schedule for pupils and teachers. *Psychology in the Schools, 8,* 330-337.

Camras, L. A. (1977). Facial expressions used by children in a conflict situation. *Child Development, 48,* 1431-1435.

Carr, E. G., Newsom, C. D., & Binkoff, J. A. (1980). Escape as a factor in the aggressive behavior of two retarded children. *Journal of Applied Behavior Analysis, 13,* 101-117.

Cone, J. D. (1978). The Behavioral Assessment Grid (BAG): A conceptual framework and a taxonomy. *Behavior Therapy, 9,* 882-888.

Cummings, E. M., Iannotti, R. J., & Zahn-Waxler, C. (1989). Aggression between peers in early childhood: Individual continuity and developmental change. *Child Development, 60,* 887-895.

Dangel, R. F., Deschner, J. P., & Rasp, R. R. (1989). Anger control training for adolescents in residential treatment. *Behavior Modification, 13,* 447-458.

Drabman, R. S., Spitalnik, R., & O'Leary, K. D. (1973). Teaching self-control to disruptive children. *Journal of Abnormal Psychology, 82,* 10-16.

Elder, J. P., Edelstein, B. A., & Narick, M. M. (1979). Adolescent psychiatric patients: Modifying aggressive behavior with social skills training. *Behavior Modification, 3,* 161-178.

Feindler, E. L., Marriott, S. A., & Iwata, M. (1984). Group anger control for junior high school delinquents.*Cognitive Therapy and Research, 8,* 299-311.

Forman, S. G. (1980). A comparison of cognitive training and response-cost procedures in modifying aggressive behavior of elementary school children. *Behavior Therapy, 11,* 594-600.

Furlong, M. J., & Wampold, B. E. (1981). Visual analysis of single-subject studies by school psychologists. *Psychology in the Schools, 18,* 80-86.

Galvin, P.P., & Singleton, R. M. (1984). *Behaviour problems: A system of management.* Windsor, Great Britain: Nfer-Nelson.

Gardner, W. I., & Cole, C. L. (1988). Self-monitoring procedures. In E. S. Shapiro & T. R. Kratochwill (Eds.), *Behavioral assessment in schools: Conceptual foundations and practical applications* (pp. 206-246). New York: Guilford.

Garrison, S. R., & Stolberg, A. L. (1983). Modification of anger in children by affective imagery training. *Journal of Abnormal Child Psychology, 11,* 115-130.

Goodenough, F. L. (1931). *Anger in young children.* Institute of Child Welfare Monograph Series No. 9. Minneapolis: University of Minnesota Press.

Goodwin, S. E., & Mahoney, M. J. (1975). Modification of aggression through modeling: An experimental probe. *Journal of Behavior Therapy & Experimental Psychiatry, 6,* 200-202.

Green, K. D., & Forehand, R. (1980). Assessment of children's social skills: A review of methods. *Journal of Behavioral Assessment, 2,* 143-159.

Hamberger, K., & Lohr, J. M. (1980). Rational restructuring for anger control: A quasi-experimental case study.*Cognitive Therapy and Research, 4,* 99-102.

Harris, A. M., & Reid, J. B. (1981). The consistency of a class of coercive child behaviors across school settings for individual subjects. *Journal of Abnormal Child Psychology, 9,* 219-227.

Horner, R. H., Day, H. M., Sprague, J. R., O'Brien, M., & Heathfield, L. T. (1991). Interspersed requests: A nonaversive procedure for reducing aggression and self-injury during instruction. *Journal of Applied Behavior Analysis, 24,* 265-278.

Hughes, J. N., & Sullivan, K. A. (1988). Outcome assessment in social skills training with children. *Journal of School Psychology, 26,* 167-183.

Humphrey, L. L., & Karoly, P. (1978). Self-management in the classroom: Self-imposed response cost versus self-reward. *Behavior Therapy, 9,* 592-601.

Kanfer, F. H. (1977). The many faces of self-control. In R. B. Stuart (Ed.), *Behavioral self-management: Strategies, techniques, and outcomes* New York: Brunner/Mazel.

Kettlewell, P. W., & Kausch, D. F. (1983). The generalization of the effects of a cognitive-behavioral treatment program for aggressive children. *Journal of Abnormal Child Psychology, 11,* 101-114.

Lochman, J. E., Burch, P. R., Curry, J. F., & Lampron, L. B. (1984). Treatment and generalization effects of cognitive-behavioral and goal-setting interventions with aggressive boys. *Journal of Consulting and Clinical Psychology, 52,* 915-916.

Lochman, J. E., Lampron, L. B., Burch, P. R., & Curry, J. F. (1985). Client characteristics associated with behavior change for treated and untreated aggressive boys. *Journal of Abnormal Child Psychology, 13,* 527-538.

Luiselli, J. K., & Slocumb, P. R. (1983). Management of multiple aggressive behaviors by differential reinforcement. *Journal of Behavior Therapy and Experimental Psychiatry, 14,* 343-347.

Mace, F. C., Page, T. L., Ivancic, M. T., & O'Brien, S. (1986). Analysis of environmental determinants of aggression and disruption in mentally retarded children. *Applied Research in Mental Retardation, 7,* 203-221.

McCullough, J. P., Huntsinger, G. M., & Nay, R. (1977). Case study: Self control treatment of aggression in a 16-year-old male. *Journal of Consulting and Clinical Psychology, 45,* 322-331.

Murphy, H. A., Hutchison, J. M., & Bailey, J. S. (1983). Behavioral school psychology goes outdoors: The effect of organized games on playground aggression. *Journal of Applied Behavior Analysis, 16,* 29-35.

Novaco, R. (1976). The functions and regulation of the arousal of anger.

American Journal of Psychiatry, 133, 1124-1128.

Novaco, R. (1977). Stress inoculation: A cognitive therapy for anger and its application to a case of depression. *Journal of Consulting and Clinical Psychology, 45,* 600-608.

Pentz, M. A. W. (1980). Assertion training and trainer effects on unassertive and aggressive adolescents. *Journal of Counseling Psychology, 27,* 76-83.

Peterson, D. R. (1968). *The clinical study of social behavior.* New York: Appleton-Century-Crofts.

Pettit, G. S., Bakshi, A., Dodge, K. A., & Coie, J. D. (1990). The emergence of social dominance in young boys' play groups: Developmental differences and behavioral correlates. *Developmental Psychology, 26,* 1017-1025.

Reid, J. B., Baldwin, D. V., Patterson, G. R., & Dishion, T. J. (1988). Observations in the assessment of childhood disorders. In M. Rutter, A.H. Tuma, & I. A. Lann (Eds.), *Assessment and diagnosis in child psychopathology* (pp. 156-195). New York: Guilford Press.

Robin, A., Schneider, M., & Dolnick, M. (1976). The Turtle Techniques: An extended case study of self-control in the classroom. *Psychology in the Schools, 13,* 449-37.

Salvia, J., & Ysseldyke, J. E. (1991). *Assessment* (5th ed.). Boston: Houghton Mifflin.

Santogrossi, D. A., O'Leary, K. D., Romanczyk, R, G., & Kaufman, K. F. (1973). Self-evaluation by adolescents in a psychiatric hospital school token program. *Journal of Applied Behavior Analysis, 6,* 277-287.

Saudargas, R. A., & Creed, V. (1980). *State-event classroom observation system.* Knoxville, TN: University of Tennessee, Department of Psychology.

Schlichter, K. J., & Horan, J. J. (1981). Effects of stress inoculation on the anger and aggression management skills of institutionalized juvenile delinquents. *Cognitive Therapy and Research, 5,* 359-365.

Shapiro, E. S. (1984). Self-monitoring procedures. In T. H. Ollendick & M. Hersen (Eds.), *Child behavioral assessment: Principles and procedures* (pp. 148-165). New York: Pergamon.

Shapiro, E. S. (1987). *Behavioral assessment in school psychology.* Hillsdale, NJ: Lawrence Erlbaum.

Shapiro, E. S., Lentz, F. E., & Sofman, R. (1985). Validity of rating scales in assessing aggressive behavior in classroom settings. *Journal of School Psychology, 23,* 69-79.

Shapiro, E. S., & Skinner, C. H. (1990). Best practices in observation and ecological assessment. In A. Thomas & J. Grimes (Eds.), *Best practices in school psychology—II* (pp. 507-518). Washington, DC: National Association of School Psychologists.

Sherburne, S., Utley, B., McConnell, S., & Gannon, J. (1988). Decreasing violent or aggressive theme play among preschool children with behavior disorders. *Exceptional Children, 55,* 166-172.

Slifer, K. J., Ivancic, M. T., Parrish, J. M., Page, T. J., & Burgio, L. D. (1986). Assessment and treatment of multiple behavior problems exhibited by a profoundly retarded adolescent. *Journal of Behavior Therapy and Experimental Psychiatry, 17,* 203-213.

Stern, J. B., & Fodor, I.G. (1989). Anger control in children: A review of social skills and cognitive behavioral approaches to dealing with aggressive children. *Child and Family Behavior Therapy, 11*(3/4), 1-20.

Turkewitz, H., O'Leary, K. D., & Ironsmith, M. (1975). Generalization and maintenance of appropriate behavior through self-control. *Journal of Consulting and Clinical Psychology, 43,* 577-583.

Wilson, R. (1984). A review of self-control treatments for aggressive behavior. *Behavioral Disorders, 9,* 131-140.

Zahavi, S., & Asher, S. R. (1978). The effect of verbal instructions on preschool children's aggressive behavior. *Journal of School Psychology, 16,* 146-153.

9 PERSONALITY ASSESSMENT OF ANGER AND HOSTILITY IN CHILDREN AND ADOLESCENTS

Thomas J. Huberty and Gregory J. Eaken

Although anger and hostility are often experienced and observed in everyday life, relatively little has been written about their characteristics, causes, and development. Bowers (1987) describes anger as a conflictive emotion that has three components: (a) physical signs evident in increased muscle tension and flow of adrenaline; (b) behavioral indicators shown in a variety of aggressive behaviors, such as tantrums, although anger is not always expressed this way; and (c) a cognitive component, which reflects the child's perceptions and interpretations of others' behavior. Although anger is often associated with negative outcomes, it can be a positive factor in helping children to socialize and to solve problems. Because anger and hostility are subjective concepts, they are difficult to assess apart from aggression, creating unique diagnostic problems for clinicians. Therefore, projective and interview techniques that address cognitions, perceptions, and conflicts may be helpful in assessing anger and hostility.

PROJECTIVE TECHNIQUES

Assumptions and Characteristics

Projective measures typically use unstructured tasks or stimuli that a person is asked to complete, such as telling stories or drawing pictures. These techniques are considered to have no "right" or "wrong" answers, but rather to reflect perceptions that a person is unable or unwilling to verbalize.

These perceptions may be about needs or feelings, for example, or about views of the world and relationships with others. Despite their frequent use (Lubin, Larsen, & Matarazzo, 1984; Prout, 1983), however, projectives have some serious limitations. The interpretations may be affected by the conditions under which they are given, because often there are no standardized directions for administration (Klopfer & Taulbee, 1976), their interpretations may be influenced by the professional orientation of the examiner (Obrzut & Boliek, 1986), and they often have poor or nonexistent norms (Anastasi, 1988).

Interpretation of Projective Techniques

Because the administration and scoring of projectives often are ambiguous, the interpretation of the data can also become difficult, and may be subject to problems of reliability and validity. In assessment of this type, there is always the problem of inference in making interpretations. Inference refers to the process of evaluating the data and interpreting what they mean with regard to the person's behavior and presenting problems. As assessment techniques become more ambiguous and subject to a wide range of interpretations, the examiner must use higher levels of inference when drawing conclusions. Inferences should serve as guides to further investigation and generation of hypotheses that may later be confirmed, modified, or rejected (Groth-Marnat, 1990). Thus, a single indicator or group of indicators on any personality measure should be viewed tentatively and subjected to a confirmatory process via other data, especially observed behavior.

It should also be noted that there is a tendency for interpretations of projective material to be focused on negative, pathological signs, as opposed to signs of normal or positive adjustment. Groth-Marnat (1990) indicates that this bias toward pathology is particularly evident in guides to interpretation of projective drawings, in which minimal attention is given to positive signs, followed by a long list of negative indicators. The examiner must be particularly sensitive to this possible bias and look for signs of positive adjustment.

Considerations Regarding Projection in Children

Although projection in adults is often considered to reflect their "true" feelings and perceptions, similar conclusions may not be warranted for children. Obrzut and Boliek (1986) indicate that clinicians should consider that a child's age, developmental status, and verbal ability may affect the both the quality and quantity of responses. Thus, what might be considered a pathological sign in adults may merely reflect immaturity in a child that may be associated with limited social knowledge and verbal skills. Klein (1986) has indicated that projective production may be confounded by intelligence, age, gender, and reading ability, again indicating the need to consider developmental variables. The rapport developed between examiner and child and the overall social situation may be important factors in responsiveness to projective material (Obrzut & Boliek, 1986), with less quality and/or quantity of production being associated with inadequate rapport.

Assessing Anger and Hostility with Projective Measures

The available research has not provided clear distinctions between anger/hostility and aggression. As discussed in other chapters in this volume, aggression cannot automatically be equated with anger and hostility. Just as it is possible that a child could be angry and not show aggressiveness, s/he may also show aggressiveness and not be experiencing hostility or anger toward a person or object. The examiner must use a high degree of inference in concluding that anger is present in projective material, little of which is supported in the research literature. Therefore, indications of anger and hostility must be viewed with caution in projective material. If such indicators do exist, the examiner is well-advised to follow them up via interviews with the child and significant others.

Projective Drawings

Projective drawings have been frequently used in assessing children and adolescents in both school and clinic settings (Cummings, 1986; Lubin et al., 1984) and historically have been used as measures of intellectual development (Goodenough, 1926; Koppitz, 1968) and to assess an individual's impulses, self- concept, conflicts, and inner states (Machover, 1949). Koppitz (1968) indicated that drawings may represent a child's fears, fantasies, attitudes, anger, or past experiences.

Koppitz (1968) also suggested that the examiner should consider three points to aid in the process of interpretation of drawings: (a) how the child drew the figure, (b) whom the child drew, and (c) the message that the child is trying to convey. The first step in interpretation is to gather an overall impression of the pictures without concern for specific details. Then, the drawings are analyzed for the presence or absence of 30 emotional indicators (EI). Although the presence of a single EI should not be considered clinically significant, 3 or more EIs may suggest emotional problems, including anger and hostility (Koppitz, 1968).

Koppitz (1983) notes that there is no direct relationship between EIs and overt behavior of a child. Some EIs appear significantly more often in drawings of aggressive and hostile children. Teeth may reflect a hostile attitude (Jolles, 1971; Klepsch & Logie, 1982; Koppitz, 1966; Machover, 1949), although Koppitz (1966) cautions that the presence of only one EI should not be overinterpreted, because some level of hostility and aggression is normal. Other indicators include: long arms, big hands, and genitals (Koppitz, 1966); clenched fists, "mitten-type" hands, or toes (Machover, 1949); and soldiers or persons with weapons and/or who are engaged in combat (Gardiner, 1969; Klepsch & Logie, 1982). Drawings also may be examined for heavy lines, re-drawing of a picture without erasing the initial attempt, and paper-turning that may suggest hostility (Jolles, 1971). It is important that production of the drawings be accompanied by asking questions about them, which will improve their interpretability. Examples of a human figure drawing and a Kinetic School Drawing and the child's comments are included in Figures 9.1 and 9.2.

According to Jolles (1971), there are some indicators of hostility on the House-Tree-Person technique (HTP): degrading details, doors with heavy locks or hinges, windows with locks, absence of windows; and two-dimensional branches that resemble clubs or fingers or a "keyhole" shape. Jolles (1971) suggests that these indicators should be used to generate hypotheses and that the clinician also should ask questions about the drawings.

Rorschach Psychodiagnostic Test

The Rorschach (Rorschach, 1921) may be helpful in assessing anger and hostility in children, and Weiner (1986) suggests that psychologists can interpret adult and child responses in a similar manner, because the psychological corollaries are independent of age. Some indicators of aggression in the Rorschach have been reported in the research literature: blood (Allison, Blatt, & Zimet, 1968; Phillips & Smith, 1953); aggressive or hostile actions in human or animal movements (Goldfried, Stricker, & Weiner, 1971; Klopfer, Mayer, & Brawer, 1970); mutilated content (Goldfried

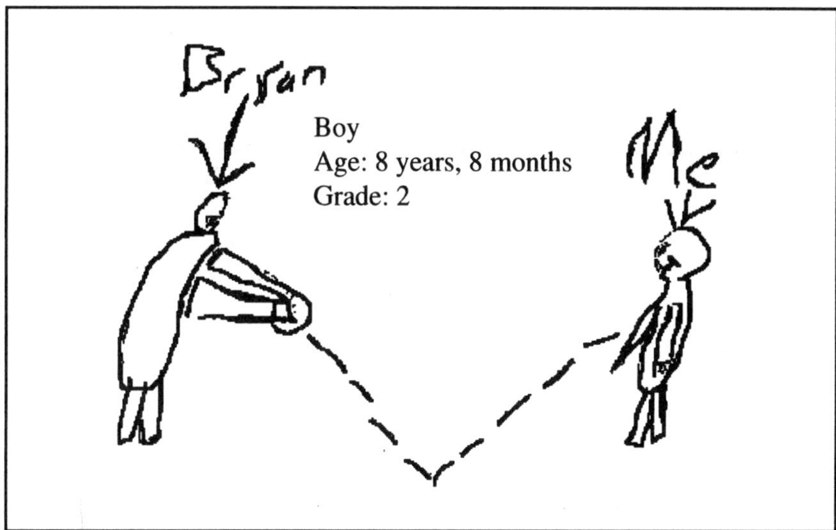

FIGURE 9. 1. KINETIC SCHOOL DRAWING
The picture depicts the client and his friend bouncing a ball at recess. The examiner asked the child to elaborate on how the boys in the picture were feeling. He responded by stating that the boys were arguing and "mad" at each other. They were attempting to bounce the ball as hard as they could so that it would hit the other boy in the face.

et al., 1971); weapons, knives, or objects used for fighting (Arnaud, 1959; Goldfried et al., 1971; Phillips & Smith, 1953); and explosions (Allen, 1978). Themes of hostility and aggression are expressed in responses referring to dangerous or threatening situations and elaboration of overt, aggressive interactions between animals and humans (Weiner, 1986). The elevation of white space (S) responses may indicate oppositional behavior and "anger affect" (Carlson & Drehmer, 1984; Exner, 1991; Weiner, 1986), although Tegtmeyer and Gordon (1983) found no differences in hostility between high and low "S" responders.

In a study of 108 children from intact and divorced families, Spigelman, Spigelman, and Englesson (1991) found that parental divorce was associated with increased levels of hostility and anxiety on the Rorschach, although these feelings may not be overt or observable. Girls demonstrated more "M" responses that suggested hostility and concerns about relationships, whereas boys' aggression was more destructive. Hostile responses appeared significantly more often in boys from divorced families than in boys from intact families. In a related manner, Owens (1984) reported that adult females who had incestuous experiences as children showed a significantly higher level of blood responses than did a control group.

Exner (1991) indicates that aggressive behavior is assigned to movement (AG) responses in the Rorschach. When more than two AG answers are given on any protocol, the clinician may hypothesize about unstable interpersonal relationships. These movement responses are related to three discrete factors: human movement, animal movement, and inanimate movement. An example of an aggressive response to Card II may be "two animals fighting and punching each other and they're bleeding." Exner (1991) reports that approximately 70% of all nonpatient subjects have AG

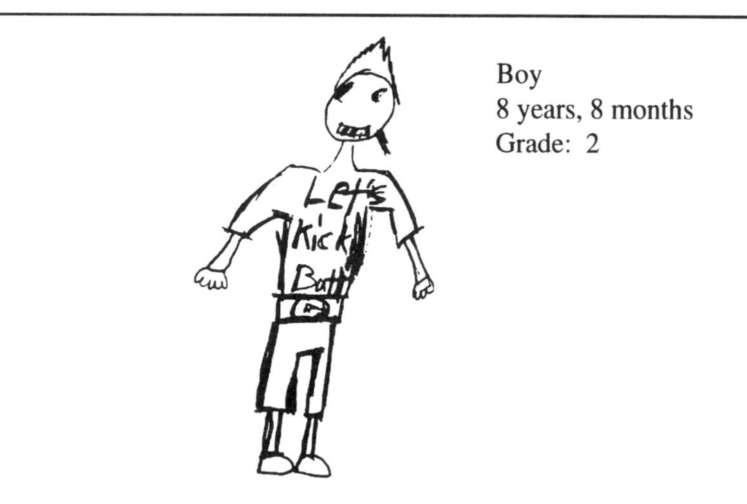

Figure 9.2. Human Figure Drawing

The human figure is a self-portrait of an 8-year-old boy who was referred for assessment due to poor anger control and excessive aggressiveness at home and school. Emotional indicators which may be suggestive of feelings of hostility and anger include teeth, heavy lines, and the overt antagonistic statement printed on the figure's T-shirt. When the psychologist queried as to how the boy was feeling, the child responded that the boy felt "mad" and was going to "fight" with his sister for calling him names.

values of 0 or 1. AG values of 2 or more are significant and suggest that interpersonal relationships are perceived as involving aggression, although it may not necessarily be antisocial in nature. Exner (1991) also recommends that the cooperative movement (COP) and AG responses be examined simultaneously. An example of a cooperative response for Card III might be "two people who are working together to lift a pot onto the table." If the COP value is less than 2 and the AG value is 2 or more, the psychologist may hypothesize that the subject is more likely to display aggressive behavior.

Thematic Approaches

The Thematic Apperception Test (TAT; Murray, 1943) presents more structured stimuli than the Rorschach and requires more elaborate verbal responses (Anastasi, 1988). Obrzut and Boliek (1986) suggest that cards 1, 3BM, 7GF, 8BM, 12M, 14, and 17BM are best suited for children, whereas cards 1, 2, 5, 7GF, 12F, 15, 17BM, 18BM, and 18GF may be more useful for adolescents. Several cards appear to have high aggressive/hostile content: 3BM, 3GF, 12M, 13MF, 14, 17BM, and 18BM (Megargee, 1967; Murstein, 1965; Obrzut & Boliek, 1986). The clinician also should be aware that the nature of the stimulus (i.e., each card) is the most influential determinant of story content (Bellak, 1986; Murstein, 1965), and that cards should be selected carefully in lieu of random selection.

Murstein (1965) also questions the assumption that cards high in hostile content can adequately differentiate between hostile and nonhostile individuals. Cards that are lower in hostile content may result in more accurate indications of emotional and personality traits related to anger/hostility. The reason for this hypothesis is that the subject is not simply responding to what is obvious in the picture. Therefore, the client may be more likely to project genuine feelings or attitudes of hostility onto more ambiguous cards, rather than simply describe the reality of what is depicted. However, Bellak (1986) comments that it is useful to note how subjects respond to cards with more obvious hostile content. For example, in Card 3BM, the object beside the person often is interpreted as a gun, and how the gun is integrated into the story may provide insights about aggressive or hostile feelings. If hostility is not evident in stories where it would be expected, the psychologist may hypothesize that anxiety is inhibiting expression of aggressive feelings (Kagan, 1956).

Fantasies about aggression are related more closely to overt aggressive behavior in adolescents than in adults (Weissman, 1964). Mussen and

Naylor (1954) found that lower SES adolescent and preadolescent delinquent boys who showed high aggression needs in the TAT showed more overt aggressive behavior than did those showing low aggressive fantasy needs. These results supported the hypothesis that boys who exhibited a high level of fantasy aggression accompanied by a small degree of fear of punishment were more overtly aggressive than boys with low fantasy aggression needs and a high level of fear of punishment.

The Children's Apperception Test (CAT; Bellak & Bellak, 1949) essentially is a downward extension of the TAT for children aged about 3 to 10. Byrd and Witherspoon (1954) found that themes of parental relationships, orality, and aggression occurred with high frequency and intensity in children aged 2 years, 8 months to 6 years, 5 months. Aggressive responses were most often associated with pictures 2, 3, and 7, and were seen to be a normal aspect of development. DeSousa (cited in Bellak, 1986) administered the CAT to emotionally handicapped students, and found that their responses included a greater occurrence of themes related to punishment, violence, aggression, weapons, accidents, and enemies. They also were more likely to perceive the environment as threatening and characters as aggressive.

Several quantitative scoring systems for the TAT and CAT have been developed. Groth-Marnat (1990) suggests that few clinicians use these systems, and the reader is referred to the research literature for discussion of these quantitative approaches (e.g., Hafner & Kaplan, 1960).

The Roberts Apperception Test for Children (RATC; McArthur & Roberts, 1982) is used with children aged 6 to 15, and was designed to overcome several perceived restrictions of other apperception tests (e.g., inadequate standardized scoring criteria and an inability of children to relate to stimulus characteristics of adult figures). The RATC manual reports a scoring system which includes five clinical scales (anxiety, aggression, depression, rejection, and unresolved) and eight adaptive scales (reliance on others, limit-setting, support to others, support of child, problem identification, and three resolutions scales).

McArthur and Roberts (1982) describe the aggression index as an attempt to measure overt aggression and its relationship to anxiety and inhibition in children. This index examines either physical or verbal expressions of anger (Obrzut & Boliek, 1986). It is divided into three parts with the first being destructive aggression, which is related to physical or verbal attacks and destruction of objects. The second part is related to aggression turned inward or directed outward. The third level focuses on constructive and adaptive uses of aggression when relating to others

(McArthur & Roberts, 1982). Cards that have been identified as eliciting aggressive responses include 3, 4, 6, 8, 9, 11, 12, 13, and 14.

Interview Techniques

One of the most established assessment techniques in psychology is the developmental and/or clinical interview. In general, interview methods vary primarily in the amount of structure. The least amount of structure is likely to be shown in the classical psychodynamic interview in which the child talks rather freely and the interviewer does not structure the assessment. At the other extreme are various structured interviews, which use an established format of questions that the interviewer follows closely, such as the Diagnostic Interview Schedule for Children (DISC; Costello, Edelbrock, Kalas, Kessler, & Klaric, 1982). Although structured interviews are very useful in formulating differential diagnoses, they are less useful in delineating internal emotional states. Groth-Marnat (1990) has indicated that highly structured interviews "...tend to overlook the idiosyncrasies and richness of the person. In many cases, these unique aspects of the person may go undetected and yet may make a significant difference in interpreting test scores or making treatment recommendations" (p. 63). Therefore, the most useful type of interview for assessing anger and hostility is the semistructured approach, in which the interviewer has some information s/he wants to obtain and identifies goals to accomplish, but does not follow a rigid approach. Most often, the explicit goal of assessing anger and hostility is to determine its presence, intensity, sources, objects or persons to whom it may be directed, and methods of coping with it. The following discussion is directed toward how the psychologist might use an interview approach to assess anger and hostility in children.

Conducting the Individual Child Interview

Step 1. Clarify what you and the child will be doing. When interviewing children, it is important to begin interviews with the objective of clarifying what will happen. Often, parents or other referral agents will not tell the child why s/he is being seen by a psychologist. It is often helpful to ask the child what s/he has been told about why the interview/assessment is being done. If the child says "I don't know," it is important to be open and direct with the child with statements such as, "Your parents tell me that there have been some problems at home lately, and they have asked me to talk with you and the rest of the family about these problems and see if we can come up with some ways to help things go better." If the child responds in a way that approximates the referral concerns, then a possible response could be: "It sounds like you have some thoughts about what is going on and why you are here, and I'd like to talk with you about what you think. I may also ask you to do some other things for me, such as draw pictures, answer some questions, and tell me stories about some pictures. I also may talk with other family members, too." Other discussion might occur, depending upon the child's understanding, verbalizations, and cooperation. There are three essential objectives in this first phase to be certain that the child understands: (a) why s/he is there, (b) what will happen during the sessions with all relevant family members, and (c) that s/he is not being singled out as being the sole source of the problems.

Step 2. Clarifying the child's perspective. In this stage of the interview, it is important to focus upon how the child views the situation and what his/her role in the problems might be. Knowledge about how the child construes the situation likely has an effect on her/his behavior and will affect how the problems are represented to the interviewer. Avoid too many direct questions with most children, because they may become reluctant to respond. A few judicious questions will help to direct the discussion to areas the interviewer wishes to explore, but the application of good listening skills and reflective comments will help to elicit cooperation and information.

With specific regard to assessing the child's anger and hostility, information that should be obtained includes:

- Is anger and hostility a problem for the child?
- What kinds of situations make the child angry?
- To whom or what is the anger directed most often?
- Is the child angry about anything now? If so, what? If not, when was the last time s/he was angry? In both instances, determine what made her/him angry.
- Is the anger long-lasting or short-lived?
- How does s/he express the anger and hostility?
- Does the child feel better or worse after expressing the anger and hostility? Why?
- Is remorse evident for feeling or expressing anger and hostility? Is the remorse appropriate given the circumstances? If not, determine if the child feels there is a reason to feel remorseful or guilty.
- How has s/he tried to control the anger and hostility? Have these techniques been effective? Why or why not?

- What are the child's plans to deal with the identified problems and her/his angry and hostile feelings?

Step 3. Determine what the child wants. In this stage, the interviewer should try to determine what the child wants to happen to address the problems. These responses will give further information about the child's perspectives on the situation. Some areas to address include:

- Is the focus on getting other people to change, because the child perceives the problems are his/her fault?
- Is s/he interested in learning how to control the anger and hostility and finding better methods of expressing it?
- Is the child willing to accept some responsibility for making changes (although perhaps accepting minimal responsibility for the problems)?
- What is the child willing to do to help her/himself deal with the anger and hostility?
- What attributes does the child have to assist in any therapeutic efforts (e.g., good language skills)?

Appendix A contains a worksheet for summarizing information that is obtained during the interview(s).

FRAMEWORK FOR ASSESSMENT

When conducting assessments of anger and hostility, it is important to have a framework from which to operate. Although somewhat similar to the data interpretation model of Maloney and Ward (1976), the framework discussed in the following section is offered as a way to conceptualize the entire assessment process.

Define Referral Questions

It is very important to clarify what information the referring party wants and the questions that are to be answered. "What is the child's present level of social-emotional functioning?" or "Does the child show a high level of anger and hostility that is affecting family relationships?" are examples of questions that should help to clarify what is to be done. Questions that are broad, inclusive, or ambiguous should be made more specific. Defining the questions to be answered often serves as a guide to the selection of assessment methods.

Determine Purpose for Assessment

There are many reasons for conducting psychological assessments, which include: screening; generating hypotheses about a person's behavior or characteristics; providing data for diagnosis or classification; determining eligibility for services; development of intervention plans; evaluating the efficacy of intervention plans; conducting research; or a combination of purposes (Huberty, 1991). The clinician should determine the purpose(s) for assessment that should be directly related to the referral questions.

Select Assessment Methods

Although this topic might sound rather elementary to the experienced psychologist, it is one that should be considered systematically. Many psychologists tend to use "standard batteries" in personality assessment (e.g., Prout, 1983). The authors take the position that the psychologist should consider the utility of a particular assessment procedure, which is a function of the purpose for which it is used and its associated psychometric adequacy (Huberty, 1989). Therefore, selection of a particular assessment method should be based upon the referral questions, how the information will be used, and its specific utility.

Conduct Assessment

When conducting a personality assessment, it is important that it be done in a multisource, multi-instrument, and multisetting format (Martin, Hooper, & Snow, 1986) to help provide comprehensiveness and to increase the opportunities for increasing reliability by aggregating several pieces of information (Epstein, 1980). In addition, we contend that the assessment should include a multitrait component (i.e., the psychologist should systematically assess a variety of characteristics, such as self-esteem, degree of anger and hostility, or anxiety, to gather as complete a picture as possible of the child and her/his circumstances).

Interpret Data

The process of interpretation of personality assessment data is one that must be approached cautiously, particularly if high-inference techniques are used. As discussed above, the psychologist must make inferences about what the data mean in order to interpret them. Many factors can influence the development of inferences, including the theoretical orientation and experience of the psychologist, the instruments used, and the behavior of the child. As these inferences are developed, the psychologist begins to develop hypotheses about the person that must be verified, such as why the child is angry and how the anger is directed. "An inference involves extrapolation; it cannot be confirmed or rejected without other information that is not present via observation" (Gambrill, 1990, p. 196). Therefore, accuracy, thoroughness, and consistency of the inferences will have important effects on the hypotheses for a specific child and their respective validity.

Formulate Hypotheses from Data

Once the inferences have been formed, the psychologist then develops hypotheses about the child, such as why the child is angry, how s/he feels about family members, or a variety of other factors. In reality, the development of inferences and hypotheses may occur almost simultaneously, and should be based upon the degree of evidence contained in the data. For example, the hypothesis that a child is angry might be derived from several themes of hostility and aggression in the TAT, comments in the interview that s/he sometimes "feels like hitting someone," and the presence of bared teeth in a human figure drawing. As the clinician evaluates each item of data, inferences are formed, and are then combined into broader inferences that lead to one or more hypotheses.

Integrate Data with Other Information

The next step in the assessment process is to integrate the obtained data with other information, such as family and developmental history, situational factors (e.g., family dysfunction, school problems), and information provided by parents and teachers (e.g., interviews, behavior rating scales, observations). By comparing the data with this objective information, the clinician essentially conducts a validity test by attempting to conclude if the interpretation and generated hypotheses are consistent with the child's behavior and current situation. If the hypotheses are not consistent with the observable behavior, then the clinician should re-examine the data and the subsequent conclusions to determine the reasons for the discrepancies. New or revised hypotheses may emerge from this re-analysis that may more adequately explain the situation and/or direct the clinician into new areas of investigation.

Accept, Reject, or Modify/Create Hypotheses

As the clinician evaluates the data and integrates them with the formed hypotheses, some hypotheses are accepted, rejected, or modified/created. In some situations, hypotheses may be modified or rejected or new hypotheses formed that require reconsideration of the assessment data, creating a "loop" back to the Hypothesis Formulation step and proceeding again through the subsequent steps.

Formulate Conclusions

The acceptance, rejection, or modification/creation of hypotheses forms the basis for the conclusions of the clinician. If a hypothesis is accepted, the clinician concludes that the assessment data do have clinical validity and conclusions are drawn. Referring back to the example above of the TAT cards, interview, and figure drawings that indicated anger, the clinician might conclude that the child does have internalized anger. At the same time, however, there may be no evidence that the anger is directed toward the parents, and the hypothesis is rejected. However, the clinician may still want to know where the anger is directed and then may modify or create new hypotheses and then re-analyze and interpret the data. In some situations, further assessment may be necessary.

Formulate Recommendations

Once the clinician has formulated conclusions, they are compared with the referral questions and recommendations are formed. The recommendations should be based upon the referral questions, the data, the conclusions, and the particular circumstances (e.g., commitment to interventions, available resources). It is not expected that every hypothesis or inference will lead directly to a recommendation, but the aggregate data should provide a basis for logical conclusions and recommendations. Appendix B is a worksheet to assist in planning and summarizing an assessment using this framework.

CASE STUDY: JEFF, AGE: 11-5, GRADE: 6

Background Information

Jeff was referred for evaluation of his social and emotional adjustment by school personnel. Presenting behavior concerns were: withdrawal, difficulty getting along with peers, not performing academically to his level of ability, short attention span, temper tantrums, social isolation, and some problems with impulse control. He is an only child and lives with his mother, following a divorce about 1 year ago. About $3^1/_2$ years earlier, Jeff had been struck by a car and was hospitalized in a coma for a day and experienced edema of the brain. A seizure disorder subsequently was diagnosed, and anticonvulsant medications (phenytoin and carbamazepine) were being taken, which controlled the seizures well. The child's neurologist was of the opinion that current stress on Jeff was contributory to his seizure disorder. His grades have deteriorated dramatically within the last year from a "B" average to primarily "Ds," and he frequently "gives up" when the work becomes difficult. His teacher reported that Jeff often had temper tantrums during the day, was extremely sensitive to criticism, and was described as "immature." His WISC-R Verbal, Performance, and Full Scale IQ scores were 98, 117, and 107, respectively. WRAT-R achievement test standard scores were: Reading = 85; Spelling = 80; and Arithmetic = 88.

Referral Questions

- What is the status of Jeff's social and emotional adjustment?
- What are the reasons for his poor academic performance and behavior problems?
- To what extent are his academic and behavioral problems attributable to his neurological history?
- What recommendations are appropriate?

Determine Purposes for Assessment

- To generate hypotheses about why Jeff was having adjustment and academic performance difficulties;
- To determine what, if any, interventions were appropriate; and
- To determine the contributions of his neurological history to his current problems.

Select Assessment Methods

Many different assessment methods were used with Jeff: Thematic Apperception Test, incomplete sentences, self-report measures (self-esteem, anxiety, and depression), behavior checklists completed by mother and teacher, observations, and semistructured interviews. An attempt was made to complete figure drawings, but Jeff did not want to draw them, and the examiner did not insist.

Conduct Assessment

Observations of Jeff were made in the classroom, physical education class, and on the playground without his knowledge that he was the object of observation. Following the observations, the clinician met with Jeff individually to conduct the interviews and to administer the various measures. Interviews with the teacher and mother were also conducted, and they completed the behavior rating scales.

Interpret Data

Due to space limitations, a complete description of the assessment data is not possible here. Therefore, selected excerpts are provided that serve as samples of the obtained data.

Observations in the individual sessions. The individual assessment required about 2.5 hours to complete and Jeff was cooperative and compliant, but seemed tired at times. He showed a rather "flat affect" and smiled infrequently, and did not engage in much spontaneous conversation. He often tried to draw the examiner off task, and frequently asked for things to be repeated. When asked to do the incomplete sentences, he began to cry, but offered no explanation for it when asked.

Observations at school. Jeff was observed for about 3 hours in the classroom and in unstructured settings, such as recess. He was observed to be compliant and following directions, but he also showed some attention problems, talked about irrelevant topics, and had difficulty sustaining effort.

Thematic Apperception Test. Cards were selected to get an overall impression of Jeff's feelings and attitudes as well as to identify the presence of angry and hostile themes. The following excerpts represent stories judged to reflect angry and hostile themes.

Card 3BM. Person is in jail for murdering somebody, killed some kid, took a knife, kept stabbing him, he'll have another knife and kill himself at the end so he won't be killed in the electric chair. (Why did he kill the person?) He killed the other person, is mad at the other person for something he did, did something to his crops [apparent reference to Card 2]. (What else can you tell me?) He had an old-fashioned lawnmower and mowed on his crops, went and killed him, took and stole it and never brought it back.

Card 4. Woman is trying to get the man to fall in love with her, but he's mad enough to kill her for bringing back a picture of a nude woman for him to look at and not her. Will take a shotgun and kill her in the heart at the very end. (What will happen then?) He'll be put in jail, after that, on the day to be crucified, they'll take him out and hang him by the neck.

Card 13B. The boy is really scared, in a ghost town, was left all alone. Parents did not want him anymore, cause he was mean. They don't want to take care of him anymore. (What will happen?) All the spirits in the ghost town change him into a ghost and they haunt the ghost town forever. He is really scared.

Card 15. He's a wicked, evil doctor who goes and looks for a tombstone, for a certain body, one of his brothers. He goes and digs it up to create the world's meanest monster to destroy every village in the world. (Why is he doing this?) Everyone hates him and wants to burn his house down, and he doesn't want that to happen. He will do it [create monster], and all the houses will be destroyed, but suddenly the monster got out of hand and he could not control it anymore and suddenly had to go back to the graveyard to dig up another body. (Why?) To create a heroic person to destroy the evil monster he created to save the world. (What happens?) Monster gets destroyed, everyone thanks him, says he will not be mean again. This is a happy ending. The end.

Incomplete sentences. The incomplete sentences form was completed by Jeff very slowly and it was necessary to encourage him to respond to all items (responses italicized).

"When the odds are against me I try to fight I'm out."

"To me the future looks terrible."

"I wish I could lose the fear of when I got hit by that car."

"Most families I know have people who don't care about them."

"My fears sometimes force me to get mad and punch the person who teased me."

"I feel that my father does not often care about me."

Self-report measures. Individual measures of depression, trait anxiety, and self-esteem were completed by Jeff. Trait anxiety was statistically and clinically significant, but depression was within the average range. Self-esteem was in the low average range, and included follow-up comments like: "I get mad once in awhile," "I still don't know why dad left me and mom," "When people bother me, I punch em if they hit me first," and "Everyone expects everything all at once."

Behavior rating scales. The teacher completed the Burks Behavior Rating Scale (Burks, 1977), and Jeff's mother completed the Child Behavior Checklist (Achenbach & Edelbrock, 1983).

Teacher's ratings. High levels of withdrawal, dependency, poor impulse control, poor anger control, acting out, distractibility, poor peer relations, and immaturity.

Mother's rating. Significant elevations on depression, hyperactivity, and social withdrawal.

Formulate Hypotheses

When considering all the available information, the following six hypotheses were developed:

- Jeff's behavior is highly influenced by his seizures.
- Jeff's behavior is influenced by the anticonvulsant medication.
- Jeff is very angry about his father leaving.
- Jeff is feeling very alone and has few friends.
- Jeff's academic performance is negatively affected by his social-emotional state.
- Jeff is experiencing some signs of depression.

Integrate Data with Other Information

Other relevant information includes a report from the neurologist that the seizures and medication should not account for Jeff's behavior. The behavior and academic problems started after the car accident and onset of seizures and shortly after the father left. Jeff does seem to have trouble concentrating and there have been some indications of crying, attention problems, and anger outbursts.

Accept, Reject, or Modify/Create Hypotheses

Hypotheses 1 and 2 about the effects of the seizures and medications are rejected, based upon the neurologist's report and the fact that the problems started after the onset of seizures. Hypothesis 3 is accepted due to references about his father's leaving. Hypothesis 4 is accepted, primarily because he spends much time alone and is not sought out by others. However, he has stated he wants more friends and he exhibits behavior designed to get their attention. Hypothesis 5 is accepted because his grades and test scores have declined, there has been a major disruption in his life recently, and there is no evidence to support the alternative hypothesis that the seizures and medications are causing the problems. Hypothesis 6 is tentatively accepted, because some of Jeff's behavior (e.g., crying, temper outbursts, attention, low self-esteem, and high anxiety) indicate depression, despite his average score on the self-report measure of depression.

Formulate Conclusions

Jeff is experiencing anger associated with his father leaving that is affecting his behavior and school performance. The seizures and medications are not related to these problems, and are not causal in nature. Jeff is anxious, depressed, lonely, and has feelings of being rejected by his father, and may be concerned that he will be left alone. The problems appear to be potentially serious and require treatment.

Formulate Recommendations

After considering the assessment information, the hypotheses, and the conclusions, recommendations then were developed.

- Continued monitoring of his neurological status.
- Involvement with a "big brother."
- Involvement with more group activities, e.g., Boy Scouts, etc.
- Individual counseling to assess his feelings of loss and anger toward his father.
- Involvement in a divorce support group for children.
- Social skills training/practice at school,with particular emphasis on developing self-control strategies, prosocial interactions, and problem-solving skills.
- Involve the mother in family therapy and in working with the school to address behavioral and academic concerns.
- Teach Jeff to identify feelings and recognize warning signs which precede angry outbursts.
- Teach Jeff relaxation techniques to help him manage his physiological responses when becoming angry.
- Teach Jeff short-term anger reduction techniques (e.g., counting to 10 or deep breathing exercises).
- Determine if academic problems are contributing to angry or aggressive reactions. If so, cooperative learning strategies, peer tutoring, or similar modifications may be helpful.

CONCLUSION

This chapter has described how the use of traditional personality assessment methods (i.e., projective techniques and interviews) can be used to assist in the assessment of anger and hostility in children and adolescents. Although there are other techniques that might be helpful to the clinician (e.g., incomplete sentences), the authors limited their discussion to major methods currently in use. The clinician must remember, however, that anger and hostility are not easily assessed, due to their subjective, internalized nature. Just as inferring anger from overt acts of aggression does not assure that a child is angry, neither does the absence of aggression assure that anger is not present. Projective techniques and interviews can be very helpful in assessing anger and hostility, but the clinician must remember that, in general, problems associated with reliability and validity make them susceptible to errors of interpretation. These techniques are best used to generate hypotheses that must be accepted, modified, or rejected, based upon using more objective information as criteria. The data are idiographic and idiosyncratic, and broad generalizations are not possible. With appropriate caution and a constant awareness of the need to validate the inferences and hypotheses, the psychologist may find projectives and interviews to be useful methods to assess anger and hostility in specific situations.

REFERENCES

Achenbach, T. M., & Edelbrock, C. S. (1983). *Manual for the Child Behavior Checklist and Revised Child Behavior Profile.* Burlington, VT: University of Vermont Department of Psychiatry.

Allen, R. M. (1978). *Student's Rorschach Manual* (rev. ed.). New York: International Universities Press.

Allison, J., Blatt, S. J., & Zimet, C. N. (1968). *The interpretation of psychological tests.* New York: Harper & Row.

Anastasi, A. (1988). *Psychological testing* (6th ed.). New York: Macmillan.

Arnaud, S. H. (1959). A system for deriving quantitative Rorschach measures of certain psychological variables for group comparison. *Journal of Projective Techniques, 23,* 403-411.

Bellak, L. (1986). *The T.A.T., C.A.T., and S.A.T. in clinical use* (4th ed.). New York: Grune & Stratton.

Bellak, L., & Bellak, S. (1949). *Children's Apperception Test.* Larchmont, NY: C.P.S.

Bowers, R. C. (1987). Children and anger. In A. Thomas & J. Grimes (Eds.), *Children's needs: Psychological perspectives* (pp. 31-36). Washington, DC: National Association of School Psychologists.

Burks, H. F. (1977). *Burks Behavior Rating Scales manual.* Los Angeles, CA: Western Psychological Services.

Byrd, E., & Witherspoon, R. L. (1954). Responses of preschool children to Children's Apperception Test. *Child Development, 25,* 35-44.

Carlson, R. W., & Drehmer, D. E. (1984). Rorschach space response and aggression. *Perceptual and Motor Skills, 58,* 987-988.

Costello, A. J., Edelbrock, C., Kalas, R., Kessler, M. D., & Klaric, S. H. (1982).*The NIMH Diagnostic Interview Schedule for Children. Unpublished interview schedule.* Department of Psychiatry, University of Pittsburgh.

Cummings, J. A. (1986). Projective drawings. In H. M. Knoff (Ed.), *The assessment of child and adolescent personality* (pp. 199-244). New York: Guilford.

Exner, J. (1991). *The Rorschach: A comprehensive system* (Vol. 2). New York: Wiley.

Epstein, S. (1980). The stability of behavior: II. Implications for psychological research. *American Psychologist, 35,* 790-806.

Gambrill, E. (1990). *Critical thinking in clinical practice.* San Francisco, CA: Jossey-Bass.

Gardiner, H. W. (1969). A cross-cultural comparison of hostility in children's drawings. *Journal of Social Psychology, 79,* 261-263.

Goldfried, M. R., Stricker, G., & Weiner, I. B. (1971). *Rorschach handbook of clinical research applications.* Englewood Cliffs, NJ: Prentice-Hall.

Goodenough, F. (1926). *Measurement of intelligence by drawings.* New York: World Book.

Groth-Marnat, G. (1990). *Handbook of psychological assessment* (2nd ed.). New York: Wiley.

Hafner, A. J., & Kaplan, A. M. (1960). Hostility content analysis of the Rorschach and T.A.T. *Journal of Projective Techniques, 24,* 137-143.

Huberty, T. J. (1989, August). Utility of personality assessment in schools: Psychometric considerations. In M. F. Schneider (Chair), *Utilizing personality assessment within the school context: Assessment to intervention.* Symposium conducted at the Annual Convention of the American Psychological Association, New Orleans, LA.

Huberty, T. J. (1991, March). *A component approach to social-emotional assessment: Practice implications.* Annual Convention of the National Association of School Psychologists, Dallas, TX.

Jolles, I. (1971). *A catalog for the qualitative interpretation of the House-Tree-Person.* Los Angeles: Western Psychological Services.

Kagan, J. (1956). The measurement of overt aggression from fantasy. *Journal of Abnormal and Social Psychology, 52,* 390-393.

Klein, R. G. (1986). Questioning the usefulness of projective psychological tests for children. *Journal of Developmental and Behavioral Pediatrics, 7,* 75-81.

Klepsch, M., & Logie, L. (1982). *Children draw and tell: An introduction to the projective uses of children's human figure drawing.* New York: Brunner/Mazel.

Klopfer, B., Mayer, M. M., & Brawer, F. B. (Eds.). (1970). *Developments in Rorschach technique* (Vol. III). New York: Harcourt, Brace, & Jovanovich.

Klopfer, W. G., & Taulbee, E. S. (1976). Projective tests. *Annual Review of Psychology, 27,* 543-567.

Koppitz, E. M. (1966). Emotional indicators on human figure drawings of shy and aggressive children. *Journal of Clinical Psychology, 22,* 466-469.

Koppitz, E. M. (1968). *Psychological evaluation of children's human figure drawings.* New York: Grune & Stratton.

Koppitz, E. M. (1983). Projective drawings with children and adolescents. *School Psychology Review, 12,* 421-427.

Lubin, B., Larsen, R. M., & Matarazzo, J. D. (1984). Patterns of psychological test usage in the United States: 1935-1982. *American Psychologist, 39,* 451-454.

Machover, K. (1949). *Personality projection in the drawing of the human figure.* Springfield, IL: Charles C. Thomas.

Maloney, M. P., & Ward, M. P. (1976). *Psychological assessment: A conceptual approach.* New York: Oxford University Press.

Martin, R. P., Hooper, S., & Snow, J. (1986). Behavior rating scale approaches to personality assessment in children and adolescents. In H. M. Knoff (Ed.), *The assessment of child and adolescent personality* (pp. 309-351). New York: Guilford.

McArthur, D. S., & Roberts, G. E. (1982). *Roberts Apperception Test for Children. Manual.* Los Angeles: Western Psychological Services.

Megargee, E. I. (1967). Hostility on the TAT as a function of defensive inhibition and stimulus situation. *Journal of Projective Techniques, 31,* 73-79.

Murstein, B. I. (1965). Projection of hostility on the TAT as a function of stimulus, background, and personality variables. *Journal of Consulting Psychology, 29,* 44-48.

Murray, H. (1943). *Thematic Apperception Test Manual.* Cambridge, MA: Harvard University Press.

Mussen, P. H., & Naylor, H. K. (1954). The relationship between overt and fantasy aggression. *Journal of Abnormal and Social Psychology, 49,* 235-240.

Obrzut, J. E., & Boliek, C. A. (1986). Thematic approaches to personality assessment with children and adolescents. In H. M. Knoff (Ed.), *The assessment of child and adolescent personality* (pp. 173-198). New York: Guilford.

Owens, T. H. (1984). Personality traits of female psychotherapy patients with a history of incest: A research note. *Journal of Personality Assessment, 48,* 606-608.

Phillips, L., & Smith, J. (1953). *Rorschach interpretation advanced techniques.* New York: Grune & Stratton.

Prout, H. T. (1983). School psychologists and social-emotional assessment techniques: Patterns in training and use. *School Psychology Review, 12,* 377-383.

Rorschach, H. (1921). *Psychodiagnostics.* (Hans Huber Verlag, Transl. 1942). Bern: Bircher.

Spigelman, G., Spigelman, A., & Englesson, I. (1991). Hostility, aggression, and anxiety levels of divorce and nondivorce children as manifested in their response to projective tests. *Journal of Personality Assessment, 56,* 438-452.

Tegtmeyer, P. F., & Gordon, M. (1983). Interpretation of white space response in children's Rorschach protocols. *Perceptual and Motor Skills, 57,* 611-616.

Weiner, I. B. (1986). Assessing children and adolescents with the Rorschach. In H. M. Knoff (Ed.), *The assessment of child and adolescent personality* (pp. 141-171). New York: Guilford.

Weissman, S. L. (1964). Some indicators of acting out behavior from the Thematic Apperception Test. *Journal of Projective Techniques and Personality Assessment, 28,* 366-375.

APPENDIX A

Worksheet for Summarizing Interview Information

NAME:_______________________________

DOB:______ **AGE:**_____

PSYCHOLOGIST:__________________________ **DATE:**_____

SUMMARIZE FROM THE CHILD'S PERSPECTIVE:

- Does the child feel that anger and hostility are a problem?
- What makes her/him angry?
- To whom or what is the anger directed most often? What is the child angry about now?
- Is the anger long-lasting or short-lived?
- How does s/he express anger?
- How does the child feel after expressing anger?
- Does the child feel remorse about being angry? If so, is it appropriate?
- What plans does the child have to deal with perceived problems and her/his angry feelings?

SUMMARIZE WHAT THE CHILD WANTS:

- Does the child feel that s/he needs to change or are the problems the fault of others?
- Is the child interested in learning how to cope with anger?
- To what extent is the child willing or able to accept responsibility for change?
- What skills or attributes does the child have to contribute to therapeutic efforts?

APPENDIX B

WORKSHEET FOR CONDUCTING ASSESSMENTS

NAME:____________________________ **DOB:**_______ **AGE:**______

PSYCHOLOGIST:____________________________ **DATE:**_________

❐ REFERRAL QUESTIONS:

❐ PURPOSES OF THE ASSESSMENT:

❐ ASSESSMENT PROCEDURES:

❐ OBSERVATIONS DURING ASSESSMENT:

❐ INTERPRETATION SUMMARY:

❐ HYPOTHESES:

❐ OTHER RELEVANT INFORMATION:

❐ HYPOTHESES ACCEPTED, REJECTED, OR MODIFIED:

❐ CONCLUSIONS:

❐ RECOMMENDATIONS:

SECTION IV

PREVENTION AND INTERVENTION STRATEGIES FOR REDUCING ANGER, HOSTILITY, AND AGGRESSION

This section of the book presents five approaches to developing anger prevention and intervention programs for youth. Chapters 10–13 describe programs that focus on a specific aspect of anger coping. Chapter 10 (Hudley) describes a reattribution training program (Brain Power) that is used to help elementary-aged boys to evaluate more accurately the intentions of their peers in ambiguous social interactions. This program is currently being implemented on a schoolwide basis as part of a grant funded by the Centers for Disease Control and Prevention. Strategies for teaching aggressive youth the social skills they need to cope with stressful situations and to express their anger more effectively are presented in Chapter 11 (Morrison & Sandowicz). A detailed description of a group counseling program designed to influence youths' anger-related attitudes and beliefs is provided in Chapter 12 (Larson). Chapter 13 (Fortman & Feldman) contains suggestions for dealing with youth who "fly off the handle" and react in an impulsive, explosive manner when angry. Finally, Chapter 14 (McLain & Lewis) presents a guide for implementing anger management for individuals with developmental disabilities. This program provides an example of an eclectic approach to anger management training.

10 THE REDUCTION OF CHILDHOOD AGGRESSION USING THE BRAINPOWER PROGRAM

Cynthia Ann Hudley

The consequences of high levels of childhood aggression can be extremely damaging to perpetrators as well as to their victims. Finding the means to reduce excessive displays of childhood aggression has thus become a top priority among practitioners and researchers alike. This chapter briefly reviews the range of interventions currently used with aggressive school-aged children. It then describes the critical elements of an experimental program designed to reduce peer-directed aggression among African-American boys and presents the evaluation research that has been conducted to date.

Minority youth are an especially compelling population of concern in research on childhood aggression, as discussed by Chan (Chapter 6). Although African-American children represent 25% of the national public school population, they comprise 40% of all suspensions and expulsions (Reed, 1988). Almost half (45%) of all suspensions and expulsions are prompted by school staff perceptions of excessive aggression, most often in the context of peer interaction (Reed, 1988). The tragedy is that although suspension may provide symptom relief for schools, it does not address the root causes of aggressive behavior and banishes those children who are most in need of the benefits of a strong academic foundation, a caring school environment, and positive peer relations.

REDUCING AGGRESSIVE BEHAVIOR: CURRENT PRACTICES

Social cognitive interventions currently used with aggressive children can typically be categorized as: (a) reducing impulsivity, (b) moderating affective interference, (c) enhancing specific social or interpersonal skills, or (d) an eclectic combination of these three basic goals.

The connection between impulsivity and aggression is founded upon the theories of Vygotsky (e.g., 1978) and Luria (e.g., 1963) regarding the role of private speech in directing behavior. Interventions to reduce impulsivity presume that strengthening the regulatory power of private speech will reduce outburst aggression by teaching children to plan and direct their own behavior. Outcome studies (Camp & Bash, 1980; Camp, Blom, Herbert, & van Doornick, 1977) for the *Think Aloud Program* (Camp & Bash, 1980), a typical example of this class of intervention, indicate mixed results. The greatest gains have been shown in the display of prosocial behaviors in the classroom and in cognitive test performance. However, treated groups did not significantly reduce displays of aggressive behavior, nor increase on teacher ratings of self-control.

Programs designed to impact affect generally focus on either reduction of intensity or affective labeling. The goal in such programs is learning to retain control of one's behavior in affectively charged situations by reducing one's own feelings of anger. Reductions in intensity of anger are achieved by either covert self-talk, which is presumed to have a calming effect (Lochman, Lampron, Gemmer, & Harris, 1987; Novaco, 1978), or the cognitive redefinition of experienced affect to some feeling other than anger (Rotheram, 1980). Outcome studies (Garrison & Stolberg, 1983; Robin, Schneider, & Dolnick, 1976) generally report inconsistent findings and suffer from significant methodological flaws including lack of attention control groups, nonrepresentative samples, and unreliable assessment instruments (Kazdin, 1985; Urbain & Kendall, 1980).

Numerous programs are available to instruct children in discrete interpersonal behaviors and strategies that can be applied in problematic social encounters. Problem-solving instruction is founded on Jahoda's theory that the competent individual is able to choose from among a variety of social problem-solving strategies in order to produce effective and appropriate interpersonal behavior (Pelligrini, 1985). Spivak and Shure's model of interpersonal cognitive problem-solving skills (Spivak, Platt, & Shure, 1976) has been extensively employed in programs designed to enhance social skills (e.g., Guerra & Slaby, 1990). A wealth of programs that teach and reinforce specific social behaviors (e.g., questioning, praising, group entry tactics) have also been employed on the assumption that excessively aggressive youth lack interaction skills (Kazdin, 1985). Outcome data suggest that the relationship between problem-solving skills and specific behavior is often inconsistent among aggressive youth, and interventions to train specific behaviors do not necessarily generalize to everyday social encounters (Kazdin, 1985).

"Comprehensive" programs may target a specific population of deviant youth (delinquent, emotionally disturbed, etc.). Goldstein and Glick's (1987) *Aggression Replacement Training Program* is typical. Designed for delinquents who are presumed to possess interlocking skill deficiencies, which cannot be remediated in isolation, the program simultaneously works to enhance social skills, reduce affective arousal and develop higher levels of moral reasoning. Outcome studies (Goldstein & Glick, 1987) reported significant reductions in acting-out behaviors and impulsivity, but no differences in prosocial behaviors when compared to attention controls and no-treatment controls among institutionalized delinquents. In a second facility, no differences were found in acting-out and impulsive behaviors, but treated subjects showed significant increases in prosocial behaviors. However, it is impossible to determine which specific treatment element is actually responsible for observed behavior change in this multiprocess intervention.

A contrasting multiple-component program of aggression reduction implemented among clients of a children's mental health center (Pepler, King, & Byrd, 1991) focused on training children, parents, and teachers in separate instructional sessions. Children participated in school-based, pullout programs of small group instruction which focused on a series of specific problem-solving (e.g., self-control) and social behavioral (e.g., joining in) skills. Parents and teachers were taught effective behavior management skills which complemented the strategies taught to the children. Evaluation studies have been mixed, with the greatest improvements reported for students' disruptive aggression in the classroom.

Attribution Retraining to Reduce Reactive Aggression

Given the convincing evidence that biased attributions play a central role in the display of reactive, hostile aggression, we next turn to a consideration of attribution retraining and the reduction of excessive levels of peer-directed aggression. As described in Chapter 2, attribution theory presents a motivational sequence in which the individual's attributions (cognitions) generate feelings of anger (affect) leading to retaliatory aggression (behavior). Correcting the distortion in this cognition-to-affect-to-behavior motivational sequence at its earliest stage should effectively minimize inappropriately experienced anger as well as reactive aggression. In other words, an intervention program of attribution retraining can be expected to reduce or eliminate biased judgments of a peer's intent. Once the bias is eliminated, treated subjects should be more likely to presume accidental causes in ambiguously caused negative outcome interactions with peers. Negative outcomes attributed to nonhostile causes would be highly unlikely to elicit anger and aggression. Thus attribution retraining provides a logical starting point in the development of an intervention package to reduce peer-directed aggression in the schools.

A school-based attribution retraining intervention would also serve as a program for primary prevention of clinical dysfunction. Such a program would provide children in regular education with the social cognitive skills necessary to interpret and respond to their social world in a functional manner. Though this single intervention is not presumed to be a panacea for a behavior that is so clearly subject to multiple determinants, it can provide an individual with alternative ways of perceiving interpersonal situations, defining acceptable responses, and enacting appropriate behavior. The result might be reduced levels of aggression, which could enhance peer relations, school adjustment, and overall developmental outcomes for children at risk due to inappropriate aggression.

However, the evidence clearly suggests that multiple interpersonal processes contribute to the display of peer-directed aggression (Dodge & Crick, 1990). Attribution retraining is but one piece of a comprehensive package of intervention strategies to reduce extreme levels of childhood aggression. The development of the program to be described here embodies a constructive treatment strategy (Kazdin, 1980) and focuses on attributional change as a starting point. By isolating the role of one social cognitive process linked to aggressive behavior (i.e., attributional bias) the specific "active" ingredient in this initial component may be more readily evaluated. Ultimately, however, this program will be most effective as a part of a comprehensive intervention program to reduce anger and aggression in the schools, which addresses various strategies discussed elsewhere in this volume.

Attribution Retraining

I have designed a three-part intervention, the *BrainPower Program,* specifically to assess the ability of attribution retraining to reduce aggressive behavior in peer interactions. The attributional treatment is a 12-lesson cognitive intervention with materials and activities appropriate for the late elementary grades (Hudley, 1991). The primary goal of the intervention is to train aggressive boys not to infer hostile peer intent in negative social encounters of ambiguous or uncertain causal origins. This retraining is accomplished by altering the participants' perceptions of controllability in negative social interactions with peers. Guided by the theoretical relationship between perceived controllability and retaliatory aggression, I inferred that aggressive young males perceive causes of negative social outcomes to be controllable (i.e., purposeful) by the peer(s) with whom they are interacting. Thus, the program focuses on training aggressive males to make more accurate attributions to uncontrollable or accidental causes for negative outcomes when a peer's intent is ambiguous.

Program Overview

There are three components in the intervention. The first component (Lessons 2–6) strengthens aggressive boys' ability to detect intentionality with accuracy. Through a variety of instructional activities participants are trained to search for, interpret, and properly categorize the verbal, physical, and behavioral cues from others in social situations. Elementary school children as a group have not yet achieved mature levels of social interpretation and insight; thus, practice in reading and interpreting the social landscape can be especially beneficial to this age group.

The second component of the intervention (Lessons 7–9) is designed to increase the likelihood that aggressive boys will make attributions of nonhostile intent when negative social encounters are ambiguous. After the participants gain some skills in the classification and interpretation of social cues, they are taught to associate the relative absence of consistent or discernible cues with attributions to "uncontrollable" or "accidental" causes.

The third component (Lessons 10–11) elaborates on the meaning of intentionality in the context of linking appropriate behavioral responses to ambiguously caused, negative outcomes. By this phase of the intervention students have gained some skills in assessing the social scene and competently judging a peer's intent. Now they practice their newly acquired skills by demonstrating the behavioral outcomes of their competent cognitive processing. Students are actually taught to generate decision rules about when to enact particular nonhostile responses (e.g., "When I don't have the information to tell what he meant, I should act as if it were an accident"). Such decision rules serve to enhance maintenance and generalization of newly acquired processing skills beyond the treatment setting.

Lesson 1 provides a general introduction to the program's rationale, benefits, and activities. The group leader and members participate in an icebreaker, and orientation to group processes and rules of conduct is provided. Lesson 12 furnishes closure for program participants by summing up the issues that have been covered, distributing certificates of completion, and evaluating the benefits of the program as perceived by students.

The BrainPower Program

Component #1—Interpreting social cues. In *Lesson 2*, students read and discuss a scenario of inappropriate retaliatory aggression caused by misattribution of intent. The leader focuses the discussion on the ways in which inferences of intent shape behavior. Students generate a definition of intent (i.e., what someone meant to do), role-play situations that might lead to misattribution of hostile intent, and discuss causes and consequences. For homework, students are expected to keep a log for the next 4 days by recording instances of errors in judgments of intent.

In *Lesson 3* children play a game with pictures and photographs in which they identify intent from facial expressions. They must select faces that illustrate the intent expressed in contrasting pairs of stimulus sentences (e.g., "I stepped on your toe because I was talking to a friend and didn't notice you sitting there" or "I stepped on your toe to get you back for what you said about me"). This activity then leads to a discussion of the types of facial cues that are useful in the accurate detection of another's intent. Students consider the look of eyebrows (e.g., turned down for anger), lips (e.g., open to show surprise), and other facial features as aids to interpreting the intent of another.

Lesson 4 addresses the importance of knowing one's own feelings. Negative outcomes often generate bad feelings that interfere with the accuracy of intention detection and lead to misattributions. After reading a series of scenarios, students complete unfinished sentences to identify feelings that would likely be elicited ("when that happened I felt _____") and information that can be gathered from the text ("when that happened I knew ________ because ______"). The discussion focuses on the difference between feelings about a situation and attending to the cues present in a situation.

By *Lesson 5*, students are generating a list of the types of cues available in a social situation, and discussing how best to use them. A set of four previously prepared videos is then presented to illustrate four types of intentions in peers: hostile, accidental, helpful, and ambiguous. (These videos can be prepared with the help of nonparticipant students at a given school site. Scripts for the scenarios can be obtained from the author.) The concept of "ambiguous" intentions is explored and contrasted with the other three types of intent.

Students bring their own ideas about the four types of intentions to the *Lesson 6* meeting. As a group, they produce a set of four videotaped scenarios. The goal is to demonstrate their understanding of the differences between prosocial, accidental, hostile, and ambiguous peer intent in social interactions.

Component #2—Understanding causal ambiguity. For *Lesson 7*, students review their video project. The leader focuses on the idea that ambiguous situations do not fit any one category. Students evaluate the usefulness of equating ambiguous with accidental intent. For homework, students receive an unfinished story of an ambiguously intended negative outcome, in which two boys are playing with a game that is about to be confiscated by a teacher. The friend hides the game, but the owner is later unable to find his friend and retrieve his property. Students are expected to write two endings for the story, one presuming a hostile intent and the other an accidental one.

Lesson 8 centers around the two endings that each student created for homework for Lesson 7. Students discuss the situation and the fact that the peer apparently disappears with the game. They assess the available social cues, which are deliberately restricted in the text of the story. Students next present their own responses. Subsequently, two prepared endings are read and discussed: uncontrollable ("My mother came for me and took me to a doctor's appointment before I could give it back") and controllable ("I just wanted to play with it some more"). The discussion focuses on helping students compare and contrast critical features of controllable and uncontrollable causes and realizing the difficulty in judging intent in the absence of cues.

In *Lesson 9* students in pairs role-play several prepared situations (e.g., a peer spills milk on you in the lunchroom). The students then classify scenes that are similar in intent, according to available cues. Discussion focuses on grouping ambiguous scenes in the accidental category. For homework students are asked to record several situations in which a peer's intent is hard to judge, including the action they took in response to the situation.

Component #3—Linking attributions and behavior. For *Lesson 10*, students present their findings and explain the category of intent for each of their situations. The leader then introduces a prepared, written scenario in which a child is pushed from behind by a peer while waiting in the lunch line. Students brainstorm and evaluate at least three behavioral alternatives. The leader makes clear the cause–effect relationship between social behavior and personal consequences.

Pairs of students role-play two ambiguous situations, alternating the role of peer in *Lesson 11*. One student role-plays the peer instigator, while the other interviews him to determine probable causes and intent. They practice generating attributions to nonhostile intent and provide appropriate endings to these stories by displaying how they would behave based on their judgments of the peer's intent.

Curriculum summary. The BrainPower Program curriculum (see Table 10.1) provides: (a) specific activities for understanding the concepts of intent and ambiguity in interpersonal interactions; (b) practice in identifying intentionality in others from a range of verbal and nonverbal social cues; (c) specific activities for distinguishing between intentional and unintentional outcomes; (d) practice in making attributions and generating decision rules about how to respond given attributional uncertainty. The program focuses entirely on peer-directed social behavior, and uses familiar playground situations typical of elementary school social life. Further, the presentation is designed to be entirely task focused, with no reference to an individual student's history of behavioral difficulties. Throughout treatment, the personal and social benefits of nonaggressive responding are emphasized in order to enhance students' motivation to use trained skills spontaneously (Bierman, 1986).

Program Implementation

The BrainPower Program is conducted as a school-based program of small group instruction (Hudley, 1991). Students are seen on a pull-out basis during the course of the regular school day. These sessions can be convened in any relatively quiet place separated from the regular classroom. The setting should have tables and chairs as well as a blackboard, overhead projector, or some other means of recording and displaying information for the entire group. Groups of six students meet twice weekly in 60-minute

TABLE 10.1. SUMMARY OF BRAINPOWER CURRICULUM

LESSON 1. Discusses goals and benefits of BrainPower Program.

LESSON 2. Focuses on the manner by which inferences of intent shape behavior.

Activity: Role-play peer interactions.

LESSON 3. Introduces the concept of nonverbal cues as an aid to intention detection.

Activity: Picture identification game.

LESSON 4. Discusses how one's own feelings may interfere with intention detection.

Activity: Unfinished sentences.

LESSON 5. Continues exploration of processes for intention detection.

Activity: View prepared videotapes.

LESSON 6. Reviews the skills necessary for accurate intention detection.

Activity: Create videotapes.

LESSON 7. Focuses on the idea that ambiguous situations do not really fit any one category.

Activity: Review videotapes.

LESSON 8. Discusses causation in social situations by contrasting controllable and uncontrollable.

Activity: Respond to unfinished story.

LESSON 9. Addresses how to detect similarities/differences and categorize situations.

Activity: Role-play peer interactions.

LESSON 10. Introduces appropriate action when responding to ambiguous situations.

Activity: Brainstorming.

LESSON 11. Reviews the behaviors for use in ambiguous or accidental situations.

Activity: Role-play peer interactions.

LESSON 12. Reviews the sequence of skills presented.

sessions for a total of 12 sessions. Each group should consist of four excessively aggressive and two average, nonaggressive students. The nonaggressive students participate in the retraining program in order to enhance the benefits for both themselves and their more aggressive peers. The presence of nonaggressives serves to: (a) negate any potential stigmatization of aggressive participants, (b) give aggressive participants the opportunity to interact with positive peer models, and (c) allow nonaggressives the opportunity to reappraise their attitudes and behaviors directed toward the aggressive students as they progress through the program. Such interaction between aggressive students and their peers is considered critical to the generalization of program effects (Asher, 1985; Bierman, 1986). These opportunities are also useful in counteracting the self-perpetuating effects that a reputation for aggressive behavior may have on aggressive children's interactions with peers (Dodge & Frame, 1982).

Evaluation Research on the BrainPower Program

The research to be reported here set out to determine if this hostile attributional bias was amenable to reduction by means of the previously described school-based intervention program of attribution retraining (Hudley & Graham, in press). The intent was not only to investigate the relationship between causal attributions and aggression, but also to enhance the social functioning of highly aggressive minority male children. Both before and after the intervention, data were collected on participants' attributional reasoning about peer provocations, teacher ratings of aggressive behavior, and number of disciplinary referrals to school administrators. For each of these dependent variables, I expected aggressive boys participating in the experimental intervention to differ from aggressives in two comparison groups in the direction of less perceived hostile peer intent, less anger, and a lower incidence of aggressive behavior. In addition, four aggressive students from the experimental treatment groups participated in separate, in-depth interviews.

Subjects. Participants were chosen from two urban, lower middle SES (20% or more students qualifying for free lunch) public schools in greater Los Angeles, enrolling predominantly African-American student populations (80% or more). For the purpose of sample selection, peer assessments and teacher ratings of aggressive behavior were collected on all students from 17 co-ed classrooms of third- through fifth-graders ($N = 529$) and for whom parental permission had been obtained. Only African-American boys ($N = 271$) were eligible to participate.

Each classroom teacher completed the aggression subscale of the Teacher Checklist (Coie, 1990) for each student enrolled in his or her class during the spring semester of 1989–90 school year. This measure is composed of eight items describing common types of childhood aggression (e.g., "this child starts fights") which the teacher rates on a 5-point scale. Higher numbers indicate greater perceived aggressiveness.

In addition, all students in the same 17 classrooms were asked to write down, with the aid of a classroom roster, the names of the three students in their class whom they liked most, the three whom they liked least, and the three who best fit each of five behavioral descriptions. Three of these descriptors portrayed aggressive behavior (i.e., "starts fights," "has a very short temper," "disrupts the group"), and two described prosocial behavior (i.e., "works well with others," "is helpful to other students").

From these data, African-American males who (a) were above the teacher median on perceived aggressiveness; (b) received a social preference score less than zero; and (c) received at least twice as many aggressive as prosocial nominations were included in the aggressive subject pool. Those who (a) were at or below the teacher median on perceived aggressiveness; (b) received a social preference score greater than zero; and (c) received at least twice as many prosocial as aggressive peer nominations were included in the nonaggressive subject pool (see Table 10.2).

The nonaggressive subjects provided a unique source of data, as the measurement of treatment effectiveness in intervention research has been redefined in recent years. Although statistically significant differences in group means signal the presence of a reliable treatment effect, they shed no

TABLE 10.2. STUDENT SELECTION CRITERIA USED IN BRAINPOWER EVALUATION

	Aggressive	Nonaggressive
Teacher Ratings	>median	≤ median
Social Preference Score	< 0	> 0
Peer Assessment	2X as many aggressive as prosocial	1.5X as many prosocial as aggressive

light on the magnitude of change for individual students. The construct of clinically significant change (Jacobsen & Truax, 1991) implies movement on the part of treated individuals out of the dysfunctional population and into the functional, or normative population (Jacobsen, 1988). To assess clinical significance most accurately, comparative data are required from a normative sample, and the design of this intervention allowed such data to be collected.

There is a related and continuing concern in the intervention research literature regarding negative effects of intervention on the normally developing child (Kazdin, 1987). Programs of primary prevention for antisocial behavior have sometimes demonstrated adverse effects on subjects' behavior (McCord, 1978), particularly among African-American youth (Hackler & Hagan, 1975). The emergence of possible deleterious effects could be closely monitored in this study, as nonaggressive youths participated fully in the program of intervention.

Procedure. During the Fall 1990 school semester, when the identified boys were fourth- through sixth-graders, 72 aggressives (*M* age = 10.5 yrs.) and 36 nonaggressives (*M* age = 10.2 yrs.) were randomly assigned to one of three treatment groups: the BrainPower attributional intervention (described earlier), an attention-training group, and a no-treatment control group. Three BrainPower and three attention-training groups met at each of the two sites, in locations away from the regular classroom. Students in both experimental and attention groups were required to attend a minimum of 10 sessions; all children fulfilled this requirement.

The groups were conducted by two African-American females, both educators with experience in small group instruction. Each experimenter, after completing 16 hours of training with the curriculum developer, individually conducted three experimental and three attention-training groups, distributed across both sites. Experimenters met with the curriculum developer on a weekly basis to monitor and discuss implementation integrity for the duration of the intervention.

Participants in both experimental and attention-training groups were told they were selected especially to assist the school in evaluating a program that might be used with students in schools throughout the city. Teachers were told that some students would receive a curriculum to assist them in getting along with peers and some students would receive an academic enrichment program. The students' group assignments were not revealed to teachers, and teachers were asked to refrain from questioning students about their respective programs.

An attention-training condition was included to control for possible effects of simple participation in a special program. The treatment, of the same 12-week duration as the attributional intervention, was based on the *Building Thinking Skills Program* (Black & Black, 1984). Using an instructional format similar to that employed in the attributional intervention, the program taught nonsocial problem-solving skills such as deductive and inductive reasoning, classifying information, and following directions. The 24 aggressive and 12 nonaggressive subjects who comprised the control group participated in pretesting and posttesting only.

Measures. Four types of instruments were used to evaluate the effects of the BrainPower program: (a) hypothetical scenarios of peer interactions, (b) behavioral rating scales completed by teachers, (c) school records of out-of-class disciplinary referrals, and (d) a laboratory task involving a negative outcome peer interaction. Data were collected prior to intervention and again at the close of the program (see Hudley & Graham, in press).

Each student was individually presented with five hypothetical interactions, resulting in a negative outcome for the subject. Situations included destruction of property (e.g., a ruined homework paper), physical harm (e.g., a hard push by a peer while playing baseball), and social rejection (e.g., a planned meeting with a peer who never showed up). In each scenario the peer's intent was systematically varied by altering the cues embedded in the story. For example, in the homework story, the child was to imagine walking onto the schoolyard and setting his notebook down, only to have an important homework paper blow out onto the ground. A peer then steps on the paper, leaving a footprint in the middle. The peer next either looks at the paper and back to the child (ambiguous), laughs and says "You lose" (hostile), apologizes and states that he did not see the paper (accidental), or explains that he was trying to save the paper from flying into the street (prosocial).

Each student received one story each of accidental, hostile, and prosocial intent and two of ambiguous intent in a single session prior to the intervention program and again at the close of intervention. For each scenario, four questions probing the student's judgment of intent (e.g., "Do you think he did this on purpose?") and three questions eliciting perceived anger (e.g., "Would you be angry with this person?") were rated on a 7-point scale. Participants also selected one from among six behaviors ranging in aggression intensity from "Have it out right then and there" to "Do something nice for him."

Teacher ratings on all participants were collected using three subscales of Coie's (1990) *Teacher Checklist*. Each student was rated on the eight-item aggression subscale also completed by the previous year's teacher for the purpose of sample selection, a five-item prosocial behavior subscale (e.g., "This child shares things in a group"), and a four-item academic performance subscale (e.g., "This child has trouble completing work"). The aggression subscale (described previously) also decomposes into derived scores for both reactive and proactive (i.e., instrumental aggression). As this intervention targeted reactive aggressive behaviors, specific scores for reactive aggression were also calculated. Each subject's current teacher completed rating scales the week prior to the onset of the program and again the week following its termination. Although teachers were aware that some students were removed from class to participate in the study, they were blind to students' intervention group assignments.

A records search was conducted at each school site to determine the number of times participants were referred to an administrator's office for formal disciplinary action. Administrative logs were reviewed for the school year immediately preceding the experimental intervention and for the school quarter immediately following the intervention (January – March). These records represent referrals for all types of infractions, including physical and verbal aggression, disruptiveness, deliberate disobedience, theft, and vandalism.

Responses to an actual peer were examined after the intervention in a laboratory task in which the aggressive child communicated with an unseen peer whose actions resulted in the subject's failure to obtain a desired goal. Both students received simple grid maps depicting various buildings and streets, and were told that they would take turns being direction giver and direction receiver. If the receiver arrived at a destination known only to the direction giver, he won a prize. On the first trial, the peer was always assigned the role of direction giver, and the subject received directions and attempted to win the prize. But the task was designed to be frustrating as, unbeknownst to either child, the peer's map was different from the subject's. Thus incorrect directions were given, the destination was not reached, and no prize was awarded.

An observer unobtrusively recorded the subject's responses, which constituted the measure of verbal aggression. After the first trial, when it was clear that the subject had not successfully completed the task, he was asked to rate his judgments of the peer's intent and his own feelings of anger on a 7-point scale. Once these measures were collected, two additional trials of the task were administered, with the two participants alternating the roles of direction giver and receiver. On both of these trials, the direction receiver successfully reached the destination, and both participants received comparable prizes.

Four participants in the experimental treatment were also interviewed individually 6 weeks after the close of the intervention program in order to supplement the quantitative data. I selected one student who received greater than expected teacher ratings of aggression and one student who received lower aggression ratings than expected from each of the two school sites.

Effect of the BrainPower Program

Hypothetical scenarios. Prior to intervention, all of these youth were quite able to incorporate intent information for those scenarios in which such information was presented. That is, only the ratings for the ambiguous scenarios differed significantly between aggressive and nonaggressive subjects. Aggressives were more likely to rate the ambiguous scenario as more hostile than any other except the hostile scenario, and nonaggressive subjects most often rated the ambiguous scenarios as similar to the accidental scenarios.

Data collected at the close of the intervention revealed a systematic change in judgments of intent, ratings of perceived anger, and endorsement of retaliatory aggressive behavior. Ratings on all three indices for nonaggressive subjects as well as aggressive subjects in the two comparison groups did not change significantly as a function of intervention type. However, aggressive subjects in the BrainPower treatment groups showed sizeable reductions in attributions of hostile intent, anger, and retaliatory behavior (see Table 10.3).

A measure of clinically significant change was also calculated to assess the ability of this treatment to facilitate the movement of excessively aggressive subjects into the average range of behavior. The pre-intervention responses of nonaggressive subjects constituted the normative sample for purposes of comparison. By using pre-intervention responses, it was also possible to evaluate changes among the nonaggressive subjects as well.

Using the standard of clinical significance, BrainPower group aggressive students showed the greatest proportion of positive changes in ratings of the ambiguous scenarios, to a level comparable to nonaggressives. Sixty percent of these aggressive subjects (n = 15) showed such reductions in attributions of hostile intent, compared to 4% (n = 1) of the attention-only

Table 10.3. Mean Ratings of Intent, Anger, and Behavior as a Function of Intervention Group and Scenario Condition.

	Causal Condition							
Group	Ambiguous		Prosocial		Hostile		Accidental	
Intent	**PRE**	**POST**	**PRE**	**POST**	**PRE**	**POST**	**PRE**	**POST**
All Nonaggres[1]	2.53_a	3.51_a	2.06	2.51_{ab}	6.31	6.05	2.37	1.63
Experiment[2]	5.31_b	2.63_a	2.55	2.05_a	6.04	6.81	2.11	1.65
AttenTrng[3]	5.18_b	5.21_b	2.65	3.10_b	6.21	6.40	2.59	2.07
NoAttCont[4]	4.63_b	4.69_b	2.22	3.14_b	6.43	6.32	2.53	2.09
Anger	**PRE**	**POST**	**PRE**	**POST**	**PRE**	**POST**	**PRE**	**POST**
All Nonaggres	3.61_a	4.00_a	2.97	2.47_{ab}	6.60	6.31	3.54	2.44
Experiment	5.51_b	3.39_a	2.50	1.78_a	6.75	6.78	3.22	2.25
AttenTrng	5.53_b	5.31_b	3.11	3.09_{ab}	6.71	6.57	3.52	2.32
NoAttCont	5.18_b	4.71_b	3.10	3.67_b	6.73	6.46	3.06	2.50
Behavior	**PRE**	**POST**	**PRE**	**POST**	**PRE**	**POST**	**PRE**	**POST**
All Nonaggres	3.23_a	3.26_{ab}	2.23	2.21	4.69	4.85_{ab}	2.66	2.64
Experiment	4.45_b	2.85_a	2.63	1.79	4.90	5.26_a	2.90	2.63
AttenTrng	4.23_b	3.81_b	2.60	2.36	4.96	4.96_{ab}	2.91	2.64
NoAttCont	3.81_{ab}	3.65_b	2.30	2.16	4.63	4.38_b	2.63	2.91

Note. Experiment(al), Atten(tion) Trng, and NoAtt(ention) Cont(rol) groups represent aggressive subjects only. Nonaggressives did not differ by group. Within variables, column means with different subscripts differ significantly at $p < .05$. Higher numbers indicate greater presumed hostile intent, reported anger, and retaliatory aggression.
[1]n = 35; [2]n = 20; [3]n = 22; [4]n = 24.

From Hudley, C., & Graham, S. (in press). An attributional intervention to reduce peer directed aggression among African-American boys, *Child Development*. Copyright by Society for the Study of Child Development, University of Chicago Press. Adapted by permission.

group and 8% ($n = 2$) of the no-attention controls. Ratings of anger and behavioral choice showed a similar pattern. No BrainPower group aggressive boys demonstrated significant negative changes, but three students (12.5%) in the no-treatment control condition and one (4%) student in the attention-only group displayed increased attributional bias, and the latter two groups also had one student whose ratings of anger increased significantly.

Among all nonaggressives, no students in the BrainPower group exhibited dysfunctional attributions of hostile intent or preferred levels of aggressive retaliation. One subject, however, significantly increased his rating of anger. Among the subjects in the comparison groups, one displayed an increase in judgments of hostile intent, and one an increase in ratings of anger. No clinically significant reductions occurred for any student in attributions of hostile intent or aggressive behavioral choice, as the great majority of these subjects' scores remained below the cutoff point from pre- to postintervention. One subject in the no-treatment condition did significantly reduce his ratings of experienced anger.

Thus, by these indicators, the BrainPower program was quite successful in reducing attributional bias among aggressive boys without producing any negative effects among nonaggressive boys. Only BrainPower group aggressives reduced their ratings of hostile intent, anger, and retaliatory aggression to a level comparable to all nonaggressive students by the end of the program. Further, the BrainPower students were the only group among aggressives who showed no significant increases on any of these measures. This intervention apparently not only reduces attributional bias but also counteracts a developmental progression in which the bias actually increases if left untreated.

Teacher ratings. Prior to the BrainPower program, all boys identified as aggressive, based on information from the previous school year, were rated by their current teachers as more aggressive overall, $F(1,94) = 52.80$, $p <.001$; more prone to aggressive retaliation, $F(1,94) = 32.75$, $p <.001$); performing less well in the classroom, $F(1,94) = 18.62$, $p <.001$; and displaying fewer prosocial behaviors toward peers, $F(1,94) = 14.44$, $p <.001$; when compared to all students designated as nonaggressive.

Following the intervention, teacher ratings for only aggressive boys in the BrainPower group were significantly lower for overall aggression, $t(19) = 2.63$, $p < .05$, and reactive aggression as well, $t(19) = 2.32$, $p < .05$, compared to their pre-intervention scores. However, even these students were still rated as significantly more aggressive than all nonaggressive subjects, $F(1,94) = 11.82$, $p <.01$. Teacher ratings of prosocial and academic behavior were unaffected by the intervention, and differences in teacher ratings were not significant for either the attention training or control group aggressive subjects, nor any of the nonaggressive subjects (see Table 10.4).

Aggressive participants in the BrainPower treatment displayed clinically significant reductions in teacher ratings of both reactive and overall aggression at a rate more than double that of either comparison group. Additionally, although aggressive boys in both comparison groups received clinically significant increases in teacher ratings for both reactive ($n = 4$) and overall

Table 10.4. Teacher Ratings of Behavior as a Function of Intervention Group.

Intervention Group		Subscale			
		Total Aggress 8 items	Reactive Aggress 3 items	Prosocial Behavior 5 items	School Behavior[a] 4 items
All Nonaggressive ($n = 35$)					
	Pre	14.44	6.14	16.97	10.47
	Post	15.41	6.29	16.06	10.44
Experimental Aggressive ($n = 20$)					
	Pre	27.55	11.05	13.05	14.80
	Post	24.05	9.55	14.65	14.40
Attention-Only Aggressive ($n = 22$)					
	Pre	24.05	10.18	14.00	14.45
	Post	26.23	12.27	14.73	14.82
No Att Control Aggressive ($n = 24$)					
	Pre	26.83	11.38	14.79	13.17
	Post	25.71	11.13	15.62	12.17

Note. Nonaggressive subjects did not differ by group.
[a]Higher numbers indicate more negative school behavior.

From Hudley, C., & Graham, S. (in press). An attributional intervention to reduce peer directed aggression among African-American boys, *Child Development*. Copyright by Society for the Study of Child Development, University of Chicago Press. Adapted by permission.

(n = 6) aggression, only one BrainPower aggressive student received clinically higher ratings of overall aggression, and no increases were observed for this group in ratings of reactive aggression. Clinically improved teacher ratings of prosocial behavior were also evident for both BrainPower and no-attention control aggressive subjects, but no effects were detected for ratings of academic performance.

One nonaggressive student each in the BrainPower and attention-only groups received clinically significant increases in teacher ratings of reactive aggression. Again, teacher ratings for these students typically remained well below cutoff levels both before and after intervention.

Office referrals. Prior to the intervention, aggressive boys were almost three times as likely to be referred to the office as were nonaggressives. Although BrainPower group aggressives displayed the greatest absolute reductions in office referrals 3 months after intervention, differences by group were not statistically significant, and differences by status remained highly significant, $F(2,94) = 14.48$, $p < .001$. Although aggressive boys continued to be referred to the office at significantly higher rates, only those in the BrainPower group showed any clinically significant changes in office referrals. Twenty percent exhibited clinically significant reductions in office referrals from pre- to postintervention, whereas only half that number demonstrated increases during the postintervention assessment period. Neither significant increases nor reductions were found for any of the nonaggressive students, as again frequencies remained stable and well below cutoff levels.

Analog task. Only aggressive subjects participated in the frustrating laboratory task, which took place 1 week after the close of intervention sessions. In judging the peer partner's intent, boys who had participated in the BrainPower program were significantly less likely to infer that the unseen peer had intentionally caused them to fail than were the two aggressive comparison groups, $F(2, 64) = 9.85$, $p < .001$, who did not differ from one another. Affect ratings showed a similar, though nonsignificant pattern. Although less intense anger was reported by BrainPower boys, none of the children reported feeling very angry at the peer.

Subjects' verbal responses during the task were subsequently classified into one of four types: *neutral*, defined as nonjudgmental statements to the peer or to the adult experimenter (e.g., "That road is a dead end"); *complaint*, which captured negative comments regarding the subject's own performance (e.g., "I can't do this"); *criticize*, defined as negative remarks to the peer about his performance (e.g., "You obviously don't know how to read a map"); and *insult*, which described negative personal comments directed toward the peer (e.g., "You're dumb").

If participants in the BrainPower group inferred less hostile intent and felt less angry, then they also should engage in fewer verbally aggressive behaviors (i.e., criticizing and insulting) that might accompany perceived hostile peer intent. The behavioral data displayed in Table 10.5 show that this was indeed the case. Neutral comments were by far the preferred verbal behavior of BrainPower students (61%), and not one of these children resorted to insult. Among the two comparison groups of boys, the four

TABLE 10.5. AGGRESSIVE SUBJECTS' ATTRIBUTIONS OF INTENT, REPORTED AFFECT, AND BEHAVIORS IN THE ANALOG TASK AS A FUNCTION OF INTERVENTION GROUP

	Intervention Group		
	Experimental Treatment[a]	Attention Training[b]	Control[c]
Variable	*M*	*M*	*M*
Intent Attributions	2.25	4.45	4.72
Reported Anger	1.65	2.48	2.62
Behaviors	$n = 31$	$n = 41$	$n = 48$
• Neutral	61%	29%	31%
• Complain	19.5%	24.5%	31%
• Criticize	19.5%	29%	23%
• Insult	0.0%	17.5%	15%

Note. Higher numbers indicate greater presumed hostility and reported anger. Behavioral data are expressed as percentages of total behaviors for each group. Total behaviors for each group are listed as the first entry in each percentage column.
[a]$n = 20$; [b]$n = 22$; [c]$n = 24$.

From Hudley, C., & Graham, S. (in press). An attributional intervention to reduce peer directed aggression among African-American boys, *Child Development*.

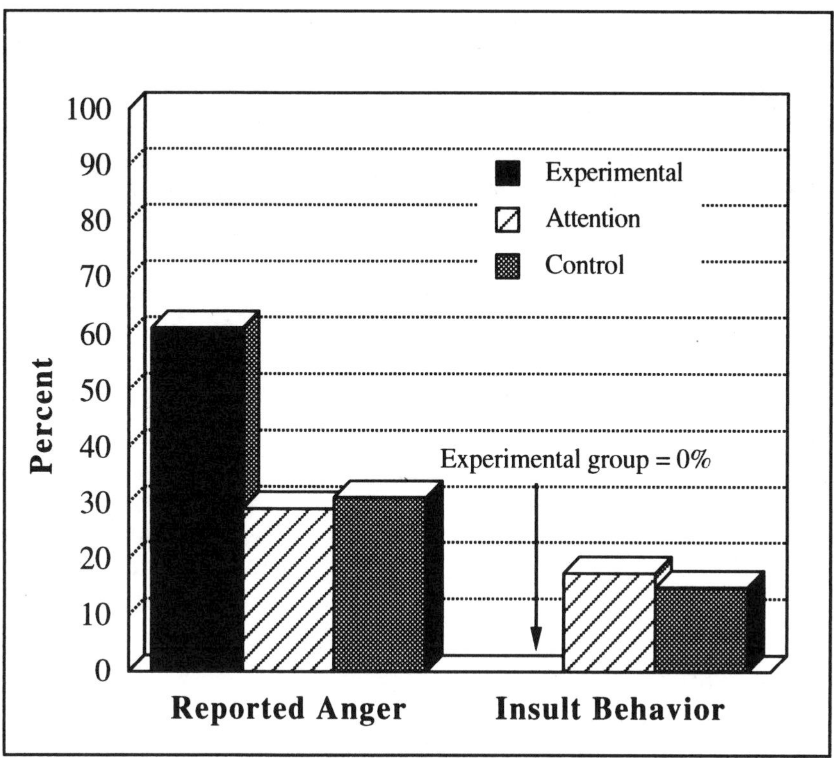

FIGURE 10.1. PERCENT C' TOTAL BEHAVIORS BY INTERVENTION GROUP.

classes of behavior were more evenly evoked, with one in six responses classified as an insult (see also Figure 10.1).

Summary of BrainPower Implementation

In sum, the hypothetical scenario judgments, teacher ratings, and office referrals for nonaggressive boys remained relatively stable from pre- to postintervention measurement. BrainPower group aggressive subjects were most likely to resemble nonaggressive subjects in their ratings of hostile peer intent, expressed anger, and behavioral preferences in the ambiguous hypothetical scenarios at postintervention. Further, BrainPower aggressives had by far the greatest proportion of clinically significant, reliable change in ratings of hypothetical scenario data. Among teacher ratings, changes in reactive aggression scores showed the greatest differences by group, again favoring the BrainPower aggressive students. Mean differences in office referral change scores did not achieve statistical significance as a function of group membership; however, only aggressive boys in the BrainPower group demonstrated clinically significant change on this variable. Finally, data from the laboratory analog task are generally consistent with other measures, indicating that BrainPower's effects generalized to an actual peer interaction.

Through the Eyes of the Students

To supplement quantitative data, individual, in-depth interviews were conducted 6 weeks after the close of the intervention program with four boys who participated in the BrainPower group (Hudley, 1991). Students were first asked to discuss the types and quality of their relationships with their peers and subsequently to describe a specific conflict or disagreement with a peer that had occurred recently. We will hear first from the two boys whose teacher and peer ratings of aggression are greater than would have been predicted, followed by the two boys whose ratings of aggression are less than would have been predicted.

Student #1. Cory, a 9-year-old, fourth-grade student, was rated by both teacher and peers as being highly aggressive. Teacher ratings were uniformly high, generally 4 or 5 on a 5-point scale, with little change in ratings observed from pre-intervention to postintervention. Postintervention information also indicated that Cory showed an increased tendency to threaten and argue with peers at school as the semester has progressed. Peers seemed to concur with the opinion that Cory's aggression is quite pronounced. After the intervention, he received a total of 37 peer nominations for aggressive behavior, distributed over three questions. He was nominated in at least one aggression question by 21 of 27 students, including all 12 boys enrolled in his class.

When describing the kinds of things he did with his various siblings and friends, Cory often spontaneously mentioned aggressive behavior. His free recall of basketball games included "kids who play sneaky and get away with fouls." He described his school friends as forming a group with him "so other kids won't feel like taking our stuff or starting anything with us." His worldview may be shaped in part by an older brother with whom he claims to spend a lot of time and who has been incarcerated for assault with a deadly weapon.

When questioned about conflicts with peers, Cory stated that the negative behavior of others is usually deliberately intended, and he made absolutely no mention of social cues that might distinguish intentional from accidental behavior. In describing his basketball experiences, for example, he categorized the fouls of opponents as purposeful, regardless of the context of the activity. Yet the fouls that he committed were always described as accidental. The behaviors that Cory described as appropriate responses to negative outcome, peer-instigated interactions were uniformly aggressive. He acknowledged that in a basketball game, one should not jeopardize the outcome of the game simply to retaliate; however, he felt strongly that he would express his displeasure to an opponent at the appropriate time. "I'd let him know, that, yeah, I see what he's doing, and we'll just see after the game." Suggested responses in other peer interactions were similarly threatening. He believed an aggressive response to be the only possible response in a negative circumstance, not based on excessive anger, but rather a notion of reciprocity. "If something happens to you, then you gotta show the other person that they can't get away with it." This young man apparently operates according to a well-defined set of values that are resistant to change from a program such as BrainPower.

Student #2. Donte, an 11-year-old fifth-grader, presents an inconsistent picture. Based on outcome measures gathered during the course of the study, Donte's teacher and classmates do not share similar perceptions of his behavior. Teacher ratings of overall aggression both pre- and postintervention were intermediate, generally 3 on a 5-point scale. The teacher rated Donte as somewhat likely to retaliate aggressively when threatened or teased (4 on a scale of 5), but showing improvement at postintervention assessment in both verbal and physical aggression. On the other hand, every single classmate of Donte's nominated him on at least one of the three aggression questions after the intervention, for a total of 49 nominations. He received the highest number of peer nominations for aggression in the entire class.

Donte insisted that he rarely had any fights, arguments, or other difficulties with peers. He commented that most other students get along well with him. The one conflict he did discuss involved a peer throwing his book bag on the ground. Donte stated that a classmate had attempted to steal notebook paper from his bag, and finding none in the bag, "just threw it down, under the lunch benches" on the playground. However, Donte had not been present when the attempted theft transpired. Further, he had no hard evidence or witnesses as to the identity of the offending classmate but was sure that he knew "exactly who was trying to get my stuff." He was absolutely certain that the peer was deliberately hostile in his intention.

In this particular instance, Donte came to his conclusion about a peer's intent in the absence of any available social cues. In fact, he stated that he had left the book bag on the bench, and it was under the bench when he returned. It was not lying open, nor were the contents damaged. When questioned directly, he was unable to cite specific information that indicated that the bag had not simply rolled off the bench, or been accidentally pushed off by someone walking by. Rather the attribution of intent to steal was based on the past experiences of "other kids who had their notebooks and paper stolen, and everybody knows who did it."

Donte also described several things he had done subsequently to the student he believed responsible for throwing his bag on the ground. These included taking his pencil, telling others not to play with him, and telling another student that "he probably took your stuff too." Apparently, Donte's preferred response to perceived negative intent is indirect aggression, or getting even later. Although he stated that he forgot about the book bag incident, his responses to specific questions indicate that he indeed exacted retribution from the peer who he assumed committed the deed. This child appears to make decisions based on schemata that are so deeply ingrained that a program of the brevity of BrainPower can be expected to have little impact.

Student #3. Albert is a 9-year-old fourth-grader who has shown evidence of positive behavioral change during his semester of participation in the experimental intervention. Teacher ratings declined from 4s to 2s on a 5-point scale, and Albert received a total of 10 postintervention nominations for aggressive behavior from classmates, distributed over three questions. His was the lowest total of aggressive nominations among all of the aggressive boys enrolled in his classroom.

Albert mentioned in connection with school activities that arguments and/or fights occurred when playing sports because there were no designated officials (e.g., umpires, basketball referees). "Everybody doesn't know the rules and nobody is there to get them straight." Of course, he felt that he had an accurate understanding of all rules.

When asked specifically about conflicts, Albert described an incident that had occurred during the immediately preceding recess period. One of his friends had pushed him down on the basketball court while they were playing on opposite teams. He stated that although he felt the push might have been deliberate, he wasn't entirely sure, because "we were both running for the ball, and I got my hands on it. He pushed me in the back, and I just fell. Maybe he didn't like it because I beat him to the ball." Almost immediately after he regained his feet, the bell rang to end recess, and both he and his friends left the court to line up with their respective classes. Albert stated that he had made no attempt at the time to retaliate. Therefore, at the time of the interview, he had not yet been able to resolve the incident with the other student. Although the outcome of the incident was negative, the peer's act might have been the result of "going for the ball to get in the last shot." However, it may just as easily have been the result of frustration in not being able to retrieve the ball from his opponent. Albert appeared to understand fully the problem of determining the peer's intent in the context of an ambiguous situation such as this. Although he did not automatically assume it was an accident, neither did he definitively presume hostile intent on the part of the peer. Albert appeared open to an attribution of accidental intent to his friend's behavior but was still seeking additional cues on which to base his behavior.

Student #4. Keith, a 10-year-old fourth-grader, received postintervention teacher and peer ratings, which suggested that his current behavior more closely resembled a nonaggressive than an aggressive child. Teacher ratings showed a marked decline from 4s and 5s to 1s and 2s on a 5-point scale. Keith received a total of only six postintervention peer nominations for aggressive behavior distributed over three questions. This is less than one third of the maximum number of nominations received by aggressive subjects in the class, and only two more than the minimum number received by nonaggressive subjects in the class.

Although Keith did not spontaneously provide any descriptions of conflicts or aggression within the peer group, violence and aggression seem to be a fact of his life. Playing at the local park is not often possible because "gang bangers are in there at certain times, smoking crack and acting wild. They take our balls and stuff if they catch us." Keith discussed disagreements with peers that arose entirely in the context of playing sports. "We might get mad at each other if someone got tripped, because you're not supposed to trip people while you're playing. Someone could get hurt." He considered tripping during a game to be an accidental occurrence most of the time, though Keith did mention being deliberately tripped while playing tackle football in his backyard because the friend was losing so badly "that he stopped me any way he could. After he tripped me I looked at him and he was kind of laughing. He didn't say sorry or anything either." In this situation, Keith reported that his behavioral response was to simply shrug it off and do nothing because aggressive retaliation would only be appropriate in this situation if the instigator has done his victim some physical harm. Keith appears to be incorporating not only social cues but also judgments about the severity of the transgression into his behavioral decisions.

Summary of case studies. The two students who were perceived by teachers and peers as less aggressive at postintervention apparently made greater efforts to utilize presented social cues in peer interactions. In contrast, excessively aggressive students were much less likely to cite available social information in explaining the need for aggressive retaliation. Instead, in justifying their aggressive behavior, both boys referred to general beliefs that peers were behaving in a deliberately hostile manner toward them. Such beliefs resemble the "paranoid expectancy" of aggression from peers which was first identified among aggressive boys by Dodge and Frame (1982).

SUMMARY AND CONCLUDING COMMENTS

Over the past 10 years, substantial evidence has documented a hostile attributional bias among highly aggressive boys (see Hudley, Chapter 2, for a review). These young men have been found to be especially likely to presume that their peers are acting toward them with deliberately hostile intentions, particularly in negative outcome situations of uncertain causal origins. These misperceptions of intent have been consistently correlated with displays of inappropriate retaliatory aggression among highly aggressive boys (Dodge & Coie, 1987). However, past research typically identified and analyzed this bias and its covariation with reactive aggression. Substantially less effort was devoted to attempts to manipulate this cognitive tendency and assess any resultant changes in aggressive behavior. Thus the question of whether this attributional bias, once established, is amenable to change has not, until now, been answered. A related question is whether the reduction of this cognitive bias also significantly reduces aggressive behavior.

The results of the BrainPower implementation reported here indicate that both questions can be answered in the affirmative, and these answers suggest a causal relationship between biased cognition and aggressive behavior. Based on the fundamental principles of attribution theory, BrainPower was designed as a program of attribution retraining that was able to reduce a cognitive bias to presume hostile peer intentions in situations that contain ambiguous social information and result in negative outcomes. So, a hostile attributional bias has been found to be amenable to cognitive retraining efforts among aggressive, African-American elementary school male students. Aggressive boys receiving the BrainPower program exhibited a marked reduction in an attributional bias to presume hostile intent on the part of peers in both hypothetical and laboratory simulations of ambiguous provocation situations. They also were less likely to endorse hostile behavioral alternatives on the judgment measures, and to engage in verbally hostile responses on a laboratory task. Furthermore, aggressive intervention subjects were rated as significantly less aggressive by their teachers who remained blind to treatment condition throughout the study. As these findings are not present among either of the two comparison aggressive groups, there is reason to believe that the particular features of the BrainPower attribution retraining program are responsible for the observed reduction in bias. This may be one of the few, if not the only intervention program with children that shows positive effects of specific attribution retraining on subsequent social behavior. As such, it supports the hypothesis that attributional bias regulates aggression.

Prior intervention research has also indicated that the presence of a "close fit between the content of the intervention and the social deficiencies of the intervention sample" may determine the success of a particular treatment (Coie, 1985, p. 149). The attribution retraining program developed for this study supports such a conclusion. The intervention targeted a specific social cognitive deficit in aggressive children (i.e., accuracy in judging the intent of others) and improvement is most evident in those areas affected by intention detection. For example, teacher ratings on general prosocial behavior and academic performance, domains of competence not pertinent to the intervention, did not change from pre- to postintervention. Nor were there changes in children's attributional inferences in the hypothetical scenarios containing clear cues of prosocial, accidental, or hostile intent. Both before and after the intervention, all of the aggressive children in our research "correctly" perceived prosocial and accidental peer provocations as unintended, and hostile provocations as maliciously caused. Aggressive children are consistently found to have the greatest problems with accurate inferences about others' intent in situations of attributional ambiguity (e.g., Dodge, 1980). This intervention was extremely effective in enhancing this particular social cognitive deficit. From a treatment perspective, focusing on one specific cognitive antecedent of aggression at a time may prove more manageable in building intervention packages that can be tailored to the specific needs of individual children than are approaches that simultaneously address multiple social cognitive processes linked to aggression.

Related to the issue of intervention and sample "fit," our program had no deleterious effects on nonaggressive participants. Their judgments of hypothetical scenarios and teacher ratings of their behavior remained stable over the duration of the program. Kazdin (1987) has cautioned those conducting programs of primary prevention to assure themselves that their treatments are not creating negative behaviors among their subjects. Increases in aggressive behavior among nonaggressive subjects are not generated by the attributional treatment reported here.

It must be acknowledged that the major outcome variables involved either hypothetical judgments or a simulation, and these data were not collected longitudinally. The single "real world," follow-up behavioral variable, office referrals, provided only modest support to the positive effect of the intervention. Three months after the intervention ended, experimental subjects were still sent to the principal's office for inappropriate behavior almost as much as they were during the school year prior to the intervention. Inasmuch as office referrals were made for any number of student transgressions (peer aggression, defiance of authority, vandalism, and theft), in retrospect it seems unlikely that this measure would be influenced by changes in attributional beliefs. At this point, therefore, follow up data are insufficient to establish the maintenance of behavior change beyond the period of posttreatment assessment. Future research must develop more sensitive indicators and include multiple measures to address the questions of maintenance and generalizability. As one alternative, naturally occurring peer interactions (e.g., playground activities) may be better contexts for observing behavioral indicators of treatment efficacy.

Although this intervention provides evidence of a relationship between cognitive change and behavior for aggressive subjects, the data with regard to emotional change are less clear. I expected anger to mediate the relation between perceived intent and aggressive action; that is, the effect on behavior of changes in judgments of intent would be accounted for by changes in reported anger. However, a stepdown analysis of the hypothetical data showed that controlling for changes in intent attributions eliminated significant group differences in reported anger for aggressive subjects. On the other hand, entering reported anger as the highest priority variable did not eliminate significant group differences in perceived intent. And in the laboratory task, reported anger (unlike perceived intent) was relatively uninfluenced by participation in the experimental intervention. It may be that the self-report measure was not sufficiently sensitive for this population which has been found to have difficulty in identifying anger within the self

(Goldstein & Glick, 1987). Thus from a treatment perspective, interventions that focus on emotional change (e.g., anger control) may not be especially effective with this population in the absence of accompanying cognitive change. Alternatively, anger may not always follow attributions to hostile intent. From a theoretical perspective, then, the role of anger as an antecedent to retaliatory peer aggression remains unclear.

As with any intervention, not all of the boys who participated in the BrainPower attributional program experienced beneficial effects. Hence, there are probably individual differences within the sample labeled as aggressive that make some children more likely than others to profit from attributional change. For example, the results of attribution retraining must be evaluated within the broader sociocultural context from which intervention participants are drawn. This was made clear in the posttreatment interviews with experimental subjects who did not benefit from the intervention. For some of our young research participants, violence and aggression may be so closely woven into their everyday life experiences that an intervention based on attributional change at the level of the individual is incapable of impacting their behavior. In addition, Dodge (1991) has suggested a distinction between children whose aggression is reactive (those who respond impulsively to perceived provocation) versus proactive (i.e., instrumental) aggression (those who instigate hostile behavior without provocation). Only the former type of aggressive boy is likely to benefit from an intervention focused on altering cognitions about peer provocation (Dodge, 1991; Dodge & Coie, 1987).

African-American boys are a highly diverse group of individuals, some of whom might benefit from an attributional change program such as the one presented here. On the other hand, for some boys labeled as aggressive this intervention would be neither viable nor appropriate. In sum, the efficacy of the BrainPower attributional retraining as an important part of treatment for childhood aggression is promising. This statement, however, must be tempered by a clear awareness of the complex array of nonattributional (and nonsocial cognitive) factors that are known determinants of aggression among African-American youth, as discussed by Chan (Chapter 6).

REFERENCES

Asher, S. (1985). An evolving paradigm in social skill training research with children. In B. Schneider, K. Rubin, & L. Ledingham (Eds.), *Children's peer relations: Issues in assessment and intervention* (pp. 157-171). New York: Springer-Verlag.

Bierman, K. (1986). Process of change during social skills training and its relationship to treatment outcome. *Child Development, 57*, 230-240.

Black, H., & Black, S. *Building thinking skills-Book 2*. Pacific Grove, CA: Midwest Publications.

Camp, B., & Bash, M. (1980). Developing self control through training in problem solving: The "Think Aloud" program. In D. Rathjen & J. Foreyt (Eds.), *Social competence: Interventions for children and adults* (pp. 24-53). New York: Pergamon Press.

Camp, B., Blom, G., Herbert, F., & von Doornick, W. (1977). Think Aloud: A program for developing self-control in young aggressive boys. *Journal of Abnormal Child Psychology, 5*, 157-169.

Coie, J. (1985). Fitting social skills intervention to the target group. In B. Schneider, K. Rubin, & J. Ledingham (Eds.), *Children's peer relations: Issues in assessment and intervention* (pp. 141-156). New York: Springer-Verlag.

Coie, J. (1990). *Teacher Checklist*. Unpublished manuscript.

Dodge, K. (1980). Social cognition and children's aggressive behavior. *Child Development, 51*, 162-170.

Dodge, K. (1991). The structure and function of reactive and proactive aggression. In D. Pepler & K. Rubin (Eds.), *The development and treatment of childhood aggression* (pp. 201-218). Hillsdale, NJ: Erlbaum.

Dodge, K., & Coie, J. (1987). Social information processing factors in reactive and proactive aggression in children's peer groups. *Journal of Personality and Social Psychology, 53*, 1146-1158.

Dodge, K., & Crick, N. (1990). Social information-processing bases of aggressive behavior in children. *Personality and Social Psychology Bulletin, 16*, 8-22.

Dodge, K., & Frame, C. (1982). Social cognitive biases and deficits in aggressive boys. *Child Development, 53*, 620-635.

Garrison, S., & Stolberg, A. (1983). Modification of anger in children by affective imagery training. *Journal of Abnormal Child Psychology, 11*, 115-130.

Goldstein, A., & Glick, B. (1987). *Aggression Replacement Training*. Champaign, IL: Research Press.

Guerra, N., & Slaby, R. (1990). Cognitive mediators of aggression in adolescent offenders: 2. Intervention. *Developmental Psychology, 26*, 269-277.

Hackler, J., & Hagan, J. (1975). Work and teaching machines as delinquency prevention tools: A four-year follow-up. *Social Science Review, 49,* 92-106.

Hudley, C. (1991). *An attribution retraining program to reduce peer directed aggression among African-American male elementary school students* [Unpublished doctoral dissertation], University of California, Los Angeles.

Hudley, C., & Graham, S. (in press). An attributional intervention to reduce peer directed aggression among African-American boys. *Child Development.*

Jacobsen, N. (1988). Defining clinically significant change: An introduction. *Behavioral Assessment, 10,* 131-132.

Jacobsen, N., & Truax, P. (1991). Clinical significance: A statistical approach to defining meaningful change in psychotherapy research. *Journal of Consulting and Clinical Psychology, 59,* 12-19.

Kazdin, A. (1980). *Research design in clinical psychology.* New York: Harper & Row.

Kazdin, A. (1985). *Treatment of antisocial behavior in children and adolescents.* Homewood, IL: Dorsey Press.

Kazdin, A. (1987). *Conduct disorders in childhood and adolescence.* Newbury Park, CA: Sage.

Lochman, J., Lampron, L., Gemmer, T., & Harris, S. (1987). Anger coping intervention with aggressive children: A guide to implementation in school settings. In P. Keller & S. Heyman (Eds.), *Innovations in clinical practice: A source book* (pp. 339-356). Sarasota, FL: Professional Resource Exchange.

Luria, A. (1963). Psychological studies of mental deficiency in the Soviet Union. In N. Ellis (Ed.), *Handbook of mental deficiency* (pp. 353-387). New York: McGraw-Hill.

McCord, J. (1978). A thirty-year follow-up of treatment effects. *American Psychologist, 33,* 284-289.

Novaco, R. (1978). Anger and coping with stress. In J. Foreyt & D. Rathjen (Eds.), *Cognitive behavior therapy: Research and applications* (pp. 135-173). New York: Plenum Press.

Pelligrini, D. (1985). Social cognition and competence in middle childhood. *Child Development, 56,* 253-264.

Pepler, D., King, G., & Byrd, W. (1991). A social-cognitively based social skills training program for aggressive children. In D. Pepler & K. Rubin (Eds.),*The development and treatment of childhood aggression* (pp.361-379). Hillsdale, NJ: Lawrence Erlbaum Associates.

Reed, R. (1988). Education and achievement of young, Black males. In J. Gibb (Ed.), *Young, Black, and male in America: An endangered species* (pp. 37-96). Dover, MA: Auburn House.

Robin, A., Schneider, M., & Dolnick, M. (1976). The Turtle Technique: An extended case study of self-control in the classroom. *Psychology in the Schools, 13*, 449-453.

Rotheram, M. (1980). Social skills training programs in elementary and high school classrooms. In D. Rathjen & J. Foreyt (Eds.), *Social competence: Interventions for children and adults* (pp. 69-112). New York: Pergamon Press.

Spivak, G., Platt, J., & Shure, M. (1976). *The problem-solving approach to adjustment*. San Francisco: Jossey-Bass.

Urbain, E., & Kendall, P. (1980). Review of social cognitive interventions with children. *Psychological Bulletin, 88*, 109-143.

Vygotsky, L. (1978). *Mind in society: The development of higher psychological processes* (M. Cole, V. John-Steiner, S. Scribner, & E. Souberman, Eds.). Cambridge MA.: Harvard University Press.

11 IMPORTANCE OF SOCIAL SKILLS IN THE PREVENTION AND INTERVENTION OF ANGER AND AGGRESSION

Gale M. Morrison and Monica Sandowicz

ANGER, AGGRESSION, AND SOCIAL SKILL DEFICITS

Anger and the expression of anger through aggressive behavior have been associated with deficits in social skills. For example, adolescents who exhibit a pattern of aggressive behavior are likely to have had inadequate socialization or poor models for self-control, which lead to difficulties in expressing their anger appropriately. In a frustrated attempt to resolve conflicts and express their emotions, they may exhibit outbursts of aggression. These adolescents lack the skills to solve day-to-day hassles in their lives. There is a critical connection between deficits in social skills and the failure to develop positive social relationships, poor peer relationships being predictive of later mental health outcomes (Cowen, Pederson, Babigian, Izzo, & Trost, 1973; Roff, Sells, & Golden, 1972). Children who have poor peer relationships (a) lack the necessary skills to form and maintain friendships and (b) exhibit an excess of aggressive-disruptive behavior (Conger & Keane, 1981; Dodge, 1983). The relationship of anger and aggression to social skills is critical because societal norms require an increasing level of anger arousal regulation as children develop.

Social Competence

When considering the effects of social skills on anger and its expression, the relationship of social skills to the broader concept of social competence should be examined. Social competence as a concept refers to a number of dimensions such as "appropriateness of social behavior vis-a-vis norms of the social setting, the presence or absence of peer relationships, evidence of specific prosocial behaviors, adult or peer judgments of behavior, and even an individual's perceptions of their own self-competence" (Siperstein, 1992, p. iv). Greenspan and Ganfield (1992) argue for the use of the term *social intelligence,* which "refers to a person's ability to understand and to deal effectively with social and interpersonal objects and events. Included in this construct are such variables as role-taking, empathic judgment, person perception, moral judgement, referential communication, and interpersonal tactics" (Greenspan, 1979, p. 483). Zigler and Trickett (1978) suggest a two-dimensional schema for conceptualizing social competence; one aspect reflects the success of the individual in meeting societal expectations and the other reflects the person's personal development or skills. A critical commonality in these definitions is the importance of the social context in which social skills are performed and the individual's ability to choose and perform social skills that fit within that context. In reference to anger and aggression, societal norms discourage the use of aggression as an expression of anger and emphasize the necessity of socially acceptable alternatives to anger expression, such as verbally appropriate expression of feelings and conflict resolution. Thus, children who are considered socially competent are more cooperative and less aggressive (Dodge, 1983) and are more likely to exhibit prosocial behaviors than their less competent peers.

Social Skills

Social *skills* can be defined as goal-oriented, rule-governed learned *behaviors* that are designed to elicit positive responses from others. These skills are situation-specific and vary according to social context (Cartledge & Milburn, 1980). Recognizing the importance of a socially normative frame of reference, Gresham (1990) provided what he termed the social validity definition of social skills:

> Social skills are situationally specific behaviors that predict important social outcomes for children and youth. In school settings, important social outcomes for children and youth include, but are not limited to: (a) peer acceptance, (b) significant others' judgments of social skill, (c) academic achievement, (d) self-concept, and (e) school adjustment. (p. 697)

In terms of Furlong and Smith's (Introduction to this volume) conceptualization of anger and its expression, aspects of both social competence and social skills are involved. That is, the social cognitive component of social competence is critical in anger-related judgments about intentionality of interpersonal events as well as in the ability to generate and evaluate response options to the experience of anger. Social skills are the behavioral responses for the appropriate expression of anger. Thus, it is important to consider both social skills and social competence when considering the dynamics of social skill deficits related to anger and aggression.

Social Skill Deficits

Gresham (1990) distinguishes between acquisition and performance deficits in social skills. Acquisition deficits occur when the child does not have the social skills in his or her repertoire; performance deficits exist when the skills are there, but the individual does not use them. Gresham and Elliott's (1984) model (see Figure 11.1) includes the concept of interfering behavior such as anxiety, impulsivity, and noncompliance. The simplest case would be where a child does not have a particular prosocial skill (acquisition deficit). This case is complicated when an interfering behavior such as aggression is present. Knowledge about the dynamics of anger and its social-cognitive component comes into play when we talk about performance deficits. With performance deficits, the child may have the appropriate skills in her or his repertoire but choose not to use them. In the case where the child may be experiencing anger, negative conclusions about intentionality and a hostile orientation may cause the interfering behavior of aggression to become the behavioral expression of the anger (performance deficit with interfering behavior). Thus, as Gresham (1990) notes, socially skilled behavior and problem behavior are not simply polar opposites of the same continuum. One can be socially skilled and exhibit problem behaviors in the same setting. The experience and cognition surrounding anger would be one explanation for this situation (see Furlong & Smith, this volume; Larson, this volume).

Thus, as we begin to think about how to intervene with problems of anger and aggression, our efforts should include the reduction or elimination of interfering behaviors and cognitions as well as the development of more appropriate thinking and more prosocial response alternatives, thus including both social-cognitive and social skill components.

Children with Social Skill Deficits

Much of the work with children who have social skill deficits has focused on children and adolescents who have learning and behavior problems such as learning disabilities, emotional and behavior disorders, or mental retardation. Children who have these disabilities often have deficits in social skills that are related to their disability and that cause them to experience difficulties in their relationships with peers. The existence of these disabilities increases the chance that they will exhibit difficulties with anger and aggression.

When describing the aggressive behavior of children or adolescents with disabilities, it is important to distinguish whether the anger and aggression exhibited is due to their initiation (predatory aggression) or to their reaction to negative comments that they may have received from their peers (reactive aggression) (Coie & Dodge, 1986). Ongoing difficulties with peer relationships could lead to either of these forms of aggression; however, effective intervention necessitates distinguishing between the two.

	Acquisition Deficit	**Performance Deficit**
Interfering Problem Behaviors Absent	Acquisition Deficit (Can't Do)	Performance Deficit (Won't Do)
Interfering Problem Behaviors Present	Acquisition Deficit with Interfering Problem Behaviors	Performance Deficit with Interfering Problem Behaviors

Figure 11.1. Model of Children's Social Skills. From Gresham, F., & Elliott, S. (1984). Assessment and classification of children's social skills: A review of methods and issues. *School Psychology Review, 13*, 292-301. Copyright 1984 National Association of School Psychologists. Adapted by permission.

Learning disabilities. Children with learning disabilities are likely to have social skill deficits in areas such as nonverbal and verbal communication, social interactions, on-task behavior, social perception, social problem-solving ability, and empathy (Bryan & Bryan, 1981; Gresham & Reschly, 1986; La Greca & Mesibov, 1981; Toro, Weissberg, Guare, & Liebenstein, 1990). Given their difficulties with academic and social development, children and adolescents with learning disabilities might be expected to experience higher levels of frustration, distress, and anger. Adelman and Smith and their colleagues (Adelman, Smith, Nelson, Taylor, & Phares, 1986) have documented that students with learning disabilities do experience higher school anger levels and negative behavior. Carlson (1987) found that LD children differed from their nonhandicapped peers in terms of their ability to generate appropriate solutions for conflict situations. However, evidence is conflicting about whether this group overall exhibits more aggressive and intrusive behavior (Bryan & Bryan 1978; Levy & Gottlieb, 1984). La Greca (1987) suggests it is possible that studies have found children with learning disabilities to exhibit more aggressive behavior because some of these children also have overlapping problems with hyperactivity (ADHD). Children with hyperactivity have documented difficulties with peer relationships, social behavior, and tendencies toward aggression (Hinshaw, Buhrmester, & Heller, 1989).

Mental retardation. Social skill deficits are also found in individuals with mental retardation. Children and adolescents with mental retardation also experience difficulties in their peer relationships due in part to deficits in social skills and the existence of negative social behaviors. For example, Healey and Masterpasqua (1992) found that interpersonal cognitive problem-solving skills could distinguish adjusted from nonadjusted classroom behavior among children with mild mental retardation. Positive adjustment was related to the ability to generate a high number of solutions to problem situations. Deficits in problem-solving skills such as generating solutions to problems are often associated with aggression.

Social skill deficits are central to the definition of mental retardation. Adaptive behavior, a closely related concept which includes social competence, is a major criterion in the definition of mental retardation (Luckkason et al., 1992). Individuals with mental retardation exhibit significant delays in the acquisition of adaptive behavior. Additionally, 39% of these individuals have problems that warrant further mental health diagnoses, thus resulting in dual diagnosis (Reiss, 1990). For example, in a study of prevalence of mental health problems in a sample of individuals with mental retardation, Reiss (1990) found that 45.8% of these individuals were rated as being "socially inadequate to the point that it is a major problem in their lives." Aggression and anger were rated as problems for up to 25% of the sample. Given that lack of social skills and challenging behavior are significant problems for this population, a good deal of work has been done in developing behavioral technology and social skill training programs for these individuals (see Meyer & Evans, 1989).

Emotional and behavior disorders. Social skill deficits are also seen in children whose major diagnosis is behavior disorder or serious emotional disturbance. In fact, an inability to build or maintain satisfactory relationships with peers and teachers is one of the five defining criteria used in the federal definition of "serious emotional disturbance" (Forness & Knitzer, 1992). As well, "inappropriate feelings under normal circumstances" may reflect extreme emotional reaction and lead to the behavioral expression of anger. However, the connection of this symptomology with aggressive or disruptive behavior is at the heart of some thorny definitional issues nationwide. Federal regulations currently stipulate that a child may not be served in this category if he or she is "socially maladjusted," social maladjustment being associated with acting-out, aggressive, and delinquent behavior. Forness (in press) points out the contradiction in the exclusion of social maladjustment (defined by some as experiencing difficulty in building and maintaining interpersonal relationships) and the inclusion of the same concept as a definitional criterion. Forty-three percent of all states currently have SED definitions that do not exclude children or youth with social maladjustment (Gonzales, 1991). Thus, the role that aggression plays in the symptomology of children identified for special education services under the SED category is dependent upon the definition accepted by the state in which the child resides. Nonetheless, a high percentage of SED students exhibit aggressive or angry behavior.

Juvenile delinquency. The use of angry, aggressive behaviors in law violations leads to the label of "delinquent." Juvenile delinquency has become an alarming concern, in particular, aggressive delinquent behaviors. Childhood aggression has been related to the severity of subsequent delinquency (Roff & Wirt, 1984). For example, according the studies conducted by the Centers for Disease Control, homicide is the second leading cause of injury-related death among all American adolescents (Fingerhut & Kleinman, 1992), and the victim and the offender tend to be of the same age (Christoffel, 1990). A substantial body of literature has documented that youth who are delinquent or aggressive display deficiencies in interpersonal, planning, aggressive management, and prosocial skills (Goldstein & Glick, 1986). Patterson, DeBaryshe, and Ramsey (1989) propose a model that highlights the early development of antisocial behavior related to ineffective parenting practices. Related to social skill development, these authors hypothesize that children's prosocial behaviors are often ignored or responded to inappropriately.

At risk. The phrase "at risk" has gained popularity in recent years for describing children who possess characteristics that have been associated with the development of various forms of maladjustment. For example, children may be considered "at risk" for developing problems with substance abuse, "at risk" for social maladjustment in the form of juvenile delinquency or "at risk" for the development of psychopathology. The literature delineating the conditions or characteristics that are predictive of these maladjustments often cites aggressive behavior as a precursor to later problems. For example, Patterson et al. (1989) describe the role of antisocial behavior in the development of psychopathology in children. Hawkins, Lishner, Catalano, and Howard (1986) include early antisocial behavior as an "at-risk" indicator for later substance abuse. On the flip side of the "at-risk" issue, Hawkins et al. describe "protective factors," which include social skills to resist drugs and to live according to society's norms. Rutter (1985) describes protective factors as those ones that "modify, ameliorate or alter a person's response" to conditions that might otherwise lead to negative outcomes. Garmezy, Masten, and Tellegen (1984) consider social competence, including skills in relating to others, as a protective factor in the development of emotional disorders. Therefore, social skills are associated with "at-risk" factors (in their absence and its association with antisocial behavior) and with protective or resiliency mechanisms. Because of the strong association of early social adjustment problems with later mental health problems, training in social skills and social problem solving is typically an integral part of prevention programs.

THEORETICAL APPROACHES APPLIED TO SOCIAL SKILLS TRAINING

Behavioral and Social Learning Approaches

Research and training in the social skills area has been heavily influenced by behavioral theory and methodology. For example, Goldstein (1981) defines social skills training as the "planned, systematic teaching of specific behaviors needed and consciously desired by the individual in order to function in an effective and satisfying manner, over an extended period of time, in a broad array of positive, negative, and neutral interpersonal contexts" (p. 162). In behavioral terms, Kanfer and Phillips (1970) outlined possible points of impact for social skills training. The *SORC* model was defined as consisting of **S**timulus Events that precede the targeted behavior (people or situations), **O**rganismic events (cognitions, emotions), **R**esponses (behavior associated with stimulus), and **C**onsequences (reinforcing events). Each of these areas can be targeted for intervention. Social learning theory (Bandura, 1977) also provides a strong theoretical background for social skills training, illustrating the concept that children learn skills by observing and interacting with parents, significant adults, peers, and others in their environment. Thus, the role models that are available to children significantly affect the behaviors children will display. If these role models routinely handle conflict situations with aggression, children are likely to repeat this behavior in their own lives. Social learning theory has been particularly helpful to practitioners in its application to methods of training such as modeling, guided practice, feedback, and transfer.

The social skills deficits model (Gresham & Elliott, 1984) presented earlier in this chapter also provides a framework for classifying intervention approaches (see Figure 11.2). One of the main assumptions of social skills training has been that children are rejected primarily because of social skills deficits. However, when dealing with children who are aggressive, techniques are needed to target the inappropriate or interfering behavior as well (Fortman & Feldman, this volume; Waas, 1987). Therefore, social skills training in relationship to anger and aggression should incorporate both approaches to reducing the interfering behaviors as well as promoting the acquisition, performance, and generalization of new skills.

It should be noted that adequate assessment is needed before training begins in order to focus the intervention on the appropriate target (skill acquisition versus skill performance) and to identify appropriate antecedents and consequences for increasing positive skills and decreasing problem behavior. Assessment procedures are not the focus of this chapter (see Stein & Karno, this volume; Furlong & Smith, this volume). Also, excellent reviews of social skills assessments are available from the following sources: Feindler (1990), Maag (1989), and Sabornie (1991).

Social Cognitive and Metabehavioral Approaches

Although social skill acquisition is a critical element to intervening with aggressive children and adolescents, the role of social cognition in the

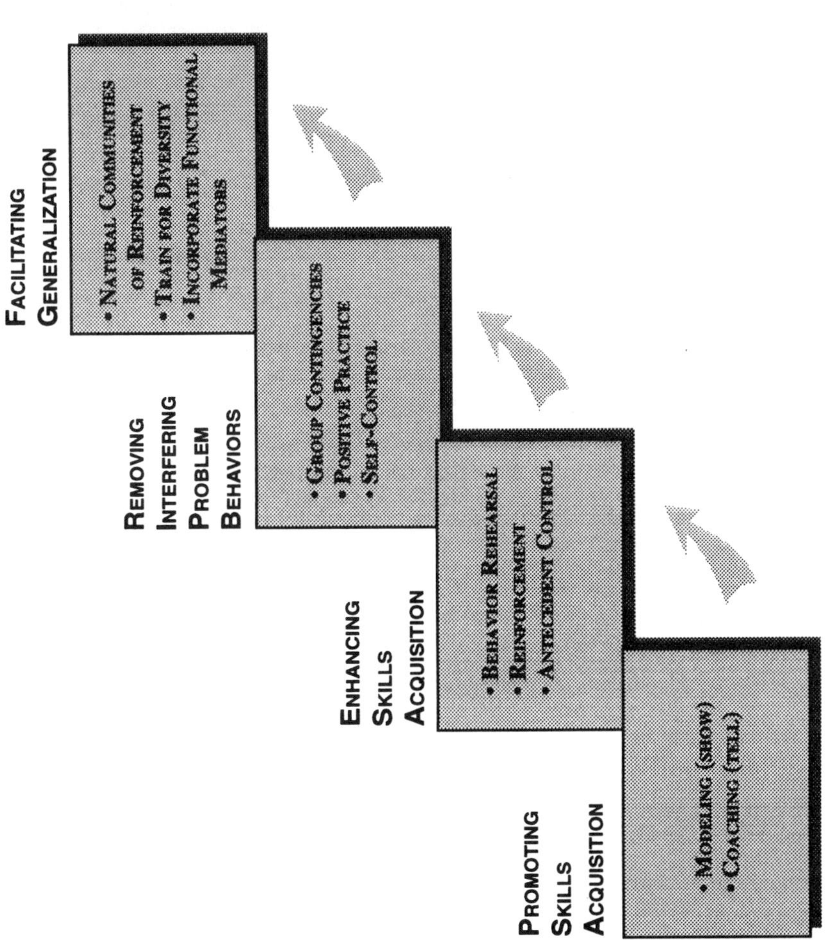

Figure 11.2. Social Skills Intervention Components. From Gresham, F., & Elliott, S. (1984). Assessment and classification of children's social skills: A review of methods and issues. *School Psychology Review, 13,* 292-301. Copyright 1984 National Association of School Psychologists. Adapted by permission.

anger–aggression relationship in social skill performance points to the importance of attending to these skills as well in the training process. Spivack, Platt, and Shure (1976) described a framework for looking at interpersonal cognitive problem-solving skills. When a problem arises, these skills can be applied to the problem solution:

- *Alternative thinking*—the ability to generate multiple alternative solutions to a problem situation;
- *Consequential thinking*—the ability to foresee the immediate as well as long-range consequences of a particular alternative;
- *Means-end thinking*—the ability to elaborate or plan a series of specific actions to attain a given goal, to devise ways around potential obstacles, and to use a realistic time framework in constructing means to a goal;
- *Social causal thinking*—the ability to recognize that one's actions and feelings are reciprocally related to the actions and feelings of others;
- *Sensitivity to problems*—the awareness of the variety of problems that arise in interpersonal relations;
- *Dynamic orientation*—the recognition that behavior may reflect motives that are not easily discerned.

Based on work with aggressive children, Dodge (1986) added to these social problem-solving concepts in proposing a social information processing model of competent social reasoning. The steps in this model include:

- *Encoding*—searching for, selecting, attending to, and storing relevant social information;
- *Interpretation*—integrating the encoded cues with memories of past experiences and inferring their meaning;
- *Response search*—generating possible behavioral responses to the situation;
- *Response decision*—considering the possible consequences of the responses generated and choosing a response that fits the situation;
- *Enactment*—enactment of the response;
- *Evaluation*—consideration of the consequences of the enactment (added to this sequence by Novaco, 1978).

The validity of this more detailed sequence is supported by the work of Dodge and his colleagues that documents specific deficits in this sequence occurring in aggressive children. For example, aggressive children search for fewer cues before inferring intentions, are biased toward interpreting the behavior of a peer as hostile, generate fewer response options, and consider fewer consequences for their response (Dodge, 1980; Dodge & Newman, 1981; Richard & Dodge, 1982).

Given the acquisition of social skills through techniques such as modeling and coaching, Svec and Bechard (1988) emphasize the importance of considering the "meta" requirements of social skill performance and acquisition. They propose a metabehavioral model for the development of social skills for aggressive adolescents that involves consideration of situation variables and task demands as important contextual delimiters of social skill performance. Effective social skill performance demands that the individual consider these aspects. Therefore, important aspects of social skills training would be teaching students how to assess situation characteristics and task demands as well as analyzing their own skills as applied to the situation. Svec and Bechard (1988) use the example of the difference in task demands and personal skills needed for a boy to call up a girl to get help with homework in contrast to calling up the same girl to ask for a date.

An additional metacognitive component in the anger–aggression relationship that is a potential area for intervention is arousal or impulse control. This type of training would attend to the development of self-instructional skills such as self-talk or verbal mediation (Meichenbaum, 1977). Novaco (1975) concluded that anger is created, maintained, and influenced by self-statements that are made in provocation. Therefore, anger control training or stress inoculation training incorporates self-instructional techniques in addition to cognitive restructuring, problem solving, relaxation, and efforts at environmental change (Feindler, 1990; Stern & Fodor, 1989). The three basic components of this type of training include:

- *Cognitive preparation*—the development of self-management skills such as relaxation and skills to assess and monitor anger reactions;
- *Skill acquisition*—discriminating circumstances where anger is justified versus those where it is not (attribution retraining) and remaining task-oriented under arousal situations;
- *Practice and application*—role play, systematic desensitization.

Cognitive-Developmental Approaches

Children gain competence and sophistication in social skills as these skills develop. They increase in their ability to make social initiations, play cooperatively, communicate effectively, and resolve conflicts (Elliott &

Ershler, 1990). In particular, children progress through stages in their ability to deal with anger and aggression. For example, Fuchs and Thelen (1988) documented that as children develop they become more capable of employing strategies to regulate their emotions. This regulation is related to the child's expectancy about the outcome of (other people's reaction to) their display of emotion. Thus, as a child develops, she becomes more capable of predicting how other people will react to her display of anger; this ability is related to the degree to which she displays her anger in certain situations.

Selman (1980) provided a developmental framework for understanding the stages of thinking about friendship and conflict resolution that is applicable to understanding the social cognitive aspects of anger and aggression. This model is based on the Piagetian stages of development, as are similar models by Turiel (1975) (friendship development) and Kohlberg (1964) (moral development).

For example, at what Selman calls *Stage 0*—momentary physical solutions to conflicts (typically preschool or kindergarten)—one way that the child deals with conflict is by simply moving to another activity and expecting that the problem will go away or be forgotten. They do not consider the feelings, motives, or attitudes of others involved in the conflict. Another approach to resolving conflicts at this stage is physical coercion or aggression. Social skills training at this stage may involve teaching physical and verbal prosocial behaviors, as well as comprehending the relationship between cause and effect in interpersonal events. Although recognizing that physical separation is one way to avoid anger and aggression, instruction may encourage the children to think about the cause-and-effect relationship between behaviors and other people's reactions.

At *Stage 1*, conflicts are viewed as one-way, caused by one person and felt by another. The resolution at this stage involves negating the action by "taking it back" or appealing to the outlook of the victim by apologizing or doing something nice. With regard to anger and aggression, children at this stage might have difficulty seeing the contribution of their own behavior to the conflict. They will be looking for overt signs from the other party that the conflict is over. In addition to perspective-taking and reasoning about cause and effect, skills to be taught are prosocial approaches that signal the end of a conflict.

Stage 2 involves cooperative solutions to interpersonal conflict. The child, at this point probably a preadolescent, begins to see conflict as a situation in which two people participate and both need to be considered in the resolution. This need to appeal to the other party requires that the participants begin to understand the attitudes and motivations of the other party and be concerned with their intent. Skills for working through anger and avoiding aggression would include being able to talk about feelings and attitudes and generate problem solutions that appeal to both parties.

The next two stages are usually seen in adolescence and adulthood. Relationships become important and a higher level of listening and negotiation is needed to work through solutions to conflict. *Stage 3*—mutual solutions to interpersonal conflict—requires participants to "work through" the conflict. The relationship between the individuals is considered more fully; therefore mutual satisfaction with the resolution is a desired outcome. At *Stage 4*—autonomous interdependent resolutions to interpersonal conflict—it is recognized that conflicts involve complex individual perspectives and beliefs as well as the interface between those perspectives. Thus, conflict resolution involves true communication.

Selman's framework provides important guidelines for understanding a child's perspective on conflicts that might lead to anger and aggression. Further, our expectations about how to approach interventions for anger and aggression need to be modulated according to the developmental level of a child's thinking about social situations. For example, although it is wise to encourage a child to think in increasingly more complex ways, there are developmental limits to the sophistication with which she can think about and interpret situations. Therefore, in the case of a conflict with peers, teaching perspective-taking skills to a preschool child would not be as effective a strategy for helping them resolve the conflict as it would be for a fourth- or fifth-grade child. A more appropriate strategy for the preschool child would be to separate them from the situation for the short term, and teach communication skills for the long term.

SOCIAL SKILL PARADIGMS

Most social skill paradigms are based on critical prosocial behaviors. Gresham and Elliott (1984) define five clusters of social behaviors: (a) cooperation, (b) assertion, (c) responsibility, (d) empathy, and (e) self-control. Assertion and self-control are particularly relevant to aggression in that they provide socially acceptable alternatives for dealing with frustrating interpersonal situations associated with anger. Although assertion and self-control are most directly related to anger-control and alternatives to aggression, other skills also contribute to avoiding or preventing anger-provoking situations.

General definitions of social skills are usually so broad that they provide little guidance about specific skills that comprise socially skilled behavior. However, the behavioral/social-cognitive frameworks described above provide some structure for social skill delineation. With respect to anger and aggression, Goldstein's programs (Goldstein & Keller, 1989) are based on a conceptualization of overt acts of aggression that involve the following steps: (a) arousal-heightening interpretation of external stimulus, (b) heightened affective arousal, (c) malcommunication, (d) mismanagement of contingencies, (e) prosocial skill deficiencies, and (f) prosocial value deficiencies. The first two steps involve the affective state of anger while the remaining steps involve skills and environmental or contextual characteristics. The steps of this sequence suggest specific approaches to managing aggression. Specific social skills are taught at the first, third, and fifth stages. Thus, social skills are implied in both the self-control or regulation of negative social behaviors and in the performance of appropriate alternative prosocial behavior.

With this sequence of aggression in mind, Goldstein and his colleagues have delineated a series of social skills that they teach in the context of their anger/aggression control programs (see Table 11.1).

METHODS OF SOCIAL SKILL TRAINING

In addition to behaviorally based techniques focused on antecedent, performance, and consequent events, there are several common techniques that are used for social skill acquisition. *Structured Learning* is a psychoeducational, behavioral approach that encompasses several of these strategies. Goldstein and his colleagues combined these strategies to teach prosocial skills as alternatives to aggression (Goldstein & Keller, 1989). The approach consists of four main components: (a) modeling, (b) role playing, (c) performance feedback, and (d) transfer of training.

Modeling

Modeling is one of the most basic procedures used to teach social behaviors. The social skill is presented through videotapes, film, verbal explanations, or live models. A four-stage sequence for modeling includes (a) presentation of the model, (b) behavioral rehearsal, (c) feedback on performance, and (d) practice in real-life situations (Cartledge & Milburn, 1980). Effective modeling procedures ensure that the steps to complex skills are presented clearly and that they are performed by models who are

TABLE 11.1. SOCIAL SKILLS COMPONENTS OF ANGER TRAINING

1. Self-instructional techniques targeting the following

- Preparation for the provocation • Impact and confrontation
- Coping with arousal • Reflecting on the provocation

2. Self-evaluation uses a set of reminders that can be used *after* a conflict situation

- Determine for themselves how well they have handled a conflict
- Reward themselves for handling it well
- Help themselves figure out how they could have handled it better

3. Relaxation Training

Self-relaxation

- Deep breathing • Backward counting • Pleasant imagery

Relaxation of Others

- Modeling calmness • Encouraging talking
- Listening openly • Showing understanding
- Reassuring the other person • Helping save face

4. Communication, Negotiation, Contracting

Preparing for Communication

- Plan on dealing with one problem at a time
- Choose the right time and place
- Consider one's plan

5. Constructive Communication Rules

- Acknowledge subjectivity • Be rational • Be direct
- Make ongoing communication checks • Focus on behavior
- Reciprocate • Disclose yourself • Be empathic
- Check it out • Pay attention to nonverbal behavior
- Avoid communication blocks

6. Negotiation Training

similar in characteristics to the learner. Coaching is a similar strategy that focuses on verbal instruction and behavioral rehearsal of the social skill being taught. Ladd and Mize (1983) identify instruction (modeling and coaching), rehearsal (covert and overt), and feedback as the critical training variables in social skill training.

They suggest that modeling should follow these guidelines:

1. Use at least two examples of different situations for each demonstration of a skill. If a given skill is taught in more than one group meeting, develop two more new modeling displays.
2. Select situations that are relevant to the trainees' real-life circumstances.
3. The main actor, that is, the trainer enacting the behavioral steps of the skill, should be portrayed as a person reasonably similar in age, socioeconomic background, verbal ability, and other salient characteristics to the people in the Structured Learning group.
4. Modeling displays should depict only one skill at a time. All extraneous content should be eliminated.
5. All modeling displays should depict all the behavioral steps of the skill being modeled in the correct sequence.
6. All displays should depict positive outcomes. Displays should always end with reinforcement to the model (Goldstein & Keller, 1989, p. 110).

Role Play

Role play is intended to provide behavioral rehearsal or practice for future use of the skill. This procedure is suggested for enacting hypothetical future rather than past events. The following aspects of the role play should be as realistic as possible: the description of the physical setting, the delineation of the events immediately preceding the role play, and the manner in which the "actors" should act. The main actor should adhere strictly to the behavioral sequence that has been modeled.

Performance Feedback

Performance feedback is given immediately following each role play. Praise, approval, and encouragement are given for the appropriate display of the target skill. This period is also a time where the other group members can give feedback and share impressions. Once the skills have been learned in group sessions, several procedures will facilitate the transfer and maintenance of training: (a) providing trainees with general principles that can be applied to multiple situations, (b) overlearning, (c) designing learning to take place in circumstances similar to those that will be encountered in the future, (d) learning the skills under a variety of stimulus conditions, and (e) arranging for reinforcement for skill performance in real-life situations.

Ladd and Mize (1983) provide a more thorough social skill training model (Cognitive-Social Learning Model of Social Skill Training) in that it considers factors that will enhance not only skill acquisition and performance, but skill maintenance and generalization as well (see Figure 11.4).

CONCEPTS OF PREVENTION AND INTERVENTION RELATED TO SOCIAL SKILL PROGRAMMING

Continuum of Prevention

It is important to distinguish between prevention and intervention programs. Prevention programs can be distinguished by three basic approaches. *Primary prevention* programs target entire populations of children and youth and develop skills that reduce the probability of the initial onset of a disorder or a negative outcome. Skills that contribute to resilience are developed and environments are modified to support this resiliency and reduce the risk or vulnerability to dysfunction. *Secondary prevention* efforts are characterized by their focus on a group of children who are identified, through certain behavioral symptoms, as at increased risk for the development of more serious dysfunction. Programming at this level is intended to treat and reverse the emerging problems. *Tertiary prevention* involves the treatment of children or adolescents who exhibit the fully developed disorder. Tertiary prevention is what is usually referred to as intervention or treatment (Hightower, Johnson, & Haffey, 1990).

Because these basic approaches focus on different groups of children at different status in regard to dysfunction, or in this case anger and aggression, programming content and methodology are likely to have different emphases. The intention of primary prevention approaches is to provide skills to groups of children before the onset of problems; thus, these programs tend to be very broad based in terms of content and geared for presentation to larger groups of children. For example, in presenting social skill information in the context of the regular classroom, the teacher or instructor will want to be concerned about issues such as classroom climate. That is, what are the norms and expectations about social relationships, how do students and teachers treat one another, and how do these climate factors

Learning Objective	Training Procedure
Enhancing Skill Concepts	1. Establishing an Intent to Learn the Skill Concept • Providing an advanced organizer • Stressing the functional relevance of the concept 2. Defining the Skill Concept in Terms of its Attributes • Conveying concept meaning • Identifying relevant and irrelevant attributes 3. Generating Exemplars • Identifying positive and negative examples 4. Promoting Rehearsal and Recall of the Skill Concept • Encouraging verbal rehearsal • Establishing a memory code 5. Refining and Generalizing the Concept • Correcting misconceptions • Identifying alternative applications
Promoting Skill Performance	1. Providing Opportunities for Guided Rehearsal • Requesting overt skill rehearsal • Conducting rehearsals in a sheltered context 2. Evaluation of Performance by the Instructor • Communicating performance standards • Providing feedback about the match between standards and performance 3. Fostering Skill Refinement and Elaboration • Recommending corrective action—concept reformulation skill modification
Fostering Skill Maintenance/ Generalization	1. Providing Opportunities for Self-Directed Rehearsal • Skill rehearsal in a series of contexts that approximates real-life situations 2. Promoting Self-Initiation of Performance • Encouraging skill usage while withdrawing performance cues or aids 3. Fostering Self-Evaluation and Skill Adjustment • Self-appraisals of skill performance • Self-monitoring of skill outcomes • Adoption of nondefeating self-attributions and affective states • Use of information from self-monitoring to modify performance

Figure 11.3. Social Skills Model and Intervention Approaches. From Ladd, G. W., & Mize, J. (1983). A cognitive-social learning model of social-skill training. *Psychological Review, 90,* 127-157. Copyright 1983 American Psychological Association. Adapted by permission.

support the skills that are being taught? Although classroom climate might also be of concern for secondary prevention programs, issues of behavior management might be of more concern given the nature of the population. Also, secondary prevention programs are more likely to target smaller groups of children, therefore more intensive strategies such as behavior management or cognitive-behavioral techniques can be more easily implemented.

Concepts of Prevention/Intervention Programming

Any description or prescription of prevention or intervention programs necessitates an examination of the assumptions about the pathways to disorder and adaptation, as these assumptions will guide our programming efforts. The chapters in Section II of this book covered some of the contextual factors associated with anger and aggression in children and adolescents. These explanations represent two different perspectives on pathways to disorder that determine or guide intervention efforts. These perspectives have been defined by Felner and Felner (1989). The specific disease prevention model relies heavily on medical and public health paradigms that suggest that dysfunction is caused by specific disease agents that interact with individual vulnerabilities. For childhood anger and aggression, some of the following "agents" have been identified: (a) hostile, abusive, or punitive parental treatment (Quinton & Rutter, 1984); (b) marital disharmony, chaotic home life, and high number of stressors (Patterson, 1982); and (c) avoidant attachment in infancy and negativistic behavior in the toddler period. Focus on within-child vulnerabilities also points to deficiencies in impulse control and social skills such as problem solving and communication. The other perspective, the antecedent condition perspective, postulates that developmental outcomes cannot be tied *directly or simplistically* to specific etiological agents. Rather, the effects of the contexts children encounter and how these contexts interact with existing child vulnerabilities must be considered as major factors in developmental outcome. Knapczyk (1988) notes that in addition to a social skill deficit in the child, aggressive behaviors can be attributed to the reciprocal relationships between setting events and the child's behavior. For example, aggressive behavior may occur in response to a particular student–peer interaction (e.g., refusal to play or interact, derogatory comments, ignoring social initiations). Patterson's theory about the development of antisocial behavior (see Patterson et al., 1989) is also an example of this perspective, emphasizing the importance of early socialization experiences in the family and in relationship to peers and schools. Given the power of these contexts, Felner and Felner (1989) suggest that "the focus of preventive interventions needs to be on the *mechanisms and processes* from which disorder and competence result, *not* the endpoint conditions" (p. 18).

Given a more complex assumption about the pathway to disordered behavior, prevention and intervention efforts might, in turn, be expected to reflect this complexity. Felner and Felner (1989) suggest three broad models that would reflect this complexity:

1. Person-focused interventions are designed to reverse the developmental deficits brought by the person to the situation.
2. Transaction-focused programs view risk as connected to the unique combination of person and environmental conditions; thus, interventions are focused on the interactions between individuals and situation. (See Larson, this volume, for an example of this type of program.)
3. Environmentally focused programs highlight elements in the social and physical environment.

Our examination of social skills programs related to anger and aggression reveals that most of these programs fall into the person-focused approach. This view assumes that the child(ren) or adolescent(s) are lacking in certain social skills, although clear difficulties may not yet be present. The approach is then to teach skills within a structured curriculum, assuming that this approach will not be harmful to those who do not need it, while helping those that do. Transactional programs attempt to incorporate situational variation as a backdrop for skill development. That is, applications in family, peer, or school contexts will be purposefully made. Our review of social skills programs will highlight where transactional approaches (in particular, peer and school-level interventions) are being used. These programs are potentially very powerful and effective given the importance of early socialization practices in social skill development. Finally, because environmentally and ecologically focused prevention approaches are critical to consider, we will be explicitly considering these factors as supports to ongoing social skill programs in our review.

REVIEW OF REPRESENTATIVE SOCIAL SKILL PROGRAMS

The following section will describe prevention and intervention programs that focus on the social skill aspect of anger and aggression management. Given that our focus is on anger and aggression, we have chosen the

Goldstein paradigm as a template for examining the array of skills taught in various curricula. The Appendix provides an overview of programs and their coverage of the skills outlined in the Goldstein "Skillstreaming" paradigm.

Our discussion of social skill programs categorizes programs into primary and secondary prevention approaches. Within these basic approaches, we will highlight the skills that relate to different stages of anger and aggression according to the sequential model presented by Goldstein and Keller (1989) described earlier in this chapter and delineated in detail in Table 11.1. Most social skill programs do not focus solely on anger or aggression; therefore, we will highlight these aspects within the larger context of the programs described.

Programs Focused on Primary Prevention

Lions-Quest programs. An example of a broad-based primary prevention program focused on the development of social skills is the Lions-Quest Skills for Growing (Quest International, 1990) developed for elementary school children. Skills for Adolescence (Quest International, 1985) is designed for middle and junior high school students; *Skills for Living* is for high school students (Quest International, 1978). The aim of the Lion's-Quest programs is to help young people develop positive social behaviors, such as self-discipline, responsibility, good judgment, and the ability to get along with others, as well as to develop positive commitments to family, school, peers, and their communities. It is assumed that children who have these prosocial skills will be better able to have healthy, successful relationships with others throughout their lives. Although this program is actually a drug and alcohol prevention program, it provides an excellent social skill development base for the prevention of other negative outcomes as well.

These programs are designed to be implemented in the classroom, with the skills taught as lessons incorporated into the regular curriculum. Content is appropriately matched to the developmental level of each age group; however, the basic social and thinking skills are taught at all levels. These basic skills include *effective communication* such as *listening, responding, resolving conflict*, and *cooperating with others. Decision-making skills,* with an emphasis on saying "no" to negative influences (drugs), and such as developing self-esteem and learning to respect one's self and others, are also covered for both age groups. The curricula provided for the older students place a greater emphasis on *strengthening peer and family relationships* and on developing *critical thinking skills.* In general, the Skills for Adolescents program is more comprehensive and complex than the Skills for Growing program, including skill training that requires greater cognitive abilities appropriate for the average adolescent's developmental level.

The social skills taught in the Lions-Quest programs suggest approaches to managing anger and aggression, and can be related to the stages of anger and aggression identified by Goldstein and Keller (1989). Unit 3, "Learning About Emotions," specifically addresses anger control and appropriate anger expression in several of its lessons. For example, one lesson focuses on exploring ways of expressing feelings of anger and frustration. The performance objectives for this session are that the student will: (a) identify experiences that produce strong feelings; (b) describe positive and negative ways of responding to feelings of anger and frustration; and (c) practice positive ways of managing feelings of anger and frustration. At the beginning of this session, the teacher introduces the topic by asking students to talk about their own experiences, to share feelings with others, and to identify some of the ways in which their peers express feelings of anger, hurt, and frustration. A basic explanation about the rationale for the importance of managing and communicating anger in a positive way is suggested also as part of the introduction. Students then participate in a 15-minute "brainstorming" activity in which they work in groups to identify several ways to "blow off steam" in a healthy, positive manner. The groups then come together to share their ideas. Five minutes is devoted at the end of the activity for processing questions. As a final step, students are given a homework assignment requiring them to list situations that create anger and frustration in their lives and to list both appropriate and inappropriate ways to express these emotions.

Other sessions covered in this unit focus on *identifying and naming emotions, understanding nonverbal communication, becoming aware of other people's feelings,* and *understanding how negative thoughts and feelings can be positive challenges.*

Program methods for promoting skill acquisition include providing an environment conducive to learning prosocial behavior, where there are opportunities to interact with peers and adults and to observe prosocial behaviors modeled by teachers. These programs are particularly noteworthy for their climate-building exercises, called energizers. These energizers are intended to provide a fun, game-like context for building awareness of, information about, and trust in the social relationships between students in the classroom.

Homework assignments, classroom activities, group interaction, community projects, and reinforcement are all strategies suggested in the Lions-Quest programs to enhance skill performance and remove interfering problem behavior. Involvement in the community also facilitates generalization of prosocial skills/behavior.

In addition to a detailed, teacher-friendly curriculum, the Quest programs also have strong administrative and parent support components. Administrators are encouraged to participate in the training of the teachers so that they can support program implementation at the school level. Specific instructions are given about how to establish parent support and involve parents constructively in program activities.

Social decision-making skills. The *Social Decision Making Skills* program (Elias & Clabby, 1989) is based on a personal-social skills model similar to the model used by Spivack et al. (1974) described earlier in this chapter. Like the *Lions-Quest Skills for Growing, Social Decision Making Skills* is an extensive curriculum guide for teaching general life-skills to elementary-age children. Its focus is on building *thoughtfulness, social awareness, responsibility,* and *a positive sense of self-worth and self-confidence* in children. The program is divided into five parts, consisting of 16 units. Part I is an introduction to the program that provides a rationale to help teachers see the importance of social decision making and its "fit" into classroom routines and school and district goals. Part II outlines the essential skills for successful social decision making and problem solving, and the major techniques for fostering these skills in students. Part III is the actual curriculum, which consists of 22 topics, grouped in the following three units: Self-Control Skills, Social Awareness and Group Participation Skills, and Improving Social Decision-Making and Problem-Solving Skills. Anger and aggression are indirectly addressed in relation to Self-Control Skills. Some of the specific skills taught as part of the Self-Control unit include: *effective communication (listening, beginning and continuing a conversation), thinking aloud, relaxation, problem solving,* and *recognizing anger cues in ourselves and others.* Problem solving as a group is also taught as part of the Social Awareness and Group Participation Unit, along with skills such as *expressing empathy towards others, giving and receiving compliments, role playing, selecting praiseworthy and caring friends,* and *asking for help and giving it to others.*

Methods for facilitating the lessons include group discussion, role playing, journal writing/worksheets, homework assignments, and other skill-related activities. Social Decision Making Skills offers a thorough set of guidelines for teachers on how to implement the program effectively. Some of the basic strategies suggested include modeling appropriate behavior, prompting, using reinforcement, and being a facilitative questioner. In addition, Part V is devoted to "Troubleshooting—Ways to Make Classroom Use Easier" and "Special Considerations for Use with Special Education Populations."

The authors do not suggest an ideal class size for teaching the Social Decision Making Skills curriculum, or appropriate grade levels for the various activities. However, they do claim that formal lessons seem to be most effective when conducted weekly, with reinforcing or follow-up activities conducted two or three times per week to maximize retention. Lesson length should be 20–30 minutes, depending on the age of the children and on whether or not they have learning or behavioral deficits. However, it is recommended in all cases that initial lessons should be 15–20 minutes, with the length gradually increased when children seem ready for it.

Affective Skill Development for Adolescents. Affective Skill Development for Adolescents (Dembrowsky, 1983) is a primary prevention program with a strong emphasis on classroom climate building. It is designed to be used ideally with a small group (8–10) of adolescents and can be implemented by both parent and teacher. The teacher's guide was developed to help teachers establish a positive climate for growth and consequently provide a nurturing, facilitative environment for students to develop healthy affective skills. The program is based on the author's belief that the students themselves play an important role in their own educational programming and that the class is neither teacher-dominated nor student-controlled; rather, it is a joint effort to learn, relate, and experience. Guidelines for conveying positive affect to students and on effective implementation of the program, in general, are provided for teachers in the beginning of the manual. Taking a social learning approach, Affective Skill Development for Adolescents incorporates activities such as role playing, relaxation, writing, group discussions, and games into the program methodology.

The curriculum itself consists of 15 units (2 supplemental) with several lessons in each unit, covering various social skills such as *communication, responsibility, assertive behavior, stress coping, identifying and appropriately expressing feelings,* and *problem solving.* In addition, there is a unit devoted to student input into curriculum content and supplemental units addressing emotional disturbance and learning disabilities. Each unit begins by stating the purpose, rationale, and unit objectives. Teachers are also provided with an orientation to each lesson and tips for teaching it effectively. Several activities are suggested and outlined in a stepwise fashion for each lesson. A Student Activity Book is to be used with the teacher's manual to facilitate the lessons.

Although its primary goal is to teach positive affective skills to adolescents in a classroom setting, the program can also be implemented at home by parents. The Parent Leader Manual was created by Dembrowsky and Brown (1983) to involve parents, in an active and supportive manner, in the educational process of their child. The parent program is divided into eight sessions. Before the first session, a home visit is required in order to acquaint eligible parents with the purposes of the program and the potential benefits and expectations for those who participate. Parents who choose to participate meet for one 2-hour session each week for 8 weeks. The meetings are structured in the following manner:

1. *Two-Way Information Exchange:* This activity promotes open communication between parents and teachers. The group leader is responsible for building a functioning parent/teacher team and for delivering messages back and forth between parents and teachers.
2. *Parent Support Group:* This activity creates a supportive atmosphere in which parents can share concerns in a nonthreatening environment. Parents are asked to report on their previous week's homework assignment. The group leader is to serve as a model for new skills, especially for giving and receiving "positive strokes."
3. *Knowledge Acquisition/Skill Development:* In this activity, parents are given specific information, introduced to specific skills, and provided with the opportunity to apply their knowledge and practice new skills with their child.

Information from each lesson will be presented by the leader through lectures, readings, overheads, video and audio recordings, and presentations by others such as teachers and diagnosticians. The eight lessons cover topics such as *communication skills, positive strokes (reinforcement), creating a positive expectancy for your child, identifying locus of control/self-responsibility, problem solving,* and *the value of limits.* Effective communication and problem solving are prosocial skills taught to participating parents, who then may model these skills at home for their child. A Parent Activity Book is also used to implement the program.

Belonging: Self and Social Discovery for Children of All Ages. This is a primary prevention program with an emphasis on facilitating group development, rather than classroom climate (Devencenzi & Pendergast, 1988). Specifically, the program's purpose is to teach prosocial (people) skills necessary for effective, positive group interaction. The program was originally designed to be used with children 8–14 years old; however, the process has been effective with older populations, including adult support and parenting groups. Exceptional children, with learning and/or emotional needs have also responded well to the process. For each group of 4–8 members, at least one adult facilitator is needed. After initial meetings, a group member is selected to share leadership with the adult facilitator; the goal is for everyone to experience being a leader. Two 45-minute sessions per week are suggested for effective teaching of the program. A comfortable, quiet environment is also recommended for successful group functioning. The *Belonging* program is composed of 12 chapters. The first 3 of these chapters provide the facilitator with step-by-step guidelines and suggestions for learning the program's process, forming a group, and getting the group started. The following steps outline the actual group process: *choosing a leader, sharing a feeling sentence, presenting a problem and/or activity,* and *sharing ideas.* People skills/topics covered in the curriculum include: *exploring self, expressing feelings, cooperating with others, recovering from disappointment (dealing with anger, fear, and sadness), handling "barbs" (physical or verbal abuse), solving problems,* and *communication.* Modeling, role playing, group discussions, homework, and other skill-related activities are used to facilitate the acquisition of these skills.

This group process has been piloted in a variety of settings. Procedures were developed to identify young people with particular life adjustment needs who could benefit from a structured social skills program offering the opportunity to learn how to interact with others successfully. The process can also be used to guide normal social development and has proven useful in support groups for children, in the classroom, for parent groups, and in rehabilitation programs.

Creative Conflict Resolution. Creative Conflict Resolution (Kreidler, 1984) is an approach to teaching prosocial skills via classroom management (peace education). Its emphasis is on teaching children conflict resolution skills rather than a general array of prosocial skills. The curriculum is designed to be taught by teachers of elementary school children (K–6). The curriculum can be integrated into the routine classroom management procedures as well as the standard subject areas. However, the ideal class size for effectively implementing this program is not identified by the author.

There are 10 chapters in the Creative Conflict Resolution guide. The first three focus on introducing the concepts of Peacemaking to the teacher and providing guidelines for resolving student vs. student and student vs. teacher conflicts. The actual curriculum is found in Chapters 4–8. Each chapter begins with information to help the teacher understand the focus of the chapter and the approach. Target skills addressed in these chapters include: *understanding conflict and its causes, problem solving, negotiating, effective communication, coping with anger and frustration, positive emotional expression, tolerance,* and *cooperation.* Each chapter offers several activities, such as role playing, group discussion, writing and drawing games, brainstorming, and relaxation exercises, for teaching a particular skill or topic. Appropriate grade levels are also suggested for each activity. In the last chapter, Kriedler offers suggestions for teaching the Creative Conflict Resolution curriculum, and provides answers to commonly asked questions about the program in general.

Learning the Skills of Peacemaking. Almost identical in focus and content to Kriedler's program is the Learning the Skills of Peacemaking program (Drew, 1987). Like Creative Conflict Resolution, its primary purpose is to teach peacemaking and conflict resolution skills to elementary-age children in a classroom setting. Although it is designed to be implemented primarily by educators, parents are encouraged to take an active part in their child's program by reinforcing the program's concepts and ideas at home and by modeling the related prosocial skills. Learning the Skills of Peacemaking focuses on four major concepts: *accepting self and others, communicating effectively, resolving conflicts,* and *understanding intercultural differences.* Peacemaking skills are presented in three "stages," with each stage integrating lessons in these four concept areas. There are 56 lessons, covering skills such as *identifying conflict, positive anger expression,* and *peaceful problem solving*. *Stage I* is "Peace Begins with Me," *Stage II* is "Integrating Peacemaking," and *Stage III* is "Exploring Our Roots and Interconnectedness." Although grade levels are suggested for some of the activities, the lessons can be adapted to meet the needs of younger or older students.

Methods used for teaching peacemaking skills include playacting, creative writing, story reading, music, the arts, and classroom discussion.

The lessons can be used twice a week to enhance the social studies and language arts curricula. However, the concepts and values of each lesson are meant to be integrated into the student's daily interactions and therefore should be used regularly throughout the week to create a peaceful classroom atmosphere.

One obvious difference between these two programs is that lessons in Learning the Skills of Peacemaking focus more on how peacemaking skills can be applied to world issues and conflict; there is an emphasis on teaching students how to generalize these skills to their lives outside of the classroom.

Fighting Invisible Tigers. The Fighting Invisible Tigers program (Schmitz & Hipp, 1987) offers a distinctive approach to teaching prosocial skills. Fighting Invisible Tigers is a 12-part course in "Lifeskills Development," with an emphasis on stress management. The purpose of the program is to raise adolescents' awareness of "lifeskills"— an assortment of behaviors that can reduce stress and help us maintain physical and psychological health. The program is offered in both a teacher and student guide *(A Student's Guide to Life in 'The Jungle').* Unlike the course structure of the teacher's program, the student book is a self-help, self-paced guide. Both guides focus on the following lifeskill areas: *physical activity, relaxation, assertiveness, supportive relationships,* and *life planning.* The student guide also addresses the skills of stress management. The 12-part course is designed to be taught by teachers within the classroom, although the materials may also be appropriate for church groups, 4-H clubs, YMCAs, or other community education agencies. The course may also be taught with the help of expert personnel such as the school nurse, school psychologist, science teacher, or college counselor. An appropriate group size is not suggested, however, the activities are structured to allow for variability in group size. Each of the 12 sessions is based on one or more of the five lifeskill areas, and is 50 minutes in length. Sessions usually begin with some presentation of content by the teacher that leads into small group exercises or discussion. Many of the learning activities engage students either in a role-play or direct experience.

Considerations in Implementing Primary Prevention Programs

The success of any program within a school system will depend somewhat on system-level factors such as support of administrators, support and help from parents, training of those involved in implementation, organization and planning, and the extent to which the program addresses "real" needs in the population. For example, classroom focus on social skill development, in particular skills related to anger and aggression reduction, might be resisted by parents or administrators who do not believe that the role of the school is to address issues other than academic development. Some may believe that handling anger and aggression is a private, individual matter to be managed by parents at home or administrators at school when the problems get out of hand. Further, regular classroom teachers may not perceive facilitating social skill development or dealing with anger and aggression as a legitimate part of their job. They may see demand for such instruction as an additional burden to their already full plate of responsibilities. Obviously, prevention programming taking place in the regular classroom can be met with resistance from a number of directions; therefore, it is critical to consider the "buy-in" of social skill training from critical consumers such as parents, administrators, and classroom teachers.

The following are some suggestions for avoiding system-level mistakes that will compromise the success of the program (Hightower et al., 1990; Morrison, 1991).

1. Start by identifying the needs of the particular school population with which you are working. Tying the program to specific needs will help support the rationale for starting the program. For example, an unusual number of fights on the playground during the first few weeks of school might be the impetus for starting a conflict resolution program.

2. Start to garner support from key school individuals from the beginning in order to foster system ownership. Key teachers, administrators, support personnel, and parents can be valuable participants in the planning process. These will be the individuals who contribute to maintaining programming commitment and effort across time.

3. In presenting the program for approval by the school system, be ready to answer the following questions:

- How will the new prevention program interfere with ongoing programs or curricula?
- Does this prevention program duplicate Ms. X's efforts?
- How will the program's effectiveness be assessed?
- Have others run similar programs?
- Who will pay for this program?
- Who will be hired and what will be their credentials? Can we use Ms. G from our staff?
- What does the teachers' union think about this program?
- Whom should parents call if they have a question?

- Why implement this program now? (Hightower et al., 1990, p. 69–70).

4. Upon approval for implementation, consider who needs to be informed and when from the following groups: administrators, teachers, support personnel, parents, community members, and media. It is particularly crucial that parents are fully informed and understand what the program is about.

5. Plan for ongoing support for program implementation. For example, teachers who are implementing a curriculum for the first time will need to be able to ask questions, seek advice, and observe other teachers in the process of doing aspects of the curriculum. A teacher might need to know how to fit the curriculum activities into his or her school day in addition to all of the other material he or she needs to cover. School-level reinforcement of the curriculum activities would support implementation efforts. For example, perhaps a schoolwide theme and all-school activities could mirror what is happening in classrooms.

6. Consider changes in school and classroom policy and climate that would support the changes and development expected of students. For example, a model, consistent and clear policy, and way of handling fighting on the playground would support a conflict resolution program. When students observe playground supervisors using problem-solving techniques to resolve conflicts on the playground, they are more likely to practice these techniques for themselves.

7. Evidence of successful implementation is important for future efforts to gain support. Evaluation efforts could cover both process (evidence of implementation) and outcome (change in student skills) areas. An example of process evidence might include student written products or videotapes of student role-playing activities. For example, one school's product of a bully/victim/bystander program was a videotape to be shown in classrooms throughout their junior high school. An example of a program outcome would be the change in the number of solutions generated by students to problem situations.

Secondary Prevention Programs

Goldstein programs. Secondary prevention programs are critical in the teaching of prosocial skills to children who have been identified as deficient in such competencies and may be at risk for developing more serious behavioral disorders. Goldstein's extensive work on anger and aggression management and social skills training has contributed significantly to the development of secondary prevention programs. In fact, three of his own creations, Skillstreaming the Elementary School Child (McGinnis & Goldstein, 1984), Skillstreaming the Adolescent (Goldstein, Sprafkin, Gershaw, & Klein, 1980) and the Prepare Curriculum (Goldstein, 1988) are some of the most comprehensive secondary prevention guides available and are currently used by teachers of both mainstream and special education classes. Both programs are quite similar in their approach, content, and methods; however, the Prepare Curriculum is much more specific, in terms of its focus and targeted population.

These programs include instruction on an array of prosocial skills presented in Table 11.1. Training for these skills is particularly crucial when skills to replace aggressive behavior are not present in the individual's behavioral repertoire (Goldstein & Keller, 1989). Goldstein and his colleagues utilize the structured learning approach described earlier in this chapter. Children or adolescents who are weak or deficient in one or more of the clusters of skills are chosen as targets for the curriculum. These authors do not recommend a specific group size; however, the size is dictated by how many individuals can be effectively involved in activities such as role play. Therefore, five to seven participants would be a good guide for group size. Sessions are conducted by two trainers who meet with the groups once or twice per week for 1-hour sessions. Pretraining preparation of the trainees includes describing the purpose of the group, the procedures that will be used, the benefits of participation, and the group rules. The effectiveness of these curricula is supported by the research done by Goldstein and other researchers on the structured learning methods, the program as a whole, and its various components (Goldstein, 1988; McGinnis & Goldstein, 1984)

Social Skills in the Classroom. Social Skills in the Classroom (Stephens, 1978) is a secondary prevention program that has been used with mildly disabled elementary-age students. This program was developed with the "directive teaching" instructional model as its foundation. In other words, skill training is oriented within a diagnostic-prescriptive model of teaching. Social skills instructors using this curriculum first model the target behavior for the students, identify the specific movements that are needed, and emphasize the conditions under which the specific target behavior is to occur. Skills levels are subsequently assessed and, based on this measurement, corrective teaching strategies are developed. These steps are also part of the structured learning instructional model followed by Goldstein's Skillstreaming programs. In fact, the Social Skills in the Classroom and Skillstreaming the Elementary School Child programs are very similar, not only in instructional approach, but in content and methodology as well. Both programs offer thorough guidelines for teaching target skills; however, Social Skills in the Classroom does not provide instructional scripts or lesson plans. Instead, the teacher must develop his or her own instructional plan based on one of three teaching strategies: social modeling, social reinforcement, and contingency management. These strategies are also used in the Goldstein programs. In addition, both curricula are comprehensive (Social Skills in the Classroom covers 136 social skills and Skillstreaming the Elementary School Child teaches 60). These programs focus on many of the same skills, such as *expressing feelings appropriately, following instructions, coping with conflict,* and *making conversation.*

In terms of instructional setting and implementers, Social Skills in the Classroom is a flexible program. Although primarily designed to be taught by teachers in the regular or special education classroom, educational consultants and school psychologists can also teach this program. The social skills can be approached as a separate curriculum to be incorporated into daily or weekly teaching schedules, or they can be taught in isolation to meet the needs of individual students.

Earlscourt Social Skills Group Program. Originally drawn from Goldstein's Skillstreaming techniques, the Earlscourt Social Skills Group Program (Pepler, King, & Byrd, 1991) is an instructional, experiential program designed to enhance the self-control and social skills of moderately aggressive, noncompliant children between the ages of 6 and 12. The Earlscourt Social Skills Group Program is a school-based program that can be implemented in either regular or special education classes. Parent training sessions are also offered as part of the program to teach parents more effective child management techniques and to facilitate their child's generalization of skills. Efforts to help children generalize learned skills to the classroom include homework assignments, teacher involvement, and the teaching of a skill to the child's entire class.

The Earlscourt Social Skills Group Program employs a group format for five to seven children at a time; both primary (ages 6–8) and junior (ages 9–12) groups are conducted. Children attend two 75-minute sessions per week for 12–15 weeks. Leaders promote a positive, therapeutic environment by encouraging a fun, club-like atmosphere, by supportive and caring leadership style, and by attention to children's needs for approval and respect.

Eight basic skills are taught: *problem solving, knowing your feelings, listening, following instruction, joining in, using self-control, responding to teasing,* and *keeping out of fights.* Group leaders utilize a variety of both behavioral and social-cognitive techniques, including self-monitoring of feelings, identifying "cues" that trigger aggressive behavior, enhancing problem-solving skills, and encouraging self-enhancing (rather than self-defeating) cognitions.

ACCEPTS. The ACCEPTS program (Walker et al., 1983) is one of the most widely used curricula for teaching prosocial skills to both mildly disabled and nondisabled elementary-level students. The lesson plans and teaching strategies are designed to be used in both regular and special education classrooms. However, the program's primary goal is to teach social-behavioral competencies to handicapped children in order to prepare them for the behavioral demands of a less restrictive, mainstream setting. A secondary goal is to teach directly skills that facilitate classroom adjustment and contribute to peer acceptance. Included in the complete package are lesson scripts for instructors, behavioral management techniques, and multistep instructional procedures based on effective teaching behaviors with mildly disabled students (i.e., direct instruction). Although teachers are the primary consumers of this curriculum, it can also be used by mental health personnel, school counselors, school psychologists, school social workers, and speech-language therapists. Instructors using ACCEPTS define the skills to be learned, provide examples (model) and counterexamples of prosocial behavior, observe students' active practice, offer performance feedback, and motivate participants to strive toward enhanced generalization of their newly acquired prosocial skills.

The ACCEPTS program is fairly comprehensive, focusing on over 25 different social skills subdivided into *classroom rules, basic interaction skills, getting along skills, friendship skills,* and *coping skills (e.g., appropriate expression of anger).* An instructional videotape that shows students actually performing the skills to be learned is also available to offer additional guidance. Optimal group size should be between 5–10 students to allow for more one-on-one student-teacher interactions; however, the program has been successfully adapted for larger groups. ACCEPTS is ideally suited for use with mildly handicapped students in mainstream classrooms.

ACCESS. The ACCESS (Walker, Todis, Holmes, & Horton, 1988) program is an upward extension of the ACCEPTS program, designed to be used with middle and high school students in special and regular classrooms. Similar in approach and format to ACCEPTS, the adolescent program emphasizes the teaching of *peer-to-peer social skills (e.g., having conversations)* and *self-management skills (e.g., using self-control).* Each lesson focuses on one particular skill from each skill area. The multistep instructional procedure implemented in the ACCEPTS program is also used to teach ACCESS lessons, with one additional step. In addition to the lesson scripts and instructional guidelines, a student study guide and situational role-play cards are included in the package. The ACCESS Student Study Guide is designed for individual student use during social skills instruction. It provides instructional content for the lessons and includes *skill acquisition and review, presentation of examples, practice, application and assessment exercises, and individual student contracts,* and *homework assignments.* The program also provides tips for behavior management and for increasing student motivation.

Although the ACCESS program can be taught successfully using one-to-one and large group interactions, the authors strongly recommend using a small group arrangement. Two to four months is normally required to move a group of students through the program, depending on students' ability levels and amount of daily instruction. Approximately 1 hour of daily ACCESS instruction is recommended.

ASSETS. ASSETS (Hazel, Schumaker, Sherman, & Sheldon-Wildgen, 1981) is a widely used and highly reputable program for teaching social skills to at-risk adolescents. This program features videocassettes that are used to teach prosocial skills such as *giving and receiving positive and negative feedback, resisting peer pressure, problem solving, negotiation, following instructions,* and *conversation.* The leader's guide of ASSETS contains over 150 pages of lesson scripts, instructional procedures, and objectives for each filmed lesson. The films keep required reading for participants to a minimum and show adolescents modeling both appropriate and inappropriate social skills in interactions with peers, teachers, parents, and adults. Participants practice the behaviors to be learned through structured role plays, and instructor feedback until the competency level is reached. The rationale for learning a specific skill is stated at the beginning of each lesson. Program evaluation includes parental feedback (judgment) of their child's progress.

Positive Adolescent Choices Training. The Positive Adolescent Choices Training (Hammond & Yung, 1991) is a violence prevention program for African-American youth, designed to promote skills to reduce anger and physical aggression. The program is accompanied by a video that provides introduction to the major target skills, modeled by African-American adolescent males. The program is ideally designed for use with groups of no more than 10 participants. Eight to 10 sessions, approximately 50 minutes each in length, are needed to complete training on the skill sequence. It is recommended that trainers should have professional experience in working with minority and disadvantaged youth. Two trainers per group are recommended. Tips are given for establishing a climate that is culturally sensitive. Although the school setting is the recommended setting for implementation, residential facilities, social services, and community- and church-sponsored groups or settings can be used.

The target skills include the following:

1. *Givin' It*—involves expressing criticism, disappointment, anger, or displeasure calmly. Use of this skill allows the participant to release strong emotions constructively and to master the skills that will prepare the youth for nonviolent verbal resolution of conflicts.
2. *Takin' It*—puts the participant on the receiving end of "Givin' It." This skill involves listening, understanding, and appropriately reacting to criticism and the anger of others.
3. *Workin' It Out*—incorporates listening, identifying problems and possible solutions, suggesting alternatives when disagreements persist, and learning to compromise.

The methods used to teach these skills to participants are based on social learning theory and include these four steps: (a) *demonstration* of the behavioral components of the target skill by an "expert"; (b) guided opportunities to *practice* the target skills; (c) praise, reinstruction, and related *feedback* on skill enactment; and (d) activities designed to *transfer* the skill to real-world settings.

The videotapes are used as a stimulus or model of correct and incorrect ways of dealing with anger. Ideally, the videos should serve as a basis for the group to develop the role-play scenarios and receive feedback on their performance of target skills. Videotaping the role plays so that participants can review them for both self-evaluation and feedback purposes is also suggested as a helpful training activity.

Other violence prevention programs. Though more of a social than educational issue, community or gang-related violence is nevertheless an important issue related to anger and aggression in children and adolescents. A diverse group of violence prevention programs has been developed by community and national organizations and is currently being implemented in schools across the country. Although these programs may differ in terms of the primary focus and targeted population, the basic goals are the same;

that is, to expand children's awareness of violence and teach them how to express their anger in an appropriate, nonviolent manner. Some of the programs are listed in the Appendix.

Efficacy of Secondary Prevention Programs

Although most of the evidence for social skill training efficacy comes from studies that do not directly target anger and aggression, there is some evidence to suggest that social skill training is effective in improving the basic social skills of aggressive youth (Feindler, 1990; Goldstein & Keller, 1989; Hughes, 1988; Stern & Fodor, 1989). However, limitations in a strict behavioral approach to training have been noted by Feindler and Ecton (1986). They highlight the following limitations in the effectiveness of behavioral interventions: (a) difficulty in completing peer reinforcement contingencies, (b) lack of powerful reinforcers, (c) low-frequency or covert aggressive behaviors that go undetected and unconsequated, and (d) inconsistent behavior change agents.

Such limitations point to the necessity of targeting social-cognitive and anger control processes as well. Interventions that include skills in interpersonal problem-solving skills in addition to social skill training have been found to be more effective than those that rely on social skill training alone (Kazdin, Esveldt-Dawson, French, & Unis, 1987; Small & Schinke, 1983). Techniques of self-instruction and other cognitive techniques have been found to be effective with aggressive children and adolescents (Kendall, 1977), with one strength being the flexibility available for adapting the intervention to the specific needs and situations of the trainee. Evidence for stress inoculation training is conflicting. Spirito, Finch, Smith, and Cooley (1981) found that this technique was effective in reducing angry and aggressive outbursts in children; whereas Schlichter and Horan (1981) did not find reduction in verbal and physical aggression for a group of institutionalized delinquents. Feindler (1990), in a review of programs for anger control, concluded that anger control interventions have documented positive changes in self-report of anger, problem-solving, and social skills but have failed to show significant changes in arousal, impulse-control, attributions, and overt aggression.

Although programs such as Goldstein's Aggression Retraining model (Goldstein, Glick, Zimmerman, & Reiner, 1987) and Feindler's *Chill-Out* program (Feindler & Ecton, 1986) have achieved success with a combination of training foci (skills, cognitions, arousal), evidence is not available that analyzes which components contribute to the program's effectiveness. A major limitation in training effectiveness is found also in the ability of trainees to generalize these skills to alternative settings. As well, reductions in aggressive behavior have not been maintained after treatment termination (Feindler, 1990; Goldstein & Keller, 1989). Goldstein (1982) found that generalization and maintenance were a function of the degree to which the investigator/trainer implemented procedures explicitly designed to enhance such transfer and/or maintenance as part of the training effort.

Because the dynamics of anger and aggression are complex, capturing their change in the context of prevention and intervention programs is very difficult. In order to ensure that change is successfully documented, thorough evaluation procedures should be implemented. For example, a first step in evaluating treatment effectiveness would be to document treatment integrity; that is, investigating whether or not the program was implemented in the way that it was designed. Also, multiple measures of effectiveness should be used. For example, are social skills successfully displayed in the treatment setting, in other settings (generalization and transfer)? Are the skills maintained across time (maintenance)? Do other people perceive improvement in social skills? Are relationships enhanced by the use of more positive social skills? The latter two questions are related to whether or not the treatment has led to socially valid changes in behavior.

CONCLUSION

This chapter has provided an overview of the definitions and constructs associated with social skills and their connection with anger and aggression, a description of groups of children who often have social skill deficits, and a description of social skill programs that represent prevention and intervention approaches. A theme that we have emphasized throughout is that social skills and social competence are contextually driven concepts. We cannot judge competence without considering the contexts in which it occurs, such as in the family, in the classroom, on the playground, or with a group of peers. In this manner, it is important to focus our intervention efforts at the transactional level; that is, we need to go beyond the social skill deficits that children and adolescents may exhibit and emphasize the interactions that these individuals have with their environment. We are suggesting that intervention or secondary/tertiary prevention program implementers begin to consider some of the characteristics that we described more often in primary prevention programs; for example, climate building activities, integration into the ongoing curriculum, and group development. Further, effectiveness of the programs would be enhanced if program components include the participation of teachers, parents, peers, and significant others in the school and neighborhood. Comprehensive, multiple strategies are needed to ensure a lasting and meaningful reduction of anger and aggression and a building of a significant repertoire of prosocial skills. Reducing anger and aggression cannot be a "one-stop" effort; it must be supported and nurtured by the total environment.

REFERENCES

Adelman, H. S., Smith, D. C., Nelson, P., Taylor, L., & Phares, V. (1986). An instrument to assess students' perceived control at school. *Educational and Psychological Measurement, 46*, 1005-1017.

Bandura, A. (1977). *Social learning theory*. Englewood Cliffs, NJ: Prentice Hall.

Bryan, T. S., & Bryan, J. (1978). Social interactions of learning disabled children. *Learning Disability Quarterly, 1*, 33-38.

Bryan, R., & Bryan, J. (1981). Some personal and social experiences of learning disabled children. In B. Keogh (Ed.), *Advances in special education* Greenwich, CT: JAI Press.

Carlson, C. I. (1987). Social interaction goals and strategies of children with learning disabilities. *Journal of Learning Disabilities, 20,* 306-311.

Cartledge, G., & Milburn, J. F. (1980). *Teaching social skills to children.* New York: Pergamon Press.

Christoffel, K. K. (1990). Violent death and injury in U. S. children and adolescents. *American Journal of Diseases of Childhood, 144*, 697-706.

Coie, J. D., & Dodge, K. A. (1986). *Hostile and instrumentally aggressive children: A social information processing perspective.* Paper presented at the Annual Meeting of the American Psychological Association, Washington, DC.

Conger , J. C., & Keane, S. P. (1981). Social skills intervention in the treatment of isolated or withdrawn children. *Psychological Bulletin, 90*, 478-495.

Cowen, E., Pederson, A., Babigian, H., Izzo, L., & Trost, M. (1973). Long-term follow-up of early detected vulnerable childrn. *Journal of Clinical and Consulting Psychology, 41,* 438-446.

Dembrowsky, C. H. (1983). *Affective skill development for adolescents–*

Teacher's manual. Jackson, WY: Constance H. Dembrosky.

Denvencenzi, J., & Pendergast, S. (1988). *Belonging: Self and social discovery for children of all ages.* San Luis Obispo, CA: Belonging.

Dodge, K. (1980). Social cognition and children's aggressive behavior. *Child Development, 51,* 162-170.

Dodge, K. A. (1983). Behavioral antecedents of peer social status. *Child Development, 54,* 1386-1399.

Dodge, K. A. (1986). A social information processing model of social competence in children. In M. Perlmutter (Ed.), *Cognitive perspectives on children's social and behavioral development: Minnesota symposium on child psychology* (Vol. 18, pp. 77-125). Hillsdale, NJ: Erlbaum.

Dodge, K. A., & Newman, J. P. (1981). Biased decision making processes in aggressive boys. *Journal of Abnormal Psychology, 90,* 372-379.

Drew, N. (1987). *Learning the skills of peacemaking.* Rolling Hills Estates, CA: Jalmar Press.

Elias, M. J., & Clabby, J. F. (1989). *Social decision-making skills: A curriculum guide for the elementary grades.* Rockville, MD: Aspen.

Elliott, S. N., & Ershler, J. (1990). Best practices in preschool social skills training. In A. Thomas & J. Grimes, *Best practices in school psychology—II* (pp. 591-606). Washington, DC: National Association of School Psychologists.

Feindler, E. L. (1990). Adolescent anger control: Review and critique. In M. Hersen, R. Eisler, & P. Miller (Eds.), *Progress in behavior modification* (Vol 26, pp. 11-59). Newbury Park, CA: Sage.

Feindler, E. L., & Ecton, R. B. (1986). *Adolescent anger control: Cognitive-behavioral techniques.* Elmsford, NY: Pergamon.

Felner, R. D., & Felner, T. Y. (1989). Primary prevention programs in the educational context: A transactional-ecological framework and analysis. In L. A. Bond & B. E. Compas (Eds.), *Primary prevention and promotion in the schools* (pp. 13-49). Newbury Park: Sage.

Fingerhut, L. A., & Kleinman, J. C. (1990). International and interstate comparisons of homicide among young males. *Journal of the American Medical Association, 263* (24), 3292-3295.

Forness, S. (1992). Broadening the cultural-organizational perspective in exclusion of youth with social maladjustment: First invited reaction to the Maag and Howell paper. *RASE, 13,* 55-59.

Forness, S., & Knitzer, J. (1992). A new proposed definition and terminology to replace "serious emotional disturbance in Individuals with Disabilities Education Act. *School Psychology Review, 21,* 12-20.

Fuchs, D., & Thelen, M. H. (1988). Children's expected interpersonal consequences of communicating their affective state and reported likelihood of expression. *Child Development, 59,* 1314-1322.

Garmezy, N., Masten, A., & Tellegen, A. (1984). The study of stress and competence in children. *Child Development, 55,* 97-111.

Goldstein, A. P. (1988). *The Prepare Curriculum.* Champaign, IL: Research Press.

Goldstein, A. P. (1982). *Psychological skills training.* New York: Pergamon.

Goldstein, A. P., & Glick, B. (1986). *Aggression replacement training: A comprehensive intervention for aggressive youth.* Champagn, IL: Research Press.

Goldstein, A. P., Glick, B., Zimmerman, D., & Reiner, S. (1987). *Aggression retraining: A comprehensive intervention for the acting out delinquent.* Champaign, IL: Research Press.

Goldstein, A. P., & Keller, H. (1989). *Aggressive behavior: Assessment and intervention.* New York: Pergamon

Goldstein, A. P., Sprafkin, R. R., Gershaw, N. J., & Klien, P. (1980). *Skillstreaming the adolescent: A structured learning approach to teaching prosocial skills.* Champaign, IL: Research Press.

Gonzales, P. (1991). *A comparison of state policy to the federal definition and a proposed definition of serious emotional disturbance.* National Association of State Directors of Special Education, 1800 Diagonal Road, Alexandria, VA 22314.

Greenspan, S., & Granfield, J. M. (1992). Reconsidering the construct of mental retardation: Implications of a model of social competence. *American Journal of Mental Retardation, 96,* 442-453.

Greenspan, S. (1979). Social intelligence in the retarded. In N. R. Ellis (Ed.), *Handbook of mental deficiency: Psychological theory and research* (2nd ed., pp. 483-531). Hillsdale, NJ: Erlbaum.

Gresham, F. M. (1990). Best practices in social skills training. In A. Thomas & J. Grimes, *Best practices in school psychology—II* (pp. 695-709). Washington, DC: National Association of School Psychologists.

Gresham, F., & Elliott, S. (1984). Assessment and classification of children's social skills: A review of methods and issues. *School Psychology Review, 13,* 292-301.

Gresham, F. M., & Reschly, D. J. (1986). Social skills deficits and low peer acceptance of mainstreamed learning disabled children. *Learning Disability Quarterly, 9,* 23-32.

Hammond, W. R., & Yung, B. R. (1991). *Dealing with anger: A violence prevention program for African American Youth.* Champaign, IL: Research Press.

Hawkins, J. D., Lishner, D. M., Catalano, R. F., & Howard, M. O. (1986). Childhood predictors of adolescent substance abuse: Toward an empirically grounded theory. *Journal of Children in Contemporary Society, 8,* 11-48.

Hazel, J. S., Schumaker, J. B., Sherman, J. A. & Sheldon-Wildgen, J. (1981). *ASSET: A social skills program for adolescents (Multimedia program).* Champaign, IL: Research Press.

Healey, K. N., & Masterpasqua, F. (1992). Interpersonal cognitive problem-solving among children with mild mental retardation. *American Journal on Mental Retardation, 96,* 367-372.

Hightower, A. D., Johnson, D., & Haffey, W. G. (1990). Best practices in adopting and prevention program. In A. Thomas & J. Grimes (Eds.), *Best practices in school psychology—II* (pp. 63-79). Washington, DC: National Association of School Psychologists.

Hinshaw, S. P., Buhrmester, D., & Heller, T. (1989). Anger control in response to verbal provocation: Effects of stimulant medication for boys with ADHD. *Journal of Abnormal Child Psychology, 17,* 393-407.

Hughes, J. (1988). *Cognitive Behavior Therapy with Children in Schools.* New York: Pergamon Press.

Kanfer, F., & Phillips, J. (1970). *Learning foundations of behavioral therapy.* New York: Wiley.

Kazdin, A., Esveldt-Dawson, K., French, N., & Unis, A. (1987). Problem-solving skills training and relationship therapy treatment of antisocial child behavior. *Journal of Consulting and Clinical Psychology, 55* (1), 76-85.

Kendall, P. (1977). On the efficacious use of verbal self-instructional procedures with children. *Cognitive Therapy and Research, 1,* 331-341.

Knapczyk, D. R. (1988). Reducing aggressive behaviors in special and regular class settings by training alternative social responses. *Behavioral Disorders, 14,* 27-39.

Kohlberg, L. (1964). Development of moral character and moral ideology. In M. L. Hoffman & L. W. Hoffman (Eds.), *Review of child development research.* New York: Russell Sage Foundation.

Kreidler, W. J. (1984). *Creative conflict resolution.* Glenview, IL: Scott,

Foresman and Company.

Ladd, G. W., & Mize, J. (1983). A cognitive-social learning model of social-skill training. *Psychological Review, 90,* 127-157.

LaGreca, A. M. (1987). Children with learning disabilities: Interpersonal skills and social competence. *Reading, Writing, and Learning Disabilities, 3,* 167-185.

LaGreca , A. M., & Mesibov, G. B. (1981). Facilitating interpersonal functioning with peers in learning disabled children. *Journal of Learning Disabilities, 14,* 197-199.

Levy, L., & Gottlieb, J. (1984). Learning disabled and non-LD children at play. *Remedial and Special Education, 5,* 43-50.

Luckkason, R. et al. (1992). *Definition and classification in mental retardation* (9th ed.). Washington, DC: AAMR.

Maag, J. W. (1989). Assessment in social skills training: Methodological and conceptual issues for research and practice. *Remedial and Special Education, 10,* 6-15.

McGinnis, E., & Goldstein, A. P. (1984). *Skillstreaming the elementary school child.* Champaign, IL: Research Press.

Meichenbaum, D. (1977). *Cognitive behavioral modification: An integrative approach.* New York: Plenum Press.

Meyer, L. H., & Evans, I. M. (1989). *Nonaversive intervention for behavior problems.* Baltimore, MD: Brookes.

Morrison, G. M. (1991). *The SCIPP Project: Skills for Consultation in Prevention Programming* (Final Report to the U.S. Office of Education: Drug Free Communities & Schools, Contract No. S184A90120).

Novaco, R. (1975). *Anger control: The development and evaluation of an experimental treatment.* Lexington, MA: D.C. Heath.

Novaco, R. W. (1978). Anger and coping with stress: Cognitive-behavioral intervention. In J. P. Foreyt & D. P. Rathjen (Eds.), *Cognitive behavioral therapy: Research and application.* New York: Plenum.

Patterson, G. R. (1982). *Coercive family process: A social learning approach* (Vol. 3). Eugene, OR: Castalia.

Patterson, G. R., Debaryshe, B. D., & Ramsey, E. (1989). A developmental perspective on antisocial behavior. *American Psychologist, 44,* 329-335.

Pepler, D. J., King, G., & Byrd, W. (1991). A social-cognitively based social skills training program for aggressive children. In D. J. Pepler & K. H. Rubin (Eds.), *The development and treatment of childhood aggression* (pp. 361-379). Hillsdale, NJ: Erlbaum.

Quest International. (1978). *Skills for living.* Granville, OH: Author.
Quest International. (1985). *Skills for adolescence.* Granville, OH: Author.
Quest International. (1990). *Skills for growing.* Granville, OH: Author.
Quinton, D., & Rutter, M. (1984). *Parenting breakdown: The making and breaking of intergenerational links.* Aldershot: Gower.
Reiss, S. (1990). Prevalence of dual diagnosis in community-based day programs in the Chicago metropolitan area. *American Journal on Mental Retardation, 94,* 578-585.
Richard, B., & Dodge, K. (1982). Social maladjustment and problem solving in school-aged children. *Jounal of Consulting and Clinical Psychology, 50,* 226-233.
Roff, M., Sells, S. B., & Golden, M. (1972). *Social adjustment and personality development in children.* Minneapolis: University of Minnesota Press.
Roff, J. D., & Wirt, R. D. (1984). Childhood aggression and social adjustment as antecedents of delinquency. *Journal of Abnormal Child Psychology, 12,* 111-126.
Rutter, M. (1985). Resilience in the face of adversity. *British Journal of Psychiatry, 147,* 598-611.
Sabornie, E. J. (1991). Measuring and teaching social skills in the mainstream. In G. Stoner, M. R. Shinn, & H. M. Walker (Eds.), *Interventions for achievement and behavior problems* (pp. 161-178). Washington, DC: National Association of School Psychologists.
Schlichter, K. J., & Horan, J. J. (1981). Effects of stress inoculation on the anger and aggression management skills of institutionalized juvenile delinquents. *Cognitive Therapy and Research, 5,* 359-365.
Schmitz, C., & Hipp, E. (1987). *A teacher's guide to fighting invisible tigers.* Minneapolis, MN: Free Spirit.
Selman, R. (1980). *The growth of interpersonal understanding: Developmental and clincal analyses.* New York: Academic Press.
Siperstein, G. N. (1992). Social competence: An important construct in mental retardation. *Journal on Mental Retardation, 96,* iii-vi.
Small, R., & Schinke, S. (1983). Teaching competence in residential group care. *Journal of Social Service Research, 7,* 1-16.
Smith, D. C., Adelman, H. S., Nelson, P., Taylor, L., & Phares, V. (1988). Anger, perceived control, and school behavior among students with learning problems. *Journal of Child Psychology and Psychiatry, 29,* 517-522.
Spirito, G., Finch, A., Smith, T., & Cooley, W. (1981). Stress inoculation

for anger and anxiety control: A case study with an emotionally disturbed boy. *Journal of Clinical Child Psychology, 10,* 67-70.

Spivack, B., Platt, J., & Shure, M. (1976). *The problem solving approach to adjustment.* San Francisco: Jossey-Bass.

Stephens, T. M. (1978). *Social skills in the classrooom.* Columbus, OH: Cedars Press.

Stern, J. B., & Fodor, I. G. (1989). Anger control in children: A review of social skills and cognitive behavioral approaches to dealing with aggressive children. *Child and Family Behavior Therapy, 11,* 1-19.

Svec, H., & Bechard, J. (1988). An introduction to a metabehavioral model with implications for social skills training for aggressive adolescents. *Psychological Reports, 62,* 19-22.

Toro, P. A. , Weissberg, R. P., Guare, J., & Liebenstein, N. L. (1990). A comparison of children with and without learning disabilities on social problem-solving skill, school behavior, and family background. *Journal of Learning Disabilities, 23,* 115-119.

Turiel, E. (1975). The development of social concepts: Mores, customs and conventions. In D. J. DePalma & F. M. Foley (Eds.), *Moral development: Current theory and research.* Hillsdale, NJ: Erlbaum.

Waas, G. A. (1987). Aggressive rejected children: Implications for school psychologists. *Journal of School Psychology, 25,* 383-388.

Walker, H. M., McConnell, S. R., Holmes, D., Todis, B., Walker, J., & Golden, H. (1983). *The Walker social skills curriculum: The ACCEPTS program.* Austin, TX: Pro-Ed.

Walker, H. M., Todis, B., Holmes, D., & Horton, G. (1988). *The Walker social skills curriculum: The ACCESS program.* Austin, TX: Pro-Ed.

Zigler, E., & Trickett, P. K. (1978). IQ, social competence, and evaluation of early childhood intervention programs. *American Psychologist, 33,* 789-798.

Appendix

Social Skills Program	Quest—Skills for Growing (K-5)	Quest—Skills for Adolescents	Prepare Curriculum (Goldstein)	Creative Conflict Resolution	Affective Development for Adolescents	Walker ACCESS Program	Belonging—Self and Social Discovery	Learning the Skills of Peacemaking	Social Skills in the Classroom	EarlsCourt Social Skills
I. Classroom Survival Skills										
1. Listening	✔	✔	✔	✔	✔	✔	✔	✔	✔	✔
2. Asking for Help	✔		✔			✔	✔		✔	✔
3. Saying Thank You	✔		✔	✔		✔	✔		✔	
4. Bringing Materials to Class					✔	✔			✔	
5. Following Instructions	✔		✔		✔	✔		✔	✔	✔
6. Completing Assignments	✔				✔	✔		✔	✔	✔
7. Contributing to Discussions	✔	✔		✔	✔	✔	✔	✔	✔	✔
8. Offering Help to an Adult	✔					✔	✔	✔	✔	
9. Asking a Question	✔		✔		✔	✔	✔		✔	✔
10. Ignoring Distractions	✔	✔			✔				✔	✔
11. Making Corrections						✔			✔	
12. Deciding on Something to Do	✔		✔			✔	✔	✔	✔	✔
13. Setting a Goal		✔	✔		✔	✔		✔		
II. Friendship Making Skills										
14. Introducing Yourself	✔	✔	✔			✔	✔		✔	
15. Beginning a Conversation	✔	✔	✔	✔	✔	✔	✔		✔	
16. Ending a Conversation	✔		✔		✔	✔	✔		✔	
17. Joining in	✔	✔	✔	✔	✔	✔	✔	✔	✔	✔
18. Playing a Game	✔	✔		✔	✔	✔	✔		✔	
19. Asking a Favor					✔		✔		✔	
20. Offering Help to a Classmate	✔	✔	✔	✔	✔	✔	✔	✔	✔	
21. Giving a Compliment	✔		✔		✔	✔		✔	✔	
22. Accepting a Compliment	✔				✔			✔	✔	
23. Suggesting an Activity	✔						✔		✔	
24. Sharing	✔	✔	✔	✔			✔	✔	✔	
25. Apologizing			✔	✔		✔		✔	✔	
III. Skills for Dealing with Feelings										
26. Knowing Your Feelings	✔	✔	✔	✔	✔	✔	✔	✔	✔	✔
27. Expressing Your Feelings	✔	✔	✔	✔	✔	✔	✔	✔	✔	✔
28. Recognizing Another's Feelings		✔		✔	✔	✔	✔	✔	✔	✔
29. Showing Understanding of Another's Feelings		✔	✔	✔	✔	✔		✔	✔	
30. Expressing Concern for Another		✔				✔		✔	✔	✔

APPENDIX

SOCIAL SKILLS PROGRAM	Fighting Invisible Tigers	Walker ACCEPTS Program	Social Decision-Making Skills	PACT	ASSETS					
I. Classroom Survival Skills										
1. Listening	✔	✔	✔	✔	✔					
2. Asking for Help	✔	✔	✔		✔					
3. Saying Thank You		✔	✔							
4. Bringing Materials to Class		✔	✔							
5. Following Instructions		✔	✔		✔					
6. Completing Assignments		✔	✔							
7. Contributing to Discussions		✔	✔		✔					
8. Offering Help to an Adult		✔								
9. Asking a Question		✔	✔							
10. Ignoring Distractions		✔								
11. Making Corrections										
12. Deciding on Something to Do	✔		✔		✔					
13. Setting a Goal	✔		✔		✔					
II. Friendship Making Skills										
14. Introducing Yourself			✔							
15. Beginning a Conversation	✔	✔	✔		✔					
16. Ending a Conversation	✔	✔	✔		✔					
17. Joining in		✔	✔		✔					
18. Playing a Game			✔							
19. Asking a Favor	✔		✔							
20. Offering Help to a Classmate		✔	✔							
21. Giving a Compliment	✔	✔	✔	✔	✔					
22. Accepting a Compliment		✔	✔		✔					
23. Suggesting an Activity		✔	✔							
24. Sharing		✔			✔					
25. Apologizing			✔	✔						
III. Skills for Dealing with Feelings										
26. Knowing Your Feelings	✔			✔						
27. Expressing Your Feelings	✔	✔		✔						
28. Recognizing Another's Feelings	✔			✔						
29. Showing Understanding of Another's Feelings	✔			✔						
30. Expressing Concern for Another	✔	✔	✔	✔						

APPENDIX

SOCIAL SKILLS PROGRAM	Quest—Skills for Growing (K-5)	Quest—Skills for Adolescents	Prepare Curriculum (Goldstein)	Creative Conflict Resolution	Affective Development for Adolescents	Walker ACCESS Program	Belonging—Self and Social Discovery	Learning the Skills of Peacemaking	Social Skills in the Classroom	Earls Court Social Skills
III. SKILLS FOR DEALING WITH FEELINGS (CONTINUED)										
31. Dealing with Your Anger	✔	✔	✔	✔	✔	✔	✔	✔	✔	✔
32. Dealing with Another's Anger	✔	✔	✔		✔	✔	✔		✔	✔
33. Expressing Affection			✔						✔	
34. Dealing with Fear			✔				✔	✔		
35. Rewarding Yourself		✔	✔			✔	✔			
IV. SKILL ALTERNATIVES TO AGGRESSION										
36. Using Self-control		✔	✔	✔	✔	✔	✔	✔	✔	✔
37. Asking Permission	✔		✔			✔	✔		✔	
38. Responding to Teasing			✔				✔	✔	✔	✔
39. Avoiding Trouble		✔	✔	✔	✔		✔	✔	✔	✔
40. Staying Out of Fights	✔		✔	✔	✔			✔	✔	✔
41. Problem Solving	✔	✔	✔	✔	✔	✔	✔	✔	✔	✔
42. Accepting Consequences		✔	✔	✔	✔	✔			✔	✔
43. Dealing with an Accusation			✔							✔
44. Negotiating	✔	✔	✔	✔	✔	✔	✔	✔	✔	✔
V. SKILLS FOR DEALING WITH STRESS										
45. Dealing with Boredom									✔	
46. Deciding What Caused a Problem	✔	✔	✔	✔			✔			✔
47. Making a Complaint		✔	✔	✔			✔		✔	
48. Answering a Complaint		✔	✔				✔		✔	
49. Dealing with Losing					✔		✔		✔	
50. Showing Sportsmanship			✔						✔	
51. Dealing with Being Left Out		✔	✔			✔	✔		✔	
52. Dealing with Embarrassment			✔							
53. Reacting to Failure			✔		✔		✔			
54. Accepting No						✔	✔		✔	
55. Saying No	✔	✔			✔	✔	✔		✔	
56. Relaxing				✔	✔		✔			
57. Dealing with Group Pressure	✔	✔	✔		✔	✔	✔		✔	
58. Dealing with Wanting Something That's Not Mine									✔	
59. Making a Decision	✔	✔	✔	✔	✔		✔	✔	✔	✔
60. Being Honest						✔		✔	✔	

Appendix

Social Skills Program	Fighting Invisible Tigers	Walker ACCEPTS Program	Social Decision-Making Skills	PACT	ASSETS
III. Skills for Dealing with Feelings (continued)					
31. Dealing with Your Anger		✔	✔	✔	
32. Dealing with Another's Anger		✔	✔	✔	
33. Expressing Affection	✔				
34. Dealing with Fear					
35. Rewarding Yourself					
IV. Skill Alternatives to Aggression					
36. Using Self-control		✔	✔	✔	
37. Asking Permission		✔	✔		
38. Responding to Teasing		✔	✔	✔	
39. Avoiding Trouble		✔	✔	✔	✔
40. Staying Out of Fights		✔	✔	✔	
41. Problem Solving	✔	✔	✔	✔	✔
42. Accepting Consequences		✔	✔		
43. Dealing with an Accusation				✔	
44. Negotiating	✔		✔	✔	✔
V. Skills for Dealing with Stress					
45. Dealing with Boredom					
46. Deciding What Caused a Problem		✔	✔	✔	
47. Making a Complaint			✔	✔	✔
48. Answering a Complaint				✔	✔
49. Dealing with Losing					
50. Showing Sportsmanship					
51. Dealing with Being Left Out		✔			
52. Dealing with Embarrassment					
53. Reacting to Failure		✔	✔	✔	
54. Accepting No		✔		✔	
55. Saying No	✔	✔		✔	
56. Relaxing	✔		✔		
57. Dealing with Group Pressure	✔	✔	✔		✔
58. Dealing with Wanting Something That's Not Mine					
59. Making a Decision	✔		✔		
60. Being Honest			✔	✔	

12 COGNITIVE-BEHAVIORAL TREATMENT OF ANGER-INDUCED AGGRESSION IN THE SCHOOL SETTING

James Larson

School-based treatment of aggressive, secondary-level students presents a particular challenge for teachers, school psychologists, and counselors. These young men and women frequently arrive at the school from homes and neighborhoods that may not just occasion aggressive behavior, but model and implicitily endorse it (Patterson, DeBaryshe, & Ramsey, 1989). Their patterns of response to provocation during their hours away from school are predictable and very frequently adaptive for the immediate situation. To be "punked" (put down) or "charged up" (physically threatened) in the streets places clear demands on those youth who do not possess alternative strategies: The youth must respond with either aggression or aggressive posturing, lest they be seen as an easy target or, even worse, afraid. To no one's surprise, many of these young people are unable or unwilling to leave these well-practiced and peer culture-approved sets of aggressive behaviors behind as they enter the school building.

If aggression and counteraggression are at times adaptive for the purposes of self-defense in the neighborhoods, they are clearly maladaptive for purposes of educational progress in school. "Official" school culture, with its bias for order, reason, and interpersonal nonviolence, runs counter to the more impulsive, action-oriented, "survival" culture of many of its students. In response, school systems have established written rules of student conduct and provided consequences in the event of their breach. The apparent expectation is that, rather than fight or otherwise disrupt in the school building, the student will inhibit out of fear for the consequence.

School psychologists and other mental health professionals are aware that students cannot enact behaviors they have not learned, nor can they even consider the behavior if it does not exist in their experiential memory (Dodge & Coie, 1987). Most students, however, know how to refrain from assaulting others in the school. To exert cognitive controls on the impulse to beat up a fellow student because he was "talking crazy" at lunch is clearly within the ability of even the most problematic youth. Indeed, one need only seat the fighters' mothers or grandmothers next to them all day long and sit back to observe the demonstrations of saint-like self-restraint. The concern for school personnel, therefore, is more than the simple inhibition and replacement of aggressive behavior.

The variable in many cases of student aggression seems to be the social-environmental context, including perceptions of who is nearby (peers/ teachers) and who is not nearby (mother/police). Students with problematic aggression are frequently lacking in the behavioral and cognitive skills necessary to inhibit within the context of the school's reinforcement-punishment paradigm. These same students will frequently report apparently honest desires and intents to be successful in school (e.g., gain passing grades, graduate), but regularly behave in a fashion that suggests little ability to make that cognitive leap from street thinking to school thinking. This hypothesized failure to differentiate and cultivate those needed skills pushes likelihood of school success further from reality.

The administrative rules of student behavior are often clearly outlined in student handbooks, repeated daily in morning announcements, and ritually intoned by stern-faced principals during student suspension conferences. What is becoming clear, however, is that punishing students for failing to perform behaviors that may not be in their repertoires in this context has doomed traditional discipline measures to failure.

STUDENTS AGAINST VIOLENCE PROGRAM

Recognizing that school-based consequences for aggressive and disruptive behavior were proving ineffective at reducing the escalating levels of interpersonal violence, the Milwaukee (Wisconsin) Public Schools instituted a wide-ranging program aimed at reducing school-context violence (Milwaukee Board of School Directors, 1988). Now in its fourth year of formal implementation and locally funded as the Students Against Violence Program, the effort involves primary, secondary, and tertiary prevention at both the elementary and secondary school levels.

A major component of this program is identification and intervention with middle and high school students experiencing high levels of problematic aggression within the school setting (Milwaukee Board of School Directors, 1988). This effort seeks to furnish cognitive-behavioral training aimed at providing the skills necessary for students to learn critical anger management and alternative response behaviors in the school setting. In Milwaukee, small group intervention with aggressive students is currently active in the majority of middle and high schools in the city. Most recently, the Long Beach (California) Unified School District has instituted a similar intervention program (Larson & McBride, 1991).

In the following section, the procedures used in Milwaukee and Long Beach to identify those students who are most likely to participate and benefit from group treatment will be discussed as a prototype for other school districts considering similar efforts. (See Figure 12.1.)

Identification of Intervention Team Members

Once the decision has been made to target and intervene with aggressive students in the school setting, the personnel, facilities, and other supportive resources must be identified and readied. Schools must decide who among the staff has the training and desire to work intensely with problematic, aggressive students. Feindler and Ecton (1986) suggest that any individual possessing "commitment, enthusiasm, and motivation" (p. 54) has the potential to become an effective group leader with aggressive adolescents. Because of the broadly based model of psychological services delivery in the Milwaukee Public Schools (Jackson, 1990a), the school psychologist is designated as the intervention team leader. In the identification of intervention personnel, schools need to consider the following staff characteristics:

1. Has the staff member received supervised training and/or does he or she have sufficient practical experience in group therapy techniques treating adolescents with externalizing behaviors?
2. Does the staff member have a cognitive or cognitive-behavioral orientation in treatment delivery?
3. Does the staff member believe in the potential value of the intervention effort?
4. Is the staff member enthusiastic about participating in the effort?
5. Does the staff member have the time in his or her schedule for the effort, and will support be forthcoming from the immediate supervisor?

1. Decision made to intervene
- Trainers are identified
- Collaboration with teachers begun with inservice

2. Member indetification procedures
- *First identification gate*: Teacher/administrator referral
- *Second identification gate*: Attendance cross check
- *Third identification gate*: Student interview
- *Fourth identification gate*: Parent permission obtained

3. Planning mechanics
- Final group members identified
- Data collection procedure in place
- Follow-up meeting with affected teachers
- Meeting time established in cooperation with teachers
- Meeting room and video equipment secured for duration

4. Intervention begins

FIGURE 12.1. STUDENTS AGAINST VIOLENCE IMPLEMENTATION STEPS.

Trained and experienced school psychologists, guidance counselors, and school social workers make up the core of potential trainers for aggression management groups. Because the model advocated here is primarily cognitive skills development and cognitive-behavioral training (as opposed to insight-focused therapy where remote causes for problems are identified), there is also reason to consider selected teachers as trainers. Special educators often have the most experience working with small groups of children with behavior problems and can be excellent resources as trainers. As with all potential staff, however, care must be taken to discourage a possible negative stigma. Students, justly or unjustly, frequently pair individual staff members with particular groups of students with whom they do not identify. Special educators may have the additional task of calming any concerns that the group members may have that they have been "classified."

Experience has demonstrated the positive benefits of a co-trainer in some adolescent group interventions, with the responsibilities split between behavioral management and training (e.g., Larson, 1990b). Teachers and inexperienced support staff can often gain needed seasoning in this co-trainer role.

Regardless of who eventually is designated for the trainer's role, it is critical that the person function from a foundation of expertise, experience, and credibility. Schools that may lack such individuals on staff are ethically bound to train or locate them elsewhere.

With the trainers identified and made sufficiently comfortable with the intervention procedure, the intervention team must set about the task of enlisting teacher support. It is likely that teachers will be the ones to write hall passes, provide make-up work, and remind students of session dates, all in support of the intervention. This important supportive role must be given the respect it is due. Prior to actually identifying the group members, the intervention team should provide inservice education to the teachers regarding both the scope and nature of the problem, as well as the type of intervention planned. Teacher input on all issues germane to the effort should be openly solicited. A schedule for providing regular feedback to the teachers regarding the skills trained and procedures used should also be arranged.

Multiple-Gating Procedure for Identifying Group Members

In large secondary schools, the number of students potentially in need of cognitive-behavioral skills training for the management of aggression can be overwhelming. Even in schools where the list of potential candidates may be smaller, basic cost-effectiveness and ethical concerns will trigger a desire to target the correct students. The initial effort should become the identification of those students in need and who are most likely to participate and benefit from the planned intervention. To accomplish this goal, the design and implementation of a multiple-gating procedure is particularly helpful.

In a multiple-gating procedure, potential student candidates are channeled through a sequence of "rule-out" gates, or screens, designed to reduce false positives until a final population with the greatest potential for benefit remains. The first gate must be sufficiently broad and encompassing to identify a pool large enough to contain within its number all of the students eventually identified for intervention. For example, following an intervention team inservice explaining the effort, these first gate candidate students may come through a large-scale teacher/administrator nomination process. Allowing individual teachers to identify their own particularly problematic students is the first step in enlisting their cooperation. The intervention team should be careful to watch for students who are nominated by multiple teachers, thus decreasing the likelihood of a narrow, teacher–student "personality" problem.

A teacher questionnaire should ask for those students who meet the following criteria:

1. The teacher has witnessed the youth in one or more physical fights in the past 6 months; or
2. The teacher is aware that the youth has been involved in at least one school-grounds fight in the past 6 months; or
3. Teacher/staff physical intervention directly prevented the youth from at least one school-grounds fight in the past 6 months; and
4. To the teacher's knowledge, the youth is in regular attendance.

A feedback system should be built into the process so that each teacher is informed as to the outcomes of their student nominees.

Larger systems can make use of any computerized data bank of student disciplinary actions. In the Milwaukee Public Schools, the computer system provides the school intervention team with the names of students who have received administrative discipline in the categories of "fighting" or "teacher assault" or "weapon possession," ranked from the most frequent violators to the least. This list is subsequently compared to the list of teacher-nominated students, partitioned by sex, and the initial pool of students is formed.

An important second gate is that of student attendance. It is not unusual for the most aggressive students to have erratic, if not miserable, attendance patterns. Experience has shown that assembling a treatment group without paying close attention to patterns of school attendance can result in two trainers doing a lot of looking at one another in an empty group room. Intervention teams are advised to track these patterns carefully and rule out those students who cannot be expected to be present reliably for the majority of the planned sessions. Those problematic but poorly attending students should be subsequently identified for individual interventions with supportive service personnel until stable attendance patterns are realized.

The third gate involves person-to-person interviews with each of the remaining students being considered for inclusion. The objectives of this interview are twofold: (a) the team must explain the nature of and rationale for the intervention to the student, answering any questions he/she may have, and securing a provisional willingness on the part of the student to participate; and (b) the team must make initial judgments regarding group composition based on impressions gleaned during the interview.

During the interview, the intervention team should outline to the student the manner in which his/her name was selected and the reason that the youth is being asked to participate. It is important that the team be completely honest from the onset and not couch the intervention in such terms as "counseling for some school problems" or "a chance to talk about your feelings." Candor is not only ethically sound practice, but sets a tone of seriousness of purpose that will need to be carried through the intervention. The following is a brief synopsis of such an explanation:

> We asked all of the teachers to give us the names of students who they believed had been in at least one fight here in school over the past 6 months. Your name was on that list. Do you recall having been in one or more fights here in school during that time? It is our belief that fighting in school, if not controlled, can lead to personal injury to yourself or others, possible legal problems, school failure, and possibly eventual drop-out. We also believe that most of the time, the decision whether or not to fight while in school is under your control. We are asking you to join with some other students in a skills training group in which we will introduce you to the techniques necessary to reduce or eliminate future school fighting. Whether or not you choose to use them will be up to you. These techniques involve anger control, thinking your way out of possible fights, and learning how to analyze and solve problems. Would such a group interest you?

The intervention team is principally looking for an initial level of understanding and cooperation, if not necessarily enthusiasm. Although the reasons may be uninspiring, such as the opportunity to get out of a class, the experience in Milwaukee has shown very few students are unwilling to show up at least for the first session.

In addition to obtaining a willingness to participate, the intervention team is also using the interview to gather an impression of the youth from a peer-status perspective. Experience has taught the lesson of homogeneity of status when working with aggressive students. Intervention team members found that when each of the group members believed the others to be of approximately equal social standing within the peer subculture, the level of cooperation rose substantially.

This is a critical insight. It is task enough to enlist the cooperation of seriously problematic students to find their way from various corners of the building to the meeting room and, once there, to work on their problems. If these students also believe that they have been grouped in a manner not in keeping with their own perceptions of peer self-concept (i.e., with lesser status, "uncool" students), that task becomes distinctly more difficult.

Additionally, recent researchers (Dodge, 1991; Dodge & Coie, 1987) have suggested differential treatment formulations for those youth whose aggression manifests principally as proactive and those whose aggression manifests as reactive. Although the initial interview may assist the intervention team in their efforts to differentiate these youth, supplementary procedures such as teacher ratings also may be required (see Dodge & Coie, 1987).

The final gate should be the securing of informed, written parental consent for each group member. Intervention team members should address this step with due care and concern for the beliefs and feelings of parents relative to their child's participation. The Milwaukee experience has demonstrated that the overwhelming majority of parents are supportive of the school's efforts to help their son or daughter. A comprehensive and clear explanation of the rationale, objectives, timeline, and procedures—consistent with the guidelines set forward by the American Psychological Association (1981) and the National Association of School Psychologists (1986)—is necessary. The issues associated with possible "negative labeling" should be addressed with the parents. Consistent with this concern, parents should be informed as to what manner of record will be kept in the student's file relative to the intervention and which individuals will have access to it. Without undue "sugar coating," when speaking with parents, intervention team members should cast the group in an affirmative, constructive light. Parents should be assured that intervention is not a punishment, but a carefully considered effort to assist the student through a difficult period in his or her school adjustment. An excellent discussion of the legal and ethical issues surrounding intervention efforts in the school setting can be found in Jacob and Hartshorne (1994).

Group Characteristics

There are no inviolable rules as to whether males and females can or should be in the same aggression intervention groups. The observation following the facilitation of numerous intervention groups in both Milwaukee and Long Beach is that same-sex groups tend to be more task oriented and less prone toward sexual posturing (J. A. McBride, personal communication, March 12, 1992). Additionally, trainers should not assume that even carefully selected group compositions will always be conducive to optimal functioning. Intervention teams should not allow one or two group members to draw so much attention as to impact the goals and objectives of the group as a whole. Permanently excusing chronically disruptive group members is markedly preferable to hoping that they won't show up. It is a wise group facilitator who knows when a mistake has been made and that the time has come to restructure or even temporarily disband the group.

Whether 6th-grade students should be in the same group as 8th-grade students, or freshman students with seniors, are questions best left to the judgment of the intervention team assembling a specific group. As noted, issues associated with relative peer status are critically important controlling variables. Although many younger students may find the company of older peers a high-status condition, the reverse frequently is not true. Mixed-age groups should be fashioned only with great care and forethought.

The number of students to be seen together in one treatment group may vary. Because the proposed intervention is more that of "training" rather than "therapy," the group may be as large as 8 to 12 members (Feindler & Ecton, 1986). As noted, the addition of a co-trainer may allow for the smoother functioning of a larger group. However, when working with a "pull-out" group, trainers should anticipate myriad potential problems as each member attempts to make his or her way from class to the group room. Too much time spent waiting for a large group to arrive (or not arrive) can frustrate efforts to function efficiently. Multiple, or successive, smaller groups may be a better choice.

A MODEL FOR THE TREATMENT OF AGGRESSION IN SCHOOLS

Identifying and assembling the most problematic aggressive youth in the school building is certainly task enough, yet the issue of what to do with them once they are assembled remains. Models exist for the group treatment of aggressive behavior in young people (e.g., Goldstein & Glick, 1987). Few researchers, however, have specifically addressed themselves to the unique circumstances associated with the treatment of school-based aggression.

John Lochman and colleagues have produced a wealth of research in recent years on the effects of cognitive-behavioral, school-based treatment of aggressive, older elementary school children. (See Lochman, Lampron, Gemmer, Harris, & Wyckoff, 1989; Lochman & Lampron, 1986; Lochman, Lampron, Gemmer, & Harris, 1986; Lochman, Nelson, & Sims, 1981.) Lochman and colleagues' Anger-Coping Program (Lochman et al., 1986) describes an 18-session, school-based group intervention designed around a cognitive processing dysfunction model (Dodge, 1986; Lochman, Nelson, & Sims, 1981). The Anger Coping Program is designed to train students in procedures such as self-instruction, problem recognition and solving, behavioral rehearsal, and goal setting. This program is readily adaptable to most school and residential situations and contains many helpful pieces of advice on working with teachers for program acceptance and generalization assistance. The Long Beach (California) Unified School District has implemented an adaptation of the Anger Coping Program in many of their elementary schools, training school psychologists, guidance counselors, and special educators as group leaders (McBride, 1991).

Feindler, Marriott, and Iwata (1984) used self-instruction, self-monitoring, modeling, and relaxation procedures to treat a population of disruptive and aggressive middle school youth in the school setting. Meeting with the small groups on a bi-weekly basis for 10 sessions, a trained therapist worked with the students developing skills in the two major areas of behavioral and cognitive controls. Students were taught aggression analysis through a self-monitoring procedure—helping them to focus on the antecedent anger cues, aggressive response, and consequent events—and later encouraged to role-play the incident, inserting the newly learned coping strategies in place of the original aggressive response.

Larson (1990a, in press) extended Feindler et al.'s (1984) research into the larger classroom setting and augmented the treatment regimen with a prerecorded video modeling procedure. Two classrooms of middle school students identified by state criteria as "at risk" for academic, behavioral, or juvenile court problems were randomly assigned to treatment or control conditions. In the treatment condition, the class received 10 sessions of anger-control and problem-solving training (Feindler et al., 1984) while the students in the control condition received attention-only sessions of equivalent length and duration. Students in the treatment condition were found to manifest significantly fewer suspensions and administrative referrals than did students in the control group.

The following is a skeletal model adapted from the work of Feindler and Ecton (1986), Feindler, Marriott, and Iwata (1984), Grant (cited in Goldstein, 1988), and Larson and McBride (1991). Within a cognitive-behavioral framework, it offers a practical training scaffold upon which individual schools may build an intervention to suit their unique needs. Drawing from Novaco's (1975, 1978) conception of a reciprocal relationship between mediating cognitions and anger, the structured intervention presented here trains aggressive students to recognize the influence that feelings of anger have over their cognitions and how those cognitions may lead to aggressive behavior. The model combines elements of anger control and social problem solving specifically oriented to address school-related, interpersonal aggression. The intervention places primary focus on student-to-student aggression; however, the issue of student-to-teacher aggression is also manifest in the training.

The intervention procedures to follow rely heavily on the use of prerecorded and in-group videotaping. The use of prerecorded video modeling in the treatment of aggressive children and youth has been advocated (Feindler & Ecton, 1986; Lochman et al., 1986;) and has been shown to extend and enhance the effects of live modeling (Thelin, Fry, Feherenbach, & Frautschi, 1979). In Milwaukee, the district elected to expand the prerecorded videotape aspect of the intervention from a few short model demonstrations used during the pilot groups to a complete, session-by-session program.

The prerecorded tape sequences provide symbolic modeling of both group processes (e.g., students are shown working with a trainer in a group setting) and targeted skill (e.g., student is shown using self-instruction to avoid a fight). Intervention teams should strongly consider producing their own video enhancement segments prior to the initiation of the intervention. Drawing the targeted students in beforehand as "production consultants" who can describe the most problematic situations in the school may help create more positive feelings about the intervention once it is started. The subsequent use of trained student actors—if possible from a different school—for the actual taping is recommended. The prerecorded tape sequences used in Milwaukee are described in the intervention sequence below and should be considered as a guide for local production efforts. Individual professionals who wish to obtain a copy of this tape, entitled *Think First*, should address their request to this author.

The following intervention procedure is organized by "sessions." A session, as intended here, should be construed to encompass either a particular time period or one or more behavioral outcomes. There is no implied mandate to complete the objectives or procedures for each session during a single class period, for instance. Intervention teams are urged to move at the pace that is best for the needs of the group, lingering in one area and moving swiftly through others as needed.

IMPLEMENTING SOCIAL-PROBLEM SOLVING TO REDUCE VIOLENCE SESSION 1

Objectives

1. Explain to students the rules and procedures of the group.
2. Enlist students as collaborators in defining treatment goals.
3. Discuss an antecedent-behavior-consequences paradigm for examining aggressive behavior.

Comment

This is the introductory session; thus, it is critical to get the students involved and invested right at the start. Trainers should attempt to establish a collaborative relationship with the group members to reduce the anticipated resistance (Meichenbaum, 1985). Trainers should avoid a teacher-to-student, unilateral approach in favor of a flexible, cooperative learning approach. Each student should be encouraged to participate in both his or her own problem analysis and in the manner in which he or she will implement the treatment. To a practical extent, trainers should utilize operant point systems for attendance and "homework" completion. In Milwaukee, buttons were made with the "no fighting" logo on them for group members to earn, and high-quality certificates of completion were printed for those who met the completion criteria. Completion criteria may be flexible (e.g., total number of sessions attended), but should be made clear to all at the onset. The availability of a snack at the conclusion of the group is always well received. Take care of all housekeeping business at this time, such as where the group will meet, procedures for missing class, obtaining hall passes, and so on.

Video

Two behavior models are demonstrated. The first model shows a young woman exhibiting an angry, aggressive response when another student steps on her notebook in class and the consequence of that angry response. It is broken down into three components: "**A**-Something Happens" then, "**B**-What You Do" then, "**C**- What Are The Consequences." The second model shows a young man being provoked to anger, but showing self-control.

Procedure

With groups of identified aggressive youth, experience has shown it helpful to play down the "nonviolence" rhetoric in favor of "choice" rhetoric. You are saying to them (literally or by implication):

> I am not going to tell you that you are a "bad" person for fighting; nor am I going to tell you never to fight, or that fighting is always wrong. This is not a "turn the other cheek" program. What you can learn, however, is how to be as powerful in your head as you are with your fists. The goal of the group is to give you that power. What we hope to teach you will allow you to make the important choices: that is, who to fight, where to fight, and when to fight. It will help you avoid getting dragged into fights that you don't want at that time, or at that place, or with that person. It will help to put the choice (power) in your hands.

Students who feel good about their "tough" persona, or need it for survival, seem to respond well to such a message. They can understand that a goal to graduate, or pass, or get out of a BD/ED program is inconsistent with suspensions for fighting. In many cases, they simply do not know how to avoid the behavior and maintain their self-concept or peer group status. Trainers should be very sensitive to this, particularly as incidences arise—and they will—during the course of the group. It has been the experience that most aggressive kids, particularly reactive aggressive kids, would much rather not fight and will act to avoid it, given the skills to do so.

Emphasize that learning self-control does NOT mean learning to be a "wimp." Greater self-control means greater power. When you are in control of yourself, you cannot be under the control of someone else. When you become aggressive—throw the first punch or decide to fight before being hit—then you have let someone else control you.

Ask. Who can remember the last time their aggression got them in serious trouble with the school, the police, or their family? (Emphasize serious trouble, that is, more trouble than the youth wanted or expected to be in.) Allow for a few anecdotes to be told; students will want to "tell their stories." Avoid passing judgment, but strive to not allow this to be a time to brag about who has been more aggressive than whom.

The A - B - C Method

Explain how any angry conflict situation can be looked at or analyzed in terms of:

A — What happened to trigger the problem?

B — What did you do in response?

C — What were the consequences to you and everyone?

Trainers should provide examples from their own lives, citing both good and bad consequences. Examples such as anger while driving a car that led to a traffic ticket will help to bring the construct to a concrete level. Use abundant visual aids. Choreographed examples with a co-leader are effective.

Example:

A— Something happened: "I was on my way to work one day and got stuck behind a very slow moving driver."

B— What I did: "I leaned on the horn and flashed my lights. When he finally turned off, I was so angry at him, I sped off so quickly that I forgot about the speed limit."

C— What were the consequences: "I got pulled over for speeding two blocks from school."

Group Discussion

The trainers should now solicit anger-induced aggression incidents from the students. The trainers should first model the format of reporting.

Each component should be preceded with its introduction, such as:

A — Something happened: "I let Robert look at my new watch in the locker room after gym, and he dropped it on the floor."

B — What I did: "I shoved him against the locker and called him a name."

C — What were the consequences: "He tried to hit me back, and we got in a fight and got suspended."

Encourage students to reflect on anger-induced incidents in the school rather than in the neighborhoods at this juncture (the former being more familiar grounds for school personnel.) Remind those students who give examples that glorify their aggressive anger that you appreciate their honesty and are glad that they now have the opportunity to learn greater self-control. Again, it will be hard to avoid allowing the discussion to become one of "who is more aggressive than whom." Note with emphasis the negative consequences (**C**) of aggression. Group members will often try to "out punch" their peers, and there are liable to be a lot of high fives going around and precious little concern for consequences, or the consequence will be glossed over or lied about. This is to be expected in some groups, as there is still considerable concern for peer status. One of your goals as leader is slowly to move self-control, or "keeping your cool," into a "status" position. Be patient. Continually emphasize that the student "chose to fight" rather than was "forced to fight," even while you may acknowledge that when you were 16, you might have made the same choice.

Closing

Experience has shown that the regular presentation of a snack to all at the close does some magical things to the most fearsome of adolescents. Although I have no data to support this, I can't help but believe it increases the likelihood of return for the next session. Announce the date of the next session and attempt to neutralize the variables that will interfere with each individual's return on that date (e.g., deliver passes, talk to teachers, etc.)

SESSION 2

Objectives

1. Introduce the "hassle log" method for student self-monitoring.
2. Discuss the concept of physiological "cues" to anger.
3. Introduce backward counting and deep breathing as anger reducers.

Comment

As groups return for the second session, trainers may note that a "sound-off" period at the outset may help to bring any existing hidden concerns out. It is often the case that group members socialize together in and out of school and that many new concerns will arise between meetings—including both lost and newly formed alliances among members. Providing group members with an opportunity to bring up personally troublesome issues in the presence of a responsible adult may be a new experience for some and may work to enhance the trainer's credibility. Again, patience is key; avoid pushing into the agenda until the group is clearly ready to do so. Staying "on schedule" at the cost of student respect for the trainer's willingness to address critical personal issues in a timely manner is no bargain.

In this session, the students will be introduced to anger "cues"—a difficult concept for them to grasp, but an important one nonetheless. Anger is a predominant precursor to many problematic forms of adolescent aggression (Feindler & Ecton, 1986). Consequently, it is important for students to have a sense of what their own anger "feels" like to them. Trainers may find that many group members have problems labeling their own feeling states and may require additional work in affective education prior to concentrating on anger. Many group members will have techniques for calming themselves when nervous or afraid, or even procedures for keeping tears at bay during times of sadness. They may, however, have considerably less skill at recognizing and controlling anger.

Video

The tape provides a model of the students together as a group, discussing what it feels like for each to lose his or her temper ("anger cues"). It concludes with a student demonstrating an anger control technique (backwards counting) under the provocation of two other students.

Procedure

Award points for attendance if appropriate. Review with students the purpose of the program. Review the A - B - C method of looking at conflict. At this point, the trainers should introduce the self-monitoring procedure, called the hassle log (adapted from Feindler & Ecton, 1986; see Figure 2). This device can serve a self-monitoring function as well as function as a memory aid to assist students in planning in-group role plays. Go over it, section by section, then have each group member fill out his or her own log on a recent conflict event. Request volunteers to present their hassle logs and answer any remaining procedural questions.

Ideally, students should leave with a blank hassle log after the group is over and fill it out shortly after a conflict event. Experience has shown this to be unrealistic. It is a rare student who leaves with a hassle log in hand at groups' end and returns it completed at the next meeting. What happens most frequently is that the group members arrive, ask for new sheets, and fill them out before or during the review. This is not all bad; it is an attempt at compliance and is best not discouraged. In self-contained groups such as an ED/BD class, a stack of hassle logs left with the teacher can be helpful.

The hassle log shown in Figure 12.2 should be re-adapted to fit local circumstances. Ease of completion is the key; problematic adolescents are unlikely to expend a great deal of academic energy on such a task. It is recommended that a reinforcement point for each successful hassle log completion be granted.

Anger Cues

The trainers should draw parallels to feelings that students commonly encounter. "What does it feel like when you feel yourself getting increasingly sad? Afraid? Embarrassed?"

Have students discuss what they do to calm themselves when they are afraid or nervous. (Note any use of self-instruction for later parallels.) Describe a scenario in which the student is at a basketball free throw line with 1 second left on the clock. He/she needs to make the free throw to first tie, then win, the game. The crowd is trying to make the player nervous. How does the player know that he/she is getting nervous? What does the player do to remain calm? How does the player keep the crowd from triggering his/her anxiety?

This is a good time to discuss what has come to be called the "I Just Ignore Them" cop-out. Students will express this particular technique to the trainers as if it were a real and effective procedure. This, of course, is because they have been told all their lives by concerned adults that it is real. From a practical standpoint, however, it is quite impossible to "ignore" an incoming perception, assuming functional sensory systems. Point out that by "ignore," students really mean that they are choosing to attend to "something else." They are probably self-instructing, or self-distracting (active), rather than ignoring (passive). Probe with the students just what it is that they are doing to "ignore."

Ask students to identify some common anger cues. Some examples include muscle tension, blood rushing to the face, heartbeat acceleration, and increased breathing rate. It may be helpful to suggest that the students visualize and describe a recent situation in school in which they could feel themselves becoming increasingly angry. Point out that getting in touch with the "cues" to anger is a critical step in getting the self-control necessary to avoid "losing your temper." It is important to get the students to begin thinking about anger and aggression as a sequential process.

FIGURE 12.2. HASSLE LOG FOR COGNITIVE-BEHAVIOR TREATMENT PROGRAM

NAME____________________________ DATE______________________

TIME: ❒ Before school ❒ AM classes ❒ Lunch
❒ PM classes ❒ After school

LOCATION:
❒ In class ❒ In the hall ❒ Restroom
❒ Gym area ❒ Front of building ❒ Administrator's office
❒ Commons ❒ Lunchroom ❒ Other________________

TRIGGER:
❒ Somebody did something I didn't like ❒ Somebody said something I didn't like
❒ Somebody took something of mine ❒ Somebody told me to do something
❒ Somebody shoved/charged me up ❒ Other________________

WHO WAS THAT SOMEBODY?
❒ Administrator ❒ Hall aide ❒ Substitute Teacher
❒ Student ❒ Teacher ❒ Other________________

WHAT DID YOU DO?
❒ Hit him/her ❒ Reported it ❒ Threatened him/her
❒ Walked away ❒ Refused to comply ❒ Complied
❒ Yelled at him/her ❒ Talked it out ❒ Talked-back/argued
❒ Broke something ❒ Other______________

HOW ANGRY WERE YOU?

1	2	3	4	5
Not angry at all		Moderately		Burning mad!!

CHECK ✔ ALL THAT APPLY:
❒ The consequences were in my best interest
❒ I would like to do the same again in a similar situation
❒ I am proud of my behavior
❒ The consequences were not in my best interest
❒ I didn't control my anger and behavior as much as I would like to
❒ I need to work harder at handling triggers like this

Anger Reducers

Now that students are learning to identify their anger cues, they can begin to make use of anger reduction techniques to help them increase their self-control. Stress that the purpose of anger reducers is to give the student time to decide how to respond most effectively. Point out that among the two easiest things to do when angry are to either fight or run. Anger reducers calm the student down enough to allow time for considering a third, more personally satisfying alternative.

Students may feel uneasy and embarrassed rehearsing the simple anger reducers below. The trainers should be prepared for this and provide a clear model of the behavior desired. Ask the students if they can think of situations in which controlling "temper" would be better for them than acting aggressively. Point out that the two anger reducers that will be introduced (below) can be accomplished privately, without anyone knowing about it.

Trainers should role-play a provoking incident, identifying anger cues and demonstrating an anger reducer. For instance, ask a student to get up to sharpen a pencil, and refuse to return to his/her seat when asked by the trainer. Trainers should then talk their way through the anger cues ("I can feel my heartbeat accelerate. I can feel the blood rushing to my face. I am thinking angry thoughts about that student"), then proceed to the anger reducer being modeled.

Anger reducer—deep breathing. Explain that taking slow deep breaths can help in maintaining control in response to anger-provoking situations. Point out that basketball players frequently use this technique at the foul line to calm themselves before attempting a shot. The technique is:

1. a long, slow inhalation;
2. immediate exhale, slowly;
3. during exhale, think the word, "Reee-laa-xxx";
4. continue to exhale, slowly, and repeat.

Anger reducer—backward counting. Point out that this technique can be done silently or in a whisper. If possible or safe, it will help to turn away from whoever is provoking the student's anger. The student may start from 100 or 50 or 20; the starting point is irrelevant as long as it leaves enough numbers to allow sufficient time to pass.

Provide opportunities for the students to rehearse these techniques with one another. Trainers will find that the students will be very creative in their role play. Keep them focused on realistic, school-related situations. It is important that the students believe in the merits of the techniques; they will not adopt new behaviors that they believe are silly or foolish for them.

Closing

Trainer should assign students to complete one hassle log prior to the next session.

SESSION 3

Objectives

1. Help students learn to identify the direct (external) and indirect (internal) provocations that are problematic in their lives.
2. Provide students with insight and training into the effects of misattribution of intent.
3. Allow students an opportunity to role-play incidents from hassle logs so as to better identify external and internal provocations.

Comment

In this session, the students have an opportunity to express aloud those events that occasion their aggression ("anger triggers"). It is also the first opportunity for the trainers to bring the students into awareness of their own internal self-talk and its possible contribution to anger ("thought triggers"). This is a critical point, for it sets up the internal self-instruction techniques to follow. Many students will have a difficult time being asked to "think about their thinking." For a few younger students, cognitive developmental delays may make it all the more difficult.

One of the crucial points associated with angry, reactive aggression has to do with what has been called "hostile attributional bias." Many chronically aggressive youth have a frequent tendency to misattribute a hostile intent where a benign one may have existed. In essence, they cognitively create anger triggers (e.g., "He did that on purpose!") from the same events that typically less aggressive youth would not (e.g., "He did it accidentally."). Although most of the literature in this area is currently with younger children, it clearly has applied value with adolescents. (For a discussion of this mechanism, see Dodge & Coie, 1987.) This meeting provides the students with an opportunity to examine the possibility of alternative attributional intent as a technique of anger and aggression control.

Session 3 offers the first opportunity for role play from the hassle log. Initially, some students will want to demonstrate aggressive behavior for purposes of peer approval. Trainers should not allow role plays of aggression. Although the hassle logs may reflect the students' inability to manage their aggression, in-group role plays should always demonstrate self-control using the techniques that have been trained. Experience has shown that students can learn to find sought-after status and approval in "keeping their cool" scenarios. A particularly aggressive student who learns to "wait until after school" has made a positive self-control gain.

Video

The session 3 video shows the group of students modeling a discussion about the things that make them angry. Role plays show anger trigger examples, including direct playful provocation, accidental physical provocation, invasion of property, and verbal provocation.

Procedure

Collect and record hassle logs, answering any questions the students may have about them. As noted earlier, students will be inclined to fill them out hurriedly just prior to the start of the session, unless other arrangements have been made.

Review by asking if anyone had attempted to apply either of the anger reducers discussed earlier. Reinforce the attempt, even if it was not ultimately successful. Encourage student(s) to role-play their hassle log, substituting, if necessary, an anger reduction technique such as deep breathing or counting backward.

Use the role play to review the A-B-C model of how conflict arises. Encourage students to identify the cues that preceded their anger.

Anger Triggers

Remind students that each conflict situation has something that (**A**) triggers someone's (**B**) angry behavior, leading to some kind of (**C**) consequence. Tell them that today we are going to list all the "triggers" we encounter in school on the chalkboard.

Write the words *Anger Triggers* on the chalkboard and ask, "What or who makes you angry?" Observe that anger triggers can be verbal (e.g., being told what to do) or they can be nonverbal (e.g., eye-rolling, gestures, or shoving).

Note. This is a brainstorming session, so all should refrain from criticizing another's anger trigger. If at least one person is angered by some person or event, then it is a valid contribution. Avoid the use of personal names, such as those of teachers or administrators. Ask, "What is it that __ does that triggers your anger?" Stimulate responses if necessary with:

- "What happens in school that triggers your anger?"
- "Can teachers trigger anger?"
- "Is there anyone you know in school whose behavior triggers your anger almost every day?"
- "Do you know people who seem to have more anger triggers than other people?
- "Do you know some who do not seem to have any?"

Thought Triggers

Ask. "Is seeing two other students talking together enough to trigger most students' anger?" (Not normally.) "What might cause it to become an anger trigger?" (If you think they are talking negatively about you.)

Point out to the students that sometimes we can trigger our own anger by thinking anger-triggering thoughts to ourselves about what we believe someone says or does. These are called *thought triggers*. Provide students with a model from the trainer's own experience.

Role play. A possible role play might be the following: The teacher has given a clear instruction that there will be no getting out of seats to sharpen pencils during the test. A student comes in late and misses that instruction. Later the student goes to the pencil sharpener.

Trainers should model a *think aloud* procedure along the lines of:

- "What's the matter with him/her?"
- "I clearly stated no pencil sharpening!"
- "She/he is trying to challenge my authority in here again!"
- "These kids never listen!" etc.

Point out that, often, thought triggers are based on faulty information, are generalizations, or are completely untrue.

The "Check It Out Game"

This is an exercise to assist the students to understand the problems that accompany misattribution of intent. The goal of the exercise is to reduce the impulsive urge to retaliate based on faulty cognitions. Discuss how intentions can be misread and provide a personal example. Ask students for their own examples of how someone else misread their intentions.

Trainers should read the first part of the incidents below. The group members then decide individually what the "intent" of the interaction was. They each describe their own ending, based on their guess. The "correct" ending is then read by the trainer.

Incident 1. Robert was getting dressed after gym. When he turned around from his locker, he saw his new $125 basketball shoes were being carried away by a new kid named Eddie. Robert yelled at him, "Hey, man! Gimme back my shoes!" Eddie's intent was: (Allow students to decide.)

Accidental. Eddie turned around, looked at the shoes he was carrying, looked around, then smiled and pointed to his own pair, exactly the same only two sizes larger, still lying under the bench. "Sorry," he said.

Incident 2. Mike was standing at his open locker talking to Tricia when Louis walked by and knocked Mike's locker closed. Mike yelled, "Hey, what are you doin', man?" Louis' intention was...

Accidental. Louis turned and looked at him, surprised. "Oh, hey! I thought you were Jerry Turner. From the back, you look just like him. I'm sorry, man. His locker is right here somewhere, too. I wasn't even looking. We do that to sort of kid around with one another. I'm sorry."

Role play. Encourage group members to devise and role-play their own provocations. Player #1 should be provoked in some fashion (shoved, gestured at, books knocked over, etc.) by player #2. Player #1 should then *think aloud* as many nonhostile—but realistic—intentions behind the alleged provocation as possible. For instance:

- "Could be an accident. I'll wait and see."
- "Maybe he's just playin."
- "Is he confusing me with someone else?"
- "We've been cool up to now. He can't mean it."

Have students volunteer to role-play events from their hassle logs. Trainers should videotape these role plays for later review by the group. Use the "stop and think aloud" technique to have the students identify any thought triggers that may have occurred after the initial anger trigger.

Closing

Close by awarding points and reinforcing effort. Use a "Looking Ahead" procedure. Go around the group and ask each member to anticipate a possible "anger trigger" situation which may arise before the next meeting.

If time permits, role-play a behavioral rehearsal of that anticipated situation, using the self-control techniques learned to date.

SESSION 4

Objectives

1. Conduct a discussion about adolescent rights with regard to rules, law, and authority figures.
2. Discuss the concept of peer pressure or peer coercion.
3. Introduce assertion techniques as alternative responses to aggression.

Comment

Adolescents often confuse what they believe to be their "right" with what is, in fact, merely what they "want." The oft heard, "He ain't got no right to…" expresses a genuine belief that some inviolable line has been crossed and the adolescent has every reason to be angry. This confusion appears to be as true for normal as well as clinical populations. The variable of concern is how the adolescent decides to respond to what he/she perceives as a violation of rights. In this session, the students will have an opportunity to verbalize what they believe to be their rights and discuss how their beliefs may conflict with those of another. Experience has shown that many adolescents hold the belief that no one, including and often most particularly teachers, may at any time physically touch or restrain them in any way. This is a belief that is fostered and made strong within the adolescent peer culture. It is also one that is dangerous to both the adolescent and the adults in school responsible for his/her well-being and safety. A teacher attempting to physically remove or restrain an angry adolescent comes in contact with this belief. The offending student is under considerable peer pressure to stand up for his (and the group's) alleged "right" not to have a teacher physically touch them in any way.

Video

The Session 4 video is a very brief modeling of three anger control assertion techniques.

Procedure

Collect and record hassle logs. Encourage students to role-play the A-B-C sequence from their hassle logs, substituting, if necessary, one of the anger control techniques discussed so far. Encourage students to identify the anger trigger and any thought triggers that may have contributed to the anger. Review with the group last session's discussion about anger triggers and thought triggers.

Rights

On the board, write the stem, "I have the right to..." Tell the students that today you are going to talk about standing up for your rights. Explain to them that tempers are often lost because people believe that their rights are being ignored or violated. Discuss with them that a "right" is something to which you are entitled, either by common agreement or by expressed rules or law.

Trainers should encourage students to finish the "I have a right to..." stem written on the board. Trainers should list these responses on the board as the students call them out. When complete, ask, "Is this a right or something that you merely want to happen?" Encourage students to back up their assertions that what they have volunteered is truly a right to which they are entitled. Trainers should be prepared for a forceful defense of long-held beliefs.

Generate a second list of teacher and staff rights with the stem, "Teachers have the right to..." Discuss how one person's rights may interfere or impact another person's rights (e.g., student's right not to be physically pushed or grabbed contrasted with teacher's right to protect the students and maintain class order. Under what conditions might it be in the student's best interest to agree to temporarily suspend his or her rights?).

How does peer pressure influence a person's decision to "stand up for their rights"? Encourage students to look at how peer pressure works (dress, language, attitude toward school, willingness to fight). Is it easy to go against the group? Is the group always right in what they appear to believe? Does the group always have your best interest in mind?

Asserting Your Rights

Introduce assertion techniques as alternatives to aggression if you believe that your rights have been violated. Explain that a response to someone violating your rights may take many forms along a continuum:

1. *Passive*—letting someone take away your rights;
2. *Assertive*—standing up for your rights while at the same time respecting the rights of the other person;

3. *Aggressive*—demanding your rights with no regard for the other person's rights.

Introduce assertion techniques as alternative responses to aggression. Students should be instructed to use these techniques as alternatives to either simple passivity (doing nothing) or aggression (violating the other's rights).

Repetition request assertion technique. This response involves a calm, monotone repetition of what you want (e.g., "Please get out of my desk"). Students should have the chance to practice the technique with a nearby peer. There is no escalation in terms of increased voice volume, threatening gestures, etc.

Escalating or nonviolent assertion technique. This is a series of responses that increase in assertiveness in order to obtain a desired outcome. The sequence begins with a minimal assertive response and ends with what can be called a final contract option in which a nonviolent threat to the other person for noncompliance with the original demand is presented. An example of a student in class is:

1st—"Please stop bothering me."
2nd—"I asked you stop bothering me."
3rd—"I want you to stop bothering me now."
4th—"If you don't stop bothering me now, I'm gonna yell 'CUT IT OUT' as loud as I can and let you deal with the teacher."

Trainers should add other techniques with which they may be familiar.

Trainers will also find that group members may have their own techniques to share. Videotape the students using the assertive techniques they have practiced and replay the tape for their observations.

Closing

Reinforce participation and assign hassle logs. Use the "Looking Ahead" procedure to rehearse the appropriate handling of potentially problematic situations.

SESSION 5

Objectives

1. Introduce students to self-instruction as a method of anger control
2. Model and discuss the use of the "reminders" technique

Comment

Self-instruction as an approach to anger and other arousal state management has been a widely researched subject for more than three decades (e.g., Meichenbaum, 1985; Novaco, 1979). Its value within a comprehensive program has been well-established. The effectiveness of self-instruction is based on the premise that external events (name-calling, pushing, taking of property) provoke anger only if these events are preceded, accompanied, or followed by self-statements of an anger-arousing nature. In other words, individuals must, in effect, tell themselves that it is time to become angry by way of applying anger-inducing meaning to the provocation. There is also research to suggest that individuals then maintain, or escalate, their anger state by labeling what they are feeling as anger (Novaco, 1975). In a similar way, individuals can learn to moderate or control their own anger by paying particular attention to how they choose to think about an anger-provoking event. In this session, students will learn a self-instruction technique known as "reminders" (Feindler & Ecton, 1986). This technique simply offers students a way to "self-instruct" or "self-coach" their way through situations in which they have to try hard to keep from becoming aggressive.

Video

The video models a brief discussion about the "reminders" technique taught in this session, then shows a model of a young man who uses thought triggers instead of reminders, culminating in aggression. The video then shows the same young man in the same circumstance using the reminders technique.

Procedure

Collect and record hassle logs. Take volunteers for role plays from the hassle logs, particularly those who may have used one of the assertiveness or one of the anger control (deep breathing, backward counting) techniques taught so far. Review the three assertiveness techniques from last session.

Reminders

Ask for student volunteers to come forward and model for the class exactly what they would do in the following situations:

1. City championship basketball game, you are at the free throw line, down by 1 point, with 1 second left on the clock. You don't want to panic and throw a "brick."
2. You are all alone, late at night in your home. You keep hearing odd noises downstairs—scraping, then a soft thumping noise, then silence. You want to keep from becoming too frightened.

Elicit from the students what it is they would be thinking or saying to themselves in these situations to stay calm. Point out that we often remind ourselves to stay calm in pressure situations by thinking them through. Ask for other examples.

Tell the students that just as we can remind ourselves to stay calm when we are nervous or frightened, we can also remind ourselves to stay calm when we are being provoked to anger. Have the students generate a list of reminders that they use in those pressure situations. Some may include: Chill, Cool it, (It, He, She) ain't worth it, Take it easy, and Go slow.

Note. Some students may find the idea of "talking to yourself" socially embarrassing and may resist the discussion. It is sometimes helpful to create a fictional situation in which the student is being pressured to become aggressive but it is very clearly in his or her best interest not to do so (e.g., another student starts "getting on your case" just before you are ready to take your last final exam of the year or just as you are ready to get on the bus for the class trip to a local amusement park).

Point out that timing is important when using the reminders technique. Remind students that they can recognize their own cues for anger. The proper time for using reminders is when they feel their temper increasing.

Closing

If time permits, ask for student volunteers to role-play scenes from their completed hassle logs, using the reminders technique. For the role plays, use overt reminders; that is, have the students say their reminder instructions aloud. The student may also be asked to replay the scene using covert (silent) reminders.

SESSION 6

Objectives

1. Review and practice the reminders self-instruction technique.
2. Introduce and discuss the *thinking ahead* procedure for anger control.

Comment

It is important for the trainers to continue to emphasize that aggression control does not mean that you are afraid to show anger or afraid to fight. In some situations, those particular qualities may be maladaptive, even dangerous. Acknowledge to the students that you are aware that they often get "double messages." Outside of school, within the peer culture, the student can get away with being more physical. Indeed, fighting prowess is a valued quality in many neighborhoods. However, regardless of what is adaptive in the neighborhood, when students enter the school building or the school bus, what may work in the neighborhoods is quickly punished. Fighting or other physical aggression as a means of problem solving is clearly not adaptive in school. Trainers should emphasize that anger and aggression control is designed to give students the ability to choose for themselves how they want to respond to an anger trigger. Remind the students that the more choices a person has to solve a problem, the more powerful that person becomes. Do not be afraid to acknowledge that fighting may be the best option for a particular student in a particular situation. On the other hand, avoid being drawn in by the frequently heard protest, "You mean if some guy comes up and starts beating on you for no reason at all, you just stand there and get beat-up?" All veteran school people know that fights don't happen like that. They are most often the result of extended transactions between individuals and often progress through many points where the opportunities for nonviolent resolution are not realized or ignored.

Video

The Session 6 video shows a brief discussion of the *thinking ahead* procedure and two video models. In the first, a young man is seen reacting in anger to the theft of his property. He is then shown in the same sequence applying the "thinking ahead" procedure. In the second model, a student is confronted with a volatile situation in which a teacher assault occurs. He is then shown in the same sequence using the thinking ahead procedure to avoid the conflict.

Procedure

Collect and record the hassle logs. Encourage students to role-play an incident from their hassle log in which they have used any of the techniques discussed so far (anger control, assertive response, reminders).

Model the use of overt reminders with a student volunteer. The trainer should angrily accuse the student of any manner of personal failings—laziness, disrespectfulness, dishonesty, etc.—while the student emits audible reminders in order to keep his/her anger under control. Suggest the use of reminders instead of reacting to the provocation.

Point out that a student has a choice after recognizing the anger trigger. He/she can either react in an angry aggressive way, which may lead to negative consequences, or he/she can emit silent, covert reminders to remain cool and decide the best course of action.

Thinking Ahead

Introduce thinking ahead as another procedure to use in conflict or anger-provoking situations. Explain that thinking ahead is a self-instruction, problem-solving technique that helps the student to estimate the possible consequences of anger or aggression in a conflict situation ahead of time. Thinking ahead uses the following contingency statement: "If I (misbehave) now, then I will (future negative consequences)."

Trainers should model some examples of if-then thinking from their own experience. Ask students to volunteer incidences from their own experience where stopping to think things out first helped them to avoid negative consequences. Ask them to predict what might have happened had they not stopped to think first.

Explain to students that fighting is often one of the consequences for not thinking ahead. Brainstorm two lists: (a) all the positive consequences of fighting and (b) all the negative consequences of fighting.

Say. "Tell me all the positive things that you can think of that people get out of fighting in school? What good comes from choosing to fight in the classroom or on school grounds?" Write down this list on the chalkboard.

- feel good (if you win)
- buddies think you're tough
- get even
- people leave you alone

Note. Most positives have the proviso "if you win..."

Next, say: "Now tell me all the negative consequences of fighting in school. What bad things can come from choosing to fight in the building or on school grounds?"

- get hurt or killed
- hurt or kill someone

• get sued
• get suspended or expelled
• bad reputation
• revenge cycle begins

The negative list will be longer than the positive. Differentiate short- and long-term consequences, noting that most positives are short term. Emphasize that reminders can allow the cool head needed to use thinking ahead, which will help you get the best possible consequences.

Closing

Allow for role plays from the hassle logs in which students use thinking ahead to avoid negative consequences.

SESSION 7

Objectives

1. Provide students with a comprehensive review of all the material introduced in Sessions 1–6 and the opportunity to practice and view their own positive models through video taping.
2. Set the stage for moving into the problem-solving sequence of the program to follow.

Comment

This session is an opportunity for students to clarify information and become more proficient with any particular technique. It is also an opportunity for the trainers to go back and work on a particular piece of the program that they believe may have special relevance to this group of students (e.g., additional work on using nonviolent assertion to get what they want). Some recent work on treatment adherence suggests very clearly that merely providing information does not change behavior with any reliable permanency (Meichenbaum & Turk, 1987). Students must have both intellectual insight and regular practice to bring the new behaviors into their repertoires. This "session" should, in fact, consist of more than one meeting time. It is critical to provide the students with as much actual practice in the techniques as is possible, given other time constraints on the program. Experience has shown that three to four review/practice sessions are optimal.

Those groups who have access to a video camera may want to dedicate much of these sessions to taping and replaying role plays from the hassle logs. Allowing the students to construct role plays and participate in the video taping is an essential feature of the program. Trainers should have technical bugs worked out ahead of time. Allow students to rehearse off-camera first. Tape only role plays that model positive use of anger management skills. Avoid giving in to a common student urging to do "before-after, uncontrolled-controlled" sequences. Rehearsing the wrong behavior can have little or no positive impact.

SESSION 8

Objectives

1. Introduce the students to the idea of structured problem solving as a way to avoid unwanted conflict and achieve personal and academic goals.
2. Discuss obstacles and goals as two common characteristics of all problems.
3. Discuss and rehearse problem definition skills.

Comment

Session 8 begins the first of three sessions on the training of problem-solving skills. This is a natural furthering of the skills taught in sessions 1–7, in which the students learned that they have the ability to exercise self-control in interpersonal conflict situations. Learning to manage anger and aggression sets the stage for making decisions about the alternative methods to resolve interpersonal problems and conflicts. Even if a student can successfully demonstrate more effective self-control, that student still needs to be provided with additional tools for decision making. Problem solving typically is seen as a sequence of defining the problem, considering the alternatives, evaluating possible consequences of those alternatives, making a decision, and acting. The next three sessions will take the students through this sequence.

Video

The Session 8 video introduces the four steps for problem solving and emphasizes to the student the need for learning the procedure.

Procedure

Students should be encouraged to continue to monitor their encounters with anger triggers through the use of the hassle log throughout the remainder of the program. Trainers will begin to have the students reframe the encounters in terms of the problem-solving skills to be taught. Explain to the students that the group is going to talk today about making decisions.

Ask. "What decisions have you made already today?" (What to wear, how to fix hair, what to eat, etc.) On the board, write the words *decision* and *problem*. Explain that we make countless decisions on what to do and how to behave all day and most are relatively easy. A decision becomes a problem when we aren't sure about what to do, or about what decision to make. On the board, write the words *goals* and *obstacles* with connecting arrows to *problem*. Point out that all problems have two characteristics in common (a) a goal, that is, something we want; and (b) one or more obstacles, or something that gets in the way of what we want. For instance, you may want to go out for basketball (goal) but your grades are too low (obstacle). Explain that solving a problem is easiest if we do it one step at a time. Make and display a *Steps for Problem Solving* poster. Have a volunteer read each of the steps aloud.

- STOP AND THINK: WHAT IS THE PROBLEM?
- WHAT CAN I DO?
- WHAT WILL HAPPEN IF?
- WHICH SHOULD I CHOOSE?
- HOW DID I DO?

The first step is to stop and think, and decide just exactly what the problem is. The important point to stress here is that if we have a problem, we have to stop and think or we may decide too quickly.

Example. You see another student in the hall with his arm around your steady girlfriend. How could you define this problem?

"I want to tell him that I don't like that (goal) but since she's there, he might want to show off and I may get into a fight (obstacle)."

Point out to the group that defining the problem accurately and in a manner that leaves open a possible solution that will avoid trouble is an important first step. The above example defines the problem accurately in a way that nonaggressive solutions are possible.

Point out that saying to yourself "stop and think" will help give you time to decide what to do. The words "stop and think" are much like a "reminder" that we learned about earlier. We are once again "reminding" ourselves not to act without defining the problem first.

Have the group define this problem. "Imagine that you are about to go into school. Just before you go inside, your cousin comes up to you and begs you to leave school with him/her to go look for some kids who were threatening him/her earlier on the way to school. You have two important tests first and second hour and you are sure you can pass them. But s/he's your cousin and if s/he goes alone, s/he could get hurt."

Role-play a scene of a young man who is mistakenly being confronted by an angry peer between classes:

- Student A—"Say, man! I heard your cousin said you were gonna kick my ass."
- Student B— "What are you talking about?"
- Student A— "You're a punk! I'll kick your ass right now!"

Ask. "What if that was you (student B), and you had never seen this other student before in your life. You take a deep breath, stop and think. How quickly can you define the problem?" ["I don't want to fight this guy here and now (goal) but he's gonna hit me if I don't think of something fast (obstacle)."]

Have various students role-play the scene. Make sure Student B takes the deep breath and self-instructs (aloud or covertly) "stop and think." Try to draw out both thoughts and feelings from the participants. Emphasize the importance of "I" statements in problem definition. In other words, the goals must be yours, and the only behavior you can change for certain is your own. It does you little good to say that your problem will be solved when someone else changes his or her behavior.

Closing

Remind students that the group will be ending soon. Collaborate with them regarding ideas for "graduation," such as certificates, party, etc.

SESSION 9

Objectives

1. Further the students' understanding of the problem-solving procedures.
2. Help the students learn to generate possible solutions to problems or tasks and consider a wide range of possible alternative courses of action.

Comment

One of the most prominent skill deficits that aggressive and/or other problematic adolescents have in common is a seeming inability to devise alternative ways of solving personal problems. The often-heard excuse, "It was the only thing I could do" displays this learning deficit. In response, exasperated teachers and parents will then begin rattling off a list of alternatives that were not considered while the adolescent stares at them in boredom. This session will give the students an opportunity to think about and practice this aspect of the problem-solving methodology.

Video

The Session 9 video introduces the second step in the problem-solving sequence with a voice-over discussion of the need to consider alternative solutions. Scenes of a youth contemplating truancy and dealing with another person's anger are shown.

Procedure

Collect and record hassle logs. Ask for student volunteers to discuss their hassle log "triggers" in terms of a problem that needs a clear definition. Encourage students to attend to using "I" statements and keeping the problem centered on what their wants and goals are. Display a *Steps for Problem Solving* poster or write the steps on the chalkboard. Review points raised in Session 8 regarding the *stop and think* procedure.

Introduction to Alternative Solutions

Tell the students that today we are going to talk about and practice the second step in effective problem solving: answering the question, "What can I do?" Explain that, too often, when confronted with a tough problem, some people simply go ahead and try to solve it with the first thing that pops into their heads. Note that this method often works for common, easy decisions, but as the problems get more complicated, picking the wrong solution can create even bigger problems. Trainers should model an incident from their own experience in which they resisted doing the first thing that came to mind and considered a better alternative.

Where Do Solutions Come From?

Ask students. "What would you do if you were put in charge of deciding":

- What new car your family should buy?
- What new bicycle your brother should buy?
- What new VCR the family should buy?

Try to elicit procedures that fall into the following:

1. Talking to others in order to obtain information.
2. Recalling things you have done before that required similar skills.
3. Imagining what someone else might do.
4. Dividing a big problem into smaller ones.
5. Using "thinking ahead" procedure.
6. "Brainstorming" with friends.

Trainers should supply these categories of procedures if they are not suggested and have them written on the board.

The "What Can I Do" Game

Divide the group members into suitable groups of two to three students per group. To each group, trainers should distribute three 3 x 5 "problem cards," chosen from the list below. Make sure each group gets the same three problems. Have each group choose a recorder who will do the writing and speaking for the group.

Say. "This is called the 'What Can I Do?' game. The object of the game is to come up with as many possible solutions to the problems on the card as you can. We call this 'brainstorming.' The only rule is that the solution must be possible; that is, you may not use magical, silly, or otherwise impossible alternatives. I will be the final judge of whether a solution is truly possible and serious. Remember: the solutions only have to be possible and real, they do not have to be good, lawful, or even smart."

The goal of this game is to get students to realize that most problems have multiple possible solutions. Allow them as much time as needed or, if you prefer, set a timer for added fun.

When all the distributed problems have been "brainstormed," have the recorder stand and read his or her group's solutions. Dismiss the silly or impossible solutions, and keep a total on the board for each group for each problem. Play the game as often as you choose, mixing the groups and changing the problems.

Problem List

This problem list is based on the work of Freedman, Rosenthal, Donahoe, Schlundt, & McFall, 1978.

1. A male, peer, stranger deliberately bumps into you in the school hall.
2. A gym teacher picks on you, makes you do extra push-ups.
3. In science class, the two kids beside you were talking. The teacher blames you and tells you to get out.
4. You are called names by some other student outside of the schoolbuilding.
5. Another student makes an insulting remark about your mother while the two of you are taking a test in English.
6. You are stopped in the hall by a hall aide after the class bell.
7. You've been grounded. A friend urges you to sneak out of the house.
8. A teacher accuses you of writing a gang symbol on the bathroom wall.
9. A friend comes by with a car he peeled and stole, and suggests you go for a ride with him.
10. A friend asks you to steal something from where you work.
11. You start your math homework but get stuck on the first problem.
12. You need more money, your parents won't give it to you, and you are too young for a work permit.
13. You are studying for a final exam. A friend wants you to go to a concert instead.
14. You are bored in history class and you want some fun.
15. It's the first nice day of spring, your friends want to skip school but you have two tests to take.

Closing

Ask if any of the students has a problem upcoming for which they would like the group to brainstorm some possible solutions. Urge the students to refer to the categories of where solutions come from written on the board as a guide. If no student volunteers, the trainer should suggest a problem "that my nephew/niece is having."

SESSION 10

Objectives

1. Help students learn the need to think about the possible outcomes of choosing one problem solution over another.
2. Give students a methodology for evaluating possible consequences.
3. Provide students with a procedure for evaluating their own choice of behavior, then self-reinforcing or dealing effectively with the failure.

Comment

Once students have had some experience with generating alternative solutions to problem situations, it is critical to give them a procedure that will lead them to the best alternative. Looking ahead to potential consequences is the most logical direction to take; however, many adolescents will need a great amount of structure to do this. As a group, adolescents tend to engage in what has been called "magical thinking." Although they may acknowledge the existence of a negative consequence, they fully believe that it will somehow not apply to them. Something will happen between the choice of behavior and the negative consequence to rescue them, and everything will work out fine. They will deny that they believe this, but they behave as if they do. School personnel are well aware of youth who firmly believe that they will graduate from high school, in spite of the fact that they are 17 years old, truant, and failing most of their classes.

This is the last formal session in the program. Experience has shown that some form of formalized "graduation" exercise is extremely well received. Having certificates made up, letters of completion sent to parents, and involving school administrators in a conclusion ceremony seems to have a genuinely positive effect on these students, who are well used to being left out of such school rituals. You are urged to pay careful attention to this aspect. In addition, trainers should plan for and schedule booster sessions with the group. Planning sessions for the third, sixth, and ninth week following completion is an adequate schedule.

Video

The Session 10 video introduces the need to consider consequences. A student is shown confronting a problem, considering the alternative solutions, and finally choosing the best alternative.

Procedure

Indicate to students that this is the last session in the program (if so chosen). Explain the procedure, if any, for distribution of rewards for attendance, hassle log completion, or other such contingencies that may have been set up at the onset of the program. Collect and record hassle logs. Ask for student volunteers to present their hassle logs, allowing the group to brainstorm alternative responses to the triggering episode. Using the *Steps for Problem Solving* poster, review the first two steps:

1. Stop and think: What is the problem?
2. What can I do?

What Will Happen If...

Stress that learning how to figure out what will happen when we choose to do something gives us increased power over what happens to us.

Example. Ask "What if you were stopped by a teacher in the hallway after the bell rang. Look at your choices of behavior and tell me what will happen if..."

1. You run off?
2. You ignore the teacher and keep walking?
3. You explain your tardiness respectfully?
4. You call the teacher a name?
5. You shove the teacher?

Example: (Ask) "What if a student next to you in class calls you a dirty name under his breath so no one but you heard him? What will happen if..."

1. You stand up and shove him over?
2. You control your anger during class and beat him up in the hall afterward?
3. You control your anger and let him slide?
4. You control your anger and try to resolve the problem later?

Write on the board and point out to students that one of the best ways of looking at possible consequences is to ask:

- "If I do (this):_____"
- What is the worst that could happen?
- What is the best that could happen?
- What is most likely to happen?

Choose some sample problem situations from the Session 9 "Problem List" (and/or have students generate their own), and for each alternative solution or response to the problem, have students apply the two consequence questions above. Have students role-play select problems, with the identified problem solver proceeding through the steps for problem solving aloud, including problem definition, considering alternatives, and evaluating consequences.

What Will I Do?

Now that students are learning to evaluate the consequences of their choices, point out that deciding which choice is best is the next step. Often, this decision will come easily if the first three steps have been followed. Use the two examples above (about being stopped by a teacher in the hall and about being called a dirty name in class).

1. Have selected students go through all four steps in a role play of the incidents, using the overt or think-aloud procedure.
2. Have them make a decision about what to do.

Self-Evaluation

Point out that it is always helpful to take some time and look carefully at the choice you made in a problem situation. When you are pleased with the consequences of your choice or when you are not pleased, take some time to look back. Ask yourself... (Trainers should write the following on the chalk board):

- Did I make the right choice?
- If so, nice job!
- If not, why?
- What should I do differently next time?

Help the students learn to analyze their choices by providing an example from the trainer's own life, one in which you did not evaluate the potential consequences adequately and later regretted your choice.

Note. At this juncture, it is important for trainers to discuss the issue of what happens if a student tries to apply what he/she has learned, but still gets in trouble. Students will frequently report back that, "I tried, but this stuff don't work." The likelihood is high that historically aggressive or problematic adolescents are going to continue to be that way out of sheer habit, at least in the short term. Emphasize that there is no magic in the program or any of the techniques for anger control or problem solving that have been discussed.

Say. "Like learning any new skill, you have to practice. And like any new skill, you will not be perfect the first time or every time thereafter. How many here hit the first free throw they ever tried? How many now hit them every time without ever missing? In the same way, learning new ways of coping with conflict and solving tough problems takes time and practice. And you won't always do it right. Mistakes are a part of life."

Provide students with a model for coping with failure.

- "I messed up, but I know why."
- "I won't make the same mistake twice."
- "I need to look at consequences more carefully."
- "Nobody's perfect. I'll do better next time."

Ask for suggestions from the students as to what kinds of self-coaching statements they can say to themselves if they make some mistakes.

Closing

At this point, formalized "completion" ceremonies can be held, with the presentation of certificates or other such recognition.

CASE EXAMPLE: CENTRAL HIGH SCHOOL

The Presenting Problem

Central High School (the name is fictionalized) is a 2,000-student, racially integrated school within the Milwaukee Public School system. Located in an area of predominantly white, middle-class residents, Central has been the scene of frequent clashes between bussed-in African-American students from the central city and neighborhood white students. Recently, administrators sought to make an impact on the school climate by targeting for intervention those comparatively few students whose chronically aggressive behavior seemed to be at the center of much of the disharmony. It was hypothesized that the verbal posturing and physical intimidation of these high-profile, volatile students, both African American and white, created an atmosphere of general anxiety among the other students. This persistent undercurrent of uneasiness seriously hampered the larger scale human relations activities and kept Central a powder keg of racial tension.

Identification of Group Members for Treatment

The building school psychologist was chosen as the intervention team leader and the process of identifying the students was put into motion. Because of their involvement in a recent series of incidents, the decision to work first with male students was made. The plan was discussed at a general faculty meeting, and teachers were asked to provide the names of student candidates. These names were matched against administrative disciplinary records and attendance records, and an initial pool of approximately 18 potential group members was established.

The intervention team, consisting of the building school psychologist, a guidance counselor assigned to the "at-risk" students, and a school psychologist with the system-wide Violence Reduction Program conducted interviews with each of the referred students. Following an explanation of the intervention goals and procedures, all of the students expressed a willingness to participate in at least the initial session, should they be selected. One student, a widely known and vocal street gang member, advised the interviewers that he would not participate if certain members of a rival gang were in the same group. (This announcement gave the intervention team members concern that the "gang variable" would have to be factored into the identification process. The decision was made to leave it up to the students in the group to express any displeasure with the affiliations of fellow group members. The gang culture, although very real and problematic in the city of Milwaukee, does not hold the sway and influence that it does in other urban areas, such as Chicago or Los Angeles.)

The interview process reduced the pool to a racially balanced group of 14 of the most seriously problematic students of generally similar "social standing" within the student peer culture. This rather informal sociometric ranking was accomplished by simply asking the students who they liked to "hang out with" and cross-checking with teacher and administrator observations. Two students were referred-out for individual counseling because of the potentially disruptive effects of their serious immaturity. Eliminated also were two students who were both 19 and had not yet even reached junior standing. These young men were targeted for immediate placement out of the school into a job training program sponsored by the state department of vocational and technical education. The remaining 14 students were subdivided into two groups of seven each, one group was put on the waiting list and the other scheduled to begin as soon as the administrative chores were accomplished.

Assessment of Treatment Effectiveness

It was decided by the intervention team to measure treatment success by monitoring administrative referrals for aggressive or disruptive behavior. An informal "baseline" was established by examining referral rates for targeted students for a 1-month period back from the start of the intervention. Referrals were continuously recorded during treatment and then again at a 1-month follow-up. As this was to be an applied effort, school personnel were most interested in the observable, more qualitative effects of the treatment. (Readers interested in the effects of controlled studies of this intervention procedure should see Eisenman, 1992, and Larson, in press.)

Pregroup Preparation

To save time, the school social worker was asked to go to the students' homes and secure the written parental consent in person. Those parents who had telephones were subsequently contacted by the building school psychologist for a follow-up conversation, further enlisting their support for the intervention effort. Of this first Central group, five of the seven students were assigned to a "school within a school" program for students who were repeating the 10th grade. Because these four all attended classes in the same area of the building, a nearby empty classroom was selected as the group meeting room. The remaining three students were more widely distributed around the building and, as expected, experienced occasional difficulties moving to and from the meeting. Providing students with special passes and informing hall security helped, but problems were inevitable, as the trainers were to find out.

For the most part, teachers were only too happy to cooperate by not penalizing the students with extra work for having missed the class ("As if he'd do it anyway..." one cynical history teacher remarked.) A degree of mutual animosity had developed between some of the teachers and the students—not at all unpredictable or incomprehensible, given the presenting problems—and this occasionally manifested as verbal sparring during the transition in or out of class. Regular feedback to the teachers from the intervention trainers helped smooth this difficulty and strengthened the team's resolve to enlist the faculty more collaboratively in the future.

The Initial Meeting

With the parent permission and other housekeeping chores in place, the identified group members were assembled for the first meeting. The students were initially suspicious concerning the motivation for their selection and almost walked out before the first bit of training could be started. Remarks such as, "We ain't the only ones causing trouble" and "Central has a lot more problems than just us" had to be dealt with. The trainers referred to the students' potential for influence and leadership as motivating factors for their selection, and informed them that other groups were sure to follow. Temporarily assuaged, if not wholly convinced, the students rather grumpily cooperated with the remainder of the first session effort. A point system that would allow them to earn credits for attendance and homework to be used toward a raffle of prizes at group's end was explained. This and the presentation of candy bars at the conclusion had a remarkable impact on their collective moods, and they all agreed to return for a second session.

The Beginning Sessions

The subsequent three sessions ran rather smoothly following that rather bumpy start. The effort to keep the group as homogeneous as possible from a peer status perspective seemed to have been effective. Indeed, the students seemed to find increased status even in the general student population through their membership in the group. The trainers had small buttons printed with a "no fighting" logo that the students could earn following their first role play. When the school administration suggested that they be made available to all students, the group members protested loudly, and the plan was scrapped. The trainers were just feeling very self-congratulatory when the first real problem arose. On his way to the group from class, one of the students got into an angry confrontation with a young hall security aide over an issue unrelated to school. Administrators had to be called to the scene, and the youth was subsequently given an administrative transfer to another school for shoving and threatening the aide.

This incident cast something of a pall over the effort. Some faculty members voiced concern that the students were "using" the group hall pass to get into the hallways to cause trouble and wondered aloud if the group was giving the young men status and privilege they did not deserve. The intervention team relayed the concerns to the students in the group and possible solutions were brainstormed. The group agreed to abandon the permanent hall pass idea and trainers arranged to escort students personally to and from the meetings. Although cumbersome and time-consuming, the trade-off for faculty support was worth it.

The serious failure of one of their number prompted the group to question the value of the treatment. After the students spent time blaming the treatment for failing to "work," the trainers allowed them an opportunity to discuss their obvious disappointment about the incident. A healthy discussion about personal responsibility for one's own behavior ensued, and by meeting's end, all were ready to move along with the next phase of the intervention.

The Final Sessions

The remainder of the sessions went comparatively without incident. The students found particular enjoyment and benefit from the use of the camcorder in the role plays. While acknowledging that the prepared video was realistic, they challenged themselves to demonstrate for the camera even greater self-control in even more realistic scenarios. Using actual incidents from their own hassle logs, they carefully rehearsed and videotaped their newly learned skills. They were so proud of their videotaped efforts, they arranged for an audience of selected administrators and teachers to view it one afternoon after school. Clearly, demonstrations of self-control had replaced the aggressive braggadocio of earlier sessions.

This is not to say, however, that equally successful generalization into the hallways and neighborhoods was an accompanying phenomenon. It was not. Of the six students who finished the group, all experienced at least one school suspension for involvement in either a fight or a major disruptive incident by 1-month follow-up. One student was later arrested for a gang-related disturbance at a community center and was waived into adult court. A second youth was expelled for threatening a teacher.

Despite these grim data, the intervention team considered the effort an overall success. Four of the original seven showed substantial decreases in administrative referrals for disruptive or aggressive behavior during a period in the school year when overall student referrals were escalating. Indeed, by year's end, one of their number emerged as a major figure in a newly formed student coalition to improve race relations in the school.

CONCLUSION

This chapter has attempted to depict how the school-based treatment of aggressive youth may be organized and implemented. Those who would take up this task, however, must remain ever cognizant of the associated obstacles to a successful intervention. Foremost among them is the presenting behavior itself. Aggression is a remarkably stable and change-resistant behavior, particularly by the time the problematic youth has reached the middle or high school level. Realistic goal setting is essential, as is a willingness to persevere in the face of apparent failure. Generalization cannot be an afterthought; it must be built into the training through the maintenance of an ongoing collaboration among teachers, trainers, and targeted students. Finally, trainers must remember that a single successful role play does not a changed behavior make. The words, "Okay, let's do it again" will bring on predictable groans, but repetition and more repetition are absolutely essential if real behavior change is to be effected.

The potential benefits to problematic students and to the school environment as a whole, however, most often make the difficulties and set-backs well worth the effort. There are equally needy populations of students within the school vying for the precious time of the supportive services staff, and each professional must allocate his or her time judiciously. School psychologists, guidance counselors, and other professionals who choose to work with this population can find both personal and professional satisfaction with their efforts. The looks of pride on the faces of tough, young students as they recount their initial success with self-control will likely stay with the trainers for a long time.

REFERENCES

American Psychological Association. (1981). Ethical principles of psychologists. *American Psychologist, 36*, 633-638.

Coie, J. D., Underwood, M., & Lochman, J. E. (1991). Programmatic intervention with aggressive children in the school setting. In D. J. Pepler & K. H. Rubin (Eds.), *Development and treatment of childhood aggression* (pp. 389-445). Hillsdale, NJ: Lawrence Erlbaum.

Dodge, K. A. (1991). The structure and function of reactive and proactive aggression. In D. J. Pepler & K. H. Rubin (Eds.), *Development and treatment of childhood aggression* (pp. 201-218). Hillsdale, NJ: Lawrence Erlbaum.

Dodge, K. A. (1986). A social information processing model of social competence in children. In M. Perlmutter (Ed.), *Cognitive perspectives on children's social and behavioral development: The Minnesota symposium on child psychology. Vol. 18* (pp. 77- 126). Hillsdale, NJ: Lawrence Erlbaum.

Dodge, K. A., & Coie, J. D. (1987). Social information-processing factors in reactive and proactive aggression in children's peer groups. *Journal of Personality and Social Psychology, 53*, 1146-1158.

Eisenman, J. M. (1992). *An anger management intervention with middle school adolescents.* Unpublished doctoral dissertation, University of Wisconsin-Milwaukee, Milwaukee, WI.

Feindler, E. L., & Ecton, R. B. (1986). *Adolescent anger control: Cognitive-behavioral techniques*. New York: Pergamon Press.

Feindler, E. L., Marriott, S. A., & Iwata, M. (1984). Group anger control training for junior high delinquents. *Cognitive Therapy and Research, 8*, 299-311.

Freedman, B. J., Rosenthal, L., Donahoe, C. P., Schlundt, D. G., & McFall, R. M. (1978). A social-behavioral analysis of skill deficits in delinquent and nondelinquent adolescent boys. *Journal of Consulting and Clinical Psychology, 46*, 1448-1462.

Goldstein, A. P. (1988). *The Prepare Curriculum.* Chanpaign, IL: Research Press.

Goldstein, A. P., & Glick, B. (1987). *Aggression replacement training: A comprehensive intervention for aggressive youth.* Champaign, IL: Research Press.

Jackson, J. H. (1990a). Best practices in urban school psychology. In A. Thomas & J. Grimes (Eds.), *Best practices in school psychology—II* (pp. 757-772). Washington, DC: National Association of School Psychologists.

Jacob, S., & Hartshorne, T. (1994). *Ethics and law for school psychologists* (2nd ed.). Brandon, VT: CPPC.

Larson, J. D. (in press). Anger and aggression management using the Think First intervention procedure. *Journal of Offender Rehabilitation.*

Larson, J. D. (1990a). Cognitive-behavioral group therapy with delinquent adolescents: A cooperative approach with the juvenile court. *Journal of Offender Rehabilitation, 16*, 47-64.

Larson, J. D. (1990b). *The effects of a cognitive behavioral anger-control intervention on the behavior of at-risk middle school students*. Unpublished doctoral dissertation, Marquette University, Milwaukee, WI.

Larson, J. D., & McBride, J. A. (1991). *Think First*. Long Beach, CA: Long Beach Unified School District.

Lochman, J. E., & Lampron, L. B. (1986). Situational social problem-solving skills and self-esteem of aggressive and nonaggressive boys. *Journal of Abnormal Child Psychology, 15*, 159-164.

Lochman, J. E., Lampron, L. B., Gemmer, T. C., & Harris, S. R. (1986). Anger-coping intervention with aggressive children: A guide to implementation in school settings. In P. Keller & S. Heyman (Eds.), *Innovations in clinical practice: A source book* (Vol. 6, pp. 339-356). Sarasota, FL: Professional Resource Exchange.

Lochman, J. E., Lampron, L. B., Gemmer, T. C., Harris, S. R., & Wyckoff, G. M. (1989). Teacher consultation and cognitive-behavioral interventions with aggressive boys. *Psychology in the Schools, 26*, 179-187.

Lochman, J. E., Nelson, W. M., III, & Sims, J. P. (1981). A cognitive-behavioral program for use with aggressive children. *Journal of Clinical Child Psychology, 10*, 146-148.

McBride, J. A. (1991). *A group counseling program for anger management for use with boys age 6-11*. Long Beach, CA: Long Beach Unified School District.

Meichenbaum, D. H. (1985). *Stress inoculation training*. New York: Pergamon Press.

Meichenbaum, D. H., & Goodman, J. (1971). Training impulsive children to talk to themselves. *Journal of Abnormal Psychology, 77*, 115-126.

Meichenbaum, D. H., & Turk, D. C. (1987). *Facilitating treatment adherence: A practitioner's guidebook.* New York: Plenum Press.

Milwaukee Board of School Directors. (1988). *Violent behavior in the schools: The problem and its solution.* Unpublished manuscript.

National Association of School Psychologists. (1986). *Principles for professional ethics.* Washington, DC: Author.

Novaco, R. W. (1979). The cognitive regulation of anger and stress. In P. Kendall & S. Hollon (Eds.), *Cognitive-behavioral interventions: Theory, research, and procedures* . New York: Academic Press.

Novaco, R. W. (1975). *Anger control: The development and evaluation of an experimental treatment*. Lexington, MA: D. C. Heath.

Patterson, G. R., DeBarsyshe, B. D., & Ramsey, E. (1989). A developmental perspective on antisocial behavior. *American Psychologist, 44*, 329-335.

Thelin, M. H., Fry, R. A., Feherenbach, P. A., & Frautschi, N. M. (1979). Therapeutic videotape and film modeling: A review. *Psychological Bulletin, 86*, 701-720.

13 CONTROLLING IMPULSIVE EXPRESSION OF ANGER AND AGGRESSION

Jay Fortman and Marcy Feldman

In this chapter we present self-control and relaxation procedures to help children control impulsive expression of anger. These procedures are intended to be used with those children and adolescents who have difficulty mediating between their affective impulses and behavioral reactions. The social skills types of procedures described by Morrison and Sandowicz (Chapter 11) potentially provide complementary strategies for these youth. In addition, the reader should be aware that other cognitive-behavioral (Bash & Camp, 1985; Kendall, 1992; Kendall, Reber, McLeer, Epps, & Ronan, 1990) and behavioral (Koegel, Koegel, & Parks, 1991) strategies provide alternative approaches for helping impulsive youth control their anger. The purpose of this chapter is to describe a general self-control approach that is applicable in school and home settings. It teaches youth to use relaxation techniques to increase self-control and reduce the frequency of impulsive anger expression.

CONTROL THROUGH RELAXATION: A PROGRAM FOR IMPULSIVE-AGGRESSIVE YOUTH

Relaxation techniques are effective in reducing the tension levels of individuals. The application of these techniques can be important for children who have poor impulse control during periods of high tension and conflict. Music, deep breathing, progressive muscle relaxation, and guided imagery have been used both separately and in combination to produce states of relaxation. Biofeedback and systematic desensitization procedures have also been used successfully in conjunction with these techniques to reduce tension levels. Uncontrolled impulsive behavior in children poses problems for them and often poses significant problems for the important adults in their lives. A relaxed state may help to slow down the impulsive response and allow the individual an opportunity to develop a more effective response to a particular situation and to make more effective use of the social skills described by Morrison and Sandowicz (Chapter 11). Therefore, teaching a variety of skills to achieve a relaxed state has potential benefits for all concerned.

In the following section, we describe the Control Through Relaxation Program, a program of relaxation skills that may be taught by counselors, teachers, and parents in either an individual or group setting. A brief description is given of some of the eight relaxation techniques used in the program, together with suggestions and guidelines about how they may be introduced to the individual who is experiencing problems with impulsive-aggressive behavior control. A more detailed explanation of each technique may be found in books listed in the references. These skills are most easily learned individually in small components that are gradually combined to create the total program. Feindler (1990) indicates that there are many different approaches to developing relaxation skills, so even though we describe a specific order for the eight different components outlined in this section this may be modified or adapted to accommodate specific individuals or groups.

Skills Used in the Control Through Relaxation Program

The relaxation skills addressed in the Control Through Relaxation Program use the following techniques and materials:

1. Music
2. Biofeedback
3. Breathing exercises
4. Positive statements and calming words
5. Closed eyes exercise
6. Daydreaming
7. Progressive relaxation
8. Systematic desensitization

When implemented, each of these techniques is developed over a period of time and requires regular practice to effectively become integrated into the child's everyday life. The number of sessions required to obtain a specific skill varies from student to student. Meeting once or twice a week in a school office or classroom is enough to teach the basics of each skill, but regular, daily practice sessions are necessary to incorporate this new skill effectively. Therefore, it is suggested that a homework assignment be given after most of the sessions and that regular practice sessions be encouraged. An initial meeting between the counselor, teacher, and parents is recommended to describe the structure and goals of the program and to encourage the participation and cooperation of these important individuals. Detailed directions in the form of hand-outs explaining the various skills are useful in communicating with parents and teachers about the different relaxation techniques (see Appendix).

There are significant advantages to be gained if the program is simultaneously implemented in more than one area of the student's life. Teaching the program in the classroom allows the impulsive-aggressive student an opportunity to practice program skills immediately while also becoming aware of the responses of his or her peer role models. A related benefit is that the child will also begin to understand that his or her responses may be more intense but are not very different from those of others. Encouraging the use of the program at home allows the whole family to become involved in the process so the child does not feel singled out, has adult role models, and generalizes these skills to other settings.

Building Rapport and Making an Assessment

As with most forms of counseling, initiating relaxation therapy involves developing a rapport with the youth. It is also valuable for the counselor/teacher to make an assessment of the individual's needs and the situations/contexts associated of anger and frustration. During the rapport-building period, the counselor /teacher elicits answers to the following questions while simultaneously examining the *cognitive* (What Thinking?), *behavioral* (Actions), and *physiological* (Body) responses to each question:

1. What makes the student angry?
2. What makes the student frustrated?
3. What makes the student happy?
4. What makes the student uptight?
5. How does the student relax?

It is important that these questions be answered specifically with attention to detail. General answers such as "I hate school" or "Life frustrates me" are not enough. The counselor may need to ask additional questions to get the necessary details. Each of these questions will have more than one response, so it may be helpful to have the individual rank order these answers. This allows the development of a personal hierarchy of anger-provoking situations. Information of this type permits the teacher/counselor to illustrate for the student the connection between certain situations and the ways that they stimulate angry feelings. With this knowledge the student can begin to learn how to express his or her feelings in these situations more effectively. Additional techniques that can be used to help students answer these questions, such as: (a) *pantomiming* (acting without words), (b) *making and using puppets* to express emotions, (c) *creating books* to illustrate feelings, and (d) *role playing* situations (acting with words), are all helpful when working with a group or with particular individuals (Canfield, 1976; Oaklander, 1978). When this assessment is extended to include the home, this information may be useful in allowing the family to understand how the impulsive person feels about specific situations, which in turn allows the student to learn to express his or her feelings more appropriately. It also allows the student to identify how different family members react to various situations. More extensive assessment can be developed using the procedures described in chapters 7, 8, and 9.

Music

Selected forms of music have been shown to produce a reduction in emotional arousal and respiration rates in individuals (Fried, 1990), with researchers frequently using classical or environmental music to produce a state of relaxation. Music helps individuals maintain their concentration during the relaxation process (Scartelli, 1984), intensifies the relaxation experience (Peach, 1984), and can enhance visual imagery. Music has often been used to enhance the biofeedback procedure (Scartelli, 1984), and music combined with deep breathing has led to a reduction in muscle tension, heart rate, and blood pressure—all of which are related to physiological responses during anger arousal.

Description. Background music played quietly during sessions helps to create a calm atmosphere and reduce tension. The choice of music is important because, contrary to expectations, the music one enjoys is not necessarily relaxing. For example, many teenagers enjoy contemporary rock music, which is not calming, likewise, the crescendos and climaxes of classical music are not designed for serenity. Several general types of music have been used but the most effective seems to be New Age music, which includes such artists as Steve Halpern, Rubycon, Asia, and so on. This music, which uses synthesizers, is effective in calming the individual because of its smooth transitions and melodies. Our experience shows that both children and young adults seem to enjoy such music within the context of relaxation training. Environmental sounds are also effective, but be aware that some sounds may be alarming to certain people (e.g., rain and thunder for people who fear lightening and ocean waves for young children and people who do not like the water). Music videos and radio are not appropriate because there is no control over programming and they are frequently interrupted by talking.

Presentation. After several rapport sessions, the child is introduced to the idea that music can affect a person's mood or change how a person is feeling. The student is asked if they are aware of the background music that has been playing during previous sessions. If not, they are asked to listen for a few minutes and encouraged to share their opinion of the music and how it made them feel (i.e., calm, relaxed, excited, and/or happy). A feeling checklist can be used with those children who are reluctant or find it difficult to identify and express their feelings. Be aware that impulsive students will want to answer immediately, so they need to be directed to listen to the music for 5 to 8 minutes, depending on the age of the child, before reactions are shared.

At the end of this session, the youth is asked to bring a selection of music of their own choice to the next meeting. This fulfills several objectives. First, choice of music is something personal and allows the individual to more effectively relate with the teacher/counselor. Second, the counselor and the student together can determine if the music is useful in relaxing and/or calming to the student.

The next session should be used to explore the music brought by the child and to discuss the feelings that it produces. At the end of this session, the counselor should suggest that the individual bring some more of her or his music to share next time and indicate that the counselor will bring some of her or his favorite music, too.

For homework, it is suggested that the student try listening to music at home and in various other locations to see if it can alter his or her mood. Headphones may be used, because they serve to block out most environmental disturbances and also seem to shut down the internal dialogue in many individuals.

In the classroom, teachers may choose to have music on during the day at times that seem to be most stressful or frustrating for the student (e.g., before and during an exam or after recess or before lunch). Some teachers may also want to encourage the students to bring their own music and discuss the effects on their mood.

At home, parent(s) may play the music during different stressful periods of the day, for example, during the morning "rush," during meals, at homework time, and in the early evening. The child and the parent should both be given the opportunity to share their music and then discuss its effects on each other's moods.

Biofeedback

Biofeedback refers to a set of procedures that provide information (feedback) about one or more biological responses. This information enables an individual to gain conscious control of their biological reactions such as muscle tension and skin temperature. Electromyographic (EMG) biofeedback and temperature feedback are examples of such procedures. EMG biofeedback involves the attachment of electrodes to the forehead to measure tension levels within the muscles of the facial area. The tension level of the facial muscles is a good indicator of the general tension level of the other muscles of the body. A visual or auditory signal serves as the feedback mechanism. Temperature biofeedback uses a digital readout, lights, or tones to provide information (Linkenhoker, 1983).

Biofeedback procedures have been incorporated into relaxation programs in order to provide children with an objective measure of their bodily states. According to Zaichowsky, Zaichowsky, and Yeager (1986), these objective measures especially motivate children to reduce their tension and temperature levels. Excessive levels of muscle tension have been associated with children who exhibit impulsive-aggressive behavior. Therefore, biofeedback can help to improve their self-control. Temperature biofeedback has been used to teach relaxation exercises. Zaichowsky et al. (1986) developed a relaxation program for 1st- through 4th-graders and used temperature biofeedback to help them practice relaxation exercises. The program included deep breathing, progressive muscle relaxation and guided imagery exercises. They reported that temperature biofeedback assisted in the acquisition of these exercises. Furthermore, the children displayed no significant differences in learning the self-control techniques. Although these studies demonstrate the effectiveness of biofeedback, others have argued that biofeedback is no more effective than less expensive relaxation procedures, such as progressive muscle relaxation (Burish, 1981; Lehrer, 1982). Dunn and Howell (1982), however, found that whereas relaxation is attained more quickly with progressive muscle relaxation, biofeedback results in a deeper, more consistent state of relaxation.

When a person's frustration level increases there are measurable physiological responses such as increased respiration rate, increased hand temperature, and increased perspiration level known as the galvanic skin response. If these responses are measured and recorded while the student is learning relaxation techniques, they may provide visible evidence to reassure the student that she or he is achieving a more relaxed state.

Description. Biofeedback consists of monitoring these various physiological responses and relaying that information back to the individual. Hand temperature appears to be the most effective measurement of tension and is the easiest to monitor. In a group situation, hand temperature "bio-strips" are useful because they are portable, complete in themselves, and have no need of any other sophisticated machines. They may also be given to the individual to take home for practice.

Presentation. Most children and young adults enjoy machines, so the introduction of the biofeedback machine can be exciting to many but may prove intimidating for a few. Some individuals are extremely wary of machines and some may ask if it is a "lie detector." A good explanation will focus on the similarity to a thermometer that takes a temperature with a finger instead of the mouth. Depending on the age of the individual, further explanations may include such physiological facts as the effect of emotions on the raising and lowering of the temperature. You may also wish to include a simple explanation of the "fight and flight" syndrome. A practical demonstration of the machine should finally dismiss any lingering concerns. This is also an opportune moment to use the individual's own music selection. Be sure to determine and discuss any changes in temperature it produces. Young children may have difficulty understanding the significance of the numbers, but they will appreciate the visual changes in the readouts. Colors and arrows are useful and exciting in highlighting these changes.

For homework, suggest that the individual monitor his or her temperature in various situations, such as at home, at school, and while watching television. Keep a record of the results (see Table 13.1). It may be difficult to get children and teenagers to keep accurate records, so a reward system may provide the necessary incentive.

During the next several sessions, discuss the homework and compare the results. Because people respond differently to various types of music, a change of the individual's music choice may improve results.

In a group situation, particularly with elementary school children, teachers may have all the students wear bio-strips for several days and record the temperature changes before and after each daily task. This allows the children to learn about how different situations create fluctuating levels of stress and frustration. A general discussion of the results allows everybody, including the impulsive youth, to understand that her or his peers experience varying levels of frustration and stress throughout the day.

At home, the family may participate by wearing bio-strips and recording their responses to various situations throughout the day. Subsequent family discussions allow the impulsive individual to realize that all of us experience stress and frustration on a regular basis.

Deep Breathing

Description. Deep breathing is often the first step used in a relaxation sequence. The act of breathing deeply serves to lower the heart rate, relax the muscles, and prepare the body to engage in relaxation exercises. Respiration rates may be divided into three categories:

Fast Pace—This is defined as shallow chest breathing with short inhalations and a rapid rate. This type of breathing speeds up the cardiovascular system and is frequently observed in high emotion producing situations.

Medium Pace—This is the normal breathing rate for most people.

Slow Pace (Deep Breathing)—This type of respiration originates at the level of the diaphragm and has a slower than normal rate. It has the advantage of slowing the cardiovascular system and appears to produce a relaxed state.

Presentation. Select some "calming" music and direct the individual to take one or two deep breaths, holding each for 3–5 seconds before exhalation. Have the individual record their temperature and note any changes.

Next explain the effects of deep breathing. For example, this skill seems to enhance clearer thinking and by increasing the oxygen supply to the brain will counteract the effects induced by fast pace breathing. Furthermore, for a short period, it may even produce a relaxed state. Thus deep breathing is a useful coping mechanism to counteract the effects of frustration, anger, and overexcitement in the everyday world.

For homework, encourage the individual to recognize when he or she encounters a situation that commonly causes frustration and advise him or her to stop and take a deep breath. The individual should carefully note the

Temperature Summary Sheet

Name ____________________

Date	Before Temperature	After Temperature	Comments

Table 13.1

effect on his or her reactions and, if wearing a bio-strip, make a note of any temperature changes.

At school, teachers may introduce the deep breathing exercise before an exam or any new task. This seems to be useful for the impulsive individual as well as other classmates because it slows them down and reminds the impulsive individual to use this skill. It also creates a positive norm for using self-control techniques in the classroom.

At home, parent(s) may remind the impulsive individual to take a deep breath before initiating tasks, such as homework, chores, and so on. In addition, family members can help by modeling such behavior in the home. This may have the added benefit of helping the family demonstrate more patience with each other by creating a relaxed mood.

Calming Words and Positive Statements

Description. Simple calming words help to produce a relaxed state, and positive statements seem to counteract the effects of negative internal dialogue. See Larson (Chapter 12) for more specific information about comprehensive cognitive approaches to anger management.

Presentation. Some simple calming words are: "*relax*" and "*calm down,*" and positive statements are: "*I am worthwhile,*" "*I am okay,*" "*I am special,*" and "*chill out.*" At the start of the session, have the individual repeat aloud one of the calming words, then note the changes in hand temperature. Have him or her repeat one of the positive statements and note the temperature changes. Discuss the effects of using positive statements and calming words. Then have the individual silently repeat a calming statement, then a positive statement and note any temperature changes for both. Typically, children of all ages have no problem with the calming words and have quick results. Results with positive statements are less promising probably because of the self-esteem variable. Selecting positive statements that feel the most natural and using these may help to begin this process.

For homework, suggest that the individual begin the day by silently repeating one of the positive statements. It is important to let the student know that though he or she may feel awkward, continued practice will make him or her more comfortable. In addition, encourage the use of the calming words in different situations (at school, at home, or in interaction with peers).

At the next session, discuss the effectiveness of this skill and assess proficiency by using the hand temperature monitor. Subsequent sessions should focus on incorporating some of the other calming aids such as deep breathing, calming words, positive statements, and music selection.

In the classroom, positive statements are an important component in developing self-esteem in students. Regular use of this skill and other self-esteem enhancers such as stating *"I am good at..." or "Who am I..."* exercises and *magic circles* (Canfield, 1976) will benefit not only the impulsive-aggressive student but all members of the class. Using the calming word during various times of the day, such as before and during an exam, after recess and toward the end of the day, will also reduce tension in the classroom and help the impulsive-aggressive individual to remember to use such words.

At home, parent(s) may use the calming words at specific times of day that have been identified as stressful or frustrating for the impulsive child. In addition, family discussions focusing on the positive events of the day will encourage him or her to focus on positive achievements.

Closed-Eyes Exercise

Description. Closing the eyes blocks outside interference and allows the individual to focus on him- or herself. The individual then can become aware of internal verbal dialogue and physical responses to situations.

Presentation. Ask the child to close her or his eyes while rehearsing various relaxation skills. Most individuals respond easily to this direction, however, a few young people may find it difficult to complete this task. To assist them, ask them to close just one eye while completing the different skills. For homework, suggest that the child practice some of the relaxation skills they have learned with his or her eyes closed in a private place at home. At the next session, review the homework assignment and then have the child attempt to run through the skills with both eyes closed.

In the classroom, the teacher can have students practice closing their eyes while in their seats or some comfortable place in the room. The whole class listens to the music while practicing the deep breathing exercise with their eyes closed. Usually, elementary school children have trouble at first, then are able to close their eyes for brief periods of time. Older students seem to have less trouble keeping their eyes closed.

Induction Process

The induction process consists of a combination of the exercises described previously in this chapter: (a) music selection, (b) deep breathing exercises, (c) calming words/positive statements, and (d) closed-eyes exercise. Using any combination of these skills before starting relaxation induction techniques will increase their effectiveness. The hand temperature monitor should also be used for each of these relaxation techniques.

Daydreaming

Guided imagery serves to create a fantasy world for children that is nonthreatening and peaceful. Fantasy "trips" can be created while children imagine peaceful and restful places, for example, a soft and fluffy cloud (Zipkin, 1985). These "trips" help children to calm down and focus on other relaxation exercises such as deep breathing and progressive muscle relaxation. Images can also be created that will help children acquire new skills. For example, children can imagine themselves reading successfully, taking a test, and controlling their aggressive behaviors (Anderson, 1980). Their fantasy worlds provide them with a safe environment in which to try out new skills vicariously and to gain the confidence needed to try these new skills in the real world. Anderson (1975, 1980) used guided imagery to teach a group of 5th-graders how to control their aggressive impulses by developing a hierarchy of 10 anger-producing situations. These situations ranged from a mildly anger-producing situation (a student receives a lunch he doesn't like) to an extremely provoking one (a student's mother is called "ugly"). The students were asked to imagine themselves in the same problem situations and encouraged to generate the best solution for each problem. Anderson found that the 5th-graders learned how to inhibit their impulsive reactions to anger. He concluded that their imaginations provided them with a safe "place" in which to practice and succeed in controlling their own behavior.

Description. The capacity for fantasy and daydreams is a valuable resource that can help children escape an unpleasant situation or master their environment. Some of the most effective techniques use an organized system of daydreaming or fantasy. This form of guided imagery is a helpful aid to relaxation and may be divided into guided and unguided scenarios (Oaklander, 1978; Singer, 1966; Stevens, 1973). Unguided daydreams allow the child to picture a peaceful location in which to feel comfortable and relaxed. Using his or her imagination, the child creates a picture of the location, places him- or herself in it, visualizes the scenery, "hears" pleasant sounds, and experiences "smells" (aromas associated with the setting). The child stays in the setting for several minutes, enjoying the sensations of peace and tranquillity until a state of complete relaxation is reached. Guided imagery follows much the same procedure except that the counselor/teacher leads the student to the location and directs the development of the fantasy. This method is particularly useful for young children or for those students who have difficulty focusing their attention. There are a number of commercial cassettes and CDs available that can help with guided daydreams, or one may choose to develop tapes or written scripts.

Presentation. The student is settled in a comfortable position in a quiet place. Start by initiating the induction process. After the student is relaxed, direct him or her in either a guided or unguided daydream. Be sure to emphasize that this is a safe and secure place. This should last for about 5 minutes. Older children can sustain this process for up to 15 minutes. Be sure to allow a little time for the student to reorient before beginning a discussion about how the student felt during and immediately after this experience. Encourage the child to label the emotions she or he experienced specifically and accurately. Discuss any changes in temperature and note whether muscles felt tense or relaxed.

During unguided daydreams children and teenagers often choose locations that are not very relaxing and that may create feelings of excitement or tension (e.g., a visit to an amusement park or a party). In this case, the counselor may suggest that they choose a more peaceful scenario such as the beach, the woods, or a park.

It seems to be most effective to experience these fantasies without a companion. Interaction with another person is not helpful and in some instances may actually detract from the experience. Several sessions may be necessary to determine which one is most relaxing and calming to the individual.

For homework, the counselor may suggest that the student try daydreaming about several different locations, keeping a record of the results and trying to determine which scenario is most successful for him/her. If a pretaped guided daydream is used, the student can take it home and listen to it at different times of the day. Encourage the student to keep details of the results to share at the next session. Some individuals may find it difficult to share the location they are daydreaming about because it is their private space and/or it creates some embarrassment for them. This privacy should be respected as long as the individual finds it necessary.

At school, the teacher may also use this skill with all his or her students. Many elementary school teachers report success in allowing students to daydream at specific times. They claim it creates a calmer atmosphere, increases focusing in the classroom, and reduces impromptu daydreaming.

At home, parent(s) may use guided imagery as a family activity. This can be easily accomplished by having all family members listen to a guided daydream or by doing an unguided daydream at a convenient time in the day.

Progressive Relaxation

Progressive muscle relaxation (Jacobson, 1962) involves the tensing and releasing of the muscle groups of the body. The purpose of this procedure is to teach children how to discriminate between feelings of tension and relaxation, a critical skill for individuals with anger control problems. This knowledge helps the individual achieve and maintain a state of relaxation. Progressive muscle relaxation exercises are available on commercially made cassettes (Zipkin, 1985) or in written scripts (Koeppen, 1974). Rossmann and Kahnweiler (1977) implemented a relaxation program incorporating deep breathing, progressive muscle relaxation, and imagery with 4th- and 5th-graders who exhibited high tension levels based on self-report measures and teacher ratings. The relaxation training was shown to reduce the children's tension levels significantly. McLain and Lewis (Chapter 14) also discuss progressive muscle relaxation procedures.

Description. An awareness of the muscle groups of the body and when they are becoming tense is one way to allow the impulsive-aggressive youth to monitor his or her frustration level. Tensing and relaxing various muscle groups in a progressive relaxation process can help decrease stress levels and control psychosomatic illnesses such as stomachaches and headaches.

Presentation. For elementary school age children, combining visual imagery with this exercise seems to be the most effective. This method gives them something concrete to achieve and holds their interest the longest. For example, have children imagine having a piece of wood at the bottom of their feet, which they push against as hard as they can, and then relax. Have them imagine a rock hanging over their stomach and tell them to keep their stomach muscles tight so that it won't crush them, and then relax. Finally, tell them to imagine a sponge in their hands from which they need to squeeze out juice, and then relax. For younger children (a) have them imagine they are robots; (b) then have it rain on them so they rust and stiffen up (tense); (c) then have them imagine that they get oiled (relaxed)—this is a useful way to teach the differences between tensed and relaxed muscles. Some older children like using visual techniques, however, others may want to be directed to tense and relax each muscle group. For all age groups, it useful to begin at the top of the head or at the toes and proceed up or down the body. Each muscle should be contracted for about 5 seconds before relaxing it.

Many individuals carry their tension and frustrations in their shoulder and neck muscles so it is useful to concentrate on these areas.

For homework, suggest that the individual practice this exercise both at home and at school. A modified version concentrating on certain strategic muscle groups, those that are chronically tense for the child, may work better in some situations.

In the classroom, teachers may use this as a warm up exercise before tasks, such as before a test, or before and after recess, or they may choose to use a shortened version that addresses only one or two muscle groups. This may help the impulsive-aggressive child to remember to use this technique and will teach him or her to integrate this into a daily schedule. In addition, having students discuss how their bodies respond in various situations and with different feelings will allow impulsive-aggressive children to better identify how their body reacts to anger-provoking situations.

At home, the parent(s) may gently remind the impulsive individual to use this skill in certain frustration-producing situations. The family could do shortened versions, such as addressing the neck and shoulders, at the dinner table before eating a meal. This may reduce the family tension and again will be good role modeling for the impulsive/ aggressive child.

Other Ways to Relax

Now that the child has discovered the value of relaxation and some effective ways to achieve it, a brain-storming session may discover some new ways to relax. Develop a list of the most successful methods of relaxation for the individual and have him or her rank them in order of effectiveness. Try out any new methods you come up with. Here are some suggestions made by elementary-age children: sports, reading, eating, and talking to friends. Older students have made these suggestions: sports, talking to friends, sleeping, and watching television.

In the classroom, teachers can develop a master relaxation list that includes contributions from various children. This is helpful for all students in understanding ways to relax, and it specifically helps impulsive children to develop a wider perspective on how others their age relax.

Systematic Desensitization

According to Warren and McLellarn (1982), systematic desensitization may be the most extensively evaluated and employed treatment in existence. This treatment procedure has been employed to reduce the aggressive behaviors of individuals. Relaxation exercises are paired with imagined anger-producing situations in order to create a response incompatible with anger. Systematic hierarchies are developed that guide the individual through progressively more intense situations. Some studies employing this procedure have shown mixed results (see Warren & McLellarn, 1982), but others have shown success in reducing the aggressive behaviors (Schloss, Smith, Santora, & Bryant, 1989; Smith 1973). Researchers have been unable to specify which components of the systemic desensitization procedure led to successful outcomes, but Kazdin and Wilcoxon (1976) suggest that differential expectancies may actually influence the outcome.

Description. This exercise uses the hierarchy of situations that produce certain emotions, gathered during the *Building Rapport* sessions. The aim here is to introduce the student to the idea gradually that he or she can gain control of these situations and consequently his or her behavior by using a combination of the relaxation techniques.

Presentation. Select one emotion from the list of anger-provoking situations. Identify the least charged situation and ask the student to imagine it happening as the induction process is initiated. Next, have the child use relaxation techniques to lessen the tension associated with the anger-provoking situation and thereby create a feeling of relaxation. All of this is accomplished while the child mentally acts out the situation. Follow this exercise with discussion of the results. Be sure to discuss any pertinent changes in hand temperature that occurred during the experience. Continue to use this technique in subsequent sessions using situations that are associated with higher levels of anger arousal. Emphasize the student's increasing control of the situation and be sure to include those techniques that seem to be the most successful. Some skills may work better in some situations than others. Allow the student to participate in the selection of those strategies believed to be most successful. When the counselor feels that the student has built up sufficient confidence in his or her abilities to use these techniques successfully, it is time to test them out in a real situation. It is important to start with situations that are lowest ranked on the anger-provocation list. In addition, the student should feel successful using relaxation skills to diffuse the situation prior to moving on to a situation of more intense anger potential. This process may take many meetings and some situations may need repeated practice.

Teachers should be aware of the feelings that are created in each situation and the intensity of anger they evoke. This information will help the teacher determine how to respond to specific situations, such as introducing a relaxation skill, and allowing the student to move away from the situation. In this manner the counselor and teacher can act as a team in helping youth better control their impulsive expression of anger. Similarly, parent(s) need to understand the different levels of anger associated with various situations at home and discuss ways that they can respond in support of their child's anger self-control efforts.

Other Hints for the Classroom

Throughout this program the role of teacher and parent has been emphasized. There are several other hints for the teacher that may help the students with impulsive-aggressive problems. It is important to evaluate the influence that any *learning disabilities* might have on the child's frustration level at school. Sometimes just a better understanding of the student's learning mode allows the teachers, parent(s), and even the student him- or herself to understand the roots of the angry and impulsive behavior pattern. In addition, adaptation of the classroom environment by organizing a *calm corner* (an area where a student may sit comfortably and relax and where music may even be available) and/or by lowering the lights in the room may help improve student attention and make it easier for students to calm down when needed. Many angry-impulsive students benefit by being allowed to leave the room when they feel the need for space and fresh air. Where they go should be arranged ahead of time for safety reasons. Teachers may have their classes role-play various situations and problem-solve how to handle each of these situations. This would allow impulsive students to become aware of how others respond to these various life situations and may encourage the development of more effective coping strategies.

CASE STUDY: NATHAN, AGE 12

This case study demonstrates the integration of various relaxation self-control techniques used with a 6th-grade boy who displayed problems with impulsive behavior and anger control both in and outside the classroom.

Background

Nathan is a 12-year-old with one older brother and parents who were divorced when he was 6 years old. He is in the custody of his mother, but visits his father bi-weekly. However, because of his father's alcohol problems this is not always practical. Both parents had several partners over the years and mother is currently in a long-term relationship. Both mother and father report that Nathan has impulsive behavior and anger problems at home and with his friends.

For the last 3 years, Nathan has received school counseling for his behavior problems at school and several behavioral modification programs have been attempted with moderate success (contracts, time-out, etc.). In addition, Nathan has been in psychotherapy for the past 2 years in an attempt to resolve the family issues and his behavioral outbursts. A review of the school records revealed that he has performed above average academically but his social skills have been unsatisfactory since 1st grade. All of his teachers have commented on problems with his peers and authority figures. Nathan was tested by the various specialists of the child study team for learning disabilities. Results indicate that he is an intellectually gifted individual who performs slightly below his expected ability level in academics. No specific learning disability was identified.

Initiating the Relaxation for Control Program

Initially, Nathan's parents, his teacher, and his psychotherapist met with the program coordinator (a school psychologist) to discuss the principles of the program and their own role in this process. They were also given literature on the various relaxation techniques to study at their leisure. An effort was made to let each individual know just how important they were to the success of this process and their active participation was encouraged. To ensure Nathan's confidence and trust in the process, open notes were used to communicate with each party. In addition, it was suggested that his teacher send home a letter to the parents of her students indicating that she was initiating a stress-relaxation program for the students with the assistance of a school psychologist.

Weeks 1 and 2. Arrangements were made for Nathan to meet weekly for 1 hour with the counselor in his office at the school. The first two sessions were used to get acquainted and to develop a rapport. Nathan was encouraged to ask questions and to answer a questionnaire on emotional responses that identified common anger-provoking situations in his life. He was cooperative and seemed to be comfortable discussing himself and his feelings. During these sessions, low-volume background music was played. When Nathan asked about the music, the counselor indicated that he enjoyed listening to music. At the end of the second session, Nathan was asked if he would like to participate in a relaxation program that would help him better control his anger and impulsive behavior. He agreed, and the details of the program were then explained to him.

Week 3. The session began by discussing the questions Nathan had about the program. He showed some concern about confidentiality (he didn't want his friends to know) and he was worried about being different. It was explained that, as with all counseling, this program was confidential and when we did work in the classroom with all the students nobody would be aware it was because he was in this program. It was mentioned that all the students would benefit by learning these skills to help control their own anger and impulsive behavior problems.

The background music was reintroduced and the counselor talked about its effects on one's mood. Nathan was asked to share his opinion. He felt that it was "kind of boring," but when asked if this music made him feel relaxed or excited, he said he seemed calm while listening to it. Several other tapes including New Age, heavy metal, and popular music were played and discussed. At the end of the session, Nathan was asked bring several of his own tapes for the next weekly meeting.

Week 4. This session was spent examining the various music tapes Nathan had selected. These included heavy metal, rap, and country music. A discussion of the mood each of these tapes induced in him was followed by several tapes selected by the counselor and further discussion of the moods they produced. At the end of the session, Nathan was asked to choose which tapes made him the most calm or the most excited. He was directed to listen to the calm tape shortly before going to school each day and as soon as he got home from school. An open letter to his parents and teacher was sent suggesting that, if possible, a selection of music should be played in their respective environments and its effects discussed.

Week 5. When Nathan came for the next session he seemed very excited. He was anxious to let the counselor know that he had seemed a little calmer this week. In addition, both his parents and the teacher had played music at school and at home. He said he had some interesting discussions with his parents about both their music selection and his own. He said that at school the other students felt the same way as he did at first about the music selection: that it was boring. However, as the week went on they began to appreciate its usefulness as a calming agent. The session continued with a demonstration of the bio-strip, which Nathan found intriguing. He enjoyed measuring his responses to the various musical pieces. For homework,

Nathan was asked to use the bio-strip while listening to various types of music at different times throughout the week and to record his responses on the summary sheet provided by the counselor. He was reminded to bring the summary sheet so that the results could be discussed at the next session.

Week 6. Nathan forgot to bring his summary sheet for the next session and with some probing it was discovered that he had not remembered to complete it. He reassured the counselor that he had experimented with the bio-strip with different types of music, but had just forgotten to record the results. He was reminded of the importance of this sheet in understanding his responses to different types of music. The session continued with a discussion of suitable situations in which to practice using the bio-strip and listening to various musical pieces. At the end of the session, Nathan was reminded again to complete the summary sheet. The counselor also indicated that he would visit Nathan's class during the week to show all the students in his class how to use the bio-strip.

During the following week, the class was introduced to the counselor and the program. After some discussion of the program and its uses, the students wer shown the bio-strip and a practical demonstration of how it measures the difference in hand temperature affected by changes in emotion. Each student received a bio-strip and, after listening to various pieces of music, there was a discussion of the temperature changes. Each student was given a summary sheet and asked to record their temperature responses to each of a variety of situations and music during the following week.

Week 7. Before reviewing the sheet, Nathan talked about his enjoyment of the classroom presentation. He realized that others found this topic fascinating too. His weekly summary sheet revealed several situations at school and one at home that caused Nathan to become tense. It was suggested that he try listening to calming music before and during these situations. Next, Nathan was taught the deep breathing exercise, and its use as a relaxation aid was discussed. His homework was to practice this skill, using it before and during situations he knew made him tense. He was also asked to use the bio-strip and to keep accurate records of the resulting temperature changes.

During the following week, the counselor visited Nathan's classroom. First, there was a general discussion of the summary sheets. Each student was requested to underline the situations that produced the most tension (a decrease in temperature) and a class list was made of these situations. It was noted that not all situations affected everybody in the same way. It was suggested that the students use calming skills such as deep breathing or relaxing music before and/or during these tension-producing situations. The students were then instructed in the deep breathing exercise. For homework, the students were asked to continue to measure and record temperature changes, while using music and the deep breathing exercise to calm them during the difficult situations.

Week 8. Nathan began by discussing his reactions to the classroom presentation at his next session. He was fascinated to discover that even the teacher's "pets" encountered difficult situations during their school day. He confided that it was helpful to have the teacher remind the students to use the deep breathing exercise when necessary. A review of Nathan's summary sheet revealed slight changes in tension. He agreed that he felt a little calmer and in more control during the preceding week.

Nathan was then introduced to the use of *positive statements and calming words*. He really seemed to enjoy the calming words and found the word "relax" to be the most useful. He then practiced combining the calming word with his deep breathing exercise. It was difficult to find a positive statement that Nathan found believable so he began by saying, "I am Okay." For homework, he was directed to use the calming word with the deep breathing exercise when encountering various situations and to record the temperature changes on the summary sheet. He was asked to wear the biostrip and record changes. A letter was sent home with details of the exercises Nathan had learned. His parents were also asked to develop a calming word for each family member and to practice the "positive statement" exercise. A family discussion of the results was also encouraged.

During discussion, in the next classroom session, the students reported on their progress with the deep breathing exercise. The general consensus was that it was useful, but sometimes it was hard to remember to use it. They were reminded that, as with any new skill, it took time and regular practice to achieve success and not get frustrated. The calming word and positive statement exercise was then introduced. Most students had no difficulty in selecting calming words, but several experienced some problems with finding a positive statement they felt comfortable using. These individuals were advised to use "I am Okay." For homework, the students were then asked to practice the calming word simultaneously with the deep breathing exercise. They were also asked to repeat the positive statement several times throughout their day. Subsequently, the teacher was asked to practice these skills with students during the day and she later reported observing some differences (more control) in her students, including Nathan, in highly stressful situations.

Week 9. During the individual session, Nathan shared that he enjoyed the classroom sessions because they made him feel less different. He found the reminders from the other students and the teacher to be helpful in remembering to use the skills. In discussing his homework, he shared that the calming statement was useful and made him slow down his deep breathing. He said he had trouble believing the positive statement and was reminded that was not a problem and to keep using the statement "I am Okay." Nathan had not remembered to do his summary sheet for that week and he was reminded to continue to complete it during the week. He was then instructed to close his eyes while relaxing. He had some difficulty keeping his eyes closed at first, but after several minutes of listening to the music and taking deep breaths he was able to keep them shut. After the exercise was completed, Nathan confided that it was difficult to close his eyes because he wanted to know what was going on and he was afraid he would fall asleep. He was reassured that nothing was happening in the room while he had his eyes closed and if he fell asleep it did not matter. For homework, Nathan was asked to close his eyes while listening to music at least once each day during the week.

The classroom session began with a discussion about the effects of the "calming word and positive statement." Most of the students agreed the calming word slowed them down and helped them take longer deep breaths. Many students continued to have difficulty with the positive statement. They felt uncomfortable saying it and often forgot to do it. The whole class practiced saying "I am okay" several times aloud. This seemed to help and the students were reminded that they just needed to repeat the statement frequently, believing it would come later. Next, all the students were directed to find a space in the classroom where they could lie down without being bothered by a classmate. They were then asked to take a deep breath and to close their eyes. Meanwhile, appropriate music was played quietly in the background. Most students were able to close their eyes without difficulty, but some found it a challenge. For homework, they were directed to close their eyes while listening to their calming music. The teacher was asked to practice this skill in the class several times during the week. She reported that she had seen several students stop and take a deep breath before encountering some situations. She had remembered to direct them to take a deep breath and relax before several tests. She also reported that Nathan seemed more relaxed and confident and there was a significant decrease in his impulsive behavior. During this week, a note came from Nathan's mother which indicated that Nathan was excited about the program and seemed more relaxed and calm at home. He was even getting along better with his brother!

Week 10. At the next meeting, Nathan reported that several times during the week the teacher had reminded the students (a) to take deep breaths before a test and (b) to stop what they were doing and close their eyes while listening to calming music. He felt this helped both him and his fellow students. Nathan was then introduced to an *unguided daydream*. Suitable music was played for a few minutes and he was directed to close his eyes and take a couple of deep breaths. Then he was asked to imagine himself in a favorite place—one where he felt secure and comfortable. A check of his temperature reading indicated that he was relaxing while he imagined being at this special location. After about 10 minutes, Nathan was asked to leave this place, come back to the room and open his eyes. Nathan discussed the experience and said he enjoyed going to this place but did not want to share where he went. For homework, Nathan was asked to practice going on a daydream trip once a day to this special place and to continue practicing the other skills.

In the classroom, the students were introduced to the use of daydreaming as a calming skill. The students were directed again to find a location in the room away from friends and to lie down. The counselor then proceeded into the induction process: deep breathing, calming words, and closed eyes. This was followed by a discussion of how it felt on this trip and what their bio-strips recorded. Most students found this relaxing, however, some found that their temperature decreased. They were asked to re-evaluate their choice of location as some places they considered to be relaxing may actually have made them excited (e.g., Disneyland or amusement parks). The teacher then indicated that they had a specific amount of time each day to daydream. For homework, each student was requested to practice daydreaming during this time period and record temperature changes. The students were also reminded to use the other skills they had learned and to change daydreaming situations if they found that their temperature kept decreasing and/or they felt excited.

Week 11. During Nathan's next visit, we discussed how the daydreaming exercise and the other relaxation skills were progressing. He felt that he was getting more control of himself. He shared that the 5–10 minutes of daydreaming allotted by his teacher allowed him an opportunity to relax and to reduce his other episodes of daydreaming during the day. Then Nathan was directed through a "guided daydream" to the woods. This was followed by a discussion of his response to this type of daydreaming. A check of his hand temperature revealed an increase indicating that he relaxed during the process. Nathan confided that he enjoyed this method more than the unguided daydreaming because he could concentrate on the trip instead of having to develop his own daydream. For homework, Nathan was given a guided daydreaming tape and asked to use it at home for himself and his family.

In the classroom, the students reported on the progress of the daydreaming exercise. Most students responded positively and freely admitted that they enjoyed the opportunity to relax. They were then introduced to the "guided daydream." Afterwards, we discussed how they felt about using this type of daydreaming to relax. About three fourths of the class enjoyed this better than the unguided daydream, while the remainder appreciated the freedom of the unguided daydream. It was suggested to the teacher that she alternate between guided and unguided daydreams for the next 2 weeks.

Week 12. This week Nathan continued with the guided and unguided daydreams, experimenting with several different daydreams. We found that the most effective guided daydream was going to the beach. Nathan was directed to listen to this daydream everyday before and after school and to continue recording his temperature changes.

Week 13. In this session, Nathan began by discussing how these new skills were helping him. He felt that they were giving him tools to calm himself and, because the class was participating, he felt better about himself and was having fewer peer problems. The *progressive relaxation* technique was described to Nathan and he was directed through the exercise. Afterwards, it was suggested that he could use a shortened version of this exercise by concentrating on one or two muscle groups if he chose. For homework, Nathan was directed to practice this skill at least once a day.

This week students in the classroom began by discussing the guided and unguided daydreams and the other skills they had learned. Most of the students really enjoyed practicing these skills and several shared that they were getting their family involved with them, too. Next the students were instructed in the progressive relaxation technique. Afterwards, we discussed how it relaxed the various muscle groups and that shortened versions could be used. The students were asked to practice this technique once a day for this week. The teacher was asked to practice the progressive relaxation in the class using a prerecorded tape or by having the students just tense and relax one or another particular muscle group. The teacher confided that her class, as a whole, seemed a lot more relaxed; the regular daydream session seemed to decrease daydreaming at other times. She also remarked that Nathan continued to remain calm.

Week 14. This session began with a review of all the skills that Nathan had learned so far and a discussion of how he felt about each. Nathan felt he could use all these different skills at various times, but could not contemplate using them all at one time. We then went over the list of situations causing him anger and fear that was compiled in the first two sessions. Some slight changes in order were made. Nathan was also given a brief description of systematic desensitization. Then the counselor initiated the induction process, passing from progressive relaxation into a guided imagery scenario. During this process, the first situation on the list (least anger-producing) was introduced. Nathan appeared to remain relaxed and a check of his bio-strip confirmed this, so the next situation on the list was introduced. This situation provoked a negative reaction from Nathan, so he was reminded to take a deep breath and use a calming word. This was successful and Nathan regained his relaxed state. The next situation again produced a negative reaction and again he was directed to relax and use a calming skill. This seemed only partially successful and so the exercise was terminated. There was a short discussion about the exercise and the outcome. For homework, he was asked to practice the various calming skills throughout the day.

In the classroom, the session began with a guided daydream followed by a discussion of its effects and its usefulness in helping the students to relax. Together the class formulated a relaxation list in which each student contributed five ways they used to relax. This list was displayed in the front of the class as a reminder of alternative ways to relax. For homework, the students were asked to research different ways that their family members used to relax.

Week 15. The next session with Nathan began with a discussion of the list compiled in class. He volunteered that he had learned several other ways to relax: reading, exercising, and talking on the phone with his friends. After a short break, the systematic desensitization procedure was initiated. Nathan progressed up the list of tension-producing situations well. Whenever he showed signs of tension, he was reminded to use one or more of his techniques to aid him in relaxing. When these did not work, the exercise was discontinued. For homework, Nathan was asked to practice the calming skills when experiencing any of these anger-producing situations and to make notes of the results.

In the final classroom meeting, there was a review of all the calming and relaxation skills. The students were reminded that these skills could be useful for all their lives, but to keep them current they would need to continue practicing them with their teacher, their parent(s), and on their own. The teacher was asked to continue to use the various calming skills everyday in the classroom. A discussion of the course with the teacher revealed that she felt the lesson to be worthwhile and that everybody, including Nathan, had benefited from it. She also felt the personal information about Nathan and his impulse triggers together with a knowledge of some skills to help him cope were useful in helping Nathan manage his impulse control problems.

Week 16. In our next session, Nathan went through his list of anger situations and was able to relax and remain calm through each one. This was followed by a review of all the calming skills and the other ways Nathan chose to relax. An appointment was scheduled to meet in 1 month to check Nathan's progress.

After this session, a meeting was arranged with Nathan's parents, his teacher, and his psychotherapist to discuss his progress. Each member felt that Nathan had made a lot of progress and was pleased with the outcome. They were all reminded that these new skills needed to be practiced and used regularly to remain effective and that their own involvement was still very important.

One month later, Nathan met with his counselor. He reported having a good month with only one really difficult situation during which, with the help of relaxation skills, he was able to retain control of himself. An appointment was made to meet in 2 months to check on Nathan's progress. This schedule of bi-monthly meetings was continued for the next 12 months, during which time Nathan maintained his overall progress.

SUMMARY

This is a highly structured program that aims to give students the skills to modify their impulsive-aggressive behavior control problems. Teaching students a series of skills that allow them to achieve a relaxed state helps to build a sense of control. This, in turn, enhances self-confidence and encourages students to feel able to take charge of situations that formerly produced only feelings of anger and frustration. When they feel confident of the effectiveness of the techniques, they no longer feel helpless and out of control. This relaxation program was designed for impulsive-aggressive youth but is not exclusive to these students. It has several useful applications for the general classroom population and may help teachers proactively control the levels of tension and frustration in the schoolroom and thereby decrease the need for after-the-fact interventions.

REFERENCES

Anderson, R. F. (1975). *Using a fantasy-modeling treatment with acting-out fifth grade boys.* Unpublished doctoral dissertation, University of Florida, Gainesville.

Anderson, R. F. (1980). Using guided fantasy with children. *Elementary School Guidance and Counseling, 14*, 39-47.

Bash, M. A. S., & Camp, B. W. (1985). *Think Aloud: Increasing social and cognitive skills—A problem-solving program for children.* Champaign, IL: Research Press.

Burish, T. G. (1981). EMG biofeedback in the treatment of stress related disorders. In C. K. Prokop & L. A. Bradley (Eds.), *Medical psychology: Contributions to behavioral medicine* (pp. 395-418). New York: Academic Press.

Canfield, J. (1976). *100 ways to improve self-esteem in the classroom.* Englewood Cliffs, NJ: Prentice-Hall.

Dunn, F. M., & Howell, R. J. (1982). Relaxation training and its relationship to hyperactivity in boys. *Journal of Clinical Psychology, 38*, 92-100.

Feindler, E. L. (1990). Cognitive strategies in anger control interventions for children and adolescents. In P. C. Kendall (Ed.), *Child and adolescent therapy: Cognitive-behavioral procedures* (pp. 66-97). New York: Guilford.

Fried, R. (1990). Integrating music in breathing training and relaxation: II. Applications. *Biofeedback and Self Regulation, 15*, 171-177.

Jacobson, E. (1962). *Progressive relaxation.* Chicago: University of Chicago Press.

Kazdin, A. E., & Wilcoxon, L. A. (1976). Systematic desensitization and nonspecific treatment effects: A methodological evaluation. *Psychological Bulletin, 83*, 729-758.

Kendall, P. C. (1992). *Stop and Think Workbook* (2nd ed.). Available from the author, 238 Meeting House Lane, Merian, PA 19066.

Kendall, P. C., Reber, M., McLeer, S., Epps, J., & Ronan, K. R. (1990). Cognitive-behavioral treatment of conduct-disordered children. *Cognitive Therapy and Research, 14*, 279-297.

Koegel, L. K., Koegel, R. L., & Parks, D. R. (1991). *How to teach self-*

management to people with severe disabilities. Santa Barbara, CA: Graduate School of Education, University of California, Santa Barbara.

Koeppen, A. S. (1974). Relaxation training for children. *Elementary School Guidance and Counseling, 9*, 14-21.

Lehrer, P. M. (1982). How to relax and how not to relax: A re-evaluation of the work of Edmund Jacobson: 1. *Behaviour Research and Therapy, 20*, 417-428.

Linkenhoker, D. (1983). Tools of behavioral medicine: Applications of biofeedback treatment for children and adolescents. *Developmental and Behavioral Pediatrics, 4*, 16-20.

Oaklander, V. (1978). *Window to our children*. Moab, UT: Real People Press.

Peach, S. C. (1984). Some implications for the clinical use of music facilitated imagery. *Journal of Music Therapy, 21*, 27-34.

Rossman, H. M., & Kahnweiler, J. B. (1977). Relaxation training with intermediate grade students. *Elementary School Guidance and Counseling, 11*, 259-266.

Scartelli, J. P. (1984). The effect of EMG biofeedback and sedative music, EMG biofeedback only, and sedative music only on frontalis muscle relaxation ability. *Journal of Music Therapy, 21*, 67-78.

Schloss, P. J., Smith, M., Santora, C., & Bryant, R. (1989). A respondent conditioning approach to reducing anger responses of a dually diagnosed man with mild mental retardation. *Behavior Therapy, 20*, 459-464.

Singer, J. (1966). *Daydreaming*. New York: Random House.

Smith, R. (1973). The use of humor in the counterconditioning of anger responses: A case study. *Behavior Therapy, 4*, 576-580.

Stevens, J. (1973). *Awareness*. New York: Bantam Books.

Warren, R., & McLellarn, R. W. (1982). Systematic desensitization as a treatment for maladaptive anger and aggression: A review. *Psychological Reports, 50*, 1095-1102.

Zaichkowsky, L. B., Zaichkowsky, L. D., & Yeager, J. (1986). Biofeedback-assisted relaxation training in the elementary classroom. *Elementary School Guidance and Counseling, 20*, 261-267.

Zipkin, D. (1985). Relaxation techniques for handicapped children: A review of literature. *The Journal of Special Education, 19*, 283-289.

Appendix. Aids to Relaxation

This is a brief summary of the different exercises and relaxation techniques your child will be learning in this program. Homework in the form of practice of the techniques will be assigned after each session. Encourage your child to share with you what he/she has learned and help him/her to remember to follow-up on the practice.

Music

Music seems to affect the neurological system. Identify several pieces of music that you find relaxing and restful. This is a personal choice, so you will need to take the time to investigate several different types of music to find what works best for you. Suggestions: Classical, New Age Music (e.g., Steve Halpern, Yanni, Asia), or Environmental sounds.

Breathing

Reducing the rate of respiration commonly produces a relaxed state. Respiration rates may be divided into three categories. *Fast Pace*—This is defined as shallow chest breathing with short inhalations and a rapid rate. This type of breathing speeds up the cardiovascular system and is frequently observed in anxiety-producing situations. *Medium Pace*—This is normal breathing rate for most people. *Slow Pace*—This type of respiration originates at the level of the diaphragm and has a slower than normal rate.

Exercise: *Take a deep breath in, feel your lungs fill up. Hold your breath for a count of five, then slowly release it. Repeat this once more.*

This exercise seems to enhance clearer thinking and by increasing the oxygen supply to the brain will counteract the effects induced by fast pace breathing. Furthermore, if prolonged, it may even produce a relaxed state.

Calming Words

Use of a specific word or term seems to help produce a more relaxed state. Words you may find useful are: *Be calm, just relax, calm down.*

Appendix, continued.

Positive Statements

Saying or even thinking negative thoughts results in anxiety and self-defeatist behavior. Training oneself to learn a sentence or statement to stop this process will help to deflect the detrimental effects, (e.g., *Stop! Everything is Okay. I am special. I am worthwhile*).

Biofeedback

When a person's frustration level increases, there are measurable physiological responses such as increased respiration rate, increase in hand temperature, and an increase in the perspiration level known as the galvanic skin response. If these responses are measured and recorded while the student is learning the relaxation techniques, they may provide visible evidence to reassure the student that he/she is achieving a more relaxed state. Biofeedback consists of monitoring these various physiological responses and relaying that information back to the individual. Research indicates that hand temperature appears to be the most effective measurement of tension and is the easiest to monitor. In a group situation hand temperature bio-strips are useful because they are portable, complete in themselves, and have no need of any other sophisticated machines. They may also be given to the individual to take home for practice.

Induction

The induction process consists of a combination of the following exercises: music selection, deep breathing exercise, calming words/ positive statements, and closed eyes exercise. Combining any of these skills before starting any of the following relaxation techniques will increase their effectiveness. The hand temperature monitor should also be attached for each relaxation technique.

Daydreaming

Take a couple of minutes in the day to stop what you are doing and imagine yourself in a place you enjoy or a situation you like to experience. There are also several prerecorded guided imagery trips available on tape or CD. These short escapes from reality may help to

Appendix, continued.

relax you and allow you to return refreshed to deal with the stressful situations of daily life.

Progressive Relaxation Exercise (tense-relax muscles)

This exercise will help you to become aware when your muscles are tense. Sit or lie in a comfortable position. Contract the muscles in your toes as hard as you can and hold it for a count of five. Relax and stretch out that muscle group. Repeat this step twice or three times before moving on to the muscles in your feet. Continue to move upwards, trying hard to isolate each group of muscles as you work with it. When you have completed each muscle group, go back and rework any muscles that still feel tense. It may be difficult, at first, to isolate the different muscle groups, but with practice you will become more proficient. This exercise may be started either at your head or your toes.

Environment

Changing various components of the environment may alter the mood of the location. Changes such as developing a "calm corner" where there is a soft chair, low lighting, and music are frequently effective. Changing the environment when the atmosphere is tense is helpful in reducing the frustration level. Role playing different situations increases the individual's repertoire for dealing with the various situations in their environment.

Time Management and Behavioral Charts

Teaching an individual how to manage time is an important technique, particularly for the impulsive student who often lacks organizational skills. Behavioral charts monitor the individual's behavior in different situations and allow an objective evaluation of the student's progress over the course of the program.

14 ANGER MANAGEMENT AND ASSERTIVENESS SKILLS: AN INSTRUCTIONAL PACKAGE FOR PERSONS WITH DEVELOPMENTAL DISABILITIES

William McLain and Ellen Lewis

This guideline and curriculum for an instructional group was developed to assist individuals with developmental disabilities who have difficulty controlling their anger in their home, work, school, or community environments. It was an outgrowth of the behavior intervention efforts at the Tri-Counties Regional Center (Santa Barbara, California) to assist persons with developmental disabilities to remain in community educational or living arrangements, to integrate physically and socially into the community, and to obtain and maintain employment.

Although there are many ways of defining anger control disorders, persons most often referred for anger control problems present with outbursts that may include yelling, hitting, cursing, property destruction, self-injurious behavior, or physical aggression. The frequency, intensity, and duration may be severe enough to threaten the placement of the individual in the classroom, home, work, or other community environments.

The authors gratefully acknowledge Don Sorensen for his technical assistance, Christine Geffner for editorial comments, Mat Mershon for participation and assistance in the case study, and Dr. Michael E. Ogle for his leadership in the development of behavior intervention services for consumers served by the Tri-Counties Regional Center. Tri-Counties Regional Center is a private, nonprofit, state-funded agency which purchases or provides service coordination, referral, diagnostic, or other needed services to persons with developmental disabilities.

In an analysis of 2,090 incident reports[1] to the Tri-Counties Regional Center over a period of 5 years, 54% were associated with the individual's inability to control physically aggressive behaviors (McLain, 1991). The prevalence of self-control problems among persons with mental retardation has been noted by other clinician/researchers (e.g., Benson, 1985). In Benson's survey of persons reporting to an outpatient clinic, 30% were referred for self-control problems.

A variety of behavior problems related to poor anger control has been observed and documented in persons who are not developmentally disabled. Among children with learning disabilities, behaviors such as inappropriate attention seeking, noncompliance, aggressive behavior, and poor peer relationships have been observed (McKibbin & King, 1983). Some children and adolescents with psychiatric diagnoses have also been found to exhibit verbal and physical aggression, property destruction, stealing, and running away (Feindler, Ecton, Kingsley, & Dubey, 1986). Young people with a range of handicapping conditions have been observed to engage in self-injurious behavior during temper outbursts. These behavior problems can result in impairment of social development (McKibben & King, 1983), loss of educational and vocational opportunities (Wodarski, Wodarski, & Kim, 1989), and a reduction in opportunities for community-integrated activities.

The curriculum that follows represents an effort to utilize the approaches that have appeared most promising for all populations, adapt them for use by persons with varying degrees of cognitive disabilities, and present them in a flexible group format that can be adjusted to the individual's abilities and learning style. The concepts are based upon behavioral and cognitive-behavioral frameworks and borrow from the work of Novaco's Stress Inoculation Therapy (1977), Benson's (1986) approach to self-instructional training and problem-solving skills, and King, Liberman, Roberts, and Bryan's work on social skills training (1977). In addition, this curriculum addresses arousal management through relaxation training, recognition of internal and external cues to manage anger, and assertiveness skills training. As such, this program is a blend of various anger management and social skills training programs described in the literature and in this volume. This approach has been successfully used with children, adolescents, and adults who possess the following prerequisite skills:

---

[1] Residential and day programs are required by law to report to the Regional Center any special incident that represents a health or safety issue for a person with a developmental disability.

• The ability to attend in a small group setting (four to eight participants) for at least 15 minutes at a time.

• The ability for receptively and expressive verbal communication, with signs or pictures or through a communication device.

The inclusion of children and adolescents who have developmental disabilities in regular education classrooms provides expanded opportunities for the use of this curriculum. Anger management and assertiveness skills training can benefit all youth in integrated settings. The curriculum is designed for use in small groups and may be implemented with the small groups consisting of a mix of nondisabled and "special needs" children or modified for use in a large classroom.

The curriculum is designed to be modified to fit the specific needs and abilities of the group members. For example, when presenting the program to a group that includes disabled and nondisabled members, or groups of adolescents who have mild disabilities and who are able to read and write, the focus should be on changing the internal thoughts that precede an anger outburst. Written homework exercises are useful with such a group. In integrated groups extra assistance or increased learning trials may benefit the individuals with disabilities. A group of children with moderate disabilities and limited abilities to read and write (and/or who may be part of an educationally integrated younger group, e.g., early elementary age) would benefit from an emphasis on role playing and rehearsal of appropriate behavior following exposure to provoking situations. The cognitive-behavioral aspects of the program may be simplified (or eliminated) in order to suit the individual's cognitive abilities. For people with severe disabilities, a focus on teaching relaxation and simple nonaggressive responses to provocation may be most beneficial. In integrated settings, the use of peer models may be beneficial for people with all levels of disabilities.

The effective and consistent use of learned anger management skills is, like many other skills, dependent upon the individual's retention, application and generalization of these skills to natural environments. Berler, Gross, and Drabman (1982) documented the difficulties of three children with learning disabilities in generalizing social skills learned in role-play situations to natural school settings. Stokes and Baer (1977) have described several approaches to insuring generalization, including programming common stimuli, sequential modification, use of language to mediate generalization, and introducing natural contingencies. This anger management program incorporates these approaches in an effort to generalize self-control and problem-solving skills from simulated to natural environments.

One of the most dependable strategies for promoting generalization involves planned training and exposure to naturally occurring contingencies in the environment (Stokes & Baer, 1977). To achieve this end it is essential to include persons from each participant's natural environment in the program. These social agents are enlisted to assist in cuing individuals to practice newly learned skills with frequency, and most important, to reinforce and support individuals when they spontaneously use these skills under naturally occurring provocations.

Facilitation of generalization and maintenance is a primary reason that training is done in a group rather than individual context, although specific group members often benefit from "booster" sessions, which could be done individually or in dyads. When anger management and assertiveness skills training is done in a group context, members are provided with opportunities to practice self-control and appropriate responses to others with whom they typically interact on a regular basis. The leadership of the group by a teacher, school counselor, or school psychologist increases the likelihood of opportunities to reinforce and shape desirable behavior outside of the formal group setting, for example, when a conflict arises on the playground or in the lunch room.

THE ANGER MANAGEMENT INSTRUCTIONAL GROUP

Forming the Group

It is usually not difficult to identify the individuals who may benefit from participation in an anger management group. These are persons who, in a school, work, or living environment, are identified by peers, teachers, school psychologists, counselors, job coaches, parents, case managers (i.e., key social agents), and often themselves as having difficulty controlling their anger. Persons appropriate for this group evidence verbal and/or physical aggression to the point that these behaviors interfere with the person's achievement of personal goals or their ability to function in these environments.

This curriculum has benefited many individuals served by the Tri-Counties Regional Center. One individual, a high school student with Down Syndrome, lost the opportunity to try out a job in the community when he had a temper outburst following a change in job coaches. Because of verbal aggression and property destruction he was sent home from school. This young man received training in anger management and assertiveness skills in both individual and small group settings. He is now beginning a new job-training program and has demonstrated the ability to remain calm under challenging circumstances. He has also demonstrated improvements in his ability to solve problems in stressful conflict situations.

When soliciting participants for the anger management group, an individual might be asked if he or she is satisfied with the way personal relationships are going. Suggesting that the individual participate in the group because of an anger problem may prove an unsuccessful strategy. When the first author suggested to a prospective participant that she may have difficulty controlling her anger, she became indignant, stormed out, and slammed the door with sufficient force to loosen the hinges. A more positive approach is introducing participation in the group as a way for the person to get the things he or she wants, have more friends, or have access to desired activities more effectively. Exploration of the individual's short-term and long-term goals is one way to accomplish this.

It is essential that the people who most frequently interact with the group participant support the intervention. Key social agents can do this by providing information, communicating with the participants about their progress, collecting data on behaviors targeted in the teaching sessions, and participating in sessions as requested by the group leader. The key social agents can promote generalization and support the individual's efforts to improve self-control by recognizing and reinforcing the skills taught in the group. Group participants are encouraged to share their progress with key social agents. These persons must be kept informed on a regular basis by the group leader about how to support the anger control intervention and about individual progress. Therefore, it is necessary to secure, preferably in writing, the permission of the participant to contact key social agents on a regular basis. Suggestions for what information should be communicated each week to these people are included at the end of each session (except 5 and 6), in the section "Notes to the Leader."

Certainly, persons with developmental disabilities present with a wide range of verbal, reading, social, and cognitive abilities. It is therefore necessary to adapt this curriculum for individuals depending on their abilities to process and retain information and monitor and reflect on their own thought processes. For persons who have difficulty with the cognitive aspects of the curriculum, instruction should focus on behavioral approaches of developing and rehearsing problem-solving skills as alternatives to temper outbursts. For persons who do not read, pictures may be used during training in a variety of ways (e.g., flowcharts, self-monitoring procedures).

The curriculum may be presented effectively with one or two group leaders. With two leaders it is possible to do a large group presentation of the session topic, then break into smaller groups for discussion and practice of individualized application of the material. The use of two leaders provides the participants with greater opportunities to practice the target behaviors, identifies individual problem situations, and allows more time for questions and discussion of the material. If two leaders are used, they should be in regular communication regarding individual participant progress. If a small group format is used, the members of the small groups should be varied from session to session in order to facilitate generalization across individuals.

Assessment and Progress Monitoring

Prior to participation in an anger management group utilizing these guidelines, preliminary assessment information should be obtained to define the behaviors of concern and guide adaptation of the curriculum. Stein and Karno (this volume) and Feindler and Ecton (1986) provide assessment protocols particularly appropriate for use in anger management programs with youth who have developmental disabilities.

The purpose of such assessment is twofold. First, the group leader can ascertain the extent of the problem in terms of the frequency, intensity, and topography of the behavior and obtain a baseline against which to measure progress. Second, the direct observation of the antecedents to anger outbursts yields information that may then be systematically used in group training sessions to teach alternative, nonaggressive responses in the face of provocation (cf. Kaufmann & Wagner, 1972).

Preliminary assessment may also include interviews with key social agents, and their direct observation and measurement of the frequency, duration, and intensity of the anger problems. Prior to the first group session key social agents in all environments should be instructed in the measurement of anger outbursts. Additional antecedent information collected by the key social agents may be useful in group sessions. Key social agents may receive instruction in collecting information in an antecedent-behavior-consequence format. The key social agent observes the individual's behavior and documents the time and place that the behavior occurred, the antecedent to the behavior (what was happening just before the behavior occurred), and a description of the observed behavior, including its duration. An account of the events immediately following the behavior (the consequences) should also be noted. Behavioral assessment may be used by the group leader to develop additional interventions in other natural environments through the rearrangement of antecedents and consequences.

Some of the sessions described in this chapter demand higher level cognitive skills than other sessions. It is essential that group leaders utilize ongoing assessment procedures to determine whether the individual is able to encode, retain, access, and utilize the specific strategies taught through the exercises and, most important, under naturally occurring conditions. By observing the youth's performance on the exercises (at the end of each session), the group leader may assess the individual's success in retaining and incorporating new skills and, if necessary, repeat sessions or provide increased opportunities for practice.

Brief interviews with participants and key social agents can be used to obtain information about the individual's medical status, sleeping and eating patterns, means of communication, and daily schedule with its concomitant demands. Information about activities and items that may motivate the individual is important when developing a menu of reinforcers for use during the program.

OVERVIEW OF TRAINING SESSIONS

Goals of the Group

The primary goal of training is to give each person the tools they need to manage their anger effectively. Inadequate anger management may result in temper outbursts, verbal or physical aggression, property destruction, self-injurious behavior, and a range of other individualized behaviors. These behaviors may occur in part because of a person's inadequate repertoire of nonaggressive problem-solving skills or because of a lack of motivation to engage in prosocial behavior. In addition, many individuals have learned that aggressive behaviors meet their needs for attention or help them escape or avoid undesirable activities. Some persons who have developmental disabilities manifest poor impulse control and simply are unable to interrupt an arousal response in the face of provocation.

The following program includes skill training and practice in desirable *social skills* (e.g., assertive behavior) and *behaviors incompatible with aggression* (e.g., relaxation) that have been demonstrated effectively to replace inappropriate social behavior (e.g., verbal or physical aggression). Through the *cognitive-behavioral* aspects of the program, individuals learn to interrupt the chain of behaviors that may lead to loss of self-control.

Structure of Sessions

The sessions are divided into two parts. The first portion of each session consists of a short presentation and discussion of a specific topic followed by exercises presented by the group leader to illustrate the use of the skill being taught during that session. The exercises are an essential component of the session if the individual is to translate the information into personal practice, that is, adopt it for daily use in natural environments. Information presented to the group is italicized and structured so as to be easy for the group to understand and retain. Of course, it is often necessary to rephrase, repeat, and in some cases greatly simplify the information to ensure that it is understood.

The second portion of each group meeting is presented in a format similar to Personal Effectiveness Training (King et al., 1977). In a small group setting (it is useful to have two leaders here to allow for even smaller groups), antecedent events are presented via narration (to set up the situation) and role-played (to present the identified antecedent) by the group leader. The participant is coached through modeling and instruction in developing an appropriate alternative response as identified for that individual. Sessions may be videotaped and the best performances of the individual selected and repeatedly played for the individual. This "self-as-a-model" approach (Hosford, 1980) is quite useful for youth with developmental disabilities.

Outline of Sessions

During *Sessions 1 and 2* the rationale for learning to manage one's anger is presented to increase motivation and commitment to the process. Individuals are then assisted with identification of individual behavior patterns and antecedents to temper outbursts. The term *antecedents* is replaced by the term "barbs" (from Kaufmann & Wagner, 1972) to simplify the idea.

Sessions 3 and 4 continue antecedent identification and cover the fundamental skills required for anger management, namely, recognizing internal cues and developing relaxation skills. Relaxation procedures consist of modified Jacobson (1938) Progressive Muscle Relaxation. The goal is to help each person identify a deep state of muscle relaxation and produce it quickly in the natural environment. *Session 5* focuses on the physiological changes that should cue an individual's self-regulatory behaviors. *Session 6* reviews all previous material in order to help participants integrate it through repetition, exercises, and instruction.

The advanced cognitive-behavioral aspects of temper control are explained in *Session 7*. Research on modifications of the cognitive-behavioral treatments for persons with developmental disabilities has been conducted by some researchers (Benson, Rice, & Miranti, 1985). These modified treatment approaches are presented and adjusted to fit the age, needs, and abilities of each group participant.

Basic assertiveness skills are taught in *Session 8* with a special emphasis on discriminating assertive from aggressive responses. Individuals begin to develop problem-solving skills that help them to discriminate which situations warrant assertive responses, differentiate appropriate from inappropriate requests from others, and practice effective communication skills.

Session 9 focuses on strategies for identifying and defining problems, generating behavioral alternatives, and evaluating the outcome of those decisions. Part of this session focuses on the positive evaluation of outcomes and constructive self-evaluation that promotes behavior change and self-esteem enhancement.

Session 10 focuses on the more subtle aspects of social skills involved with assertiveness responses. Topics such as dealing with repeated criticism, reinforcing others for desirable behaviors and communicating feelings without blaming are practiced. Making requests for behavior change from others is incorporated into a sequence of behaviors.

Session 11 (the final session) reviews all material and role-play situations. Individuals are encouraged to set personal goals and continue anger management strategies on their own.

Additional Considerations

This outline can be modified to include additional strategies or to extend the number of sessions for difficult topics. There should be ongoing evaluation of the need for individual, topic-specific sessions to augment the group sessions. Special modifications for presentation of material to group members who, for example, do not read, is the responsibility of the group leader. The group leader should assess, through questions and role plays, the amount of time needed for individuals to master the material and extend the number of sessions per topic as needed. Individuals may develop anger management strategies that do not follow the exact skills presented here; the group leader should allow this if the strategies are useful for the participant.

If this program is used in integrated settings, it is suggested that participants have equal opportunities to model appropriate behavior (for example, the nondisabled students do not show the "special needs" students the right way to do everything) and to brainstorm on appropriate solutions to problems. Students should also be reminded to support each other in their newly acquired skills outside of the training sessions, and to refrain from presenting "barbs" without authorization.

Group leaders may choose to create incentive systems to motivate individuals to attend sessions and complete homework assignments. One option is to require participants to contribute a set amount of money at the beginning of the course. The money is then distributed to each member for attendance and homework completion at each session. Money that is left over at the end of the training course may be used to have a "graduation party" for those who have successfully met their goals for managing anger. Incentives may also be arranged to occur in natural settings during and after the training period when key social agents observe an individual using a strategy practiced in training. Group members may reinforce each other as they see each other use appropriate problem-solving skills in natural settings. This is another reason for regular communication with key social agents regarding the current training topic and weekly goals of each person. A case study illustrating the use of the program in a classroom with students who have moderate to severe handicaps is included at the end of the chapter. The case study includes examples of how the curriculum was adapted to fit the anger management needs of young people with a variety of cognitive abilities and problem behaviors.

SESSION 1: RATIONALE FOR TRAINING

Topic: Why Is It Important to Learn to Control Your Anger?

This discussion should focus on problems created by poor anger control. Discuss each of these facts with the group:

1. When people lose their jobs it's usually because they can't get along with their boss or co-workers, not because they can't do the work.

2. If you hurt someone and the police are called, the person you have hit may wish to press charges, which can result in you having to go to court. If it has happened before, you can go to juvenile hall, or you may have to move to a different place. If you get really mad and you can't calm down, you may have to go a special hospital called a psychiatric facility so that you won't hurt yourself or others.

3. You may lose friends or relationships. Your family or friends may not want to spend much time with you. This can be very lonely.

4. You can lose your job and lose the chance to get a new job. If your boss fires you because you fight with others, you may not get a good report for your next job.

5. You may be kicked out of school for a few days (suspension) or be sent to a different school (expulsion) if you can't get along with others around you.

6. You may not be allowed to continue to ride a bus independently if you have problems with your temper while you are riding the bus. This cuts down on your independence.

7. People who stay angry may get sick more often and may even die at a younger age. Getting angry is hard on your body.

8. When you yell a lot or hit others you might have to move out of places where you like to live.

9. Most of you have decided you want to have a happier, better life by learning ways to control your anger and solve problems better.

Exercise: Impact on Anger

Have individuals list and discuss events in their lives in each area that have been affected by their anger:

- School
- Transportation
- Legal
- Friends
- Jobs
- Relationships
- Roommates
- Family

Homework

List the things that happen this week that make you feel angry and write down or tell someone how you handled them.

Notes to the Leader

❒ Provide practice for the homework assignment in class by demonstrating from your personal life an event you might include on the worksheet.

Have each individual complete at least one entry and assist as necessary. Fade prompts so that the individual is able to demonstrate independent completion of an item.

❒ Contact the key social agents in the participants' home, school, or work environments and share with them any pertinent information that came out of the first session. Give them information about the homework assignment, and ask them to provide social reinforcement to the group member following daily completion of the homework.

SESSION 2: WHAT IS ANGER?

Topic #1: How This Group Will Work

1. Give an explanation of how the group will be structured with discussion and group role playing. Let people know that in the group they will have the opportunity to talk about things that bother them. Set up ground rules for turn taking and interrupting in group discussions.

2. Explain the idea of confidentiality of information shared in the group; information about other group members is not to be shared outside of group without their explicit permission. The group leader, of course, is bound by the same guidelines for confidentiality. Explain that there will be visitors to the group who will participate in the role-play sessions and that they too are bound to strict confidentiality. None of the "barbs" discussed in the group are to be used outside of the group unless there has been a clear request from the group leader for this to happen. The group leader may not share specific information about the participants without their permission.

3. The group is there to learn how to manage anger and no person will produce perfect responses in each role play or group discussion. Therefore, criticism, teasing, or ridicule have no place in group interactions (unless structured in a "barb" role-play situation). Group members should practice finding positive aspects of a member's attempts and reinforce the attempts. This is how people will learn best.

Topic #2: Anger Is a Normal Part of the Range of Human Emotions

Discuss the difference between anger and aggression by making the following points:

1. An emotion is a feeling that we have. Can you name some emotions? Anger is a human emotion that is not by itself "bad." It can help save our

life if we are in danger. Anger can help us work to change the things that make us mad. Anger is a problem when we get so mad we hurt people by hitting them, yelling at them, or saying things we don't really mean. Aggression is the way some people show angry feelings. Aggression includes yelling at people, hitting, kicking, telling people that you are going to hurt them, or trying to frighten them in any way. Aggression does not solve problems. It often gets people into trouble and makes people lose friends.

2. This group is here because you can learn to control your anger and learn better, more effective ways to solve problems than getting angry. This does not mean that you will never get angry after you are part of this group. You may learn how to control your anger so that you can solve problems in ways that are more positive for you and the other people in your life. When you learn to control your anger, you will learn to understand better what it was that made you mad.

3. One of the best ways to learn these skills is to watch other people control their anger and solve problems with words, and then practice in this group and, most important, practice in your everyday life.

4. Lots of people who find it hard to control their anger believe that it is always someone else's fault when they get mad. When people talk about what made them mad they usually "point the finger" at someone else or find someone to blame for their anger outburst. In this group you will hear over and over again that (a) you are responsible for your own feelings and your own behavior and (b) you are not responsible for anybody else's feelings or behavior.

Exercise: Responsible Statements

- Do a responsible statement exercise where each group member asks another member, "Who are you responsible for?" The desired response is, "Myself." The person who responds then asks the question of someone else.
- Ask group members for situations when people interact and quiz group members about whether these people are taking responsibility for their behavior or the behavior of others.
- Check homework and allow group members to share part of their homework if they desire. Allow some time for discussion of the situations that came up during the week for group members. Identify situations that illustrate the issue of personal responsibility.

Notes to the Leader

❐ In the second exercise, encourage and prompt the use of real-life situations of which you are aware. These situations may occur just prior to or during the training session, as group members interact informally with each other, or may come out of participants' homework assignments.

❐ In both exercises model the desired behavior only as necessary. As group members demonstrate competence with the exercises, throw in "error responses" and see if group members are able to identify them. If not, have the other leader model a response to the "error response."

❐ Check in with the key social agents regarding any challenging situations that may have come up for the group member during the week. See if the member's report matches the report from the key social agent.

❐ If you have decided to set up a monetary reward system, present the following during the session:

> *Each of you will be asked to give a certain amount of money if you decide to be part of this group. This is your choice and will help you follow through on attendance and homework assignments. Each week that you come to the group, you will get some of the money that you put in. If you finish your homework assignment you will get more money. If you come to all of the sessions and finish all of your homework assignments, you will get all of your money back. Any money that is left at the end of the classes will be used to give a graduation party for the people who finish the whole program.*

SESSION 3: IDENTIFYING ANTECEDENTS

Topic #1: What Are "Barbs?"

1. *Barbs* are the things that happen, inside you or outside of you, right before you get mad. Has anyone ever seen a barbed wire fence? (Draw a picture.) The barbs are the little prickles on the fence. If you touch them they can poke you or hurt you. In this class we call barbs the things that happen just before we get angry. Barbs are things that may hurt us or make us feel angry. They may be things people say like somebody telling us we haven't done a very good job, or they may be things we tell ourselves inside our head, like "he's not going to get away with that." Here are some other barbs that happen inside of us: pictures in our minds, things we say to ourselves, or physical feelings such as menstrual cramps, sore throat, tiredness, tight muscles, breathing quickly, upset stomach, fast heartbeat, and so on.

2. Some barbs that happen outside of us are things that people do or say, or other things that happen around us that we can see and feel. Some examples are a teacher telling you that you did something wrong, your mom or dad asking you to do something you don't like, a friend making a face at you, a stranger swearing at you or giving you the finger. Examples of barbs from our environment might include being in a room that is too hot or too noisy.

Topic #2: Why Identify Angry Antecedents to Angry Outbursts?

1. People who get mad easily usually do it when certain things happen. It may be hard to be told that you have done a bad job or to be told to do a job that you don't like. It may be confusing to be told to do different things by two different people. Usually the things that upset people are different for each person. Something that doesn't bother one person may easily upset another person. Sometimes it depends on the day or time. Something that doesn't bother you one day might bother you on another day. The purpose of this next exercise is to find out exactly the things that people say or do that make you get really angry.

Exercise: What Makes Me Angry?

• Make a list of things people have said to you that make you angry. Include who says them, where, when, and the way that they say them. The teacher may need to help with this list.

• Put the items that make you most angry at the top of the list and so on to the things that make you less angry.

• Make a list of the things you say to yourself or things you see in your mind when these things happen. For example, you may say things like:

a. "He can't talk to me that way"
b. "That isn't fair"
c. "I never get what I want"
d. "People never see things my way"
e. "I'm going to get even"
f. "I'm going to punch her in the nose" or
g. "That jerk."

• These types of statements are *trouble* statements that we will learn to change into *coping* statements. For now it is most important to know when you're telling yourself these types of things and then stop them. These trouble statements will not help you to control your anger.

Homework

• Write down the date, time, and barb any time you get angry this week. Use the Anger Diary (see Figure 14.1) to write this information. If you would like to use a tape recorder to record this information, talk to me after the session.

Notes to the Leader

❐ It may be easier for people to put barbs in order if each one is written on a 3 x 5 index card. Often what is the strongest barb at one time will not elicit as strong a response, even the very next meeting. By putting the barbs on cards, the participants can re-order them according to how they are feeling each session. The experiences that they have had during the time between sessions may influence the order of their barbs.

❐ Check to see if what the participant reports as barbs fit with the information that you have collected from key social agents. If you notice any striking differences, it may warrant further investigation and/or direct observation.

❐ The group leader should again model the homework exercise with a clear example. People who are unable to read or write may use a tape recorder or pictures to track their anger.

SESSION 4: RELAXATION RESPONSE

The following is an abbreviated version of Jacobson's (1938) Progressive Muscle Relaxation. Because the most important aspect of relaxation is that the youth can use it unnoticed, particularly in the classroom, this procedure will always pair the subaudible cue of the word *relax* with each exhale during the relaxation. The goal is for individuals to be able to relax without having to tense each muscle group. When the sensation of relaxation is consistently paired with the word "relax," the word will begin to induce relaxation by itself.

When narrating these exercises always (a) pace your instruction—a slow presentation will allow time for deeper relaxation and may have a slightly hypnotic effect; (b) have the individual breathe deeply following the tension release, hold the breath and say "relax" to him- or herself; and (c)

ANGER DIARY			
DATE	TIME	SITUATION	WHAT YOU THOUGHT AND DID

repeat each muscle group two to three times before moving to the next muscle group.

1. Sit so that you are comfortable. Rest your hands on your lap, palms up. Focus on your hands. Make a fist with both hands, like this. Hold tight. Now relax and open your hands. Relax each arm completely. Let your arms feel very heavy. Now relax them some more. Take a deep breath and "relax."

2. Now focus on your shoulders. Hold all of the muscles in your shoulders very tight, like this. Now relax and let your shoulders hang down, very heavy. Take a deep breath and say "relax" to yourself.

3. Focus on your neck. Move your head a little bit forward and up. Hold it until you can feel your neck getting tight. Now let your neck relax.

4. Focus on your face. Squint your eyes. Wrinkle your nose. Clench your teeth. Tighten your mouth. Hold tight. Relax. Relax your eyelids, letting them feel very heavy. Relax your cheeks, and lips, forehead. Take a deep breath, and say "relax" as you exhale.

5. Focus on your stomach. Make your stomach tense by lifting your feet a little bit off the ground. Feel the tense feeling. Hold it. Now let your feet down. Relax, take a deep breath and say "relax" as you exhale.

6. Focus on your back muscles. Tighten your back by sitting up very tall and pulling your back away from the chair. Hold it. Now sink down and relax. Take a deep breath and relax even more. Breathe deeply and each time you exhale feel yourself sink just a bit deeper into relaxation than before.

7. Now focus on your leg muscles. Point your toes and tighten all the muscles in your legs. Hold it. Now relax your toes, let your legs hang down and let all the tension just melt away. Practice deep breathing on your own.

8. Now take a minute and see if you can let your entire body relax as completely as possible. See if you can find any tension in your body and simply release it. Let it go and continue to deep breathe, relaxing just a bit deeper each time you exhale.

9. I am going to come around and see if you are really relaxed. If you are very relaxed, your arms and legs should feel limp, like noodles that have been cooked, soft and floppy. I will try to lift your arm. If you are relaxed, it should be very heavy for me. If your arm does not feel relaxed, I will have you try to lift my arm and I will show you what a relaxed arm feels like.

Exercise: Relaxation Role Play

- Practice relaxation in identified role-play situations without having to use tension/release. Use real-life items reported in participants' homework.

• Now we're going to use these relaxation skills. I'm going to give each of you a barb. As I give you the barb, I want you to tell yourself "relax" on the inside, take a deep breath, and let yourself completely relax. When you feel very relaxed, answer me.

• Now we'll practice using relaxation when you get more than one barb all at once. I'm going to give each of you more than one barb. I want you to keep practicing relaxation as you answer me.

Homework

• Practice relaxation the way we did in class today (tension/release) until you can become very relaxed without having to tighten each part of your body (i.e., skip directly to the "release" part). You will know that you are very relaxed when your arms and legs feel very heavy.

Notes to the Leader

❒ Make sure that you are training relaxation in a conducive setting. It should be quiet, with dim lighting if possible, or outdoors in a quiet area. Group members should be seated comfortably or stretched out on mats or grass. There should be no interruptions.

❒ Ask group members to notice during relaxation if there are any parts of their body that are particularly difficult to relax. Have them direct their attention to those areas until they are able to relax those areas, too.

❒ Communicate with key social agents and, with group members' permission, invite them to specific meetings. Share the current barbs that the person is working on, and their progress with relaxation training. Ask the key social agent to allow the group member to practice relaxation with them and to show them what they have learned following this session. Ask the key social agent to provide positive social reinforcement to the participant when they are observed to demonstrate the use of relaxation techniques, especially under stressful conditions.

SESSION 5: RECOGNIZING BODY CUES

Topic: Review of the Internal Antecedents Identified in Session #3

1. Today we are going to help you learn to find the things that happen inside your body when you are just starting to get angry. When some people get

angry, they feel their muscles get tight and hard. Other people feel their heart start to pound or they clench their teeth together very tightly. Everybody is different. I want you to find out what happens when you get angry.

Exercise: Relaxation

• Have the group members practice the relaxation response and develop the deepest state of relaxation possible for each individual.

• When you are very deeply relaxed lift your finger to signal me.

• I am going to come around to each of you and describe the thing that you said made you most angry. Pretend that this is really happening to you now. As you think about it notice what happens to your body. Are any muscles getting tense? Is your stomach getting upset or tight? Is your heart beating faster? Is your jaw tight? Do you feel like you are getting a headache?

• Repeat the exercise several times for different scenes. Use real-life situations that have been reported in homework or in members' barb lists.

• Survey the members of the group after having them open their eyes and have them describe the sensations they experienced. Write them on a blackboard and draw pictures.

• Use the most salient body responses as a cue to begin a self-control procedure.

• Draw the flowchart for anger management (see Figure 14.2) for those persons who are able to read. Simplify the flowchart as needed, depending on your student's cognitive abilities. Use pictures instead of words for those persons who are not able to read. Proceed up to the point where the person identifies their bodily response, makes a coping/self-instructional statement, and then relaxes.

• Present group practice exercises by narrating various real-life scenes for the group and follow each scene with group discussion about identifying internal cues, making self-coping statements and relaxing.

Notes to the Leader

❐ Some people may have difficulty identifying their body responses. It may help them if you can give them observational feedback such as, "I notice that your face gets very red when you seem to be upset about something. What happens inside when that happens?"

❐ Discuss physical manifestations of tension and stress such as headaches and stomachaches.

1. Anticipate conflict situation
2. Relax...make self-control statements
3. BARB
   - Catch any body tension and relax
   - Catch "trouble" statements...Replace with control statements
4. If person is angry, Actively listen
5. Problem Solve
   - What is situation?
   - What can I do?
   - What will happen if I do this?
6. Select Behavior
   - Continue active listening
   - Make "I" statements
   - Make direct request for change
   - Ask for time to think
7. Evaluate How You Did
   - Did you stay relaxed? Good!
   - Did you catch and eliminate trouble statements? Nice Job!
   - Did you make an assertive statement?
     - a. With neutral voice tone?
     - b. With nonthreatening posture?
   - Are there any things you would change if you could do it again?
   - Congratulate yourself on the things you were able to do well!

Figure 14.2. Anger Management Steps

❒ Explore the use of soft, slow music before, during, and after relaxation exercises. Talk with the group about how certain kinds of music may create certain moods and feelings and they can use music to lower their arousal level or to stay relaxed. If possible, use headphones to enhance the relaxing effects of music.

SESSION 6: REVIEW

Topic: Review of Sessions 1–5

Session 1— Rationale for Training.

- Anger in itself is not "bad."
- How we handle anger determines whether it is a problem.
- Each individual is responsible for his or her feelings and behavior.
- Uncontrolled anger can create many problems in school, work, home, and social environments. Review what individual problems each person has had.

Session 2—What is Anger?

- Review of anger diary

Session 3—Identifying Antecedents.

- Review with the group what barbs are, what each individual's barbs are, and why we are tracking them.
- Review with each individual member what they have identified as specific "trouble" statements.

Session 4—Relaxation Response.

- Review relaxation procedures and practice in group.
- Review applications in real life.

Session 5—Recognizing Body Cues.

- Review body cues that anger should be managed, and practice using relaxation procedure.
- Review anger diary for information on body cues.
- Review the flowchart up to this point and practice exercises used in previous sessions.

SESSION 7: RECOGNIZING SELF-STATEMENTS

Topic #1: Recognizing "Trouble" Statements

1. *Trouble* statements happen when you say to yourself how unfair a situation is, or how another person is wrong. Describe how making trouble

statements will interfere with the individual's relaxation, recognizing internal cues, and problem solving.

2. *Coping* statements happen when you say to yourself something that helps you feel better and solve a problem, like "That person is probably just having a bad day. I can handle this."

Exercise: Identifying Coping Statements

• See if you can tell which of these statements is a *coping* or *trouble* statement:

a. "That guy is such a jerk."
b. "No way can I do this assignment."
c. "I'm starting to get mad but I'm going to handle this like a pro."
d. "If I punch him it won't solve the problem and I'll just get in trouble."
e. "Yep, this person wants me to change the way I work."
f. "If she says another word I'm going to scream."
g. "How could he be so stupid?"
h. "Hmmmm...I wonder how I could deal with this situation."
i. "I hate him."
j. "Time to take a deep breath and use the old noodle."

Topic #2: Review of Previously Identified Self-Statements (from Session #3)

1. Determine if they are *coping* or *trouble* statements.

2. Save the statements that are coping statements.

3. Decide what new coping statements you could use to replace the old *trouble* statements. Make a personalized list of coping statements that each participant will practice in the next exercise.

4. Enlist the help of other group members in brainstorming positive, alternative coping statements.

Exercise: Making Self-Statements

• I want you to pretend that_____________ (describe antecedent) is happening with ______________(group member's name), and when she gives you the barb, I want you to say just like you were thinking out loud (insert individual's selected statement). OK?

• Provide any positive/corrective feedback and have the person immediately repeat the role play, saying the coping statement silently.

Notes to the Leader

❐ Use a situation from real life for the exercise. Ask other group members to act as observers and to give their feedback, too.

❐ Check in again with key social agents. Find out if they are seeing any changes in the group member's behavior. Let them know how the person is progressing in the group. Enlist their assistance if the person needs additional practice on any specific part of the program up to this point. Ask the key social agent to model some coping statements for the participant in the natural setting.

SESSION 8: ASSERTIVENESS SKILLS I

Topic: What is Assertive Behavior?

1. Assertive behavior is (a) figuring out what your own feelings are (e.g., anger, admiration, sadness); (b) figuring out what are the behaviors of others that you would like changed; and (c) asking directly for change that keeps your rights and respects the rights of others. People have the right not to be yelled at, threatened, ridiculed, or hit.

Exercise #1: Discrimination Training, Assertive vs. Aggressive Responses

• Group leaders should model examples of assertive or aggressive behaviors along the following parameters and have individuals identify which is being demonstrated.

• *Posture* (e.g., aggressive: both hands on hips or clenched fists; assertive: arms folded or hands in pockets).

• *Tone of voice* (e.g., aggressive: loud; assertive: conversational).

• *Facial expression* (e.g., aggressive: scowl or glare; assertive: neutral or smile).

• *Verbal content* (e.g., aggressive: a *trouble statement*; assertive: making an *"I"* statement—a request for change).

Topic #2: Active Listening Skills

1. These skills will help by slowing you down so that you don't say or do anything before you have decided how you really want to handle the problem.

2. It is important not to interrupt when another person is talking, especially if the other person is angry.

3. Look at the person while they talk so they know you are listening.

4. Restate the problem in your own words to make sure that you understand what the problem is.

Exercise #2: Relaxation Exercise

- Now let's put everything together. We'll do relaxation, use a nice tone of voice and a pleasant expression on your face, and use good listening. I'm going to give you one of the barbs. When I say __________ I want you to take a deep breath and relax, then restate what I say the way that we practiced before. Make sure you don't sound or look angry. We will tell you the good things that you do. Everybody will have a chance to practice this many times because it is very important.
- We will work on things to say to solve the problem next time.

Notes to the Leader

❐ If possible, videotape this session. After the session, edit the videotape so that you retain the best demonstrations of the active listening behaviors. Consider doing some additional videotaping in natural settings in ways that don't draw attention to the individual, attempting to capture similar behaviors by the participants or by people they know. Plan to view the videotape and allow time for discussion in an additional session or at the beginning of the next session.

❐ Talk with the key social agents about reinforcing assertive behavior, even if the group member is making a choice that the key social agent may not agree with. Encourage the key social agents to give specific praise for the target behaviors described in Exercise 2 as they occur in natural settings. It may be necessary to do some attitude assessment and education with key social agents about individual rights and the importance of teaching people to make choices. In supporting this program the key social agent has a responsibility to respect those choices.

SESSION 9: PROBLEM-SOLVING STRATEGIES

Topic: What to Do When You Are Having a Problem

1. Use the antecedent information from previous sessions for members to practice selecting a behavioral response to provocation.

2. Ask yourself the question, "What is the problem?"

3. Then ask, "What can I do?" Think of at least three different ways you could handle the problem.

4. Then ask, "What will happen if I...?" and decide which is the best thing to do. Pay special attention to things that you could say or do that might cause more trouble instead of solving the problem.

5. Then choose a plan that will not make the situation worse and that is most likely to get you what you want (see exercise "Asking for Behavior Change"). Try out the plan.

6. How did you do with your plan? Did you get what you wanted? Did you get something that works for you and for the other people around you?

7. Here are just a few examples of things you might do to deal with the problem (we'll be talking more about this in our next session):

- ask the person to stop
- ignore the person and walk away
- ask a teacher to help

Exercise: Handling Barbs

• I want each of you to think of the barb that is on the top of your list today. Think of at least three different ways you could handle the situation. We will talk about them with the group and you can decide which the best option is. You may get some ideas from listening to how other people handle their barbs.

Homework

• Find situations where you can use these skills and practice them over the next week. Bring back a story about your experience to share at the next session.

Notes to the Leader

❒ Individual role playing occurs with the group, or in pairs coached by the group leader utilizing direct instruction, modeling, behavior rehearsal, feedback, shaping, and positive reinforcement (see Figure 14.3).

❒ For the people in the group who cannot read, use a picture flowchart that includes the information in the topic above (selecting a behavioral response to provocation).

❒ Some people might have difficulty thinking of three different ways to handle a situation—try two first.

❒ This is an important session for the key social agents to attend as participants. Make sure they are aware of the skills the individuals are practicing in the sessions.

❒ When possible, conduct practice sessions in the actual environment where the individual tends to have problems. This may be done when other students or individuals are not present.

SESSION 10: ASSERTIVENESS SKILLS II

Topic: Review Session #7 Skills

1. Discriminating assertive from aggressive responses (practice with various role-played responses in group).
2. Relaxation during provocation (practice with the antecedent information identified previously).
3. Active listening (practice with antecedent information identified previously).

Exercise: Asking for Behavior Change

• This section may require much practice for some people. It may be necessary to simplify this exercise substantially. This may be done by developing a short, nonaggressive request for behavior change in others and teaching the response through repeated modeling and behavior rehearsal.

• Today we're going to practice what to say to people when their behavior makes you angry. This is a way of asking them to change their behavior after you have stayed calm and actively listened to their complaint.

• Make an "I" statement about how you feel when they do _______. Do this without blaming them for how you feel. Your feelings are your responsibility. For example, "I feel nervous when your voice gets louder."

• Nicely tell them how you would like them to treat you. Don't demand. Try, "I would like it better if you could talk to me with a quieter voice."

• Putting this together. Here is something that you might say if a teacher scolded you in front of other students:

> "Ms. Jones, I feel nervous when you raise your voice. Would it be possible to talk to me alone if I'm doing something wrong?"

• Have participants identify situations from their own list of barb situations and practice including each of the three parts. The group members should provide positive feedback to each other on the correct portions of each performance.

Figure 14.3. Using Modeling and Behavioral Rehearsal

1. Instruct

A. Rationale—Give a rationale to individual for working on the target behavior. Explain the specific behavior's usefulness and how it may be used to avoid or solve problems or "get things you want." Describe the "modeling" procedure as a way of "showing" individual exactly what you want him or her to do.

B. Description—Describe the setting conditions in which it would be appropriate to use the target behavior. Describe how the behavior should look and/or sound when it is successfully learned.

2. Modeling

A. Demonstrate—Have the individual observe you as you demonstrate the behavior with another person.

B. Repeat—Repeat the demonstration several times, pointing out an important aspect of the target behavior after each demonstration. You should draw attention to things such as voice volume, content, eye contact, tone of voice, and posture (including the use of the hands).

3. Behavioral Rehearsal

A. Describe—Reiterate the setting condition you will present that should cue the individual to emit the behavior.

B. Present—Present the stimulus and, if necessary, prompt the desired behavior.

4. Feedback

A. Shape—Point out the positive aspects of the performance, citing all correct components performed. Omit description of undesirable aspects of the behavior. Use short statements containing one aspect of the target behavior at a time.

FIGURE 14.3. CONTINUED.

B. Instruct—Ask the individual to repeat the performance and give instructions for correct behavior where the performance was lacking. You do not need to describe how the performance was inadequate.

C. Recycle—If necessary model the desired performance again by recycling back to step 2 until the response closely resembles the target behavior. At this point move to Step 5 for generalization.

5. GENERALIZE

A. Antecedents—Introduce the other similar setting conditions requiring the target behavior that were identified in the assessment. This may include new persons presenting the provocation, small changes in the content or tone of the provocation, or slight variations of the original stimulus setting. Begin with the least anxiety-arousing situations and proceed to more stressful or different conditions.

B. Recycle—Repeat Steps 2-5 as needed during the generalization programming. When all setting conditions and variations of the provocation reliably elicit the desired response move to Step 6.

6. MAINTENANCE

A. Inform—Be sure all of the key social agents in the individual's environment are aware of the new target behavior so the behavior can be reinforced when it occurs naturally. They may wish to prompt the new skill if they observe a provocation and the individual does not spontaneously use the new behavior.

Notes to the Leader

❒ Find out what current real-life situations fit into this training topic. If possible, role-play these, then actually go out and coach the participant through a real interaction with someone in the natural setting. Prompt only as much as necessary to assist the person to make an assertive request for change. Then come back to the group and talk about how it worked or didn't work and what might be done differently the next time.

❒ Contact key social agents and communicate about the progress of group members on the current topic. Ask that they provide positive social reinforcement to members for making nonaggressive requests for change under natural circumstances.

SESSION 11: REVIEW

Topic: Putting It all Together—Review the Flowchart Combining all of the Components and Practice Using Antecedent Information in Role Plays

1. Preparation: prepare for the situation using relaxation, coping, and planning statements.

2. Use body cues (tension, nervousness) to relax and change trouble statements to coping statements.

3. Use problem solving and anticipate probable outcomes of choices.

4. You may choose any one or more of these to use at the same time: Active Listening, use "I" statements, description of behaviors you want changed, and direct request for behavior change. You may ask for more time to say or do something. If you feel like you can't control your anger you may go to another place so that you can practice relaxation and assertive responses.

5. Evaluate performance in positive terms and identify things to alter in future conflicts.

6. Ask group members to choose one or two specific goals in terms of their implementation of what they have learned in the program.

Notes to the Leader

❒ If possible, arrange to observe the group members in a variety of natural settings and at different times. Let the members know that you will be stopping by to see how well they remember and use what we have been working on. Give group members feedback during observations when you see them using target behaviors effectively.

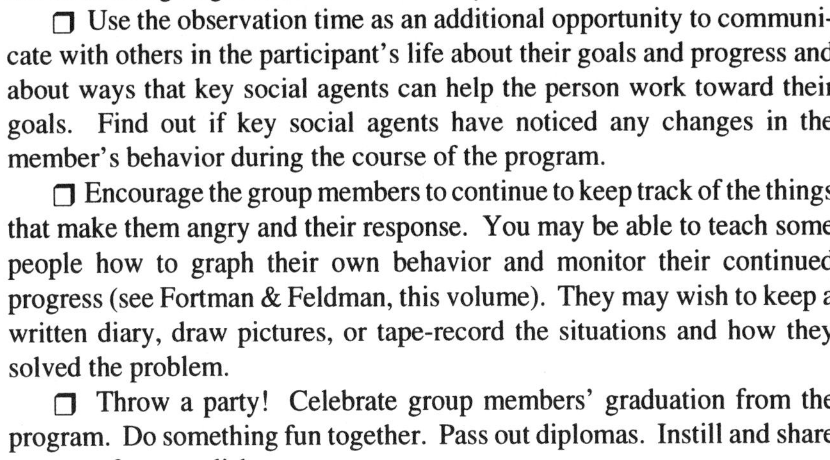

❒ Use the observation time as an additional opportunity to communicate with others in the participant's life about their goals and progress and about ways that key social agents can help the person work toward their goals. Find out if key social agents have noticed any changes in the member's behavior during the course of the program.

❒ Encourage the group members to continue to keep track of the things that make them angry and their response. You may be able to teach some people how to graph their own behavior and monitor their continued progress (see Fortman & Feldman, this volume). They may wish to keep a written diary, draw pictures, or tape-record the situations and how they solved the problem.

❒ Throw a party! Celebrate group members' graduation from the program. Do something fun together. Pass out diplomas. Instill and share a sense of accomplishment.

CASE STUDY

The Anger Management and Assertiveness Skills Training curriculum has been used successfully with developmentally disabled adults in day programs, and in independent-living residential facilities. To illustrate its use and application with adolescents in a school setting, the curriculum was run during a summer school session in a community-based special education class in a public high school.

Ten students with severe disabilities attended the summer school program. Their ages ranged from 15 to 20 years. Six of the students were classified as having mental retardation, two students as multihandicapped, one student was classified as severely learning disabled (autistic), and one student had a health impairment. Spanish was the primary language for two of the students. Three of the students described above also had seizure disorders. Academic level ranged from 1st to 5th grade. Four of the students were living in licensed care facilities at the time of the case study. The rest of the students were living with their families.

The teacher for the classroom had 10 years of teaching experience in Special Education, 5 years at this school. She had several of these students in her classroom for the preceding school year, some of the students for more than 1 year. In addition to the teacher, two classroom assistants were present during the sessions.

The teacher reported that prior to the anger management and assertiveness skills training, she had observed aggressive behaviors indicative of anger (such as hitting, kicking, spitting, throwing objects, and yelling) in 7 of the 10 students. She also stated that at least one verbal argument occurred between students daily. She considered poor anger management and consequent behaviors to be a problem for the majority of the students in her classroom.

The teacher collected baseline data for the first 8 days of the summer session, prior to anger management training. During this time, the frequency of physical and verbal aggression was recorded for all students in the class. Five of the ten students displayed verbal and/or physical aggression during the baseline period. Physical aggression included pushing, hitting, throwing objects at people, and kicking. Verbal aggression included yelling and making threats of physical harm to others. Both types of aggression were considered to be problem behaviors and were combined to obtain the following rates:

Student	*# of incidents/8 school days*	*Average*
1	5/8	.63/day
2	7/8	.88/day
3	2/8	.25/day
4	3/8	.38/day
5	4/8	.50/day

The Anger Management and Assertiveness Skills Training curriculum was run during the first hour of each morning for 11 consecutive school days during the latter part of the summer school session. The primary trainer was a bilingual graduate student who had run the program in adult day and small (2–3 persons) independent living residential programs.

The teacher was present during all sessions and assisted with presentation of material, reminded students to complete homework assignments, and encouraged students to bring real-life, anger-management conflict situations to the sessions. The teacher also demonstrated various skills during several of the training sessions. In addition, she was primary communicator with key social agents and obtained consent prior to the beginning of training. Near the end of training, she sent home a request for feedback on students' behavior in home settings.

The two classroom assistants also participated in training. One assistant provided support to the behavior specialist in explaining the session content to the Spanish-speaking students. The other assistant gave occasional feedback and comments to the group during sessions. All teaching staff provided positive reinforcement for anger management skills observed during the rest of the day, usually in community settings.

The training followed the 11-session format. Each session was simplified to fit the cognitive and communicative abilities of the group members. Just within the group, there was great variation in these abilities, so often the same material was presented in a variety of ways: demonstrated with modeling, role play, and behavior rehearsal, presented verbally in English and Spanish, written on the blackboard, and illustrated with a pictorial flowchart.

Individual antecedents were identified and tracked throughout training. Often, antecedents to anger outbursts were specific interactions between students that the teacher assisted in describing. A female student became angry with a male student when he splashed her at the pool. A student who uses a wheelchair became angry when another student who was pushing him would not take him where he wanted to go.

Homework from the previous day was reviewed each day. The students were encouraged to assist each other by demonstrating relaxation exercises both in class and outside of class. Three students in particular became quite skilled and motivated to lead relaxation exercises. The students worked together to identify and develop "coping" statements and strategies for challenging situations.

One student role-played assertive statements to a van driver who (according to the student report) did not properly secure his wheelchair to the van. This student was able to communicate assertively with the van driver following the role-play session. When the driver did not respond appropriately, the class assisted this student in problem solving and then role playing a telephone call to the driver's supervisor. The student made the phone call independently and was able to give the driver's supervisor an account of unsafe (and anxiety-producing) driving practices. The supervisor agreed to talk with the driver. This student succeeded, with training and support, in identifying and changing problem statements to coping statements, rehearsing and implementing effective communication, and solving a real problem without having a temper outburst.

There was one report of verbal aggression (1/11 days = .09/day) reported or observed for all 10 students during school hours in the training period. Requests for feedback from students' families and care providers yielded one response: a parent reported noticing a difference in her son's behavior—"E. seems to talk more and say why he's mad instead of sulking or hitting people." The teacher is now planning to use components of the program in her teaching on a regular basis.

There are aspects of this case study that vary from the model provided. One key feature in the curriculum is the involvement of key social agents. Because of time constraints, additional key social agent contact and involvement was not possible at the time. Parents and care providers were aware of the general nature of training, but were not aware of the specific daily topics covered. When this program is run throughout the school year, it is expected that additional participation and communication with key social agents will maximize the success of the program for individual students.

A trained behavior specialist who had prior experience with the program was available to present the material and to modify it spontaneously in order to best meet individual needs. This may be quite a different experience for a teacher or school counselor who uses the material for the first time, with or without assistance, and possibly with a group of unfamiliar students. Familiarity with the materials and with the students, their needs, and behaviors will optimize the successful use of the curriculum.

REFERENCES

Benson, B., Rice, C. J., & Miranti, S. V. (1985). Effects of anger management training with mentally retarded adults in group treatment. *Journal of Consulting and Clinical Psychology, 55*, 728-729.

Benson, B. (1986). Anger management training. *Psychiatric Aspects of Mental Retardation Reviews, 55*, 51-55.

Berler, E. S., Gross, A. M., & Drabman, R. S. (1982). Social skills training with children: Proceed with caution. *Journal of Applied Behavior Analysis, 15*, 41-53.

Feindler, E. L., & Ecton, R. B. (1986). *Adolescent anger control: Cognitive-behavioral techniques*. New York: Pergamon Press.

Feindler, E. L., Ecton, R. B., Kingsley, D., & Dubey, D. R. (1986). Group anger-control training for institutionalized psychiatric male adolescents. *Behavior Therapy, 17*, 109-123.

Hosford, R. (1980). Self-as-a-model: A cognitive social learning technique. *The Counseling Psychologist, 9*, 45-62.

Jacobson, E.(1938). *Progressive relaxation*. Chicago: University of Chicago Press.

Kaufmann, L., & Wagner, B. R. (1972). Systematic treatment technology for temper control disorders. *Behavior Therapy, 3*, 84-90.

King, L. W., Liberman, R. P., Roberts, J., & Bryan, E. (1977). Personal effectiveness: A structured therapy for improving social and emotional skills. *Behavioural Analysis and Modification, 2*, 82-91.

McKibbin, E., & King, J. (1983). Activity group counseling for learning-disabled children with behavior problems.*The American Journal of Occupational Therapy, 37*, 617-623.

McLain, W. (1991). *An analysis of special incident reports in the Tri-Counties*. Carpinteria, CA: Tri-Counties Regional Center. Unpublished manuscript.

Novaco, R. W. (1977). Stress inoculation: A cognitive therapy for anger and its application to a case of depression. *Journal of Consulting and Clinical Psychology, 45*, 600-608.

Stokes, T. F., & Baer, D. M. (1977). An implicit technology of generalization. *Journal of Applied Behavior Analysis, 10*, 349-367.

Wodarski, J. S., Wodarski, L. A., & Kim, T. W. (1989). Comprehensive employment preparation for adolescents with developmental disabilities: An empirical paradigm. *Adolescence, 24*, 821 836.

SUBJECT INDEX

A

B

C

D

E

F

R

S